Fodor's

NEW YORK CITY

11/14

WELCOME TO NEW YORK CITY

From Wall Street's skyscrapers to the neon of Times Square to Central Park's leafy paths, New York City pulses with an irrepressible energy. History meets hipness in this global center of entertainment, fashion, media, and finance. World-class museums like MoMA and unforgettable icons like the Statue of Liberty beckon, but discovering the subtler strains of New York's vast ambition is equally rewarding: ethnic enclaves and shops, historic streets of dignified brownstones, and trendy bars and eateries all add to the urban buzz.

TOP REASONS TO GO

★ **Landmarks:** With towering edifices and awe-inspiring bridges, the skyline says it all.

★ **Shopping:** Whether you're in the market for top designers or inexpensive souvenirs.

★ **Food:** Dim sum to pizza and everything in between, NYC has what you're craving.

★ **Museums:** Art is it, with museums like the Guggenheim and galleries all over town.

★ **The Dazzle:** From the lights of Broadway to celebrity sightings, NYC is full of stars.

★ **Brooklyn and Elsewhere:** Cool neighborhoods and restaurants are a subway ride away.

Fodor's NEW YORK CITY

Design: Tina Malaney, *Associate Art Director*; Erica Cuoco, *Production Designer*

Photography: Jennifer Arnow, *Senior Photo Editor*; Mary Robnett, *Photo Researcher*

Maps: Rebecca Baer, *Senior Map Editor*; Mark Stroud (Moon Street Cartography), *Cartographers*

Production: Angela L. McLean, *Senior Production Manager*; Jennifer DePrima, *Editorial Production Manager*

Sales: Jacqueline Lebow, *Sales Director*

Business & Operations: Chuck Hoover, *Chief Marketing Officer*; Joy Lai, *Vice President and General Manager*; Stephen Horowitz, *Head of Business Development and Partnerships*

Writers: Kelsy Chauvin, Jessica Colley Clarke, David Farley, Elissa Garay, Laura Itzkowitz, Kristen Iversen, Christina Knight, Megan Eileen McDonough, Marisa Meltzer, Chris Molanphy, Jacinta O'Halloran, Matt Rodbard, Josh Rogol, Emily Saladino, Sarah Spagnolo, Kate Thorman

Editors: Amanda Sadlowski, Caroline Trefler, Alexis Kelly

Production Editor: Jennifer DePrima

28th Edition

ISBN 978-1-101-87994-8

ISSN 0736–9395

All details in this book are based on information supplied to us at press time. Always confirm information when it matters, especially if you're making a detour to visit a specific place. Fodor's expressly disclaims any liability, loss, or risk, personal or otherwise, that is incurred as a consequence of the use of any of the contents of this book.

PRINTED IN THE UNITED STATES OF AMERICA

10 9 8 7 6 5 4 3 2 1

CONTENTS

CONTENTS

MAPS

ABOUT THIS GUIDE

Fodor's Recommendations

Everything in this guide is worth doing—we don't cover what isn't—but exceptional sights, hotels, and restaurants are recognized with additional accolades. **Fodor's Choice ★** indicates our top recommendations; and **Best Bets** call attention to notable hotels and restaurants in various categories. Care to nominate a new place? Visit Fodors.com/contact-us.

Trip Costs

We list prices wherever possible to help you budget well. Hotel and restaurant price categories from **$** to **$$$$** are noted alongside each recommendation. For hotels, we include the lowest cost of a standard double room in high season. For restaurants, we cite the average price of a main course at dinner or, if dinner isn't served, at lunch. For attractions, we always list adult admission fees; discounts are usually available for children, students, and senior citizens.

Hotels

Our local writers vet every hotel to recommend the best overnights in each price category, from budget to expensive. Unless otherwise specified, you can expect private bath, phone, and TV in your room. For expanded hotel reviews, facilities, and deals visit Fodors.com.

Top Picks	Hotels &
★ **Fodor's** Choice	**Restaurants**
	🏨 Hotel
Listings	⤵ Number of
✉ Address	rooms
✉ Branch address	🍽 Meal plans
☎ Telephone	✗ Restaurant
🖷 Fax	🗘 Reservations
⊕ Website	🏛 Dress code
🖅 E-mail	⊟ No credit cards
🖃 Admission fee	$ Price
☉ Open/closed	
times	**Other**
Ⓜ Subway	⇨ See also
✛ Directions or	☞ Take note
Map coordinates	🏌 Golf facilities

Restaurants

Unless we state otherwise, restaurants are open for lunch and dinner daily. We mention dress code only when there's a specific requirement and reservations only when they're essential or not accepted.

Credit Cards

The hotels and restaurants in this guide typically accept credit cards. If not, we'll say so.

EUGENE FODOR

Hungarian-born Eugene Fodor (1905–91) began his travel career as an interpreter on a French cruise ship. The experience inspired him to write *On the Continent* (1936), the first guidebook to receive annual updates and discuss a country's way of life as well as its sights. Fodor later joined the U.S. Army and worked for the OSS in World War II. After the war, he kept up his intelligence work while expanding his guidebook series. During the Cold War, many guides were written by fellow agents who understood the value of insider information. Today's guides continue Fodor's legacy by providing travelers with timely coverage, insider tips, and cultural context.

EXPERIENCE
NEW YORK CITY

NEW YORK CITY TODAY

The phrase "in a New York minute" exists for a reason: in this frenetic city, things really do change in a flash. With the constant ebb and flow, it can be hard to keep up. Here is just some of what New Yorkers are talking about.

Politics

As it always has, New York City remains a confluence of political ideals that lean toward the liberal side, while balancing the enormous egos and ambitions of its elected officials. In 2014, Democrat Bill de Blasio took over as mayor from Republican-turned-Independent Michael Bloomberg—the fourth-longest-serving NYC mayor in history, with 12 years in office. From the start, Mayor de Blasio faced challenges to employ his populist values and put into action his plans for economic equality across the five boroughs. He's had to pick up where billionaire Bloomberg left off, attempting to rein in some of the seemingly limitless large-scale real estate development and private-public partnerships his predecessor facilitated, while still keeping more favored policies that improved public transit, schools, and parks intact. It doesn't help that de Blasio and Governor Andrew Cuomo are reputed to have their own friction, leaving city and state leadership somewhat at odds with each other. But it's all a familiar song for New Yorkers, who have endured more than their fair share of political strife in both the long and short term. On the bright side, New Yorkers possess a strong survival instinct to get along with each other—it applies to politics just as much as to daily subway commutes.

Economy

A few quick positive economic indicators: New York is experiencing its biggest hotel expansion in a generation, attracting a host of new brands—from high-end boutiques to budget chains—all across the city. The city has 108 hotels in the pipeline to open by 2017, with about half of these properties slated for the outer boroughs—a key indicator of the recent visitor trend to visit, and stay in, boroughs beyond Manhattan. And tourists keep on coming: 2015 had a record number of visitors—over 58 million, up from the previous year's 56 million, and the city is expecting to exceed that number by the end of 2016.

WHAT'S NEW?

The Pier 57 development at West 15th Street in Hudson River Park originally opened in 1952 as a shipping terminal. Today, the pier's 12 acres are under construction with the intent to introduce new retail, dining, and entertainment programming, as well as the new Google headquarters, in 2017.

Lincoln Center will receive a $500 million gut renovation to create an exciting new concert venue to house the New York Philharmonic and to address evolving performances and audiences. Thanks to a new donor, the hall has a new name: David Geffen Hall. There are plans to begin construction in 2019.

The South Street Seaport is undergoing a $514 million makeover that includes replacing the existing complex at Pier 17 with a sleek new

Battle of the Boroughs

While visitors are discovering all things Brooklyn right now, New Yorkers are steadily refocusing their trend-spotting gaze on Queens. And it's no wonder—the borough has long-standing residential communities, cheap ethnic eats, established attractions like MoMA PS1, the second-biggest Chinatown in the country, Long Island City's skyline views, and a hop-skip-jump subway ride to Midtown. Add less-expensive-than-Manhattan (and Brooklyn) hotel rooms and rents, the current and projected development boom, and proposed projects like the QueensWay (aka "the Queens High Line"), and it seems Queens is where it's at for 2017, 2018, and beyond.

The Arts

Some of the biggest movers and shakers in the New York art scene will be moving and/or shaking off dust after recent renovations, perhaps suggesting that the art world will be more focused on exhibition spaces than the exhibitions themselves. In 2015, the Whitney Museum of American Art debuted its state-of-the-art new space in the Meatpacking District, complete with terraces opening onto the High Line and stunning views of the Hudson.

Meanwhile, the Metropolitan Museum of Art opened the Met Breuer in spring 2016 inside the Whitney's old digs to display its growing collection of contemporary art as it refines plans to gut-renovate its Modern Wing. The Tenement Museum is expanding to re-create the life of immigrants in New York post–World War II, expected to debut in summer 2017. The American Museum of Natural History is planning a six-story addition to improve navigation and add facilities for research and education, while the Lowline is gaining steam to open in 2020 as the city's only "underground park" inside a converted historic trolley terminal.

---

retail and dining complex, featuring a 60,000-square-foot landscaped rooftop. The reopening is scheduled for summer of 2017.

Coney Island's New York Aquarium is open but currently undergoing a $150 million renovation. New features will include a roof deck and a walk-through coral tunnel with sharks swimming overhead. It's set to open in 2017.

Staten Island is hoping to become a tourist destination as it redevelops its waterfront to include a mall, a giant observation wheel, an open-air pedestrian boardwalk, restaurants, and a hotel. The first spin on the Wheel is scheduled for mid-2017.

PLANNER

When to Go

New York City weather is a study in extremes. Much of winter brings bone-chilling winds and an occasional traffic-snarling snowfall, but you're just as likely to experience mild afternoons sandwiched by frigid temperatures.

In late spring and early summer, streets fill with parades and street fairs, and free outdoor performances pop up from river to river. Late August is sweltering, sometimes bringing subway station temperatures over 100°F (thankfully the trains themselves are climate-controlled). This is why autumn brings palpable excitement, with stunning yellow-and-bronze foliage complementing the dawn of a new cultural season. Between October and May, museums mount major exhibitions, most Broadway shows open, and opera, ballet, and concert seasons begin.

Getting Around

On Foot. The best way to explore New York is on foot. No matter what neighborhood you're headed to, you'll get a better sense of it by wandering around; you can check out the architecture, pop into cool-looking shops and cafés, and observe the walk-and-talk of the locals. And if you get lost, New Yorkers are actually very helpful with directions.

By Bike. Since Citi Bike's bike-sharing program rolled out in 2013, ridership has gradually increased and New York City's program now boasts the largest fleet of bikes in the nation—with plans for the system to double in size by 2017. The city is slowly acclimating to this popular new mode of transportation (both with its bike lanes and attitudes), but it's still no Amsterdam—yet. Ride off-peak if possible, keep out of Midtown, and stay alert at all times.

By Public Transportation. New York's subway system is probably the most efficient and cost-effective way to get around, and it's one of few in the world that runs 24 hours a day. The subway is safe, but be smart: try to avoid riding alone (especially late at night) and stand near others on the platform or by a stairwell.

If you prefer to stay above ground, and you're not in a rush, consider taking a bus. They're particularly good if you need to travel crosstown in Manhattan, plus they're all equipped with real-time GPS to track when the next bus arrives at each stop (check out the website: ⊕ *bustime. mta.info*). What a city bus lacks in efficiency (especially at rush hour), it makes up for in people-watching and city views.

By Taxi. If you'd rather be comfy than thrifty, hail a yellow cab. You'll also spot some apple-green "Boro Taxis" that service the outer boroughs and therefore won't make pickups south of East 96th Street or West 110th. A taxi is available if the center panel of the roof light is lit and the side panels are dark. It's best to give your destination address using cross streets: ask to be taken to "55th and Madison" rather than "545 Madison." Avoid trying to hail a cab between 4 and 4:30 pm, when drivers change shifts. And remember that the subway is often faster than a cab, especially when it rains or during rush hour.

E-hail Car Services. Uber, Lyft, Gett, and SheRides are some of the app-based car services available in Manhattan. ⇨ *For more information about getting around, check out the Travel Smart chapter.*

A Guide to the Grid

The map of Manhattan is, for the most part, easy to follow: north of 14th Street, streets are laid out in a numbered grid pattern. Numbered streets run east and west (crosstown), and broad avenues, most of them also numbered, run north (uptown) and south (downtown). The main exception is Broadway, which runs the entire length of Manhattan on a diagonal. Below 14th Street, street patterns get somewhat askew. In the West Village, West 4th Street intersects West 11th Street, Greenwich Street runs roughly parallel to Greenwich Avenue, and Leroy Street turns into St. Luke's Place for one block and then becomes Leroy again. There's an East Broadway and a West Broadway, both of which run north–south, and neither of which is an extension of Broadway, leaving even locals scratching their heads.

Street Smarts

You'll look and probably feel less conspicuous if you replace paper maps with apps. If you have a smartphone or tablet, download a subway map app from the MTA's website to help you plan your trip (by fastest route or fewest train changes), find nearby stations, and stay up-to-date on service disruptions. Most NYC attractions have their own apps to help you make the most of your time, so download accordingly before you visit. Even better, download just one app—the Fodor's NYC app—for attraction overviews and suggestions of what's nearby.

New York City is a safe metropolis, but it's still a city, so keep flashy jewelry out of sight on the street, and keep your extra cash and credit cards in your hotel safe.

When in bars or restaurants, don't hang your purse or bag on the back of a chair.

Expect to have yourself and your possessions inspected thoroughly in such places as museums, sports stadiums, and major attractions. Police officers reserve the right to check your bags before you pass through a subway turnstile.

We suggest politely ignoring panhandlers on streets and subways, people who offer to hail you a cab, and limousine and gypsy-cab drivers who (illegally) offer rides.

Opening Hours

Subways and buses run around the clock, as do plenty of restaurants. Some shops and services have longer hours than you'll find elsewhere in the United States, so you can get late-night groceries, buy souvenirs, or even get your nails done. In general, you can safely assume that most shops are open seven days a week, from about 10 to 7 or 8 Monday through Saturday, and from noon to 6 on Sunday. Bars generally close at either 2 or 4 am, though some after-hours clubs are open later.

Money-Saving Tips

Consider buying a CityPass, a group of tickets to six top-notch attractions in New York: the Empire State Building, the Guggenheim Museum or Top of the Rock, the American Museum of Natural History, the Metropolitan Museum of Art (including the Cloisters), Circle Line Cruises or admission to Liberty and Ellis islands, and the 9/11 Memorial & Museum or the *Intrepid* Sea, Air & Space Museum. The $114 pass, which saves you almost half the cost of each individual ticket (and all that time on ticket lines), is good for nine days from first use.

Sign up for social-discount shopping sites like Groupon, Gilt City, Amazon Local, and LivingSocial a month before your visit to New York to score discounts on everything from trendy restaurants and clubs to beauty treatments and attractions.

WHAT'S WHERE

Numbers refer to chapters.

2 **Lower Manhattan.** The Financial District, NY Harbor, and TriBeCa. Heavy-duty landmarks anchor the southern tip of Manhattan, including Wall Street and the waterfront parks of Battery Park City. Ferry terminals dispatch boats to Staten Island, Governors Island, Ellis Island, and the Statue of Liberty. The the 9/11 Memorial & Museum, One World Trade Center, and the Brooklyn Bridge are also found here.

3 **SoHo, NoLIta, Little Italy, and Chinatown.** Luxe shops dominate in SoHo these days, while NoLIta, to the east, has lots of boutiques and restaurants. Little Italy is a shrinking zone of touristy eateries (though some maintain old-school authenticity). Farther south, Chinatown teems with street vendors selling knockoff handbags and side streets with Chinese herb shops and dim-sum joints.

4 **The East Village and the Lower East Side.** Once a gritty neighborhood of artists and punks, the East Village is now a gentrified melting pot of NYU students, young professionals, and old-timers, but it still feels like a neighborhood. You'll find some of the best people- and pooch-watching from a bench in Tompkins Square Park. The once seedy, now trendy Lower East Side has live-music clubs, indie clothing shops, and wine bars.

5 **Greenwich Village and the West Village.** Artists with rent-controlled apartments, out-and-proud gays, and university students still live in the Village, but because those town houses have become so expensive, residents also include wealthy media moguls, celebrities, and socialites. From 14th Street south to Houston (pronounced *how-ston* here), and from the Hudson River east to 5th Avenue, the blocks are a jumble of jazz clubs, restaurants, former speakeasies, and rainbow flags.

6 **Chelsea and the Meatpacking District.** With hundreds of galleries in a seven-block radius, Chelsea is still the center of the city's contemporary-art scene, even if real estate development has forced some galleries to relocate elsewhere in the city or to Brooklyn. To the south, the Meatpacking District has evolved into a swanky clubbing and restaurant scene by night and—with the High Line, the new Whitney Museum of American Art, and high-end boutiques—a prime daytime destination too.

7 **Union Square, the Flatiron District, and Gramercy Park.** Bustling Union Square Park hosts the city's best greenmarket. On the 14th Street edge are broad steps where break dancers and other performers busk for onlookers. Nearby, private and elegant Gramercy Park is surrounded by storied mansions and town houses.

WHAT'S WHERE

8 Midtown East and Murray Hill. Midtown from 5th Avenue to the East River is the refined big sister of flashy Midtown West, with grand hotels, posh shopping, the Chrysler Building, and Grand Central Terminal. Murray Hill is a mix of quiet tree- and town-house-lined streets and attractions like the Empire State Building and the Morgan Library.

9 Midtown West. Head to 42nd Street to see Times Square in all its neon and mega-screen glory. Towering office buildings line Broadway up to Columbus Circle at the edge of Central Park. At Rockefeller Center are the famous ice rink and Christmas tree (in season), and nearby are swank shops like Saks and Bergdorf Goodman.

10 The Upper East Side. The Upper East Side is home to more millionaires than any other part of the city. Tucked into this stretch of 5th Avenue are the Museum Mile and Madison Avenue's haute boutiques.

11 The Upper West Side with Central Park and the Cloisters. Wide sidewalks and ornate prewar buildings set the tone, and the American Museum of Natural History and Lincoln Center are big draws. Nearby is the pastoral heart of New York, Central Park, the place to come to escape the bustle of the city with its small zoo, sports fields, carousel, and even a castle. Much farther north is the Cloisters, a branch of the Metropolitan Museum of Art housing medieval works in a reconstructed monastery.

12 Harlem. A hotbed of African American and Hispanic American culture for almost a century, Harlem still sizzles. The brownstone-lined blocks are being refurbished, boutiques and restaurants are popping up, and a few music venues from the 1920s and '30s are still in full swing.

13 Brooklyn. New York's largest borough counts among its stars Prospect Park, the Brooklyn Museum, Brooklyn Botanic Garden, and Brooklyn Academy of Music. Its distinctive neighborhoods include Brooklyn Heights, Williamsburg, DUMBO, Park Slope, Coney Island, and Brighton Beach.

14 Queens, the Bronx, and Staten Island. Queens is known for its ethnic communities and cuisine, Arthur Ashe Stadium, and Citi Field. The Bronx may be best known for Yankee Stadium, but the New York Botanical Garden and Bronx Zoo also score home runs. Staten Island's best-known feature might be the ferry, but there are reasons to stick around, including a children's museum and New York City's only historic town and farm: Historic Richmond Town.

The Cloisters
W. 123rd St.
W. 122nd St.
W. 120th St.
W. 118th St.
W. 116th St.
W. 114th St.
W. 112th St.
W. 110th St.
W. 108th St.
W. 106th St.
W. 104th St.
W. 102nd St.
W. 100th St.
W. 98th St.
W. 96th St.
W. 94th St.
W. 92nd St.
W. 90th St.
W. 88th St.
W. 86th St.
W. 84th St.
W. 82nd St.
W. 80th St.
W. 78th St.
W. 76th St.
W. 74th St.
W. 72nd St.
W. 70th St.
W. 68th St.
W. 66th St.
W. 64th St.
W. 62nd St.
W. 61st St.
W. 59th St.
W. 57th St.
W. 55th St.
W. 54th St.
W. 52nd St.
W. 50th St.
W. 48th St.
W. 46th St.
W. 44th St.
W. 42nd St.
W. 40th St.
W. 38th St.
W. 36th St.
W. 34th St.
W. 32nd St.

Henry Hudson Parkway

Hudson River

Morningside Park

Riverside Park

Manhattan Ave.
Amsterdam Ave.
Columbus Ave.
Broadway
West End Ave.
Riverside Dr.

Frederick Douglass Blvd. (8th Ave.)
St. Nicholas Ave.
6th Ave.
Central Park W.
Central Park W.

HARLEM

12

Marcus Garvey Park

EAST HARLEM

Harlem Meer

UPPER WEST SIDE

11

CENTRAL PARK

Jacqueline Kennedy Onassis Reservoir

The Lake

American Museum of Natural History

Metropolitan Museum of Art

E. 123rd St.
E. 121st St.
E. 119th St.
E. 117th St.
E. 110th St.
E. 109th St.
E. 107th St.
E. 105th St.
E. 103rd St.
E. 101st St.
E. 99th St.
E. 97th St.
E. 95th St.
E. 93rd St.
E. 91st St.
E. 89th St.
E. 87th St.
E. 86th St.
E. 85th St.
E. 83rd St.
E. 81st St.
E. 79th St.
E. 77th St.
E. 75th St.
E. 73rd St.
E. 72nd St.
E. 71st St.
E. 69th St.
E. 67th St.
E. 65th St.
E. 63rd St.
E. 61st St.
E. 59th St.
E. 57th St.

W. 118th St.
W. 115th St.
W. 113rd St.
W. 111th St.

5th Ave.
Madison Ave.
Park Ave.
Lexington Ave.
Third Ave.
Second Ave.
First Ave.
York Ave.
Fifth Ave.
Madison Ave.
Park Ave.
Lexington Ave.
Third Ave.

UPPER EAST SIDE

10

FDR Dr.

Roosevelt Island

Queensboro Br.

Sutton Pl.

MIDTOWN WEST

Time Warner Center
Columbus Circle
Central Park South

Lincoln Center

Ninth Ave.
Eighth Ave.
Seventh Ave.
Avenue of the Americas ("Sixth Ave.")
Broadway
Tenth Ave.
Eleventh Ave.

MIDTOWN EAST

Rockefeller Center

9

Times Square

Bryant Park

Public Library

Grand Central Terminal

E. 55th St.
E. 53rd St.
E. 51st St.
E. 49th St.
E. 47th St.
E. 45th St.
E. 43rd St.
E. 41st St.
E. 39th St.
E. 37th St.

8

MURRAY HILL

West Side Highway

Javits Convention Center

Port Authority Bus Terminal

Madison Square Garden

Penn Station

Empire State Building

Herald Square

Fifth Ave.
Madison Ave.
Park Ave.
Second Ave.
First Ave.

East River

0   1/2 mile
0   800 meters

THE BRONX
14

Westchester
Nassau

QUEENS
14

MANHATTAN

Hudson River

NEW JERSEY
14

BROOKLYN
13

STATEN ISLAND
14

ATLANTIC OCEAN

NEW YORK CITY
TOP ATTRACTIONS

Metropolitan Museum of Art

(A) The largest art museum in the Western Hemisphere, the Met is a mecca for art lovers. Treasures from all over the world and every era of human creativity make up its collection. If you need a breather, you can always retire to the Temple of Dendur or the rooftop café.

Times Square

(B) Times Square is the most frenetic part of New York City: a cacophony of languages and flashing lights, outré street performers, shoulder-to-shoulder crowds, and back-to-back billboards. These days it's also a pedestrian-friendly zone, so you won't have to take your eyes off the excitement to watch for traffic.

Empire State Building

(C) It may not be the tallest building in New York anymore (One World Trade Center now claims that title), but its status as most iconic will never change. Take in the panoramic views of the city from its observatories, or just enjoy it from afar—after dark it's illuminated by colored lights that correspond to different holidays and tributes.

Museum of Modern Art

(D) Airy and spacious, with soaring, high-ceiling galleries suffused with natural light and masterpieces that include Warhol's *Campbell's Soup Cans* and van Gogh's *Starry Night,* this one-of-a-kind museum designed by Japanese architect Yoshio Taniguchi is as famous for its architecture as for its collections.

Brooklyn Bridge

(E) New York's most famous bridge first connected Manhattan and Brooklyn in 1883, and it still serves many thousands of pedestrians, vehicles, skaters, and bicyclists a day. Crossing its span is an essential New York experience.

Statue of Liberty

(F) Presented to the United States in 1886 as a gift from France, Lady Liberty is a near-universal symbol of freedom and democracy, standing 152 feet tall atop an 89-foot pedestal on Liberty Island.

American Museum of Natural History

(G) The towering reassembled dinosaur skeletons that greet you when you enter this museum might stop you in your tracks, but there's much more to see, including exhibits of ancient civilizations, the live Butterfly Conservatory (October–May), a hall of oceanic creatures overseen by a 94-foot model of a blue whale, and space shows at the Rose Center for Earth and Space.

Central Park

The literal and spiritual center of Manhattan, Central Park has 843 acres of meandering paths, tranquil lakes, ponds, and open meadows. For equestrians, softball and soccer players, strollers, skaters, bird-watchers, boaters, picnickers, and outdoor performers, it's an oasis of fresh air and greenery amid the city's hustle.

9/11 Memorial and Museum

The National September 11 Memorial and Museum at the World Trade Center is a moving tribute to the lives lost on 9/11. The free memorial features two large waterfalls and recessed pools, marking the footprints of the Twin Towers. The belowground museum commemorates the lives of those lost through personal artifacts, multimedia displays, and first-person accounts.

The High Line

A botanical garden, a bridge to nowhere, a local hangout, and a work of art using the city's architecture, greenery, and people as part of its composition, this once-abandoned railroad track rises above the west side of Chelsea.

LIKE A LOCAL

New Yorkers love this city, and with good reason: there's no other place like it on earth. Living here can be challenging, from high rents to simply battling crowds for a table at weekend brunch. But locals have plenty of tricks up their collective sleeve that you too can enjoy.

Getting Around

Hit the ground walking

Spend a day in a New Yorker's shoes and you'll quickly realize that New Yorkers walk, and they walk fast. Pounding the pavement is often the fastest way to get around, but remember: move quickly. If you can't keep up the pace or you need to check your smartphone or take a photo, step to the side of the sidewalk and get out of the way.

Take the subway

If you truly want to look like a local you'll skip the double-decker bus tours and get yourself a MetroCard—it's cheaper than a cab and usually faster. The subway runs 24 hours a day, seven days a week. There are maps posted in all stations, but locals are more than happy to show off their knowledge if you need directions. Even seasoned New Yorkers ask for or confirm directions, so don't be shy. If you're traveling with a smartphone, apps like NYC Subway Map will help you figure out the best route. As for safety, the same advice applies here as to traveling in any major city: be alert, watch your bag, and avoid traveling solo late at night.

E-hail a taxi cab

Many visitors to the city expect to find locals summoning taxis with a loud whistle or a brash "Hey, Taxi!" But in reality, locals prefer to hail cabs with a raised arm or with a smartphone app. Several e-hail services are available in the city, but Uber and Lyft are the most popular. Once you've signed up, a simple tap will search for a car and track it in real time; you pay with a saved credit card. Uber is the best-known service, but its "surge pricing" for high-traffic times like holidays and inclement weather have not endeared it to locals (the practice may soon be banned). If you're a woman traveling solo, or you prefer a female driver, you can hail a car from the city's newest e-hailing app—and the only car service app tailored to the needs of women—SheRides.

Food and Drink

Drink decent coffee

There might be a chain coffee shop on every corner in New York City, but you won't find many locals there. The so-called "city that never sleeps" is fueled with coffee, but not just any coffee. Locals are particular (some might say snobby) about coffee, so wait those few extra minutes for the best freshly roasted beans and pour-over brews. Join discerning locals at gourmet hot spots like Blue Bottle Coffee, Everyman Espresso, Joe the Art of Coffee, La Colombe, Ninth Street Espresso (which has locations other than 9th Street), Stumptown, and Third Rail Coffee. Most offer the added bonus of homemade pastries and treats.

Follow that truck

New Yorkers have an appetite for the food trucks parked around the city, offering everything from Korean tacos and falafel to vegan doughnuts and Belgian waffles. Twitter feeds and blogs track their whereabouts (try ⊕ *NYCTruckFood.com*).

Support local farmers

New Yorkers do eat in on occasion, and when they do, they shop local. Local greenmarkets like the Union Square farmers' market offer a range of fresh fruit and vegetables, as well as locally sourced meats, fish, and specialty foods. If you don't have a kitchen to prepare a meal, shop for the makings of a great picnic. Join hungry locals to shop the stands on Monday, Wednesday, Friday, and Saturday from 8 am to 6 pm.

Skip the food fair

Beloved food festivals like Smorgasburg and Hester Street Fair are a huge local draw, especially on warm summer weekends. But now that the word is out and the lines are long, locals are heading back indoors to the city's new crop of highly curated food courts. Indoor markets like Gotham West Market, Gansevoort Market, Chelsea Market, and Hudson Eats feature artisan vendors and affordable meals, and sometimes live music and extended hours.

Do brunch

Weekend brunch is a lifestyle here, so brace yourself for an ultimate foodie experience featuring eggs Benedict, bagels with cream cheese and smoked salmon, fruit-filled pancakes, decadent French toast, gourmet burgers, or fried chicken and waffles, accompanied by mimosas, Bloody Marys, or specialty brunch cocktails. Most places start serving at 11 am, and the more popular spots will have a line, so either plan to wait or get there early. These days, just about every restaurant worth its menu serves brunch on the weekends, even if it doesn't serve lunch during the week.

Entertainment

Take in a show

You won't cross paths with many locals in Times Square, but New Yorkers are not so jaded as to ignore the wealth of the city's theatrical and musical offerings—they just don't like paying full price for the experience. Do as locals do and find

discounted tickets at social buying sites like Groupon, Gilt City, and Living Social, or score deals at discount ticket booth TKTS (though you'll make better use of your time if you line up at the less-trafficked booths in Brooklyn or South Street Seaport than the one in Times Square). ■ TIP➔ Use the free TKTS app for up-to-date ticket availability at each of the city's three booths. You can also try to score discounted rush tickets: show up at the theater when the box office opens on the day of the performance (some of these deals are limited to students—be sure to look up the ticket policy in advance); the most popular shows offer rush tickets as a random lottery, so actually getting to see a show isn't guaranteed Otherwise, we favor the Off-Off-Broadway experience, staying in the know with sites like ⊕ *OffOffOnline.com.*

Support the arts

Take advantage of the city's amazing museums, but make like a local and go during off-hours, like weekday mornings, to avoid the crowds. If you visit regularly, become a member of your favorite museums (as much to skip lines as to support the arts). Many museums have free or pay-as-you-wish nights (or days), but they can be very crowded. Another popular (and free) local art activity is skipping the major museums altogether and hopping from gallery to gallery in Chelsea or SoHo. In Chelsea, Thursday nights are usually when the galleries open their doors to art lovers (often with free wine and snacks).

NEW YORK CITY SPORTS TEAMS

No city in the world can claim such a long and storied sports heritage as the Big Apple. Indeed, even the term "Big Apple" is rooted in sports history, as a reference to 1920s horse racing in and around the city. With more than a dozen professional sports teams—many of them playing in major leagues—this town is downright fanatical about competition, not to mention being home to some of the greatest all-time players and sporting events: Jackie Robinson and Babe Ruth made baseball history, and Roger Federer won five straight U.S. Open championships; the 1958 NFL championship is considered "the greatest game ever played." There are big-time sports happening almost every day in the five boroughs. And even if you can't catch an event live, you can surely find it playing in a local bar, where you may encounter fans unlike those anywhere else, sports-logo tattoos and all.

Baseball

Few teams are more synonymous with a city than the Yankees are with New York. The team has one of baseball's best all-time win records, as well as the best regular-season win percentage (.569 as of 2015). They play at Yankee Stadium in the Bronx, and their famous players include Yogi Berra, Joe DiMaggio, Lou Gehrig, Reggie Jackson, Derek Jeter, Roger Maris, and Babe Ruth. They currently have a total 27 World Series titles, and 40 American League pennants. Over in Queens, the New York Mets play at Citi Field, with a proud fan base and legacy all their own. Famous past players include Dwight Gooden, Keith Hernandez, Willie Mays, and Darryl Strawberry. While they don't boast quite as many titles as the Yankees (only two World Series championships and five National League pennants), they're considered the

city's scrappy underdog, and all of New York cheered when they made it to the World Series in fall 2015 (eventually losing to the Kansas City Royals). Although the two teams are in different leagues, they play each other several times a year in what's known as a subway series, making the inter-city rivalry as fierce as ever.

Basketball

In addition to witnessing the **New York Knicks** in action, catch an NBA game at Madison Square Garden from October to June to get an eyeful of the celebrities often in attendance. The Knicks 2015–16 season left a little to be desired, but with two NBA championships, eight conference titles, and greats like Carmelo Anthony, Patrick Ewing, and Walt Frasier on their past roster, it's hard to escape the team's legacy in the basketball world and throughout the city. But since 2012, they've had rivals in the city, with the **Brooklyn Nets** returning to NYC's most populous borough. Games are played in the eye-catching, green-roofed Barclays Center, with former team-owner Jay-Z often in attendance at the games.

Football

Loyalty is a big thing with NYC sports fans, and some **New York Giants** fans are so loyal they even claim to bleed Giants' blue, whereas **New York Jets** fans' rallying cry "J-E-T-S Jets Jets Jets!" is so mighty that if you listen closely on game days, you can almost hear it from across the Hudson River. Both teams play in New Jersey, at MetLife Stadium, from September through February. The Giants have won four Super Bowls (most recently in 2011 against the New England Patriots) and 11 conference titles, led by such players as Eli Manning, Michael Strahan, and Lawrence Taylor. The lower-key

Jets, meanwhile, are known as the city's underdog, with only one Super Bowl title (all the way back in 1968) and four division titles. They still rack up big names like Curtis Martin, Don Maynard, and Joe Namath.

Hockey

Back in 1928, the **New York Rangers** were the first American team to win the NHL's championship Stanley Cup, and today's fans are just as eager as back then to get it back, when they play each season at Madison Square Garden. Famous players like Brian Leetch, Henrik Lundqvist, and Mark Messier have helped the team win a total of two Stanley Cups and two conference titles. Meanwhile, the **New York Islanders** relocated from their suburban Long Island stadium to their new home at Brooklyn's Barclays Center in 2015. Since they haven't won a Stanley Cup since the early 1980s, maybe Brooklyn will help them get their mojo back. Their pre-1980s glories include four Stanley Cups and five conference titles.

Soccer

Soccer fans can choose between the city's two Major League Soccer teams during its March through October season: the **New York Red Bulls** and **New York City Football Club,** who began to sway fair-weather fans upon their 2013 formation by playing in the hallowed baseball grounds of Yankee Stadium. Meanwhile, devoted Bulls fans get to enjoy the soccer-specific Red Bull Arena in Harrison, New Jersey, near Newark.

Other Sports

If you can't pick a team, consider a less contentious sport, like tennis—the **U.S. Open** brings the best in tennis to the USTA Billie Jean King National Tennis Center in Queens in late summer. You could also try to catch a matchup in smaller-scale college games, rugby, minor-league baseball, or even **Gotham Girls** roller derby. Or just plan an early November trip to witness the NYC Marathon, the largest marathon in the world, with more than 50,000 runners from around the globe.

SITTING IN A TV AUDIENCE

Tickets to tapings of TV shows are free, but can be hard to get, especially on short notice. Most shows accept advance requests by email, phone, or online—but for the most popular shows, you might have to wait a few months. Same-day standby tickets are often available, but be prepared to wait in line for several hours, sometimes starting at 5 or 6 am, depending on how hot the show is, or the wattage of that day's celebrity guests. Remember that standby tickets do not guarantee a seat in the audience.

The Shows

The Daily Show with Trevor Noah. Jon Stewart may have moved on, but host Trevor Noah is glad to welcome you to free tapings of *The Daily Show* just like his predecessor did. Reservations can be made online only, with tickets released gradually for future shows, so check the website often to RSVP for your preferred date. Only the person whose name is on the reservation is allowed in, along with a photo I.D., and all audience members must be at least 18. The big caveat is that a reservation doesn't guarantee entry, so get in line early. Check-in starts at 2:30 pm and ends at 4 pm. ⊠ *733 11th Ave., Midtown West* ⊕ *www.cc.com/shows/the-daily-show-with-trevor-noah* ⊠ *Free* Ⓜ *A, C, E to 50th St.*

Good Morning America. Robin Roberts and George Stephanopoulos host this early-morning news and entertainment show. It airs live, weekdays from 7 to 9 am, and ticket requests (required only if you want a studio tour after the show) should be made online four to six months in advance. Gather before 7 am on the corner of West 44th Street and Broadway to participate in outdoor segments. ⊠ *7 Times Sq., 44th St. and Broadway, Midtown West* ⊕ *www.abcnews.*

go.com/GMA/part-times-square-audience/story?id=12883468 Ⓜ *1, 2, 3, 7, N, Q, R, S to Times Sq.–42nd St.*

Late Night with Seth Meyers. *Saturday Night Live* alum Seth Meyers took the reins as host of *Late Night* on NBC in 2014, when former host Jimmy Fallon departed for the *Tonight Show*. Tickets are available online up to two months in advance. Same-day standby tickets are handed out at 9 am at the NBC Experience Store (49th Street entrance). If all else fails, monologue-rehearsal tickets are available at the NBC Experience Store at 12:30. Guests must be 16 or older to be in the audience. ⊠ *30 Rockefeller Plaza, Midtown West* ☎ *212/664–3056* ⊕ *www.showclix.com/event/latenightseth* Ⓜ *B, D, F, M to 47th–50th Sts./Rockefeller Center.*

The Late Show with Stephen Colbert. After hosting the *Late Show* for 22 years, David Letterman passed the torch to former *Colbert Report* host, Stephen Colbert, in 2015. While Colbert's fictional conservative persona did not follow him to his new gig at the Ed Sullivan Theater, his loyal audience did, so expect competition for tickets. The show is usually taped daily at 5:30 pm; check the website and the show's social media for updated details and new ticket releases. Standby tickets are available on a lottery system; be there at 1 pm to add your name to the list, and return at 4:15 to see if you got lucky. You must be 18 or older to sit in the audience. ⊠ *Ed Sullivan Theater, 1697 Broadway, between 53rd and 54th Sts., Midtown West* ☎ *212/975–5853* ⊕ *www.colbertnewshub.com/ticket-information-2* Ⓜ *1 to 50th St.; C, E to 50th St.; B, D, E to 7th Ave.*

Live! with Kelly and Michael Sparks fly on this morning program, which books an eclectic roster of cohosts and guests. Tickets are available online about six weeks in advance. Standby tickets become available weekdays at 7 am at ABC Studios. Children under 10 are not permitted in the audience. ⊠ *7 Lincoln Sq., between W 67th St. and Columbus Ave., Midtown West* ☎ *212/456–3054* ⊕ *livekellyandmichael.dadt.com* Ⓜ *1 to 66th St.–Lincoln Center.*

Saturday Night Live. After four decades of laughs, *SNL* continues to push buttons, nurture comedic talents, and captivate audiences—all "live from New York." Standby tickets (only one per person) are distributed at 7 am on the day of the show at the West 49th Street entrance to 30 Rockefeller Plaza. You may ask for a ticket for either the dress rehearsal (8 pm) or the live show (11:30 pm). Requests for advance tickets (two per applicant) must be submitted by email only in August to *snltickets@nbcuni.com*; recipients are determined by lottery. You must be 16 or older to sit in the audience. ⊠ *NBC Studios, 30 Rockefeller Plaza, between W. 49th and W. 50th Sts., Midtown West* ☎ *212/664–3056* ⊕ *www.nbc.com/tickets* Ⓜ *B, D, F, M to 47th–50th Sts./Rockefeller Center.*

Today. The *Today Show* doesn't have a studio audience, but if you get yourself to the corner of Rockefeller Center and West 49th Street before dawn, with posterboard and markers (fun signs always get camera time), comfortable shoes (you'll be on your feet for hours), and a smiley, fun attitude, you might get on camera. America's first morning talk-news show airs weekdays from 7 to 10 am in the glass-enclosed, ground-level NBC studio. ⊠ *Rockefeller Plaza, W. 49th St., Midtown West* ⊕ *www.today.com* Ⓜ *B, D, F, M to 47th–50th Sts./Rockefeller Center.*

The Tonight Show Starring Jimmy Fallon. In early 2014, *Saturday Night Live* veteran Jimmy Fallon packed up his impressions and sketches, his roster of star friends, and his house band (the Roots) and moved from *Late Night* to the *Tonight Show*, filling the big comedic shoes of Jay Leno and Johnny Carson before him. He also moved the show back to New York, where it had resided until 1972. Visit the website to reserve free tickets; they're released during the first week of the month prior to the show. ■TIP➔ Each month's ticket release date and time is announced exclusively on the show's Twitter feed (@FallonTonight). ⊠ *30 Rockefeller Plaza, Studio 6B, Midtown West* ☎ *212/664–3506* ⊕ *www.tonightshow.com/tickets* Ⓜ *B, D, F, M to 47th–50th Sts./Rockefeller Center.*

FREE AND CHEAP

Sometimes it seems like everything in New York costs too much, but in fact the city has tons of free or cheap things to do—you just need to know where to look for them. Note that NYC is at its most free in summer when there are all sorts of outdoor events, but you can find a "wealth" of freebies all year round.

Free Art
The $25 admission fee to the **Metropolitan Museum of Art**, the $22 fee to the **American Museum of Natural History**, and the $16 admission to the **Brooklyn Museum** are actually *suggested* donations. Smaller donations may get some eye-rolling from the cashier, but it's a small price to pay for access to world-famous works of art. The **Museum at FIT**, "the most fashionable museum in the city" at the Fashion Institute of Technology, is home to a collection of some 50,000 garments and accessories from the 18th century to the present. It's free, off the beaten museum path, and fabulous. Another less trafficked—and free—gem, the **American Folk Art Museum**, features traditional folk art as well as contemporary works by self-taught artists. The museum's diverse collection includes everything from drawings, paintings, and ceramics to mummylike sculptures, decorative furniture, and a beautifully stitched quilt made by female slaves on a Southern plantation. The **National Museum of the American Indian (Smithsonian Institution)**, in a majestic Beaux Arts building on the south side of Bowling Green in Lower Manhattan, is a small museum (by New York standards), but it offers free admission as well as free music and dance performances and an extensive permanent collection of textiles, ceremonial objects, and decorative arts. Decidedly on the beaten path, and for good reason, **MoMA** is free on Friday between 4 and 8 pm, when the

$25 entry fee is waived. Arrive as close to 4 as you can, and once you get your ticket (the line is long but fast), avoid the crowds by working your way down from the fifth floor. If you want to avoid the crowds altogether—and get ahead of the art game—take a gallery crawl in and out of the scores of **galleries in Chelsea** for free access to up-and-coming and superstar artists alike. Unlike major museums, galleries are rarely crowded (except for Thursday, when they often host openings with free wine and cheese). You'll also find trendy art scenes in SoHo, and Williamsburg and Bushwick, in Brooklyn.

Free Entertainment
If you don't see enough movie stars wandering around New York City, you can catch them on a big screen—under the stars—with a free summer flick. There are free screenings all across the five boroughs in summer, from Brooklyn Bridge Park to Bronx Terminal Market (⊕ *www. nycgovparks.org/events/free_summer_ movies*). In Manhattan, take your blanket and picnic basket to **Bryant Park**: a tradition since 1992, watching films alfresco surrounded by tall Midtown buildings is a summertime rite of passage for New Yorkers. Be prepared to stake out a good spot on the lawn early in the day. Movie schedules are posted at ⊕ *www. bryantpark.org*.

If you prefer live entertainment, catch tango dancers and jazz musicians outside Lincoln Center at the annual, free, monthlong **Out of Doors** festival, held in August. It includes more than 100 performances. You can also experience free music performances, film screenings, and artist conversations at Lincoln Center's **David Rubenstein Atrium**; check the online calendar before you visit. **Central Park**

SummerStage is your free ticket to big-name performers like Afrobeat bandleader Seun Kuti and Columbia University's own Vampire Weekend. There are also a few concert series in Brooklyn, most notably in Prospect Park for summer's **Celebrate Brooklyn!** festival.

Catch rising stars in music, drama, and dance at the **Juilliard School**'s free student concerts (check ⊕ *www.juilliard.edu* for a calendar of events). Free tickets are available at the Juilliard box office for theater performances; standby tickets are available an hour before the show.

One of the city's most beloved events (and the hottest free ticket in town) is **Shakespeare in the Park,** which usually features celebrities practicing their olde-English acting skills in outdoor performances in Central Park. Get in line very early at the Public Theater for a shot at tickets, or head to the Delacorte Theater in Central Park. ⊕ *www.shakespeareinthepark.org.*

Like your theater a little less scripted? Get gratis giggles at the **Upright Citizens Brigade Theatre**'s improv comedy shows, where professional comedians, including UCB cofounder and *Saturday Night Live* alumna Amy Poehler, are sprinkled in with amateurs during the performances. Many of the shows are just $5; some are free. ⊕ *www.ucbtheatre.com.*

Another way to save your pennies for dinner is to catch a free reading at one of the city's bookstores—big (Barnes & Noble) and small (Housing Works Bookstore Café). Or you can get your fix of free words at KGB in the East Village, where authors have been reading since 1993. In Brooklyn, Pete's Candy Store and Franklin Park (both bars) have reading series.

Free Rides

One of the best free rides in the city is on the **Staten Island Ferry.** A one-way trip takes 30 minutes and offers magnificent views of the Statue of Liberty, Ellis Island, and the southern tip of Manhattan—plus there's inexpensive beer and snacks. Note that you have to disembark at St. George Terminal in Staten Island before your return trip. Another cheap/sometimes-free ferry sure to (ahem) float your boat is the seven-minute ferry ride from Lower Manhattan to **Governors Island,** a 172-acre island oasis in the heart of New York Harbor. You can visit the former military base turned sculpture park and public playground daily from late May to late September to bike, picnic, wander forts, take in views of Lower Manhattan, and enjoy a variety of cultural offerings and festivals. Ferries are free on weekend mornings and $2 round-trip (for adults) on all weekday and weekend-afternoon ferries. Give your sea legs a rest and take to the sky for an almost-free aerial ride on the **Roosevelt Island Tramway.** For the price of a subway ride ($2.75), you can glide over the East River on the only commuter cable in North America and score stunning city views while you're at it. The trip takes only a few minutes (board at the East 59th Street and 2nd Avenue station) so you have plenty of time to explore Roosevelt Island and FDR Four Freedoms Park before you make the return trip.

NYC'S WATERFRONT PARKS

If Central Park makes you think, "Been there, done that," head to one of the city's many waterfront parks. Many New Yorkers are just now discovering some of these green getaways, too.

Battery Park City

Built on landfill jutting out into the Hudson River, Battery Park City is a high-rise residential neighborhood split in two by the World Financial Center and its marina. The Hudson River Park promenade borders Battery Park City along the West Side Highway. There are several reasonably priced outdoor restaurants with stunning views of the Statue of Liberty. If you have kids, don't miss the excellent Teardop Park, with its huge slide, and the park's newest attraction, SeaGlass, an aquatic-themed carousel ride that simulates a descent to the ocean's floor.

Getting Here

By subway: South Battery Park: 1, R to Rector Place; 4, 5 to Bowling Green. North Battery Park: 1, 2, 3, A, C to Chambers Street; E to World Trade Center. By bus: M9, M20, M22.

Brooklyn Bridge Park

Over in Brooklyn, a former industrial site running along a narrow stretch of Brooklyn waterfront from Vinegar Hill to Brooklyn Heights has been turned into a 1.3-mile-long park featuring grassy lawns, rocky outcrops, bike paths, playgrounds, sports fields, basketball courts, and a carousel. There are picnic areas, seasonal food stands by high-profile restaurants, music and film festivals in summer, water-taxi service to Governors Island, and thousands of visitors and locals taking advantage of it all. Perhaps the best feature of this new hipster destination is one that's been here all along: the picture-postcard views of the Brooklyn and Manhattan Bridges and the Manhattan skyline.

Getting Here

By subway: A, C to High Street; F to York Street. Instead of taking the subway, you could take a water taxi (⊕ www.nywatertaxi.com) to Fulton Ferry Landing, the East River Ferry (⊕ www.nywaterway.com) to Fulton Ferry Landing, or by walking across the Brooklyn Bridge.

The East River Park

This recently landscaped waterfront park, stretching from Montgomery Street to 12th Street along the Manhattan side of the East River, is one of the Lower East Side's best-kept secrets, with ball fields, bike paths, tennis courts, playgrounds, gardens, and picnic areas—along with impressive views of the Brooklyn skyline and the Williamsburg Bridge. You have to cross a footbridge over the FDR Drive to get to the park.

Getting Here

By subway: J, M, Z to Essex Street; F to 2nd Avenue.

Governors Island

A recent addition to the city's parks scene, this little island feels like a small town just 800 yards from the tip of Manhattan. Tourists love the unparalleled views of the New York Harbor and Lower Manhattan, and locals love the out-of-city experience. The 172-acre park, built in part from landfill from subway excavations, was a base for the U.S. Army and Coast Guard for almost two centuries. Until 2003, it was off-limits to the public, which could be why the 19th-century homes here are so well preserved. The island is open to the public daily from May to October, with programs including art showings, concerts, and family events. You can take a bike over on the ferry or rent one on the island. For more information, including updated ferry schedules and a calendar of activities, go to ⊕ *www.govisland.org.*

Getting Here

A $2 seven-minute ferry ride (free on weekend mornings) takes passengers to Governors Island from a dock at the restored, cast-iron Battery Maritime Building (10 South Street), next to the Staten Island Ferry. Get to the ferry by subway: 1 to South Ferry; 4, 5 to Bowling Green; or R to Whitehall Street. By bus: M1 (weekdays only), M6, M9, and M15.

The High Line

Once an elevated railroad track that serviced the long-ago factories along the lower west side, the High Line was converted into a park (really more of a promenade) that integrates landscaping with rail-inspired design and provides a fresh perspective on the city. Vegetation here includes 210 species of plants, trees, and shrubs intended to reflect the wild plants that flourished for decades after the tracks were abandoned in 1980. The park—30 feet above street level—is open between Gansevoort Street in the Meatpacking District and 34th Street in Midtown. Sweeping views of the Hudson River, an extended sight line of the Meatpacking District, and the Whitney Museum of American Art are the highlights. For information on tours, public programs, and a calendar of events, go to ⊕ *www.thehighline.org* or call ☎ *212/500–6035.* Note that the park is often extremely crowded, especially on afternoons and weekends.

Getting Here

The High Line is accessible at Gansevoort and every two blocks between 14th and 30th Streets with elevator access at 14th, 16th, 23rd, 30th, and 34th Streets (no

bikes allowed). It's two blocks west of the subway station at 14th Street and 8th Avenue, served by the A, C, E, and L. You can also take the C, E to 23rd Street and walk two blocks west. The 1, 2, 3 stops at 14th Street and 7th Avenue, three blocks away. By bus: M11 to Washington Street, M11 to 9th Avenue, M14 to 9th Avenue, M23 to 10th Avenue, M34 to 10th Avenue.

The Hudson River Park

This 5-mile greenway park hugs the Hudson River from 59th Street to Battery Park. Although the park has a unified design, it's divided into seven distinct sections that reflect the different Manhattan neighborhoods just across the West Side Highway. Along with refurbished piers with grass and trees, there are also attractions like the *Intrepid* Sea, Air & Space Museum at Pier 86 across from 46th Street. A few blocks south, the Circle Line and World Yacht offer boat tours of the Hudson. At Piers 96 and 40, the Downtown Boat House (⊕ *www.downtownboathouse.org*) offers free kayaking. There's a mammoth sports center, **Chelsea Piers**, between Piers 59 and 61, and a playground, mini-golf course, and beach volleyball court at Pier 25. The park also sponsors free tours and classes, including free fishing. For a calendar of events and activities, go to ⊕ *www. hudsonriverpark.org.* North of Hudson River Park is one of Manhattan's better-known parks, **Riverside Park.**

Getting Here

Hudson River Park is on the far west side of the city, adjacent to the West Side Highway. Crosstown buses at 14th, 23rd, and 42nd Streets will get you close, but you'll still have to walk a bit. It's worth it.

NEW YORK CITY WITH KIDS

From space shuttles to vintage trains, climbing walls to climbing coasters, not to mention zoos, parks, playgrounds, kid-centric shows, and more—the city that never sleeps has plenty of ways to tire out your kids.

Museums

There's a museum for every age, interest, and attention span in New York City. Some are aimed squarely at the younger set, but you shouldn't limit yourself or your kids to "children's" museums; most—especially the big players like MoMA, the Guggenheim, the Met, and the Whitney—offer programs to engage younger visitors (just ask at the admission desk). That said, sometimes toddlers want play places designed specifically for them, like the play center and interactive exhibits created for the under-five set at the **Children's Museum of Manhattan** and the arts-and-crafts rooms and ball pit at the **Children's Museum of the Arts**. The **American Museum of Natural History** is a top choice for kids of all ages and interests, visitors and locals alike: the giant dinosaurs and the huge blue whale alone are worth the trip, as is the live Butterfly Conservatory (October through May). You'll also find an IMAX theater, ancient-culture displays, and fabulous wildlife dioramas. The space shows at the Hayden Planetarium (tickets sold separately) are a big bang with kids. Nearby, the often overlooked **DiMenna Children's History Museum**—in the New-York Historical Society—invites kids (ages eight and up) to connect to the lives of real New York children from the past through hands-on activities that include video games, cross-stitching, and interactive maps. The **Lower East Side Tenement Museum** also offers a glimpse into the lives of early New Yorkers, in this case immigrant families. Guided tours (for ages six and up) visit restored tenement apartments where costumed "residents" bring history to life. You can also explore the history of public transit in NYC—from horsepower to the subway—at the **New York Transit Museum**. Housed in an old subway station in downtown Brooklyn, this museum has an old bus to pretend-drive, vintage subway cars, and retro ads and maps. Also in Brooklyn is the **Brooklyn Children's Museum**, which, although a trek from the subway, has great hands-on exhibits (best suited for under-eights) like an interactive greenhouse. The **Intrepid Sea, Air & Space Museum**, an aircraft carrier turned museum, houses the world's fastest jets, a Cold War–era submarine, the first space shuttle, the interactive Exploreum Hall, flight simulators, and more. When museums try to make learning fun, they often fall flat, but the new kid museum on the block, the **Museum of Mathematics**, makes learning kaleidoscopic—and yes, fun—through interactive puzzles, games, displays, and hands-on tools like square-wheel tricycles.

Parks and Playgrounds

If you're looking for space to let off steam in Manhattan, the 843-acre **Central Park** is a good start. You can row boats on the lake, ride a carousel, explore the zoo, rent bikes, picnic, or just wander and enjoy the park's musicians, performers, and 21 playgrounds.

Head to **DUMBO** (short for Down Under the Manhattan Bridge Overpass) for family-friendly **Brooklyn Bridge Park**, a picnic-perfect waterfront park with several inventive playgrounds, Jane's Carousel, the Brooklyn Ice Cream Factory, a public swimming pool, and a variety of kid-centric music, arts, and kite-flying festivals.

If it's too hot, too cold, or the kids just want sporting time in one easy location, head to **Chelsea Piers**, between 18th and 23rd Streets along Manhattan's Hudson River. With a climbing wall, batting cages, ice-skating rinks, basketball and volleyball courts, indoor soccer fields, bowling, sailing, golf, gymnastics, and an Explorer Center with a ball pit and slides, it's a five-block energy outlet for local and visiting kids of all ages.

Attractions

With all the screeching and honking, wild colors, and crazy behavior, New York City can feel like one big zoo, but if the kids want the real deal, there's a zoo in every borough of NYC. The **Bronx Zoo** is the city's—and country's—largest metropolitan wildlife park, and home to more than 4,000 animals, including endangered and threatened species. Plan to spend a whole day here so your kids don't have to choose between Congo Gorilla Forest and the Siberian cats at Tiger Mountain. Manhattan's **Central Park Zoo** is small but popular, and known to little kids as the setting for the animated *Madagascar* films. You'll find red pandas, snow leopards, a penguin house, performing sea lions, grizzly bears, and a petting zoo. You can get face-to-face with even more interesting creatures in **Coney Island**, where the whole family can enjoy a walk along Coney Island's famous boardwalk to take in the beach, Luna Park's amusement rides, the land-marked Cyclone wooden roller coaster (54-inch height requirement), minor-league baseball games at the Cyclones' stadium (MCU Park), Nathan's hot dogs, and the **New York Aquarium**, where the new *Ocean Wonders: Sharks!* exhibit is slated to open in 2016. If adorable creatures of the robotic variety are called for, hit the **Sony Wonder Technology Lab**. The line to get into this futuristic fantasy world might be long (entry is free) but a talking robot keeps everyone entertained while you wait. Inside, kids can program their own robots; record their own digital music, movies, and games; and perform open-heart surgery using haptic technology.

Shows

Once upon a time, it seemed like the only truly kid-friendly show on Broadway was *The Lion King*. These days, adults could gripe that Broadway is selling itself to the youngest bidder—but who's complaining when the shows are so adult-friendly, too. *The Lion King* is still a firm favorite with kids, but it has solid competition with the likes of *Aladdin, Matilda, Wicked,* and Off-Broadway shows like *Stomp*, the *Gazillion Bubble Show,* and *Blue Man Group*. Kids shows are popular, so it's rare to find tickets at TKTS booths; book ahead if possible. Preteens and teens who are too cool for the Disney musical experience might appreciate Sam Eaton's mind-boggling display of magic and mentalism in **The Quantum Eye**, Off-Broadway at Theatre 80 in St. Mark's Place. The **New Victory Theater** is New York City's only theater dedicated to presenting family-friendly works; tickets are affordable, and shows are entertaining, never condescending, and, yes, cool. Kids ages three–nine can partake of music, dance, comedy, storytelling, and dancing at Just Kidding at **Symphony Space,** a performing arts center on Broadway and West 95th Street that inspires and entertains with established and emerging family-friendly artists. Interacting is encouraged.

NEW YORK CITY MUSEUMS, AN OVERVIEW

From the grand institutions along Fifth Avenue's museum mile and an underground museum in a converted subway station in Brooklyn to the dramatic new Whitney Museum in the Meatpacking District, New York City is home to an almost overwhelming collection of artistic riches, so it's a good idea to plan ahead. This overview includes museums listed elsewhere in the book; check the index for full listings.

Major Museums

It's hard to create a short list of top museums in New York City, because, well, there are just so many of them. That said, ambitious art lovers will likely focus on the big five. One of the most visited museums in the world, a must is the **Metropolitan Museum of Art** (known locally as "the Met," not to be confused with the Metropolitan Opera, also known as "the Met"). Its collection consists of more than 2 million works of art representing 5,000 years of history. From its world-famous dinosaur exhibits, its halls of fossils, gems, and human evolution, and its planetarium, the **American Museum of Natural History** is one of the most celebrated museums in the world. Both the **Museum of Modern Art (MoMA)** and the **Solomon R. Guggenheim Museum** are known for their incredible spaces—MoMA, a maze of glass walkways, was designed by Yoshio Taniguchi, while the nautilus-like Guggenheim is a masterwork of Frank Lloyd Wright—as well as for their superlative collections of contemporary art and space-specific shows. The **Whitney Museum of American Art**, which moved from its Upper East Side home to the Meatpacking District in 2015, is the city's hottest museum ticket, as much for its High Line and Hudson views as for its expansive indoor and outdoor exhibition spaces.

Other Top Museums

There are many other important museums in the city. The **Frick Collection,** an elegant museum in the neoclassical mansion of industrialist Henry Clay Frick, is especially worthy of a visit. The **Morgan Library and Museum** is another mansion-museum founded on the vast and varied collections of a magnate—in this case J. P. Morgan. The **American Folk Art Museum** is dedicated to American folk art and the work of contemporary self-taught artists. The **New Museum** is the only museum dedicated solely to contemporary art in Manhattan. There are several museums to satisfy design lovers, including the **Museum of American Illustration and Museum of Comic and Cartoon Art at the Society of Illustrators,** the **Museum of Arts and Design,** the **Museum at FIT,** the **Skyscraper Museum,** and the **Cooper Hewitt, Smithsonian Design Museum,** packed with hands-on activities for grown-ups. Speaking of lovers, the provocative, adults-only **Museum of Sex** explores the history, evolution, and cultural significance of sex, while the **Museum of American Finance** satisfies our curiosity about money and Wall Street.

New York–Specific Museums

It's appropriate that the city's oldest museum, the **New-York Historical Society,** is dedicated to the city itself. Founded in 1805, this neighbor of the American Museum of Natural History offers a unique and comprehensive overview of New York's history, as well as quirky and compelling exhibits. Other NY–centric museums include the **Museum of the City of New York,** the **Lower East Side Tenement Museum,** the **Merchant's House Museum,** the **Fraunces Tavern Museum,** the **Ellis Island Immigration Museum,** the **New York City Police Museum,** the **New York City Fire**

Museum, the **9/11 Memorial & Museum**, and the **New York Transit Museum**.

Culturally Specific Museums

New York City is often referred to as a melting pot, which explains the profusion of culture-specific museums dedicated to sharing the broad and specific stories, struggles, and experiences of certain cultural and ethnic groups—often overlooked in mainstream museums. **El Museo del Barrio** focuses on Latin American and Caribbean art and features a popular collection of hand-carved wooden folk-art figures from Puerto Rico. The **Hispanic Society of America Museum and Library** houses paintings by Goya, Velázquez, and El Greco, as well as an unsurpassed collection of Spanish, Portuguese, and Latin American artifacts. The **National Museum of the American Indian (Smithsonian Institution)** explores the diversity of Native American peoples through cultural artifacts, and regular music and dance performances. The **Jewish Museum**, the **Museum of Jewish Heritage**, and the **Museum at Eldridge Street** explore Jewish culture and art, and the Jewish experience in New York. The **Asia Society and Museum**, the **Museum of Chinese in America (MOCA)**, the **Japan Society**, and the **Rubin Museum of Art** are dedicated to the art and experiences of Asian communities. Other notable ethnic- or culture-specific museums include the **Leslie-Lohman Museum of Gay and Lesbian Art**, the **Ukrainian Museum**, and the **Studio Museum in Harlem** (for artists of African descent locally, nationally, and internationally).

Museums Farther Afield

The **Brooklyn Museum** is the second-biggest museum in New York City and home to an impressive collection of European and American paintings and sculptures, an outstanding Egyptian collection, the Elizabeth A. Sackler Center for Feminist Art, and a memorial sculpture garden of salvaged architectural elements from throughout New York City. A visit to Queens means innovative and experimental art at **MoMA PS1** and the small museum and garden of the **Noguchi Museum**, dedicated to the art of Isamu Noguchi, a prominent Japanese-American sculptor. Other top museums in Queens include the **Museum of the Moving Image** and the **Queens Museum of Art**. The enchanting **Cloisters Museum and Gardens** (an outpost of the Met museum) in Fort Tryon Park in Upper Manhattan is a bit of a trek relative to other city museums but it's almost guaranteed that you'll find it worth the trip.

Children's Museums

Some kids' museums are fun just for the kids, like the **Children's Museum of the Arts**, the **Children's Museum of Manhattan**, and the **Brooklyn Children's Museum**, but many are fun for the entire family. Kids of all ages will appreciate the fleet of jets, the flight simulator, and other hands-on activities, the space shuttle *Enterprise,* and the *Growler* submarine at the *Intrepid* **Sea, Air & Space Museum**. Other crowd-pleasers include **Madame Tussauds New York** and the **Museum of Mathematics**. The **DiMenna Children's History Museum** (at the New-York Historical Society) has interactive exhibits geared to help kids connect with children throughout New York's history.

Galleries

There are countless art galleries in Manhattan and Brooklyn worth visiting; check neighborhood chapters for specific listings. It can also depend on what shows are on at what times, so we also recommend checking the listings in *New York Magazine* and the *New York Times.*

GREAT
ITINERARIES

It's challenging, but not impossible to take in the big sights of New York City in a bite-size amount of time. Of course, with more major attractions than almost any other city on earth, New York can prove a hard town to know where to start. Here are two compact plans to sample the very best of the Big Apple, whether it's for one day or five days.

NEW YORK CITY IN 1 DAY

In one day, the best way to soak up Manhattan is to start early, and mix together a bit of both downtown and Midtown. So grab New York's breakfast of champions—coffee and a bagel—and prepare yourself for the subway morning rush hour on your way to **Battery Park**. From this southernmost tip of the island, you'll see the **Statue of Liberty, Ellis Island,** and the **Staten Island Ferry Terminal**. Head up Broadway past **Bowling Green** and the famous *Charging Bull* statue on your way to **Wall Street**. Turn right at the 1846 Gothic Revival–style **Trinity Church** to view giant George Washington at **Federal Hall**, across from the **New York Stock Exchange**. Stroll north, then take a left on Liberty Street to the **World Trade Center** site, home to the **National 9/11 Memorial** and the 104-story **One World Trade Center**. Make your way to the top of the new WTC building for a bird's-eye view of Manhattan.

Take a train uptown to spend the afternoon browsing the **Metropolitan Museum of Art**, stopping for lunch in the rooftop garden, which also gives you a nice view of the city. Take a quick stroll through nearby **Central Park** afterwards, and then take a walk downtown to 42nd Street, passing through **Times Square**—best experienced after dark. If you time it right, you

may even have time to catch an 8 o'clock Broadway show.

NEW YORK CITY IN 5 DAYS

Five days in New York is enough to explore much of the city's culture and sights, along with a few culinary highlights. The first and most important stop is to any subway-station kiosk to buy a seven-day, unlimited-ride MetroCard for $31—it'll help you make your trip much more affordable and easier to get around the city.

Day 1: Lower Manhattan, SoHo, and Chelsea

With its four centuries of history, lower Manhattan is a prime starting point for your trip. Kick off Day 1 with a visit to **Battery Park**, Wall Street, and **One World Trade Center**, along with a stop at the **National 9/11 Memorial**. If you get there early enough, you might have time to hop on a ferry and visit either Liberty Island, home to the **Statue of Liberty**, or **Ellis Island**, the entryway for immigrants coming to America throughout the 1800s. If you're not able to visit, you'll still be able to glimpse them from Manhattan's most southern tip.

Afterwards, drift north towards Canal Street to discover **SoHo** and its unique cast-iron architecture and shops, and continue your walk even further uptown into Chelsea (a subway ride might be in order here) to walk the **High Line** at sunset. Afterwards, gallery-hop around Chelsea's many art galleries. If you're big on nightlife, the nearby Meatpacking District has plenty of hopping bars and clubs to get your dance on into the wee hours of the morning.

Day 2: Grand Central, Fifth Avenue, Rockefeller Center, and Times Square

Start Day 2 with breakfast at **Grand Central Terminal,** one of NYC's most majestic spaces, where you can gaze up at its ceiling's sparkling constellations and down at the throngs of commuters whizzing through. Head north on **Fifth Avenue** to check out **Rockefeller Center** (if winter, that will include the ice-skating rink). Pop into the **NBC Experience Store** and book a tour through several classic NBC sets. On a clear day, visit the tower's observation deck for a perfect view of the **Empire State Building** and beyond.

Then make a pit stop at the **Museum of Modern Art (MoMA)** to check out one of the world's best modern art museums; must-see exhibits include Andy Warhol's soup cans and "Starry Night" by Vincent van Gogh. After you get your art fill, veer southwest toward **Times Square** to join travelers (and some locals) who converge on the "crossroads of the world" to bask in Broadway's bright lights.

Day 3: Brooklyn Bridge, Chinatown, Lower East Side, and the East Village

For Day 3, begin at **Brooklyn Bridge Park** to view the picturesque lower Manhattan skyline. There you can walk across the **Brooklyn Bridge** to **Chinatown** and its many tasty eateries. Cross Canal Street and walk east past the regal **Manhattan Bridge Arch,** into the **Lower East Side.** The **Tenement Museum** is among the city's most interesting, historic experiences, so plan an hour or two there.

Then stroll north through the **East Village** and **Alphabet City,** with a break in **Tompkins Square Park** for a nice dose of people-watching. Grab a drink at one of the many bars, or treat yourself to a cannoli at an old-school Italian bakery.

Day 4: Museum Mile, Central Park, and the Upper West Side

Infuse some of NYC's best art and history into Day 4 at one of several truly great institutions along the Museum Mile on the Upper East Side. You can invest a couple of hours (or the whole day) exploring the **Metropolitan Museum of Art, Guggenheim,** and many more. You can also start (or end) your museum-hopping on the Upper West Side with the **American Museum of Natural History.** Regardless of where you start, make sure you spend a few hours checking out **Central Park** and its many points of interest, like Bethesda Terrace, the carousel, and Belvedere Castle.

As you exit the park on the west side, walk to Broadway for a taste of some of the Upper West Side's authentic delicatessen delights, and top off the evening in Harlem for a show at the historic **Apollo Theater.**

Day 5: Union Square, Washington Square Park, West Village

On Day 5, start at **Union Square,** home to a greenmarket (and seasonal holiday crafts market), and surrounded by stores big and small. Don't miss the "18 miles of books" (new and used) for sale at the Strand on Broadway, a local literary institution. Stroll down to **Washington Square Park** to hear buskers playing their hearts out and watch NYU kids hanging out between classes.

Walk towards Bleecker Street, and wander along the winding lanes of the West Village. On Christopher Street, see the historic **Stonewall Inn,** a pivotal site in the gay-rights movement, and other famous watering holes frequented by artistic luminaries throughout the decades.

NEW YORK CITY FESTIVALS

There's always *something* going on New York City, but if you want to put a finger on the real pulse of New York, you should participate in a *big something* while you're here. Summer is an especially good time for festivals. Here are a few of our favorites:

Spring

Spring means the start of baseball season with home openers, usually in the first week of April, for both of New York's Major League teams: the Yankees and the Mets.

Sakura Matsuri Cherry Blossom Festival. New Yorkers come out of hibernation en masse every spring to witness the extremely popular annual Sakura Matsuri Cherry Blossom Festival at the Brooklyn Botanic Garden. In addition to the blooming cherry trees, there are Taiko drumming performances, Japanese pop bands, samurai swords, martial arts, tea ceremonies, and more. ⊠ *New York* ⊕ *www.bbg.org* Ⓜ *2, 3 to Eastern Parkway–Brooklyn Museum; 2, 3, 4, 5 to Franklin Ave.*

Tribeca Film Festival. Founded by Jane Rosenthal and Robert De Niro to contribute to the long-term recovery of Lower Manhattan after 9/11, the Tribeca Film Festival has become one of the most prominent film festivals in the world. There are upward of 250 films, more than 1,000 screenings, and even more buzz. It typically takes place mid-to-late April. ⊠ *New York* ⊕ *www.tribecafilm.com.*

Summer

With festivals and events on city streets, at the beaches, and in almost every city park, New Yorkers take full advantage of the long summer days and nights. Free outdoor movie festivals are a huge draw in summer: choices include sci-fi movies with a view of Brooklyn Bridge Park (⊕ *www. brooklynbridgepark.org*); indie movies

on city rooftops (⊕ *www.rooftopfilms. com*); and classics screened every Monday night in Midtown's Bryant Park (⊕ *www. bryantpark.org*).

Celebrate Brooklyn! Launched in 1979 to bring people back into Prospect Park after years of neglect, Celebrate Brooklyn! is one of the city's most popular, free, outdoor performing arts festivals, and *the* place to catch excellent live music in the great Brooklyn outdoors. The artists and ensembles reflect the borough's diversity, ranging from internationally acclaimed performers to up-and-coming musicians. The lineup also includes kids' shows, movies with live music, ballet, and more. Performances are rain or shine and free (there is a suggested donation of $3), with the exception of ticketed benefit concerts, which directly support the festival. Seats for free shows are first come, first served. Local restaurants provide the food. Get there early and bring a blanket to sit on. ⊠ *Prospect Park Bandshell, 9th St. and Prospect Park W entrance, Park Slope* ⊕ *www.bricartsmedia.org/performing-arts/celebrate-brooklyn* ⊠ *Free* Ⓜ *F, G to 7th Ave.; 2, 3 to Grand Army Plaza.*

Midsummer Night Swing. If dancing in the street is your thing, join the Midsummer Night Swing festival, an outdoor music and dance party in Lincoln Center Plaza that occurs from late June to early July. Take lessons with pros or just strut your natural moves on the dance floor. ⊠ *New York* ⊕ *www.midsummernightswing.org* Ⓜ *1 to 66th St.*

Museum Mile Festival. For one day every June, thousands of locals and visitors celebrate the Museum Mile Festival when 10 museums along 5th Avenue open their doors for free. ⊠ *New York* ⊕ *www. museummilefestival.org.*

Summer Streets. On three consecutive Saturdays every August, you can join hundreds of thousands of locals to let loose on nearly 7 miles of pedestrianized arterials for Summer Streets. From the Brooklyn Bridge to Central Park, along Park Avenue and connecting streets, New Yorkers hit the car-free streets to rock climb, zip line, dance, work out, experience art, or just ramble along the city's streets in a new way—all for free. ⊠ *New York* ⊕ *www.nyc.gov/summerstreets.*

Other popular summer festivals and events include Coney Island's **Mermaid Parade,** the **New York International Fringe Festival, SummerStage,** and **Shakespeare in the Park.**

Fall

Brooklyn Book Festival. The Brooklyn Book Festival is a huge, (mostly) free public event with an array of established and emerging authors, readings, panels, discussions, parties, games, and signings—all held in clubs, parks, theaters, and libraries across Brooklyn every September. ⊠ *New York* ⊕ *www.brooklynbookfestival.org.*

Feast of San Gennaro. Every year, thousands of locals and visitors flock to Little Italy for the 11-day Feast of San Gennaro in mid-September. This festival is a mix of religion, delicious food, colorful parades, and live entertainment. Don't miss the cannoli-eating competition at the end of the week. ⊠ *New York* ⊕ *www. sangennaro.org.*

New York City Marathon. Even if you're not joining the more than 50,000 runners taking a 26.2-mile jog through New York's five boroughs on the first Sunday in November, you'll want to experience the electric atmosphere and the very best of New York with the 2 million spectators. ⊠ *New York* ⊕ *www.tcsnycmarathon.org.*

Other top fall events include the **Village Halloween Parade, Macy's Thanksgiving Day Parade,** and the **Rockefeller Center Tree Lighting Ceremony.**

Winter

Sure, it can be icy-cold in New York in winter, but locals know that the best way to stay warm is by hopping from one event to another.

Holiday Train Show. The New York Botanical Garden's Holiday Train Show is one of the city's top seasonal attractions, especially for families. You'll find electric trains, more than 150 miniature replicas of city landmarks (made out of twigs and bark), and magical landscapes—all housed in a conservatory, so winter weather can't dampen your spirits. ⊠ *New York* ⊕ *www.nybg.org.*

To ring in the **Lunar New Year,** the streets of Chinatown give way to food vendors hawking traditional eats, colorful costumes and decorations, and a major parade of elaborate floats, marching bands, and dragon troupes running from Little Italy through Chinatown and Lower Manhattan. Festivities also take place in Sunset Park in Brooklyn and in the Flushing neighborhood of Queens (⊕ *www. betterchinatown.com*).

Find your groove for five days each January at **Winter Jazzfest NYC,** happening at venues around the city. If you want to join in on a little local tomfoolery, join tens of thousands of "Santafied" locals who tear up the town for **SantaCon** (⊕ *nycsantacon.com*), or sign up for a **No Pants Subway Ride** in January (⊕ *www. improveverywhere.com*).

BEST TOURS IN NEW YORK CITY

Sometimes a guided tour is the way to go, even if you usually prefer to fly solo. It can be a great way to investigate out-of-the-way areas, to get an insider's perspective on where locals eat and play in the city, and to learn about interesting aspects of the city's history, inhabitants, or architecture. Whether you want the classic hop-on, hop-off bus tour to get oriented in the city, or a more personal, interest-specific walk, you'll find it here. ■TIP➔ Some of the bigger tour companies offer discounts if you book in advance online.

Boat Tours

Circle Line Sightseeing Cruise. In good weather, a Circle Line Sightseeing Cruise around Manhattan Island is one of the best ways to get oriented in the city. A "Best of NYC" 2½-hour, $41 cruise runs at least once daily. Shorter, cheaper options are available too, including the 30-minute thrill ride, the Beast. ⊠ *Pier 83, W. 42nd St., Midtown West* ☎ *212/563–3200* ⊕ *www.circleline42. com* ✆ *From $29.*

Manhattan By Sail. Looking for a more historical experience? Manhattan By Sail has an 82-foot yacht dating from the 1920s that makes daily 90-minute public sails and Sunday brunch sails from mid-April through mid-October. Themed sailings include a wine-tasting sail, lobster-and-beer-lovers sail, and a jazz sail against stunning moonlit views. They also offer two-hour sunset sails in June, July, and August. Reservations are advised. ⊠ *North Cove Marina at World Financial Center, Lower Manhattan* ☎ *212/619–0907* ⊕ *www. manhattanbysail.com* ✆ *From $25.*

Bus Tours

Big Bus New York. Like its double-decker competitors, Big Bus offers various hop-on, hop-off open-top tours of the city, but its most popular ticket is a two-day pass that includes loops that cover downtown, uptown, and Brooklyn, as well as a night tour and a free sightseeing cruise with Hornblower Cruises from Pier 15 at the South Street Seaport. ⊠ *Ticket desk, B.B. King Blues Club & Grill, 237 W. 42nd St., Midtown West* ☎ *212/685–8687* ⊕ *www. bigbustours.com/newyork* ✆ *From $47.*

Gray Line New York Sightseeing. Gray Line runs various hop-on, hop-off double-decker bus tours, including a downtown Manhattan loop, an upper Manhattan loop, a Brooklyn loop, and evening tours of the city. Packages include 48-hour and 72-hour options plus entrance fees to attractions. ⊠ *777 8th Ave., between 46th and 47th Sts., Midtown West* ☎ *800/669–0051* ⊕ *www.newyorksightseeing.com* ✆ *From $54.*

Walking Tours

Big Onion Walking Tours. The wisecracking, PhD candidates of Big Onion Walking Tours lead themed tours such as "Upper East Side: A Clash of Titans," "Immigrant New York," and "The Official Gangs of New York," as well as famous multiethnic eating tours and guided walks through neighborhoods from Harlem to the Financial District and Brooklyn. Tours run daily and last about two hours; there's an additional $5 tacked on for tours that include making various stops to eat. ⊠ *New York* ☎ *888/606–9255* ⊕ *www.bigonion.com* ✆ *$20.*

Levy's Unique New York. With tours that include "Jewish Gangsters of the Lower East Side," "Staten Island: Sailors, Suburbs & Secrets," and "Graffiti to Galleries: Street Art in NYC," family-run Levy's tours are anything but the usual top attractions hit list (although you can visit those, too). Guides are knowledgeable and personable, and will cater to specific interests. All tours are private so the more the merrier (and it's cheaper the more people that are on the tour). ⊠ *New York* ⊕ *www.levysuniqueny.com* ✉ *From $300.*

Like A Local. Walk like a local, talk like a local, and best of all eat like a local with a highly curated tour from Like A Local. Tours include the Flatiron Food tour, which is a lovely walk from the Flatiron District to Union Square with a lot of tasty stops, photo ops, local history, and private kitchen visits along the way. If you're looking to feel like a hip local in Brooklyn, take the Sunday Funday tour of Williamsburg. ⊠ *New York* ⊕ *www.likealocaltours.com* ✉ *From $50.*

The Municipal Art Society of New York. The Municipal Art Society conducts a series of walking tours that emphasize the architecture, history, and changing faces of particular neighborhoods. Options include "Empire to Penn," "The Bronx's Urban Art," and "Storefront: the Disappearing Face of New York." An official daily walking tour of Grand Central explores the 100-year-old terminal's architecture, history, and hidden secrets. Tours begin in the main concourse at 12:30 and last 75 minutes. Tickets can be purchased in advance online or from the ticket booth in the main concourse. ⊠ *111 W. 57th St., New York* ☎ *212/935–3960,* *212/935–3960 for recorded info* ⊕ *www. mas.org/tours* ✉ *From $20.*

New York City Cultural Walking Tours. Alfred Pommer's walking tours cover such topics as buildings' gargoyles, the TriBeCa Historic District, and the Upper East Side Millionaire's Mile. Two-hour public tours run on some Sundays from March to December (no reservations needed); private tours can also be scheduled. ⊠ *New York* ☎ *212/979–2388* ⊕ *www.nycwalk. com* ✉ *$25.*

New York Food Tours. Options from the New York Food walking tours include "The Freakiest and Funniest Food" and a "Tastes of Chinatown" tour. Prices range from $75 for a 2½-hour East Village food and culture tour to $125 for a 3½-hour multicultural bar-hopping tour. ⊠ *New York* ☎ *347/559–0111* ⊕ *www. foodtoursofny.com* ✉ *From $75.*

Specialty Tours

Bike and Roll. From Central Park to the Brooklyn Bridge, there's a lot of ground to cover; do yourself a favor and use wheels. Bike and Roll NYC offers guided bike (and Segway) tours of the city with a range of distances and levels of difficulty. The Bike and Boat tour is a scenic ride from Lower Manhattan's Battery Park across the Brooklyn Bridge to Brooklyn Heights. From Brooklyn, there's a NY Water Taxi ride to Midtown Manhattan and then a final bike ride south along the Hudson River. Other tour options include New York at Night, 9/11 Memorial, and Central Park. Rates include bike rentals, helmets, and water. ⊠ *New York* ☎ *212/260–0400* ⊕ *www. bikenewyorkcity.com* ✉ *From $50.*

Boroughs of the Dead. From tours taking in haunts of the East and West Village to 19th-century true-crime tours to Manhattan's only dedicated Edgar Allan Poe walking tour, the Boroughs of the Dead two-hour tours suggest that the inhabitants of this city truly never sleep—even when they're dead. Don't wait for Halloween to explore the historical crime, gore, and paranormal activities of Manhattan and Brooklyn. No capes, costumes, or gimmicks here: just dark, haunting history. ⊠ *New York* ☎ *646/932–0680* ⊕ *www. boroughsofthedead.com* ✉ *From $20.*

Shop Gotham. If you're on a mission to shop till you drop, you won't want to waste time with a map. The fashion-savvy guides at Shop Gotham will save you time and money by guiding you to the best boutiques of SoHo and NoLIta and elsewhere, getting you exclusive shop discounts, and also offering styling advice. Tours last two to three hours. Private tours are available, too. ⊠ *New York* ☎ *212/209–3370* ⊕ *www.shopgotham. com* ✉ *From $40.*

A Slice of Brooklyn. You can manage fine without a guide to hold your hand through Rockefeller Center and past the decked-out windows of 5th Avenue, but if you're interested in experiencing a more local holiday light tradition, take A Slice of Brooklyn's bus tour to the festive (and blinding) neighborhood light scene that is Brooklyn's Dyker Heights. The 3½-hour tour, offered nightly in December, introduces you to some of Brooklyn's less touristed neighborhoods. Other tours include the Original Brooklyn Pizza Tour, a 4½-hour bus tour of iconic Brooklyn pizza joints, and tours of quintessential Brooklyn neighborhoods.

⊠ *New York* ☎ *212/913–9917* ⊕ *www. asliceofbrooklyn.com* ✉ *From $50.*

Free Tours

Big Apple Greeter. This free volunteer-led tour service pairs visitors with knowledgeable locals who share insights and tips and cater tours to specific interests. It's like having a friend in town who squires you around and pays for his or her own lunch. Request a greeter at least three weeks before your visit by filling in the online form. ⊠ *New York* ☎ *212/669–8159* ⊕ *www.bigapplegreeter.org* ✉ *Free.*

Central Park Conservancy. The Central Park Conservancy offers free one- to two-hour guided tours that provide an introduction to the different areas of Central Park: its woodlands, romantic vistas, Conservatory garden, Seneca Village, and secret corners and off-the-beaten-path walks. Volunteer-led Welcome Tours meet at different points in the park, so check the website for details. Premier tours are ticketed ($15) and provide a more in-depth experience. ⊠ *New York* ☎ *212/794–6564* ⊕ *www.centralparknyc.org* ✉ *Free.*

Free Tours by Foot. The walking, photography, food, and biking tours of Manhattan and Brooklyn hosted by Free Tours by Foot are technically free (you pay what you feel the tour was worth, if anything, upon completion), but there is a rental fee for bike and bus tours—still significantly cheaper than most other bike and bus tours. Highlights include a sunset walking tour of the High Line, a Harlem food tour, and a journey through the storied past of the East Village. Reservations are required for all tours. ⊠ *New York* ☎ *646/450–6831* ⊕ *www.freetoursbyfoot.com* ✉ *Free (suggested donation).*

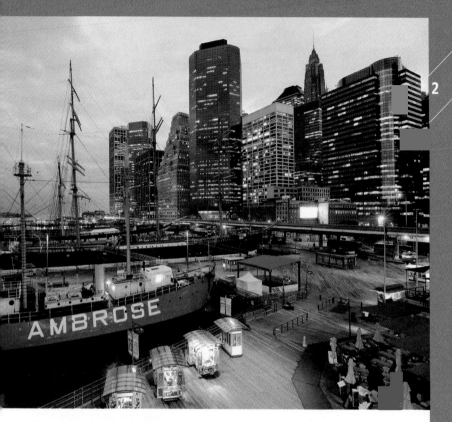

LOWER MANHATTAN

GETTING ORIENTED

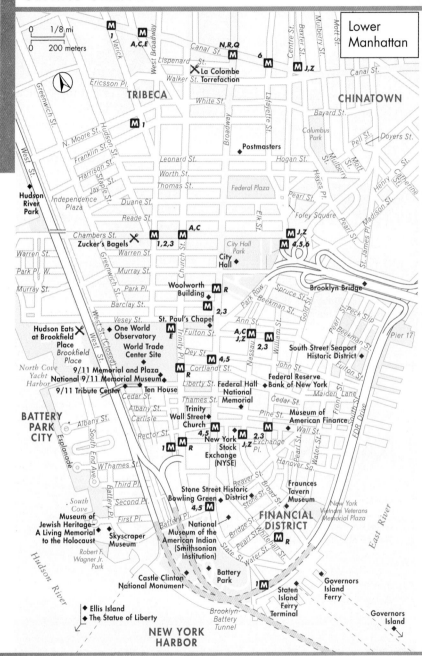

Lower
Manhattan

0   1/8 mi
0   200 meters

TRIBECA

CHINATOWN

La Colombe
Torrefaction

Postmasters

Hudson
River
Park

Independence
Plaza

Zucker's Bagels

City
Hall

City Hall
Park

Woolworth
Building

Brooklyn Bridge

St. Paul's Chapel

Hudson Eats
at Brookfield
Place

Brookfield
Place

North Cove
Yacht
Harbor

One World
Observatory

World Trade
Center Site

9/11 Memorial and Plaza
National 9/11 Memorial Museum

9/11 Tribute Center

Ten House

South Street Seaport
Historic District

Federal Reserve
Bank of New York

Museum of
American Finance

BATTERY
PARK
CITY

Federal Hall
National
Memorial

Trinity
Church

Wall Street

New York
Stock
Exchange
(NYSE)

Fraunces
Tavern
Museum

New York
Vietnam Veterans
Memorial Plaza

Stone Street Historic
District

Bowling Green

FINANCIAL
DISTRICT

South
Cove

Museum of
Jewish Heritage–
A Living Memorial
to the Holocaust

Skyscraper
Museum

Robert F.
Wagner Jr.
Park

National
Museum of the
American Indian
(Smithsonian
Institution)

Castle Clinton
National Monument

Battery
Park

Governors
Island Ferry

Staten
Island
Ferry
Terminal

Ellis Island
The Statue of Liberty

Brooklyn-
Battery
Tunnel

Governors
Island

Hudson River

East River

NEW YORK
HARBOR

MAKING THE MOST OF YOUR TIME

Visit the Financial District during the weekend and you might feel like a lone explorer in a canyon of buildings; even on weeknights the decibel level of the neighborhood reduces significantly after about 6. Weekdays, however, the sidewalks bustle so much that you can expect to be jostled if you stand still too long. End your visit by watching the sunset over the Hudson River.

The sights of the New York Harbor are some of the most quintessential of New York, but be prepared for long lines for Ellis Island and the Statue of Liberty, especially on weekends. TriBeCa is one of the quieter neighborhoods in Manhattan, being mostly residential. There are pleasant shops, restaurants, and local bars, but the neighborhood tends not to be a tourist attraction unless the film festival is going on.

COFFEE AND QUICK BITES

Hudson Eats at Brookfield Place. The upscale food court and terrace in the Brookfield Place complex has the best of NYC's fast and casual food options ranging from Blue Ribbon Sushi to Black Seed Bagels to Dos Toros Tacos and more. ⊠ *West St., between Vesey and Liberty Sts., Battery Park* ☎ *212/978–1698* ⊕ *www.brookfieldplaceny.com* Ⓜ *E to World Trade Center; R to Cortlandt St.*

La Colombe Torrefaction. In this loftlike space just below Canal Street, expect excellent espresso drinks and impressive latte art. Unlike other coffee shops plagued by laptops and customers clad in headphones, La Colombe does not have Wi-Fi. ⊠ *319 Church St., at Lispenard St., TriBeCa* ☎ *212/343–1515* ⊕ *www.lacolombe.com* Ⓜ *A, C, E to Canal St.*

Zucker's Bagels. This is one of the few places left in the city that still serves hand-rolled, kettle-boiled New York bagels. Coffee is from La Colombe. ⊠ *146 Chambers St., TriBeCa* ☎ *212/608–5844* ⊕ *www.zuckersbagels.com* Ⓜ *1, 2, 3 to Chambers St.*

TOP EXPERIENCES

Visiting the National 9/11 Memorial

Riding the Staten Island Ferry

Touring Ellis Island and the Statue of Liberty

Snapping a photo in front of Wall Street's bull

Strolling through Hudson River Park

BEST FOR KIDS

Castle Clinton and Battery Park

South Street Seaport Museum

GETTING HERE

Many subway lines connect to the Financial District. The grand Fulton Center—opened in 2014—is serviced by nine different subway lines (2, 3, 4, 5, A, C, J, Z, R) and puts you within walking distance of City Hall, South Street Seaport, and the World Trade Center site. To get to the Brooklyn Bridge, take the 4, 5, or 6 to Brooklyn Bridge–City Hall.

For sights around New York Harbor, take the R to Whitehall Street, or the 4 or 5 to Bowling Green. (Note that you can also reach the Harbor area via the 1 train to South Ferry; it also stops in the heart of TriBeCa, at Franklin Street.)

Lower Manhattan, or "all the way downtown" in the parlance of New Yorkers emphatically giving directions to tourists, has long been where the action—and transaction—is. Originally the Dutch trading post called New Amsterdam (1626–47), this neighborhood is home to historic, cobblestone streets next to soaring skyscrapers. This mix of old and new, the bustle of Wall Street, and a concentration of city landmarks all lure visitors to the southern tip of Manhattan.

FINANCIAL DISTRICT

Updated by
Kelsy Chauvin

Little from Manhattan's Colonial era is left in Lower Manhattan (apart from a precious few structures built in the 1700s), but you can still sense history in the South Street Seaport's 19th-century brick facades and in pedestrianized Stone Street's picnic tables. There's life to be found within the skyscraper canyons of Wall Street and lower Broadway, as locals move into the neighborhood and fill the bar stools in candlelit watering holes. Bounded by the East and Hudson Rivers to the east and west, respectively, and by Chambers Street and Battery Park to the north and south, the Financial District is best appreciated by getting lost in its streets.

You'll want to see what's here, but above all you'll want to see what's not, most notably in that empty gulf among skyscrapers: the World Trade Center site where two 1-acre pools represent the footprints of the fallen Twin Towers.

TOP ATTRACTIONS

FAMILY **Battery Park.** Jutting out at the southernmost point of Manhattan, tree-filled Battery Park is a respite from the narrow, winding, and (on weekdays) bustling streets of the Financial District. Even if you don't plan to stay for long, carve out a few minutes of sightseeing time to sit on a bench and take in the view, which includes the Statue of Liberty and Ellis Island. On clear days you can see all the way to Port Elizabeth's cranes, which seem to mimic Lady Liberty's stance; to Governors Island, a former Coast Guard installation now managed by the National Park Service; a hilly Staten Island in the distance; and the old railway terminal in Liberty State Park, on the mainland in Jersey City, New Jersey. Looking away from the water and toward Lower Manhattan's skyscrapers, there's a feeling that you're at the beginning of the city, and a sense of all the possibility it possesses just a few blocks in.

The park's main structure is **Castle Clinton National Monument,** the ticket office site and takeoff point for ferries to the Statue of Liberty and Ellis Island. This monument was once 200 feet off the southern tip of the island located in what was called the Southwest Battery, and was erected during the War of 1812 to defend the city. (Its sister fort, Castle Williams, sits across the water on Governors Island.) As dirt and debris from construction were dumped into the harbor, the island expanded, eventually engulfing the landmark. Later, from 1855 to 1890, it served as America's first official immigration center (Ellis Island opened in 1892).

Inside Battery Park are several monuments and statues, including Fritz Koenig's *The Sphere,* which for three decades stood on the plaza at the World Trade Center as a symbol of peace. Damaged but still intact after the towers collapsed, the sculpture was installed in Battery Park and will remain there indefinitely.

To the west is the **Staten Island Ferry Terminal,** and to the east is Robert F. Wagner Jr. Park, with its flat, tidy lawn and wide benches from which to view the harbor or the stream of runners, cyclists, and skaters on the promenade. ⊠ *Battery Park* ☎ *212/417–2000* ⊕ *www.nycgovparks.org/ parks/batterypark* Ⓜ *4, 5 to Bowling Green; 1 to South Ferry.*

Fodor'sChoice
★
Brooklyn Bridge. "A drive-through cathedral" is how the journalist James Wolcott described the Brooklyn Bridge, one of New York's noblest and most recognized landmarks, perhaps rivaling Walt Whitman's comment that it was "The best, most effective medicine my soul has yet partaken." The bridge stretches over the East River, connecting Manhattan and Brooklyn. A walk across its promenade—a boardwalk elevated above the roadway, shared by pedestrians, skaters, and cyclists—takes about 40 minutes and delivers exhilarating views. If you start from Lower Manhattan, you'll end up in the heart of Brooklyn Heights (you can also take the subway to the Brooklyn side and walk back to Manhattan). It's worth noting that on evenings and weekends when the weather is nice, the narrow path gets pretty congested; it's most magical, and quietest, early in the morning. ⊠ *East River Dr., Lower Manhattan* Ⓜ *4, 5, 6 to Brooklyn Bridge–City Hall; J, Z to Chambers St.; A, C to High St. (in Brooklyn).*

National 9/11 Memorial Museum. Beside the reflecting pools on the 9/11 Memorial Plaza is the glass pavilion of the Memorial Museum. The museum descends some 70 feet down to the bedrock the Twin Towers were built on, and displays a poignant, powerful collection of artifacts, memorabilia, photographs, and multimedia exhibits, as well as a gallery that takes visitors through the history of events surrounding both the 1993 and 2001 attacks. There's also a memorial wall with portraits of those who died, pieces of the Towers' structural steel and foundations, and remnants of the "Survivors Stairs," which allowed hundreds of people to escape the buildings that fateful September day. Current access to the museum is through the Memorial Plaza from the intersections of Liberty and Greenwich Streets, Liberty and West, or West and Fulton. The 9/11 Memorial Museum Store (*20 Vesey Street; 877/643–4911*) sells souvenirs, apparel, books, and other mementos; partial proceeds go to museum operations. ⊠ *180 Greenwich St., Financial District* ☎ *212/266–5211* ⊕ *www.911memorial.org/museum* ⊠ *$24 (free Tues. 5–8 pm)* ⊗ *Sun.–Thurs. 9–8, Fri. and Sat. 9–9* Ⓜ *R to Cortlandt St.; 2, 3, 4, 5, A, C, J, Z to Fulton Center; E to World Trade Center.*

New York Stock Exchange (NYSE). Unfortunately, you can't tour it, but it's certainly worth ogling. At the intersection of Wall and Broad Streets, the Exchange is impossible to miss. The neoclassical building, designed by architect George B. Post, opened on April 22, 1903. It has six Corinthian columns supporting a pediment with a sculpture titled *Integrity Protecting the Works of Man,* featuring a tribute to the then-sources of American prosperity: Agriculture and Mining to the left of Integrity; Science, Industry, and Invention to the right. The Exchange was one of the world's first air-conditioned buildings. ⊠ *11 Wall St., Financial District* ☎ *212/656–3000* ⊕ *www.nyse.com* Ⓜ *1 to Rector St.; R to Rector St.; 2, 3, 4, 5 to Wall St.; J, Z to Broad St.*

Fodor'sChoice ★ **9/11 Memorial and Plaza.** Opened just in time for the 10th anniversary of 9/11, the somber Memorial was designed by Michael Arad and Peter Walker and occupies a large swath of the 16-acre World Trade Center complex, forming what's known as the Memorial Plaza. It's comprised of two recessed, 30-foot-tall waterfalls that occupy the giant, square footprints where the Twin Towers once stood. Every minute, some 60,000 gallons of water cascade down the sides and then down into smaller square openings in the center of the pools. At nearly an acre in size each, they are said to be the largest man-made waterfalls in North America. Edging the Memorial pools are bronze panels inscribed with the names of the nearly 3,000 people who were killed in the attacks at the WTC site, in Flight 93's crash in Pennsylvania, at the Pentagon, and the six people who died in the World Trade Center bombing in 1993. Because the names are arranged by affiliation rather than alphabetically, it can be difficult to locate names—visit the Memorial's website or use on-site kiosks to find the location of a particular name. Visitors are allowed to place tribute items in front of the Memorial pools as well as on the name panels. Across the plaza are benches, grassy strips, and more than 400 swamp white-oak trees harvested from within a 500-mile radius of the site, as well as from Pennsylvania and near Washington, D.C. There's also a single Callery pear tree known as the "survivor tree," which, after being nearly destroyed on September 11, 2001, was nursed, revived, and replanted here in 2010. Visits to the 9/11 Memorial are free as an open-access public plaza. Enter the National 9/11 Museum via the pavilion on the plaza. ⊠ *180 Greenwich St., Financial District* ☎ *212/266–5211 for reservation help* ⊕ *www.911memorial.org* ⊠ *Free* ⊗ *daily 7:30 am–9 pm* Ⓜ *R to Cortlandt St.; 2, 3, 4, 5, A, C, J, Z to Fulton St.; E to World Trade Center.*

9/11 Tribute Center. This project of the September 11th Families' Association opened five years after 9/11 to put the events of that day into context—at the time, there was little to see beyond a big construction site. The four rooms of exhibits, which include a wall with hundreds of photographs of those lost on that day, are a good complement to the broader mission of the separate National 9/11 Memorial and Museum. Same-day tickets are available for daily 75-minute-long walking tours, which are meant for adults and children age 10 and up. The tour route includes a visit to the Memorial as well as other major sites related to the events of 9/11. Next door to the Tribute Center is "Ten House," the firehouse closest to Ground Zero, which was nearly destroyed on 9/11. ⊠ *120 Liberty St., Financial District* ☎ *866/737–1184* ⊕ *www.tributewtc.org* ⊠ *$20 (for tour of 9/11 Memorial and access to 9/11 Tribute Center)* ☉ *Mon.–Sat. 10–6, Sun. 10–5 (last tickets sold 30 mins before closing); walking tours Sun.–Thurs. 11–3, Fri. and Sat. 10:30–3* Ⓜ *2, 3, 4, 5, A, C, J, Z to Fulton St.; E to World Trade Center; N, R to Cortlandt St.*

FAMILY **One World Observatory.** Be whisked to the top of the tallest building in the Western Hemisphere in the world's fastest elevators for incredible views of Manhattan, Brooklyn, and beyond. The observatory occupies the 100th, 101st, and 102nd floors of One World Trade Center, and the experience includes panoramic vistas, exhibits, and personal stories about the construction of this monumental skyscraper, plus a dramatic two-minute video of time-lapse images of Lower Manhattan through the centuries. There are three dining options on the 101st floor, including a casual café and a sit-down restaurant. ⊠ *One World Trade Center, 285 Fulton St., Financial District* ☎ *844/696–1776* ⊕ *oneworldobservatory.com* ⊠ *$32* ☉ *May–Labor Day, daily 9 am–midnight; Labor Day–May, daily 9–8 (check website for holiday and extended hours)* Ⓜ *R to Cortlandt St.; E to World Trade Center; 2, 3, 4, 5, A, C, J, Z to Fulton Center.*

South Street Seaport Historic District. Had this charming cobblestone corner of the city not been declared a historic district in 1977, the city's largest concentration of early-19th-century commercial buildings would have been destroyed. Today, the area is largely filled with tourists, and if you've been to Boston's Quincy Market or Baltimore's Harborplace, you may feel a flash of déjà vu—the same company leased, restored, and adapted the existing buildings, resulting in a blend of quasi-authentic historic district with a slightly homogenous shopping zone.

At the intersection of Fulton and Water Streets, the gateway to the seaport, is the *Titanic* **Memorial,** a small white lighthouse that commemorates the sinking of the RMS *Titanic* in 1912. Beyond the lighthouse, Fulton Street turns into a busy pedestrian mall. On the south side of Fulton is the seaport's architectural centerpiece, **Schermerhorn Row,** a redbrick terrace of Georgian- and Federal-style warehouses and countinghouses built from 1811 to 1812. Some upper floors house gallery space, and the ground floors are occupied by shops, bars, and restaurants. Cross South Street (once known as the Street of Ships) under an elevated stretch of FDR Drive to **Pier 16,** where historic ships are docked, including the *Pioneer,* a 102-foot schooner built in 1885;

the *Peking,* the second-largest sailing bark in existence; the iron-hulled *Wavertree*; and the lightship *Ambrose.* The Pier 16 ticket booth provides information and sells tickets to the museum, ships, tours, and exhibits. Pier 16 also is the departure point for various seasonal cruises.

To the north is **Pier 17,** a multilevel dockside shopping mall that closed in 2013 for redevelopment, and is planned to open in summer 2017 with a 60,000-square-foot landscaped rooftop, indoor and outdoor restaurants and bars, and year-round performance venues. Pier 17 was the longtime home of the Fulton Fish Market, which first opened in 1807. Starting in 1939 it was housed in the New Market Building, just north of the Seaport, but that closed in 2005 when operations were moved to a new 400,000-square-foot facility in Hunt's Point in the Bronx. ⊠ *South Street Seaport* ☎ *212/732–8257 for event and shopping info* ⊕ *www.southstreetseaport.com* Ⓜ *2, 3, 4, 5, A, C, J, Z to Fulton Center.*

Stone Street Historic District. Amid skyscrapers, the low-rise, two-block oasis of bars and restaurants along historic Stone Street feels more like a village than the center of the financial universe. In the summer, tables spill out into the cobblestone street and the mood is convivial, especially on Thursday and Friday nights. This was Manhattan's first paved street and today the cluster of buildings along here, with South William and Pearl Streets, and Coenties Alley, make up the Stone Street Historic District. ⊠ *Stone, S. William, and Pearl Sts., and Coenties Alley, Financial District* Ⓜ *R to Whitehall St.; 4,5 to Bowling Green.*

Ten House. Located just across Liberty Street from the World Trade Center site, the "Ten House" firehouse is officially known as Ladder Company 10 and Engine Company 10. On the morning of September 11, 2001, firefighters on duty here were among the first to respond to New York's terrorist attacks. The companies lost six heroes that day. The "Ten House Bravest Memorial" stands inside the firehouse to commemorate their ultimate sacrifice, and that of other Ten House heroes. Around the corner on Greenwich Street, the 56-foot long, bronze bas-relief "FDNY Memorial Wall" serves as a tribute to 343 firefighters who perished on 9/11. ⊠ *124 Liberty St., Financial District* ⊕ *www. fdnytenhouse.com* Ⓜ *2, 3, 4, 5, A, C, J, Z to Fulton St.; E to World Trade Center; N, R to Cortlandt St.*

World Trade Center Site. On September 11, 2001, terrorist hijackers steered two jets into the World Trade Center's Twin Towers, setting them ablaze and causing their collapse, killing 2,753 people and injuring countless others. The 16 acres of fenced-in rubble and debris that slowly evolved into a construction zone known as "Ground Zero" quickly became a memorial unto itself, a place where visitors and those who lost loved ones could mourn and reflect on what was the single-most-deadly foreign attack ever to happen on American soil. Exactly a decade later, the 9/11 Memorial Plaza opened, giving thousands of annual visitors a solemn, dedicated place to commemorate the events of that infamous day. After many delays, the accompanying underground National 9/11 Museum opened in 2014, on the same bedrock once used to support the Twin Towers' foundation. It serves as a fitting, if somber home to a vast array of artifacts from 9/11 and its aftermath.

The names of those lost on September 11th are commemorated on Memorial Plaza, at the former site of the Twin Towers.

The Memorial Plaza's twin reflecting pools are bordered by four distinct skyscrapers: the 1,776-foot One World Trade Center, and Towers 2, 3, and 4, each designed by renowned architects and rising 80-plus, 80, and 72 stories, respectively. The site also includes the WTC Transportation Hub designed by Santiago Calatrava. Known for a time as the "Freedom Tower," the 104-story One WTC has a roof that's 1,368 feet tall—a height identical to the original 1 WTC, the "north tower." (The south tower, or original 2 WTC, stood 1,362 feet tall.) An illuminated antenna further increases the new skyscraper's height to 1,776 feet to commemorate America's founding, and earning its title as the tallest building in the Western Hemisphere. Designed by award-winning architect David Childs, the new One WTC opened to tenants in late 2014. One World Observatory, on its 100th, 101st, and 102nd floors, opened in May 2015. With its angular, mirrored-glass facade, the Fumihiko Maki–designed 4 WTC anchors the southeastern corner of the complex, and was the first tower to open on the site, in late 2013. On its north side, 3 WTC is under construction and slated to open in 2018. At the site's northeast corner, 2 WTC construction restarted after several major delays, and is now expected to open in 2020. Between Towers 2 and 3 stands the eye-catching, $3.9 billion WTC Transportation Hub, which serves as the terminal for New Jersey's PATH trains and an underground link to Brookfield Place, as well as 10 subway lines and the Fulton Center transit complex. Inspired by the image of a bird in flight, the iconic hub features massive white steel "wings" extending from its riblike substructure. A largely column-free interior and glass-paneled roof allows natural light into the terminal's lower floors. The multilevel hub connects underground to Towers 2, 3 and 4, and offers more than 360,000 square feet of shops and restaurants. As you plan your visit, set aside time to check out other key parts of the 9/11 story, such as St. Paul's Chapel, the Tribute Center, and the "Ten House" firehouse on Liberty Street. ⊠ *Between Church and West Sts. and Vesey and Liberty Sts., Financial District* ⊕ *www.wtc.com* Ⓜ *R to Cortlandt St.; E to World Trade Center; 2, 3, 4, 5, A, C, J, Z to Fulton Center.*

WORTH NOTING

Bowling Green. Perhaps most recognized as the home of Arturo Di Modica's 7,000-pound, bronze *Charging Bull* statue (1989), Bowling Green, at the foot of Broadway, became New York's first public park in 1733. Legend has it that before that, this was the site upon which Peter Minuit purchased the island of Manhattan from the Native Americans, in 1626, supposedly for what amounted to 24 U.S. dollars. On July 9, 1776, a few hours after citizens learned about the signing of the Declaration of Independence, rioters toppled a statue of British King George III that had occupied the spot for 11 years; much of the statue's lead was melted down into bullets. In 1783, when the occupying British forces fled the city, they defiantly hoisted a Union Jack on a greased, uncleated flagpole so it couldn't be lowered; patriot John Van Arsdale drove his own cleats into the pole to replace it with the Stars and Stripes. The copper-top subway entrance across State Street is the original one, built in 1904–05. ⊠ *Broadway at Whitehall St., Financial District* Ⓜ *4, 5 to Bowling Green.*

City Hall. What once marked the northernmost point of Manhattan today houses the office of the mayor, and serves as a gathering place for demonstrators and the news crews who cover their stories. This is the oldest City Hall in the country, a striking (but surprisingly small) building dating back to 1803. If the history of local politics and architecture is your thing, free tours are available (sign up in advance online). Inside, highlights include the Rotunda where President Lincoln lay in state in 1865 under a soaring dome supported by 10 Corinthian columns; the Victorian-style **City Council Chamber;** and the **Governor's Room,** an elegantly preserved space with portraits of historic figures, as well as a writing table that George Washington used in 1789 when New York was the U.S. capital. If nothing else, take a moment to snap a photo of the columned exterior and see the small but lovely City Hall Park, bound by Broadway to the west and Chambers Street to the north. This park is a shady respite to stop, enjoy the fountain, and take a breather from the Lower Manhattan hubbub. ⊠ *City Hall Park, Financial District* ☎ *212/788–2656 for tour reservations* ⊕ *www.nyc. gov/html/artcom/html/tours/city_hall.shtml* ⊠ *Free* ☉ *Tours available some weekdays (reserve online or by phone)* Ⓜ *2, 3 to Park Pl.; R to City Hall; 4, 5, 6 to Brooklyn Bridge–City Hall; A, C to Chambers St.; J, Z to Chambers St.*

Federal Hall National Memorial. It's a museum now, but this site has quite a notable claim: George Washington was sworn in here as the first president of the United States, in 1789, when the building was the Federal Hall of the new nation. The museum within covers 400 years of New York City's history, with a focus on the life and times of what

The Gangs of Five Points

In the mid-19th century, the Five Points area was perhaps the city's most notorious and dangerous neighborhood. The confluence of five streets—Mulberry, Anthony (now Worth), Cross (now Park), Orange (now Baxter), and Little Water (no longer in existence)—had been built over a drainage pond that was filled in the 1820s. When buildings began to sink into the mosquito-filled muck, middle-class residents abandoned their homes. Buildings were then chopped into tiny apartments that were rented to the poorest of the poor, who at this point included newly emancipated slaves and Irish immigrants fleeing famine. Newspaper accounts at the time tell of daily robberies and other violent crimes. With corrupt political leaders like William Marcy "Boss" Tweed more concerned with lining their pockets than patrolling the streets, keeping order was left to the club-wielding hooligans portrayed in Martin Scorsese's *Gangs of New York*. The neighborhood, finally razed in the 1880s to make way for Columbus Park, has left a lasting legacy: in the music halls where different ethnic groups grudgingly came together, the Irish jig and the African American shuffle combined to form a new type of fancy footwork called tap dancing. Today, this is the heart of Chinatown. Residents gather in Columbus Park for tai chi in the morning and rowdy board games in the afternoon.

is now the city's Financial District. You can spot this building easily—it was modeled on the Parthenon, and a statue of George Washington is planted proudly on its stately steps. Free guided tours are available 10–3 on weekdays. ⊠ *26 Wall St., at Nassau St., Financial District* ☎ *212/825–6990* ⊕ *www.nps.gov/feha* ⊠ *Free* ☉ *Weekdays 9–5* Ⓜ *2, 3 to Wall St.; J, Z to Broad St.*

Federal Reserve Bank of New York. With its imposing mix of sandstone, limestone, and ironwork, the Federal Reserve looks the way a bank ought to: strong and impregnable. The gold ingots in the subterranean vaults here are worth roughly $350 billion—reputedly a third of the world's gold reserves. Forty-five-minute tours (conducted twice a day and requiring reservations made at least five days in advance) include a visit to the gold vault, the trading desk, and "FedWorks," a multimedia exhibit center where you can track hypothetical trades. Visitors must show an officially issued photo ID, such as a driver's license or passport, and pass through scanners to enter the building. The Fed advises arriving 20 minutes before your tour to accommodate security screening. Photography is not permitted. ⊠ *33 Liberty St., between William and Nassau Sts., Financial District* ☎ *212/720–6130* ⊕ *www.newyorkfed. org* ⊠ *Free, including tours* ☉ *Tours weekdays at 1 and 2 (reservations required)* Ⓜ *2, 3, 4, 5, A, C, J, Z to Fulton St.*

Fraunces Tavern Museum. This former tavern, where General George Washington celebrated the end of the Revolutionary War in 1783, is now a museum covering two floors above a restaurant and bar. Here, in his pre-presidential days, Washington bid an emotional farewell to his officers upon the British evacuation of New York. Today, this historic landmark has two fully furnished period rooms—including the Long Room, site of Washington's address—and other modest displays of 18th- and 19th-century American history. These days, you'll find more tourists and Wall Street types than revolutionaries in the tavern and restaurant on the ground floor, but a cozy Colonial atmosphere and decent hearty meal are available. ⊠ *54 Pearl St., at Broad St., Financial District* ☎ *212/425–1778* ⊕ *www.frauncestavernmuseum.org* 🖾 *$7* ☉ *Weekdays noon–5, weekends 11–5* Ⓜ *R to Whitehall St.; 4, 5 to Bowling Green; 1 to South Ferry; J, Z to Broad St.*

Museum of American Finance. Pre-9/11, a visit to the New York Stock Exchange was the ultimate high; the energy of the floor and the proximity to so much power couldn't be beat. Post-9/11, security prohibits tours of the Exchange, but you can still get a feel—albeit a less exhilarating feel—for what makes the financial world go 'round (and sometimes down) by visiting this museum. Located in the grandiose former banking hall of the Bank of New York, this Smithsonian affiliate is home to artifacts of the financial market's history; interactive exhibits on the financial markets, banking, entrepreneurship, and Alexander Hamilton; and well-executed temporary exhibits. ⊠ *48 Wall St., at William St., Financial District* ☎ *212/908–4110* ⊕ *www.moaf.org* 🖾 *$8* ☉ *Tues.– Sat. 10–4* Ⓜ *2, 3 to Wall St.*

Museum of Jewish Heritage—A Living Memorial to the Holocaust. In a granite 85-foot hexagon at the southern end of Battery Park City, this museum's mission is to educate visitors on the "broad tapestry of Jewish life in the 20th and 21st centuries—before, during, and after the Holocaust." Architects Kevin Roche and John Dinkeloo designed the six-sided museum to be symbolic of the Star of David, with three floors of exhibits demonstrating the dynamism of Jewish culture. Visitors enter through a gallery that provides context for the early-20th-century artifacts on the first floor: an elaborate screen hand-painted for the fall harvest festival of Sukkoth, tools used by Jewish tradesmen, and wedding invitations. Original documentary films play throughout the museum. The second floor details the rise of Nazism and anti-Semitism, and the ravages of the Holocaust. A gallery covers the doomed final voyage of the SS *St. Louis,* a ship that crossed the Atlantic twice in 1939, carrying German Jewish refugees in search of safe haven. Signs of hope are also on display, including a trumpet that Louis Bannet (the "Dutch Louis Armstrong") played for three years in the Auschwitz-Birkenau inmate orchestra. The third floor covers postwar Jewish life. Recent temporary exhibits have explored the history of American Jews who tried to rescue European Jews leading up to and during the Holocaust, as well as the rich Jewish history of Oswiecim, the town the Germans called Auschwitz. The museum's east wing has a theater, memorial garden, library, galleries, and café. A free audio guide, with narration by Meryl Streep and Itzhak Perlman, is available at the admissions desk. ⊠ *36 Battery Pl., Battery Park City, New York* ☎ *646/437–4202* ⊕ *www. mjhnyc.org* 🖾 *$12 (free Wed. 4–8)* ☉ *Thurs. and Sun.–Tues. 10–5:45, Wed. 10–8, Fri. and eve of Jewish holidays 10–3* Ⓜ *4, 5 to Bowling Green; 1 to Rector St.; R to Rector St.*

National Museum of the American Indian (Smithsonian Institution). Massive granite columns rise to a pediment topped by a double row of statues at the impressive Beaux Arts Alexander Hamilton U.S. Custom House (1907), which is home to the New York branch of the Smithsonian museum (the other branch is in Washington, D.C.). Inside, the oval stairwell and rotunda embellished with shipping-theme murals (completed in the 1930s) are worth a long pause. The permanent exhibit, "Infinity of Nations," is an encyclopedic survey of Native American cultures from across the continent, with the entire museum housing more than 825,000 art pieces and artifacts dating from ancient to modern times. The venue presents changing exhibits, videos and films, dance, music, and storytelling programs. ⊠ *1 Bowling Green, between State and Whitehall Sts., Financial District* ☎ *212/514–3700* ⊕ *www.nmai. si.edu* ▧ *Free* ⊙ *Mon.–Wed. and Fri.–Sun. 10–5, Thurs. 10–8* Ⓜ *4, 5 to Bowling Green; 1 to Rector St.; R to Whitehall St.; J, Z to Broad St.; 4, 5 to Wall St.*

Skyscraper Museum. Why get a crick in your neck—or worse, risk looking like a tourist—while appreciating New York City's famous skyline, when you can visit the Skyscraper Museum instead? At this compact museum with a lofty spirit, you can appreciate highly detailed, hand-carved miniature wood models of Midtown and Lower Manhattan; explore the past, present, and future of the skyscraper—from New York City's Empire State Building to Dubai's Burj Khalifa (taller than the Empire State Building and Chicago's Willis Tower combined); and examine both the history of the Twin Towers at the World Trade Center and the ongoing reconstruction at Ground Zero. The museum's exhibits are always evolving, so expect models of current or future buildings, videos, drawings, floor plans, and talks that reveal the influence of history, real estate, and individuals on shaping city skylines. ⊠ *39 Battery Pl., across from Museum of Jewish Heritage, Financial District* ☎ *212/968–1961* ⊕ *www.skyscraper.org* ▧ *$5* ⊙ *Wed.–Sun. noon–6* Ⓜ *4, 5 to Bowling Green.*

St. Paul's Chapel. For more than a year after the 2001 World Trade Center attacks, the chapel's fence served as a shrine for visitors seeking solace. People from around the world left tokens of grief and support, or signed one of the large dropcloths that hung from the fence. After serving as a 24-hour refuge where rescue and recovery workers could eat, pray, rest, and receive counseling, the chapel, which amazingly suffered no damage, reopened to the public in fall 2002. The powerful ongoing exhibit, titled "Unwavering Spirit: Hope & Healing at Ground Zero," honors the efforts of rescue workers in the months after September 11 with photos, drawings, banners, and other items sent to them as memorials. Open since 1766, St. Paul's is the oldest public building in continuous use in Manhattan. ⊠ *209 Broadway, at Fulton St., Financial District* ☎ *212/602–0800* ⊕ *www.trinitywallstreet.org/about/st-pauls* ⊙ *Mon.–Sat. 10–6, Sun. 7–6* Ⓜ *2, 3, 4, 5, A, C, J, Z to Fulton St.; E to World Trade Center.*

Trinity Wall Street Church. Alexander Hamilton is buried under a white-stone pyramid in this historic church's graveyard, not far from a monument commemorating steamboat inventor Robert Fulton (buried in the

Liberty Enlightening the World, as the Statue of Liberty is officially named, was given by France to the United States in 1886 to mark the U.S. centennial.

Livingston family vault with his wife). The church (the third on this site) was designed in 1846 by Richard Upjohn. Its most notable feature is the set of enormous bronze doors designed by Richard Morris Hunt to recall Lorenzo Ghiberti's portal for the Baptistery in Florence, Italy. *Trinity Root,* a 12½-foot-high, 3-ton sculpture by Steven Tobin cast from the sycamore tree struck by debris on 9/11 behind St. Paul's Chapel, was installed in front of the church in 2005. A museum inside outlines the church's storied history. ⊠ *74 Trinity Pl., entrance at Broadway and the head of Wall St., Financial District* ☎ *212/602–0800* ⊕ *www.trinitywallstreet.org* ⊙ *Weekdays 7–6, Sat. 8–4, Sun. 7–4; museum: weekdays 9–5:30, weekends 9–3:45* Ⓜ *2, 3, 4, 5 to Wall St.; 1, N, R to Rector St.; J, Z to Broad St.*

NEW YORK HARBOR

The southern tip of Manhattan has often served as a microcosm for a city that offers as many first shots as it does second chances, so it's appropriate that the key point of departure for the Statue of Liberty and Ellis Island is here. This experience should never be dismissed as too touristy. Unlike any other, the excursion is a reminder that New York is a city of immigrants and survivors.

FAMILY
Fodor's Choice
★

Ellis Island. Between 1892 and 1924 approximately 12 million men, women, and children first set foot on U.S. soil at the Ellis Island federal immigration facility. By the time the facility closed in 1954, it had processed ancestors of more than 40% of Americans living today. The island's main building, now a national monument, is now known as the **Ellis Island National Museum of Immigration,** and tells the story not just of Ellis Island but of immigration from the Colonial era to the present day, through numerous galleries containing artifacts, photographs, and taped oral histories. The centerpiece of the museum is the white-tile Registry Room (also known as the Great Hall). It feels dignified and cavernous today, but photographs show that it took on a multitude of configurations through the years, always packed with humanity. While you're there, check out the Registry Room's tall, arched windows and try to imagine what passed through immigrants' minds as they viewed Lower Manhattan's skyline to one side and the Statue of Liberty to the other.

Because there's so much to take in, it's a good idea to make use of the museum's interpretive tools. Check at the visitor desk for free film tickets, ranger tour times, and special programs. The audio tour (included in the price of your ferry ticket) takes you through the exhibits, providing thorough, engaging commentary interspersed with recordings of immigrants themselves recalling their experiences.

Along with the Registry Room, the museum's features include the ground-level Peopling of America Center, a major expansion to the Ellis Island Museum that explores immigration to the United States before and after Ellis Island became a portal for immigrants. Interpretative graphics and poignant audio stories give first-hand accounts of the immigrant's journey—from making the trip and arriving in the United States to their struggle and survival after they arrived. There's also the American Family Immigration Center, where you can search Ellis Island's records for your own ancestors; and the American Flag of Faces, an interactive display filled with a montage of images of immigrants submitted online (submit yours at *FlagofFaces.org*). Outside is the American Immigrant Wall of Honor, which has the names of more than 600,000 immigrant Americans against the backdrop of the Manhattan skyline.

There is no admission fee for either the Statue of Liberty or Ellis Island, but the ferry ride (which goes round-trip from Battery Park to Liberty Island to Ellis Island), costs $18. Ferries leave from Battery Park every 30 to 40 minutes depending on the time of year (buy your tickets online at *www.statuecruises.com*). There are often long lines, so arrive early, especially if you have a reserved-time ticket. There is a pleasant indoor-outdoor café on Ellis Island. ⊠ *Battery Park* ☎ *212/561–4588 Ellis Island, 212/561–4500 Wall of Honor information, 877/523–9849* ⊕ *www.ellisisland.org* ✉ *Free; ferry $18 round-trip (includes Liberty Island)* ☉ *Daily 9–5:15; last ferry at 3:30, extended hrs in summer.*

FAMILY

Fodor's Choice

★

Governors Island. Governors Island is open to the public from May to October: get there via a short, free ferry ride. It's essentially a big, charming park that looks like a small New England town—it's popular with locals for biking and running trails, summer festivals, art shows, concerts, and family programs. Wouter Van Twiller, a representative for Holland, supposedly purchased the island for his private use, in 1637, from Native Americans for two ax heads, a string of beads, and a handful of nails. It was confiscated by the Dutch government a year later, and for the next decade its ownership switched back and forth between the Dutch and British until the Brits gained firm control of it in the 1670s. The island was officially named in 1784 for His Majesty's Governors and used by the American military until the 1960s, when the Coast Guard took it over. After their facilities were abandoned in 1995, the island was purchased by the city in 2002 and started welcoming visitors in 2003. The Governors Island ferry departs from the Battery Maritime Building and from Brooklyn's Pier 6. It is a favorite summertime excursion for New Yorkers. ⊠ *Battery Maritime Building (for Manhattan ferry), 10 South St., Battery Park* ⊕ *www.govisland. com* ⊠ *Free* ⊙ *May–Oct., Fri. 10–5, weekends 10–7* Ⓜ *1 to South Ferry; 4, 5 to Bowling Green; R to Whitehall St.*

Fodor's Choice   **Staten Island Ferry.** Every day, some 70,000 people ride the free ferry
★   to Staten Island, one of the city's outer boroughs, and you should be one of them. Without paying a cent, you get phenomenal views of the Lower Manhattan skyline, the Statue of Liberty, and Ellis Island during the 25-minute cruise across New York Harbor. You also pass tugboats, freighters, and cruise ships—a reminder that this is very much still a working harbor. The boat embarks every 15 to 30 minutes (24 hours a day, 365 days a year) from the Whitehall Terminal at Whitehall and South Streets, near the east end of Battery Park. You must disembark once you reach the opposite terminal, but you can just get back in line to board again if you don't plan to stay. ⊠ *4 Whitehall St., Battery Park* ☎ *212/639–9675* ⊕ *www.siferry.com* ⊠ *Free* Ⓜ *1 to South Ferry; R to Whitehall St.; 4, 5 to Bowling Green.*

Fodor's Choice   **The Statue of Liberty.** For millions of immigrants, the first glimpse of
★   America was the Statue of Liberty, growing from a vaguely defined figure on the horizon into a towering, stately colossus. Visitors approaching Liberty Island on the ferry from Battery Park may experience a similar sense of wonder.

Liberty Enlightening the World, as the statue is officially named, was presented to the United States in 1886 as a gift from France. The 152-foot-tall figure was sculpted by Frederic-Auguste Bartholdi and erected around an iron skeleton engineered by Gustave Eiffel. It stands atop an 89-foot pedestal designed by Richard Morris Hunt, with Emma Lazarus's sonnet "The New Colossus" ("Give me your tired, your poor, your huddled masses . . .") inscribed on a bronze plaque at the base. Over the course of time the statue has become precisely what its creators dreamed it would be: the single-most-powerful symbol of American ideals and, as such, one of the world's great monumental sculptures. Inside the statue's pedestal is a museum that's everything it should be: informative, entertaining, and quickly viewed. Highlights include the original flame (which was replaced because of water damage), full-scale replicas of Lady Liberty's face and one of her feet, Bartholdi's alternate designs for the statue, and a model of Eiffel's intricate framework. You're allowed access to the museum as part of one of the free tours of the promenade (which surrounds the base of the pedestal) or the observatory (at the pedestal's top).

On a typical weekday, five ferries make roughly 110 trips back and forth between Staten Island and Manhattan, transporting about 70,000 passengers.

There is no admission fee for either the Statue of Liberty or Ellis Island, but the ferry ride (which goes round-trip from Battery Park to Liberty Island to Ellis Island) costs $18, $21 for access to the statue's crown. Ferries leave from Battery Park every 30 to 40 minutes depending on the time of year (buy your tickets online at *www.statuecruises.com*). There are often long lines, so arrive early, especially if you have a reserved-time ticket. There is a pleasant indoor-outdoor café on Liberty Island.

The tours are limited to 3,000 participants a day. The only way to guarantee entry is with an advance purchase of a Reserve Ticket with Monument or Pedestal Pass, which should be purchased at least a few days and ideally longer before your visit (they can be reserved up to 180 days in advance by phone or online). No tickets are sold on the island; however, tickets are sold daily at Castle Clinton Monument in Battery Park, and at Liberty State Park in New Jersey. Visitors who are unable to acquire a Reserve Ticket with Monument Pass can still be issued a No Monument Access Pass, allowing them to walk around the island on the ground level without access to the statue. Approximately 240 people are allowed to visit the crown each day via a set of narrow, double-helix stairs. Tickets are available online, but are usually sold out up to three or four months ahead of the visit, so book early. If you can't get tickets to the crown, you can get a good look at the statue's inner structure on the observatory tour. From the observatory itself there are fine views of the harbor and an up-close view of Lady Liberty. If you're on one of the tours, you'll go through a security check more thorough than any airport screening, and you'll have to deposit any bags in a locker. ✉ *Liberty Island,*

Lower Manhattan ☎ *212/363–3200, 877/523–9849 ticket reservations* ⊕ *www.libertyellisfoundation.org* ✉ *Free; ferry $18 round-trip (includes Ellis Island), crown tickets extra $3* ⊙ *Daily 9:30–5; last ferry at 3:30, extended hrs in summer.*

TRIBECA

Tucked on the west side south of Canal Street, residential TriBeCa (the *Tri*angle *Be*low *Ca*nal Street) has a quieter vibe than most other Manhattan neighborhoods. Walk the photogenic streets, especially the stretch of Federal row houses on Harrison Street, and you'll understand why so many celebrities own apartments here. The two-block-long Staple Street, with its connecting overhead walkway, is a favorite of urban cinematographers. Although TriBeCa's money is often hidden behind grand cast-iron facades, you can get a taste of it at posh neighborhood restaurants, cocktail bars, and boutiques, or at the star-studded TriBeCa Film Festival every spring.

FAMILY **Hudson River Park.** The quiet green spaces of New York City are trea-
Fodor's Choice sured by locals, and one of the best options is Hudson River Park, a
★ 5-mile path from Battery Place to 59th Street. This riverside stretch has been renovated into a landscaped park, incorporating the piers that jut out into the Hudson, with walking and cycling paths, a seasonal minigolf course, dog runs, and skate parks. The TriBeCa portion consists of Piers 25 and 26 and has picnic spaces, playgrounds, and a sand volleyball court. The areas adjacent to the West Village (Piers 45 and 46) and near Chelsea (Piers 63 and 64) are equally attractive, with lots of spots for leisure and recreation. ⊠ *TriBeCa* ☎ *212/627–2020* ⊕ *www.hudsonriverpark.org* Ⓜ *1 to Franklin St. for TriBeCa section of the park.*

Postmasters. This gallery, first opened in the East Village in 1984, shows new and established conceptual artists of all ages. Past exhibits have included Claude Wampler's *Pomerania*—a series of photographs, sculptures, video, and drawings examining the artist's relationship with her pet Pomeranian. ⊠ *54 Franklin St., between Broadway and Lafayette St., TriBeCa* ☎ *212/727–3323* ⊕ *www.postmastersart.com* ✉ *Free* ⊙ *Tues., Wed., Fri., Sat. 11–6, Thurs. 11–8* Ⓜ *6, J, N, Q, R, Z to Canal St.*

SOHO, NOLITA, LITTLE ITALY, AND CHINATOWN

GETTING ORIENTED

SoHo, NoLlta,
Little Italy, and
Chinatown

W. 1st St.
E. 1st St.
3rd Ave.
Sullivan St.
West Broadway
Broadway
W. Houston St.
E. Houston St.
B,D,F,M
Aroma
Espresso Bar
Puck Building
New York
Earth Room
St. Patrick's
Old Cathedral
NOLITA
Forsyth St.
Prince St.
R,N
Prince St.
Greene St.
Mercer St.
Mulberry St.
Mott St.
Elizabeth St.
Bowery
Sara D. Roosevelt
Park
SOHO
New York City
Fire Museum
Donald Judd
House
Spring St.
DeSalvio
Playground
Saigon Vietnamese
Sandwich Deli
Spring St.
C,E
Cleveland Pl.
6
Kenmare St.
J,Z
Chrystie St.
Thompson St.
Broadway
Crosby St.
Lafayette St.
LITTLE
ITALY
Broome St.
Broome St.
Drawing
Center
Wooster St.
Mott Street
Grand St.
B,D
Ronald Feldman
Fine Arts
Grand St.
Mott St.
Elizabeth St.
Leslie + Lohman
Museum of Gay
and Lesbian Art
The Museum of Chinese
in America (MOCA)
Baxter St.
Hester St.
Bowery
Howard St.
A,C,E
Canal St.
Centre St.
Lispenard St.
N,R,Q
Most Precious
Blood Church
Canal St.
Mahayana
Buddhist
Temple
Walker St.
6
J,Z
CHINATOWN
Mulberry St.
Bayard St.
White St.
TRIBECA
W. Broadway
Church St.
Franklin St.
Broadway
Lafayette St.
Collect
Pond Park
Columbus
Park
Mosco
St.
Pell St.
Doyers St.
Leonard St.
Hogan Pl.
Worth St.
Worth St.
Kimlau
Square
Thomas St.
Foley
Square
Centre St.
Duane St.
Thomas
Paine Park
Reade St.

0   1/8 mi
0   200 meters

MAKING THE MOST OF YOUR TIME

If you're coming to SoHo and NoLIta to shop, there's no need to rush out the door—most shops don't open until 10 or 11 am, and many stay open until the early evening. If art is your thing, avoid Sunday since most galleries are closed. SoHo, with national chains lining its section of Broadway, is almost always a madhouse on weekend afternoons (unless it's raining), but weekdays are somewhat less frenetic. NoLIta, with less traffic, fewer chains, and more boutiques, is calmer and less crowded.

Little Italy is a small area nowadays, having lost ground to a growing Chinatown. Note that foodwise, most of the checkered-tablecloth spots in Little Italy itself are touristy, with mediocre food.

If you're visiting New York in mid-September, you'll time it right for the Feast of San Gennaro—a huge street fair in honor of the patron saint of Naples—along with thousands of others, who enjoy exploring the many food and souvenir booths and playing games of chance. Given that few Italian Americans live in the area anymore, it's not exactly like visiting old Napoli, but it is a fun way to take in the sights while sampling cannoli or sausage and peppers.

Chinatown bustles with local shoppers pretty much any time of day, but there are more tourists on the weekends, when it gets so busy you may have to duck into a shop or restaurant just for a break from all the sidewalk jostling.

TOP EXPERIENCES

Browsing boutiques and people-watching in SoHo and NoLIta

Ogling the out-of-the-ordinary produce and seafood in Chinatown

Gallery-hopping in SoHo

Eating dim sum in Chinatown

Sipping a cocktail in NoLIta

GETTING HERE AND AROUND

SoHo (*South of Houston*) is bounded by Houston Street, Canal Street, 6th Avenue, and Lafayette Street. To the east, NoLIta (*North of Little Italy*) is contained by Houston, the Bowery, Kenmare, and Lafayette Street. Plenty of subways service the area: take the 6, C, or E to Spring Street; the N or R to Prince Street; or the B, D, F, or M to Broadway–Lafayette Street. For Chinatown, farther south, take the 6, J, N, Q, R, or Z to Canal Street, or the B or D to Grand Street.

COFFEE AND QUICK BITES

Aroma Espresso Bar. With large corner windows perfect for observing the well-dressed tide of humanity crossing West Houston, this busy branch of the international coffee chain serves sandwiches, soups, and pastries. ⊠ *145 Greene St., at W. Houston St., SoHo* ☎ *212/533–1094* ⊕ *www.aroma.us* Ⓜ *B, D, F, M to Broadway/Lafayette St.; N, R to Prince St.*

Saigon Vietnamese Sandwich Deli. Predating the *banh mi* craze by perhaps a decade, this storefront keeps hungry gallery-hoppers, shoppers, and locals happy with its complicated and delicious sandwiches, all served on baguettes. ⊠ *369 Broome St., between Mott and Elizabeth Sts., SoHo* ☎ *212/219–8341* ⊕ *www.vietnamese-sandwich. com* ⊟ *No credit cards* Ⓜ *J, Z to Bowery; 6 to Spring St.; B, D to Grand St.*

Sightseeing
★★★
Nightlife
★★★
Dining
★★★★
Lodging
★★★
Shopping
★★★★★

SoHo, NoLIta, Little Italy, and Chinatown are all jam-packed with humanity, all the more perfect for people-watching as you shop, nibble, and wander. Parts of SoHo and NoLIta are destinations for super-trendy shopping as well as popular chains and department stores: the boutiques are often overpriced but undeniably glamorous (keep a lookout for sales). Little Italy and Chinatown are more about local shopping and Instagram-worthy food shops and stalls.

SOHO

Updated by
Kelsy Chauvin

Once the epicenter of the New York art scene, SoHo today is now more synonymous with shopping. A bit of bohemia still exists on the cobblestone side streets, where there are charming restaurants with sidewalk seating and some of the art galleries that haven't scattered elsewhere. The main thoroughfares tend to have sidewalks lined with tables of handmade jewelry, hats, purses, and art. If you take the time to look, there's a local vibe here beneath the glitzy boutiques—like elderly residents speaking Italian on the corners around Sullivan Street and Thompson Street, who reveal the neighborhood's Italian past.

Donald Judd House. A five-story cast-iron building from 1870, 101 Spring Street was the New York home and studio of artist Donald Judd. Although the neighborhood used to be home to many single-use cast-iron buildings, this is the only one that remains—and is a designated historic building. Judd bought it in 1968, and today, guided 90-minute tours explore Judd's living and working spaces and include art installations as they were arranged by Judd prior to his death in 1994 (note: climbing stairs is required). ⊠ *101 Spring St., SoHo* ☎ *212/219–2747* ⊕ *www.juddfoundation.org* ✉ *$25* ۞ *Tues.–Sat., by guided tour only* Ⓜ *N, R to Prince St.; 6 to Spring St.*

Drawing Center. At this nonprofit organization the focus is on drawings—contemporary and historical. Works shown in the three galleries

CLOSE UP

SoHo and NoLIta Architecture

3

There are plenty of beautiful people in SoHo and NoLIta, but tilt your eyes up, beyond the turn-of-the-20th-century cast-iron "bishop's crook" lampposts, and discover some of New York's most impressive architecture. Look down, and see Belgian-brick cobblestones lining some of the streets. Along Broadway and the neighboring streets of SoHo, you see "vault lights" in the sidewalk: starting in the 1850s, these glass lenses were set into sidewalks so daylight could reach basements.

The **King of Greene Street,** at 72–76 Greene, between Grand and Canal, is a five-story, Renaissance-style 1873 building with a magnificent projecting porch of Corinthian columns and pilasters. These days it's unmistakably painted in high-gloss ivory. Over at 28–30 Greene Street is the **Queen of Greene Street,** a graceful 1873 cast-iron beauty that exemplifies the Second Empire style with its dormers, columns, window arches, projecting central bays, and roof.

The **Haughwout Building,** at 488–492 Broadway, north of Broome, is best known for what's no longer inside—the world's first commercial passenger elevator, invented by Elisha Graves Otis. The building's exterior is worth a look, though: nicknamed the "Parthenon of Cast Iron," the five-story, Venetian palazzo–style structure was built in 1857 to house department-store merchant E.V. Haughwout's china, silver, and glassware store. Each window is framed by Corinthian columns and rounded arches.

Built in 1904, the **Little Singer Building,** at 561 Broadway, is a masterpiece of cast-iron styling, its delicate facade covered with curlicues of wrought iron. The L-shape building's second facade is around the corner on Prince Street.

Charlton Street, not technically in SoHo but across 6th Avenue in the West Village, is Manhattan's longest stretch of Federal-style redbrick row houses dating from the 1820s and '30s. The high stoops, paneled front doors, leaded-glass windows, and narrow dormer windows are all intact. King and Vandam Streets also have historic houses. Much of this area was the site of a mansion called Richmond Hill, and in the late 18th century the surrounding area was a beautiful wild meadow from where you could see the nearby "hamlet" of Greenwich Village.

Over in Little Italy/NoLIta, the magnificent old **Police Headquarters** building at 240 Centre Street, between Broome and Grand, might be familiar from Martin Scorsese's *Gangs of New York.* The 1909 Edwardian baroque–style structure with its striking copper dome was the headquarters of the New York City Police Department until 1973. Designed to "impress both the officer and the prisoner with the majesty of the law," it was converted into luxury condos in 1988 and is known today as the Police Building Apartments.

The 1885 Romanesque Revival **Puck Building,** at 295 Lafayette Street, on the southeast corner of Houston, is a former magazine headquarters and now a busy event space and home to REI's New York flagship store. Look for the statue of Puck just over the door: his gilding contrasts with the deep-red brick.

SoHo has one of the world's greatest concentrations of cast-iron buildings, created in response to fires that wiped out much of Lower Manhattan in the mid-18th century.

often push the envelope on what's considered drawing; many projects are commissioned by the center. ✉ *35 Wooster St., between Broome and Grand Sts., SoHo* ☎ *212/219–2166* ⊕ *www.drawingcenter.org* 🎟 *$5* 🕓 *Wed. and Fri.–Sun. noon–6, Thurs. noon–8* Ⓜ *1 to Canal St.; A, C, E to Canal St.; 6, J, N, Q, R, Z to Canal St.*

Leslie + Lohman Museum of Gay and Lesbian Art. Founded in 1987, this nonprofit museum has roots in the collection of its founders, Charles Leslie and Fritz Lohman, two lifelong champions of LGBTQ artists. The well-curated exhibits are usually photographic (and sometimes sexually charged), though the museum's impressive archive leads to new exhibitions in various media as often as eight times a year. The museum underwent a major renovation in 2016, adding a gift shop and further expanding its exhibition and programming spaces. ✉ *26 Wooster St., between Grand and Canal Sts., SoHo* ☎ *212/431–2609* ⊕ *www.leslielohman.org* 🎟 *Free* 🕓 *Tues., Wed., and Fri.–Sun. noon–6, Thurs. noon–8* Ⓜ *1 to Canal St.; A, C, E to Canal St.; 6, J, N, Q, R, Z to Canal St.*

New York City Fire Museum. In the former headquarters of Engine 30, a handsome Beaux Arts building dating from 1904, retired firefighters volunteer their time in the morning and early afternoon to answer visitors' questions. The collection of firefighting tools from the 18th century to the present includes hand-pulled and horse-drawn engines, speaking trumpets, pumps, and uniforms. A memorial exhibit with photos, paintings, children's artwork, and found objects relating to the September 11, 2001, attacks is also on view—a poignant reminder and tribute to the 343 firefighters who died on 9/11. ✉ *278 Spring St., between Hudson* *and Varick Sts., SoHo* ☎ *212/691–1303* ⊕ *www.nycfiremuseum.org* ▧ *$8* ⊙ *Daily 10–5* Ⓜ *C, E to Spring St.; 1 to Houston St.*

New York Earth Room. Noted "earthworks" artist Walter De Maria's 1977 avant-garde installation consists of 140 tons of gently sculpted soil (22 inches deep). It fills 3,600 square feet of a second-floor gallery maintained by the Dia Art Foundation since 1980. As the *New York Times* put it in 1999, "a loamy smell definitely permeates the space." You can't touch or walk on the dirt, nor can you take its photo. If you like this installation, check out De Maria's equally odd and impressive work, *The Broken Kilometer,* an 18.75-ton installation that consists of five columns of a total of 1,000 meter-long brass rods, which cover the wood floors of an open loft space. It's a few blocks away at 393 West Broadway, and has the same hours as the Earth Room. ✉ *141 Wooster St., 2nd fl., between W. Houston and Prince Sts., SoHo* ☎ *212/989–5566* ⊕ *www.diaart.org/ sites/main/earthroom* ▧ *Free* ⊙ *Mid-Sept.–mid-June, Wed.–Sun. noon–3 and 3:30–6* Ⓜ *N, R to Prince St.; B, D, F, M to Broadway–Lafayette St.*

Ronald Feldman Fine Arts. Founded in 1971 and in SoHo since the 1980s, this gallery represents more than 30 international contemporary artists; exhibits include contemporary painting, sculpture, installations, drawings, and prints. The space also hosts performances and has a large selection of Andy Warhol prints, paintings, and drawings. ✉ *31 Mercer St., between Grand and Canal Sts., SoHo* ☎ *212/226–3232* ⊕ *www.feldmangallery.com* ▧ *Free* ⊙ *Winter, Tues.–Sat. 10–6; summer, Mon.–Thurs. 10–6, Fri. 10–3* Ⓜ *1 to Canal St.; A, C, E to Canal St.; 6, J, N, Q, R, Z to Canal St.*

NOLITA

Many locals would say that the spirit of old SoHo is somewhat alive in NoLIta, a charming neighborhood with an artistic spirit, independently run boutiques and restaurants, and a local vibe. The streets here are less frantic and crowded than either SoHo or Chinatown, and each block could provide hours of roaming and ducking into small shops, nursing a cappuccino at a sidewalk café, or lingering over a meal surrounded by stylish New Yorkers. This is downtown, so the prices aren't cheap, but the quality is high and the experience unique.

St. Patrick's Old Cathedral. If you've seen *The Godfather,* you've had a peek inside New York's first Roman Catholic cathedral—the interior shots of the infamous baptism scene were filmed here. Dedicated in 1815, this church lost its designation as the seat of New York's bishop when the current St. Patrick's opened uptown, in 1879. The unadorned exterior of the cathedral gives no hint of the splendors within, which include an 1868 Henry Erben pipe organ. The interior dates from the 1860s, after a large fire gutted most of the original structure. The enormous marble altar surrounded by hand-carved niches (*reredos*) houses an extraordinary collection of sacred statuary and other Gothic exuberance. Sunday Mass in English is at 9:15 and 12:45. ✉ *263 Mulberry St., corner of Mott and Prince Sts., NoLIta* ☎ *212/226–8075* ⊕ *www.oldcathedral.org* ⊙ *Daily 8–5 (hrs vary)* Ⓜ *N, R to Prince St.; 6 to Bleecker St.*

LITTLE ITALY

Just east of Broadway, the tangle of pedestrian-friendly blocks surrounding Mulberry Street between NoLIta and bustling Canal Street are still a cheerful salute to all things Italian, although over the decades Little Italy has been whittled down by the sprawl of nearby Chinatown. There are red, green, and white street decorations on permanent display, and specialty grocers and cannelloni makers still dish up delights, though it's all a bit touristy these days—if it's a great Italian meal you want, you might be wise to look elsewhere. Still, Little Italy is fun to walk around, and several of the classic food stores on Grand Street are worth a stop if you're after an edible souvenir, like classic cannoli and espresso. For a bigger and more bustling Little Italy, head up to Arthur Avenue in the Bronx *(see Chapter 14)* to find several good, affordable restaurants and a cornucopia of authentic Italian goods made for New Yorkers and tourists alike.

Every September, Little Italy's Mulberry Street is home to the giant Feast of San Gennaro, a busy 11-day festival that sizzles with old–New York flavors—sausages and onions included. (Don't miss John Fasullo's braciole, an iconic sandwich filled with fillet of pork roasted over a coal pit and topped with peppers and onions).

Most Precious Blood Church. The National Shrine of San Gennaro, a replica of the grotto at Lourdes, is the high point of Most Precious Blood Church's richly painted interior. The church becomes a focal point during the annual Feast of San Gennaro. Sunday Mass is in English at 9 and noon. ⊠ *113 Baxter St., between Canal and Hester Sts., Little Italy* ☎ *212/226–6427* Ⓜ *6, J, N, Q, R, Z to Canal St.*

CHINATOWN

Chinatown is a living, breathing, anything-but-quiet ethnic enclave with vibrant streets full of food shops selling exotic produce and seafood, Chinese restaurants and bakeries, Buddhist temples, herbalists, discount massage parlors, and barbershops. A quarter of the city's Chinese residents live here, in a neighborhood that started as a seven-block area, but now covers some 40-plus blocks above and below Canal Street (encroaching on what was once a thriving Little Italy). Head to **Mott Street,** south of Canal—Chinatown's main thoroughfare—where the first Chinese immigrants (mostly men) settled in tenements in the late 1880s. Walk carefully, as the sidewalks can be slick from the ice underneath the eels, blue crabs, snapper, and shrimp that seem to look back at you as you pass by. You can create a movable feast here with delicious soup dumplings, Peking duck, yellow custard cake, and bubble tea—each at a different place in the neighborhood. A city tourist-information kiosk on a traffic island where Canal, Baxter, and Walker Streets meet can help you with tours, and also has a map that's very useful for unraveling the area's tangled and angled streets.

Columbus Park. People-watching is the thing to do in this park. If you swing by in the morning, you'll see men and women practicing tai chi; the afternoons bring intense games of mah-jongg. In the mid-19th

Some of the storefronts and signage in Chinatown are bilingual—but some are just in Chinese.

century the park was known as Five Points—the point where Mulberry Street, Anthony (now Worth) Street, Cross (now Park) Street, Orange (now Baxter) Street, and Little Water Street (no longer in existence) intersected—and was notoriously ruled by dangerous Irish gangs. In the 1880s a neighborhood-improvement campaign brought about the park's creation. More recently, the park was spruced up by a major capital renovation. ✉ *Chinatown* ⊕ *www.nycgovparks.org/parks/M015* Ⓜ *6, J, N, Q, R, Z to Canal St.*

Kimlau Square. Ten streets converge at this labyrinthine intersection criss-crossed at odd angles by pedestrian walkways. Standing on an island in this busy area is the **Kimlau Arch,** named for Ralph Kimlau, a bomber pilot who died in World War II; the arch is dedicated to all Chinese Americans who "lost their Lives in Defense of Freedom and Democracy." A statue on the square's eastern edge pays tribute to a Qing Dynasty official named Lin Zxeu, the Fujianese minister who sparked the Opium War by banning the drug. ✉ *Chatham Sq., Bowery and E. Broadway, Chinatown* ⊕ *www.nycgovparks.org/parks/kimlausquare* Ⓜ *4, 5, 6 to Brooklyn Bridge–City Hall; J, Z to Chambers St.*

Mahayana Buddhist Temple. This bright and beautiful Buddhist temple is at a very busy corner, at the foot of the Manhattan Bridge Arch on the Bowery, where gilded lions guard its entrance. Inside you'll find a 16-foot-tall Buddha seated on a lotus flower (allegedly the largest Buddha in the city), incense-burning urns, hand-painted prints, and a gift shop on the second floor. ✉ *133 Canal St., at the Bowery, Chinatown* ☎ *212/925–8787* ⊕ *en.mahayana.us* ✉ *Donations accepted* ☉ *Daily 8:30–6* Ⓜ *B, D to Grand St.*

The Museum of Chinese in America (MOCA). Founded in 1980, this museum is dedicated to preserving and presenting the history of the Chinese people and their descendants in the United States. Its current building, which opened in 2009 near the boundary between Chinatown and Little Italy (technically, many would say it's in Little Italy), was designed by Maya Lin, architect of the Vietnam Veterans Memorial in Washington, D.C. MOCA's core exhibit on Chinese American history, "With a Single Step: Stories in the Making of America," includes artworks, personal and domestic artifacts, historical documentation, and films. Chinese laundry tools, a traditional general store, and antique business signs are some of the unique objects on display. Rotating exhibits, some of which examine the sometimes turbulent relations between Asian Americans and other citizens, are on display in the second gallery. MOCA sponsors workshops, walking tours, lectures, and family events. ⊠ *215 Centre St., between Grand and Howard Sts., Chinatown* ☎ *212/619–4785* ⊕ *www.mocanyc.org* ✉ *$10* ◷ *Tues., Wed., and Fri.–Sun. 11–6, Thurs. 11–9* Ⓜ *6, J, N, Q, R, Z to Canal St.*

THE EAST VILLAGE AND THE LOWER EAST SIDE

GETTING ORIENTED

The East Village
and the
Lower East Side

M 4,5,6,L,
N,Q,R

M L

M L

E. 14th St.

E. 13th St.

Broadway

Fourth Ave.

E. 12th St.

Third Ave.

Second Ave.

First Ave.

E. 11th St.

St. Mark's Church
in-the-Bowery

X Veniero's
Pastry

Museum of
Reclaimed
Urban Space →

Stuyvesant St.

E. 10th St.

Astor Place
Subway Station

E. 9th St.

M R

St. Mark's Place

Tompkins
Square Park

Astor Pl.

Astor Pl.

M 6

Fourth Ave.

Lafayette St.

Third Ave.

Taras Shevchenko Pl.

E. 7th St.

Alphabet
City

E. 6th St.

Ukrainian
Museum

EAST VILLAGE

Avenue A

Avenue B

Merchant's
House Museum

E. 5th St.

Cooper
Square

E. 4th St.

Gt. Jones St.

E. 3rd St.

GREENWICH
VILLAGE

E. 2nd St.

The Hole

M 6

Bleecker St.

E. 1st St.

Il Laboratorio
del Gelato

Katz's Delicatessen X

X

Essex St.

Norfolk St.

Suffolk St.

F
M

E. Houston St.

B,D,F,M
M

Lafayette St.

Chrystie St.

Eldridge St.

Forsyth St.

Allen St.

Orchard St.

Ludlow St.

Sperone
Westwater

Stanton St.

International
Center of
Photography

Bowery

Gallery
Onetwentyeight

Prince St.

New
Museum

LOWER
EAST SIDE

Rivington St.

Essex Street
Market

← SOHO

NOLITA

M 6 Spring St.

Mulberry St.

Mott St.

Elizabeth St.

Delancey St.

M J,M,Z,F

Lower East Side
Tenement Museum

J,Z M

Broome St.

0   1/8 mile

0   200 meters

Museum at
Eldridge Street

MAKING THE MOST OF YOUR TIME

Houston Street runs east–west and neatly divides the East Village (north of Houston) and the Lower East Side (south of Houston). The eastern boundary of the East Village and Lower East Side is the East River; the western boundary is 4th Avenue and the Bowery. So many communities converge in these neighborhoods that each block can seem like a neighborhood unto itself.

The East Village lets loose on weekends, when nightlife-seekers descend on the area, filling up the bars and spilling onto the sidewalks. Weekday evenings are less frenetic, with more of a local vibe—although the term "local" around here always means a large number of students from New York University. Daytime is great for shopping in local boutiques, and brunch on weekends generally means lines for hot spots like Prune and Back Forty, which fill with patrons lingering over coffee.

The Lower East Side does not tend to be an early-riser destination any day of the week. Although there's plenty to see during the day, nightfall offers a more exciting vision: blocks that were previously empty rows of pulled-down gates transform into clusters of throbbing bars. On Rivington and Stanton and their cross streets, stores, bars, and cafés buzz all week.

GETTING HERE AND AROUND

For the East Village, take the N or R subway line to 8th Street–New York University (NYU), the 6 to Astor Place, or the L to 3rd Avenue. To reach Alphabet City, take the L to 1st Avenue or the F to 2nd Avenue. For the Lower East Side, head southeast from the 2nd Avenue stop on the F, or take the F, M, J, or Z to the Delancey Street–Essex Street stop.

TOP EXPERIENCES

People-watching on St. Marks Place or at Tompkins Square Park

Shopping at boutiques and vintage clothing stores

Visiting the Lower East Side Tenement Museum

4

COFFEE AND QUICK BITES

Il Laboratorio del Gelato. Seasonal flavors make this gelato la crème de la crème. There are 48 flavors offered each day. ⊠ *188 Ludlow St., ot E. Houston St., Lower East Side* ☎ *212/343–9922* ⊕ *www.laboratoriodelgelato.com* ⊟ *No credit cards* Ⓜ *F to 2nd Ave.*

Katz's Delicatessen. Given Katz's location and its equally lost-in-time vibe, this deli goes as well with visits to the Tenement Museum as a Cel-Ray soda goes with pastrami. ⊠ *205 E. Houston St., at Ludlow St., Lower East Side* ☎ *212/254–2246* ⊕ *www.katzsdelicatessen.com* ⊟ *No credit cards* Ⓜ *F to 2nd Ave.*

Veniero's Pastry. This Italian bakery has been churning out cookies, coffee, and elaborate cakes and tarts since 1894— and the late hours it keeps only sweetens the deal. The fruit-topped minicheesecakes are always a good idea. ⊠ *342 E. 11th St., between 1st and 2nd Aves., East Village* ☎ *212/674–7070* ⊕ *www.venierospastry.com* ⊟ *No credit cards* Ⓜ *L to 1st Ave.*

Sightseeing
★★

Nightlife
★★★★★

Dining
★★★★★

Lodging
★★

Shopping
★★★★

Vibrant, bold, and bohemian: the streets of the East Village and the Lower East Side are some of the most electric in New York City. Both neighborhoods have a deep immigrant past, and have evolved into nighttime destinations where you can dance till dawn any day of the week. This area of downtown is tamer than it used to be (as the arrival of Whole Foods and several glass-and-chrome condos attests), but a gritty edge lives on in the dive bars, sultry live music venues, and experimental restaurants. Spend time wandering these side streets, and you'll be struck by the funky pastiche of ethnicities whose imprints are visible in the neighborhood's shops, eateries, and, of course, people.

EAST VILLAGE

Updated by
Kelsy Chauvin

Many opposites coexist peacefully in the East Village: dive bars and craft-cocktail dens, Ukrainian diners and the latest chef-driven restaurant, stylish boutiques and counterculture stores. Famous for its nightlife, the East Village has become increasingly more upscale in recent years with St. Marks Place trading in some of its grit for a hodgepodge of students, well-earning postgrads, and international expats. At its roots, the neighborhood is a community of artists, activists, and social dissenters—and though this is still the essential vibe here, the finish is much more polished these days.

East of 1st Avenue is Alphabet City, once the city's seedy drug haunt but now an ever more gentrified neighborhood. There is still a young, artistic (and sometimes seedy) vibe in and around Tompkins Square Park.

Keep Your Eyes Peeled

The East Village's reputation for quirkiness is evinced not only by its residents and sites but also in the many incongruous structures that somehow coexist so easily that they often go unnoticed. Keep your eyes open as you explore the streets. You never know what might turn up: the Hells Angels' Headquarters, for example, tucked into a residential block of 3rd Street between 1st and 2nd Avenues, surrounded by a bevy of showstopping bikes; the architectural "joke" on New York City atop the Red Square building on Houston Street at Norfolk, where a statue of Lenin points to the sky and a clock has lost its notion of time; or the shingled Cape Cod–style house perched on the apartment building at the northwest corner of Houston and 1st Avenue, one of the city's many unique rooftop retreats (it's best viewed from the east). Two privately owned, nearly hidden, but airy "marble" cemeteries (New York Marble Cemetery and the New York City Marble Cemetery) established in the 1830s on 2nd Avenue between 2nd and 3rd Streets hold the remains of thousands in underground, marble-lined vaults thought to prevent the spread of disease in a time marked by cholera epidemics. The gardens are surrounded by 12-foot walls made of Tuckahoe marble, and are entered through wrought-iron gates. Although rarely open to the public, they can be visited by appointment.

TOP ATTRACTIONS

Alphabet City. The north–south avenues east of 1st Avenue, from Houston Street to 14th Street, are all labeled with letters, not numbers, which gives this area its nickname: Alphabet City. Avenues A, B, and C are full of restaurants, cafés, stores, and bars that run from the low-rent and scruffy to the pricey and polished—the streets are more mixed than in other neighborhoods downtown. Parts of Avenues A and B run along Tompkins Square Park. A close-knit Puerto Rican community makes its home around Avenue C, also called "Loisaida" (a Spanglish creation meaning "Lower East Side"). Although it's still filled with many Latino shops and bodegas, it's also now home to some trendy restaurants and bars. Avenue D remains rough around the edges—in part because of the uninterrupted row of housing projects that are on its east side. The East River Park, farther east, provides some nice views of Williamsburg and other parts of Brooklyn. To reach the park, cross Avenue D and take one of the pedestrian bridges that crosses FDR Drive at East 10th or East 5th Street, or cross the road at East Houston Street. ⊠ *East Village* Ⓜ *L to 1st Ave.; F to 2nd Ave.*

St. Marks Place. The longtime hub of the edgy East Village, St. Marks Place is the name given to idiosyncratic East 8th Street between 3rd Avenue and Avenue A. During the 1950s, beatniks Allen Ginsberg and Jack Kerouac lived and wrote in the area; the 1960s brought Bill Graham's Fillmore East (nearby, at 105 2nd Avenue), and Andy Warhol's Dom and the Electric Circus nightclub (both at Nos. 19–25), where the Velvet Underground performed. The studded, pink-haired, and shaved-head punk scene followed, and there's a good chance of still seeing some pierced rockers and teenage Goths on the block. Farther down, at No. 33, is where the punk store Manic Panic first foisted its lurid hair dyes and makeup on the world. At No. 57 stood the short-lived Club 57, a church basement that attracted such '80s stalwarts as Keith Haring, Ann Magnuson, Klaus Nomi, Kenny Scharf, and Fab Five Freddy.

These days, there's not much cutting edge left. Some of the grungy facades lead to luxury condos, and the area has become a Little Japan, with several ramen and dumpling shops, some sake bars, and lots of young Asian students. The blocks between 2nd and 3rd Avenues can feel like a shopping arcade, crammed with body-piercing and tattoo salons, and shops selling cheap jewelry, sunglasses, incense, and wacky T-shirts. The cafés and bars from here over to Avenue A attract customers late into the night—thanks partly to lower drink prices than in other downtown neighborhoods. ⊠ *8th St., between 3rd Ave. and Ave. A, East Village* Ⓜ *6 to Astor Pl.; N, R to 8th St.–NYU.*

FAMILY **Tompkins Square Park.** This leafy park fills up year-round with locals partaking in picnics and drum circles, and making use of the playground and the dog run. Free Wi-Fi (strongest on the north side of the park) joins the shade, benches, and an elegant 1891 water fountain (donated by a teetotaling benefactor) as some of the best amenities here. There are movie screenings and music gatherings throughout the summer, a year-round farmers' market on Sunday, and an annual Halloween dog-costume event. But it wasn't always so rosy in the park: in 1988, police followed then-mayor David Dinkins's orders to evict the many homeless who had set up makeshift homes here, and homeless rights and antigentrification activists fought back with sticks and bottles. The park was reclaimed and reopened in 1992 with a midnight curfew, still in effect today. ⊠ *From 7th to 10th St., between Aves. A and B, East Village* ⊕ *www.nycgovparks. org/parks/tompkinssquarepark* Ⓜ *6 to Astor Pl., L to 1st Ave.*

WORTH NOTING

Astor Place Subway Station. At the beginning of the 20th century, almost all of the city's Interborough Rapid Transit (IRT) subway entrances resembled the one here—an ornate cast-iron replica of a Beaux Arts kiosk marking the subway entrance for the uptown 6 train. This traffic-island entrance, which was—and still is—the stop nearest to the venerable Cooper Union college, is now on the National Register of Historic Places. Inside, plaques of beaver emblems line the tiled station walls, a reference to the fur trade that contributed to John Jacob Astor's fortune. Milton Glaser, the Cooper Union graduate who originated the "I [heart] NY" logo, designed the station's murals. ⊠ *8th St. and 4th Ave., traffic island, East Village* Ⓜ *6 to Astor Pl.*

The Hole. Run by Kathy Grayson, the former director of the highly influential Deitch Projects, this contemporary-arts gallery generally hosts two simultaneous shows a month. Its artists lean more toward the up-and-coming rather than the establishment. The on-site Hole Shop carries lots of quirky zines, posters, books, and art objects. ⊠ *312 Bowery, between Bleecker and E. Houston Sts., East Village* ☎ *212/466–1100* ⊕ *www.theholenyc.com* ☉ *Wed.–Sun. noon–7* Ⓜ *6 to Bleecker St.; B, D, F, M to Broadway–Lafayette St.*

Merchant's House Museum. Built in 1832, this redbrick house, combining Federal and Greek Revival styles, provides a glimpse into the domestic life of the period 30 years before the Civil War. Retired merchant Seabury Tredwell and his descendants lived here from 1835 until 1933. The home became a museum in 1936, with the original furnishings and architectural features preserved; family memorabilia are also on display. The fourth-floor servants' bedroom, where the Tredwell family's Irish servants slept and did some of their work, offers a rare and intimate look at the lives of Irish domestics in the mid-1800s. ⊠ *29 E. 4th St., between the Bowery and Lafayette St., East Village* ☎ *212/777–1089* ⊕ *www.merchantshouse.org* ✉ *$10* ☉ *Thurs.–Mon. noon–5; guided tours Thurs.–Mon. at 2, and Thurs. at 6:30* Ⓜ *N, R to 8th St.–NYU; 6 to Astor Pl.; B, D, F, M to Broadway–Lafayette St.*

Museum of Reclaimed Urban Space. Opened in late 2012, this self-described "living archive of urban activism" covers the vexatious postwar period in New York, during which the city's public housing was often woefully mismanaged and hundreds of apartments lay abandoned and crumbling. Zines, photographs, and videos fill the small exhibit space inside a tenement's storefront and its basement. Squatters, community gardens, the Tompkins Square riots, and the renaissance of bicycling in the city are all given their due, as is Occupy Wall Street. Tours of community gardens, activist landmarks, and other squats, both legal and otherwise, are also run by the museum. ⊠ *C-Squat, 155 Ave. C, between 9th and 10th Sts., East Village* ☎ *973/818–8495* ⊕ *www.morusnyc.org* ✉ *$5 suggested donation; tours $20* ☉ *Thurs.–Sun. and Tues. 11–7* Ⓜ *L to 1st Ave.*

St. Mark's Church in-the-Bowery. This charming 1799 fieldstone country church, which is Episcopalian, stands on what was once Governor Peter Stuyvesant's *bouwerie*, or farm. It's Manhattan's second-oldest church, and both Stuyvesant and Commodore Matthew Perry are buried in vaults here. Check out the gorgeous modern stained-glass windows on the balcony, which replaced the more traditional windows (like those on the ground level) after a fire in the late '70s. Over the years St. Mark's has hosted many avant-garde arts events, including readings by poet Carl Sandburg and dance performances by Martha Graham and Merce Cunningham. The tradition of art partnerships has continued with Danspace, the Poetry Project, New York Theatre Ballet, and LocoMotion, which give performances throughout the year. Services are held Sunday at 11. ⊠ *131 E. 10th St., at 2nd Ave., East Village* ☎ *212/674–6377* ⊕ *www.stmarksbowery.org* Ⓜ *6 to Astor Pl.; L to 3rd Ave.; N, R to 8th St.–NYU.*

Stuyvesant Street. This diagonal slicing through the block bounded by 2nd and 3rd Avenues and East 9th and 10th Streets is unique in Manhattan: it's the oldest street laid out precisely along an east–west axis. Among the handsome 19th-century redbrick row houses are the Federal-style **Stuyvesant-Fish House** at No. 21, built as a wedding gift for a great-great-granddaughter of the Dutch governor Peter Stuyvesant, and **Renwick Triangle,** an attractive group of Anglo-Italianate brick and brownstone residences, that face Stuyvesant and East 10th Streets. ⊠ *Stuyvesant St., East Village* Ⓜ *6 to Astor Pl.; N, R to 8th St.–NYU.*

Ukrainian Museum. From the late 19th century through the end of World War II, tens of thousands of Ukrainians made their way to New York City—and particularly to "Little Ukraine," as much of the East Village was known. This museum, which opened in 2005, examines Ukrainian Americans' dual heritage, with a permanent collection made up of folk art, fine art, and documentary materials about the immigrants' lives. Ceramics, jewelry, hundreds of brilliantly colored Easter eggs, and an extensive collection of Ukrainian costumes and textiles are the highlights. ■TIP→ To continue the experience, sample a little Ukrainian food at nearby Veselka diner. ✉ *222 E. 6th St., between 2nd and 3rd Aves., East Village* ☎ *212/228–0110* ⊕ *www.ukrainianmuseum.org* ✉ *$8* ☉ *Wed.–Sun. 11:30–5* Ⓜ *6 to Astor Pl.; N, R to 8th St.–NYU.*

LOWER EAST SIDE

The Lower East Side (or simply LES) is a center of all things cool: arts and nightlife, restaurants and cafés, boutiques and salons. What was once the "Gateway to America"—and home to waves of Irish, German, Jewish, Hispanic, and Chinese immigrants—is now a quickly gentrifying neighborhood where modern high-rises, the ultracontemporary New Museum, and low-key hangouts all exist in the same corner of Manhattan.

On Saturday night, the scene can be as raucous as in a college town, especially on Rivington and Orchard Streets. But Ludlow Street, one block east of Orchard, has become the main drag for twentysomethings with attitude, its boutiques wedged between bars and small restaurants.

The best time to experience the neighborhood's past is by day. The excellent Lower East Side Tenement Museum movingly captures the immigrant legacy of tough times and survival instincts. You might not find many pickles being sold from barrels anymore, but this remains a good place to nosh on delicious Jewish food like matzo-ball soup, corned beef, and knishes from Katz's Delicatessen or Russ & Daughters.

TOP ATTRACTIONS

FAMILY

Fodor's Choice

★

Lower East Side Tenement Museum. Step back in time and into the partially restored 1863 tenement building at 97 Orchard Street, where you can squeeze through the preserved apartments of immigrants, learn about the struggles of past generations, and gain historical perspective on the still contentious topic of immigration. This is America's first urban living-history museum dedicated to the life of immigrants. The museum itself is only accessible by guided tour, each run at various times each day and limited to 15 people, so it's a good idea to buy tickets in advance. The building tour called "Hard Times" visits the homes of Natalie Gumpertz, a German-Jewish dressmaker (dating from 1878), and Adolph and Rosaria Baldizzi, Catholic immigrants from Sicily (1935). "Sweatshop Workers" visits the Levines' garment shop/apartment and the home of the Rogarshevsky family from Eastern Europe (1918). "Irish Outsiders" explores the life of the Moores, an Irish-American family living in the building in 1869, and shows a re-created tenement backyard. "Shop Life" looks at the various

The Tenement Museum offers a fascinating glimpse into the lives of early-20th-century immigrants.

businesses operating on local streets, including a German-style bar, a kosher butcher, an auctioneer, and, in the 1970s, a discount underwear store. ■TIP→ A two-hour extended experience tour with a chance for in-depth discussion is hosted daily, as are walking tours of the neighborhood; most tours don't allow kids under five. ⊠ *103 Orchard St., at Delancey St., Lower East Side* ☎ *877/975–3786* ⊕ *www.tenement.org* ⌨ *Most tours $25* ⊙ *Fri.–Wed. 10–6:30, Thurs. 10–8:30; last tour at 5* Ⓜ *B, D to Grand St.; F to Delancey St.; J, M, Z to Essex St.*

New Museum. This seven-story, 60,000-square-foot structure—a glimmering, metal-mesh-clad assemblage of off-center squares—caused a small neighborhood uproar when it was built in 2007, with some residents slow to accept the nontraditional building. Not surprisingly, given the museum's name and the building, shows are all about contemporary art: previous exhibitions have included the popular *Carsten Höller: Experience*, featuring an adult-size tubular metal slide connecting the fourth and second floors, and a sensory-deprivation tank, among other things. If you're visiting on the weekend, check out the seventh-floor Skyroom and its panoramic views. ■TIP→ From 10 to noon on the first Saturday of every month, the museum runs free family-oriented programs and events designed for kids ages 4 to 12. Thursday's pay-what-you-wish night always brings a fun-loving, hipster-heavy crowd out of the woodwork. ⊠ *235 Bowery, at Prince St., Lower East Side* ☎ *212/219–1222* ⊕ *www.newmuseum.org* ⌨ *$16 (pay-what-you-wish Thurs. 7–9)* ⊙ *Tues., Wed., and Fri.–Sun. 11–6, Thurs. 11–9* Ⓜ *6 to Spring St., F to 2nd Ave.*

WORTH NOTING

Gallery Onetwentyeight. Inside this narrow space, artist Kazuko Miyamoto directs crisp and provocative group and solo shows. ⊠ *128 Rivington St., between Essex and Norfolk Sts., Lower East Side* ☎ *212/674–0244* ⊕ *www.galleryonetwentyeight.org* ⊗ *Wed.–Sat. 1–7, Sun. 1–5* Ⓜ *F to Delancey St.; J, M, Z to Essex St.*

International Center of Photography. Founded in 1974 by photojournalist Cornell Capa (photographer Robert Capa's brother), this top-notch photography museum and school has a collection of over 150,000 original prints spanning the history of photography from daguerreotypes to large-scale pigment prints. The museum left its Midtown space in early 2015 to relocate to a new outpost on the Bowery in 2016. Check the website for updates. ⊠ *250 Bowery, between E. Houston and Prince Sts., Lower East Side* ☎ *212/857–0000* ⊕ *www.icp.org* Ⓜ *6 to Spring St., F to 2nd Ave.*

Museum at Eldridge Street. The exterior of this 1887 Orthodox synagogue-turned-museum (and community space) is the first to be built by the many Eastern European Jews who settled in the Lower East Side in the late 19th century, and is a striking mix of Romanesque, Gothic, and Moorish motifs. Inside is an exceptional hand-carved ark of mahogany and walnut, a sculptured wooden balcony, jewel-tone stained-glass windows, vibrantly painted and stenciled walls, and an enormous brass chandelier. The museum can be viewed as part of an hour-long tour, which begins downstairs where interactive "touch tables" teach all ages about Eldridge Street and the Lower East Side. The crowning piece of the building's decades-long restoration is a stained-glass window by artist Kiki Smith and architect Deborah Gans, which weighs 6,000 pounds and has more than 1,200 pieces of glass. ⊠ *12 Eldridge St., between Canal and Division Sts., Lower East Side* ☎ *212/219–0302* ⊕ *www. eldridgestreet.org* ⊠ *$12* ⊗ *Sun.–Thurs. 10–5, Fri. 10–3; tours on the hr* Ⓜ *F to East Broadway; B, D to Grand St.*

Sperone Westwater. Founded in 1975 in SoHo, and after spending nearly a decade in Chelsea, Sperone Westwater now finds itself a major part of the "artification" of the Lower East Side. In 2010, the gallery moved into this nine-story building, which it commissioned for itself—a vote of confidence in both its Bowery surroundings and the continued importance of its artists, which have included Bruce Nauman, William Wegman, Gerhard Richter, and a host of blue-chip minimalists. The narrow building, designed by Norman Foster, rivals the New Museum (a few doors down) for crisp poise: in 2011 New York's Municipal Art Society deemed it the best new building of the year. Its Big Red Box, essentially a huge roomlike freight elevator visible from the street, is a major contributor to the building's personality. ⊠ *257 Bowery, between E. Houston and Stanton Sts., Lower East Side* ☎ *212/999–7337* ⊕ *www.speronewestwater.com* ⊗ *Tues.–Sat. 10–6* Ⓜ *6 to Spring St., F to 2nd Ave.*

GREENWICH VILLAGE AND THE WEST VILLAGE

GETTING ORIENTED

Greenwich Village
and the West Village

MEATPACKING
DISTRICT

A,C,E,L   1,2,3
W. 14th St.

Seventh Ave. S.

W. 13th St.
W. 12th St.
W. 11th St.

High Line Park

Little W. 12th St.

Gansevoort St.

Grounded

Greenwich Ave.

Eighth Ave.

W. 4th St.

Waverly Pl.

Patchin Place

Hudson
River
Park◆

Horatio St.

Jane St.

W. 12th St.

Greenwich St.

Bethune St.

Bank St.

Abingdon
Square

W. 11th St.

Hudson St.

Ga-
Stre

Sheridan
Square

Joe

West St.

Perry St.

Charles St.

Washington St.

W. 10th St.

Christopher St.

Grove St.

Christopher Park

Hudson River

West St.

WEST
VILLAGE

P PATH

Commerce St.

Bedford St.

75 1/2
Bedford St.

Bleecker St.

Leroy St.

Cornelia

0   1/8 mi
0   200 meters

Barrow

Greenwich St.

Morton St.

Leroy St.

Children's Museum
of the Arts

Carmine St.

Downing

TOP EXPERIENCES	MAKING THE MOST OF YOUR TIME
People-watching in Washington Square Park	A visit to Washington Square Park, in the heart of Greenwich Village, is a must for people-watching and relaxing on a bench (you might also catch some live music performances). There are lots of restaurants and shops in the neighborhood, though they do tend to cater primarily to New York University students.
Strolling and window-shopping along the picturesque streets of the West Village	
Relaxing in a café	The West Village—basically from 7th Avenue to the Hudson River—is more residential, and a bit quieter, with carefully tended, tree-lined streets that make the neighborhood a perfect place to roam, camera in hand. Everything from upscale boutiques to cheap pizza joints line Bleecker Street and Greenwich Avenue.
Walking by the water in Hudson River Park	
Eating your way down Bleecker Street	
	The windy streets of the West Village often seem mazelike, even to many New Yorkers, because most of the streets here are named rather than numbered, and they were established before Manhattan laid out its street-grid system back in 1811. Assume that you're going to get a little bit lost—that's part of the fun—but don't hesitate to ask for directions.

5

COFFEE AND QUICK BITES

Caffe Reggio. Usually packed, this café dates back to the 1920s, making it one of the oldest coffeehouses in the city. ⊠ *119 MacDougal St., between W. 3rd and Carmine Sts., Greenwich Village* ☎ *212/475–9557* ⊕ *www.caffereggio.com* ▭ *No credit cards* Ⓜ *A, B, C, D, E, F, M to W. 4th St.*

Grounded. At this welcoming café, both the pastries and the people-watching are a cut above. ⊠ *28 Jane St., between 8th and Greenwich Aves., West Village* ☎ *212/647–0943* ⊕ *www.groundedcoffee.com* Ⓜ *A, C, E to 14th St.; L to 8th Ave.; 1, 2, 3 to 14th St.*

Joe (West Village). The coffee is exquisitely prepared at this small corner café, the first of what is now a small chain. ⊠ *141 Waverly Pl., at Gay St., Greenwich Village* ☎ *212/924–6750* ⊕ *www.joenewyork.com* Ⓜ *A, B, C, D, E, F, M to W. 4th St.; 1 to Christopher St.–Sheridan Sq.*

GETTING HERE AND AROUND

The West 4th Street subway stop—serviced by the A, B, C, D, E, F, and M lines—puts you on the west side of Greenwich Village. Farther west, the 1 train has stops at Houston Street and at Christopher Street–Sheridan Square. The L stops at 8th Avenue, and the A, C, and E trains stop at 14th Street, which is the northern boundary of the West Village.

BEST FOR KIDS

Hudson River Park

Washington Square Park

Taking time out for pizza or dessert

Sightseeing
★★★

Nightlife
★★★★

Dining
★★★★★

Lodging
★★★

Shopping
★★★★

The charming, tree-lined streets of the Village are beloved by New Yorkers (whether they can afford to live there or not) for their cozy restaurants and cafés, chic cocktail bars, and inviting boutiques. Long the home of writers, artists, bohemians, and bon vivants, "the Village" is made up of Greenwich Village proper (the area surrounding Washington Square Park) and the West Village, from 7th Avenue to the Hudson River. Greenwich Village, in prime New York University (NYU) territory, has lots of young people, while the West Village is primarily residential, with lots of well-to-do couples and families and a substantial community of older gay men and some lesbians. Both sections have a relaxed, downtown vibe and a distinctly New York style in their bookstores, corner bars, and trendy restaurants.

GREENWICH VILLAGE

Updated by
Kelsy Chauvin

Many would argue that Washington Square Park is still the beating heart of downtown, a magnet for all kinds of life. People come here to hear live music, stretch out on a picnic blanket, let the pooch loose at the dog run, or bring kids to the playground. The park anchors Greenwich Village, where you can encounter just about every variety of New Yorker, from skateboarders and students to white-collar workers on break to people who look like they've lived in the park for years, playing chess and checkers at the stone tables. This is also a historic part of the neighborhood, with the grand Washington Memorial Arch looking north to two blocks of lovingly preserved Greek Revival and Federal-style town houses known as "the Row."

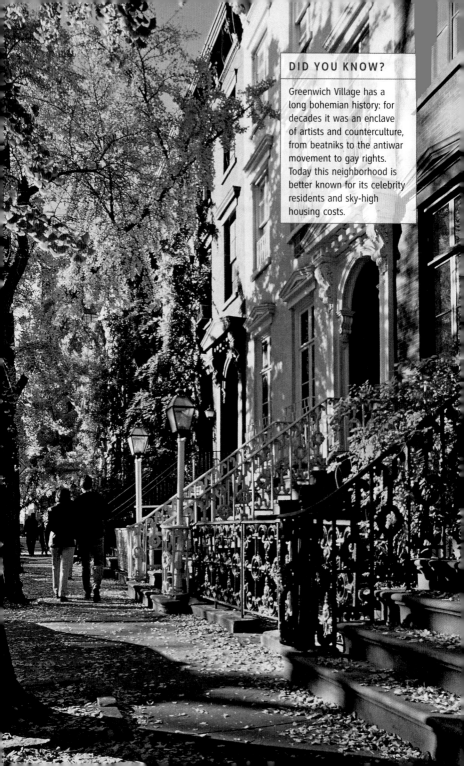

CLOSE UP

Halloween in the Village

All things weird and wonderful, all creatures great and small, all costumes clever and fantastical, New York City has them all—and on All Hallows' Eve they strut through the streets in New York's Village Halloween Parade. White-sheeted ghouls seem dull compared with fishnets and leather, sequins and feathers posing and prancing along 6th Avenue in this vibrant display of vanity and insanity.

In 1974 mask-maker and puppeteer Ralph Lee paraded his puppets from house to house, visiting friends and family along the winding streets of his Greenwich Village neighborhood. His merry march quickly outgrew its original, intimate route and now, decades later, it parades up 6th Avenue, from Spring Street to 16th Street, attracting upwards of 60,000 creatively costumed exhibitionists, artists, dancers, and musicians, hundreds of enormous puppets, scores of bands, and more than 2 million spectators. Anyone with a costume can join in, no advance registration required, although the enthusiastic interaction between participants and spectators makes it just as much fun simply to watch. It's a safe "street event" for families and singles alike (though, be aware you will be entering very dense crowds), and a joyful night unlike any other.

The parade lines up along 6th Avenue between Canal and Spring Streets from 6:30 to 8:30 pm. The walk actually starts at 7, but it takes about two hours to leave the staging area. It's best to arrive from the south to avoid the crush of participants. Get there a few hours early if possible. Costumes are usually handmade, clever, and outrageous, and revelers are happy to strike a pose. The streets are crowded along the route, with the most congestion below 14th Street. Of course, the best way to truly experience the parade is to march, but if you're not feeling the face paint, it's possible to volunteer to help carry the puppets. For information, visit ⊕ *www. halloween-nyc.com.*

Bountiful doesn't even begin to describe Greenwich Village's yield of creative genius. In the late 1940s and early 1950s, abstract expressionist painters Jackson Pollock, Lee Krasner, Mark Rothko, and Willem de Kooning congregated here, as did Beat writers Jack Kerouac, Allen Ginsberg, and Lawrence Ferlinghetti. The 1960s brought folk musicians and poets, notably Bob Dylan and Joan Baez. Its bohemian days may be long gone, but there is still a romantic allure lingering along tree-lined streets and at the back of the cafés, behind the frenetic clamor of NYU students and the polished veneer of multimillion-dollar town houses.

TOP ATTRACTIONS

Bleecker Street. Walking the stretch of Bleecker Street between 5th and 7th Avenues provides a smattering of just about everything synonymous with Greenwich Village these days: NYU buildings, record stores, Italian cafés and food shops, pizza and takeout joints, bars and nightclubs, and funky boutiques. A lazy afternoon here may consist of sampling some of the city's best pizza, grabbing an espresso, and soaking up the downtown fashion scene. Notable along the Greenwich Village length of the street is Our Lady of Pompeii Church, at Bleecker and Carmine, where Mother Cabrini, a naturalized Italian immigrant who became the first American citizen to be canonized, often prayed. Foodies love the blocks between 6th and 7th Avenues for the specialty purveyors like Murray's Cheese (at No. 254). West of 7th Avenue, where Bleecker crosses the border into the West Village, things get more upscale, with fashion and home-furnishings boutiques featuring antiques, eyeglasses, handbags, shoes, and designer clothing. ⊠ *Greenwich Village* Ⓜ *A, B, C, D, E, F, M to W. 4th St.*

FAMILY
Fodor's Choice
★

Washington Square Park. NYU students, street musicians, skateboarders, jugglers, chess players, and those just watching the grand opera of it all generate a maelstrom of activity in this physical and spiritual heart of Greenwich Village. The 9¾-acre park had inauspicious beginnings as a cemetery, principally for yellow-fever victims—an estimated 10,000–22,000 bodies lie below (a headstone was even unearthed in 2009). At one time, plans to renovate the park called for the removal of the bodies, but local resistance prevented this from happening. In the early 1800s the park was a parade ground and the site of public executions; the notorious Hanging Elm still stands at the northwest corner of the square. Today that gruesome past is all but forgotten, as playgrounds attract parents with tots in tow, dogs go leash-free inside the popular dog runs, and everyone else seems drawn toward the large central fountain.

The triumphal European-style **Washington Memorial Arch** stands at the square's northern flank, marking the start of 5th Avenue. The original wood-and-papier-mâché arch, originally situated a half block north, was erected in 1889 to commemorate the 100th anniversary of George Washington's presidential inauguration. The arch was reproduced in Tuckahoe marble in 1892, and the statues—*Washington as General Accompanied by Fame and Valor* on the left, and *Washington as Statesman Accompanied by Wisdom and Justice* on the right—were added in 1916 and 1918, respectively. ⊠ *5th Ave., between Waverly Pl. and 4th St., Greenwich Village* Ⓜ *A, B, C, D, E, F, M to W. 4th St.*

WORTH NOTING

Gay Street. A curved, one-block lane lined with small row houses, Gay Street was probably named after an early landowner and definitely had nothing to do with gay rights. In the 1930s, this tiny thoroughfare and nearby Christopher Street became famous nationwide after Ruth McKenney began to publish somewhat zany autobiographical stories based on what happened when she and her sister moved to No. 14 from Ohio. The stories, first published in the *New Yorker*, birthed many adaptations, including the 1953 Broadway musical *Wonderful Town* (revived in 2004) and the 1942 and 1955 movies *My Sister Eileen*. ⊠ *Between Christopher St. and Waverly Pl., Greenwich Village* Ⓜ *1 to Christopher St.–Sheridan Sq.; A, B, C, D, E, F, M to W. 4th St.*

Patchin Place. This narrow, gated cul-de-sac off West 10th Street between Greenwich and 6th Avenues has 10 diminutive 1848 row houses. Around the corner on 6th Avenue is a similar dead-end street, **Milligan Place,** with five small houses completed in 1852. The houses in both

Out and On Display: George Segal's sculptures of two gay couples in Christopher Park embody LGBT pride in Greenwich Village.

quiet enclaves were originally built for waiters who worked at 5th Avenue's high-society Brevoort Hotel, long since demolished. Later Patchin Place residents included writers Theodore Dreiser, e. e. cummings, Jane Bowles, and Djuna Barnes. Milligan Place became popular among playwrights, including Eugene O'Neill. ⊠ *Off W. 10th St., Greenwich Village* Ⓜ *A, B, C, D, E, F, M to W. 4th St.*

The Row. Built from 1833 through 1837, this series of Greek Revival and Federal row houses along Washington Square North, between University Place and MacDougal Street, once belonged to merchants and bankers, then to writers and artists such as John Dos Passos and Edward Hopper. Many are now owned by NYU and used for housing and offices. Although the facades remain beautifully preserved, the interiors have been drastically altered over the years. ⊠ *1–13 and 19–26 Washington Sq. N, between University Pl. and MacDougal St., Greenwich Village* Ⓜ *A, B, C, D, E, F, M to W. 4th St.*

Washington Mews. A rarity in Manhattan, this pretty, brick-covered street—really a glorified alley—is lined on one side with the former mews (stables) of the houses on the Row on the south side of the block. Although the street is private, gated and owned by New York University, which uses many of the buildings for clubs and offices, it's open to pedestrian traffic from 7 am to 11 pm and is a lovely, historic strip for a stroll. ⊠ *From Washington Sq. N to 8th St., between 5th Ave. and University Pl., Greenwich Village* Ⓜ *A, B, C, D, E, F, M to W. 4th St.; N, R to 8th St.–NYU.*

Bleecker Street's Little Italy

Little Italy can be besieged by slow-moving crowds, touristy shops, and restaurant hosts hollering invitations to dine inside. Bleecker Street between 6th and 7th Avenues, on the other hand, with its crowded cafés, bakeries, pizza parlors, and old-world merchants, offers a more pleasurable, equally vital alternative to the traditional tourist trap.

For an authentic Italian bakery experience, stop by Pasticceria Rocco (No. 243) for wonderful cannoli, cream puffs, and cookies packed up, or order an espresso and linger over the treats.

Step into the past at the old-style (and now high-end) butcher shops, such as Ottomanelli & Sons (No. 285) and Faicco's Pork Store (No. 260), where locals have bought their sausage, prime beef, and custom-cut pork since 1900.

The sweet (or stinky) smell of success is nowhere more evident than at Murray's Cheese (No. 254). The original shop, opened in 1940 by Murray Greenberg (not Italian), was not much larger than the display case that stocked the stuff. Now it's a fromage-fiend's emporium, with everything from imported crackers and bamboo cutting boards to a full-service sandwich counter. Samples of cheese, salami, gelato, and other goodies are frequently served. Educational cheese-tasting classes are also held in the upstairs classroom (sign up online in advance).

There are also a few popular pizzerias along this strip; Kesté Pizza & Vino (No. 271) serves Neapolitan pies that some would argue rival even Da Michele in Naples. It's also the official location in the United States for the Associazione Pizzaiuoli Napoletani, whose mission is to promote pizzas made in the Neapolitan tradition, using Neapolitan products. Brick-oven favorite John's Pizzeria (No. 278) is a classic New York pizza joint—pies only, no slices!

WEST VILLAGE

Small curving streets, peculiar alleys, and historic town houses—it's easy to see why the tree-lined streets of the West Village (which are primarily residential) are in such high demand. A stroll here reveals charming cafés, carefully disheveled celebrities out and about, and well-dressed children playing in the parks. Visitors come here to feel like a local, to daydream about a life in New York. Unlike 5th Avenue or SoHo, the pace is slower, allowing shoppers to enjoy the peaceful streets and independent and designer stores. This is the place to come for unusual finds as well as global-brand goods. The West Village section of Bleecker Street is a particularly good place to indulge all sorts of shopping appetites; high-fashion foragers prowl the stretch between West 10th Street and 8th Avenue. Hudson Street and Greenwich Avenue are also prime boutique-browsing territories.

Christopher Street has long been the symbolic heart of New York's gay and lesbian community, though places like Chelsea, Hell's Kitchen, and parts of Brooklyn attract more gay and lesbian residents these days. On Christopher Street, among the cafés and adult shops, is one of the city's most acclaimed Off-Broadway theaters, the Lucille Lortel, where major playwrights like David Mamet, Eugene Ionesco, and Edward Albee have their own sidewalk markers. Nearby, at 51–53 Christopher Street, is the site of the Stonewall Inn and the historic Stonewall riots, one of the most famous, catalyzing events in the LGBT civil rights movement. Across the street is a gated triangle named Christopher Park, where commemorative statues of two life-sized gay and lesbian couples have posed for photos since 1992.

TOP ATTRACTIONS

Hudson River Park. ⇨ *See the listing in the TriBeCa section of Chapter 2.*

WORTH NOTING

FAMILY **Children's Museum of the Arts.** The CMA encourages children ages 1 to 15 to get creative through a variety of mediums. Along with the requisite children's museum offerings like pencils, chalk, and paint, you'll find a clay bar; a media lab with mounted cameras and a recording studio; a small slide and colorful ball pond that kids can play in; an airy exhibition space with rotating exhibits (and workshops inspired by exhibits); a permanent collection of children's art from more than 50 countries; and classes in ceramics, origami, animation, filmmaking, and more. Check the website for a busy calendar of events. ⊠ *103 Charlton St., between Hudson and Greenwich Sts., West Village* ☎ *212/274–0986* ⊕ *www. cmany.org* 🖾 *$12* ⊘ *Mon. noon–5, Thurs. and Fri. noon–6, weekends 10–5* Ⓜ *C, E to Spring St.; 1 to Houston St.*

Christopher Park. You might have to share a bench in this tiny park with George Segal's life-size sculptures of a lesbian couple. Titled *Gay Liberation,*the white-painted bronzes were cast in 1980 but not installed until 1992, and also include a gay male couple, captured mid-chat. ⊠ *Bordered by W. 4th, Grove, and Christopher Sts., West Village* Ⓜ *1 to Christopher St.–Sheridan Sq.; A, B, C, D, E, F, M to W. 4th St.*

75½ Bedford Street. Rising real-estate prices inspired the construction of New York City's narrowest house—just 9½ feet wide and 32 feet deep—in 1873. Built on a lot that was originally a carriage entrance of the Isaacs-Hendricks House next door, this sliver of a building's past residents include actor John Barrymore and poet Edna St. Vincent Millay. ⊠ *75½ Bedford St., between Commerce and Morton Sts., West Village* Ⓜ *A, B, C, D, E, F, M to W. 4th St.*

CHELSEA AND THE MEATPACKING DISTRICT

GETTING ORIENTED

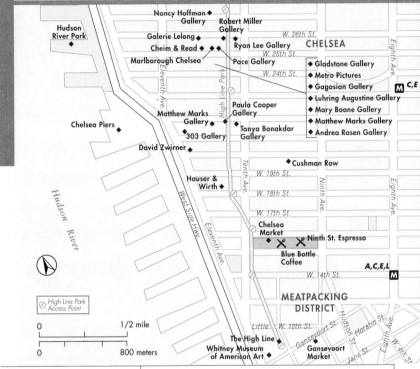

GETTING HERE AND AROUND

The A, C, E, L, 1, 2, and 3 trains stop at 14th Street for both the Meatpacking District and Chelsea. The latter neighborhood is further served by the C, E, F, M, and 1 lines at 23rd Street and by the 1 train at 28th Street. PATH trains also stop at 14th Street and 23rd Street.

MAKING THE MOST OF YOUR TIME

Plan your visit to the High Line around food: work up an appetite first by walking downtown along the High Line from 34th Street and then to Chelsea Market, Gansevoort Market, or the food carts peppering the southern reaches of the park (from 15th to 17th Street) for a bite, or pick up food on your way *to* the High Line for a picnic there. There are also seasonal food vendors on the High Line for impromptu snacking.

Chelsea has a dual life: typical gallery hours are Tuesday to Saturday 10–6, but at night the neighborhood changes into a party town, with bars (gay and straight) and high-profile nightclubs that don't rev up until after 11.

To truly appreciate the Meatpacking District, make a 9 pm or later dinner reservation at a hot restaurant, then hit the bars to see the glitterati.

If shopping is your pleasure, weekdays are great; come after noon, though, or find most spots shuttered.

Chelsea and the Meatpacking District

6

COFFEE AND QUICK BITES

Blue Bottle Coffee. If you're serious about coffee, fresh-baked pastries, eco-friendly practices, and good old-fashioned service, stop in at this trendy coffee shop, or its seasonal outpost on the High Line. ⊠ *450 W. 15th St., Chelsea* ⊕ *www. bluebottlecoffee.com* Ⓜ *A, C, E to 14th St.; L to 8th Ave.*

Donut Pub. Care for a red-velvet doughnut or an old-fashioned cruller with your coffee? A 5 am sugar fix after a night clubbing in the Meatpacking District? Pull up a stool—it's open 24/7. ⊠ *203 W. 14th St., at 7th Ave., Chelsea* ☎ *212/929–0126* ⊕ *www.donutpub.com* Ⓜ *1, 2, 3 to 14th St.; A, C, E to 14th St.; L to 8th Ave.*

Ninth Street Espresso. The Chelsea Market outpost of Ninth Street Espresso is popular all day, though the lines in the morning are longest. ⊠ *Chelsea Market, 9th Ave., between 15th and 16th Sts., Chelsea* ☎ *212/228-2930* ⊕ *www. ninthstreetespresso.com* Ⓜ *A, C, E to 14th St.; L to 8th Ave.*

TOP EXPERIENCES

Gallery-hopping in Chelsea

Walking along the High Line

Exploring the Whitney Museum of American Art: the new building has light-filled galleries and wonderful views from the terraces

Checking out the Meatpacking District's nightlife

Eating your way through Chelsea Market or Gansevoort Market

Shopping the ultrachic boutiques in the Meatpacking District

BEST FOR KIDS

Chelsea Piers

The High Line

Hudson River Park

Sightseeing
★★★

Nightlife
★★★★★

Dining
★★★★★

Lodging
★★★

Shopping
★★★★

Chelsea long ago usurped SoHo as the epicenter of New York contemporary art galleries, but the opening of the High Line above 10th Avenue gave a new life to this part of the city, catalyzing new development and quickly turning the area into one of the city's most popular attractions. Momentum surged with the 2015 arrival of the Whitney Museum of American Art, which firmly established the area as a major art hub and destination—and one of the city's hottest real estate markets. Rising rents have meant fewer small galleries and, indeed, fewer small anything. With the onslaught of tech and media companies relocating here, you'll find more hackers than butchers, more chain stores than independent boutiques, and a constantly changing neighborhood.

MEATPACKING DISTRICT

By Jacinta O'Halloran

Concentrated in a few blocks of what is essentially the West Village, between the Hudson River and 9th Avenue, from Little West 12th Street to about West 17th Street, the Meatpacking District used to be the center of the wholesale meat industry for New York City. There are few meat markets left in this now rather quaint cobblestone area, but it's definitely a figurative meat market at night, when the city's trendiest frequent the equally trendy restaurants and bars here. The area is also home to some of the city's swankiest retailers, with high-profile fashion designers and labels like Christian Louboutin, Diane von Furstenberg, Ted Baker London, and Tory Burch, as well as lesser-known boutiques like Warby Parker, Kilian, and The Kooples.

Gansevoort Market. Named after a food market that existed here in the 1800s, this 8,000-square-foot food hall—with its carefully curated list of vendors and vine-covered, skylit dining space—is like the younger, cooler, lesser-known sister of nearby tourist-mobbed Chelsea Market. Opened in late 2014, the market is slowly filling up with a mix of artisan purveyors selling everything from overstuffed lobster rolls, sweet and savory stuffed brioche-muffin hybrids, and American-style macarons to tacos served from a VW van, homemade bread from Gansevoort Bakery, and a variety of pork fare from the Pig Guy. When weather permits, the garage-door facade rolls up to expose the market to the cobblestone streets outside. ⌧ *52 Gansevoort St., between Greenwich and Washington Sts., Meatpacking District* ☎ *212/247–1701* ⊕ *www.gansmarket. com* ☉ *Daily 8 am–9 pm* Ⓜ *A, C, E, to 14th St.; L to 8th Ave.*

Fodor's Choice
★
Whitney Museum of American Art. After four decades on the Upper East Side, the Whitney shook off its stone Marcel Breuer shell in early 2015 and relocated to this steel, glass, and light-filled Renzo Piano–designed building in the Meatpacking District. Unlike its notoriously aloof Chelsea gallery neighbors, the museum welcomes visitors with a lively plaza, bold works of contemporary and modern American art, terraced outdoor spaces, and expansive windows. There are eight floors with more than 50,000 square feet of state-of-the-art gallery space, 13,000 square feet of outdoor space facing the High Line, a restaurant on the ground floor, and a café on the eighth floor. ■TIP→ **Start your visit at the top, on the eighth floor, and work your way down via the outdoor terraces, the interior stairs, or the elevators, which usually have works of art as well.** The galleries house rotating exhibitions of postwar and contemporary works from the permanent collection that include artists such as Jackson Pollock, Jim Dine, Jasper Johns, Mark Rothko, Chuck Close, Cindy Sherman, and Roy Lichtenstein. Notable pieces often on view include Hopper's *Early Sunday Morning* (1930), Bellows's *Dempsey and Firpo* (1924), Alexander Calder's beloved *Circus*, and several of Georgia O'Keeffe's dazzling flower paintings. The Whitney experience is as much about the setting as the incredible artwork. The outdoor terraces on floors 6, 7, and 8 are connected by exterior stairs that provide a welcome reprieve from crowded galleries; the balconies also offer rotating exhibits along with stunning views of the city skyline, including the Empire State Building and One World Trade Center. Free tours of the collection and current exhibitions are offered daily; check the website for more information. After 7 pm on Friday the price of admission is pay what you wish. ■TIP→ **Skip the long lines and buy tickets in advance, and note that you can not buy same-day tickets online. They must be purchased the day before and are available up to midnight.** ⌧ *99 Gansevoort St., between Washington St. and 10th Ave., Meatpacking District* ☎ *212/570–3600* ⊕ *www.whitney.org* 🎟 *$22* ☉ *Mon., Wed., and Sun. 10:30–6, Thurs.–Sat. 10:30–10* Ⓜ *A, C, E to 14th St.; L to 8th Ave.*

6

CHELSEA

Most of Chelsea's art galleries are found from about 20th to 27th Streets, primarily between 10th and 11th Avenues. The range of contemporary art on display includes almost every imaginable medium and style; if it's going on in the art world, it'll be in one of the 300 or so galleries here.

TOP ATTRACTIONS

FAMILY **Chelsea Market.** This former Nabisco plant—where the first Oreos were baked in 1912—now houses more than three dozen vendors carrying everything from gourmet food and wine, to oils, vinegars, teas, spices, gift baskets, and kitchen supplies; there's also an Anthropologie store, wine bar, barbershop, shoeshine stand, and one of New York City's last independent bookstores (Posman Books). Renowned specialty purveyors including L'Arte del Gelato, Fat Witch Bakery, Amy's Bread, and Ninth Street Espresso flank the interior walkway that stretches between 9th and 10th Avenues. Be sure to wander into the 15th Street Arcade, where a bunch of great kiosks sell everything from fresh mini-doughnuts to Australian meat pies, Brooklyn-made caramels, and authentic Mexican street food. The market's funky industrial design—a tangle of glass and metal for an awning, a factory pipe converted into an indoor waterfall—complements the eclectic assortment of shops. ■ TIP→ There is some seating inside, but if the weather's nice, take your goodies to the High Line. ⊠ 75 9th Ave., between 15th and 16th Sts., Chelsea ☎ 212/652–2117 ⊕ www.chelseamarket.com ⊗ Mon.–Sat. 7 am–9 pm, Sun. 8–8 Ⓜ A, C, E to 14th St.; L to 8th Ave.

David Zwirner. In 2013, Zwirner further solidified his commitment to contemporary art, and his place in the ranks of the most successful galleries in the art world, with this vast, purpose-built, five-story exhibition and project space, created to complement the programming of the gallery's three existing West 19th Street locations a block away. Zwirner's galleries show works in all mediums by artists like Dan Flavin, Donald Judd, Blinky Palermo, Jeff Koons, Gordon Matta-Clark, Doug Wheeler, and Yayoi Kusama. In 2016, Zwirner presented its first exhibition of Sigmar Polke's work, now exclusively represented by the gallery. Since his death in 2010, the German-born artist's eclectic, multidisciplinary works have been the subject of critically acclaimed retrospectives at major museums around the world. ⊠ 537 W. 20th St., between 10th and 11th Aves., Chelsea ☎ 212/517–8677 ⊕ www.davidzwirner.com ⊠ Free ⊗ Tues.–Sat. 10–6 Ⓜ C, E to 23rd St.

Gagosian Gallery. This enterprising modern gallery has two large Chelsea branches (the other is at 522 West 21st Street, between 10th and 11th Avenues) and three galleries on the Upper East Side, as well as 10 more outposts in cities around the world. Perhaps the most powerful dealer in the business, Gagosian Gallery shows works by heavy hitters such as Pablo Picasso, Jean-Michel Basquiat, Urs Fischer, Richard Serra, and pop-art icon Roy Lichtenstein. ⊠ 555 W. 24th St., at 11th Ave., Chelsea ☎ 212/741–1111 ⊕ www.gagosian.com ⊠ Free ⊗ Tues.–Sat. 10–6 Ⓜ C, E to 23rd St.

Gladstone Gallery. The international roster of artists at this gallery's two Chelsea locations includes painter Ahmed Alsoudani, sculptor Anish Kapoor, photographer Sharon Lockhart, and multimedia artists Matthew Barney and Cecilia Edefalk. The other location is 530 West 21st Street, between 10th and 11th Avenues. ⊠ *515 W. 24th St., between 10th and 11th Aves., Chelsea* ☎ *212/206–9300* ⊕ *www.gladstonegallery.com* ⊡ *Free* ☉ *Tues.–Sat. 10–6* Ⓜ *C, E to 23rd St.*

Hauser & Wirth. On the site of the former Roxy nightclub and roller rink on West 18th Street, this Hauser & Wirth gallery is the opposite of its narrow town-house location on the Upper East Side. The space is huge (23,000 square feet), cavernous, and begs for sprawling exhibits and large-scale works. Emerging and established contemporary artists in the powerful Hauser & Wirth fold that show here include Dieter Roth, Paul McCarthy, Eva Hesse, and Jason Rhoades. In 2018, the gallery will relocate to a new building on West 22nd Street and will have two floors of galleries, office space, and a bookstore. ⊠ *511 W. 18th St., between 10th and 11th Aves., Chelsea* ☎ *212/790–3900* ⊕ *www.hauserwirth. com* ⊡ *Free* ☉ *Tues.–Sat. 10–6* Ⓜ *C, E to 23rd St.*

FAMILY
Fodor's Choice
★

The High Line. Once a railroad track carrying freight trains, this elevated space has been transformed into one of the city's top attractions—a 1½-mile landscaped "walking park," with curving walkways, picnic tables and benches, public art installations, and views of the Hudson River and the Manhattan skyline. Running from Gansevoort Street in the Meatpacking District (at the Whitney Museum of Art) to West 34th Street, the High Line somehow manages to host about 5 million visitors a year and still feel like a wonderful retreat from the hubbub of the city.

One of the main draws of the High Line is the landscaping, which is carefully choreographed and yet wild and untamed at the same time. Visitors can see many of the original species that grew in the rail beds, as well as shrubs, trees, grasses, and perennials chosen for their hardiness and sustainability. The landscape is restless and always changing, with each week bringing new colors, textures, and scents; check the website before you visit to see what's in bloom.

Chelsea Market Passage, between 15th and 16th Streets, is accented with Spencer Finch's stained-glass art and home to public art displays, video programs, music performances, and sit-down events.

A particularly popular feature that illustrates the High Line's greatest achievement—the ability to see the city with fresh eyes—is the 10th Avenue Square (between 16th and 17th Streets). This viewing window with stadium seating and large picture windows frames the ever-moving and -changing city below as art, encouraging viewers to linger, watch, pose, and engage with the city in a new way.

The 25-by-75-foot billboard located within a parking lot next to the High Line at 18th Street and 10th Avenue presents a series of art installations on view for a month at a time.

The best way to fully appreciate the High Line is to walk the full length of the elevated park in one direction (preferably from Gansevoort Street uptown so that you can end with panoramic views of the city and Hudson River) and then make the return journey at street level, taking in the Chelsea neighborhood, and eats, below. ■TIP→ Nearby Chelsea Market and Gansevoort Market are convenient places to pick up fixings for a picnic lunch.

✉ *10th Ave., from Gansevoort St. to 34th St., Chelsea* ☎ *212/206–9922* ⊕ *www.thehighline.org* ⊙ *Dec.–Mar., daily 7–7; Apr., May, Oct., and Nov., daily 7 am–10 pm; June–Sept., daily 7 am–11 pm* Ⓜ *A, C, E to 14th St.; L to 8th Ave.; 1, 2, 3 to 14th Sts.; 1 to 23rd St. or 28th St.; 7 to Hudson Yards.*

Hudson River Park. ⇨ *See the listing in the TriBeCa section of Chapter 2.*

Marlborough Chelsea. With galleries in London, Monaco, and Madrid, the Marlborough empire also operates two of the largest and most influential galleries in New York City, as well as a shared annex on the Lower East Side. The Chelsea location (the other is on 57th Street) shows the latest work of modern artists, with a focus on sculptural forms, such as the boldly colorful paintings of Andrew Kuo. Red Grooms, Richard Estes, and Magdalena Abakanowicz are just a few of the 20th-century luminaries represented. ✉ *545 W. 25th St., between 10th and 11th Aves., Chelsea* ☎ *212/463–8634* ⊕ *www.marlboroughgallery.com* ✆ *Free* ⊙ *Tues.–Sat. 10–6* Ⓜ *C, E to 23rd St.*

Mary Boone Gallery. Based in SoHo in the late '70s, when it was a hot showcase for younger artists, the Mary Boone Gallery relocated to Midtown (745 5th Avenue, near 58th Street) in 1996 and then opened this additional branch in a former garage in Chelsea in 2000. The Chelsea space allows for large-scale works and dramatic installations. Over the years, Boone has shown and represented artists including Jean-Michel Basquiat, Jeff Koons, Julian Schnabel, Ross Bleckner, and Ai Weiwei. Boone continues to show established artists such as Barbara Kruger, Pierre Bismuth, and Francesco Clemente, as well as relative newcomers such as Jacob Hashimoto and Hilary Harkness. ✉ *541 W. 24th St., between 10th and 11th Aves., Chelsea* ☎ *212/752–2929* ⊕ *www.maryboonegallery.com* ✆ *Free* ⊙ *Tues.–Sat. 10–6* Ⓜ *C, E to 23rd St.*

Matthew Marks Gallery. A hot venue for both the New York and international art crowd, openings at any of the four Matthew Marks galleries are always an interesting scene—there are three other locations along 22nd Street between 10th and 11th Avenues. Swiss artist Ugo Rondinone made his U.S. debut here, as did Andreas Gursky. Luigi Ghirri, Darren Almond, Jasper Johns, Robert Adams, Nan Goldin, Ellsworth Kelly, and a cast of illustrious others also show here. ✉ *523 W. 24th St., between 10th and 11th Aves., Chelsea* ☎ *212/243–0200* ⊕ *www.matthewmarks.com* ✆ *Free* ⊙ *Tues.–Sat. 10–6* Ⓜ *C, E to 23rd St.*

Fodor'sChoice **Museum at FIT.** What this small, three-gallery museum housed in the
★ Fashion Institute of Technology (FIT) lacks in size, staging, and effects, it more than makes up for in substance and style. You don't find interactive mannequins, elaborate displays, or overcrowded galleries at the self-declared "most fashionable museum in New York City," but you do find carefully curated exhibits, an impressive permanent collection that includes more than 50,000 garments and accessories from the 18th century to the present, and dedicated followers and students sketching and leaning in to wow over seams and sequins. The Fashion and

Chelsea Galleries 101

Good art, bad art, edgy art, downright disturbing art—it's all here waiting to please and provoke in the contemporary art capital of the world. For the uninitiated, the concentration of nearly 300 galleries within a seven-block radius can be overwhelming, and the sometimes cool receptions on entering and the deafening silence, intimidating. Art galleries are not exactly famous for their customer service, but you don't need a degree in art appreciation to stare at a canvas or installation.

There's no required code of conduct, although most galleries are library quiet and cell phones are seriously frowned on. Don't worry, you won't be pressured to buy anything; staff will probably be doing their best to ignore you.

Galleries are generally open Tuesday through Saturday from 10 to 6. Gallery hop on a Saturday afternoon—the highest-traffic day—if you want company. You can usually find a binder with the artist's résumé, examples of previous work, and exhibit details (usually including prices) at the front desk; if not, ask. Also ask whether there's information you can take with you.

You can't see everything in one afternoon, so if you have specific interests, plan ahead. Find gallery information and current exhibit details by checking the listings in the *New Yorker* or the weekend section of the *New York Times*. Learn more about the galleries and the genres and artists they represent at ⊕ *www.artincontext.org*.

Textile History Gallery, on the main floor, provides ongoing historical context with a rotating selection of historically and artistically significant objects from the museum's permanent collection (exhibits change every six months), but the real draw here is the special exhibitions in the lower-level gallery. Recent examples include *Denim: Fashion's Frontier*, an exploration of the history of denim from work wear to haute couture, and *Fashion Underground: The World of Susanne Bartsch*, featuring almost 100 over-the-top looks from the queen of the New York City nightclub scene in the '80s. Gallery FIT, also located on the main floor, is dedicated to student and faculty exhibitions. ✉ *227 W. 27th St., at 7th Ave., Chelsea* ☎ *212/217–4558* ⊕ *www.fitnyc.edu/museum* ✆ *Free* ☉ *Tues.–Fri. noon–8, Sat. 10–5* Ⓜ *N, R to 28th St.*

Pace Gallery. The impressive roster of artists represented by the Pace Gallery includes a variety of upper-echelon artists, sculptors, and photographers, including Alexander Calder, Tara Donovan, Chuck Close, Sol LeWitt, and Robert Rauschenberg. Pace has three spaces along West 25th Street in Chelsea (including its new eight-story flagship gallery currently under construction at No. 540), as well as a Midtown location (at 32 East 57th Street). ✉ *508 W. 25th St., between 10th and 11th Aves., Chelsea* ☎ *212/989–4258* ⊕ *www.thepacegallery.com* ✆ *Free* ☉ *Tues.–Sat. 10–6* Ⓜ *C, E to 23rd St.*

Paula Cooper Gallery. SoHo pioneer Paula Cooper moved to Chelsea in 1996 and enlisted architect Richard Gluckman to transform a warehouse into a dramatic space with tall ceilings and handsome skylights.

There are now two galleries (the other is at 521 West 21st Street) that showcase the minimalist works of artists such as Carl Andre, Sam Durant, Hans Haacke, Donald Judd, and Dan Flavin. ✉ *534 W. 21st St., between 10th and 11th Aves., Chelsea* ☎ *212/255–1105* ⊕ *www.paulacoopergallery.com* ✉ *Free* ⊙ *Tues.–Sat. 10–6* Ⓜ *C, E to 23rd St.*

Ryan Lee Gallery. In 2014, the Ryan Lee Gallery moved from its year-old, street-level location a few doors down to this new third-floor, 8,000-square-foot space, thereby doubling its physical space and—thanks to its elevated exhibition space, RLWindow, which can be viewed from the High Line—increasing its visibility by millions. RLWindow shows innovative and experimental projects by contemporary artists; recent exhibits turning heads on the High Line have included video installations from Rashaad Newsome and Rudy Burckhardt. ✉ *515 W. 26th St., between 10th and 11th Aves., Chelsea* ☎ *212/397–0742* ⊕ *www.ryanleegallery.com* ✉ *Free* ⊙ *Tues.–Sat. 10–6* Ⓜ *C, E to 23rd St.*

WORTH NOTING

Andrea Rosen Gallery. Artists on the cutting edge, such as Felix Gonzalez-Torres, video artists Ryan Trecartin and Lizzie Fitch, sculptor Andrea Zittel, and painter and installation artist Matthew Ritchie, are on view here. Rosen has a second space, Gallery 2 (at 544 West 24th Street), just down the street from the gallery headquarters, with more experimental shows that place less emphasis on commercial appeal or success. ✉ *525 W. 24th St., between 10th and 11th Aves., Chelsea* ☎ *212/627–6000, 212/627–6100 for Gallery 2* ⊕ *www.andrearosengallery.com* ✉ *Free* ⊙ *Tues.–Sat. 10–6* Ⓜ *C, E to 23rd St.*

Casey Kaplan. While many galleries are fleeing Chelsea's high rents for less pricey and more artist-friendly neighborhoods like the Lower East Side or the Upper East Side, Casey Kaplan chose to mark its 20th anniversary in 2015 by moving just a few blocks, into a new 10,000-square-foot, two-story storefront space on West 27th Street. The Kaplan gallery represents contemporary artists from Europe and the Americas. ✉ *121 W. 27th St., between 6th and 7th Aves., Chelsea* ☎ *212/645–7335* ⊕ *www.caseykaplangallery.com* ✉ *Free* ⊙ *Tues.–Sat. 10–6* Ⓜ *1 to 28th St.*

Cheim & Read. This prestigious gallery represents artists such as Louise Bourgeois, William Eggleston, Joan Mitchell, Jenny Holzer, Donald Baechler, and Jack Pierson. ✉ *547 W. 25th St., between 10th and 11th Aves., Chelsea* ☎ *212/242–7727* ⊕ *www.cheimread.com* ✉ *Free* ⊙ *Tues.–Sat. 10–6* Ⓜ *C, E to 23rd St.*

FAMILY **Chelsea Piers.** This sports-and-entertainment complex along the Hudson River between 17th and 23rd Streets, a phenomenal example of adaptive reuse, is the size of four 80-story buildings laid out flat. There's pretty much every kind of sports activity going on both inside and out, including golf (check out the multitier, all-weather, outdoor driving range), sailing classes, ice-skating, rock climbing, soccer, bowling, gymnastics, and basketball. Plus there's a spa, elite sport-specific training, and film studios. Chelsea Piers is also the jumping-off point for some of the city's various boat tours and dinner cruises. ✉ *Piers 59–62,*

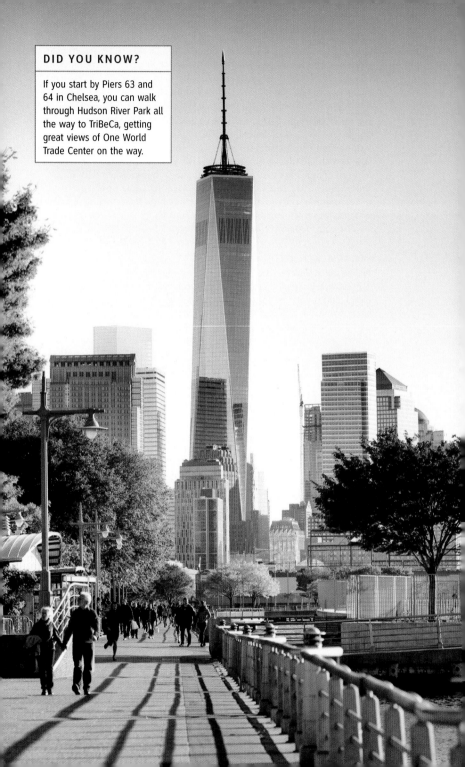

DID YOU KNOW?

If you start by Piers 63 and 64 in Chelsea, you can walk through Hudson River Park all the way to TriBeCa, getting great views of One World Trade Center on the way.

Hudson River from 17th to 23rd Sts. (entrance at 23rd St.), Chelsea ☎ *212/336–6666* ⊕ *www.chelseapiers.com* Ⓜ *C, E to 23rd St.*

Cushman Row. Built in 1840 for merchant and developer Don Alonzo Cushman, this string of redbrick beauties between 9th and 10th Avenues represents some of the country's best examples of Greek Revival row houses. Original details include small wreath-encircled attic windows, deeply recessed doorways with brownstone frames, and striking iron balustrades and fences. Note the pineapples, a traditional symbol of welcome, on top of the black iron newels in front of No. 416. ⊠ *406–418 W. 20th St., between 9th and 10th Aves., Chelsea* Ⓜ *C, E to 23rd St.*

Galerie Lelong. This large gallery presents challenging installations, including work by many Latin American artists. Look for art by Yoko Ono, Alfredo Jaar, Andy Goldsworthy, Cildo Meireles, Ana Mendieta, Hélio Oiticica, Nalini Malani, and Petah Coyne. ⊠ *528 W. 26th St., between 10th and 11th Aves., Chelsea* ☎ *212/315–0470* ⊕ *www.galerielelong.com* 🖃 *Free* ☉ *Tues.–Sat. 10–6* Ⓜ *C, E to 23rd St.*

Luhring Augustine Gallery. Owners Lawrence Luhring and Roland Augustine have been working with established and emerging artists from Europe, Japan, and America since 1985. In 2012, Luhring Augustine opened a Brooklyn outpost (at 25 Knickerbocker Avenue in Bushwick) for large-scale installations and long-term projects. ⊠ *531 W. 24th St., between 10th and 11th Aves., Chelsea* ☎ *212/206–9100* ⊕ *www.luhringaugustine.com* 🖃 *Free* ☉ *Tues.–Sat. 10–6* Ⓜ *C, E to 23rd St.*

Metro Pictures. The hottest talent in contemporary art shown here includes Cindy Sherman, Olaf Breuning, Louise Lawlor, Trevor Paglen, Camille Henrot, and B. Wurtz. ⊠ *519 W. 24th St., between 10th and 11th Aves., Chelsea* ☎ *212/206–7100* ⊕ *www.metropicturesgallery.com* 🖃 *Free* ☉ *Tues.–Sat. 10–6* Ⓜ *C, E to 23rd St.*

Nancy Hoffman Gallery. Contemporary painting, sculpture, drawing, photography, and video works by an impressive array of international artists are on display in this light-filled space with high ceilings and a sculpture garden. Artists range from Viola Frey, known for her heroic-scale ceramic male and female figures, to well-established artists and a strong group of young artists embarking on their first solo shows. ⊠ *520 W. 27th St., between 10th and 11th Aves., Chelsea* ☎ *212/966–6676* ⊕ *www.nancyhoffmangallery.com* 🖃 *Free* ☉ *Sept.–July, Tues.–Sat. 10–6; Aug., weekdays 10–5* Ⓜ *C, E to 23rd St.*

Robert Miller Gallery. Robert Miller was a titan of the New York art world, and he founded this gallery in 1977 (he passed away in 2011). It continues to represent some of the biggest names in modern painting and photography, including Diane Arbus, Patti Smith, Mayumi Terada, and the estate of Lee Krasner. ⊠ *524 W. 26th St., between 10th and 11th Aves., Chelsea* ☎ *212/366–4774* ⊕ *www.robertmillergallery.com* 🖃 *Free* ☉ *Sept.–June, Tues.–Sat. 10–6; July, weekdays 10–6; Aug., by appointment only* Ⓜ *C, E to 23rd St.*

Rubin Museum of Art. This sleek and serene museum spread over six floors is the largest in the Western Hemisphere dedicated to the art of the Himalayas, India, and neighboring regions. The pieces shown here include paintings on cloth, metal sculptures, and textiles dating from the 2nd century onward. Many of the works from areas such as Tibet, Nepal, southwest China, and India relate to Buddhism, Hinduism, Bon, and other eastern religions. In late 2015, the museum expanded its fourth-floor Tibetan Buddhist Shrine room to allow for a more immersive experience, with art and ritual objects presented as they would be in an elaborate household shrine. A pleasant café and gift shop is on the ground floor. ■TIP➜ Admission is free Friday 6–10 pm. ✉ *150 W. 17th St., near 7th Ave., Chelsea* ☎ *212/620–5000* ⊕ *www.rmanyc.org* ✉ *$15* ☉ *Mon. and Thurs. 11–5, Wed. 11–9, Fri. 11–10, weekends 11–6* Ⓜ *1 to 18th St.*

Tanya Bonakdar Gallery. Contemporary artists such as Olafur Eliasson, Uta Barth, Ernesto Neto, Lisa Oppenheim, and Sarah Sze, who represented the United States at the 55th Venice Biennale, are shown here. ✉ *521 W. 21st St., between 10th and 11th Aves., Chelsea* ☎ *212/414–4144* ⊕ *www.tanyabonakdargallery.com* ✉ *Free* ☉ *Tues.–Sat. 10–6* Ⓜ *C, E to 23rd St.*

303 Gallery. International cutting-edge artists shown here include up-and-coming New York artist Jacob Kassay, photographer Doug Aitken, and installation artists Karen Kilimnik and Jane and Louise Wilson. In 2016, 303 Gallery moved to its long-awaited new home on West 21st Street after a temporary stint under the High Line at 24th Street. The gallery's new space anchors the first two floors and mezzanine of a new Norman Foster luxury high-rise. ✉ *551 W. 21st St., between 10th and 11th Aves., Chelsea* ☎ *212/255–1121* ⊕ *www.303gallery.com* ✉ *Free* ☉ *Sept.–July, Tues.–Sat. 10–6* Ⓜ *C, E to 23rd St.*

UNION SQUARE, THE FLATIRON DISTRICT, AND GRAMERCY PARK

Visit Fodors.com for advice, updates, and bookings

GETTING ORIENTED

Union Square,
the Flatiron District,
and Gramercy Park

B,D,F
M,N,Q,R
Herald
Square

E. 34th St.

E. 33rd St.

6

W. 32nd St.

Broadway

Fifth Ave.

Madison Ave.

Park Ave. S.

Lexington Ave.

E. 32nd St.

E. 31st St.

E. 30th St.

E. 29th St.

N,R

W. 28th St.

Museum
of Sex

6

E. 28th St.

Little
India

W. 27th St.

W. 26th St.

Museum of Mathematics

E. 27th St.

E. 26th St.

W. 25th St.

Appellate Division
Courthouse

Madison
Square Park

E. 25th St.

Third Ave.

Second Ave.

W. 24th St.

Eataly

Metropolitan Life
Insurance Company Tower

E. 24th St.

F,M

W. 23rd St.

N,R

E. 23rd St.

W. 22nd St.

Flatiron Building

6

**FLATIRON
DISTRICT**

E. 21st St.

Broadway

E. 22nd St.

Avenue of the Americas
(Sixth Ave.)

Fifth Ave.

W. 20th St.

Gramercy
Park

E. 20th St.

W. 19th St.

GRAMERCY PARK

E. 19th St.

W. 18th St.

Irving Farm
Coffee Roasters

E. 18th St.

W. 17th St.

Irving
Place

E. 17th St.

W. 16th St.

Union Square Park
and Greenmarket

Park Ave. S.

Irving Pl.

Stuyvesant
Square

W. 15th St.

**UNION
SQUARE**

L,F,M

W. 14th St.

L,N,Q,R
4,5,6

E. 14th St.

L

W. 13th St.

E. 13th St.

Third Ave.

W. 12th St.

Fifth Ave.

University Pl.

Broadway

The Strand

E. 12th St.

0   1/8 mile

E. 11th St.

0   200 meters

E. 10th St.

MAKING THE MOST OF YOUR TIME

Union Square seems like it's busy at just about every time of day and night, with people hanging out on the steps, eating lunch, or watching street performers, but market days—Monday, Wednesday, Friday, and Saturday—are even busier. Early weekday mornings are quietest, before the market is set up, though without all the people, the area loses some of its allure.

This is definitely an area for strolling, shopping, and eating, so plan your visit around a meal—or several.

If you're planning to eat at the Shake Shack in Madison Square Park, come before noon to avoid long lines.

COFFEE AND QUICK BITES

Eataly. There are multiple restaurants, take-out shops, a Nutella bar, and cafés, as well as a rooftop brewery at Mario Batali's Italian food emporium. You can also shop for gourmet Italian chocolates, coffees, gelati, and pastries. ✉ *200 5th Ave., at 23rd St., Flatiron District* ☎ *212/229–2560* ⊕ *www.eataly.com* Ⓜ *N, R to 23rd St.*

Irving Farm Coffee Roasters. Steps from Union Square, this busy little café (known to locals as 71 Irving) roasts its own beans—always a good sign—and serves good people-watching along with sandwiches, muffins, and snacks. ✉ *71 Irving Pl., Union Square* ☎ *212/995–5252* ⊕ *www.irvingfarm.com* Ⓜ *4, 5, 6, L, N, Q, R to 14th St.–Union Sq.*

TOP EXPERIENCES

Strolling in Union Square Park and checking out the produce and other goodies at the greenmarket

Browsing the miles of books in the Strand bookstore

Strolling from Irving Place to Gramercy Park, and around the perimeter of this historic, private park

GETTING HERE AND AROUND

Union Square is a major subway hub, with the 4, 5, 6, L, N, Q, and R lines all converging here. For Madison Square Park and the Flatiron District, take the N or R train to 23rd Street (this lets you out on Broadway). The 6 stops at 23rd and 28th Streets (on Park Avenue South).

SEASONAL HIGHLIGHTS

Union Square Holiday Market. From Thanksgiving to Christmas, this outdoor market has more than 150 vendors selling unique, often locally made products. ⊕ *www.urbanspacenyc.com*

Madison Square Eats. This monthlong pop-up food market happens twice a year (spring and fall) across the street from Madison Square Park, and includes popular vendors like the Red Hook Lobster Pound, Fire Belly Korean BBQ, and Roberta's Pizza. ⊕ *www.madisonsquarepark.org/mad-sq-eats*

7

Sightseeing
★★★★
Nightlife
★
Dining
★★★
Lodging
★★★
Shopping
★★★★

Union Square is a hub of seemingly never-ending activity and people-watching, a distinction amplified by the bordering quieter neighborhoods of Gramercy and the Flatiron District. When that certain brand of New Yorker says they don't like to travel above 14th Street, they're usually thinking about Union Square as the cutoff.

UNION SQUARE

Updated
by Jacinta
O'Halloran

The energy of Union Square reaches its peak during greenmarket days (Monday, Wednesday, Friday, and Saturday), when more than 140 regional farmers and food purveyors set up shop on the square's north and west sides to peddle everything from produce to meat and fresh fish to baked goods. The market is a great place to rub elbows with—and get elbowed by—local shoppers and chefs, and a great source for tasty souvenirs (locally produced honeys, jams, pickles, and cheeses) as well as lunch. Find a bench in the park to savor your goodies and take in the scene. Political rallies sometimes happen here, too.

Even on a nonmarket day, Union Square regularly has vendors of all kinds, selling everything from art to jewelry to T-shirts. New York University students, nannies with their charges, visitors, and other locals gather in this open space that can at times feel more like an outdoor version of Grand Central Terminal than a park. Just south of Union Square, on Broadway at 12th Street, is the Strand, a giant bookstore that attracts book lovers like a magnet.

Union Square Park and Greenmarket. A park, farmers' market, meeting place, and the site of rallies and demonstrations, this pocket of green space sits in the center of a bustling residential and commercial neighborhood. The name "Union" originally signified that two main roads—Broadway and 4th Avenue—crossed here. It took on a different meaning in the late 19th and early 20th centuries, when the square became a rallying spot for labor protests; many unions, as well as fringe political parties, moved their headquarters nearby.

Union Square is at its best on Monday, Wednesday, Friday, and Saturday (8–6), when the largest of the city's greenmarkets gathers farmers and food purveyors from the tristate area. Browse the stands of fruit and vegetables, flowers, plants, fresh-baked pies and breads, cheeses, cider, New York State wines, fish, and meat. Between Thanksgiving and Christmas, there is a popular market where artisans sell gift items and food in candy-cane-stripe booths toward the square's southwest end.

> **TIME OUT!**
>
> Union Square's most love-it-or-hate-it feature is the *Metronome* sculpture with its bank of cascading numbers. Half art installation, half timepiece, it sits above Nordstrom Rack, and is actually a clock that counts both time elapsed and time remaining in the day. At noon and midnight huge bursts of steam emerge.

New York University dormitories, theaters, and cavernous commercial spaces occupy the handsomely restored 19th-century commercial buildings that surround the park, along with chain coffee shops and restaurants. The run of diverse architectural styles on the Decker Building at 33 Union Square West is as imaginative as its former contents: this was once home to Andy Warhol's studio. The building at 17th Street and Union Square East, now housing the New York Film Academy and the Union Square Theater, was the final home of Tammany Hall, an organization famous in its day as a corrupt and powerful political machine. Statues in the park include those of George Washington, Abraham Lincoln, Mahatma Gandhi (often wreathed in flowers), and the Marquis de Lafayette (sculpted by Frederic Auguste Bartholdi, designer of the Statue of Liberty). Plaques in the sidewalk on the southeast and southwest sides chronicle the park's history from the 1600s to 1800s. After years of legal battles, the once-crumbling pavilion in the northern end of the park was reincarnated in summer 2014 as an upscale, seasonal restaurant: The Pavilion. The restaurant provides alfresco dining (from April to October) with ingredients sourced from the surrounding greenmarket. ⊠ *From 14th to 17th St., between Broadway and Park Ave. S, Union Square* Ⓜ *4, 5, 6, L, N, Q, R to 14th St.–Union Sq.*

FLATIRON DISTRICT

The Flatiron District—anchored by Madison Square Park on the north and Union Square to the south—is one of the city's busiest neighborhoods, particularly along 5th Avenue and Park Avenue South. Once known as Ladies' Mile because of the fashionable row of department stores where women routinely shopped, the area is still a favorite for lady-spotting because of the number of modeling agencies and photography studios here. Lovely Madison Square Park, a pleasant green space hemmed in by the neighborhood's notable architecture—from the triangular Flatiron to the dazzling, gold-pyramid-topped New York Life Building and Metropolitan Life Tower, with its elegant clock face—is the best place to savor the view. Sit and admire the scene with a burger and shake from the park's always-busy Shake Shack, or takeout from

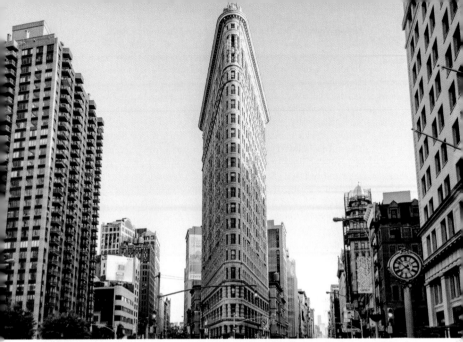

The wedge-shape Flatiron Building got its nickname because of its resemblance to the shape of a clothes iron; its original name is the Fuller Building.

the mother (or "mamma mia") of all Italian markets, Eataly, across the street from the west side of the park.

TOP ATTRACTIONS

Flatiron Building. When completed in 1902, the Fuller Building, as it was originally known, caused a sensation. Architect Daniel Burnham made ingenious use of the triangular wedge of land at 23rd Street, 5th Avenue, and Broadway, employing a revolutionary steel frame that allowed for the building's 22-story, 286-foot height. Covered with a limestone-and-white-terra-cotta facade in the Italian Renaissance style, the building's shape resembled a clothing iron, hence its nickname. When it became apparent that the building generated strong winds, gawkers would loiter at 23rd Street hoping to catch sight of ladies' billowing skirts. Local traffic cops had to shoo away the male peepers—one purported origin of the phrase "23 skidoo." There is a small display of historic building and area photos in the lobby, but otherwise you have to settle for appreciating this building from the outside, at least for now; the building may be converted to a luxury hotel when current occupant leases expire in late 2018. ⊠ *175 5th Ave., bordered by 22nd and 23rd Sts., 5th Ave., and Broadway, Flatiron District* Ⓜ *N, R to 23rd St.*

FAMILY **Madison Square Park.** The benches of this elegant tree-filled park afford great views of some of the city's oldest and most charming skyscrapers—the Flatiron Building, the Metropolitan Life Insurance Tower, the gold-crowned New York Life Insurance Building, and the Empire State Building—and serve as a perfect vantage point for people-, pigeon-, and dog-watching. Add free Wi-Fi, the newly renovated Shake Shack, temporary art exhibits, and free summer and fall concerts, and you realize that a bench here is definitely the place to be. New York City's first baseball games were played in this 7-acre park in 1845 (though New Jerseyans are quick to point out that the game was actually invented across the river in Hoboken, New Jersey). On the north end of the park, an imposing 1881 statue by Augustus Saint-Gaudens memorializes Civil War naval hero Admiral David Farragut. An 1876 statue of Secretary of State William Henry Seward (the Seward of the term "Seward's Folly," coined when the United States purchased Alaska from the Russian Empire in 1867) sits in the park's southwest corner, though it's rumored that the sculptor placed a reproduction of the statesman's head on a statue of Abraham Lincoln's body. ⊠ *From 23rd to 26th St., between 5th and Madison Aves., Flatiron District* ☎ *212/520–7600* ⊕ *www.madisonsquarepark.org* Ⓜ *N, R to 23rd St.*

WORTH NOTING

Appellate Division Courthouse. Sculpted by Frederick Ruckstull, figures representing Wisdom and Force flank the main portal of this imposing Beaux Arts courthouse, built in 1899. Melding the structure's purpose with artistic symbolism, statues of great lawmakers line the roof balustrade, including Moses, Justinian, and Confucius. In total, sculptures by 16 artists adorn the ornate building, a showcase of themes relating to the law. This is one of the most important appellate courts in the country: it hears more than 3,000 appeals and 6,000 motions a year, and also admits approximately 3,000 new attorneys to the bar each year. Inside the courtroom is a stunning stained-glass dome set into a gilt ceiling. The main hall and the courtroom are open to visitors weekdays from 9 to 5. All sessions, which are generally held Tuesday to Thursday at 2 pm, are open to the public (visitors can call the main number ahead of time to be sure court is in session). ⊠ *27 Madison Ave., entrance on 25th St., Flatiron District* ☎ *212/340–0422* ⊕ *www.courts.state.ny.us/courts/ad1* ☉ *Weekdays 9–5* Ⓜ *N, R, 6 to 23rd St.*

Metropolitan Life Insurance Company Tower. When it was added to the original building on this site in 1909, the 700-foot tower resembling the campanile of St. Mark's in Venice made this 1893 building the world's tallest; it was surpassed in height a few years later (by the Woolworth Building). It was stripped of much of its classical detail during renovations in the early 1960s, but remains a prominent feature of the Midtown skyline today. The clock's four faces are each three stories high, and their minute hands weigh half a ton each. If the view from the park doesn't quite cut it, you can now reserve a room in the skyline itself: in 2015, Marriott International and Ian Schrager opened a 273-room luxury hotel, the New York Edition Hotel, in the long-vacant clocktower portion of the building. ⊠ *1 Madison Ave., between 23rd and 24th Sts., Flatiron District* Ⓜ *N, R, 6 to 23rd St.*

FAMILY **Museum of Mathematics** (*MoMath*). There's no exact formula to get kids excited about math, but the sleek, two-floor Museum of Mathematics (MoMath)—the only cultural institution devoted to math in all of North America—comes close to finding the perfect fun-to-math ratio. Kids can ride square-wheel trikes, create human fractal trees, build virtual 3-D geometric shapes (which can be printed out on a 3-D printer for a fee), use lasers to explore cross sections of objects, solve dozens of puzzles, and generally bend their minds while they unknowingly multiply brain cells (sshh!). MoMath's newest exhibition, Robot Swarm, allows kids to explore swarm robotics and interact with two dozen small (Roomba-like), glowing robots, using simple math rules. Exhibits are best suited to kids ages six and up, but preschoolers can still enjoy many of the interactive exhibits, like the Math Square, a light-up floor programmed with math games, simulations, and patterns. ■ TIP➡ The museum closes at 2:30 pm the first Wednesday of every month. Save $1 by ordering tickets in advance online. ⊠ *11 E. 26th St., between 5th and Madison Aves., Flatiron District* ☎ *212/542–0566* ⊕ *www.momath.org* ✉ *$16* ⊙ *Daily 10–5* Ⓜ *N, R to 28th St.*

Museum of Sex. Ponder the profound history and cultural significance of sex at this 14,000-square-foot museum while staring at vintage pornographic photos, S&M paraphernalia, antimasturbation devices from the 1800s, explicit film clips, vintage condom tins, and a collection of artwork. The Spotlight on the Permanent Collection gallery features revolving artifacts and ephemera, as well as a "Jump for Joy" bounce house (of inflated breasts) that was originally part of a recent exhibition, *Funland: Pleasures & Perils of the Erotic Fairground.* Other recent exhibits have probed such topics as desire on the Internet and the sex lives of animals, as well as a translation of the campground setting as a surreal adult playground, complete with tents, campfire, and park rangers. The subject matter is given serious curatorial treatment, though the gift shop is full of fun sexual kitsch. Only patrons over 18 are admitted. ■ TIP➡ After visiting the museum's exhibitions, sate your appetite with a kinky cocktail or gourmet coffee and pastry in the museum's Play bar and Nice & Sweet café. ⊠ *233 5th Ave., New York* ☎ *212/689–6337* ⊕ *www.museumofsex.com* ✉ *$17.50* ⊙ *Sun.–Thurs. 10–9, Fri. and Sat. 11–11* Ⓜ *N, R to 28th St.*

GRAMERCY PARK

The haste and hullabaloo of the city calms considerably in the residential neighborhood of Gramercy Park. Dignified Gramercy Park, named for its 1831 gated garden ringed by historic buildings and private clubs, is an early example of the city's best creative urban planning. Just north of the park is Ian Schrager's reincarnation of the Gramercy Park Hotel on Lexington Avenue. South of the park, running north to south from 14th Street, is Irving Place, a short street honoring Washington Irving, which feels calm, green, exclusive, and has a combination of old and new eateries, stores, and architecture. Pete's Tavern (⇨ *Nightlife*), on Irving Place since 1864, maintains its claim as the oldest original bar in the city. Two famous writers, O. Henry (*Gift of the Magi*) and Ludwig Bemelmans (*Madeline*), were "inspired" here, probably by the amazing eggnog or Pete's House Ale.

Gramercy Park. You may not be able to enter this private park (the only truly private park in Manhattan—only those residing around it have keys), but a look through the bars in the wrought-iron fence that encloses it is worth your time, as is a stroll around its perimeter. The beautifully planted 2-acre park, designed by developer Samuel

B. Ruggles, dates from 1831, and is flanked by grand examples of early-19th-century architecture and permeated with the character of its many celebrated occupants.

When Ruggles bought the property, it was known as Krom Moerasje ("little crooked swamp"), named by the Dutch settlers. He drained the swamp and set aside 42 lots for a park to be accessible exclusively to those who bought the surrounding lots in his planned London-style residential square. The park is still owned by residents of the buildings surrounding the square, although neighbors from the area can now buy visiting privileges. Guests of the Gramercy Park Hotel also enjoy coveted access to this private park. In 1966 the New York City Landmarks Preservation Commission designated Gramercy Park a historic district. Notable buildings include No. 15, a Gothic Revival brownstone with black granite trim designed by Calvert Vaux, which was once home to Samuel Tilden, governor of New York. A secret passageway to 19th Street permitted Tilden to evade his political enemies. It is now home to the 100-year-old National Arts Club. Next door at No. 16 Gramercy Park South lived the actor Edwin Booth, perhaps most famous for being the brother of Lincoln's assassin. In 1888 he turned his Gothic-trim home into the Players Club, a clubhouse for actors and theatrical types who were not welcome in regular society. A bronze statue of Edwin Booth as Hamlet has pride of place inside the park. ■TIP→ Alexander Calder's iconic, monumental outdoor sculpture *Janey Waney* (1969) is installed inside the park and can be viewed through the railings. ⊠ *Lexington Ave. and 21st St., New York* Ⓜ *4, 5, 6, L, N, Q, R to 14th St.–Union Sq.; 6 to 23rd St.*

MIDTOWN EAST

GETTING ORIENTED

Midtown East

N,Q,R

N,Q,R,4,5,6

E. 59th St.

E. 58th St.

Edwynn Houk Gallery

E. 57th St.

Trump Tower

Pace Gallery (Midtown)

E. 56th St.

Sony Wonder Technology Lab

Little Collins

E. 55th St.

Third Ave.

Second Ave.

E. 54th St.

E,M

Seagram Building

E,M

First Ave.

E. 51st St.

MIDTOWN EAST

Beekman Place

St. Patrick's Cathedral

E. 50th St.

E. 49th St.

Fifth Ave.

Madison Ave.

Park Ave.

Lexington Ave.

E. 48th St.

E. 47th St.

Japan Society

Helmsley Building

E. 46th St.

E. 45th St.

United Nations Headquarters

Grand Central Terminal

E. 44th St.

Grand Central Market

E. 43rd St.

Ford Foundation Building

4,5,6,7,S

Chrysler Building

FDR Drive

7

E. 42nd St.

Tudor City

Bryant Park

E. 41st St.

Daily News Building

Queens-Midtown Tunnel

E. 40th St.

E. 39th St.

MURRAY HILL

E. 38th St.

East River

E. 37th St.

Morgan Library and Museum

E. 36th St.

B. Altman Building/ New York Public Library— Science, Industry, and Business Library (SIBL)

E. 35th St.

E. 34th St.

Empire State Building/ NY SKYRIDE

6

E. 33rd St.

0   1/4 mi

Koreatown

E. 32nd St.

Curry Hill

0   1/4 km

MAKING THE MOST OF YOUR TIME

The east side of Midtown is somewhat more laid-back than the west side, but there's still lots to keep you busy. Wherever you're headed, try to make sure you at least pass through Grand Central Terminal, which celebrates its 105th birthday in 2018—it's a madhouse on weekday mornings or in the early evening, right after work, but extremely quiet on weekends, an ideal time to visit.

If you're planning to visit the Empire State Building, try to do so either early or late in the day—morning is the least crowded time, and late at night the city lights are dazzling. Allow at least two hours for a visit to the observation deck.

It's also worth making time for a quick trip out of the United States to visit the "international zone" of the United Nations; take a tour of the recently renovated buildings and mail a postcard with a unique U.N. stamp.

TOP EXPERIENCES

Standing in the center of Grand Central Terminal's main concourse and taking in the fiber-optic map of the constellations overhead

Strolling down 5th Avenue, where some of the world's top luxury brands have flagship stores, especially around the holidays when store windows are dressed to impress

Viewing rare manuscripts at the Morgan Library

Enjoying panoramic views of the city at dusk from the top of the Empire State Building

Soaking in peace and serenity while ogling the neo-Gothic architecture, stained glass, and sculptures at iconic St. Patrick's Cathedral

Dining with locals in Koreatown and Curry Hill

GETTING HERE

To get to the east side of Midtown, take the 4, 5, 6, or 7 to Grand Central. The S, or Shuttle, travels back and forth between Grand Central and Times Square.

You can reach the Empire State Building via the B, D, F, M, N, Q, and R trains to 34th Street or the 6 to 33rd Street. The 6 also stops at 23rd and 28th Streets.

COFFEE AND QUICK BITES

Grand Central Market. The lower level of Grand Central is a cornucopia of gourmet eating options, including Ciao Bella Gelato, Murray's Cheese, and Joe the Art of Coffee. ✉ *Grand Central Terminal main entrance, 42nd St., at Park Ave., Midtown East* ⊕ *www.grandcentralterminal. com/market* ▭ *No credit cards* Ⓜ *4, 5, 6, 7, S to Grand Central–42nd St.*

Little Collins. This Australian import pays as much attention to what it puts on your plate—try the avocado and feta on toast—as what it pours in your coffee mug—try the flat white. ✉ *667 Lexington Ave., near 56th St., Midtown East* ☎ *212/308–1969* ⊕ *www.littlecollinsnyc. com* ▭ *No credit cards* Ⓜ *4, 5, 6 to 59th St.; N, Q, R to Lexington Ave./59th St.; E, M to Lexington Ave./53rd St.*

8

Sightseeing
★★★★★
Nightlife
★★
Dining
★★★★
Lodging
★★★★★
Shopping
★★★★★

Fifth Avenue is Manhattan's dividing line, marking the division of east and west sides, but the avenue itself seems to connote so much of what the city's East Side is all about. This is where some of the city's most iconic buildings are found, including the Empire State Building, in the Murray Hill neighborhood.

MIDTOWN EAST

By Jacinta
O'Halloran

In terms of architecture, Midtown East has some of the city's most notable gems, including the stately Chrysler Building, considered an Art Deco triumph, and the bustling Beaux Arts masterpiece, Grand Central Terminal. At night the streets here are relatively quiet, but the restaurants are filled with expense-account diners celebrating successes. Some of the most formal dining rooms and expensive meals in town can be found here. The lower section of 5th Avenue is also a shopper's paradise, home to megabrand flagships such as Louis Vuitton, Yves Saint Laurent, and Chanel, and some of the world's most famous jewelry stores, including Tiffany, Van Cleef & Arpels, and Harry Winston. Upscale department stores like Bloomingdale's and Saks Fifth Avenue are also around here.

TOP ATTRACTIONS

Chrysler Building. A monument to modernity and the mighty automotive industry, the former Chrysler headquarters wins many New Yorkers' vote for the city's most iconic and beloved skyscraper (and the world's tallest for 40 days, until the Empire State Building stole the honor). Architect William Van Alen, who designed this 1930 Art Deco masterpiece, incorporated car details into its form: American eagle gargoyles made of chromium nickel sprout from the 61st floor, resembling hood ornaments used on 1920s Chryslers; winged urns festooning the 31st floor reference the car's radiator caps. Most breathtaking is the pinnacle, with tiered crescents and spiked windows that radiate out like a magnificent steel sunburst. View it at sunset to catch the light gleaming off the tip. Even better, observe it at night, when its peak illuminates the sky. The inside is sadly off-limits, apart from the amazing time-capsule lobby replete with chrome "grillwork," intricately patterned wood elevator doors, marble walls and floors, and an enormous ceiling mural saluting transportation and human endeavor. ⊠ *405 Lexington Ave., at 42nd St., Midtown East* Ⓜ *4, 5, 6, 7, S to 42nd St./Grand Central.*

Fodor's Choice **Grand Central Terminal.** Grand Central is not only the world's largest (76
★ acres) and the nation's busiest railway station—nearly 700,000 commuters and subway riders use it daily—but also one of the world's most magnificent, majestic public spaces. Past the glimmering chandeliers of the waiting room is the jaw-dropping **main concourse,** 200 feet long, 120 feet wide, and 120 feet (roughly 12 stories) high, modeled after an ancient Roman public bath. In spite of it being completely cavernous, Grand Central manages to evoke a certain sense of warmth rarely found in buildings its size. Overhead, a twinkling fiber-optic map of the constellations covers the robin's-egg-blue ceiling. To admire it all with some sense of peace, avoid visiting at rush hour.

To escape the crowds, head up one of the sweeping staircases at either end, where three upscale restaurants occupy the balcony space. Any would make an enjoyable perch from which to survey the concourse, but for a real taste of the station's early years, head beyond the western staircase to the **Campbell Apartment,** a clubby cocktail lounge housed in the restored private offices and salon of 1920s tycoon John W. Campbell. Located around and below the main concourse are fantastic shops and eateries—this is, of course, home to the eponymous Grand Central Oyster Bar—making this one of the best, if somewhat labyrinthine, "malls" in the city.

To best admire Grand Central's exquisite Beaux Arts architecture, start with its ornate south face on East 42nd Street, modeled after a Roman triumphal arch. Crowning the facade's Corinthian columns and 75-foot-high arched windows, a graceful clock keeps time for hurried commuters. In the central window stands an 1869 bronze statue of Cornelius Vanderbilt, who built the station to house his railroad empire. Also noteworthy is the 1½-ton, cast-iron bald eagle displaying its 13-foot wingspan atop a ball near the corner of 42nd Street and Vanderbilt Avenue.

Grand Central still functions primarily as a railroad station, and might resemble its artless crosstown counterpart, Penn Station, were it not for Jacqueline Kennedy Onassis's 1975 public information campaign to save it as a landmark. Underground, more than 60 ingeniously integrated railroad tracks carry trains upstate and to Connecticut via Metro-North Commuter Rail. The subway connects here as well. The **Municipal Art Society** (*212/935–3960; www.mas.org/tours*) leads an official daily walking tour to explore the 100-year-old terminal's architecture, history, and hidden secrets. Tours begin in the main concourse at 12:30 and last 75 minutes. Tickets ($20) can be purchased in advance online (*www.docentour.com/gct*) or from the ticket booth in the main concourse. Alternatively, rent a headset ($9) and take a self-guided audio tour at your own pace. Headsets and maps are available

8

Department stores like Saks Fifth Avenue go all out for their holiday displays come December.

at GCT Tour windows on the main concourse and tours last about 45 minutes. ⊠ *Main entrance, 42nd St. and Park Ave., Midtown East* ☎ *212/935–3960* ⊕ *www.grandcentralterminal.com* Ⓜ *4, 5, 6, 7, S to Grand Central–42nd St.*

FAMILY **Sony Wonder Technology Lab.** Have kids in tow? The free Sony Wonder Technology Lab in the Sony Building lets them program robots, remix songs, perform virtual heart surgery, learn about new technologies inspired by nature, and see their dance moves performed by favorite Sony-animated characters in real time through motion capture. A fascinating evolutionary timeline explores how technology keeps getting faster, sharper, smaller, and more portable. The lab also shows classic and contemporary films for both young and adult audiences in its HD theater on Thursday and Saturday. ■**TIP➔ Admission is free, but reservations are strongly recommended; they can be made a minimum of seven days and up to three months from the time of visit.** A limited number of same-day tickets are available on a first-come, first-served basis. ⊠ *550 Madison Ave., at 56th St., Midtown East* ☎ *212/833–8100* ⊕ *www.sonywondertechlab.com* ⏱ *Tues.–Sat. 9:30–5:30* Ⓜ *E, M to 5th Ave./53rd St.*

St. Patrick's Cathedral. This Gothic-style edifice—the largest Catholic cathedral in the United States, seating approximately 2,400 people—is among Manhattan's most striking churches, with its double spires topping out at 330 feet. "St. Pat's," as locals call it, holds a special place in the hearts of many New Yorkers and provides a calm and quiet refuge in the heart of buzzy Midtown, despite the throngs of tourists (the cathedral receives more than 5.5 million visitors annually).

The church dates back to 1858–79, but thanks to an extensive $177 million rehabilitation project, completed in late 2015 and christened with a papal visit and mass, the cathedral no longer shows its age. The three-year renovation left no stone or detail unturned, from the stone faces of the 80-foot spires that tower above 5th Avenue to the cleaned and glazed (for UV protection) 3,700 stained-glass panels and the newly revealed skylights that had been covered with roofing for decades, down to the newly added panels of the confessional, carefully carved to match existing woodwork. In addition to cosmetic work and restorations, the building now has a state-of-the-art sprinkler system as well as a heating and cooling system that reduces energy consumption by 30%. Highlights of this brightened and refreshed cathedral include the almost-90-year-old organ in the choir gallery with its—newly cleaned—7,855 pipes and the famous rose window (considered stained-glass-artist Charles Connick's greatest work). Also check out the statues in the alcoves around the nave, including a modern depiction of the first American-born saint, Mother Elizabeth Ann Seton. Don't miss the ornately carved bronze double doors on your way in and out: each weighs 9,200 pounds and features sculptures of saints.

The church's *Pietà* sculpture is three times larger than the *Pietà* at St. Peter's in Rome. Daily masses are open and free to the public (check the website for schedule) with the exception of Midnight Mass on Christmas Eve, which is a ticketed event. Free guided tours are held at 10 am most days (call ahead to confirm). ✉ *5th Ave., between 50th and 51st Sts., Midtown East* ☎ *212/753–2261 for rectory* ⊕ *www. saintpatrickscathedral.org* ⊘ *Daily 6:30 am–8:45 pm* Ⓜ *E, M to 5th Ave./53rd St.*

United Nations Headquarters. Officially an "international zone" and not part of the United States, the U.N. Headquarters is a working symbol of global cooperation. Built between 1947 and 1961, the headquarters sit on a lushly landscaped, 18-acre tract on the East River, fronted by flags of member nations. The United Nations celebrated its 70th anniversary in 2015 with the completion of a seven-year overhaul that retained the 1950s look and feel (and in some cases, green carpet) of the complex, while incorporating state-of-the-art technology to upgrade the heat, sound, and security systems and to improve its overall performance. The $2.1 billion renovation returns the historic campus to its original design, in the process addressing contemporary concerns, like accessibility, energy efficiency, and blast-proofing, as well as adding some not exactly *new* conveniences, like sprinklers. The General Assembly Building reopened in early 2015 after its 16-month renovation, which included replacing the gold-leafed background of the iconic U.N. emblem that had become caked with tar and nicotine—as had the walls and ceiling of the hall—after decades of cigar and cigarette smoke (city law did not apply here, so smoking was not outlawed until 2008). The only way to enter the U.N. Headquarters is with the 45-minute guided tour (given in 20 languages; reservations can be made through the website), which includes the **General Assembly** and major council chambers. While the tour covers a lot of educational ground, it does not cover a lot of physical ground; council chambers may be closed on any given day, and you cannot enter the Secretariat building. Also, you can no longer wander the grounds, rose garden, or riverside promenade. Arrive 30 minutes before the start of your tour for security screening. If you ordered tickets online, be sure to bring your printout. The newly renovated Conference Building, which includes the original chambers of the Security Council, the Trusteeship Council, and the Economic and Social Council, as well as gifts from U.N. Member States, like the mosaic representation of Norman Rockwell's *Golden Rule*, are all back on public display. The tour also includes displays on war, peacekeeping, nuclear nonproliferation, human rights, and refugees, and passes corridors overflowing with imaginatively diverse artwork. Free tickets to assemblies are sometimes available on a first-come, first-served basis before sessions begin; pick them up in the General Assembly lobby. The complex's buildings (the slim, 505-foot-tall green-glass **Secretariat Building;** the much smaller, domed **General Assembly Building;** and the **Dag Hammarskjöld Library**) evoke the influential French modernist Le Corbusier (who was on the team of architects that designed the complex), and the surrounding park and plaza remain visionary. The public concourse has a gift shop, a bookstore, and a post office where you can mail postcards with U.N. stamps; you can also get your passport stamped with the U.N. stamp. ⊠ *Visitor entrance, 1st Ave. at 46th St., Midtown East* ☎ *212/963–8687* ⊕ *visit.un.org* ☝ *Tour $18 (plus $2 online surcharge)* ⊗ *Tours weekdays 9:15–4:15 (tours in English leave every 30 mins; for other languages, check schedule online)* ☞ *Children under 5 not admitted* Ⓜ *4, 5, 6, 7, S to Grand Central–42nd St.*

WORTH NOTING

Daily News Building. The landmark lobby of this Art Deco tower contains an illuminated 12-foot globe that revolves beneath a black glass dome. Around it, spreading across the floor like a giant compass and literally positioning New York at the center of the world, bronze lines indicate mileage to various international destinations. Movie fans may recognize the building as the offices of the fictional newspaper *The Daily Planet* in the original *Superman* movie. On the wall behind the globe you can check out a number of meteorological gauges, which read New York City's weather—especially fun on a windy day when the meters are whipping about. The *Daily News* hasn't called this building home since the mid-1990s; only the lobby is open to the public (but that's enough). ■**TIP→** The globe was last updated in 1967 so part of the fun here is seeing how our maps have changed; note Manchuria and East and West Germany. ⊠ *220 E. 42nd St., between 2nd and 3rd Aves., Midtown East* ☎ *212/210–2100* Ⓜ *4, 5, 6, 7, S to Grand Central–42nd St.*

Edwynn Houk Gallery. The impressive stable of 20th-century photographers represented and shown here includes Sally Mann, Robert Polidori, Nick Brandt, Lalla Essaydi, Annie Leibovitz, Herb Ritts, Mona Kuhn, and Elliott Erwitt. The gallery also has prints by masters Edward Weston and Alfred Stieglitz. ⊠ *745 5th Ave., 4th fl., between 57th and 58th Sts., Midtown East* ☎ *212/750–7070* ⊕ *www.houkgallery.com* ☝ *Free* ⊗ *Tues.–Sat. 11–6* Ⓜ *N, R, Q to 5th Ave./59th St.*

Ford Foundation Building. While most Midtown office lobbies remain off-limits to visitors, the Ford Foundation Building's is a welcome respite from high-traffic Midtown sidewalks and nearby attractions like Grand Central Station and the United Nations Headquarters. Built in 1967 as the Ford Foundation's New York City headquarters, and designed by Kevin Roche John Dinkeloo and Associates (also responsible for several galleries and wings at the Metropolitan Museum of Art, the renovation of the Central Park Zoo, and many other iconic attractions), this landmark, 12-story transparent glass cube is one of Midtown's most notable buildings, thanks to its open, C-shape office floors overlooking an incredibly lush, secret—but public—garden. While most office buildings fulfill their green quota with a few potted plants and maybe a fountain in the courtyard, this light-filled atrium is a veritable oasis, complete with soaring trees, cascading plants, walking paths, three tiers of plantings, and a small pool. Whether you're an urban gardener or just a weary visitor, pause in this rare patch of quiet in the heart of the city—you'll likely have this tropical scene to yourself. The atrium can be accessed from the 42nd or 43rd Street entrance during office hours (10–4). ⊠ *320 E. 43rd St., between 1st and 2nd Aves., Midtown East* ☏ *212/573–5000* ⊕ *www.fordfoundation.org* Ⓜ *4, 5, 6, 7, S to Grand Central–42nd St.*

Helmsley Building. This Warren & Wetmore–designed 1929 landmark was intended to match neighboring Grand Central Terminal in bearing, and succeeded, with a gold-and-copper roof topped with an enormous lantern (originally housing a 6,000-watt light) and distinctive dual archways for traffic on Park Avenue. The building's history gets quirky. When millionaire real estate investor Harry Helmsley purchased the building in 1977, he changed its name from the New York Central Building to the New York General Building in order to save money by replacing only two letters in the facade (only later did he rename it after himself). During a renovation the following year, however, he actually gilded the building, applying gold paint even to limestone and bronze—it was removed by a succeeding owner. In 2010, after a $100 million renovation, the Helmsley Building, no longer under Helmsley ownership (so technically 230 Park, or "the building formerly known as the Helmsley Building and informally still known as the Helmsley Building"), became the first prewar office tower to receive LEED Gold certification for energy efficiency. Despite being blocked from view from the south by the MetLife Building (originally, the Pan Am Building), the Helmsley Building remains a defining—and now "green," as opposed to gold—feature of one of the world's most lavish avenues. ⊠ *230 Park Ave., between 45th and 46th Sts., Midtown East* Ⓜ *4, 5, 6, 7, S to 42nd St./Grand Central.*

Japan Society. The stylish, serene lobby of the Japan Society has interior bamboo gardens linked by a second-floor waterfall. Works by well-known Japanese artists are exhibited in the second-floor gallery. Past shows have included "For a New World to Come"—a comprehensive exhibit of Japanese photography from the late 1960s that examines how experiments in the medium of photography laid the foundation for contemporary art in Japan, and the "Life of Cats"—an exploration of cats as depicted in Japanese paintings, prints, and decorative objects dating from the 17th to the early 20th century. The society's annual performing arts season (from September through March) offers works by established and emerging artists in dance, music, and theater. In July, the museum hosts an annual film festival, Japan Cuts, showcasing contemporary Japanese cinema. ⊠ *333 E. 47th St., between 1st and 2nd Aves., Midtown East* ☎ *212/832–1155* ⊕ *www.japansociety. org* 🖾 *Gallery $12* ⊙ *Gallery Tues.–Thurs. 11–6, Fri. 11–9, weekends 11–5; building hrs vary* Ⓜ *4, 5, 6, 7, S to Grand Central–42nd St.; E, M to Lexington Ave./53rd St.; 6 to 51st St.*

Pace Gallery (Midtown). This leading contemporary art gallery—with three outposts in Chelsea, two in London, and one each in Beijing and Hong Kong—focuses on such modern and contemporary artists as Julian Schnabel, Mark Rothko, James Turrell, and Tara Donovan. ⊠ *32 E. 57th St., 2nd fl., between Park and Madison Aves., Midtown East* ☎ *212/421–3292* ⊕ *www.thepacegallery.com* 🖾 *Free* ⊙ *Tues.–Sat. 10–6* Ⓜ *N, Q, R to 5th Ave./59th St.*

Seagram Building. Ludwig Mies van der Rohe, a pioneer of modern architecture, built this boxlike bronze-and-glass tower in 1958. The austere facade belies its wit: I-beams, used to hold buildings up, here are merely attached to the surface, representing the *idea* of support. The Seagram Building's innovative ground-level plaza, extending out to the sidewalk, has since become a common element in urban skyscraper design, but at the time it was built, it was a radical announcement of a new, modern era of American architecture. Most visitors are distracted by more elaborate figures in the city skyline, but the Seagram is a must-visit for architecture buffs. With its two giant fountains and welcoming steps, it's also a popular lunch spot with Midtown workers. Visit late in the afternoon to avoid crowds. ⊠ *375 Park Ave., between 52nd and 53rd Sts., Midtown East* ⊕ *www.375parkavenue.com* Ⓜ *6 to 51st St.; E, M to Lexington Ave./53rd St.*

Trump Tower. The tallest all-glass building in Manhattan when it was completed in 1983, this skyscraper's ostentatious atrium flaunts that decade's unbridled luxury, with three well-trafficked dining options (a café, grill, and bar), expensive boutiques (including Ivanka Trump's Fine Jewelry store), and gaudy brass everywhere. You half expect the pleasant-sounding waterfall streaming down to the lower-level food court to flow with champagne. ⊠ *725 5th Ave., at 56th St., Midtown East* ☎ *212/832–2000* ⊕ *www.trump.com* Ⓜ *N, Q, R to 5th Ave./59th St.; E, M to 5th Ave./53rd St.*

Tudor City. Before Donald Trump, there was Fred F. French. In 1925 the prominent real-estate developer became one of the first to buy up a large number of buildings—more than 100, in fact, most of them tenements—and join their properties into a single new development. He designed a collection of nine apartment buildings and two parks in the "garden city" mode, which placed a building's green space not in an enclosed courtyard, but in the foreground. French also elevated the entire development 70 feet (40 stone steps) above the river and built a 39-by-50-foot "Tudor City" sign, best viewed from 42nd Street walking east, atop one of the 22-story buildings. The development's residential towers opened between 1927 and 1930, borrowing a marketable air

The restoration and cleaning of Grand Central in the late 1990s uncovered the elaborate astronomical design on the ceiling of the main concourse.

of sophistication from Tudor-style stonework, stained-glass windows, and lobby design flourishes. An official city landmark, Tudor City has featured in numerous films, and its landmark gardens—sometimes compared to Gramercy Park, but without the key—remain a popular lunch spot among office workers. The neighborhood was designated a historic district in 1988. ⊠ *From 40th to 43rd St., between 1st and 2nd Aves., Midtown East* Ⓜ *4, 5, 6, 7, S to Grand Central–42nd St.*

MURRAY HILL

Murray Hill stretches roughly from 30th to 40th Street between 5th and 3rd Avenues and is a mix of high-rises, restaurants, and bars filled mostly with a postcollege crowd. The small but solid enclave of Little India (also known as "Curry Hill"), primarily around Lexington and 28th Street, is a good area to sample authentic cuisine and shop for traditional clothing and other goods in a handful of boutiques. Farther north, a few side streets are tree lined and town-house filled, with some high-profile haunts, including the Morgan Library and Museum with its vast book stacks and rare manuscripts. Probably the main reason to visit this neighborhood is to see New York's biggest icon, the Empire State Building.

TOP ATTRACTIONS

FAMILY
Fodor's Choice
★

Empire State Building. With a pencil-slim silhouette, recognizable virtually worldwide, the Empire State Building is an Art Deco monument to progress, a symbol for New York City, and a star in some great romantic scenes, on- and off-screen. Its cinematic résumé—the building has

The lights on the top of the Empire State Building often change to support different holidays and causes.

appeared in more than 250 movies—means that it remains a fixture of popular imagination, and many visitors come to relive favorite movie scenes. You might just find yourself at the top of the building with *Elf* look-alikes or even the building's own *King Kong* impersonator.

Built in 1931 at the peak of the skyscraper craze, this 103-story limestone giant opened after a mere 13 months of construction. The framework rose at an astonishing rate of 4½ stories per week, making the Empire State Building the fastest-rising skyscraper ever built. Unfortunately, your rise to the observation deck might not be quite so record breaking.

There are three lines to get to the top of the Empire State Building: a line for tickets, a line for security, and a line for the elevators. Save time by purchasing your tickets in advance (*esbnyc.com*). You can't skip the security line, but you can skip to the front of both the ticket line and the line for elevators by purchasing an Express ticket to the 86th floor ($65). ■TIP→ **If you don't want to pony up for express service, do yourself a favor and skip that last elevator line at the 80th floor by taking the stairs.**

If this is your first visit, keep yourself entertained during your ascent with a free multimedia tour (available in eight languages), which offers images, maps, quizzes, and historical tidbits to supplement displays as you make your way to the top.

The 86th-floor observatory (1,050 feet high) has both a glass-enclosed area (heated in winter and cooled in summer) and an outdoor deck spanning the building's circumference. Don't be shy about going outside into the wind (even in winter) or you'll miss half the experience. Also, don't be deterred by crowds; there's an unspoken etiquette when it comes to sharing the views and backdrop, and there's plenty of city to go around. Bring quarters for the high-powered binoculars—on clear days you can see up to 80 miles—or bring binoculars of your own so you can get a good look at some of the city's rooftop gardens. If it rains, the deck will be less crowded and you can view the city between the clouds or watch the rain travel sideways around the building from the shelter of the enclosed walkway.

The views of the city from the 86th-floor deck are spectacular, but the views from 16 stories up on the 102nd-floor observatory are even more so—and yet, fewer visitors make it this far. Instead of rushing back to elevator lines, ask yourself when you'll be back again and then head up to the enclosed 102nd floor. The ticket for both the 86th-floor and 102nd-floor decks costs $52, but you will be rewarded with peaceful, bird's-eye views of the entire city. Also, there are fewer visitors angling for photo ops, so you can linger a while and really soak in the city and experience.

Even if you skip the view from up top, be sure to step into the lobby and take in the ceiling, beautifully restored in 2009. The gilded gears and sweeping Art Deco lines, long hidden under a drop ceiling and decades of paint, are a romantic tribute to the machine age and part of the original vision for the building. ⌧ *350 5th Ave., at E. 34th St., Murray Hill* ☎ *212/736–3100, 877/692–8439* ⊕ *www.esbnyc.com* ✆ *$32; $52 for 86th-fl. and 102nd-fl. decks* ⊙ *Daily 8 am–2 am; last elevator up leaves at 1:15 am* Ⓜ *B, D, F, N, Q, R, M to 34th St./Herald Sq.; 6 to 33rd St.*

Morgan Library and Museum. The treasures inside this museum, gathered by John Pierpont Morgan (1837–1913), one of New York's wealthiest financiers, are exceptional: medieval and Renaissance illuminated manuscripts, old-master drawings and prints, rare books, and autographed literary and musical manuscripts. Other crowning achievements on paper include letters penned by John Keats and Thomas Jefferson; a summary of the theory of relativity in Einstein's own elegant handwriting; three Gutenberg Bibles; drawings by Dürer, Leonardo da Vinci, Rubens, Blake, and Rembrandt; the only known manuscript fragment of Milton's *Paradise Lost;* Thoreau's journals; and original manuscripts and letters by Charlotte Brontë, Jane Austen, Thomas Pynchon, and many others. Recent exhibits have included *Ernest Hemingway: Between Two Wars*, featuring notebooks, correspondence, personal items, and early drafts of short stories, and *Warhol by the Book*, an exhibition of Warhol's book projects from his early student days through his later years as a cultural icon.

The library shop is housed within an 1852 Italianate brownstone, once the home of Morgan's son, J. P. Morgan Jr. Outside on East 36th Street, the sphinx in the right-hand sculptured panel of the original library's facade is rumored to wear the face of architect Charles McKim. ⌧ *225 Madison Ave., at 36th St., Murray Hill* ☎ *212/685–0008* ⊕ *www. themorgan.org* ✆ *$18 (free Fri. 7–9)* ⊙ *Tues.–Thurs. 10:30–5, Fri. 10:30–9, Sat. 10–6, Sun. 11–6* Ⓜ *B, D, F, M, N, Q, R to 34th St.–Herald Sq.; 6 to 33rd St.*

The Lights of the Empire State Building

At night the Empire State Building lights up the Manhattan skyline with a colorful view as awe-inspiring from a distance as the view from the top. The colors at the top of the building are changed regularly to reflect seasons, events, and holidays, so New Yorkers and visitors from around the world always have a reason to look at this icon in a new light.

The building's first light show was in November 1932, when a simple searchlight was used to spread the news that New York–born Franklin Delano Roosevelt had been elected president of the United States. Douglas Leigh, sign designer and mastermind of Times Square's kinetic billboard ads, tried to brighten up prospects at the "Empty State Building" after the Depression by negotiating with the Coca-Cola Company to occupy the top floors. He proposed that Coca-Cola could change the lights of the building to serve as a weather forecast and then publish a small guide on its bottles to decipher the colors. Coca-Cola loved this idea, but the deal fell through after the bombing at Pearl Harbor, when the U.S. government needed office space in the building.

In 1956 the revolving "freedom lights" were installed to welcome people to America; then in 1964 the top 30 floors of the building were illuminated to mark the New York World's Fair. Douglas Leigh revisited the lights in 1976, when he was made chairman of City Decor to welcome the Democratic Convention. He introduced the idea of color lighting, and so the building's tower was ablaze in red, white, and blue to welcome the convention and mark the celebration of the American Bicentennial. The color lights were a huge success, and they remained red, white, and blue for the rest of the year.

Leigh's next suggestion of tying the lights to different holidays, a variation on his weather theme for Coca-Cola, is the basic scheme still used today. In 1977 the lighting system was updated to comply with energy conservation programs and allow for a wider range of colors. Leigh further improved this new system in 1984 by designing an automated color-changing system so vertical fluorescents in the mast could be changed.

The Empire State Building's LED light system can produce intensely saturated full-color light and dimmable cool white light, allowing for an astonishing and flexible range of dramatic or subtle lighting effects.

For a full lighting schedule, visit ⊕ www.esbnyc.com.

—Jacinta O'Halloran

WORTH NOTING

FAMILY **B. Altman Building/New York Public Library–Science, Industry and Business Library (SIBL).** In 1906, department-store magnate Benjamin Altman gambled that his fashionable patrons would follow him uptown from his popular store in the area now known as the Ladies' Mile Historic District. His new store, one of the first of the grand department stores on 5th Avenue, was designed to blend in with the mansions nearby. Note in particular the beautiful entrance on 5th Avenue. In 1996 the New York Public Library (NYPL) set up a high-tech library here. A

33-foot-high atrium unites the building's two floors: the lending library off the lobby and the research collections below. Downstairs, a wall of electronic ticker tapes and TVs tuned to business-news stations beams information and instructions to patrons. A free hour-long tour is given Thursday at 2; meet at the reception desk. ⊠ *188 Madison Ave., between 34th and 35th Sts., Murray Hill* ☎ *917/275–6975* ⊕ *www. nypl.org* ⊘ *Mon., Fri., and Sat. 10–6, Tues.–Thurs. 10–8* Ⓜ *B, D, F, M, N, Q, R to 34th St.–Herald Sq.; 6 to 33rd St.*

Curry Hill. An affectionate play on the name of the neighborhood, Curry Hill is an aromatic three-block cluster of Indian restaurants and one of the city's most exciting dining destinations. There are nearly 25 Indian restaurants peppered (or is it spiced?) around Lexington Avenue between 26th and 28th Streets, and while the neighborhood is popular with in-the-know New Yorkers, it is decidedly off the beaten tourist track. You'll find culinary offerings from a variety of regional cuisines, be it a filling *biryani* or a quick *chaat* (savory snack). Highlights include a *saag paneer* (spinach dish with cheese) or a bowl of curry at one of the neighborhood's founding restaurants, Curry in a Hurry (28th and Lex); sweet-and-sour *bamia kuhta* (lamb stew) or potato-and-beet fritters at Jewish-Indian restaurant Haldi (Lexington between 27th and 28th); and *kati* rolls (meat or veggie filling wrapped in flatbread) and other urban Indian street snacks at Desi Galli (Lexington between 27th and 28th). Don't leave the neighborhood without sampling a *dosa*, a fermented crêpe often filled with spiced potato and served with dipping sauces, and shopping the spice markets. Too full to walk? Curry Hill is a great place to score a ride as Indian cab drivers regularly stop here for food. ⊠ *Lexington Ave., between 26th and 28th Sts., Murray Hill* Ⓜ *6 to 28th St.; N, R to 23rd St.*

Koreatown. Despite sitting in the shade of the Empire State Building, and within steps of Herald Square, Koreatown (or "K-Town," as it's locally known) is not a tourist destination. In fact, it feels decidedly off the beaten track and insulated, as though locals wryly planted their own place to eat, drink, be merry, and get a massage—right under the noses of millions of tourists. Technically, Koreatown runs from 31st to 36th Street between 5th and 6th Avenues, though the main drag is 32nd Street between 5th and Broadway. Labeled Korea Way, this strip is home to 24/7 Korean barbecue joints, karaoke bars, and spas, all piled on top of each other. Fill up on *kimchi* (spicy pickled cabbage), *kimbap* (seaweed rice), and red-bean doughnuts (delicious), try some authentic Asian karaoke, and then top off your Koreatown experience by stepping into a jade-igloo sauna (at Juvenex Spa, 25 West 32nd Street). Expect a big bang for your buck, to rub elbows with locals, and bragging rights over visitors who followed the crowds to Chinatown. ⊠ *From 31st to 36th St., between 5th and 6th Aves., Murray Hill* Ⓜ *B, D, F, M, N, Q, R to 34th St.–Herald Sq.; 6 to 33rd St.*

FAMILY **NY SKYRIDE.** Although some parents blanch when they discover both how much it costs and how it lurches, the NY SKYRIDE, on the second floor of the Empire State Building, is New York's only aerial-tour simulator, and much cheaper than an actual aerial tour of New York. Narrated by actor Kevin Bacon, the ride takes a 30-minute virtual tour of New York, soaring by the Brooklyn Bridge, the Statue of Liberty, Central Park, Times Square, Yankee Stadium, and other top attractions along the way. There's also a brief but poignant trip back in time to visit the World Trade Center's Twin Towers—a sight sure to drive you straight into the arms of the first "I [Heart] NY" T-shirt vendor you see after leaving the building. It's a fun way to get a sense of the city's highlights, though teenagers may find the technology a little dated. When you purchase a SKYRIDE–Empire State Building combo ticket, you visit the SKYRIDE first, then join the line for the observation deck at the elevators, skipping up to half the wait. ☒ *Empire State Building, 33rd St. entrance, Murray Hill* ☏ *212/279–9777, 888/759–7433* ⊕ *www. skyride.com* ☐ *$42; $64 combo Skyride and observatory* ☉ *Daily 8 am–10 pm* Ⓜ *B, D, F, M, N, Q, R to 34th St.–Herald Sq.; 6 to 33rd St.*

MIDTOWN WEST

GETTING ORIENTED

Midtown West

Central Park

Columbus Circle   **M** A,B,C,D,1

Central Park South

N,Q,R   **M**

W. 58th St.

W. 57th St.   *N,Q,R*   **M**   **M** F   Hirschl & Adler Galleries ◆

◆ Tibor de Nagy Gallery

Carnegie Hall   Marlborough Gallery (Midtown) ◆   ◆ Marian Goodman Gallery

◆ David Findlay Jr. Gallery

W. 56th St.   Zibetto ✕ Espresso Bar

W. 55th St.

Broadway

Avenue of the Americas

The Museum of Modern Art (MoMA)

W. 54th St.

B,D,E   **M**   *W. 53rd St.*   The Paley Center for Media   **M** *E,M*

W. 52nd St.

W. 51st St.   NBC Studios ◆

Eighth Ave.   *Seventh Ave.*   Radio City Music Hall ◆   Top of the Rock ◆   Fifth Ave.

C,E   **M**   **M** 1   *W. 50th St.*   The Rink at ◆ ◆ Rockefeller Center ✕ Rockefeller Center

HELL'S KITCHEN   *N,Q,R*   **M**   *W. 49th St.*   Blue Bottle Coffee

W. 48th St.   **M** *B,D,F,M*   ◆ Christie's

Restaurant Row   *W. 47th St.*

←◆ Intrepid Sea, Air and Space Museum   *W. 46th St.*

W. 45th St.

W. 44th St.

TIMES   ◆ TKTS booth   *W. 43rd St.*
SQUARE

Madame Tussauds New York   ◆ Times Square

A,C,E   **M**   **M** 7

◆   *N,Q,R,S* **M**   *W. 42nd St.*   *B,D,F,M*   **M**
1,2,3,7

W. 41st St.   ◆ Bryant Park   ◆ New York Public Library

The New York Times Building ◆   *W. 40th St.*

Broadway

W. 39th St.   ✕ Café Grumpy

W. 38th St.

0 _____ 1/4 mi

0 _____ 1/4 km   *W. 37th St.*

MAKING THE MOST OF YOUR TIME

Most people think of Times Square when they think of Midtown, but there's a lot more going on here. The Museum of Modern Art (MoMA) is one of the neighborhood's top attractions and definitely worth a visit, as is Bryant Park, a cool oasis for Midtown's workers and locals. If you have enough time, hop in a cab and head over to 12th Avenue to visit the space shuttle *Enterprise* at the *Intrepid* Sea, Air & Space Museum.

Times Square is almost always a frenetic mass of people staring up at the lights and the giant televisions. If you're in a hurry to get somewhere, try to avoid walking—or cabbing—through here. If staying in Midtown, you can take advantage of the prime location and rise early to be first in line at landmarks, museums, or the TKTS booth for discount day-of theater tickets (⇨ *Chapter 19: Performing Arts*).

TOP EXPERIENCES

Summer film screenings at dusk in Bryant Park

Skating at Rockefeller Center

Checking out the views from the Top of the Rock; opinions vary on whether the better views are from here or from the Empire State Building. Either way, if you go at night, the city spreads out below in a mesmerizing blanket of lights.

Soaking in the art and serenity of MoMA's sculpture garden

GETTING HERE

You can get to Midtown via (almost) all the subways; many make numerous stops throughout the area. For Midtown West, the 1, 2, 3, 7, A, C, E, N, Q, and R serve Times Square and West 42nd Street. The S, or Shuttle, travels back and forth between Times Square and Grand Central Station. The B, D, F, and M trains serve Rockefeller Center.

COFFEE AND QUICK BITES

Blue Bottle Coffee. Known for their meticulous brewing, freshly roasted organic beans (prepared in a Brooklyn roastery), and delicious treats and pastries (also rushed in fresh from Brooklyn), the Rock Center outpost of this cult California coffee favorite is the perfect refueling spot amid the chaos of Midtown. ✉ *1 Rockefeller Plaza, Concourse level, Midtown West* ☎ *510/653–3394* ⊕ *www.bluebottlecoffee.com* 🚫 *No credit cards* Ⓜ *B, D, F, M to 47–50th Sts./Rockefeller Center; E, M to 5th Ave./53rd St.*

Café Grumpy. Stop by this Garment District outlet of the New York minichain and turn any sign of grumpiness into a smile with coffee roasted at the Greenpoint, Brooklyn, location. All pastries are baked at the Lower East Side branch: the black-pepper-and-cardamom banana bread is a standout. ✉ *200 W. 39th St., Midtown West* ☎ *646/499-8747* ⊕ *www.cafegrumpy.com* 🚫 *No credit cards* Ⓜ *1, 2, 3, 7, N, Q, R, S to Times Sq.-42nd St.*

Zibetto Espresso Bar. You won't find any seats, but you will find arguably the best espresso in New York. ✉ *1385 6th Ave., at 56th St., Midtown West* ☎ *646/707-0505* ⊕ *www.zibettoespressobar.com* 🚫 *No credit cards* Ⓜ *F to 57th St.*

9

Sightseeing
★★★★★
Nightlife
★★★
Dining
★★★★★
Lodging
★★★★★
Shopping
★★★★★

Big is the buzz in Times Square, where giant TV screens, towering skyscrapers, and Broadway theaters play starring roles alongside megastores like Hershey's and Toys "R" Us. Love it or hate it, Times Square is the flashy and flashing heart of Midtown. A visit to New York demands a photo op in Times Square. Just don't forget that there's also a lot more to see and experience on this side of Midtown.

Updated
by Jacinta
O'Halloran

Luckily, you needn't go far from Times Square to get away from the crowds. Head over to 9th Avenue—also known as Hell's Kitchen (where the food is heavenly)—and calmer side streets, home to a mixed bag of locals, many of whom work in the theater industry. There are lots of eclectic restaurants, pretheater dining options, and cute boutiques for shopping. Head over to the Avenue of the Americas (6th Avenue), and discover Bryant Park's Zen green space, stretched out like a yoga mat at the back door of the New York Public Library (another refuge from Midtown madness).

You can score good seats to some of the hottest Broadway and Off-Broadway shows for half the going rate at the TKTS booth in Duffy Square at 47th Street and Broadway *(see Performing Arts)*. Although people think of Broadway as the heart of the theater scene, few theaters actually line the thoroughfare. For some of the grande dames, head west on 45th Street. There are several Broadway beauties here, including the **Booth**, the **Schoenfeld**, the **Jacobs**, the **Music Box**, and the **Imperial**. On the southern side of 45th Street there's the pedestrians-only **Shubert Alley**, distinguished by colorful posters advertising the latest hit plays and musicals, and the **Shubert Theatre**, one of Broadway's most lustrous gems. Head west along 44th Street to see the **Helen Hayes**, the **Broadhurst**, the **Majestic**, and the **St. James.**

You might be surprised to learn that Chelsea is not the only gallery hub in the city; 57th Street between 5th and 6th Avenues is home to some of the city's most prestigious galleries, including Marian Goodman, the Pace Gallery, and Tibor de Nagy Gallery.

Bryant Park is one of the best places to bring your lunch and people-watch in the city.

TOP ATTRACTIONS

FAMILY **Bryant Park.** This lovely green space spread out among landmarks and skyscrapers is one of Manhattan's most popular parks. Tall London plane trees line the perimeter of the sunny central lawn, overlooking stone terraces, formal flower beds, gravel pathways, and a smattering of kiosks selling everything from sandwiches to egg creams (in season). The garden tables scattered about fill with lunching office workers and folks enjoying the park's free Wi-Fi (signs show you how to log on). In summer you can check out free live jazz and "Broadway in Bryant Park" musical theater performances, as well as author readings. Most popular of all is the Summer Film Festival: locals leave work early to snag a spot on the lawn for the outdoor screenings each Monday at dusk. At the east side of the park, near a squatting bronze cast of Gertrude Stein, is the stylish Bryant Park Grill, which has a rooftop garden, and the adjacent open-air Bryant Park Café, open seasonally. The 5th Avenue terrace is home to a different food truck at lunchtime every day during the week. On the south side of the park is an old-fashioned **carousel** ($3) where kids can ride fanciful rabbits and frogs instead of horses, and attend storytellings and magic shows. Big kids can play with the park's selection of lawn and tabletop games, which includes everything from quoits and Scrabble to Chinese checkers and Scandinavian kubb. Come November the park rolls out the artificial frozen **"pond"** (*Oct.–Mar., daily 8 am–10 pm; skate rental $15–$19*) for ice-skating. Surrounding the ice rink are the Christmas-market-like stalls of the **Holiday Shops**, selling handcrafted goods and local foods. ⊠ *6th Ave., between 40th* *and 42nd Sts., Midtown West* ☏ *212/768–4242* ⊕ *www.bryantpark. org* ☉ *Hrs vary by month; see website for exact times* Ⓜ *B, D, F, M to 42nd St.–Bryant Park; 7 to 5th Ave.*

FAMILY **Intrepid Sea, Air & Space Museum.** The centerpiece of the *Intrepid* Sea, Air & Space Museum complex is the 900-foot *Intrepid* aircraft carrier, Manhattan's only floating museum. The carrier's most trying moment of service, the day it was attacked in World War II by kamikaze pilots, is recounted in a multimedia presentation. The museum faced its own trying period when forced to close for several months due to extensive flooding after 2012's Superstorm Sandy. Fortunately, the *Intrepid*'s unparalleled collection of aircraft was not damaged in the storm. While repairs to electrical and safety systems are still ongoing, and plans to build a permanent home for the space shuttle *Enterprise* are pending, the museum is fully operational. The space shuttle *Enterprise,* NASA's first prototype orbiter, joined the Intrepid in July 2012 and is temporarily housed in a climate-controlled bubble tent on the flight deck of the *Intrepid,* but visitors can check out plans for its eventual permanent home, on the interactive wall outside the Space Shuttle Pavilion. While *Enterprise* never flew in space, it is presented in a dramatic darkened display with blue lighting to evoke the atmosphere of flight. Images and displays share the shuttle's history and that of NASA's 30-year space shuttle program.

The interactive Exploreum contains 18 hands-on exhibits. You can experience a flight simulator, transmit messages in Morse code, and see what it was like to live aboard the massive carrier. An engrossing new exhibit focuses on the *Intrepid*'s three tours of duty in Vietnam between 1966 and 1969. History is brought to life through artifacts that include the shared diary of junior pilots who were roommates onboard; a calendar counting down days until the crew members could return home; oral histories and personal effects of prisoners of war; anti-aircraft weaponry used by North Vietnamese forces; and aircraft that served during the war. Docked alongside the *Intrepid,* and also part of the museum, is the *Growler,* a strategic-missile submarine. Ticket booths and gift shops have been relocated to the museum's plaza while the visitor welcome center is being rebuilt. ■TIP➜ **Before you visit, download the Intrepid's new, free Explore Enterprise app to unlock additional trivia, history, and behind-the-scenes video at trigger points in exhibits throughout the museum. There are also frequent ticket discounts if you purchase through the museum website.** ✉ *Pier 86, 12th Ave. at 46th St., Midtown West* ☏ *212/245–0072, 877/957–7447* ⊕ *www. intrepidmuseum.org* 🎫 *$24; $31 combo ticket with Space Shuttle* ☉ *Apr.–Oct., weekdays 10–5, weekends 10–6; Nov.–Mar., daily 10–5; last admission 1 hr before closing* Ⓜ *A, C, E to 42nd St.–Port Authority.*

Fodor'sChoice **The Museum of Modern Art (MoMA).** Housing one of the world's finest
★ collections of modern art, the Museum of Modern Art (MoMA) is renowned for its permanent exhibits, which include masterpieces by Picasso, van Gogh, Monet, and Dalí, as well as its first-rate—and highly buzzed about—exhibitions on modern art, photography, and film. Located minutes from Rockefeller Center, and slowly expanding along 53rd Street to accommodate both its growing collection and audience,

MoMA's current building design features a maze of glass walkways to permit art viewing from many angles; a high-end restaurant and bar, The Modern; and a cinema that offers curated international film selections and talks.

The museum spans six levels, with an impressive lineup of special exhibits on the skylighted top floor; painting and sculpture on Levels 5 and 4; architecture, design, drawings, and photography on 3; and contemporary galleries, prints, and books on Level 2. It's best to explore the museum from top to bottom, beginning with the museum's main attractions and ending on Level 1 at a favorite resting spot, the Abby Aldrich Rockefeller Sculpture Garden. Designed by Philip Johnson, it features Barnett Newman's *Broken Obelisk* (1962–69). The glass wall lets visitors look directly into the surrounding galleries from the garden, where there's also a reflecting pool and trees. Plans for an expansion into the space next door (which, controversially, meant tearing down the American Folk Art Museum) include additional gallery space, a retractable glass wall, an expanded lobby, and the opening of its entire first floor, including the sculpture garden, as a free public space. Construction is already under way, with an expected completion date in 2019. ■TIP➡ Entrance between 4 and 8 pm on Friday is free, but expect long lines. ✉ *11 W. 53rd St., between 5th and 6th Aves., Midtown West* ☎ *212/708–9400* ⊕ *www.moma.org* ✍ *$25* ��� *Sat.–Thurs. 10:30–5:30, Fri. 10:30–8* Ⓜ *E, M to 5th Ave./53rd St.; F to 57th St.; B, D, E to 7th Ave.*

Radio City Music Hall. ⇨ *See the listing in Chapter 19: Performing Arts.*

FAMILY **The Rink at Rockefeller Center.** Set in the shadow of the giant Rockefeller Center Christmas tree, the city's most iconic ice-skating rink is a quintessential experience for visitors and a longstanding tradition for many locals. Skaters swoop or stumble across the ice while crowds gather at street level to watch the spins and spills. General-admission skating is on a first-come, first-served basis, so it is best to come early, and on weekdays, to avoid crowds. First Skate tickets ($45–$55, reserved online) allow 7 am access to the rink, followed by a complimentary hot chocolate or coffee and pastry or breakfast. VIP Skate packages ($60–$125) allow guests to skate past the long lines and include skate rental, 90 minutes of ice time, and hot chocolate and cookies. Other packages include Christmas Show and VIP Skate (from $102), which includes orchestra seating for the Radio City Christmas Spectacular as well as admission to the rink, skate rental, and refreshments; and Engagement on Ice packages ($350–$1,000), which provide exclusive ice time, a romantic backdrop, and a variety of romantic add-ons to seal the deal. The rink is a café in summer. ✉ *30 Rockefeller Plaza, Midtown West* ⊕ *www.therinkatrockcenter.com* ✍ *$25–$32; $12 skate rental* ☉ *Oct.–Apr., daily 8:30 am–midnight* Ⓜ *B, D, F, M to 47th–50th Sts./ Rockefeller Center; E, M to 5th Ave./53rd St.*

Rockefeller Center. If Times Square is New York's crossroads, Rockefeller Center is its communal gathering place, where the entire world converges to snap pictures, skate on the ice rink, peek in on a taping of the *Today* show, shop, eat, and take in the monumental Art Deco structures

Ice-skating under the sculpture of Prometheus, at Rockefeller Center, is a winter ritual for many local and visiting families.

and public sculptures from the past century. Totaling more than 100 shops and 50 eateries (including Thomas Keller's Bouchon Bakery), the complex runs from 47th to 52nd Streets between 5th and 7th Avenues. Special events and huge pieces of art dominate the central plazas in spring and summer. In December an enormous twinkling tree towers above the ice-skating rink, causing huge crowds of visitors from across the country and the globe to shuffle through with necks craned and cameras flashing. The first official tree-lighting ceremony was held in 1933.

The world's most famous ice-skating rink *(The Rink at Rockefeller Center)* occupies Rockefeller Center's sunken lower plaza October through April and converts to a café in summer. The gold-leaf statue of the fire-stealing Greek hero **Prometheus**—Rockefeller Center's most famous sculpture—hovers above, forming the backdrop to zillions of photos. Carved into the wall behind it, a quotation from Aeschylus reads, "Prometheus, teacher in every art, brought the fire that hath proved to mortals a means to mighty ends." The lower plaza also provides access to the marble-lined corridors underneath Rockefeller Center, which house restaurants, a post office, and clean public restrooms—a rarity in Midtown.

Rising from the Lower Plaza's west side is the 70-story (850-foot-tall) Art Deco **GE Building**, a testament to modern urban development. Here Rockefeller commissioned and then destroyed a mural by Diego Rivera (upon learning that it featured Vladimir Lenin). He replaced it with the monumental *American Progress* by José María Sert, still on view in the lobby, flanked by additional murals by Sert and English artist Frank Brangwyn. Up on the 65th floor is the landmark **Rainbow**

Art in Rockefeller Center

The mosaics, murals, and sculptures that grace Rockefeller Center—many of them Art Deco masterpieces—were part of John D. Rockefeller Jr.'s plans. In 1932, as the steel girders on the first of the buildings soared heavenward, he put together a team of advisers to find artists who could make the project "as beautiful as possible." Some artists scoffed at the idea of decorating an office building: Picasso declined to meet with Rockefeller, and Matisse replied that busy businessmen wouldn't be in the "quiet and reflective state of mind" needed to appreciate his art. Those who agreed to contribute, including muralists Diego Rivera and José María Sert, were relatively unknown, though a group of American artists protested Rockefeller's decision to hire "alien" artists. More than 50 artists were commissioned for 200 works.

As Rockefeller Center neared completion in 1932, Rockefeller still needed a mural for the lobby of the main buildings and he wanted the subject to be grandiose: "human intelligence in control of the forces of nature." He hired Rivera. *Man at the Crossroads*, with its depiction of massive machinery moving mankind forward, seemed exactly what Rockefeller wanted—until it was realized that a portrait of Soviet Premier Vladimir Lenin surrounded by red-kerchiefed workers occupied a space in the center. Rockefeller, who was building what was essentially a monument to capitalism, was less than thrilled. When Rivera was accused of propagandizing, he famously replied, "All art is propaganda."

Rivera refused to remove the offending portrait and, in early 1934,

as Rivera was working, representatives for Rockefeller informed him that his services were no longer required. Within a half hour, tar paper had been hung over the mural. Despite negotiations to move it to the Museum of Modern Art, Rockefeller was determined to get rid of the mural once and for all. Not content to have it painted over, he ordered ax-wielding workers to chip away the entire wall. He commissioned a less offensive one (by Sert) instead.

Rivera had the last word, though: he re-created the mural in the Palacio de Bellas Artes in Mexico City, adding a portrait of Rockefeller among the Champagne-swilling swells ignoring the plight of the workers.

The largest of the original artworks that remains is Lee Lawrie's 2-ton sculpture, *Atlas*. Its building also stirred up controversy, as it was said to resemble Italy's fascist dictator, Benito Mussolini. The sculpture, depicting a muscle-bound man holding up the world, drew protests in 1936. Some even derided Paul Manship's golden *Prometheus*, which soars over the ice-skating rink, when it was unveiled the same year. Both are now considered to be among the best public artworks of the 20th century.

Lawrie's sculpture *Wisdom*, over the main entrance of 20 Rockefeller Plaza, is another gem. Also look for Isamu Noguchi's stainless-steel plaque *News* over the entrance of the Bank of America Building at 50 Rockefeller Plaza and Attilio Piccirilli's 2-ton glass-block panel *Youth Leading Industry* over the entrance of the International Building.

9

Room, a glittering big-band ballroom dating to 1934; it serves a showy and very expensive brunch on Sunday, and dinner and entertainment on Monday nights. Higher up, **Top of the Rock** has what many consider the finest panoramic views of the city. ⊠ *30 Rockefeller Plaza, Midtown West* ⊕ *www.rockefellercenter.com* Ⓜ *B, D, F, M to 47th–50th Sts./ Rockefeller Center; E, M to 5th Ave./53rd St.*

Times Square. Hands down, this is the most frenetic part of New York City, a cacophony of flashing lights and shoulder-to-shoulder crowds that many New Yorkers studiously avoid. Originally named after the *New York Times* (whose headquarters have since relocated nearby), the area has seen many changes since the first subway line, which included a 42nd Street station, opened in 1904. You won't find speakeasies and unsavory clubs around here nowadays; it's a vibrant, family-friendly destination, with a newly resurfaced pedestrianized stretch of Broadway with granite benches, and stadium seating behind discount-theater-ticket-seller TKTS, all under the glare of brand names like MTV and M&Ms. If you like sensory overload, the chaotic mix of huge underwear billboards, flashing digital displays, and on-location television broadcasts will give you your fix, while naked cowboys, seminude painted ladies, Elmo clones, fake Buddhist monks, and other street performers will shake you down— some quite aggressively—for tips. The focus of the entertainment may have shifted over the years, but showtime is still the heart of New York's theater scene, and there are 40 Broadway theaters nearby. The Times Square Visitor Center is closed, but you can still learn about Broadway's history and architecture with a 90-minute walking tour ($30) of the area by Manhattan Walking Tours (*www.manhattanwalkingtour.com*); the guided Broadway Walking tour (*daily at 9:30, 11:30, and 2; www. walkinbroadway.com*) includes audio headsets and 30 stops, and leaves from the Actor's Chapel on West 49th Street, between Broadway and 8th Avenue. ⊠ *Broadway between 42nd and 44th Sts., Midtown West* ☎ *212/768–1560 for Times Square Alliance* ⊕ *www.timessquarenyc.org* Ⓜ *1, 2, 3, 7, N, Q, R, S to Times Sq.–42 St.*

Fodor's Choice ★ **Top of the Rock.** Rockefeller Center's multifloor observation deck, the Top of the Rock, on the 69th and 70th floors of the building, provides views that rival those from the Empire State Building (some would say they're even better because the views include the Empire State Building). Arriving just before sunset affords a view of the city that morphs before your eyes into a dazzling wash of colors, with a bird's-eye view of the tops of the Empire State Building, the Citicorp Building, and the Chrysler Building, and sweeping views northward to Central Park and south to the Statue of Liberty. Timed-entry ticketing eliminates long lines. Indoor exhibits include films of Rockefeller Center's history and a model of the building. Glass elevators lift you to the 67th-floor interior viewing area, and then an escalator leads to the outdoor deck on the 69th floor for sightseeing through nonreflective glass safety panels. Then, take another elevator or stairs to the 70th floor for a 360-degree outdoor panorama of New York City on a deck that is only 20 feet wide and nearly 200 feet long. Especially interesting is a Plexiglas screen on the floor with footage showing Rock Center construction workers dangling on beams high above the streets; the brave can even "walk"

Some of the world's most famous paintings hang in the MoMA, including Monet's *Water Lilies*.

across a beam to get a sense of what it might have been like to erect this skyscraper. A Sun & Stars ticket ($47) allows you to visit twice and see the city as it rises and sets in the same day. ⊠ *30 Rockefeller Plaza, 50th St. entrance, between 5th and 6th Aves., Midtown West* ☎ *212/698–2000, 212/698–2000* ⊕ *www.topoftherocknyc.com* 🖃 *$32* ⊗ *Daily 8–midnight; last elevator at 11 pm* Ⓜ *B, D, F, M to 47th–50th Sts./Rockefeller Center; E, M to 5th Ave./53rd St.*

WORTH NOTING

Christie's. One of the first items to be auctioned at the New York outpost of this infamous auction house, when it opened in 2000, was the "Happy Birthday" dress worn by Marilyn Monroe when she sang to President Kennedy (it sold for more than $1.2 million, in case you were wondering). Yes, the auction house has come a long way since James Christie launched his business in England by selling two chamber pots, among other household goods, in 1766. You could easily spend an hour or more wandering the free, museumlike galleries, where on any given day, you find impressive works of art, estate jewelry, furniture, and other rarely displayed letters and objects of interest that are usually housed in (and most likely, soon to be returned to) private collections. The lobby's specially commissioned abstract Sol LeWitt mural alone makes it worth visiting the 310,000-square-foot space. Hours vary by sale, so call ahead to confirm. ⊠ *20 Rockefeller Plaza, 49th St. between 5th and 6th Aves., Midtown West* ☎ *212/636–2000* ⊕ *www.christies.com* 🖃 *Free* ⊗ *Weekdays 9:30–5, weekend hrs vary; hrs vary for specific exhibits* Ⓜ *B, D, F, M to 47th–50th Sts./Rockefeller Center; E, M to 5th Ave./53rd St.*

David Findlay Jr. Gallery. This well-established gallery concentrates on contemporary and 20th-century American artists from Whistler to Herman Cherry, Byron Brown, and David Aronson, and specializes in the New York School. ✉ *724 5th Ave., 8th fl., between 56th and 57th Sts., Midtown West* ☎ *212/486-7660* ⊕ *www.davidfindlayjr.com* ✉ *Free* ⊙ *Mon.–Sat. 10–5:30* Ⓜ *N, Q, R to 5th Ave./59th St.*

Hirschl & Adler Galleries. Although this gallery has a selection of European works, it's best known for American paintings, prints, and decorative arts. The celebrated 19th- and 20th-century artists whose works are featured include Stuart Davis, Childe Hassam, Camille Pissarro, and John Singleton Copley. Each year, the gallery presents up to a dozen special exhibits exploring historical themes of works culled from its collection. ✉ *730 5th Ave., 4th fl., at 57th St., Midtown West* ☎ *212/535-8810* ⊕ *www.hirschlandadler.com* ✉ *Free* ⊙ *Tues.–Fri. 9:30–5:15, Sat. 9:30–4:45* Ⓜ *N, Q, R to 5th Ave./59th St.*

FAMILY **Madame Tussauds New York.** Sit in the Oval Office with President Obama, strike a fierce pose alongside *Hunger Games* heroine Katniss Everdeen, croon with Pharell Williams and Taylor Swift, pucker up to your favorite heartthrob, be it Justin Bieber or Justin Timberlake, or enjoy a royal chat with the Duke and Duchess of Cambridge, William and Kate. Much of the fun here comes from photo opportunities—you're encouraged to pose with and touch the more than 200 realistic replicas of the famous, infamous, and downright super. The Marvel 4D Experience includes wax likenesses of heroes like the Hulk, Captain America, Ironman, and Thor, as well as a short animated movie shown on a 360-degree screen that surrounds the viewer. Other interactive options at the museum include a karaoke café, a celebrity walk down the red carpet, and a Sports Zone where you can see how you measure up to sporting legends like Lionel Messi, Serena Williams, Derek Jeter, and Eli Manning. Closing hours vary during peak seasons, so call ahead to verify. ✉ *234 W. 42nd St., between 7th and 8th Aves., Midtown West* ☎ *866/841-3505* ⊕ *www.madame-tussauds.com* ✉ *$37 (discounts available online)* ⊙ *Sun.–Thurs. 10–8, Fri. and Sat. 10–10* Ⓜ *1, 2, 3, 7, N, Q, R, S to Times Sq.–42nd St.; A, C, E to 42nd St.–Port Authority.*

Marian Goodman Gallery. Perhaps the most respected contemporary art dealer in town, the Marian Goodman Gallery has been introducing top European artists to American audiences for over 40 years. The stable of excellent contemporary artists in the Goodman fold includes Gerhard Richter, Jeff Wall, John Baldessari, William Kentridge, Chantal Akerman, and Steve McQueen. ✉ *24 W. 57th St., between 5th and 6th Aves., Midtown West* ☎ *212/977-7160* ⊕ *www.mariangoodman.com* ✉ *Free* ⊙ *Mon.–Sat. 10–6* Ⓜ *F to 57th St.*

Marlborough Gallery (Midtown). The Marlborough Gallery has an international reputation, representing modern artists such as Magdalena Abakanowicz, Beverly Pepper, Red Grooms, and photo-realist Richard Estes. Look for sculptures by Tom Otterness, whose whimsical bronzes are found in several subway stations. There are also two downtown branches (in Chelsea and on Broome Street). ✉ *40 W. 57th St.,* *between 5th and 6th Aves., Midtown West* ☎ *212/541–4900* ⊕ *www. marlboroughgallery.com* ✉ *Free* ⊘ *Mon.–Sat. 10–5:30* Ⓜ *F to 57th St.*

NBC Studios. You can join the gawking crowds watching news tapings outside the NBC studios (which are housed in the Art Deco GE Building on Rockefeller Plaza), or you can get even closer to the action (without having to elbow anyone) by taking a recently revamped tour behind the scenes of the legendary NBC studios. Tours depart every 30 minutes daily and delve into the history of television and into the studios of some of the network's top shows, like *Saturday Night Live, The Tonight Show Starring Jimmy Fallon,* and *Nightly News with Lester Holt.* Tours start at the Shop at NBC Studios (49th Street between 5th and 6th Avenues). ✉ *30 Rockefeller Plaza, between 5th and 6th Aves. at 49th St., Midtown West* ☎ *212/664–3700* ⊕ *www.thetouratnbcstudios. com* ✉ *$33* ⊘ *Tours depart every 30 mins weekdays 8:30–2, weekends 8:30–5* ☞ *Children under 6 not permitted* Ⓜ *B, D, F, M to 47th–50th Sts./Rockefeller Center.*

New York Public Library Main Branch. In 2011 the "Library with the Lions" celebrated its centennial as a masterpiece of Beaux Arts design and as one of the great research institutions in the world, with more than 6 million books, 12 million manuscripts, and 3 million pictures. Expect changes, if not to the look, then to the feel, of the building as it attempts to become more welcoming and useful for its next 100 years of use, all without selling its soul, of course. After years of deliberation and negotiation with a very attached public, renovation plans now include the creation of more public space and amenities as well as state-of-the-art collections storage beneath Bryant Park. For now, the library remains open to visitors. The marble staircase at the library's grand 5th Avenue entrance is an excellent perch for people-watching, before or after you explore the opulent interior.

The library's bronze front doors open into **Astor Hall,** which leads to several special exhibit galleries and, to the left, a stunning periodicals room with wall paintings of New York publishing houses. Ascend the sweeping double staircase to a second-floor balconied corridor overlooking the hall, with panels highlighting the library's development. Make sure to continue up to the recently restored, magisterial **Rose Main Reading Room**—297 feet long (almost two full north–south city blocks), 78 feet wide, and just over 51 feet high; walk through to best appreciate the rows of oak tables and the extraordinary ceiling. Several additional third-floor galleries show rotating exhibits on print and photography (past exhibits have included old New York restaurant menus and a 1455 Gutenberg Bible). Free hour-long tours leave Monday–Saturday at 11 and 2, and Sunday at 2 from Astor Hall. Women's bathrooms are on the ground floor and third floor, and there's a men's bathroom on the third floor. ✉ *5th Ave., between 40th and 42nd Sts., Midtown West* ☎ *212/930–0800 for exhibit info* ⊕ *www.nypl.org* ⊘ *Mon. and Thurs.–Sat. 10–6, Sun. 1–5, Tues. and Wed. 10–8; exhibitions until 6* Ⓜ *B, D, F, M to 42nd St.–Bryant Park; 7 to 5th Ave.*

The New York Times Building. This 52-story building with its distinctive, ladderlike ceramic rods is a testament to clean-lined modernism. The architect, Renzo Piano, extended the ceramic rods beyond the top of the building so that it would give the impression of dissolving into the sky. One of the skyscraper's best features—and the one that's open to the public—is the building's lobby atrium, which includes an open-air moss garden with 50-foot paper birch trees and a wooden footbridge; a 560-screen media art installation titled *Moveable Type*, streaming a mix of the newspaper's near-real-time and archival content; and the New York flagship store of minimalist home-goods designer MUJI. You never know which famous journalists you'll spy on the coffee line in Dean & DeLuca. Unfortunately, tours are not offered. ⊠ *620 8th Ave., between 40th and 41st Sts., Midtown West* ☎ *212/984–8128* ⊕ *www. newyorktimesbuilding.com* Ⓜ *A, C, E to 42nd St.–Port Authority; 1, 2, 3, 7, N, Q, R, S to Times Sq.–42nd St.*

The Paley Center for Media. With three galleries of photographs and artifacts that document the history of broadcasting, a computerized catalog of more than 150,000 television and radio programs, and public seminars, lectures, and programs, the Paley Center for Media examines the past and constantly evolving present state of media. The past is the main draw here. If you want to see a performance of "Turkey Lurkey Time" from the 1969 Tony Awards, for example, type the name of the song, show, or performer into a computer terminal, then proceed to one of the semiprivate screening areas to watch your selection. People nearby might be watching classic comedies from the '50s, miniseries from the '70s, or news broadcasts from the '90s. Possibly the most entertaining part of these TV shows from yesteryear is the fact that the original commercials are still embedded in many of the programs. If ads are your thing, you can also skip the programming altogether and watch compilations of classic commercials. ⊠ *25 W. 52nd St., between 5th and 6th Aves., Midtown West* ☎ *212/621–6800* ⊕ *www.paleycenter. org* 🖃 *$10* ⊙ *Wed., Fri., and weekends noon–6, Thurs. noon–8* Ⓜ *E, M to 5th Ave./53rd St.; B, D, F, M to 47th–50th Sts./Rockefeller Center.*

Tibor de Nagy Gallery. Founded in 1950, this gallery shows works by 20th-century artists such as Biala, Nell Blaine, Jane Freilicher, and Shirley Jaffe. Instrumental in bringing many of America's finest Abstract Expressionist artists to public attention in the mid-20th century, the gallery now shows abstract and realistic work. ⊠ *724 5th Ave., 12th fl., between 56th and 57th Sts., Midtown West* ☎ *212/262–5050* ⊕ *www. tibordenagy.com* ⊙ *Tues.–Sat. 10–5:30* Ⓜ *N, Q, R to 5th Ave./59th St.*

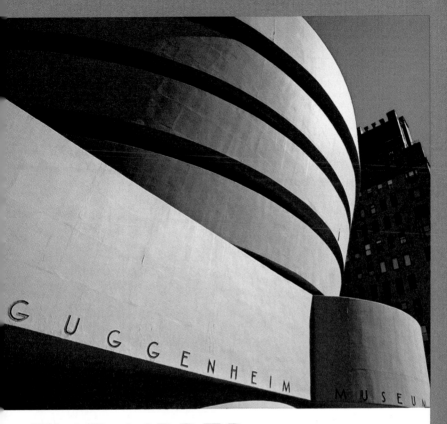

THE UPPER
EAST SIDE

GETTING ORIENTED

Upper East Side

E. 97th St.
E. 96th St.
6
E. 95th St.
El Museo ◆ ◆ Museum of the
del Barrio   City of New York
E. 94th St.
E. 93rd St.
◆ The Jewish Museum
E. 92nd St.
◆ Cooper-Hewitt,
Smithsonian Design Museum
E. 91st St.
E. 90th St.
Solomon R. Guggenheim
◆ Museum
E. 89th St.
Gracie
Mansion
E. 88th St.
■ Museum Mile
E. 87th St.
Neue Galerie
New York
4,5,6
Carl Schurz
Park
Café
Sabarsky ✕ ◆
E. 86th St.
E. 85th St.
Two Little
Red Hens ✕
E. 84th St.
E. 83rd St.
E. 82nd St.
◆ The Metropolitan
Museum of Art
E. 81st St.
E. 80th St.
Peter Findlay
Gallery
◆ Acquavella Galleries
E. 79th St.
Mitchell-Innes
& Nash
Lady M
Cake Boutique
E. 78th St.
6
E. 77th St.
Castelli
Gallery
✕ Gagosian Madison Avenue
E. 76th St.
◆ Gagosian Gallery
E. 75th St.
The Met Breuer ◆ ✕ Joe (Upper
East Side)
E. 74th St.
◆ Jane Kahan
E. 73rd St.
Van Doren
Waxter
UPPER
EAST SIDE
E. 72nd St.
◆ Frick Collection
E. 71st St.
◆ Asia Society
and Museum
E. 70th St.
E. 69th St.
E. 68th St.
6
E. 67th St.
◆ Blum & Poe
New York
E. 66th St.
E. 65th St.
E. 64th St.
F
E. 63rd St.
Museum of American
Illustration
E. 62nd St.
Mount Vernon Hotel
Museum and Garden
E. 61st St.
Roosevelt Island Tram
N,Q,R
M
N,Q,R,4,5,6
E. 59th St.
E. 58th St.

0   1/4 mile
0   400 meters

East River

Roosevelt
Island

East River

FDR Dr.

Roosevelt Island Tram

Four Freedoms
Park

Queensboro Bridge

CENTRAL PARK
Fifth Ave.
Madison Ave.
Park Ave.
Lexington Ave.
Third Ave.
Second Ave.
First Ave.
York Ave.
East End Ave.

MAKING THE MOST OF YOUR TIME

The Upper East Side lends itself to a surprising variety of simple but distinct itineraries: exploring the landmarks on Museum Mile; languorous gallery grazing; window-shopping on Madison Avenue; or, for just-out-of-college kids, barhopping on 2nd Avenue. If it's the museums you're after, make sure to plan at least a few hours per museum—with some snack or coffee breaks. There's a lot to see, so we advise visiting not more than one museum a day. The Upper East Side's town houses, boutiques, consignment stores, and hidden gardens are easy to miss unless you take some time to wander.

GETTING HERE

Take the Lexington Avenue 4 or 5 express train to 59th or 86th Street. The 6 local train also stops at 59th, 68th, 77th, 86th, and 96th Streets. From Midtown, the F train lets you out at Lexington Avenue at 63rd Street, where you can transfer to the 4, 5, or 6 after a short walk (and free transfer). From the Upper West Side, take one of the crosstown buses, the M66, M72, M79, M86, or M96. You can also take the N or R train to 59th Street and Lexington Avenue.

TOP EXPERIENCES

Exploring any of the world-class museums here, followed by a relaxing, restorative lunch

Gallery-hopping the UES's so-unhip-it's-now-hip art scene (plus they're free)

Window-shopping on Madison Avenue

Appreciating the views from the cable car on the ride to Four Freedoms Park on Roosevelt Island

COFFEE AND QUICK BITES

Joe (Upper East Side). One of the city's best coffee chains, Joe has the kind of quality caffeine and sweets to fuel you up and down Museum Mile (and maybe even around the park). ⊠ *1045 Lexington Ave., between 74th and 75th Sts., Upper East Side* ☎ *212/988–2500* ⊕ *www. joenewyork.com/locations/ lexington* Ⓜ *6 to 77th St.*

Lady M Cake Boutique. The signature here is the Mille Crepes cake: 20 crêpes stacked together with a delicious cream filling. Thank us later. ⊠ *41 E. 78th St., at Madison Ave., Upper East Side* ☎ *212/452–2222* ⊕ *www. ladym.com* Ⓜ *6 to 77th St.*

Two Little Red Hens. With first-rate coffee and delicious cupcakes, cheesecake, and cookies to match, this little bakery is a legend with locals. ⊠ *1652 2nd Ave., at 86th St., Upper East Side* ☎ *212/452– 0476* ⊕ *www.twolittleredhens. com* Ⓜ *4, 5, 6 to 86th St.*

10

Sightseeing
★★★
Nightlife
★
Dining
★★
Lodging
★★
Shopping
★★★★

To many New Yorkers, the Upper East Side connotes old money and high society. Alongside Central Park, between 5th and Lexington Avenues, up to East 96th Street, the trappings of wealth are everywhere apparent: posh buildings, Madison Avenue's flagship boutiques, and doormen in braided livery. It's also a key destination for visitors, because some of the most fantastic museums in the country are here.

Updated
by Jacinta
O'Halloran

There's a reason this stretch of Manhattan is called "Museum Mile": this is where you'll find the **Metropolitan Museum of Art**, the **Solomon R. Guggenheim Museum**, the **Cooper Hewitt, Smithsonian Design Museum**, as well as a number of art galleries. For a local taste of the luxe life, catwalk down Madison Avenue for its lavish boutiques; strolling the platinum-card corridor between 60th and 82nd Street is like stepping into the pages of a glossy magazine. Many fashion houses have their flagships here and showcase their lush threads in exquisite settings.

Venture east of Lexington Avenue and encounter a less wealthy—and more diverse—Upper East Side, inhabited by couples seeking some of the last (relatively) affordable places to raise a family south of 100th Street, as well as recent college grads getting a foothold in the city (on weekend nights 2nd Avenue resembles a miles-long fraternity and sorority reunion). One neighborhood particularly worth exploring is northeast-lying Yorkville, especially between 78th and 86th Streets east of 2nd Avenue. Once a remote hamlet with a large German population, its several remaining ethnic food shops, 19th-century row houses, and—one of the city's best-kept secrets—**Carl Schurz Park**, make for a good half-day's exploration, as does catching a glimpse of the most striking residence there, **Gracie Mansion**.

If art galleries appeal, there are some elegant ones on the Upper East Side. In keeping with the tony surroundings, the emphasis here is on works by established masters.

TOP ATTRACTIONS

Asia Society and Museum. The Asian art collection of Mr. and Mrs. John D. Rockefeller III forms the core of this museum's holdings, which span from Pakistan to Java and date back to the 11th century BC, including Hindu stone sculpture, Tibetan Buddhist paintings, Vietnamese ceramics, Han Dynasty bronzes, and Japanese woodblock prints. Founded in 1956, the society has a regular program of lectures, films, and performances, in addition to changing exhibitions of traditional and contemporary art. Trees grow in the glass-enclosed, skylighted Garden Court Café, which serves an eclectic Asian lunch menu and weekend brunch. Call ahead to reserve afternoon tea service, available 2–5 pm. Admission is free Friday 6–9 pm (September to July). A free audio tour is included with admission, or you can take a free guided tour at 2 daily and 6:30 Friday. ✉ *725 Park Ave., at 70th St., Upper East Side* ☎ *212/288–6400* ⊕ *www.asiasociety.org/ny* ☑ *$12* ☉ *Tues.–Thurs. and weekends 11–6, Fri. 11–9* Ⓜ *6 to 68th St.–Hunter College.*

Blum & Poe New York. This contemporary art gallery may be a relative newbie on the Upper East Side art scene (it opened in spring 2014), but as one of L.A.'s top art galleries, Blum & Poe was very quick to settle into its renovated town house on East 66th Street—a cozy space compared to its sprawling, 21,000-square-foot L.A. counterpart—and to establish itself in the New York art world. Recent exhibits have featured artists including Hugh Scott-Douglas, Kishio Suga, Yun Hyong-Keun, and Zhu Jinshi. ✉ *19 E. 66th St., at 5th Ave., Upper East Side* ☎ *212/249–2249* ⊕ *www. blumandpoe.com* ☉ *Tues.–Sat. 10–6* Ⓜ *6 to 68th St.–Hunter College.*

Cooper Hewitt, Smithsonian Design Museum. Reopened in late 2014, after a three-year, $81 million overhaul, the Cooper Hewitt, Smithsonian Design Museum is a slick, 21st-century museum in a century-old mansion. It marries old and new, digital and physical, and the result is an ornate, historic home (once the residence of industrialist Andrew Carnegie) outfitted with the latest technologies and amenities for a highly interactive experience. You don't just *look* at design here; you play with it, engage it, and then take it home. On arrival at the museum, visitors receive a digital pen that acts as a key to the museum's entire collection of more than 200,000 objects, everything from antique cutlery and Japanese sword fittings to robotics and animation. Museum highlights include giant touch-screen tables where visitors can summon random-yet-relevant items from the museum's collection by drawing a squiggle or a shape; the Immersion Room, where visitors can view and save their favorite wallpapers from the museum's incredible collection or create their own designs (which can be projected onto the gallery walls); and the Process Lab where visitors get hands-on to solve design dilemmas and enhance everyday design objects. The focus on design and discovery extends to "SHOP," where limited-edition objects created in collaboration with contemporary designers and influenced by exhibitions are for sale. There is a café, too. Guided tours run daily at 11:30 and 1:30 on weekdays and 1 and 3 on weekends. Admission is pay-what-you-wish Saturday evening from 6 to 9. ✉ *2 E. 91st St., at 5th Ave., Upper East Side* ☎ *212/849–8400* ⊕ *www.cooperhewitt.org* ☑ *$18 ($16 online)* ☉ *Sun.–Fri. 10–6, Sat. 10–9* Ⓜ *4, 5, 6 to 86th St.*

10

El Museo del Barrio. *El barrio* is Spanish for "the neighborhood" and the nickname for East Harlem, a largely Spanish-speaking Puerto Rican and Dominican community. El Museo del Barrio, on the edge of this neighborhood, focuses on Latin American and Caribbean art, with some 10% of its collection concentrated on works by self-taught artists from New York, Puerto Rico, the Caribbean, and Latin America. The more than 6,500-object permanent collection includes over 400 pre-Columbian artifacts, sculpture, photography, film and video, and traditional art from all over Latin America. The collection of 360 *santos,* carved wooden folk-art figures from Puerto Rico, is popular. El Museo hosts performances, lectures, films, and cultural events, including a monthlong Día de los Muertos celebration. ■**TIP**➜ **Admission to El Museo del Barrio gains you free entrance to the neighboring Museum of the City of New York.** ✉ *1230 5th Ave., between 104th and 105th Sts., Upper East Side* ☎ *212/831–7272* ⊕ *www.elmuseo.org* ✉ *$9 suggested donation* ☉ *Tues.–Sat. 11–6* Ⓜ *6 to 103rd St.*

Fodor'sChoice
★

Frick Collection. Henry Clay Frick made his fortune amid the soot and smoke of Pittsburgh, where he was a coke (a coal fuel derivative) and steel baron, but this lovely museum, once Frick's private New York residence, is decidedly removed from soot. With an exceptional collection of works from the Renaissance through the late 19th century that includes Édouard Manet's *The Bullfight* (1864), a Chinard portrait bust (1809), three Vermeers, three Rembrandts, works by El Greco, Goya, Van Dyck, Hogarth, Degas, and Turner, as well as sculpture, decorative arts, and 18th-century French furniture, everything here is a highlight. The Portico Gallery, an enclosed portico along the building's 5th Avenue garden, houses the museum's growing collection of sculpture. Controversial plans to expand the museum, and eliminate a gated garden to add a six-story structure, are currently being revised due to public resistance. If new proposals are approved, construction could begin in late 2017; the museum plans to remain open during renovations. An audio guide, available in several languages, is included with admission, as are the year-round temporary exhibits. The tranquil indoor garden court is a magical spot for a rest. Children under 10 are not admitted, and those ages 10–16 with an adult only. ✉ *1 E. 70th St., at 5th Ave., Upper East Side* ☎ *212/288–0700* ⊕ *www.frick.org* ✉ *$20* ☉ *Tues.–Sat. 10–6, Sun. 11–5* Ⓜ *6 to 68th St.–Hunter College.*

Gagosian Madison Avenue. If you are looking for ambitious works by the world's most acclaimed artists in a gallery that easily competes with the city's top museums, you have to visit Gagosian. Perhaps the most powerful art dealer in the world, Larry Gagosian has galleries in London, Paris, Rome, Athens, and Hong Kong, as well as five galleries in New York (three of which are on the Upper East Side). The Madison Avenue location, the contemporary art empire's headquarters, is a multifloor gallery that has shown works by big names like Warhol, Pollock, Miró, Calder, Twombly, and Hirst. Because Gagosian likes to dominate the real estate market the way he dominates the art market, he also has spaces at nearby 976 Madison Avenue, as well as it newest uptown outpost (with a decidedly downtown feel)—a storefront space on Park Avenue and 75th Street. ✉ *980 Madison Ave., near 76th*

St., Upper East Side ☎ *212/744–2313* ⊕ *www.gagosian.com* ✉ *Free* ⊙ *Tues.–Sat. 10–6* Ⓜ *6 to 77th St.*

Gracie Mansion. The official mayor's residence, Gracie Mansion was built in 1799 by shipping merchant Archibald Gracie, and enlarged in 1966. Nine mayors have lived here since it became the official residence in 1942, though Michael Bloomberg broke with tradition and chose to stay in his own 79th Street town house during his three terms as mayor. He poured millions into renovations at Gracie Mansion without spending a single night there. In January 2014, the newly prepped, polished, and spruced-up mansion became home to newly elected Mayor Bill de Blasio and his family—and the renovations resumed, this time to the roof, chimney, and railings. The "People's House"—with all its history and colorful rooms furnished over centuries and packed with American objets d'art—finally reopened its doors (and tours) to the people in late 2015. As well as a spruced-up interior and exterior, visitors can see that the resident first family of New York City has been busy adding its personal touch to the 200-year-old mansion, swapping out much of the artwork to better reflect the city's diversity. The collection now includes a bill of sale for a slave, a portrait of Frederick Douglass, and Native American artifacts. Tours are offered once weekly and reservations must be made online; plan at least two weeks in advance, if possible. ✉ *Carl Schurz Park, East End Ave. at 88th St., Upper East Side* ☎ *212/676–3060* ⊕ *www1.nyc.gov/gracie* ✉ *Free* ⊙ *Tues. tours at 10, 11, 2, and 3* Ⓜ *4, 5, 6 to 86th St.*

The Jewish Museum. In a Gothic-style 1908 mansion, the Jewish Museum draws on a large collection of art and ceremonial objects to explore Jewish identity and culture spanning more than 4,000 years. The two-floor permanent exhibition "Culture and Continuity: The Jewish Journey" displays nearly 800 objects complemented by interactive media. The wide-ranging collection includes a 3rd-century Roman burial plaque, 20th-century sculpture by Elie Nadelman, and contemporary art from artists such as Marc Chagall and Man Ray. Don't leave without checking out the museum's recently opened café, Russ & Daughters: an outpost of the almost century-old Jewish specialty store and downtown NYC institution. ✉ *1109 5th Ave., at 92nd St., Upper East Side* ☎ *212/423–3200* ⊕ *www.thejewishmuseum.org* ✉ *$15 (free Sat., pay-what-you-wish Thurs. 5–8)* ⊙ *Sat.–Tues. 11–5:45, Thurs. 11–8, Fri. 11–4 (Fri. until 5:45 Mar.–Nov.)* Ⓜ *6 to 96th St.*

The Met Breuer. A great addition to the Metropolitan Museum of Art's already stunning collection, the Met Breuer offers art lovers four floors of rotating exhibits focusing on modern and contemporary art from the 20th and 21st centuries. The former site of the Whitney Museum (now in Chelsea), the building was designed by Marcel Breuer (pronounced BROY-er) and also offers performances, art commissions, and educational programs. A ticket to the Met Breuer also includes admission to the Met a few blocks away on Fifth Avenue and the Cloisters further uptown. ✉ *945 Madison Ave., at 75th St., Upper East Side* ☎ *212/731–1675* ⊕ *www.metmuseum.org/visit/met-breuer* ✉ *$25 suggested donation (includes the Met)* ⊙ *Tues., Wed., and weekends 10–5:30, Thurs. and Fri. 10–9* Ⓜ *6 to 77th St.*

The Temple of Dendur in the Metropolitan Museum of Art is one of the highlights of the museum's Egyptian art collection.

The Metropolitan Museum of Art. With more than 6 million visitors annually, dozens of new exhibitions each year, and more than 2 million works of art representing 5,000 years of history, the colossal and iconic Metropolitan Museum of Art is the city's top attraction and one of the world's top art museums. With so much to see, you could easily wander the Met's labyrinthine corridors for days, so it's a good idea to plan ahead.

A major star of the museum is the **Temple of Dendur** (circa 15 BC), in a huge atrium to itself and with a moatlike pool of water to represent its original location near the Nile. The temple was commissioned by the Roman emperor Augustus to honor the goddess Isis and the sons of a Nubian chieftain. Egypt gave the temple as a gift to the United States in 1965; it would have been submerged after the construction of the Aswan High Dam. The Egyptian collection as a whole covers 4,000 years of history, with papyrus pages from the Egyptian Book of the Dead, stone sarcophagi inscribed with hieroglyphics, and tombs.

Other highlights include the Met's revitalized **American Wing** (aka the New American Wing Galleries for Paintings, Sculpture, and Decorative Arts) which uses 30,000 square feet of airy, skylit space to showcase—in themed and chronological order—one of the best and most extensive collections of American art in the country, as well as the **Anna Wintour Costume Center,** which hosts the annual Met Gala fundraiser and fashion extravaganza to mark the opening of the Costume Center's annual fashion exhibit. The visually stunning **Islamic galleries,** a suite of 15 galleries, feature a collection that traces the course of Islamic civilization over a span of 13 centuries and include an 11-foot-high 14th-century *mihrab* (prayer niche); a 16th-century Persian carpet that was presented to the Habsburg Emperor Leopold I by Peter the Great of Russia; a Syrian Ottoman reception room decorated with poetic verses; and glass, ceramics, and metalwork from Egypt, Syria, Iraq, and Iran.

If you're hungry, there are several options inside the museum for a meal or snack, including the ground-floor self-service cafeteria; the Petrie Court Cafe and Winebar on the first floor; and the Great Hall Balcony Bar on the second-floor balcony overlooking the Great Hall (Friday and Saturday evenings). ■ TIP➔ **The Roof Garden ($), open May–October, has fabulous views of Central Park and the city skyline.** Admission includes same-day admission to the museum's newly opened modern and contemporary art outpost—the Met Breuer (Madison Avenue and 75th Street), as well as same-week entrance to the Cloisters Museum and Gardens in northern Manhattan. ⊠ *1000 5th Ave., at 82nd St., Upper East Side* 🕿 *212/535–7710* ⊕ *www.metmuseum.org* 🖃 *$25 suggested donation; $7 for audio guide* ☉ *Sun.–Thurs. 10–5:30, Fri. and Sat. 10–9* Ⓜ *4, 5, 6 to 86th St.*

Museum of the City of New York. The city's present, past, and future is explored through quirky, engaging exhibits on subjects such as architecture, fashion, history, and politics in a Colonial Revival building designed for the museum in the 1930s. Exhibitions such as "New York's Yiddish Theater: From the Bowery to Broadway" and "New York At Its Core" explore the sweep and diverse faces of the city's history through artifacts, photography, archival film, and interactive digital experiences. Don't miss *Timescapes,* a 25-minute media projection that innovatively illustrates New York's physical expansion and population changes, or "Activist New York," an ongoing exploration of the city's history of social activism. You can also find New York–centric lectures, films, and walking tours here. In late 2015, the museum completed the last phase of a three-part, $95 million renovation to upgrade and modernize the entire facility. Improvements included a new climate-control system, an updated lobby and terrace, a redesigned gift shop, the addition of a state-of-the-art auditorium and a new café, and restored historical elements throughout the building. When finished touring the museum, cross the street and stroll through the Vanderbilt Gates to enter the Conservatory Garden, one of Central Park's hidden gems. ⊠ *1220 5th Ave., at 103rd St., Upper East Side* 🕿 *212/534–1672* ⊕ *www.mcny.org* 🖃 *$14 suggested donation* ☉ *Daily 10–6* Ⓜ *6 to 103rd St.*

Neue Galerie New York. Early-20th-century German and Austrian art and design are the focus here, with works by Gustav Klimt, Wassily Kandinsky, Paul Klee, Egon Schiele, Josef Hoffmann, and other designers from the Wiener Werkstätte taking center stage. The Neue Galerie was founded by the late art dealer Serge Sabarsky and cosmetics heir and art collector Ronald S. Lauder. It's in a 1914 wood- and marble-floored mansion designed by Carrère and Hastings, which was once home to Mrs. Cornelius Vanderbilt III. An audio guide is included with admission. Children under 12 are not admitted, and teens 12–16 must be accompanied by an adult. **Café Sabarsky,** in an elegant, high-ceiling space on the first floor, is a destination in its own right for Viennese coffee, cakes, strudels, and Sacher tortes. ■ TIP➔ **Admission is free 6–8**

10

pm on the first Friday of the month. ⊠ *1048 5th Ave., at 86th St., Upper East Side* ☎ *212/628–6200* ⊕ *www.neuegalerie.org* 🖾 *$20* ☉ *Thurs.– Mon. 11–6* ☞ *Children under 12 not admitted* Ⓜ *4, 5, 6 to 86th St.*

Fodor'sChoice **Solomon R. Guggenheim Museum.** Frank Lloyd Wright's landmark nautilus-
★ like museum building is renowned as much for its famous architecture as for its superlative collection of art and well-curated shows. Opened in 1959, shortly after Wright's death, the Guggenheim is acclaimed as one of the greatest buildings of the 20th century. Inside, under a 96-foot-high glass dome, a ramp spirals down, past the artworks of the current exhibits (the ramp is just over a quarter-mile long, if you're wondering). The museum has strong holdings of Wassily Kandinsky, Paul Klee, Marc Chagall, Pablo Picasso, and Robert Mapplethorpe.

Wright's design was criticized by some who believed that the distinctive building detracted from the art within, but the interior nautilus design allows artworks to be viewed from several different angles and distances. Be sure to notice not only what's in front of you but also what's across the spiral from you. On permanent display, the museum's Thannhauser Collection is made up primarily of works by French impressionists and postimpressionists van Gogh, Toulouse-Lautrec, Cézanne, Renoir, and Manet. Perhaps more than any other 20th-century painter, Wassily Kandinsky, one of the first "pure" abstract artists, has been closely linked to the museum's history: beginning with the acquisition of his masterpiece *Composition 8* (1923) in 1930, the collection has grown to encompass more than 150 works. The museum is pay-what-you-wish on Saturday from 5:45 to 7:45. Lines can be long, so arrive early. The last tickets are handed out at 7:15.

Even if you aren't planning to eat, be sure to stop at the museum's modern American restaurant, the Wright (at 88th Street), for its stunning design by Andre Kikoski. If planning to eat, note that hours are limited and prices high. ■TIP➔ Escape the crowded lobby by taking the elevator to the top and working your way down the spiral. ⊠ *1071 5th Ave., between 88th and 89th Sts., Upper East Side* ☎ *212/423–3840, 212/423–3500* ⊕ *www.guggenheim.org* 🖾 *$25* ☉ *Sun.–Wed. and Fri. 10–5:45, Sat. 10–7:45* Ⓜ *4, 5, 6 to 86th St.*

WORTH NOTING

Acquavella Galleries. The 19th- and 20th-century museum-quality art inside this five-story, marble-floored French neoclassical mansion tends to be big name, from impressionists through pop artists, including Picasso, Lucian Freud, Jean-Michel Basquiat, James Rosenquist, and Wayne Thiebaud. ⊠ *18 E. 79th St., between 5th and Madison Aves., Upper East Side* ☎ *212/734–6300* ⊕ *www.acquavellagalleries. com* 🖾 *Free* ☉ *Weekdays 10–5* Ⓜ *6 to 77th St.*

FAMILY **Carl Schurz Park.** Facing the East River, this park, named for a German immigrant who was a prominent newspaper editor in the 19th century, is so tranquil you'd never guess you're directly above the FDR Drive. Walk along the promenade, where you can take in views of the river and the Roosevelt Island Lighthouse across the way. To the north are Randall's and Wards Islands and the RFK Bridge (aka the Triborough Bridge)—as well as the more immediate sight of locals pushing strollers, riding bikes, or walking their dogs. If you use the 86th Street entrance, you'll find your-self near the grounds of a Federal-style wood-frame house that belies the grandeur of its name: Gracie Mansion. ⊠ *From 84th to 90th St., between East End Ave. and the East River, Upper East Side* 🕾 *212/459–4455* ⊕ *www.carlschurzparknyc.org* Ⓜ *4, 5, 6 to 86th St.*

Castelli Gallery. One of the most influential dealers of the 20th century, Leo Castelli helped foster the careers of many important artists, including one of his first discoveries, Jasper Johns. Castelli died in 1999, but the gallery continues to show works by Roy Lichtenstein, Andy Warhol, Ed Ruscha, Jackson Pollock, Robert Morris, and other heavies. ⊠ *18 E. 77th St., between 5th and Madison Aves., Upper East Side* 🕾 *212/249–4470* ⊕ *www.castelligallery.com* 🎟 *Free* ☉ *Tues.–Sat. 10–6* Ⓜ *6 to 77th St.*

Jane Kahan. This welcoming gallery represents some lofty works. In addition to tapestries by modern masters like Pablo Picasso, Joan Miró, and Alexander Calder—one of this gallery's specialties—works by late-19th- and early-20th-century modern artists like Fernand Léger and Marc Chagall are showcased. ⊠ *922 Madison Ave., 2nd fl., between 73rd and 74th Sts., Upper East Side* 🕾 *212/744–1490* ⊕ *www.janekahan. com* 🎟 *Free* ☉ *Labor Day–Memorial Day, Tues.–Sat. 10–6; Memorial Day–Labor Day, weekdays 11–5* Ⓜ *6 to 77th St.*

Mitchell-Innes & Nash. This sleek spot represents the estates of Roy Lichtenstein, Alberto Burri, Nancy Graves, and Jack Tworkov as well as other impressionist, modern, and contemporary masters. ⊠ *1018 Madison Ave., between 78th and 79th Sts., Upper East Side* 🕾 *212/744–7400* ⊕ *www.miandn.com* 🎟 *Free* ☉ *Weekdays 10–5* Ⓜ *6 to 77th St.*

FAMILY **Mount Vernon Hotel Museum and Garden.** Built in 1799, this former carriage house became a day hotel (a sort of country club) in 1826. Now restored and owned by the Colonial Dames of America, it provides a glimpse of the days when the city ended at 14th Street and this area was a country escape for New Yorkers. A 45-minute tour (the only way to see the museum and garden) passes through the eight rooms that display furniture and artifacts of the Federal and Empire periods. Many rooms have real artifacts such as clothes, hats, and fans that children can handle. There is a lovely adjoining garden, designed in an 18th-century style. Tours are on demand and can be geared to specific interests. Arrive at least a half hour before closing time to allow for tour. ⊠ *421 E. 61st St., between York and 1st Aves., Upper East Side* 🕾 *212/838–6878* ⊕ *www.mvhm.org* 🎟 *$8* ☉ *Tues.–Sun. 11–4* Ⓜ *4, 5, 6 to 59th St.; N, Q, R to Lexington Ave./59th St.*

10

Museum of American Illustration. Founded in 1901, the museum of the Society of Illustrators presents its annual "Oscars," a juried international competition, from January to March. The best in children's book illustration is showcased October through November. In between are eclectic exhibitions on science fiction, fashion, politics, and history illustrations. In 2012, the Society of Illustrators incorporated the holdings of the Museum of Comic and Cartoon Art (MoCCA) into its collections. MoCCA's collection is housed in its own gallery on the second floor and continues its workshops, programs, and comic festival (MoCCA

Fest). ■TIP➜ Admission is free on Tuesday 5–8. ✉ *128 E. 63rd St., between Lexington and Park Aves., Upper East Side* ☎ *212/838–2560* ⊕ *www.societyillustrators.org* 🎫 *$10* ⊙ *Tues. 10–8, Wed.–Fri. 10–5, Sat. noon–4* Ⓜ *F to Lexington Ave./63rd St.; 4, 5, 6 to 59th St.; N, Q, R to Lexington Ave./59th St.*

Peter Findlay Gallery. Covering 19th- and 20th-century works by European artists, this gallery shows pieces by Mary Cassatt, Paul Klee, and Alberto Giacometti. ✉ *16 E. 79th St., 2nd fl., Upper East Side* ☎ *212/644–4433* ⊕ *www.findlay.com* ⊙ *Weekdays 1:30–5* Ⓜ *6 to 77th St.*

FAMILY **Roosevelt Island.** The 2-mile-long East River slice of land that parallels Manhattan from 48th to 85th Streets is now a quasi-suburb of more than 14,000 people, and the vestiges of its infamous asylums, hospitals, and prisons make this an offbeat trip for the historically curious. At its southern tip are the eerie ruins of a **Smallpox Hospital,** built in 1854 in a Gothic Revival style by the prominent architect James Renwick Jr. (Among many other works, Renwick also designed St. Patrick's Cathedral.) Neighboring the hospital ruins is the recently opened **Four Freedoms Park,** a memorial to Franklin Delano Roosevelt designed by famed architect Louis I. Kahn. The monument to President Roosevelt is essentially a large, open granite box with a giant bust of FDR, and a wall inscribed with the words of the wartime Four Freedoms speech. Visitors can stroll the stone walkways and the symmetrical tree-lined pebble paths that run along the manicured lawn and enjoy unique views of the United Nations and East River. Individual or group guided walking tours ($20) of FDR Four Freedoms Park are available daily; check website to reserve. At the island's north tip is a small park with a lighthouse built in 1872 by island convicts. Cornell University's new state-of-the-art, sustainable Tech campus is currently under construction on the island, and will open in phases beginning late 2017. You can get to the island by subway, but why would you when you can take the five-minute ride on the **Roosevelt Island Tramway,** the only commuter cable car in North America, which lifts you 250 feet in the air for impressive views of Queens and Manhattan. A visitor center (open May to September), made from an old trolley kiosk, stands to your left as you exit the tram. Free red buses service the island. ✉ *Tramway entrance, 2nd Ave., between 59th and 60th Sts., Upper East Side* ☎ *212/688–4836 for visitor center* ⊕ *www.fdrfourfreedomspark.org* 🎫 *$2.75 (one-way subway fare)* ⊙ *Park Wed.–Mon. 9–5. Tram Sun.–Thurs. 6 am–2 am, Fri. and Sat. 6 am–3:30 am; leaves approximately every 15 mins* Ⓜ *F to Roosevelt Island.*

Van Doren Waxter. The gallery formerly known as the Greenberg Van Doren Gallery changed its name and moved to this historic town house on a tree-lined street, just a block from the Met Museum's new outpost at the former Whitney Museum. Solo and group shows of postwar artists as well as emerging young artists are exhibited here. ✉ *23 E. 73rd St., between Madison and 5th Aves., Upper East Side* ☎ *212/445–0444* ⊕ *www.vandorenwaxter.com* 🎫 *Free* ⊙ *Tues.–Sat. 10–6* Ⓜ *6 to 77th St.*

THE UPPER WEST SIDE

GETTING ORIENTED

105th–123rd St. (top map)

86th–104th St. not shown on map

59th–85th St. (bottom map)

The Upper West Side

Grant's Tomb

INWOOD The Cloisters Museum and Gardens

W.121st St.
W.120th St.
W.119th St.
W.118th St.
W.117th St.

HARLEM

Barnard College

Broadway

Columbia University

Amsterdam Ave.

Morningside Ave.

Morningside Dr.

Morningside Park

B,C

W.116th St.

W.115th St.
W.114th St.
W.113rd St.

W.115th St.
W.114th St.
W.113th St.

St. Nicholas Ave.

Cathedral Church of St. John the Divine

W.112nd St.
W.111st St.

Hungarian Pastry Shop
Cathedral Pkwy.

B,C Central Park N.

W.109th St.
W.108th St.

Central Park

W.107th St.
W.106th St.
W.105th St.

Riverside Park

Henry Hudson Parkway

Broadway

86th–104th Streets Not Shown

Children's Museum of Manhattan

W.85th St.

W.84th St.
W.83rd St.

Great Lawn

Riverside Park

W.82nd St.
W.81st St.

B,C

79th St. Boat Basin

Zabar's Cafe

W.80th St.
W.79th St.
W.78th St.
W.77th St.

American Museum of Natural History

Promenade

Riverside Drive

UPPER WEST SIDE

Broadway

Amsterdam Ave.

Columbus Ave.

New-York Historical Society

W.76th St.

Hudson River

Fairway ◆ Beacon Theatre

W.75th St.
W.74th St.

The Lake

Verdi Square

W.73rd St.

The Dakota

B,C

Statue of Eleanor Roosevelt

1,2,3 W.72nd St.
72nd St. Subway Station

W.71st St.
W.70th St.
W.69th St.
W.68th St.
W.67th St.

Central Park West

Sheep Meadow

West Side Highway

West End Ave.

American Folk Art Museum

W.66th St.
W.65th St.

Central Park see detail map

Lincoln Center for the Performing Arts

W.64th St.

W.62nd St.

W.61st St.
W.60th St.

Time Warner Center

A,B,C,D,1

Bouchon Bakery

W.59th St.

Central Park South

Columbus Circle

Museum of Arts and Design ◆

0   1/4 mile
0   400 meters

MAKING THE MOST OF YOUR TIME

Broadway is one of the most walkable and interesting thoroughfares on the Upper West Side because of its broad sidewalks and aggressive mix of retail stores, restaurants, and apartment buildings. If you head north from the Lincoln Center area (around 65th Street) to about 81st Street (about 1 mile), you'll get a feel for the neighborhood's local color, particularly above 72nd Street. Up here you'll encounter residents of every conceivable age and ethnicity either shambling or sprinting, street vendors hawking used and newish books, and such beloved landmarks as the 72nd Street subway station, the Beacon Theatre, the produce mecca Fairway (the cause of perhaps the most perpetually congested block), and Zabar's (a food spot that launches a memorable assault on all five of your senses—and your wallet). The Upper West Side's other two main avenues—Columbus and Amsterdam—are more residential but also have myriad restaurants and shops.

If you're intrigued by having the city's only Ivy League school close at hand, hop the 1 train to 116th Street and emerge on the east side of the street, which puts you smack in front of Columbia University and its Graduate School of Journalism. Pass through the gates and up the walk for a look at a cluster of buildings so elegant you'll understand why it's an iconic NYC setting.

GETTING HERE

The A, B, C, D, and 1 subway lines take you to Columbus Circle. From there, the B and C lines run along Central Park. The 1 train runs up Broadway, making local stops. The 2 and 3 are express trains that also go along Broadway.

TOP EXPERIENCES

Strolling through Riverside Park past the boat basin

Exploring Central Park

Standing below the gigantic blue whale at the American Museum of Natural History

Taking in the views, gardens, and medieval masterpieces at the Cloisters Museum and Gardens

COFFEE AND QUICK BITES

Bouchon Bakery. In Columbus Circle's busy Time Warner shopping center, this take-out bakery outpost of the sit-down restaurant serves excellent sandwiches, quiches, pastries, and coffee. There are a few seats. ✉ *10 Columbus Circle, 3rd fl., Upper West Side* ☎ *212/823-9366* ⊕ *www.thomaskeller.com* Ⓜ *1, A, B, C, D to 59th St.–Columbus Circle.*

Hungarian Pastry Shop. Linger over a danish and bottomless cups of coffee with the Columbia kids and professors at this old-world (cash only) café and bakery. ✉ *1030 Amsterdam Ave., at 111th St., Upper West Side* ☎ *212/866-4230* Ⓜ *1 to Cathedral Pkwy.–110th St.*

Zabar's Cafe. Fast-track the Zabar's experience with a gourmet coffee and sandwich, pickled lox, or slice of cheesecake. ✉ *2245 Broadway, at 80th St., Upper West Side* ☎ *212/787-2000* ⊕ *www.zabars.com* Ⓜ *1 to 79th St.*

Sightseeing
★★★
Nightlife
★★
Dining
★★
Lodging
★
Shopping
★★★★

Updated
by Jacinta
O'Halloran

The Upper West Side is one of the city's quieter, more residential neighborhoods, with wide sidewalks and a (relatively) slower pace. The Cloisters, in Inwood, has the Metropolitan Museum's medieval collection.

The tree-lined side streets of the Upper West Side are lovely, with high stoops leading up to stately brownstones. Central Park, of course, is one of the main attractions here, no matter the season or time of day, though locals know that Riverside Park, along the Hudson River, can be even more appealing, with smaller crowds.

The Upper West Side also has its share of cultural institutions, from the 16-acre **Lincoln Center** complex, to the impressive and quirky collection at the **New-York Historical Society,** to Columbus Circle's **Museum of Arts and Design** and the much-loved, soon-to-be-expanded **American Museum of Natural History.**

Most people think the area north of 106th Street and south of 125th Street on the West Side is just an extension of the Upper West Side. Technically it's Morningside Heights, largely dominated by Columbia University along with a cluster of academic, religious, and medical institutions, including Barnard College and the **Cathedral Church of St. John the Divine.**

TOP ATTRACTIONS

Fodor'sChoice   **American Museum of Natural History.** The largest natural history museum
★   in the world is also one of the most impressive sights in New York. Four city blocks make up its 45 exhibition halls, which hold more than 30 million artifacts from the land, sea, and outer space. With so many wonders, you can't see everything on a single visit, but you can easily hit the highlights in half a day. Most visitors begin with the iconic and amazing assembly of **dinosaur and mammal fossils** taking up the entire fourth floor. Highlights include a T. Rex, an Apatosaurus (formerly called a Brontosaurus), and the Titanosaur, a recently discovered species that is so long at 122 feet, it can't even fit all the way inside its exhibit hall (its head sticks out the door to greet you). The specimens are not in chronological order, but put together based on their shared characteristics. The **Rose Center for Earth and Space** is another must-see. *Dark*

Universe, in the Hayden Planetarium, puts Hollywood effects to shame as it explores the cosmos and just how little we really know about it. Head for the third floor to check out the Komodo dragon lizards and a 23-foot-long python in **Reptiles and Amphibians;** a brief but interesting comparison between apes, monkeys, and humans in the **Primates Hall;** and the upper gallery of the famed **Akeley Hall of African Mammals.**

The small **Hall of Biodiversity** includes a shady replica of a Central African Republic rain forest. Within a few yards are 160 species of flora and fauna—and also evidence of the forest's destruction. The **Milstein Hall of Ocean Life,** designed to emit an underwater glow, is home to another museum icon—the 94-foot model of a blue whale, suspended from the ceiling. The hall focuses on the vast array of life in the ocean that covers our planet. The AMNH offers various programs and special exhibits throughout the year that allow for a more interactive experience. Between October and May, don't miss the warm, plant-filled Butterfly Conservatory, where blue morphos, monarchs, and other butterflies flit and feed. Ten minutes is probably enough time to enjoy it. Also in October, the AMNH hosts the Margaret Mead Film & Video Festival, the longest-running premiere showcase for international documentaries in the United States. Tickets are made available one month prior to the festival, and online at www.amnh.org/mead. The Rose Center's monthly One Step Beyond series is the perfect place to bust out your moonwalk and enjoy a few "cosmicpolitans"; the event features live bands, DJs, VJs, cocktails, and dynamic visuals. If you just don't want to go home, the museum also offers a hugely popular Night-at-the-Museum sleepover program for kids age 6–13 as well as a separate sleepover program for adults. Learn more about special programs at *amnh.org/plan-your-visit.*

If you're hungry, there are several options in the museum, including a cafeteria ($) on the ground floor that serves sandwiches and burgers. The Petrie Court Café, at the back of the first-floor European Sculpture Court, has waiter service. The Roof Garden (open May–Oct.) has contemporary sculpture exhibits, but most people take the elevator here to have a drink or snack while checking out the views of Central Park and the skyline. ⊠ *Central Park W at W. 79th St., Upper West Side* ☎ *212/769–5100* ⊕ *www.amnh.org* ✉ *$22 suggested donation, includes admission to Rose Center for Earth and Space; $27 includes an IMAX or space show* ☉ *Daily 10–5:45* Ⓜ *B, C to 81st St./Museum of Natural History.*

Cathedral Church of St. John the Divine. The largest Gothic-style cathedral in the world, even with its towers and transepts still unfinished, this divine behemoth comfortably asserts its bulk in the country's most vertical city. The seat of the Episcopal diocese in New York, it acts as a sanctuary for all, giving special services that include a celebration of New York's gay and lesbian community as well as the annual Blessing of the Bikes (mid-April), when cyclists of all faiths bring their wheels for a holy-water benediction. Built in two long spurts starting in 1892, the cathedral remains only two-thirds complete. What began as a Romanesque Byzantine–style structure under the original architects, George Heins and Christopher Grant Lafarge, shifted upon Heins's death in

AMNH on Film

Does the inside of AMNH look familiar? It should. The museum is a popular location for movies filming in New York. In *Spider-Man 2* (2004), Peter Parker (Tobey Maguire) has yet another bad day wrestling with his secret identity while in the Rose Center. Larry (Ben Stiller) is chased through the halls by a T. Rex and outsmarts a monkey in the Hall of African Mammals while working as a night security guard in *Night at the Museum* (2006). AMNH plays a roll in *Night at the Museum: Battle* of the Smithsonian (2009) and *Night at the Museum: Secret of the Tomb* (2014), too. In the coming-of-age film *The Squid & the Whale* (2005), Walt Berkman (Jesse Eisenberg) comes to a revelation that he is the squid and his father is the whale in front of the Hall of Ocean Life's famous diorama. And then there's *The Devil Wears Prada* (2006) where Andrea (Anne Hathaway) wins over Miranda (Meryl Streep) by remembering the names of high-society guests while attending a benefit here.

1911 to French Gothic under the direction of Gothic Revival purist Ralph Adams Cram. You can spot the juxtaposition of the two medieval styles by comparing the finished Gothic arches, which are pointed, with the still-uncovered arches, which are rounded in the Byzantine style.

To get the full effect of the cathedral's size, approach it from Broadway along 112th Street (all the while doing your best to avoid the sight of the two unholy 15-story rental towers cozying up to—and obscuring— the 113th Street side of the cathedral). Above the 3-ton central bronze doors is the intricately carved **Portal of Paradise,** which depicts St. John witnessing the Transfiguration of Jesus, and 32 biblical characters. Step inside to the cavernous nave: more than 600 feet long, it holds some 5,000 worshippers, and the 162-foot-tall dome crossing could comfortably contain the Statue of Liberty (minus its pedestal). The **Great Rose Window** is the largest stained-glass window in the United States; it's made from more than 10,000 pieces of colored glass.

At the end of the nave, surrounding the altar, are seven chapels expressing the cathedral's interfaith tradition and international mission—with menorahs, Shinto vases, and dedications to various ethnic groups. The **Saint Saviour Chapel** contains a three-panel bronze altar in white gold leaf with religious scenes by artist Keith Haring (his last work before he died in 1990). Outside in the cathedral's south grounds is the eye-catching **Peace Fountain.** It depicts the struggle of good and evil in the form of the archangel Michael decapitating Satan, whose head hangs from one side. Encircling it are whimsical animals cast in bronze from pieces sculpted by children.

On the first Sunday of October, in honor of St. Francis of Assisi, the patron saint of animals, the church holds its usual Sunday service with a twist: the service is attended by men, women, children, dogs, cats, rabbits, hamsters, and the occasional horse, sheep, or ant farm. In past years upward of 3,500 New Yorkers have shown up to have their pets blessed. A procession is led by such guest animals as elephants, camels,

llamas, and golden eagles. Sunday services are at 8, 9, 11, and 4. "High-light Tours" and "Vertical Tours" are offered throughout the week; check the website for details and to reserve. ✉ *1047 Amsterdam Ave., at 112th St., Upper West Side* 🕾 *212/316–7540, 866/811–4111 for tour reservations* ⊕ *www.stjohndivine.org* 💬 *$10 suggested donation; tours $12–$20* ⊙ *Daily 7:30–6; visitor center daily 9–5; tours Mon. at 11 and 2, Tues.–Sat. at 11 and 1, Sun. at 1* Ⓜ *1 to Cathedral Pkwy.–110th St.*

Fodor's Choice
★
Lincoln Center for the Performing Arts. *See the listing in Chapter 19.*

Fodor's Choice
★
New-York Historical Society. Manhattan's oldest (and perhaps most under-the-radar) museum, founded in 1804, boasts one of the city's finest research libraries in addition to a contemporary glass facade, sleek interactive technology, a children's museum, restaurant, and inventive exhibitions that showcase the museum's eclectic collections and unique voice. While the permanent collection of more than 6 million pieces of art, literature, and memorabilia sheds light on America's history, art, and architecture, the special exhibitions showcase the museum's fresh—and often surprising—insight on all things New York. The Henry Luce III Center for the Study of American Culture (due to reopen by 2017) on the fourth floor of the museum will include a new Center for the Study of Women's History, with permanent and rotating exhibits that examine and celebrate New York's central role in women's history, especially for New Yorkers like Eleanor Roosevelt, Zora Neale Hurston, and Margaret Sanger. The **DiMenna Children's History Museum** on the lower level invites children to become "history detectives" and explore New York's past through interactive displays, hands-on activities, and the stories of iconic New York children through the centuries. The Historical Viewfinder allows kids to see how certain New York sites have changed over time. Unlike most other children's museums, this museum is geared to mature elementary and middle schoolers, not toddlers. Caffé Storico, the light-filled restaurant on the first floor (with a separate entrance), serves upscale Italian food at lunch and dinner and is open for weekend brunch. ✉ *170 Central Park W, Upper West Side* 🕾 *212/873–3400* ⊕ *www.nyhistory.org* 💬 *$20 (pay-as-you-wish Fri. 6–8 pm)* ⊙ *Tues.–Thurs. and Sat. 10–6, Fri. 10–8, Sun. 11–5* Ⓜ *B, C to 81st St.–Museum of Natural History.*

WORTH NOTING

American Folk Art Museum. After a near-death, or rather, near- *debt* experience in late 2011, the American Folk Art Museum left its home of 10 years on 53rd Street (since razed and taken over by MoMA) and returned to its humble rental near Lincoln Center. Here, the focus returns to its incredible collection of contemporary self-taught artists of the 20th and 21st centuries, including the single largest collection of reclusive Chicago artist Henry Darger, known for his painstakingly detailed collage paintings of fantasy worlds. Past exhibitions have included "Art Brut in America: The Incursion of Jean Dubuffet," which featured 200 works of art and explored the introduction of art brut (art created completely outside the boundaries of the art world and culture, often by children or the mentally ill) to America. The gift shop has an impressive collection of handcrafted items. ⊠ *2 Lincoln Sq., Columbus Ave. at 66th St., Upper West Side* ☎ *212/595–9533* ⊕ *www.folkartmuseum.org* ☞ *Free* ☉ *Mon.–Thurs. and Sat. 11:30–7, Fri. noon–7:30, Sun. noon–6* Ⓜ *1 to 66th St.–Lincoln Center; A, B, C, D to 59th St.–Columbus Circle.*

FAMILY **Children's Museum of Manhattan.** In this five-story exploratorium, children ages one–seven are invited to paint their own masterpieces, float boats down a "stream" (weather permitting), rescue animals with Dora and Diego (in an exhibition created in collaboration with Nickelodeon), and walk through giant interactive human organs to explore the connections between food, sleep, and play. Special exhibits are thoughtfully put together and fun. Seasonal programs include a Grinch Holiday workshop. Art workshops, science programs, and storytelling sessions are held daily. ■ TIP➔ **Admission is free 5–8 pm on the first Friday of every month.** ⊠ *212 W. 83rd St., between Broadway and Amsterdam Ave., Upper West Side* ☎ *212/721–1223* ⊕ *www.cmom.org* ☞ *$12* ☉ *Tues.– Fri. and Sun. 10–5, Sat. 10–7* Ⓜ *1 to 79th St.*

Columbus Circle. This busy traffic circle at Central Park's southwest corner anchors the Upper West Side and makes a good starting place for exploring the neighborhood if you're coming from south of 59th Street. The central 700-ton granite monument (capped by a marble statue of Christopher Columbus) serves as a popular meeting place. To some people, Columbus Circle is synonymous with the **Time Warner Center** building (*212/823–6300; www.theshopsatcolumbuscircle.com*) and its several floors of shops and restaurants, including takeout-friendly Bouchon Bakery and Whole Foods—both perfect places to pick up picnic fixings to take to Central Park. It's also home to the Rose Hall performing arts complex, part of Jazz at Lincoln Center. ⊠ *Broadway at 58th St. to 60th St., Upper West Side* Ⓜ *1, A, B, C, D to 59 St.– Columbus Circle.*

The Dakota. One of the first residences built on the Upper West Side, the château-style Dakota (1884) remains an architectural fixture with its lovely gables, gaslights, copper turrets, and central courtyard. Celebrity residents have included Boris Karloff, Rudolf Nureyev, José Ferrer, Rosemary Clooney, Lauren Bacall, Leonard Bernstein, Gilda Radner, and Connie Chung, but none more famous than John Lennon, who in 1980 was shot and killed at the Dakota's gate by a deranged fan. Visitors are not welcome in the lobby and there are no tours of the building. Fortunately, the elaborate exterior is best admired from across the street. ⊠ *1 W. 72nd St., at Central Park W, Upper West Side* Ⓜ *B, C to 72nd St.*

Grant's Tomb (*General Grant National Memorial*). Walk through upper Riverside Park and you're sure to notice this towering granite mausoleum (1897), the final resting place of Civil War general and two-term president Ulysses S. Grant and his wife, Julia Dent Grant. As the old joke goes, who's buried here? Nobody—they're *entombed* in a crypt beneath a domed rotunda, surrounded by photographs and Grant memorabilia. Once a more popular sight than the Statue of Liberty, this pillared Classical Revival edifice feels more like a relic of yesteryear, but it remains a moving tribute. The words engraved on the tomb, "Let Us Have Peace," recall Grant's speech to the Republican convention upon his presidential nomination. Surrounding the memorial are the so-called "rolling benches," which are swoopy and covered with colorful mosaic tiles that bring to mind the works of architect Antoni Gaudí's Park Güell, in Barcelona. Made in the 1970s as a public art project, they are now as beloved as they are incongruous with the grand memorial they surround. ■TIP→ Free public talks are available in the visitor center (across the street from the tomb), Wednesday through Monday at 11:15, 1:15, and 3:15. ⊠ *Riverside Dr. at 122nd St., Upper West Side* 🕾 *212/666–1640* ⊕ *www.nps.gov/gegr* 🚇 *Free* ⊘ *Wed.–Sun. 9–5* Ⓜ *1 to 116th St. St.*

Museum of Arts and Design (*MAD*). In a funky-looking white building across from the Time Warner Center, the Museum of Arts and Design celebrates joyful quirkiness and personal, sometimes even obsessive, artistic visions. The art is human scale here, much of it neatly housed in display cases rather than hanging on the walls, with a strong focus on contemporary jewelry, glass, ceramic, fiber, wood, and mixed-media works. Thursday evening is pay-what-you-wish. ⊠ *2 Columbus Circle, 59th St. at 8th Ave., Upper West Side* 🕾 *212/299–7777* ⊕ *www. madmuseum.org* 🚇 *$16* ⊘ *Tues., Wed., and weekends 10–6, Thurs. and Fri. 10–9* Ⓜ *1, A, B, C, D to 59th St.–Columbus Circle.*

FAMILY　**Riverside Park.** Surrounded by concrete and skyscrapers in Manhattan, you might not realize that there is an expansive green space running along the water just blocks away. Riverside Park—which, along with the Riverside Park South extension, runs along the Hudson from 58th to 156th Streets—dishes out a dose of tranquillity. The original sections of Riverside Park, designed by Frederick Law Olmsted and Calvert Vaux of Central Park fame and laid out between 1873 and 1888, have a waterfront bike and walking paths. There are several access points to the park, including one at West 72nd Street and Riverside Drive (look for the statue of Eleanor Roosevelt), where you reach the waterfront path by an underpass beneath the West Side Highway. You can then head north along the Hudson River, past the 79th Street Boat Basin, where a flotilla of houseboats bobs in the water. Above it, a ramp leads to the Rotunda, home in summer to the Boat Basin Café, a dog-friendly open-air café that serves lunch and dinner in the warmer months (from March-ish through October). The 91st Street Garden, planted by community gardeners, explodes with flowers in most seasons and is a level up from the water: leave the riverside path near 92nd Street by taking another underpass and then heading up the path on the right. ⊠ *From 58th to 156th St., between Riverside Dr. and the Hudson River, Upper West Side* ⊕ *www. nycgovparks.org/parks/riversidepark* Ⓜ *1, 2, 3 to 72nd St.*

CENTRAL PARK

More than 38 million people visit Central Park each year; on an average summer weekend day, a quarter of a million children and adults flood these precincts, frolicking in the 21 playgrounds and 26 ballfields, and collapsing on more than 9,000 benches, which would span 7 miles if

you lined them up. There are more than 55 monuments and sculptures in the park, and countless ways to have fun.

TOP ATTRACTIONS

Fodor'sChoice
★

Bethesda Fountain. Few New York views are more romantic than the one from the top of the magnificent stone staircase that leads down to the ornate, three-tiered Bethesda Fountain. The fountain was built to celebrate the opening of the Croton Aqueduct, which brought clean drinking water to New York City. The name Bethesda was taken from the biblical pool in Jerusalem that was supposedly given healing powers by an angel, which explains the statue *The Angel of the Waters* rising from the center. The four figures around the fountain's base symbolize Temperance, Purity, Health, and Peace. Beyond the terrace stretches the lake, filled with swans, gondolas, and amateur rowboat captains. At its western end is the Boathouse, home of an outdoor café for on-the-go snacks, and a pricier restaurant for more leisurely meals. ⊠ *Mid-park at 72nd St. transverse, Central Park* Ⓜ *B, C to 72nd St.*

FAMILY
Fodor'sChoice
★

Central Park. Central Park's creators had a simple goal: to design a place where city dwellers could go to forget the city. Even though New York eventually grew far taller than the trees planted to hide it, this goal has never faltered. A combination escape hatch and exercise yard, Central Park is an urbanized Eden that gives residents and visitors alike a bite of the apple. Indeed, without the Central Park's 843 acres of meandering paths, tranquil lakes, ponds, and open meadows, New Yorkers (especially Manhattanites) might be a lot less sane.

The busy southern section of Central Park, from 59th to 72nd Street, is where most visitors get their first impression. But no matter how many people congregate around here, you can always find a spot to picnic, ponder, or just take in the greenery, especially on a sunny day. Playgrounds, lawns, jogging and biking paths, and striking buildings populate the midsection of the park, from 72nd Street to the Reservoir. You can soak up the sun, have a picnic, have your photo taken at Bethesda Fountain, visit the penguins at the Central Park Zoo, or join the runners huffing counterclockwise on the dirt track that surrounds the reservoir. North of the reservoir and up to 110th Street, Central Park is less crowded and feels more rugged. Not many people know that there's a swimming pool in the northeast corner of the park, which becomes a skating rink in winter—and it's much less crowded than Volker Rink in the southern part of the park. To find out about park events and a variety of walking tours, visit the website of the Central Park Conservancy.

If you're taking the subway to the park's southernmost parts, then the stops at either Columbus Circle (at the west side) or 5th Avenue/59th Street are handy. If headed for points north, the B, D, A, and C subway lines travel along Central Park West, while the 4, 5, and 6 lines travel along Lexington Avenue, three blocks east of 5th Avenue and the park.

There are many paved pedestrian entrances into the park, from 5th Avenue, Central Park North (110th Street), Central Park West, and Central Park South (59th Street) Four roads, or transverses, cut through

the park from east to west—66th, 79th, 86th, and 96th Streets. The East and West drives are both along the north–south axis; Center Drive enters the south edge of the park at 6th Avenue and connects with East Drive around 66th Street. Along the main loop, lampposts are marked with location codes that include a letter—always "E" (for east) or "W" (for west)—followed by numbers, the first two of which tell you the nearest cross street. For example, E7803 means you're near 78th Street; above 99, the initial "1" is omitted, so W0401 is near West 104th Street. Download the free Central Park app in advance of your visit for a GPS-enabled map to help you navigate the park. The app also includes an audio guide, self-guided tours, and current events in the park. If you haven't packed a picnic and you want a snack, you can usually find one of those rather tired-looking food carts selling pretzels and ice-cream sandwiches. But these days, there are often more interesting specialty-food carts around, too, mostly in the southern half of the park, so keep on the lookout—your taste buds will thank you. Other reliable options include the café next to the Boathouse Restaurant (mid-park at 74th Street), or the park's branch of Le Pain Quotidien (mid-park at 69th Street). Both serve sandwiches, soup, pastries, and other satisfying on-the-go grub (and Le Pain also has free Wi-Fi). If you're looking for something a little more iconic, you can stop for brunch, lunch, or dinner at the Tavern on the Green, which reopened in summer 2014.

As part of a park-wide restoration project named Central Play, all 21 playgrounds will receive an update over the next few years. A playground at East 110th Street, in the park's northeast corner, has already undergone renovation and features interconnected circular spaces that have swings, play structures, and water features. The Wild West playground at West 93rd Street and the East 79th Street playground reopened in spring 2015 after a full renovation, and work continues throughout the park. ⊠ *Central Park* ☎ *212/794–6564 Dairy Visitor Center, 212/360–2727 for schedule of walking tours, 646/310–6600 Central Park Conservancy* ⊕ *www.centralparknyc.org* Ⓜ *A, B, C, D, 1 to Columbus Circle; N, Q, R to 5th Ave.–59th St.*

Central Park Conservancy. Five visitor centers—the Dairy (mid-park at 65th Street), Belvedere Castle (mid-park at 79th Street), the Chess & Checkers House (mid-park at 64th Street), the Charles A. Dana Discovery Center (at the top northeast corner of the park on the shore of Harlem Meer), and the North Meadow Recreation Center (mid-park, near 96th Street)—have directions, park maps, event calendars, and volunteers who can give you guidance. ⊠ *Dairy Visitor Center, 65th St. transverse, Central Park* ☎ *212/310–6600 Central Park Conservancy, 212/310–6600 Dairy Visitor Center* ⊕ *www.centralparknyc.org.*

FAMILY **Central Park Zoo.** Even a leisurely visit to this small but delightful menagerie takes only about an hour (unless, of course, you fall under the spell of the zoo's adorable first king penguin chick, born in early 2015, or the spry snow leopard cub, Malala, born here in mid-2014). There are more than 130 species here, but no space for animals like zebras and giraffes to roam; the biggest specimens here are Betty and Veronica—two lovable grizzly bears who joined the zoo in late 2014. Don't miss the sea lion feedings, possibly the zoo's most popular attraction, daily

Many Beatles fans come to Strawberry Fields to pay their respects to John Lennon, who was murdered across the street at the Dakota apartments.

at 11:30, 2, and 4. Clustered around the central Sea Lion Pool are separate exhibits for each of the Earth's major environments: penguins and polar bears live at Polar Circle; the highlights of the open-air Temperate Territory are the chattering monkeys; and the Rain Forest contains the flora and fauna of the tropics. The Tisch Children's Zoo (no additional ticket required) gives kids the opportunity to feed sheep, goats, cows, and pigs. The 4-D theater ($7) shows 15-minute-long family-friendly films like "Ice Age: Dawn of the Dinosaurs, the 4-D Experience" that feature sensory effects like wind, mist, bubbles, and scents. ✉ *Entrance at 5th Ave. and E. 64th St., Central Park* ☎ *212/439–6500* ⊕ *www. centralparkzoo.org* 🎫 *$12; $18 Total Experience (includes 4-D show)* 🕐 *Apr.–early Nov., weekdays 10–5, weekends 10–5:30; early Nov.– Mar., daily 10–4:30* ☞ *Children under 12 not admitted without adult* Ⓜ *6 to 68th St./Hunter College; N, Q, R, to 5th Ave./59th St.; F to Lexington Ave./63rd St.*

Great Lawn. This 14-acre oval has endured millions of footsteps, thousands of ball games, hundreds of downpours, dozens of concerts, and even the crush attending one papal Mass. Yet it's the stuff of a suburbanite's dream—perfectly tended turf (a mix of rye and Kentucky bluegrass), state-of-the-art drainage systems, automatic sprinklers, and careful horticultural monitoring. The area hums with action on weekends and most summer evenings, when its softball fields and picnicking grounds provide a much-needed outlet for city folk (and city dogs) of all ages. ✉ *Mid-park between 81st and 85th Sts., Central Park* ⊕ *www. centralparknyc.org* Ⓜ *B, C to 81st St./Museum of Natural History.*

Strawberry Fields. This memorial to John Lennon, who penned the classic 1967 song "Strawberry Fields Forever," is sometimes called the "international garden of peace." The curving paths, shrubs, trees, and flower beds create a deliberately informal landscape reminiscent of English parks. Every year on December 8, Beatles fans mark the anniversary of Lennon's death by gathering around the star-shape, black-and-white "Imagine" mosaic set into the pavement. Lennon's 1980 murder took place across the street at the Dakota apartment building, where he lived. ⊠ *Just off W. 72nd St., Central Park* ⊕ *www.centralparknyc.org* Ⓜ *B, C to 72nd St.*

INWOOD

Well north of Harlem, at the very northern tip of Manhattan, Inwood is essentially the upper Upper West Side, with Fort Tryon Park lying just to its south.

The Cloisters Museum and Gardens. Perched on a wooded hill in Fort Tryon Park, near Manhattan's northwestern tip, the Cloisters Museum and Gardens houses the medieval collection of the Metropolitan Museum of Art and is a scenic destination in its own right. Colonnaded walks connect authentic French and Spanish monastic cloisters, a French Romanesque chapel, a 12th-century chapter house, and a Romanesque apse. One room is devoted to the 15th- and 16th-century Unicorn Tapestries, which date to 1500—a must-see masterpiece of medieval mythology. The tomb effigies are another highlight. Two of the three enclosed gardens shelter more than 250 species of plants similar to those grown during the Middle Ages, including flowers, herbs, and medicinals; the third is an ornamental garden planted with both modern and medieval plants, providing color and fragrance from early spring until late fall. Concerts of medieval music are held here regularly (concert tickets include same-day admission to the museum). The outdoor Trie Café is open 10 to 4:15 Tuesday through Sunday, from April to October, and serves sandwiches, coffee, and snacks. ■ TIP➔ Admission includes same-day entry to the Metropolitan Museum of Art's main building on 82nd Street as well as its new contemporary art outpost—the Met Breuer—on 75th Street. ⊠ *99 Margaret Corbin Dr., Fort Tryon Park, Upper West Side* ☎ *212/923–3700* ⊕ *www.metmuseum.org* ⊠ *$25 suggested donation* ⊗ *Mar.–Oct., daily 10–5:15; Nov.–Feb., daily 10–4:45* Ⓜ *A to 190th St.*

HARLEM

GETTING ORIENTED

Harlem

THE BRONX

TOP EXPERIENCES

Shopping at the monthly Sugar Hill Market

Visiting the Studio Museum in Harlem

Spending an evening at the iconic Apollo Theater

Donning your Sunday best for jazz brunch

MAKING THE MOST OF YOUR TIME

Harlem's simplest pleasures are free. Take time to walk the areas around Strivers' Row, Hamilton Heights, Sugar Hill, and 116th Street to see some impressive—and often fanciful—architecture. Hear the sweet sounds of a choir practice as you stroll by any of Harlem's churches (which number in the hundreds). See well-curated exhibits showcasing the work of contemporary artists of African descent at the Studio Museum in Harlem (open Thursday–Sunday), or visit the Morris-Jumel Mansion for a trip back in time to Colonial New York.

GETTING HERE AND AROUND

The 2 and 3 subway lines stop on Lenox Avenue; the 1 goes along Broadway, to the west; and the A, B, C, and D trains travel along St. Nicholas and 8th Avenues (note: the B train does not run on weekends). And yes, as the song goes, the A train is still usually "the quickest way to Harlem."

The city's north–south avenues take on different names in Harlem: 6th Avenue is called both Malcolm X Boulevard *and* Lenox Avenue; 7th Avenue is Adam Clayton Powell Jr. Boulevard (named for the influential minister and congressman); and 8th Avenue is Frederick Douglass Boulevard. West 125th Street, the major east–west street and Harlem's commercial center, is also known as Dr. Martin Luther King Jr. Boulevard.

COFFEE AND QUICK BITES

Levain Bakery. From coffee and cakes to breads and scones, this bakery has something for every sweet tooth. It's the cookies, however, that make them famous. Choose from varieties such as chocolate chip walnut and dark-chocolate chocolate chip; they're big enough to share, but after one bite you may not want to. ✉ *2167 Frederick Douglass Blvd., between 116th and 117th Sts., Harlem* ☎ *646/455–0952* ⊕ *www.levainbakery.com* Ⓜ *B, C to 116th St.*

Manhattanville Coffee. It may be on a quiet corner, but this coffee shop is always buzzing. The vintage-inspired space appeals to laptop-toting locals with a large communal table, tufted leather couches, and free Wi-Fi. The super-friendly staff, Intelligentsia coffee, gourmet pastries, and grilled cheese sandwiches make this a neighborhood favorite. ✉ *142 Edgecombe Ave., at 142nd St., Harlem* ☎ *646/781–9900* ⊕ *www.manhattanvillecoffee. com* Ⓜ *A, B, C, D to 145th St.; B, C to 135th St.*

Sightseeing
★★
Nightlife
★★★★
Dining
★★★
Lodging
★★
Shopping
★★

Harlem is known throughout the world as a vibrant center of African American culture, music, and life. The neighborhood invites visitors to see historic jewels such as the Apollo Theater, architecturally splendid churches, cultural magnets like the Studio Museum in Harlem and the Schomburg Center for Research in Black Culture, as well as an ongoing list of new and renovated sites and buildings.

Updated by
Jessica Colley
Clarke

A stroll along Harlem's 125th Street reveals the electric energy of the neighborhood, from impromptu drum circles to a bustling farmers' market to sidewalk vendors hawking bootleg DVDs, incense, and African shea butter. This east–west stretch is the heart of the neighborhood, and home to some of the best people-watching in Manhattan. Bill Clinton's New York office is at 55 West 125th Street, and the legendary Apollo Theater stands at No. 253. A large number of chains (Starbucks, Red Lobster, H&M) make it hard to distinguish 125th Street from the city's other heavily commercialized areas, but there are still a few things that set it apart: the wide number of languages spoken, the aroma of West African spices for sale, and stylish locals who take pride in their fashion.

To get a feel for Harlem, spend time visiting its past and present. On 116th Street, particularly between St. Nicholas and Lenox Avenues (Malcolm X Boulevard), you'll find some of the area's most interesting religious buildings, from ornate churches to a green-domed mosque.

Along Lenox Avenue and Frederick Douglass Boulevard, between 110th and 130th Streets are chic restaurants, bars, and a few boutiques offering everything from bespoke cocktails and live music to Harlem-inspired gifts and high-end menswear.

TOP ATTRACTIONS

Apollo Theater. ⇨ *See the listing in Chapter 19, Performing Arts.*

Hamilton Heights. To taste this neighborhood's Harlem Renaissance days, walk down tree-lined Convent Avenue and cross over to **Hamilton Terrace** to see a time capsule of elegant stone row houses in mint condition. One of the neighborhood's most beautiful blocks, it's popular with film and TV crews. The **Hamilton Grange National Memorial,** founding father Alexander Hamilton's Federal-style mansion, is located at the southern end of the block, on 141st Street. Turn west and continue down Convent Avenue to see the looming Gothic spires (1905) of **City College.** The stately Oxford-inspired buildings here are New York to the core: they are clad with the schist rock unearthed when the city was building the IRT line (1 train). Next, head southwest to visit **Strivers' Row.** ⊠ *Convent Ave., between 138th and 150th Sts., Harlem* Ⓜ *A, B, C, D to 145th St.*

FAMILY **Morris-Jumel Mansion.** During the Revolutionary War, General Washington used this wooden, pillared 8,500-square-foot house (1765) as his headquarters, and when he visited as president in 1790, he brought along John Quincy Adams, Thomas Jefferson, and Alexander Hamilton. Inside rooms are furnished with period decorations; upstairs, keep an eye out for the hand-painted wallpaper (original to the house) and a "commode chair," stuck in a corner of the dressing room. Outside, behind the house, is a Colonial-era marker that says it's 11 miles to New York—a reminder of what a small sliver of Manhattan the city was at that time. East of the house is the block-long Sylvan Terrace, a row of crisp two-story clapboard houses built in 1882. ⊠ *65 Jumel Terr., north of 160th St., between St. Nicholas and Edgecombe Aves., Harlem* ☎ *212/923–8008* ⊕ *www. morrisjumel.org* ⊠ *$10; guided tour $12* ☉ *Tues.–Fri. 10–4, weekends 10–5; guided tours Sat. at noon* Ⓜ *C to 163rd St.*

Strivers' Row. This block of gorgeous 1890s Georgian and Italian Renaissance Revival homes earned its nickname in the 1920s from less affluent Harlemites who felt its residents were "striving" to become well-to-do. Some of the few remaining private service alleys, used when deliveries arrived via horse and cart, lie behind these houses and are visible through iron gates. Note the gatepost between Nos. 251 and 253 on 138th Street that reads, "Private Road. Walk Your Horses." These houses were built by the contractor David H. King Jr., whose works also include the base for the Statue of Liberty and the oldest parts of the Cathedral Church of St. John the Divine. When they failed to sell to whites, the properties on these blocks were sold to African American doctors, lawyers, and other professionals; composers and musicians W. C. Handy and Eubie Blake were also among the residents. If you have the time, detour a block north to see the palazzo-style group of houses designed by Stanford White, on the north side of 139th Street. ⊠ *138th and 139th Sts., between Adam Clayton Powell Jr. and Frederick Douglass Blvds., Harlem* Ⓜ *B, C to 135th St.; A, B, C, D to 145th St.*

Fodor'sChoice ★ **Studio Museum in Harlem.** Contemporary art by African American, Caribbean, and African artists is the focus of this small museum with a light-filled sculpture garden. Three artists in residence present their works

D.I.Y. Harlem Gospel Tours

Over the past decade, the popularity of Sunday gospel tours has surged. While some in the community see it as an opportunity to broaden horizons and encourage diversity, others find tours disruptive and complain that tourists take seats away from regular parishioners (churches regularly fill to capacity). If you plan on attending a service, here are some tips:

Most churches have Sunday services at 11, but you may need to arrive as much as two hours early (depending on the church) to get in. Dress nicely (no shorts, sneakers, or jeans); be as quiet as possible; do not leave in the middle of the service; and do not take photos or videos or use your cell phone. Most important, remember that parishioners do not consider the service, or themselves, tourist attractions or entertainment.

A bus tour is generally an inauthentic (and more expensive) way to experience Harlem. Explore the neighborhood and churches on your own, or join a small tour like those led by **Harlem Heritage Tours** (☎ 212/280–7888 ⊕ www.

harlemheritage.com). Their tours ($39) get high marks from past clients and are run by guides who were born and raised in Harlem. Groups are no larger than 25 people.

The following are some of the uptown churches with Sunday services:

Abyssinian Baptist Church (☎ 212/862–7474 ⊕ www.abyssinian. org) is one of the few churches that does not allow tour groups. Services for visitors are held at 11; arrive at least two hours ahead of time. **Canaan Baptist Church of Christ** (☎ 212/866–0301 ⊕ www.cbccnyc. org) has services at 10. **Convent Avenue Baptist Church** (☎ 212/234–6767 ⊕ www.conventchurch.org) has services at 8, 11, and 5. **First Corinthian Baptist Church** (☎ 212/864–5976 ⊕ www.fcbcnyc.org) has services at 7:30, 9:30, and 11:30.

Greater Refuge Temple (☎ 212/866–1700 ⊕ www.greaterrefugetemple.org) has services at 11 and 4. **Memorial Baptist Church** (☎ 212/663–8830 ⊕ www.mbcvisionharlem.org) has services at 8 and 11.

each year, and summer hosts the lively Uptown Fridays! featuring DJs, cocktails, and a fashionable crowd. The gift shop is small but packs a punch; don't miss its fantastic collection of coffee-table books. ⊠ *144 W. 125th St., between Lenox Ave. and Adam Clayton Powell Jr. Blvd., Harlem* ☎ *212/864–4500* ⊕ *www.studiomuseum.org* ☜ *$7 suggested donation (free Sun.)* ☉ *Thurs. and Fri. noon–9, Sat. 10–6, Sun. noon–6* Ⓜ *2, 3 to 125th St.; A, B, C, D to 125th St.*

Fodor's Choice **Sugar Hill Market.** This monthly market, held on the ground floor of ★ an art gallery's brownstone space, features a mostly consistent roster of Harlem-based designers. Expect to find handmade items including vegan soaps, pottery, gourmet jams, and clothing fusing modern silhouettes with colorful Ghanaian fabrics. The market's founder (who happens to have a fashion background) creates limited-edition Harlem T-shirts that make great souvenirs. ⊠ *La Maison d'Art, 259 W. 132nd St., between Frederick Douglass and Adam Clayton Powell Jr. Blvds.,*

The Studio Museum features contemporary art by African American, Caribbean, and African artists.

Harlem ✛ *Located on the ground floor of a brownstone; look for the sandwich board on the sidewalk* ⊕ *sugarhillmarketnyc.blogspot.com* Ⓜ *B, C, 2, 3 to 135th St.; A, B, C, D to 125th St.*

WORTH NOTING

The Butcher's Daughter. After five years in Detroit, Monica Bowman (yes, she really is a butcher's daughter) moved her gallery to this quiet block in Harlem. The glass-front space is minimal, allowing the exhibits, which change every six weeks and showcase emerging and established fine artists from across the United States, to really shine. ⊠ *318 W. 142nd St., between Edgecombe Ave. and Frederick Douglass Blvd., Harlem* ☎ *917/634–1354* ⊕ *www.thebutchersdaughtergallery.com* 🎫 *Free* ⊙ *Tues.–Sat. 11–6* Ⓜ *A, B, C, D to 145th St.*

Gitler & _____. This sliver of a gallery gets its name from owner and curator Avi Gitler, who uses the tight space to showcase up-and-coming artists from around the world and across genres. ⊠ *3629 Broadway, between 149th and 150th Sts., Harlem* ☎ *No phone* ⊕ *www.gitlerand. com* 🎫 *Free* ⊙ *Weekends 1–6, Mon. 3–8* Ⓜ *1 to 145th St.*

FAMILY **Hamilton Grange National Memorial.** Founding father Alexander Hamilton and his wife raised eight kids in this Federal-style country home, which he called his "sweet project." Located on Hamilton's 32 acres, the Grange, named after his father's childhood home in Scotland, has moved three times since it was built in 1802. It now stands in St. Nicholas Park and gives a lesson in Hamilton's life, from his illegitimate birth in the West Indies and his appointment as the nation's first Secretary of

Harlem's Jazz Age

It was in Harlem that Billie Holiday got her first singing job, Duke Ellington made his first recording, and Louis Armstrong was propelled to stardom. Jazz was king during the Harlem Renaissance in the 1920s and '30s, and though Chicago and New Orleans may duke it out for the "birthplace of jazz" title, New York was where jazz musicians came to be heard.

In the 1920s, socialites made the journey uptown to Harlem's Cotton Club and Connie's Inn (131st Street and 7th Avenue) to hear "black" music. Both clubs were white-owned and barred blacks from entering, except as performers. (The rules changed years later.) Connie's introduced New Yorkers to Louis Armstrong. The Cotton Club—Harlem's most popular nightspot by far—booked such big names as Fletcher Henderson, Coleman Hawkins, Duke Ellington, Cab Calloway, and Ethel Waters. After shows ended at the paying clubs, musicians would head to after-hours establishments with black patrons, such as Small's Paradise, Minton's Playhouse (which reopened in 2013), and Basement Brownies, where they'd hammer out new riffs into the wee hours.

the Treasury to his authorship on *The Federalist Papers* and his death following a duel with Vice President Aaron Burr. The house's ground floor, formerly servants' quarters, hosts an interactive exhibit that includes a short film on Hamilton's life. Upstairs a parlor, study, dining room, and two guest rooms are open to view; note the beautiful piano, which belonged to his daughter Angelica. ⊠ *414 W. 141st St., between St. Nicholas and Convent Aves., Harlem* ☎ *646/548–2310* ⊕ *www.nps. gov/hagr/index.htm* ⊠ *Free* ⊗ *Wed.–Sun. 9–5; self-guided tours of the furnished rooms noon–1 and 3–4 only; 30-min ranger-led tours at 10, 11, 2, and 4* Ⓜ *1 to 137th St.–City College; A, B, C, D to 145th St.*

FAMILY
Fodor's Choice
★
The Hispanic Society of America Museum and Library. This is the best collection of Hispanic and Spanish art outside El Prado in Madrid, with paintings, sculptures, textiles, manuscripts, music, and decorative arts from ancient Iberia through the 20th century. On the first floor, Joaquín Sorolla y Bastida's *Vision of Spain* fills the entire Sala Bancaja; stand in the middle and admire the 13 massive, colorful paintings, capturing everything from Holy Week penitents to fishermen in Catalonia. A smaller room houses intricately carved marble pieces from bishops' tombs. Upstairs, there's a room filled with antique iron doorknockers, two rooms of earthenware from Spain and Mexico, and notable pieces by Goya, El Greco, Murillo, Velázquez, and Zurbarán. The entrance is on Broadway, between 155th and 156th Streets, up the steps to the left. ⊠ *Audubon Terr., 613 W. 155th St., Harlem* ☎ *212/926–2234* ⊕ *www. hispanicsociety.org* ⊠ *Free* ⊗ *Tues.–Sun. 10–4:30* Ⓜ *1 to 157th St.*

Masjid Malcolm Shabazz (*Mosque*). Talk about religious conversions. In the mid-'60s, the Lenox Casino was transformed into this house of worship and cultural center, and given bright yellow arches and a huge, green onion dome that loudly proclaims its presence in a neighborhood

The Hispanic Society of America Museum and Library celebrates the work of Hispanic and Spanish artists.

of churches. Once functioning as Temple No. 7 under the Nation of Islam with a message of pro-black racism, the mosque was bombed after the assassination of Malcolm X, who had preached here. It was then rebuilt and renamed in honor of the name Malcolm took at the end of his life, El-Hajj Malik Shabazz; its philosophy now is one of inclusion. These days the Sunni congregation has a large proportion of immigrants from Senegal, many of whom live in and around 116th Street. Next door is Graceline Court, a 16-story luxury condominium building that cantilevers somewhat awkwardly over the mosque. Farther east on 116th Street is the outdoor **Malcolm Shabazz Harlem Market,** where you can find African and African-inspired jewelry, art, clothing, and fabrics. On weekends with nice weather more vendors open. ⊠ *102 W. 116th St., at Malcolm X Blvd. (Lenox Ave.), Harlem* ☎ *212/662–2200* ⊕ *www.masjidmalcolmshabazz.com* Ⓜ *2, 3 to 116th St.*

Sugar Hill. Standing on the bluff of Sugar Hill overlooking Jackie Robinson Park, outside the slightly run-down **409 Edgecombe Avenue,** you'd never guess that here resided such influential African Americans as NAACP founder W.E.B. DuBois and Supreme Court Justice Thurgood Marshall, or that farther north at **555 Edgecombe** (known as the "Triple Nickel"), writers Langston Hughes and Zora Neale Hurston and jazz musicians Duke Ellington, Count Basie, and others lived and played. It's also here that for nearly 20 years musician Marjorie Eliot has been hosting jazz concerts in her apartment, 3F, at 3:30 pm every Sunday. Farther down, at No. 345, you can't miss the **Benzinger House** with its flared mansard roof. Amid all this history, the modern-looking **Sugar Hill Children's Museum of Art & Storytelling,** at 155th Street and St.

Nicholas Avenue, gathers local families for programs that encourage the creative spirit of children. Its design has earned it the nickname "the Sugar Cube Building." ⊠ *From 145th to 155th Sts., between Edgecombe and St. Nicholas Aves., Harlem* Ⓜ *A, B, C, D to 145th St.*

Tatiana Pagés Gallery. This Chilean-born, Dominican Republic–raised designer and collector doesn't have a long commute to work—she lives next door to her namesake gallery. Set on a quiet corner near Strivers' Row, the gallery (Pagés's first) exhibits contemporary art and design, with an emphasis on Caribbean and Latin American art. ⊠ *2605 Frederick Douglass Blvd., at 139th St., Harlem* ☎ *646/415–8093* ⊕ *www.tatianapagesgallery.com* ⊠ *Free* ⊗ *Tues.–Fri. 11–7, Sat. noon–7* Ⓜ *A, B, C, D to 145th St.; B, C to 135th St.*

BROOKLYN

GETTING ORIENTED

TOP EXPERIENCES

Eating and barhopping in Williamsburg

Screaming at the top of the Cyclone roller coaster in Coney Island

Smelling the roses, and everything else, at the Brooklyn Botanic Garden

Catching a show at BAM or Barclays Center

Walking across the Brooklyn Bridge

Picnicking in Brooklyn Bridge Park

Being awestruck by architecture in Brooklyn Heights or street art in Bushwick

GETTING HERE

Brooklyn is very accessible by subway from Manhattan; check the listings for subway info. Brooklyn Heights, Downtown Brooklyn, DUMBO, and Williamsburg are the closest neighborhoods to Manhattan. Coney Island and Brighton Beach are the farthest; budget about an hour each way if you're traveling from Midtown.

MAKING THE MOST OF YOUR TIME

The best way to get to Brooklyn is by its most majestic bridge. Walking along the wooden pedestrian path of the Brooklyn Bridge—a classic New York experience—takes about 30 minutes, worth it for the panoramic views of the skylines and the harbor. On summer weekends the path is crowded, unless you go early in the morning. Exit the bridge onto Cadman Plaza on the Brooklyn side, then walk southwest to get to Brooklyn Heights, a charming neighborhood of 19th-century brownstone homes, or walk north into the hip neighborhood of DUMBO.

13

QUICK BITES

Jacques Torres Chocolate. French-born Torres is New York's adopted Willy Wonka. Here, he dishes out drool-worthy truffles and bonbons, and hot chocolate rich enough to make a Swiss miss blush. Festively wrapped bars and baskets make sweet souvenirs, but the shop also has a café with marble-top tables for those whose chocolate cravings simply cannot wait. ⊠ *66 Water St., DUMBO* ☎ *718/875–1269* ⊕ *www.mrchocolate.com* Ⓜ *A, C to High St.; F to York St.*

Juliana's Pizza. Skip the lines at the more famed Grimaldi's and walk next door. Here you'll find what many Brooklynites think of as the "real" Grimaldi's. Opened in 2011 by Patsy and Carol Grimaldi (who sold both their original restaurant and the naming rights more than 10 years earlier), Juliana's serves up deliciously charred New York–style coal-oven pizza, made by a master pizzaiolo in a brick oven that is generations old. ⊠ *19 Old Fulton St., DUMBO* ☎ *718/596–6700* ⊕ *julianaspizza.com* ⌧ *Reservations not accepted* Ⓜ *F to York St.*

Sightseeing
★★★
Nightlife
★★★★
Dining
★★★★ ★
Lodging
★ ★
Shopping
★★★

Updated by
Josh Rogol

Hardly Manhattan's sidekick, Brooklyn is a destination in its own right, with many diverse neighborhoods and a seemingly endless number of compelling sights and fabulous places to eat and drink and shop.

Across the East River from Manhattan, on Long Island's western edge, Brooklyn is one of New York City's five boroughs. At 71 square miles, it's more than three times the size of Manhattan, and with more than 2½ million people, if it were a city it would be the fourth largest in the United States, in terms of population. Brooklyn *was* a city until the end of the 19th century, with its own widely circulated newspaper (*The Brooklyn Eagle*), its own expansive park (Prospect Park), and its own baseball team that would eventually be called the Brooklyn Dodgers. In 1883 it also got its own bridge: the Brooklyn Bridge, which drew the attention of the entire country.

Brooklyn Heights and **DUMBO** are easily accessible from Manhattan by subway or via the Brooklyn Bridge; both neighborhoods have compelling but very different architecture (brownstones versus 19th-century warehouses), and fabulous views of Manhattan. **Carroll Gardens, Cobble Hill, Boerum Hill**, and **Fort Greene** all have plenty of lovely streets to stroll with thriving restaurant and bar scenes. The latter also has the Brooklyn Academy of Music. **Williamsburg** is the epicenter of trendsetting Brooklyn, which is overflowing into up-and-coming **Bushwick** and **East Williamsburg. Park Slope** and **Prospect Park** welcome with laid-back, family-friendly activities, while **Prospect Heights** and **Crown Heights** are home to heavy hitters like the Barclays Center, the Brooklyn Botanic Gardens, Weeksville Heritage Center, and the Brooklyn Children's Museum. **Coney Island** and **Brighton Beach** have Brooklyn's subway-accessible beaches, boardwalks, and amusement parks, including the legendary Cyclone roller coaster.

CLOSE UP

Brooklyn Is Book Country

Brooklyn has been a mecca for writers and literature since the days of *Uncle Tom's Cabin,* written by a preacher's daughter in Brooklyn Heights. Since then, writers have flocked here for the cheap rent and quiet streets. Henry Miller, Norman Mailer, Truman Capote, Arthur Miller (with Marilyn Monroe), Paul and Jane Bowles, Carson McCullers, James Purdy, and Walt Whitman created more than one masterpiece here.

Today, amid the gentrification, Brooklyn continues to lure famous and near-famous writers and musicians from all over the world.

Perhaps reflecting the plethora of writers in the neighborhood, the borough has a relatively high density of both used and new bookstores, and also several small presses, including Melville House, a publisher with a storefront.

And with all these writers so close by, it only makes sense that Brooklyn has a fabulous book festival, to boot. The Brooklyn Book Festival happens every year at Borough Hall, on the third weekend in September. Authors gather for readings and signings, and independent publishers display their wares.

13

BROOKLYN HEIGHTS

Brooklyn Heights is quintessential "brownstone Brooklyn." It's the oldest neighborhood in the borough, and the original village of Brooklyn; almost the entire neighborhood is part of the Brooklyn Heights Historic District. This is still very much the neighborhood of shady lanes, cobblestone streets, centuries-old row houses, and landmark buildings that Walt Whitman rhapsodized about, and the magnificent postcard views of the Manhattan skyline and the Brooklyn Bridge have inspired countless artists and photographers since. In the early to mid-20th century, Brooklyn Heights was a bohemian haven, home to such writers as Arthur Miller, Truman Capote, Henry Miller, Alfred Kazin, Carson McCullers, Paul Bowles, Marianne Moore, Norman Mailer, and W.E.B. DuBois.

The majestic **Brooklyn Bridge** has one foot in Brooklyn Heights, near DUMBO, and a walk across it either to or from Lower Manhattan is one of the classic New York experiences.

TOP ATTRACTIONS

Fodor'sChoice ★ **Brooklyn Bridge.** (⇨ *Chapter 2*) *F to York St.; A, C to High St.*

FAMILY
Fodor'sChoice ★
Brooklyn Bridge Park. What started as a scenic but small hilltop park beneath the Manhattan Bridge has turned into a sweeping feat of green urban renewal stretching from the Manhattan Bridge in DUMBO to the Brooklyn Bridge and south all the way to Pier 6, carpeting old industrial sites along the waterfront with scenic esplanades and lush meadows. The park has playgrounds, sports fields, food concessions, a beach, a pop-up pool, and lots of grass for lounging. You can access the park at various points, including Main Street, for the Main Street Playground; Old Dock Street, off Water Street, for the wonderfully

restored **Jane's Carousel**; Old Fulton Street, for the popular Fulton Ferry Landing and Pier 1; Old Squibb Park Bridge, off Columbia Heights, for Piers 1 and 2; and Joralemon Street, for Piers 5 and 6. ⊠ *Brooklyn waterfront, between Manhattan Bridge and Pier 6, Brooklyn Heights* ☏ *718/222–9939* ⊕ *www.brooklynbridgepark.org* Ⓜ *2, 3 to Clark St.; A, C to High St.; F to York St.*

FAMILY

Fodor'sChoice

★

Brooklyn Heights Promenade. Strolling this mile-long path, famous for its magnificent Manhattan views, you might find it surprising to learn that its origins were purely functional: the promenade was built as a sound barrier to protect nearby brownstones from highway noise. Find a bench and take in the skyline, the Statue of Liberty, and the Brooklyn Bridge; the setting is especially impressive in the evening, when the lights of Manhattan sparkle across the East River. Below are the Brooklyn–Queens Expressway and Brooklyn Bridge Park. ⊠ *Between Remsen and Cranberry Sts., Brooklyn Heights* Ⓜ *2, 3 to Clark St.; A, C to High St.; R to Court St.*

Fodor'sChoice

★

Brooklyn Historical Society. Four centuries' worth of art and artifacts bring Brooklyn's story to life at this marvelous space. Housed in an 1881 Queen Anne–style National Historic Landmark building—one of the neighborhood's gems—the society surveys the borough's changing identity through permanent exhibits that include interactive displays, landscape paintings, photographs of the area, portraits of prominent Brooklynites, and fascinating memorabilia. The gift shop is a highlight on its own, featuring an eclectic assortment of Brooklyn-themed books and tchotchkes. Check the website for details about the stellar lineup of temporary exhibitions. ⊠ *128 Pierrepont St., at Clinton St., Brooklyn Heights* ☏ *718/222–4111* ⊕ *www.brooklynhistory.org* ✉ *$10 suggested donation* ☉ *Wed.–Sun. noon–5* Ⓜ *2, 3, 4, 5 to Borough Hall; R to Court St.; A, C, F to Jay St.–MetroTech.*

"Fruit" Streets. Brooklyn Heights is filled with stately brownstones and brick homes, and the quiet blocks of Pineapple, Cranberry, and Orange Streets contain some of the most picturesque ones. A few homes made of wood still exist, too, although they've been banned in the Brooklyn Heights area since the mid-19th century because of the fire hazard. The wood-frame house at 24 Middagh Street, a typical example built in the Federal style, dates to the 1820s. Middagh Street was named for the ancestors of one Lady Middagh, who, so the legend goes, thought that naming streets after wealthy families was pretentious. She removed the existing street signs and installed her own fruit-themed ones. The city confiscated them, but she kept replacing the city's signs until her choices were made official. To ponder the irony that despite her initiative Middagh Street still exists, stroll west (toward the East River) on Orange or Cranberry to the Fruit Street Sitting Area, the connector between Brooklyn Heights Promenade and Columbia Heights. ⊠ *Pineapple, Orange, and Cranberry Sts., Brooklyn Heights* Ⓜ *2, 3 to Clark St.; A, C to High St.*

Brooklyn Heights is well-known for its multitude of picturesque brownstones.

WORTH NOTING

Brooklyn Borough Hall. Built in 1848 as Brooklyn's city hall, this Greek Revival landmark, adorned with Tuckahoe marble, is one of the borough's handsomest buildings. The statue of Justice atop its cast-iron cupola was part of the original plan but wasn't installed until 1988. Today the building serves as the office of Brooklyn's borough president and the home of the Brooklyn Tourism & Visitors Center. ⊠ *209 Joralemon St., between Court and Adams Sts., Brooklyn Heights* ☎ *718/802–3846* ⊗ *Weekdays 10–6* Ⓜ *2, 3, 4, 5 to Borough Hall; R to Court St.; A, C, F, R to Jay St.–MetroTech.*

FAMILY **New York Transit Museum.** Step down into an old 1930s subway station to experience this entertaining museum's displays of vintage trains and memorabilia. You can wander through trains and turnstiles and sit behind the wheel of a former city bus (it's not only the kids who do this). Original advertising, signage, and upholstery make this feel like a trip back in time. The gift shop carries subway-line socks, decorative tile reproductions, and other fun stuff. ⊠ *Boerum Pl., at Schermerhorn St., Brooklyn Heights* ☎ *718/694–1600* ⊕ *www.mta.info/museum* ⊠ *$7 adults, $5 children* ⊗ *Tues.–Fri. 10–4, weekends 11–5* Ⓜ *2, 3, 4, 5 to Borough Hall; A, C, G to Hoyt–Schermerhorn Sts.; A, C, F, R to Jay St.–MetroTech.*

Brooklyn Heights,
Downtown Brooklyn,
and DUMBO

0   1/4 mile

0   1/4 km

DOWNTOWN BROOKLYN

Downtown Brooklyn is modern and bustling, and other than a few notable restaurants, there isn't much to attract visitors—but it's convenient to the Brooklyn Bridge and Brooklyn Heights, and walking distance to neighborhoods like Cobble Hill, Boerum Hill, and DUMBO.

NEED A BREAK?

Ganso. Duck inside this narrow Japanese ramen shop, grab a stool at the counter, and order a steaming bowl of the Spicy Soboro Miso ramen. It's a miso broth that's combined with Sapporo noodles and two types of pork, topped off with an *ajitama* (soft-boiled) egg. Wash down the addictive blend of spice and noodles with a can of Ginga Ninja IPA or any other of Ganso's featured local and Japanese craft beers. ⊠ *25 Bond St., Downtown Brooklyn* ☎ *718/403–0900* ⊕ *gansonyc.com/ganso-ramen* Ⓜ *2, 3 to Hoyt St.; A, C, G to Hoyt-Schermerhorn Sts.; 2, 3, 4, 5 to Nevins St.; B, Q, R to DeKalb Ave.*

DUMBO

For sheer jaw-dropping drama, few city walks are as cinematic as strolling the DUMBO waterfront. The photogenic area pairs 19th-century warehouses and refurbished industrial buildings on cobblestone streets with rumbling trains and soaring bridges overhead. (The latter gives the district its name, an acronym of Down Under the Manhattan Bridge Overpass.) Across the East River, the glittering Manhattan skyline provides epic views and popular backdrops for wedding proposals, fashion shoots, and innumerable selfies. Major galleries and performance hubs imbue the neighborhood with artistic élan, and the adjacent Navy Yard is a booming example of Brooklyn's revitalized industrial waterfront.

An integral part of DUMBO is the Brooklyn Bridge Park, and its renovated piers and rolling green spaces. Crowds of locals and tourists alike flock to its riverfront benches and tiny beaches to sunbathe or simply to ponder the magnificence of one of the city's finest views.

DUMBO Walls. Keep an eye out for the walls under and around the Manhattan Bridge and the BQE, where eight walls display artwork by big names including CAM, Shepard Fairey, and MOMO. The project is sponsored by the DUMBO Improvement District and Two Trees Management Co. along with the New York City Department of Transportation Urban Art Program and the Jonathan LeVine Gallery. ⊠ *DUMBO* Ⓜ *F to York St.*

Smack Mellon. The transformation of an industrial boiler house into an edgy arts compound is quintessential DUMBO. This 12,000-square-foot structure now hosts large-scale, avant-garde exhibitions. They also run a prestigious residency program. Don't be surprised if you pass a binder-clutching bride-to-be on your way in: the 5,000-square-foot gallery is also a popular wedding venue. ⊠ *92 Plymouth St., DUMBO* ☎ *718/834–8761* ⊕ *www.smackmellon.org* ☾ *Wed.–Sun. noon–6* Ⓜ *A, C to High St.; F to York St.*

Fodor'sChoice
★
The Stable Building. Many Brooklynites mourned the loss of the Galapagos Art Space when it closed shop and moved to Detroit; fortunately, the site continues its arts legacy, and the building now houses four first-floor gallery spaces, which were previously part of the 111 Front Street gallery collective. Minus Space shows artists specializing in "reductive abstract art" (simple materials, precise craftsmanship, monochromatic or limited color, repetition of shapes). United Photo Industries (UPI) shows work by emerging photographers and those working in new photography styles. The Klompching Gallery focuses on fine-art photography. Masters Projects represents artists working in all sorts of media, including paint, mixed media, street art, photography, and installations. Gallery hours vary, but weekday and Saturday afternoons are your best bet to visit; most are closed Monday. ⊠ *16 Main St., at Water St., DUMBO* ☾ *Gallery hrs vary* Ⓜ *2, 3 to Clark St.; A, C to High St.; F to York St.*

13

Carroll Gardens, Cobble
Hill, Boerum Hill, and
Fort Greene

NEED A BREAK?

One Girl Cookies. Snag a window seat overlooking cobblestone Main Street and tuck into a variety of whoopie pies, cakes, and bite-size cookies each named for a different woman in Dawn's (the founder and baker) family. Try the Penelope, a butter cookie covered in chopped nuts filled with apricot preserves, or the Juliette, a chocolate-cinnamon ganache sandwiched between two hazelnut cookies. ⊠ *33 Main St., DUMBO* ☎ *212/675–4996* ⊕ *onegirlcookies.com/dumbo* Ⓜ *F to York St.; A, C to High St.*

CARROLL GARDENS

Named for Charles Carroll, the only Catholic signatory of the Declaration of Independence, and the lush front gardens that line the neighborhood's brownstones, Carroll Gardens was a well-kept secret until the 1980s. Traditionally an Italian neighborhood, many old-school vestiges, including some that have served the area for well over a half century, still remain. Court and Smith Streets are the backbone of the community, and now feature a mix of top-notch restaurants and bistros, handsome cocktail lounges and craft-beer bars, and boutiques selling the most current styles, to go along with original mom-and-pop bakeries and butcher shops. A recent influx of French expats makes the neighborhood's annual Bastille Day festival and petanque (like lawn bowling but played on sand using heavy metal balls) tournament a high point each July.

QUICK
BITE

Brooklyn Farmacy. In 2010 Peter Freeman and his sister Gia opened Brooklyn Farmacy, a 1950s-style soda fountain, in a storefront that was a working pharmacy decades before. The sibling duo is serving up classic Brooklyn egg creams, sparkling sodas, and seasonal sundaes in a space that transports you back in time. The egg creams are made, of course, with Fox's U-bet chocolate syrup, while the delectable sundaes require their own menu. Visit during the week (before the after-school rush), when you can score a seat at the counter and dive headfirst into the Mr. Potato Head sundae, featuring vanilla ice cream covered with potato chips, peanut butter, warm caramel, and whipped cream. ⊠ *513 Henry St., Carroll Gardens* ☎ *718/522–6260* ⊕ *www.brooklynfarmacyandsodafountain.com* ⌁ *Reservations not accepted* Ⓜ *F, G to Carroll St.*

COBBLE HILL

Cobble Hill stands out for its 19th-century architecture, leafy and compact park, and more recently, for escalating real estate prices. Dutch residents called the area Cobleshill in reference to a Revolutionary War–era land mound, which was flattened by British soldiers to prevent strategic use by George Washington's troops. These days, most of the 22-block neighborhood is landmarked as Brooklyn's second-oldest district, a mix of brick town houses, brownstones, and Victorian schoolhouses, where only the Gothic Revival churches exceed a 50-foot height limit. Historically working-class, the neighborhood has adopted all the trappings of haute Brooklyn, especially along busy Court Street.

BOERUM HILL

Understated elegance defines Boerum Hill, where redbrick town houses and brownstones line quiet, tree-lined thoroughfares from 4th Avenue to Smith Street and Schermerhorn to Baltic. The neighborhood saw an influx of immigrants in the late 1800s, with completion of the Brooklyn Bridge and the emergence of trolley cars, but fell into disrepair after World War II. Now fully gentrified, the setting is laden with beautiful cafés and plays host to Atlantic Antic, NYC's largest street festival and unofficial fall kick-off, each September. Despite its air of sophistication, Boerum Hill presents moments of levity, namely artist Susan Gardner's sparkly mosaic-covered brownstone at 108 Wyckoff Street.

NEED A
BREAK?

Two8Two Burger. Burgers, beers, and fries. That's what you'll get at this low-key burger joint. Among stroller-toting parents and neighborhood regulars, you can sidle up to the bar (or grab a table in back) and sink your teeth into a burger patty that was ground that morning by local butcher Los Paisanos. The headliner is the two8two burger, topped with roasted poblano chilies, cheddar cheese, and two8two sauce (a combination of mayo, ketchup, and spices). The bar features a variety of craft beers on tap, including a couple of local selections, as well as the chipotle-habanero Bloody Mary—it's as hot as it sounds. ⊠ *282 Atlantic Ave., Boerum Hill* ☎ *718/596–2282* ⊕ *www.two8twoburger.com* Ⓜ *F, G to Bergen St., A, C, G to Hoyt–Schemerhorn Sts.*

FORT GREENE

Art institutions, flatteringly lit eateries, and the sort of showstopping architecture that sends real estate agents into early retirement make Fort Greene irresistible. Bookended by the Pratt Institute and the former Williamsburg Savings Bank Tower (now 1 Hanson Place)—a four-sided clock tower that was once the borough's tallest building and remains a local landmark—the neighborhood has a central location and an illustrious past. Climb the 96 steps or the grassy slopes of Fort Greene Park and you'll be greeted by vistas of the Manhattan skyline, while standing in the silhouette of the 149-foot tall Prison Ship Martyrs' Monument—dedicated to the thousands of Americans who died on British prison ships during the Revolutionary War. Everyone from Walt Whitman to Spike Lee has called these iconic streets home.

FAMILY

Fodor's Choice

★

Brooklyn Flea. The country's chicest flea market is a collection of antiques dealers, artisanal woodworkers, culinary craftsmen (try the roasted garlic achaar!), vintage clotheshorses, and so much more. Held Saturdays, April through October, in an outdoor lot in Fort Greene and on Sundays in Williamsburg, the Flea has launched many brick-and-mortar businesses throughout New York City. It's also spawned an all-culinary offshoot, Smorgasburg, along the waterfront in Williamsburg and in Prospect Park, as well as the Berg'n food hall. If you're looking for the Flea or Smorgasburg during the winter, head to Industry City (D, N, R to 36th Street) in Sunset Park, where the two share an indoor space. ⊠ *176 Lafayette Ave., Fort Greene* ⊕ *www.brooklynflea.com* Ⓜ *C to Lafayette Ave.; G to Clinton–Washington Aves.*

WILLIAMSBURG

These days, it's impossible to walk through North Brooklyn without encountering something new. Fabulous boutiques, vintage shops, and forward-thinking restaurants crop up constantly, lending an energy that verges on overwhelming. The neighborhood has certainly glossed itself up in recent years, evinced by pricey cocktail bars, high-rise waterfront condos, and expensive boutiques. But Williamsburg's past is also endlessly intriguing: for much of the 20th century this industrial area on the East River was home to a mix of working-class Americans. Rising Manhattan rents in the 1990s sent an influx of East Village artists and musicians onto the L train, and since then the area has rapidly, albeit creatively, gentrified. And while some side streets may appear graffitied and creepy, rest assured that there's likely to be a DIY concert-gallery space in one of those seemingly abandoned factories.

Williamsburg's 70-plus galleries are distributed randomly, with no single main drag. Plan your trip ahead of time using the online **Brooklyn Art Guide** at ⊕ *www.wagmag.org.* (You can also pick up a copy at neighborhood galleries and some cafés.) Hours vary widely, but most are open weekends (call ahead). Although serendipitous poking is the best way to sample the art, longtime gallery Pierogi is a must-see.

FAMILY **City Reliquary.** Subway tokens, Statue of Liberty figurines, antique seltzer bottles, and other artifacts you might find in a time capsule crowd the cases of this museum that celebrates New York City's past and present. Temporary exhibits here have included one about doughnut shops and another about Jewish gangsters of the Lower East Side. ⊠ *370 Metropolitan Ave., Williamsburg* ☎ *718/782–4842* ⊕ *www.cityreliquary.org* ⊠ *$5* ☉ *Thurs.–Sun. noon–6* Ⓜ *L to Lorimer St.; G to Metropolitan Ave.; J, M, Z to Marcy Ave.*

Pierogi Gallery. Nope, it's not a restaurant; it's a hip art gallery showcasing multimedia artists. If you can't make it in person, virtual visitors can browse the Flat Files, an online collection of the portfolios of more than 900 young artists. **The Boiler** (*191 N. 14th Street*), an affiliated but more expansive space nearby, hosts large-scale exhibitions and performances. ⊠ *177 N. 9th St., between Bedford and Driggs Aves.,*

Williamsburg ☎ *718/599–2144* ⊕ *www.pierogi2000.com* ⊙ *Pierogi, Tues.–Sun. 11–6; The Boiler, Thurs.–Sun. noon–6* Ⓜ *L to Bedford Ave.*

Crif Dogs. This Williamsburg outpost—the original is in the East Village— brings to life hot dog masterpieces that New Yorkers once could only dream of. The dogs are smoked and deep-fried, and then turned into creations like the Chihuahua (a bacon-wrapped dog layered with avocado and sour cream) or the pièce de résistance, the Jon-Jon Deragon (a dog with a schmear of cream cheese, scallions, and everything-bagel seeds sprinkled on top). Open until 2 am on weekdays and 4 am on Fridays and Saturdays, there's no better late-night snack in the borough. ✉ *555 Driggs Ave., Williamsburg* ☎ *718/302–3200* ⊕ *www.crifdogs.com* Ⓜ *L to Bedford Ave.*

Urban Oyster Tours. For a glimpse into Brooklyn's illustrious past as the nation's brewing capital (once home to 48 breweries), book a spot on the **Brewed in Brooklyn** walking tour ($65 per person). The journey starts with a tour and tasting at **Brooklyn Brewery** (79 N. 11th Street), followed by a stroll through historic Brewers Row with stops that include a 19th-century German brewery once operated by Otto Huber, lunch at Danny's Pizzeria, and, of course, a craft beer at each watering hole along the way. Other popular tour offerings include the Williamsburg Fermented Craft Beer Crawl and the Neighborhood Eats: Brownstone Brooklyn tour, which is without a doubt the best way to sample the eclectic bites of BoCoCa (Boerum Hill, Cobble Hill, Carroll Gardens) in one afternoon. ✉ *Williamsburg* ☎ *347/618–8687* ⊕ *www. urbanoyster.com.*

BUSHWICK

Bushwick is young and cool, but also gritty and very industrial—working factories make everything from wontons to plastic bags—but it's definitely where to go if you're interested in street art: check out the Bushwick Collective and the streets surrounding it. The neighborhood also has pockets of cafés and restaurants, including Roberta's—making some of the best Neopolitan-style pizza this side of the Atlantic.

Fodor's Choice ★ **The Bushwick Collective.** For evidence of art's ability to transform individuals and their surroundings, visit this colorful outdoor street-art gallery curated by Joseph Ficalora. The Bushwick native came of age during the neighborhood's period of decline, which he experienced first-hand in the early 1990s when his father was murdered. Following his mother's death in 2011, he channeled his grief over both losses into developing this space where street artists are commissioned to create temporary works of art. Pixel Pancho of Turin and Baltimore-based Gaia are among the established artists whose contributions have helped turn urban streets into an arts destination. Many works are also by up-and-comers. ✉ *Troutman St. at St. Nicholas Ave., Bushwick* Ⓜ *L to Jefferson St.*

56 Bogart (The BogArt). Many young Bushwick galleries showcase edgy and experimental work—visiting this converted warehouse is an easy

On a walk through Bushwick and East Williamsburg, you'll find plenty of dynamic local street art.

way to see a lot of art, of varying quality, in one shot. The BogArt, as the space is commonly known, contains large studios for working artists, and more than a dozen galleries on the main and lower levels. Standouts include Robert Henry Contemporary, Theodore:Art, Fresh Window, Momenta Art, and NurtureArt. ■TIP→ Gallery hours vary, but the best time to visit is on Friday and weekends, when most of them are open. ⊠ *56 Bogart St., Bushwick* ☎ *718/599–0800* ⊕ *www.56bogartstreet. com* ▭ *Free* Ⓜ *L to Morgan Ave.*

EAST WILLIAMSBURG

Industrial East Williamsburg, between Williamsburg and Bushwick, has become an enclave of street art, up-and-coming art galleries, cafés, and restaurants.

Luhring Augustine. Probably the neighborhood's most established gallery, this annex of the Chelsea original is worth a stop to see whatever show is up and to appreciate the soaring space and its cantilevered ceiling. ⊠ *25 Knickerbocker Ave., East Williamsburg* ☎ *718/386–2746* ⊕ *www. luhringaugustine.com* ⏱ *Sept.–June, Thurs.–Sun. 11–6; July and Aug., Wed.–Sat. 11–5:30* Ⓜ *L to Morgan Ave.*

Fodor'sChoice
★
The Wick & The Well. Step inside this 19th-century German brewery for a glimpse into Brooklyn's age-old love affair with lager beer, and its more recent affection for warehouse parties. The Otto Huber brewery, once a powerhouse of the old brewers' row prior to Prohibition, now houses both a craft-beer bar (The Well) featuring 60 drafts and more than 100 bottles (most of them local), and a music venue (The Wick) that

packs in well over 600 people for shows ranging from metal to hip-hop and everything in between. If the weather is nice, take a few minutes to explore the massive beer garden in back and the graffiti-adorned walls of the building's exterior. ⊠ *272 Meserole St., East Williamsburg* ☏ *347/338–3612* ⊕ *www.thewellbrooklyn.com; www.thewicknyc.com* Ⓜ *L to Montrose Ave.*

PARK SLOPE

Full of young families, dog walkers, double-wide strollers, and impeccably curated shops, the neighborhood that literally slopes down from Prospect Park can feel like a veritable Norman Rockwell painting. Add to all that a slew of laptop-friendly coffeehouses and turn-of-the-20th-century brownstones—remnants of the days when Park Slope had the nation's highest per-capita income—and it's no surprise that academics and writers have flocked here. Park Slope's busiest drags, 5th and 7th Avenues, present plenty of shopping and noshing opportunities. Head to the elegant, 585-acre Prospect Park for long strolls or bicycle rides past lazy meadows, shady forests, and lakes designed by Olmsted and Vaux of Central Park fame (look out for free summertime concerts). Adjacent is Brooklyn Botanic Garden, which features a variety of public classes and the springtime Cherry Blossom Festival. Also perched on the park is the Brooklyn Museum, lauded for collections of American, Egyptian, and feminist art.

TOP ATTRACTIONS

FAMILY **LeFrak Center at Lakeside.** The highlight of this restored 26-acre space in Prospect Park is the all-season ice- and roller-skating rink; also check out the new walkways, the reconstructed esplanade near the lake, and the Music Island nature reserve, all of which were part of the original Olmsted and Vaux plans. Themed roller-skating night takes place on Friday, May through October; in winter, the rink hosts hockey and curling clinics for all ages. There's also a café and snack bar. ⊠ *Prospect Park, 171 East Dr., Prospect Park* ☏ *718/462–0100* ⊕ *www.lakesidebrooklyn.com* ☜ *Skating $6 weekdays, $8 weekends; rentals $6* ⊙ *Ice rink: Mon.–Thurs. 10–6:30, Fri. 10–9, Sat. 11–9, Sun. 11–6:30* Ⓜ *B, Q, S to Prospect Park; Q to Parkside Ave.*

QUICK BITE

Smorgasburg. More than a hundred of New York City's best and brightest cooks and culinary artisans unite in Prospect Park (replacing the Brooklyn Bridge Park Pier 5 location) every Sunday to form the city's hottest foodie flea market. An offshoot of the Brooklyn Flea, this food bazaar extravaganza has launched countless culinary crazes (ramen burger, anyone?), and most vendors are small-scale, homegrown operators. Lines can grow long and vendors can sell out as the afternoon goes on, so head over early in the day if possible. There is also an outpost on the Williamsburg waterfront (between Kent Avenue and N. 7th Street) on Saturdays, as well as smaller Smorgasburgs in Queens, at Coney Island, at the South Street Seaport, and at Central Park SummerStage events. The latest addition to

Park Slope,
Prospect Heights,
and Crown Heights

this grub empire is a collaboration with the Winter Flea, held weekends year-round at Industry City in Sunset Park. The larger Smorgasburgs are seasonal and generally take place from May through October, but check the website to confirm. ⊠ *Breeze Hill, Prospect Park* ⊕ *www.brooklynflea. com* ⊙ *May–Oct., Sat. and Sun. 11–6* Ⓜ *Q, S to Prospect Park; F, G to 15th St.-Prospect Park.*

FAMILY
Fodor'sChoice
★

Prospect Park. Brooklyn residents are passionate about Prospect Park, and with good reason: lush green spaces, gently curved walkways, summer concerts, vivid foliage in autumn, and an all-season skating rink make it a year-round getaway. In 1859 the New York Legislature decided to develop plans for a park in the fast-growing city of Brooklyn. After landscape architects Frederick Law Olmsted and Calvert Vaux completed the park in the late 1880s, Olmsted remarked that he was prouder of Prospect Park than of any of his other works—Manhattan's Central Park included. Many critics agree that this is their most beautiful work. On weekends, those not jogging the 3.35-mile loop gravitate to the tree-ringed Long Meadow to fly kites, picnic, or play cricket, flag football, or frisbee. The park's north entrance is at Grand Army Plaza, where the Soldiers' and Sailors' Memorial Arch (patterned on the Arc de Triomphe in Paris) honors Civil War veterans. On Saturdays year-round, a greenmarket at the plaza throngs with shoppers.

A good way to experience the park is to walk the Long Meadow and then head to the eastern side, where you'll find the lake and most attractions, including the Lefferts Historic House, Prospect Park Audubon Center, and the LeFrak Center. The extravagant Prospect Park Carousel, built in 1912, still thrills the kids. The annual Celebrate Brooklyn! festival takes place at the Prospect Park Bandshell from early June through mid-August. Films are occasionally shown on a 50-foot-wide outdoor screen, one of the world's largest. ⊠ *450 Flatbush Ave., Prospect Park* ☎ *718/965–8951* ⊕ *www.prospectpark.org* 🎫 *Carousel $2 per ride* ⊙ *Carousel: Apr.–June, Sept., and Oct., Thurs.–Sun. noon–5; July–Labor Day, Thurs.–Sun. noon–6* Ⓜ *2, 3 to Grand Army Plaza; F, G to 7th Ave. or 15th St.–Prospect Park; B, Q to 7th Ave.*

QUICK BITES

City Subs. Just a five-minute walk from the Barclays Center, this neighborhood darling (formerly City Sub) brought a smile to the face of many Brooklynites when the shop reopened in this new location in the fall of 2015. The sandwiches are made-to-order, so get creative and invent your own, or go with one of the 29 suggested combos, each named for a different local thoroughfare. ⊠ *82 5th Ave., Park Slope* ☎ *718/636–1777* ⊕ *citysubsbrooklyn.com* ⊙ *Closed Sun.* Ⓜ *2, 3 to Bergen St.*

WORTH NOTING

FAMILY **Lefferts Historic House.** A visit to this Dutch Colonial farmhouse, built in 1783 and moved from nearby Flatbush Avenue to Prospect Park in 1918, is a window into how Brooklynites lived in the 19th century, when the area was predominately farmland. Rooms are furnished with antiques and reproductions from the 1820s, when the house was last redecorated. ⊠ *Prospect Park, 452 Flatbush Ave., at Empire Blvd., Prospect Park* ☎ *718/789–2822* ⊕ *www.prospectpark.org/lefferts* 🎫 *$3 suggested donation* ⊙ *Weekends noon–4; call for details on seasonal hrs and holidays* Ⓜ *B, Q, S to Prospect Park.*

FAMILY **Old Stone House.** The original of this reconstructed Dutch farmhouse was built in 1699 and survived until the 1890s. It played a central role in the Battle of Brooklyn, one of the largest battles of the Revolutionary War, and the small museum here focuses on the events of that week in 1776. The museum also depicts the early life of Dutch setters in the area and the years of British occupation in New York, until 1783. Music, art, plays, and other events take place year-round, including a ball game to celebrate the Brooklyn Baseball Club, which started here and gave rise to the Brooklyn Dodgers. ⊠ *Washington Park/J.J. Byrne Playground, 336 3rd St., between 4th and 5th Aves., Park Slope* ☎ *718/768–3195* ⊕ *www.theoldstonehouse.org* 🎫 *$3 suggested donation* ⊙ *Weekends 11–4 and by appt.* Ⓜ *R to Union St.; F, G, R to 4th Ave.–9th St.*

The boathouse in Prospect Park, built in 1905, was one of the first buildings in New York City to be declared a historic landmark.

PROSPECT HEIGHTS

An influx of creative young professionals and impressive eats has lifted Prospect Heights out from the shadow of nearby Park Slope. Swing by Grand Army Plaza on a Saturday to hit the borough's flagship farmers' market, where cooking demos and fresh produce entice the food-loving hoards. Or gorge on everything from lobster rolls to Korean tacos at the plaza's Food Truck Rally held on select Sundays, May through October. Vanderbilt Avenue and Washington Avenue are the main drags for restaurants and bars.

FAMILY **Barclays Center.** This rust-tinted spaceship of an arena houses two sports franchises—basketball's Brooklyn Nets and, as of fall 2015, ice hockey's New York Islanders. With a capacity rivaling Madison Square Garden, Barclays is now a regular stop for national tours, from circuses and ice capades to glossy pop stars and bearded indie rockers. Also impressive are the Barclays food vendors: a solid roster of local restaurateurs, including Williamsburg Pizza, Paisano's Butcher Shop, and Calexico. ⊠ *620 Atlantic Ave., at Flatbush Ave., Prospect Heights* ☎ *917/618–6100* ⊕ *www.barclayscenter.com* Ⓜ *2, 3, 4, 5, B, D, N, Q, R to Atlantic Ave.–Barclays Ctr.; G to Fulton St.; C to Lafayette Ave.; LIRR to Atlantic Terminal.*

FAMILY **Brooklyn Botanic Garden.** A gem even among New York's superlative
Fodor'sChoice botanical sites, this verdant 52-acre oasis charms with its array of "gar-
★ dens within the garden"—an idyllic Japanese Hill-and-Pond garden, a nearly century-old rose garden, and a Shakespeare garden. The Japanese cherry arbor turns into a breathtaking cloud of pink every spring, and

the Sakura Matsuri two-day cherry blossom festival is the largest public-garden event in America. There are entrances on Eastern Parkway, near the Prospect Park B, Q, S subway station, and on Washington Avenue, behind the Brooklyn Museum. A variety of free garden tours are available with admission; check the website for seasonal details. ✉ *150 Eastern Pkwy., Prospect Heights* ☎ *718/623–7200* ⊕ *www.bbg.org* 🎫 *$12 (free all day Tues., Sat. before noon, and weekdays mid-Nov.–mid-Feb.)* 🕑 *Mar.–Oct.: grounds Tues.–Fri. 8–6, weekends 10–6; conservatory Tues.–Sun. 10–5:30. Nov.–Feb.: grounds Tues.–Fri. 8–4:30, weekends 10–4:30; conservatory Tues.–Sun. 10–4. Closed Mon. except major holidays* Ⓜ *2, 3 to Eastern Pkwy.–Brooklyn Museum; 2, 3, 4, 5 to Franklin Ave.; S to Botanic Garden; B, Q to Prospect Park.*

FAMILY
Fodor'sChoice
★
Brooklyn Museum. First-time visitors may well gasp at the vastness of New York's second-largest museum (after Manhattan's Metropolitan Museum of Art) and one of the largest in America at 560,000 square feet of exhibition space. Along with changing exhibitions, the colossal Beaux Arts structure houses one of the best collections of Egyptian art in the world and impressive collections of African, pre-Columbian, and Native American art. It's also worth seeking out the museum's works by Georgia O'Keeffe, Winslow Homer, John Singer Sargent, George Bellows, Thomas Eakins, and Milton Avery—all stunners in a collection that ranges from Egyptian antiquities to Colonial paintings with very contemporary, cutting-edge special exhibits. The monthly (except for September) "First Saturday" free-entry night is a neighborhood party of art, music, and dancing, with food vendors and several cash bars. ✉ *200 Eastern Pkwy., at Washington Ave., Prospect Heights* ☎ *718/638–5000* ⊕ *www.brooklynmuseum.org* 🎫 *$16 suggested donation (free 1st Sat. of month), $23 combo ticket with Brooklyn Botanic Garden* 🕑 *Wed., Fri., and weekends 11–6, Thurs. 11–10; 1st Sat. of month 11–11* Ⓜ *2, 3 to Eastern Pkwy.–Brooklyn Museum.*

BED-STUY AND CROWN HEIGHTS

Crown Heights and nearby Bedford-Stuyvesant (known as Bed-Stuy) are vast and historic neighborhoods with a tumultuous past. Long since the 1991 riots that escalated tensions between the area's Hasidic and black communities, these days Crown Heights is more likely to inspire thoughts of diverse stoops and row houses, rapid gentrification, and authentic Caribbean fare. Crown Heights is also home to the Brooklyn Children's Museum and Weeksville Heritage Center.

FAMILY
Brooklyn Children's Museum. What's red, yellow, and green, and shaped like a spaceship? The Brooklyn Children's Museum. Nestled in a residential area and abutting a pretty city park, the attention-grabbing exterior suits this interactive space designed for kids—one of a few places in New York City where "little people" can run and touch and play with abandon indoors. Exhibits range from a working greenhouse to Totally Tots, where daily afternoon programming includes art experiences for kids five and under. The cornerstone is World Brooklyn, a warren of rooms dedicated to various NYC cultures—from an Italian pizza shop to a Hispanic bakery—and a replica MTA bus for fun photo ops. Feel

free to bring strollers and heavy coats: the museum may be a long walk from the subway, but the coat check takes everything free of charge. The museum has plans to expand to the DUMBO waterfront, aiming to open a new studio annex in the fall of 2016, where children and their families can discover art with the help of teaching artists. ✉ *145 Brooklyn Ave., at St. Marks Ave., Crown Heights* ☎ *718/735–4400* ⊕ *www. brooklynkids.org* ☞ *$11; free Thurs. 2–6* ☉ *Tues., Wed., and Fri.–Sun. 10–5; Thurs. 10–6* Ⓜ *C to Kingston–Throop Aves.; 3 to Kingston Ave.; A, C to Nostrand Ave.*

13

FAMILY **Weeksville Heritage Center.** Devoted to honoring the history of the 19th-century African American community of Weeksville, one of the first communities of free blacks in New York, founded by James Weeks, this Crown Heights museum comprises a new industrial-modern building by Caples Jefferson Architects, botanical gardens, and three houses that date as far back as 1838. The restored homes, located along historic, gravel Hunterfly Road, are now period re-creations depicting African American family life in the 1860s, 1900s, and 1930s. Tours (Tuesday, Thursday, and Friday at 3 pm, or by appointment for groups of six or more; $5) lead visitors through bedrooms, kitchens, and sitting rooms accented by objects such as original clothing irons and ceramics found in the area at student-led archeological digs. Throughout the year, the venue hosts exhibits that honor the neighborhood's history. ✉ *158 Buffalo Ave., Crown Heights* ☎ *718/756–5250* ⊕ *www. weeksvillesociety.org* ☉ *Tues.–Fri. 9:30–4:30* Ⓜ *A, C to Utica Ave.; 3, 4 to Crown Heights–Utica Ave.*

CONEY ISLAND

Coney Island is practically synonymous with the sounds, smells, and sights of a New York City summer: hot dogs and ice cream, suntan lotion, roller coasters, excited crowds, and weathered old men fishing.

Named Konijn Eiland (Rabbit Island) by the Dutch for its wild rabbit population, the Coney Island peninsula has a boardwalk, a 2½-mile-long beach, amusement parks, and the **New York Aquarium,** which is currently undergoing a $157 million face-lift that will showcase the much-anticipated exhibit, "Ocean Wonders: Sharks!" Nathan's Famous (*1310 Surf Avenue*) is the quintessential hot dog spot.

Among the other entertainments out here are the freakish attractions at **Coney Island Circus Sideshow** and the heart-stopping plunge of the granddaddy of all roller coasters—the **Cyclone.** The Mets' minor-league baseball team, the Cyclones, plays at MCU Park, where music concerts are also held in summer. The area's banner day is during the raucous Mermaid Parade, held in June. A fireworks display lights up the sky Friday night from late June through Labor Day.

TOP ATTRACTIONS

FAMILY **The Cyclone.** This historic wooden roller coaster first thrilled riders in 1927 and it'll still make you scream. Anticipation builds as the cars slowly clack up to the first unforgettable 85-foot plunge—and the look on your face is captured in photos that you can purchase at the end of

A stroll on the boardwalk at Coney Island is a New York summer tradition.

the ride. The Cyclone may not have the speed or the twists and turns of more modern rides, but that's all part of its rickety charm. It's one of two New York City landmarks in Coney Island; the other is Deno's Wonder Wheel. ⊠ *Luna Park, 834 Surf Ave., at W. 10th St., Coney Island* ☎ *718/373–5862* ⊕ *www.lunaparknyc.com* ⊠ *$9* ⊙ *Seasonal hrs vary, but generally Apr. and May, weekends (plus daily Apr. 3–12); June–Aug., daily; Sept. and Oct., weekends (after Labor Day)* Ⓜ *F, Q to W. 8th St.–NY Aquarium; D, F, N, Q to Coney Island–Stillwell Ave.*

FAMILY
Fodor's Choice
★

New York Aquarium. The oldest continually operating aquarium in the United States is run by the Wildlife Conservation Society; its mission is to save wildlife and wild places worldwide through science, conservation action, and education. The aquarium occupies 14 acres of beachfront property and is home to 266 aquatic species. At the Sea Cliffs, you can watch penguins, sea lions, sea otters, seals, and walrus frolic: the best action is at feeding time. The Conservation Hall and Glovers Reef building is home to marine life from Belize, Fiji, and all over the world, including angelfish, eels, rays, and piranhas. The new *Ocean Wonders: Sharks!* exhibit will bring hundreds more species, including nurse sharks, to the aquarium. Expected to be completed sometime in 2017, along with the reopening of facilities damaged by Hurricane Sandy in 2012, the highlight will be a coral-reef tunnel that provides 360-degree views of this underwater universe. ■ TIP→ Purchase tickets online for discounted rates. ⊠ *602 Surf Ave., at W. 8th St., Coney Island* ☎ *718/265–3474* ⊕ *www. nyaquarium.com* ⊠ *$11.95* ⊙ *Labor Day–Memorial Day, daily 10–4:30; Memorial Day–Labor Day, 10–6* Ⓜ *F, Q to W. 8th St.–NY Aquarium; D, F, N, Q to Coney Island–Stillwell Ave.*

QUICK BITES

Nathan's Famous. Nathan Handwerker, a Polish immigrant, founded this Coney Island hot dog stand in 1916, and what followed can only be described as a quintessential American success story. With a $300 loan and his wife Ida's secret spice recipe, Nathan set up shop and his success was almost instantaneous—Al Capone, Jimmy Durante, and Cary Grant became regulars early on, President FDR served Nathan's dogs to the king and queen of England, local-girl Barbra Streisand had them delivered to London, and Walter Matthau asked that they be served at his funeral. The century-old recipe still works: the hot dogs have good, firm texture and a snap when you bite. Buns are soft and the crinkle fries are hot, crispy, and perfectly creamy on the inside. ■TIP➔ The biggest day of the year at Nathan's is always July 4th, when competitive eaters and fans converge on Surf Avenue to crown that year's hot-dog-eating champion. In a contest that's an all-out sprint from start to the finish, the record for dogs and buns downed in 10 minutes is a nearly unimaginable 69. ⊠ *1310 Surf Ave., at Stillwell Ave., Coney Island* ☎ *718/333–2202* ⊕ *www.nathansfamous.com* Ⓜ *D, F, N, Q to Coney Island–Stillwell Ave.*

FAMILY

Fodor's Choice

★

Riegelmann Boardwalk. Built in 1923, just one year before legendary Totonno's Pizzeria opened its doors on nearby Neptune Avenue, this famous wood-planked walkway is better known as the Coney Island Boardwalk, and in summer it seems like all of Brooklyn is out strolling along the 2½-mile stretch. The quintessential walk starts at the end of the pier in Coney Island, opposite the Parachute Jump—you can see the shoreline stretched out before you, a beautiful confluence of nature and city. From here to Brighton Beach is a little over a mile and should take about a half hour at a leisurely amble. Those modernistic, rectangular structures perched over the beach are new bathrooms and lifeguard stations. ⊠ *Between W. 37th St. and Brighton 15th St., Coney Island* Ⓜ *D, F, N, Q to Coney Island–Stillwell Ave.; F, Q to W. 8th St.–NY Aquarium; B, Q to Brighton Beach; Q to Ocean Pkwy.*

WORTH NOTING

Coney Island Circus Sideshow. The cast of talented freaks and geeks who keep Coney Island's carnival tradition alive include sword swallowers, fire-eaters, knife throwers, contortionists, and Serpentina the snake dancer. Every show is an extravaganza, with 10 different acts to fascinate and impress. ⊠ *Sideshows by the Seashore, 1208 Surf Ave., at W. 12th St., Coney Island* ☎ *718/372–5159* ⊕ *www.coneyisland.com/sideshow.shtml* ⊡ *$10* ⊙ *Apr.–Sept.* Ⓜ *F, Q to W. 8th St.–NY Aquarium; D, F, N, Q to Coney Island–Stillwell Ave.*

FAMILY

Deno's Wonder Wheel Amusement Park. The star attraction at Deno's is the towering 150-foot tall Wonder Wheel. The Ferris wheel first opened in 1920, making it the oldest ride in Coney Island, and the spectacular views from the top take in a long stretch of the shoreline. Other rides for tots here include the Dizzy Dragons, the Pony Carts, and a brightly painted carousel. ⊠ *1025 Boardwalk, at W. 12th St., Coney Island*

☎ *718/372–2592* ⊕ *www.wonderwheel.com* ✉ *$7 per ride (5 rides for $30)* ⊙ *Late Mar.–Oct., hrs vary* Ⓜ *F, Q to W. 8th St.–NY Aquarium; D, F, N, Q to Coney Island–Stillwell Ave.*

BRIGHTON BEACH

A pleasant stroll just down the boardwalk from Coney Island is Brighton Beach, named after Britain's beach resort. In the early 1900s Brighton Beach was a resort in its own right, with seaside hotels that catered to rich Manhattan families visiting for the summer. Since the 1970s and '80s Brighton Beach has been known for its 100,000 Soviet émigrés. To get to the heart of "Little Odessa" from Coney Island, walk about a mile east along the boardwalk to Brighton 1st Place, then head up to Brighton Beach Avenue. To get here from Manhattan directly, take the B or Q train to the Brighton Beach stop; the trip takes about an hour from Midtown Manhattan.

FAMILY
Fodor's Choice
★

Brighton Beach. Just steps from the subway, this stretch of golden sand is the showpiece of Brooklyn's ocean-side playground. Families set up beach blankets, umbrellas, and coolers, and pickup games of beach volleyball and football add to the excitement. Calm surf, a lively boardwalk, and a handful of restaurants for shade and refreshments complete the package. That spit of land in the distance is the Rockaway Peninsula, in Queens. ⊠ *Brighton Beach Ave., between Ocean Pkwy. and Brighton 14th St., Brighton Beach* Ⓜ *B, Q to Brighton Beach; Q to Ocean Pkwy.*

Brighton Beach Avenue. The main thoroughfare of "Little Odessa" can feel more like Kiev than Manhattan. Cyrillic shop signs advertise everything from salted tomatoes and pickled mushrooms to Russian-language DVDs and Armani handbags. When the weather's good, local bakeries sell sweet honey cake, cheese-stuffed *vatrushki* danishes, and chocolatey rugelach from sidewalk tables. ⊠ *Brighton Beach Ave., between Ocean Pkwy. and Brighton 6th St., Brighton Beach* Ⓜ *B, Q to Brighton Beach.*

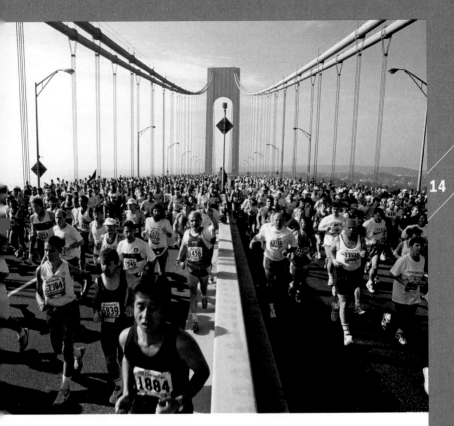

QUEENS, THE BRONX, AND STATEN ISLAND

GETTING ORIENTED

Queens, the Bronx, and Staten Island

MAKING THE MOST OF YOUR TIME

Queens is rich with museums and authentic ethnic cuisine. A day spent hopping around Long Island City and Astoria enables you to take in the PS1 Contemporary Art Center, the Museum of the Moving Image, and the Noguchi Museum. Then jump on the 7 train and sample international dishes at neighborhood eateries in Jackson Heights or Flushing.

It's easy to spend a full day at either of the Bronx's treasures: the New York Botanical Garden or the Bronx Zoo. To visit both, start early and plan a late lunch or early dinner in the Arthur Avenue area.

Many tourists' only sight of Staten Island is during a round-trip ride on the ferry, but the borough beckons with unexpected offerings in its small museums and historic neighborhoods.

GETTING HERE

Queens is served by many subway lines. To get to Astoria, take the N, Q, R, or M train. For Long Island City, take the E, M, G, or 7 train. To get to Jackson Heights, take the 7 train to the 74th Street–Broadway stop. You can also take the E, F, M, or R train to Jackson Heights–Roosevelt Avenue. The 7 also brings you out to the attractions of Flushing Meadows Corona Park, and Citi Field.

The Bronx is serviced by the 1, 2, 4, 5, 6, B, and D trains. The attractions in the Bronx are spread out across the borough, though, so you need to take different lines to get where you want to go, and it's not necessarily convenient to make connections across town. The B, D, and 4 trains all go to Yankee Stadium, and the B and D continue uptown to the vicinity of Arthur Avenue. The 2 and 5 trains take you close to the Bronx Zoo and Arthur Avenue.

From the scenic (and free) Staten Island Ferry you can catch a local bus or hop in a taxi to hit up attractions that are further afield. Tell the driver where you're going, and ask about the return bus schedule or taxi pickup.

TOP EXPERIENCES

Sampling ethnic eats in Queens

Catching a game at Yankee Stadium or Citi Field

Taking a free ride on the Staten Island Ferry

Soaking up modern art at Long Island City museums

14

QUICK BITES

Pugsley Pizza. Dig in to delicious and piping-hot pies at this fun, family-run neighborhood favorite and hangout for nearby Fordham University students; it's been a locals' go-to for quality slices for nearly 30 years. ⊠ *590 E. 191st St., Belmont* ☎ *718/365–0327* Ⓜ *4, B, D to Fordham Rd.*

SingleCut Beersmiths. Named for a body style of guitar, this craft brewery has a taproom that also serves food (like empanadas, flatbread pizzas, and brats), free tours, and live music on Friday nights. ⊠ *19-33 37th St., Astoria* ☎ *718/606–0788* ⊕ *www.singlecutbeer.com* Ⓜ *N, Q to Astoria–Ditmars Blvd.*

White Bear. The wontons at this tiny hole-in-the-wall are worth the trek to New York's other Chinatown, in Flushing. Order the No. 6: a dozen wontons with hot sauce for $5. ⊠ *135-02 Roosevelt Ave. (entrance on Prince St.), Flushing* ☎ *718/961–2322* ⊟ *No credit cards* Ⓜ *7 to Flushing–Main St.*

Sightseeing
★★★
Nightlife
★★★
Dining
★★★★
Lodging
★
Shopping
★★★★

Many tourists miss out on Queens, the Bronx, and Staten Island—the three boroughs of New York City other than the biggies for tourism, Manhattan and Brooklyn—and that's a shame. There are some noteworthy restaurants, museums, and attractions, and the subway's handful of express trains means that they're closer than you might think.

QUEENS

Updated by
Elissa Garay

Just for the museums and restaurants alone, a short 15-minute trip from Midtown on the 7, E, or M train to **Long Island City** or a slightly longer ride on the N, Q, M, or R train to **Astoria** is truly worth it. In Long Island City, major must-sees are **MoMA PS1** and the **Noguchi Museum.** No trip to Astoria—once nicknamed "Little Athens"—is complete without sampling some of the city's finest Greek and Mediterranean fare and a stop at the **Museum of the Moving Image.**

Jackson Heights boasts a diverse cornucopia of culture and cuisine and is home to one of the city's busiest Indian shopping districts. It's a wonderful place to spend an afternoon browsing shops and dining in one of the many authentic ethnic restaurants.

Top reasons to trek out to **Flushing** and **Corona** include seeing a ball game at the New York Mets' stadium, **Citi Field,** spending time at the expansive **Flushing Meadows Corona Park,** especially if traveling with kids, and devouring a wide array of Asian dim sum in Flushing's Chinatown.

ASTORIA

Head to Astoria for authentic Greek restaurants, shops, and grocery stores. Here you can buy kalamata olives and salty sheep's (or sheep-and-goat's) milk feta from store owners who can tell you where to go for the best gyro or spanakopita (spinach pie). **Taverna Kyclades** is well known for its classic Greek seafood dishes that attract diners from all five boroughs, while just a few blocks up the road, SingleCut Beersmiths

TIPS FOR QUEENS ADDRESSES

Addresses in Queens can seem confusing at first. Not only is there 30th Street and 30th Avenue, but also 30th Drive and 30th Road, all next to one another. But the system is actually logical. Sequentially numbered avenues run east-to-west, and sequentially numbered streets run north-to-south. If there are any smaller roads between avenues, they have the same number as the nearest avenue and are called roads or drives. Thus, 30th Road is one block south of 30th Avenue. Similarly, smaller side roads between streets are called places or lanes. Additionally, most addresses have two pairs of numbers, separated by a hyphen. The first pair indicates the nearest cross street, and the second gives the location on the block. If this all still seems confusing to you, there's good news: locals are used to giving directions to visitors.

14

runs free brewery tours and pours some tasty ales and lagers. Astoria, named for John Jacob Astor—America's first multimillionaire—has been the center of Greek immigrant life in New York City for more than 60 years. Today substantial numbers of Arab, Asian, Eastern European, Irish, and Latino immigrants have also joined the dwindling Greek and Italian populations that call Astoria home. The presence of the Greek community is evident on strips like Broadway, between 31st and Steinway Streets. Another busy thoroughfare is 30th Avenue, with almost every kind of food store imaginable. Astoria is also home to the nation's only museum devoted to the art, technology, and history of film, TV, and digital media. The Museum of the Moving Image has a dynamic hands-on exhibition that allows visitors to immerse themselves in the creative process of making movies and television shows.

Fodor's Choice ★ **Museum of the Moving Image.** Like switching to a wide-screen television, the Museum of the Moving Image is twice as nice as it was before the 2011 expansion and renovation. The Thomas Leeser design includes a three-story addition, new theaters, and a modern entryway. The museum is full of Hollywood and television memorabilia, but the core exhibition, *Behind the Screen,* demonstrates how movies and TV shows are produced and shown, including stations where visitors can create their own short animation, experiment with sound effects, or view the behind-the-scenes editing process of a live Mets baseball game. A wide range of films, from classic Hollywood to avant-garde works to foreign-festival hits, are generally shown weekend evenings and afternoons, and there are other special programs including film retrospectives, lectures, and workshops. ⊠ *36-01 35th Ave., at 37th St., Astoria* ☎ *718/777–6888* ⊕ *www.movingimage.us* ✉ *$12 (free Fri. after 4)* ☉ *Wed. and Thurs. 10:30–5, Fri. 10:30–8, weekends 11:30–7* Ⓜ *M, R to Steinway St.; N, Q to 36th Ave.*

Food Market Mania

CLOSE UP

Queens has always ranked high for its eclectic and authentically ethnic culinary landscape, and its foodie-friendly appeal has only been bolstered in recent years by a slate of new food markets. In Long Island City, **LIC Flea & Food** (⊠ *5-25 46th Ave.; ⊕ www.licflea.com*) runs on weekends between April and October. It features some 85 stands that range from food to handmade items, as well as a beer garden pouring Queens-brewed beers on tap from Rockaway Brewing Company, Finback Brewery, and more. The 2015-debuted **Queens Night Market** (⊕ *www.queensnightmarket. com*) is an outdoor market held Saturday evenings, late April through October in Flushing. It's reminiscent of Asia's popular food markets, and

you can expect to find about 80 vendors serving flavorful (and often adventurous) ethnic fare such as ceviche, Peking duck buns, Trinidadian shark sandwiches, and more. Finally, a beach trip to the Rockaways anytime between Memorial Day and Labor Day rewards visitors with the **Riis Park Beach Bazaar** (⊕ *www. riisparkbeachbazaar.com*). Launched in 2015, it features some half-dozen local food-and-drink vendors (try fried-chicken waffle cones from The Brooklyn Star or ice cream from Brooklyn-based Ample Hills Creamery), cultural offerings (like free weekend concerts), beach activities (volleyball, kite flying, etc.), and assorted handicrafts vendors on the waterfront at Jacob Riis Park Beach.

QUICK BITE

The Queens Kickshaw. Run by a local husband-and-wife team, the menu at this cozy spot uses fresh, high-quality ingredients in every recipe. Come here for specialty coffee, a vast variety of grilled-cheese sandwiches, and craft ales and ciders. It's close to the Museum of the Moving Image, and open for breakfast, lunch, and dinner (with brunch and late-night hours on the weekends); there's live music Friday evenings. ⊠ *40-17 Broadway, at 41st St., Astoria* ☎ *718/777–0913* ⊕ *www.thequeenskickshaw.com* Ⓜ *M, R to Steinway St.*

LONG ISLAND CITY

Long Island City (LIC) is the art capital of Queens, with MoMA PS1, which presents experimental and innovative contemporary work; the Noguchi Museum, showcasing the work of Japanese American sculptor Isamu Noguchi in a large, peaceful garden and galleries; and the Socrates Sculpture Park, with large outdoor installations fronting the East River.

Worth noting for art buffs, the free LIC Art Bus shuttles guests between Socrates Sculpture Park, the Noguchi Museum, SculptureCenter, and MoMA PS1 on Saturday and Sunday afternoons between mid-May and mid-September. It runs every 45 minutes between 1 and 6 pm.

0 · 1/4 mile

0 · 400 meters

Astoria and
Long Island City

TOP ATTRACTIONS

Fodor's Choice **MoMA PS1.** A pioneer in the "alternative-space" movement, PS1 rose
★ from the ruins of an abandoned school in 1976 as a sort of commu-
nity arts center for the future. MoMA PS1 focuses on the work of
currently active experimental and innovative artists. Long-term installations include work by Sol LeWitt, James Turrell, and Pipilotti Rist.
Every available corner of the enormous building is used; discover art not
only in former classrooms-turned-galleries, but also on the rooftop, in
the boiler room, and even in some bathrooms. Also inside the museum
is **M. Wells Dinette,** a café designed to resemble a school classroom,
with daily specials listed on the chalkboard and lunch served at your
"desk." On summer Saturdays, MoMA PS1 presents "Warm Up," an
outdoor dance party series that attracts a hip art-school crowd, held in
the courtyard noon–9. Similarly, their "Sunday Sessions" are held on
Sundays from fall through spring (hours vary) in the VW Performance
Dome and include various artistic installations, scholarly lectures, and
special performances. ⊠ *22–25 Jackson Ave., at 46th Ave., Long Island
City* ☎ *718/784–2084* ⊕ *www.momaps1.org* ⊠ *$10 suggested donation
(free with MoMA entrance ticket, within 14 days of visit); Warm Up
$18 in advance, $20 at the door; Sunday Sessions $15* ⊙ *Thurs.–Mon.
noon–6* ⊂ *M. Wells Dinette closed Tues. and Wed.* Ⓜ *7 to Court Sq.;
E, M to Court Sq.–23rd St.; G to 21st St.*

CLOSE UP

Queens Brew-and-Booze Boom

Queens has plenty on tap for craft-beer lovers with the borough's recent influx of seven inventive microbreweries. There are four breweries in Long Island City alone: **Rockaway Brewing Company** (✉ 46-01 5th St. ⊕ rockawaybrewco. com); **Transmitter Brewing** (✉ 53-02 11th St. ⊕ www.transmitterbrewing. com); **Big Alice Brewing** (✉ 808 43rd Rd. ⊕ bigalicebrewing.com); and **LIC Beer Project** (✉ 39-28 23rd St. ⊕ licbeerproject.com). In Astoria, try **SingleCut Beersmiths** (✉ 19-33 37th St. ⊕ www. singlecutbeer.com); in Glendale, hit up **Finback Brewing** (✉ 7801 77th Ave. ⊕ www.finbackbrewery. com), or try the 2016-debuted beer garden at **Queens Brewery** (✉ 1539 Covert St. ⊕ www.queensbrewery. com) for an assortment of cool brews. Prefer spirits to suds? The makers of Queens Courage gin, **Astoria Distilling Company** (✉ Falchi Building, 31-00 47th Ave. ⊕ astoriadistilling.com), recently opened a tasting room in Long Island City; its 2015-debuted operation is the first craft distillery to operate in Queens since Prohibition days.

The Noguchi Museum. In 1985 the Japanese American sculptor Isamu Noguchi (1904–88) transformed this former industrial plant into a place to display his modernist and earlier works. A peaceful central garden is surrounded by galleries, and there are some 200 pieces in stone, metal, clay, and other materials on display. Temporary exhibits have examined his collaborations with others, such as industrial designer Isamu Kenmochi, architect and inventor R. Buckminster Fuller, and choreographer Martha Graham. The museum is about a mile from subway stops; check the website for complete directions. ■ **TIP ➜ There are extended evening hours on the first Friday of the month, from May through September.** ✉ 9-01 33rd Rd., at Vernon Blvd., Long Island City ☎ 718/204–7088 ⊕ www.noguchi.org ⬆ $10 (free 1st Fri. of month) ⊗ Wed.–Fri. 10–5, weekends 11–6 Ⓜ N, Q to Broadway.

WORTH NOTING

Gantry Plaza State Park. Mosey down to this 12-acre waterfront park for sweeping views of Midtown Manhattan across the East River. The atmospheric stretch comes with piers, manicured lawns, Adirondack chairs and well-designed benches, and interesting relics that nod to Long Island City's industrial past, including restored towering old gantries (once used as shipping lifts between barges and rail cars) that fringe the river and a massive Pepsi-Cola sign that once stood atop a factory here. ✉ 4-09 47th Rd., at Center Blvd., Long Island City ☎ 718/786–6385 ⊕ nysparks.com/parks ⬆ Free ⊗ Daily 8 am–10 pm Ⓜ 7 to Vernon Blvd.–Jackson Ave.

LIC Flea & Food. On Saturdays and Sundays between April and October, the outdoor LIC Flea & Food market welcomes visitors to peruse stands from some 85 vendors selling foodie fare and handcrafted wares. Sample snacks from many Queens-based food vendors hawking everything from ethnic eats like Filipino *lumpias* (spring rolls) to fresh-baked bundt

The Noguchi Museum is dedicated to the work of visionary sculptor Isamu Noguchi.

cakes. Wash it all down at the alfresco beer garden, selling Queens-brewed beers from Rockaway Brewing Company, Finback Brewery, and more. ✉ *5-25 46th Ave., at 5th St., Long Island City* ☎ *718/224–5863* ⊕ *www.licflea.com* ⊗ *Apr.–Oct., weekends 11–7* Ⓜ *7 to Vernon Blvd.–Jackson Ave.; G to 21st St.; E, M to Court Sq.–23rd St.*

Rockaway Brewing Company. At the epicenter of the Queens microbrew boom, this laid-back brewery offers a taproom serving up tasty hand-crafted brews (take-home growlers and cans are available) and free brewery tours on weekends. ✉ *46-01 5th St., at 46th Ave., Long Island City* ☎ *718/482–6528* ⊕ *rockawaybrewco.com* Ⓜ *7 to Vernon Blvd.–Jackson Ave.; G to 21st St.; E, M to Court Sq.–23rd St.*

SculptureCenter. Founded by artists in 1928 to exhibit innovative contemporary work, SculptureCenter now occupies a former trolley repair shop that was renovated by artist Maya Lin and recently updated and expanded by Andrew Berman Architect; it's not far from MoMA PS1. Indoor and outdoor exhibition spaces sometimes close between shows; call ahead before visiting. ✉ *44-19 Purves St., at Jackson Ave., Long Island City* ☎ *718/361–1750* ⊕ *www.sculpture-center.org* ✉ *$5 suggested donation* ⊗ *Thurs.–Mon. 11–6* Ⓜ *7, G to Court Sq.; E, M to Court Sq.–23rd St.; N, Q to Queensboro Plaza.*

FAMILY **Socrates Sculpture Park.** In 1986 local artist Mark di Suvero and other residents rallied to transform what had been an abandoned landfill and illegal dump site into this 4½-acre waterfront park devoted to public art. Today a superb view of the East River and Manhattan frames changing exhibitions of contemporary sculptures and multimedia installations. Free public programs include art workshops and an annual outdoor international film series (Wednesday evenings in July and August). ■**TIP➔ Socrates is open 365 days a year, but the best time to visit is during warmer months.** Check online for a list of current and upcoming exhibitions. ✉ *32-01 Vernon Blvd., at Broadway, Long Island City* ✛ *From subway, walk about 8 blocks west on Broadway* ☎ *718/956–1819* ⊕ *www.socratessculpturepark.org* 🔊 *Free* ⊙ *10 am–sunset* Ⓜ *N, Q to Broadway.*

JACKSON HEIGHTS

Much more than just a hub for traditional Indian delicacies, Jackson Heights resembles a giant international food court. Even in the diverse borough of Queens, it stands out for being a true multicultural neighborhood. In just a few blocks surrounding the three-way intersection of Roosevelt Avenue, 74th Street, and Broadway are shops and restaurants catering to the area's strong Tibetan, Nepalese, Bangladeshi, Colombian, Mexican, and Ecuadorian communities. Built as a planned "garden community" in the late 1910s, the area boasts many prewar apartments with elaborate block-long interior gardens as well as English-style residences. Celebs who grew up in the area include Lucy Liu and Gene Simmons. It's also the birthplace of the board game Scrabble.

QUICK BITE

✕ **Kababish.** For freshly baked *naan* (Indian-style flatbread) and grilled kebabs, pop in to this wee Jackson Heights takeout-only eatery. Kababish churns out authentic Indian, Pakistani, and Bangladeshi takeout. Everything is made to order, so consider calling ahead to avoid a wait. ✉ *70-64 Broadway, at 72nd St., Jackson Heights* ☎ *718/565–5131* Ⓜ *7 to 74th St.–Broadway; E, F, M, R to Jackson Heights–Roosevelt Ave.*

FLUSHING AND CORONA

To New Yorkers, making the trip to Flushing usually means catching a baseball game at Citi Field or hunting down the best the Far East has to offer in its vibrant Chinatown. The historic town of Flushing is a microcosm of a larger city, with a bustling downtown area, fantastic restaurants, and the bucolic Flushing Meadows Corona Park nearby. Flushing may seem like a strange name for a neighborhood, but it's an English adaption of the original (and hard-to-pronounce) Dutch name Vlissingen (the Dutch named it for a favorite port city in the Netherlands).

Next door, quiet Corona could easily be overlooked, but that would be a mistake, with attractions like the Queens Zoo, Queens Museum, and New York Hall of Science spilling over into the neighborhood from within Flushing Meadows Corona Park. Here you also find two huge legacies: the Louis Armstrong House Museum and the cooling Italian ices at neighborhood institution The Lemon Ice King of Corona.

TOP ATTRACTIONS

FAMILY

Fodor's Choice

★

Citi Field. Opened in 2009, the Mets' newest stadium was designed to hark back to Ebbets Field (where the Dodgers played in Brooklyn until 1957), with a brick exterior and lots of fun features for fans of all ages, from a batting cage and Wiffle-ball field to the original giant apple taken from the team's old residence, Shea Stadium. Even those who aren't Mets fans but simply love baseball should come to see the Jackie Robinson Rotunda, a soaring multistory entrance and history exhibit dedicated to the Dodgers player who shattered baseball's color barrier. While here, don't miss the chance to taste your way through the more-than-fabulous food court, Taste of the City, set behind center field (on the Field Level), where you'll find Shake Shack burgers, Blue Smoke ribs, close to 40 beer varieties at the Big Apple Brews stand, and even lobster rolls and tacos. Still feeling nostalgic for the old Shea? Stop by the Mets Hall of Fame & Museum, or check out the plaques designating the spots where Shea's old home plate, pitching mound, and bases were in what's now parking lot D. ■**TIP→** One-hour ballpark tours are conducted at least once per month, weather permitting; see mets.com/tours for up-to-date schedule and ticketing info. ⊠ *123-01 Roosevelt Ave., at 126th St., Flushing* ☎ *718/507–8499* ⊕ *newyork.mets.mlb.com* Ⓜ *7 to Mets–Willets Point.*

FAMILY **Flushing Meadows Corona Park.** Standing in the lush grass of this park, you'd never imagine that it was once a swamp and dumping ground. But the gleaming Unisphere (an enormous 140-foot-high steel globe) might tip you off that this 898-acre park was also the site of two World's

Fairs. Take advantage of the park's barbecue pits, seasonal boat rentals, sports fields, and big cultural festivals, but don't forget that there's an art museum, science hall, zoo, theater, carousel, indoor pool, ice-skating rink, pitch-and-putt golf and minigolf course, and even a model-airplane field. There's way too much to see here to pack into a day, so aim to hit a few primary spots, noting that while several are clustered together on the northwest side of the park, visitors should be prepared for long peaceful walks in between. The flat grounds are ideal for family biking; bike rentals are available at two locations from March to October. The park is open from 6 am to 9 pm, 365 days a year (like most city parks, it's advisable to exercise caution when visiting outside of sunlight hours). ⊠ *Between 111th St./Grand Central Pkwy. and Van Wyck Expressway/ College Point Blvd., Flushing* ⊕ *www.nycgovparks.org/parks/fmcp* ☞ *Free parking available* Ⓜ *7 to 111th St. or Mets–Willets Point.*

FAMILY **New York Hall of Science.** At the northwestern edge of Flushing Meadows Corona Park, the New York Hall of Science has more than 400 hands-on exhibits that make science a playground for inquisitive minds of all ages. Climb aboard a replica of John Glenn's space capsule, throw a fastball and investigate its speed, explore Charles and Ray Eames's classic Mathematica exhibition, or check out the newest exhibit, *Connected Worlds,* which demonstrates the interconnectedness of ecosystems via animation and motion-activated displays. ⊠ *47-01 111th St., at 48th Ave., Corona* ☎ *718/699–0005* ⊕ *www.nysci.org* 💲 *$15 (free Fri. 2–5 pm and Sun. 10–11 am)* ⊗ *Weekdays 9:30–5, weekends 10–6* ☞ *3-D Theater, Rocket Park Mini Golf, and Science Playground require additional fees; parking $10* Ⓜ *7 to 111th St.*

Queens Museum. Between the zoo and the Unisphere in Flushing Meadows Corona Park lies the Queens Museum. Don't miss the astonishing Panorama of the City of New York, a nearly 900,000-building model of NYC made for the 1964 World's Fair. There are also rotating exhibitions of contemporary art and a permanent collection of Louis Comfort Tiffany stained glass. The museum recently doubled in size after a major expansion project, which resulted in more exhibitions, a café, and areas for family activities. There are free guided tours on Sunday afternoons. ⊠ *Flushing Meadows Corona Park, New York City Building, Corona* ⟟ *From the subway, the museum is about a 15-minute walk southwest through Flushing Meadows Corona Park* ☎ *718/592–9700* ⊕ *www. queensmuseum.org* 💲 *$8 suggested donation* ⊗ *Wed.–Sun. noon–6* ☞ *Free (limited) parking* Ⓜ *7 to Mets–Willets Point.*

FAMILY **Queens Zoo.** Also in Flushing Meadows Corona Park is the intimate Queens Zoo, dedicated to the animals of North and South America. The 11-acre facility features puma, Andean bears, Canadian lynx, and *pudu*—the world's smallest deer species. The zoo also maintains a farm with domesticated animals like sheep, goats, horses, rabbits, and more. ⊠ *53-51 111th St., at 53rd Ave., Corona* ☎ *718/271–1500* ⊕ *www. queenszoo.com* 💲 *$8* ⊗ *Apr.–Oct., weekdays 10–5, weekends and holidays 10–5:30; Nov.–Mar., daily 10–4:30. Last ticket sold 30 mins before closing* Ⓜ *7 to 111th St.*

The big matches for the U.S. Open happen at Arthur Ashe Stadium, part of the USTA Billie Jean King National Tennis Center.

USTA Billie Jean King National Tennis Center. Each year, from late August through early September, 700,000 fans come here for the U.S. Open, which claims the title of highest-attended annual sporting event in the world. The rest of the year, the 34 courts (19 outdoor and 12 indoor, all DecoTurf, plus 3 stadium courts) are open to the public for $24–$68 hourly. Make reservations up to two days in advance. ⊠ *Flushing Meadows Corona Park, Flushing* ⚓ *Walk 3 mins down the ramp from the subway* ☎ *718/760–6200* ⊕ *www.ntc.usta.com* ☉ *Daily 6 am–midnight; closed major holidays and 1 month around U.S. Open* ☞ *Limited free parking available* Ⓜ *7 to Mets–Willets Point.*

WORTH NOTING

Louis Armstrong House Museum. For the last 28 years of his life the famed jazz musician lived in this modest three-story house in Corona with his wife Lucille. Take a 40-minute guided tour, and note the difference between the rooms vividly decorated by Lucille in charming midcentury style and Louis's dark den, cluttered with phonographs and reel-to-reel tape recorders. Although photographs and family mementos throughout the house impart knowledge about Satchmo's life, it's in his den that you really begin to understand his spirit. Exclusive to the museum, guests can also tune in to intimate audio clips of Louis playing the trumpet or telling jokes on his home-recorded private tapes. The museum also hosts Armstrong-related special events and a "Hot Jazz / Cool Garden" summer concert series; check their website for details. ⊠ *34-56 107th St., at 37th Ave., Corona* ☎ *718/478–8274* ⊕ *www.louisarmstronghouse.org* 🎫 *$10, includes guided house tour* ☉ *Tues.–Fri. 10–5, weekends noon–5; mandatory tours depart hourly (last tour at 4 pm)* Ⓜ *7 to 103rd St.–Corona Plaza.*

NEED A BREAK?

✕ **The Lemon Ice King of Corona.** If you're looking for an authentic Queens experience, there are few as true as eating an Italian ice from The Lemon Ice King of Corona on a hot summer day. A neighborhood institution of more than 60 years, there are dozens of flavors to dig into (just note there are no seats). ✉ *52-02 108th St., at 52nd Ave., Corona* ☎ *718/699–5133* ⊕ *www.thelemonicekingofcorona.com* Ⓜ *7 to 111th St.*

THE ROCKAWAYS

"Hitch a ride to Rockaway Beach" by taking the A train to its southernmost terminus, where the transformation of the once-neglected Rockaways (an area spanning several neighboring beach communities along the skinny Rockaway Peninsula) into a sort of Williamsburg-on-the-waterfont is fully underway. Its anti-Hamptons hipster beach scene is back on track following damage sustained during Hurricane Sandy, back in 2012. Throughout beach season (late May through mid-September), buzzy restaurants and beach bars draw crowds (including the new Riis Park Beach Bazaar at Jacob Riis Park), as do the sandy shores, with plenty of water activities beyond swimming, like surfing, Jet Skiing, and even whale- and dolphin-watching cruises.

Riis Park Beach Bazaar. Launched in 2015, this outdoor fair features about a half-dozen local food-and-drink vendors (try fried-chicken waffle cones from **The Brooklyn Star** or ice cream from Brooklyn-based **Ample Hills Creamery**), cultural offerings (like free weekend concerts), beach activities (volleyball, kite flying, etc.), and assorted handicrafts vendors on the waterfront at **Jacob Riis Park Beach.** Facilities and vendors are generally open from Memorial Day through Labor Day, with most activity unfolding on weekends. ✉ *Jacob Riis Park, Gateway National Recreation Area, 16702 Rockaway Beach Blvd., Rockaway Park, Queens* ⊕ *www.riisparkbeachbazaar.com* ⊙ *Memorial Day–Labor Day, daily 11 am–late; Labor Day–Memorial Day, Fri. 4 pm–late; weekends 10 am to late.*

QUICK BITE

✕ **Bungalow Bar & Restaurant.** This casual waterfront restaurant and bar serves up beach-friendly frozen drinks and signature seafood-centric dishes like lobster grilled cheese. Pull up a chair on the bustling outdoor deck facing Jamaica Bay to wind down with sunset views, paired with live music or DJs most summer nights. ✉ *377 Beach 92nd St., at Beach Channel Dr., Queens* ☎ *718/945–2100* ⊕ *www.bungalowbarny.com* Ⓜ *A Shuttle to Beach 90th St.*

THE BRONX

Whether you're relaxing at a ball game, indulging in fresh mozzarella and cannoli on Arthur Avenue, or scoping out exotic species at the zoo, there's plenty of fun to be had here. Named for the area's first documented European settler, Jonas Bronck, the Bronx is often the city's most misunderstood borough. Its reputation as a gritty, down-and-out

Two bronze rhinoceros statues stand at the entrance to the Keith W. Johnson Zoo Center at the Bronx Zoo. They're modeled after a rhino named Bessie, who lived at the zoo from 1923 to 1962.

place is a little outdated, and there's lots of beauty if you know where to look. There is more parkland in the Bronx than in any other borough, as well as one of the world's finest botanical collections, the largest metropolitan zoo in the country, and, of course, Yankee Stadium.

TOP ATTRACTIONS

FAMILY

Fodor's Choice

★

Bronx Zoo. When it opened its gates in 1899, the Bronx Zoo had less than 800 animals. But today, with 265 acres and more than 10,000 animals (representing 700-plus species), it's the largest metropolitan zoo in the United States. Get up close and personal with exotic creatures in outdoor settings that re-create natural habitats; you're often separated from them by no more than a moat or wall of glass. Don't miss the **Congo Gorilla Forest**, a 6½-acre re-creation of a lush African rain forest with two troops of western lowland gorillas, as well as mandrills, okapis, and red river hogs. At **Tiger Mountain** an open viewing shelter lets you get incredibly close to Siberian tigers, who frolic in a pool and lounge outside (even in cold weather). As the big cats are often napping at midday, aim to visit in the morning or evening. In the $62 million exhibit **Madagascar!**, the formality of the old Lion House has been replaced with a verdant re-creation of one of the most threatened natural habitats in the world. Here you see adorable lemurs and far-from-adorable hissing cockroaches.

Go on a mini-safari via the **Wild Asia Monorail,** May through October, weather permitting. As you wend your way through the forest, see Asian elephants, Indo-Chinese tigers, Indian rhinoceroses, *gaur* (the world's largest cattle), Mongolian wild horses, and several deer and antelope species. Try to visit the most popular exhibits, such as Congo Gorilla

Forest, early to avoid lines later in the day. In winter the outdoor exhibitions have fewer animals on view, but there are also fewer crowds, and plenty of indoor exhibits to savor. Also note that there is an extra charge for some exhibits. If you want to see everything, you'll save money by purchasing the Total Experience ticket. ✉ *2300 Southern Blvd., near 187th St., Belmont* ☎ *718/220–5100* ⊕ *www.bronxzoo.com* ✍ *General admission $16.95–$19.95 (extra charge for some exhibits); Total Experience $23.95–$33.95; free entry Wed. ($15 suggested donation; some attractions extra)* ☉ *Apr.–Oct., weekdays 10–5, weekends and holidays 10–5:30; Nov.–Mar., daily 10–4:30. Last entry to exhibits is 30 mins before closing* ☞ *Check website for seasonal discounts available when purchasing tickets online. Parking $16* Ⓜ *2, 5 to Pelham Pkwy. or BxM11 express bus to Bronx River entrance.*

FAMILY

Fodor'sChoice

★

New York Botanical Garden. Considered one of the leading botany centers in the world, this 250-acre garden is one of the best reasons to make a trip to the Bronx. Built around the dramatic gorge of the Bronx River, the Garden is home to lush indoor and outdoor gardens and acres of natural forest, and offers classes, concerts, and special exhibits. Be astounded by the captivating fragrance of the Peggy Rockefeller Rose Garden's 4,000 plants of more than 650 varieties; see intricate orchids that look like the stuff of science fiction; relax in the quiet of the forest or the calm of the Conservatory; or take a jaunt through the Everett Children's Adventure Garden: a 12-acre, indoor-outdoor museum with a boulder maze, giant animal topiaries, and a plant discovery center.

The Garden's roses bloom in June and September, but there's plenty to see year-round. The Victorian-style **Enid A. Haupt Conservatory** houses re-creations of misty tropical rain forests and arid African and North American deserts, as well as exhibitions such as the annual Holiday Train Show and Orchid Show. The **All-Garden Pass** gives you access to the Conservatory, Rock Garden (Apr.–Oct.), tram tour, Everett Children's Adventure Garden, and other special exhibitions. ✉ *2900 Southern Blvd., Belmont* ☎ *718/817–8700* ⊕ *www.nybg.org* 🎫 *All-Garden Pass $20–$30. Grounds only admission is free Sat. 9–10 and all day Wed. (available otherwise only to NYC residents for $13)* ☉ *Tues.–Sun. 10–6 (mid-Jan.–Feb. 10–5); some holiday Mon. 10–6 (check online)* 🚗 *Parking $15* Ⓜ *B, D to Bedford Park Blvd.; 4 to Bedford Park Blvd.–Lehman College; then walk about 8 blocks downhill to the Garden (or take the Bx26 bus). Metro-North (Harlem local line) to Botanical Garden.*

14

FAMILY

Fodor'sChoice

★

Yankee Stadium. See the "Bronx Bombers" in action at their 2009-debuted, $1.5 billion Yankee Stadium (set right across the street from the site of the original stadium, aka "the House that Ruth Built"), which got off to a good start, with the Yankees winning the World Series in its inaugural year. Tickets can be pricey, but the experience is like watching baseball in a modern-day coliseum. It's quite opulent: a traditional white frieze adorns the stadium's top; inside, limestone-and-marble hallways are lined with photos of past Yankee greats; lower-level seats have cushions, cup holders, and easy access to a boffo "meatery," NYY Steak. History buffs and hard-core fans should visit the Yankees Museum (set on the main level and open till the end of the eighth inning), filled with historical team memorabilia, and Monument Park (closes 45 minutes prior to first pitch), with plaques of past Yankee legends, by center field. ■TIP➔ Pregame and off-season one-hour stadium tours are held on a near-daily basis year-round; visit the Yankees website for more info on times and ticketing. ✉ *1 E. 161st St., at River Ave., Bronx* ☎ *718/293–4300* ⊕ *newyork.yankees.mlb.com* ☉ *Baseball season runs Apr.–Oct.* Ⓜ *4, B, D to 161st St.–Yankee Stadium.*

WORTH NOTING

Arthur Avenue (Belmont). Manhattan's Little Italy is sadly overrun with mediocre restaurants aimed at tourists, but Belmont, the Little Italy of the Bronx, is a real, thriving Italian-American community. Unless you have family in the area, the main reason to come here is for the food: eating it, buying it, looking at it fondly through windows, and chatting with shopkeepers so you can get recipe advice.

Nearly a century after pushcarts on Arthur Avenue catered to Italian-American workers constructing the zoo and Botanical Garden, the area teems with meat markets, bakeries, cheese makers, and shops selling kitchenware (espresso machines, pasta makers, etc.). There are long debates about which store or restaurant is the "best," but thanks to generations of Italian grandmothers, vendors here don't dare serve anything less than superfresh, handmade foods.

Although the area is no longer solely Italian—many Latinos and Albanians share this neighborhood now—Italians dominate the food scene. The covered **Arthur Avenue Retail Market** is a terrific starting point. It houses some dozen vendors. Regulars mostly shop on Saturday afternoon; many stores are shuttered on Sunday and after 5 pm. ⊠ *Arthur Ave. between Crescent Ave./184th St. and 188th St., and 187th St. between Lorillard Pl. and Cambreleng Ave., Belmont* ⊕ *www.bronxlittleitaly.com* Ⓜ *4, B, D to Fordham Rd., then it's about a 15-min walk (or take Bx12 bus).*

QUICK BITE

✕ **Artuso Pastry.** Step inside this neighborhood mainstay near Arthur Avenue for a drool-worthy selection of cakes, cookies, and pastries, including the signature cannolis. Artuso's has been run by the same Italian-American family for nearly 70 years, and the impassioned proprietors and community feel only add flavor to the shop's outstanding selection of sweets. ⊠ *670 E. 187th St., at Cambreleng Ave., Belmont* ☎ *718/367–2515* ⊕ *artusopastry.com* Ⓜ *4, B, D to Fordham Rd., walk 15 mins east.*

Edgar Allan Poe Cottage. The beloved American poet-writer's legacy is detailed at this historic house museum, tucked into a bustling section of the Bronx. The small farmhouse, dating to 1812, housed Poe, his young, ailing wife, Virginia, and his mother-in-law during the last years of his life from 1846 to 1849. Rooms are filled with reproduction period pieces, as well as a handful of personal effects that may have inspired the enduring poems Poe wrote here, like "Annabel Lee" and "The Bells." The surrounding green space in Poe Park lends well to the transporting back-in-time feel of a visit here. Audio and guided tours are included with admission. ⊠ *2640 Grand Concourse, at East Kingsbridge Rd., Bronx* ☎ *718/881–8900* ⊕ *bronxhistoricalsociety.org/poe-cottage* ⊠ *$5* ⊗ *Thurs. and Fri. 10–3, Sat. 10–4, Sun. 1–5* Ⓜ *4, B, D to Kingsbridge Rd.*

OFF THE BEATEN PATH

Wave Hill. Drawn by stunning views of the Hudson River and New Jersey's dramatic Palisades cliffs, 19th-century Manhattan millionaires built summer homes in the Bronx neighborhood of Riverdale. One of the most magnificent, Wave Hill, is today a 28-acre public garden and cultural center that attracts visitors from all over the world. Along with exquisite gardens, grand beech and oak trees tower above wide lawns, while an elegant pergola overlooks the majestic river view, and benches on curving pathways provide quiet respite. Open year-round, Wave Hill House (1843) and Glyndor House (1927) host art exhibitions, Sunday concerts, wellness-minded activities, and gardening workshops. Even England's Queen Mother stayed here during a visit, back when the estate was privately owned (it's no longer open to overnight guests). It's worth the schlep. ⊠ *W. 249th St., at Independence Ave., Riverdale* ☎ *718/549–3200* ⊕ *www.wavehill.org* ⊠ *$8 (free Tues. and Sat. 9–noon)* ⊗ *Mid-Mar.–Oct., Tues.–Sun. 9–5:30; Nov.–mid-Mar., Tues.–Sun. 9–4:30; closed Mon. except select holidays. Free garden tours Sun. at 2* ☞ *Parking $8* Ⓜ *1 to Van Cortlandt Park–242nd St. (free hourly shuttle service between 9:10 am and 3:10 pm); A to Inwood–207th St., then Bx7 or Bx20 bus to W. 252nd St.*

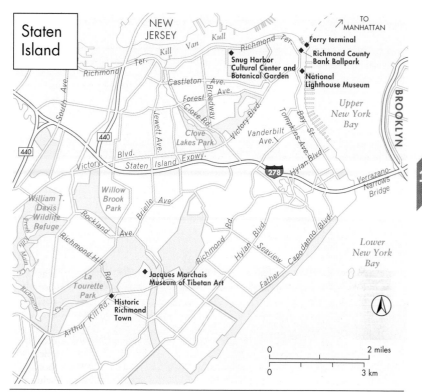

Staten
Island

NEW
JERSEY

Van Kull

Kill

Ter.

Richmond

Richmond Ter.

Ferry terminal

Richmond County
Bank Ballpark

Snug Harbor
Cultural Center and
Botanical Garden

National
Lighthouse Museum

Castleton Ave.

Forest Ave.

Broadway

Clove Rd.

Jewett Ave.

*Clove
Lakes Park*

Victory Blvd.

*Vanderbilt
Ave.*

Tompkins Ave.

Bay St.

Hylan Blvd.

Upper
New York
Bay

BROOKLYN

440

440

Blvd.

Victory

Staten Island Expwy.

278

Willow
Brook
Park

Brielle Ave.

Rockland Ave.

Richmond Hill Rd.

William T.
Davis
Wildlife
Refuge

Richmond Rd.

Hylan Blvd.

Seaview

Capodanno Blvd.

Father

Verrazano-
Narrows
Bridge

14

Lower
New York
Bay

La
Tourette
Park

Jacques Marchais
Museum of Tibetan Art

Historic
Richmond
Town

Arthur Kill Rd.

South Ave.

0 _____ 2 miles

0 _____ 3 km

STATEN ISLAND

A free 25-minute ferry voyage from the southern tip of Manhattan to
Staten Island provides one of the city's best views of the Statue of Liberty
and the downtown Manhattan skyline. Upon arrival in the St. George
neighborhood, it's hard to miss the **waterfront promenade**, with its Manhattan skyline views and "Postcards" 9/11 memorial, or the Richmond
County Bank Ballpark, the home of the **Staten Island Yankees** (⊕ *www.
siyanks.com*), where minor leaguers in pinstripes affectionately known
as "Baby Bombers" dream of one day playing in the major leagues
in the Bronx. Also in St. George, come 2017, look out for the debut
of two major attractions: the **Empire Outlets** (⊕ *www.empireoutletsnyc.
com*), the city's first outlets mall with more than 100 planned shops,
a hotel, and waterfront dining options. The 630-foot-high **New York
Wheel** (⊕ *newyorkwheel.com*), meanwhile, will be the tallest observation wheel in the world, accommodating up to 1,440 people per ride.

When venturing beyond the borough's northernmost tip, you will find
that Staten Island is full of surprises. Along with suburban sprawl, there
are wonderful small museums, including a premier collection of Tibetan
art; walkable woodlands; and a historic village replicating New York's
rural past. From the ferry terminal, grab an S40 bus to the **Snug Harbor**

DID YOU KNOW?

Many New Yorkers consider the Staten Island Ferry the ultimate inexpensive date. Its decks provide romantic waterfront views of the Statue of Liberty and Lower Manhattan without costing a cent (and beer is a bargain).

Cultural Center (less than 10 minutes) or take the S74 and combine visits to the **Jacques Marchais Museum of Tibetan Art** and **Historic Richmond Town.**

Legally part of New York City since 1898, Staten Island is in many ways a world apart. The city's most suburban borough (sometimes called the "Forgotten Borough" by locals), is geographically more separate, less populous, politically more conservative, and ethnically more homogeneous than the rest of the city.

TOP ATTRACTIONS

Jacques Marchais Museum of Tibetan Art. At the top of a hill sits this replica of a Tibetan monastery containing one of the largest collections of Tibetan and Himalayan sculpture, paintings, and artifacts outside Tibet. Meditate with visiting Buddhist monks, or just enjoy the peaceful views from the terraced garden. ⊠ *338 Lighthouse Ave., Lighthouse Hill* ☎ *718/987–3500* ⊕ *www.tibetanmuseum.org* ⧈ *$6* ⊘ *Apr.–Dec. 22, Wed.–Sun. 1–5; Feb. and Mar., Fri.–Sun. 1–5; Jan., by appt. only* Ⓜ *S74 bus to Lighthouse Ave. (35- to 45-min ride from ferry terminal) and walk uphill 15 mins; cab fare from ferry terminal is about $20.*

FAMILY

Fodor'sChoice
★

Snug Harbor Cultural Center and Botanical Garden. Once part of a retirement center for sailors, this 83-acre cultural center is now a popular spot to engage with contemporary art and historical collections. Enjoy the **Children's Museum** (*www.sichildrensmuseum.org; $6*), or take a stroll through lush gardens. (Note that all on-site attractions can be visited—and, if applicable, ticketed—independently of each other.)

Made up of 26 landmarked buildings, nine botanic gardens, 10 acres of wetlands, and a 2-acre farm, Snug Harbor is also home to a new outpost of the **Staten Island Museum** (*www.statenislandmuseum.org; $5*), with exhibits spanning art, history, and science; the **New York Chinese Scholar's Garden** (*$5*); as well as dance and music studios, art galleries, and residency programs. Main Hall—the oldest building on the property, dating to 1833—is home to the **Eleanor Proske Visitors Center** (*free*) and the **Newhouse Center for Contemporary Art** (*$5*), which exhibits artworks connected to Snug Harbor's history. Next door, the **Noble Maritime Collection** (*www.noblemaritime.org; suggested donation*) maintains historic collections specific to Staten Island and Snug Harbor's maritime past. ⊠ *1000 Richmond Terr., between Snug Harbor Rd. and Tysen St., Livingston* ⊕ *From the Staten Island Ferry terminal, take the S40 bus 2 miles (about 7 mins) to the Snug Harbor Rd. stop. Otherwise, grab a car service at the ferry terminal (the ride should cost about $8)* ☎ *718/448–2500* ⊕ *www.snug-harbor.org* ⧈ *Grounds and Botanical Gardens free; $8 Chinese Scholar's Garden and Newhouse Center combo ticket; free parking* ⊘ *Grounds and Botanical Gardens daily dawn–dusk; Children's Museum Tues.–Fri. 11–5, weekends 10–5, school holidays 10–6; Staten Island Museum weekdays 11–5, Sat. 10–5, Sun. noon–5; New York Chinese Scholar's Garden Wed.–Sun. 10–5; visitor center and Newhouse Center for Contemporary Art Wed.–Sun. 10–5; Noble Maritime Collection Thurs.–Sun. 1–5 or by appt.; check websites for seasonal hrs* ☞ *Packing a picnic is recommended.*

14

WORTH NOTING

FAMILY **Historic Richmond Town.** Think of a small-scale version of Virginia's Colonial Williamsburg (the polar opposite of Brooklyn's scene-y Williamsburg), and you'll understand the appeal of Historic Richmond Town, NYC's only living-history museum. This 100-acre village, constructed from 1695 to the 19th century, was the site of Staten Island's original county seat. Fifteen of the site's 27 historic buildings are open to the public; more than $12 million has been raised for ongoing renovations to many of the structures. Highlights include the Gothic Revival **Courthouse,** the one-room **General Store,** and the **Voorlezer's House,** the oldest schoolhouse in America (it served as a residence and place of worship, in addition to an elementary school). Also on-site is the **Staten Island Historical Society Museum,** built in 1848 as the second county clerk's and surrogate's office, which now houses Staten Island artifacts plus changing exhibits about the island.

You may see staff in period dress demonstrate Early American crafts and trades such as tinsmithing or basket making, though the general era meant to be re-created is 1820–1860. December brings a month-long Christmas celebration; check the website for other special events and educational programs held throughout the year. ✉ *441 Clarke Ave., at St. Patrick's Pl., Richmondtown* ✛ *Take the S74 bus (30–45 mins) or a car service (about $20) from the ferry terminal* ☎ *718/351–1611* ⊕ *www.historicrichmondtown.org* ⌨ *$8 (free Fri.); free parking* ☺ *Wed.–Sun. 1–5; guided tours Wed.–Fri. at 2:30, weekends at 2 and 3:30* Ⓜ *S74 bus to Richmond Rd./St. Patrick's Pl.*

National Lighthouse Museum. Just a short stroll from the ferry terminal, this museum sheds "light" on lighthouse history throughout America. It's housed in a 1912 foundry that was once part of an 18-building complex for the U.S. Lighthouse Service General Depot, which was the center of all lighthouse operations in the country from 1864–1939. Only six structures remain, including underground vaults, an administration building where architects designed the country's lighthouses, and buildings where Fresnel lenses were assembled. Self-guided visits through the small museum take in exhibits and artifacts surrounding the history, technology, and keepers behind lighthouses, illustrating the role they collectively played in American maritime history. ✉ *200 Promenade, at Lighthouse Point, St. George* ✛ *5-min walk south of Staten Island Ferry terminal* ☎ *718/390–0040* ⊕ *lighthousemuseum. org* ⌨ *$5* ☺ *Daily 11–5.*

WHERE TO EAT

EAT LIKE A LOCAL

A handful of foods are associated with New York City: apples (big ones, obviously), pizza, pastrami, hot dogs, bagels—the list of earthly delights is long and delicious. These, generally speaking, are what the locals tend to talk about.

FOOD TRUCKS

The food-truck movement is officially on. It seems there's a special truck for everything from ethnic eats to fresh-baked sweets. The southern end of Washington Square, near NYU, is a prime location, with trucks lined up serving the cuisines of Holland, Colombia, Cambodia, and Mexico, but you can find food trucks parked all over town, some with legendary followings and Twitter feeds to help you find them. Thompson Hotels, which has several properties in New York, even has a Food Truck Concierge.

PIZZA

There are few things more Big Apple than a slice of pizza, its bottom crust crispy from the coal oven. There are take-out joints for slices and sit-down restaurants that only serve pies; some are thin crust, some are thick, some even have fried dough, and everyone has a favorite. There's no question that pizza will always be synonymous with New York, but the crust is being elevated to a real art form these days. Some people say the reason the pizza here is so good is because of the excellent quality of the New York water.

SOUL FOOD IN HARLEM

Sylvia Woods, the "Queen of Soul Food" and proprietor of the eponymous Harlem restaurant, may have ascended to that great soul food restaurant in the sky, but the cuisine lives on in this historic neighborhood—in fact, more now than ever, since celeb-chef Marcus Samuelsson moved into the area, opening the Red Rooster, a global eatery that gives a big nod to soul food.

CHINESE FOOD

There's Chinese food and then there's New York's downtown Chinatown Chinese food, which some visitors might find head-scratchingly unfamiliar. That's because Chinatown boasts a diverse population from China's many regions, which means menus are going to look deliciously foreign to the uninitiated. Go ahead, point and order something you've never heard of. Restaurants serving dim sum, which are basically different kinds of small fried or steamed dumplings, are popular for weekend breakfast.

BURGERS

Hamburgers will forever be a part of the Big Apple dining landscape. But it so happens that it's never been a better time to be a burger eater, and nearly every restaurant—American or not—has some kind of burger on its menu. If you're a discriminating burger lover, look for the name Pat LaFrieda, a meat purveyor

par excellence. Just don't expect to save any money; it's not unusual to see a $20 hamburger on a menu.

GASTROPUBS

The gastropub phenomenon, imported from London, began with the Spotted Pig in the West Village, and within a few years, every neighborhood had one. And why not? Blending a casual pub atmosphere with way-better-than-average pub grub is a fun and tasty combination that's hard to beat.

BANH MI SANDWICHES

The banh mi sandwich has grabbed the attention of Big Apple eaters in recent years and has not let go. This French-influenced Vietnamese sandwich consists of pork, pâté, carrots, cilantro, and jalapeño peppers stuffed into a baguette. This is a delicacy worth seeking out, so check the menus at our top Asian restaurant picks.

LOCAVORE

The focus on local food and beverages has definitely taken hold at NYC restaurants. Menus flaunt the nearby provenance of their meat and produce, whether it's from upstate New York or from the restaurant's rooftop garden. Wine lists frequently include excellent Long Island wines, as well as bourbon and other spirits brewed as close as the Brooklyn Navy Yards or the Hudson Valley.

15

Updated by
David Farley

Ready to take a bite out of New York? Hope you've come hungry. In a city where creativity is expressed in innumerable ways, the food scene takes center stage, with literally thousands of chances to taste what Gotham is all about. Whether lining up at street stands, gobbling down legendary deli and diner grub, or chasing a coveted reservation at the latest celebrity-chef venue, New Yorkers are a demanding yet appreciative audience.

Every neighborhood offers temptations high, low, and in between, meaning there's truly something for every taste, whim, and budget. No matter how you approach dining out here, it's hard to go wrong. Planning a day of shopping among the glittering flagship boutiques along 5th and Madison? Stop into one of the Upper East Side's storied restaurants for a repast among the "ladies who lunch." Clubbing in the Meatpacking District? Tuck into a meal at eateries as trendy as their patrons. Craving authentic ethnic? From food trucks to hidden joints, there are almost more choices than there are appetites. Recent years have also seen entire food categories, from ramen to meatballs to mac 'n' cheese, riffed upon and fetishized, and at many restaurants you find an almost religious reverence for seasonal, locally sourced cuisine.

And don't forget—New York is still home to more celebrity chefs than any other city. Your chances of running into your favorite cookbook author, Food Network celeb, or paparazzi-friendly chef are high, adding even more star wattage to a restaurant scene with an already through-the-roof glamour quotient. Newfound economic realities, however, have revived appreciation for value, meaning you can tap into wallet-friendly choices at every level of the food chain. Rest assured, this city does its part to satisfy your appetite. Ready, set, eat.

PLANNING

CHILDREN

Although it's unusual to see children in the dining rooms of Manhattan's most elite restaurants, dining with youngsters in New York does not have to mean culinary exile. Many of the restaurants reviewed in this chapter are excellent choices for families, and are marked as such.

RESERVATIONS

It's always a good idea to plan ahead. Some renowned restaurants like Per Se, Daniel, Brooklyn Fare, and Momofuku Ko are booked weeks or even months in advance. If that's the case, you can get lucky at the last minute if you're flexible—and friendly. Most restaurants keep a few tables open for walk-ins and VIPs. Show up for dinner early (5:30) or late (after 10), and politely inquire about any last-minute vacancies or cancellations.

Occasionally, an eatery may take your credit-card number and ask you to call the day before your scheduled meal to reconfirm: don't forget or you could lose out, or possibly be charged for your oversight.

WHAT TO WEAR

New Yorkers like to dress up, and so should you. Whatever your style, dial it up a notch. Have some fun while you're at it. Pull out the clothes you've been saving for a special occasion and get glamorous. Unfair as it is, the way you look can influence how you're treated—and where you're seated. Generally speaking, jeans and a button-down shirt suffice at most table-service restaurants in the $ to $$ range. In reviews, we note dress only when a jacket or jacket and tie are required. If you have doubts, call the restaurant and ask.

TIPPING AND TAXES

In most restaurants, tip the waiter 15%–20%. (To figure out a 20% tip quickly, just move the decimal point one place to the left on your total and double that amount.) Tip at least $1 per drink at the bar, and $1 for each coat checked. Never tip the maître d' unless you're out to impress your guests or expect to pay another visit soon.

SMOKING

Smoking is prohibited in all enclosed public spaces in New York City, including restaurants and bars.

HOURS

New Yorkers seem ready to eat at any hour. Many restaurants stay open between lunch and dinner, some have late-night seating, and still others serve around the clock. Restaurants that serve breakfast often do so until noon or later. Restaurants in the East Village, Lower East Side, SoHo, TriBeCa, and Greenwich Village are likely to remain open late, whereas Midtown spots and those in the Theater and Financial districts and uptown generally close earlier. Unless otherwise noted, the restaurants listed in this guide are open daily for lunch and dinner.

15

PRICES

Be sure to ask the price of the daily specials recited by the waiter; the charge for specials at some restaurants is noticeably out of line with the other prices on the menu. Beware of the $10 bottle of water; ask for tap water instead, and always review your bill.

If you eat early or late, you may be able to take advantage of a prix-fixe deal not offered at peak hours. Most upscale restaurants have great lunch deals.

Credit cards are widely accepted, but many restaurants (particularly smaller ones downtown) accept only cash. If you plan to use a credit card, it's a good idea to confirm that it is acceptable when making reservations or before sitting down to eat.

WHAT IT COSTS AT DINNER				
	$	$$	$$$	$$$$
RESTAURANTS	under $13	$13–$24	$25–$35	over $35

Restaurant prices are the average cost of a main course at dinner or, if dinner is not served, at lunch.

15

CHECK BEFORE YOU GO

The nature of the restaurant industry means that places open and close in a New York minute. It's always a good idea to phone ahead and make sure your restaurant is still turning tables.

RESTAURANT REVIEWS

Listed alphabetically within neighborhoods. Use the coordinate (⊕ 1:B2) at the end of each listing to locate a property on the corresponding map at the end of the chapter.

LOWER MANHATTAN

FINANCIAL DISTRICT

The southern tip of the island, once skyscraper laden and nightlife starved, has been getting buzzier in the last few years. Exciting new bars and restaurants have opened, but the old dependable steak houses and bistros are still here.

$$$$
STEAKHOUSE
✗ **Delmonico's.** The oldest continually operating restaurant in New York City (since 1837), austere Delmonico's is steeped in cultural, political, and culinary history. Lobster Newburg and Baked Alaska were invented here—and are still served. Inside the stately mahogany-panel dining room, tuck into the classic Delmonico's steak, a 20-ounce boneless rib eye smothered with frizzled onions, and don't forget to order creamed spinach on the side. The cheesy spaetzle with pancetta is also sinfully sublime. The dining room gets busy early with an after-work Wall Street crowd, making reservations essential. $ *Average main: $37 ⊠ 56 Beaver St., at William St., Financial District* ☎ *212/509–1144* ⊕ *www.delmonicosny. com* ⏱ *Closed Sun. No lunch Sat.* ☙ *Reservations essential* Ⓜ *2, 3 to Wall St.; R to Whitehall St.; 4, 5 to Bowling Green; J, Z to Broad St.* ⊕ *1:D4.*

BEST BETS FOR NEW YORK CITY DINING

With thousands of restaurants to choose from, how do you decide where to eat? Fodor's writers and editors have selected their favorite restaurants by price, cuisine, and experience in the Best Bets lists below.

Fodor's Choice ★

Babbo Ristorante, $$$
Bar Boulud, $$$
Bergen Hill, $$
The Breslin Bar and Dining Room, $$$
Burger Joint, $
Café Sabarsky, $$
Candle 79, $$
The Cecil, $$$
Charlie Bird, $$$
Clinton St. Baking Co., $$
Colonie, $$
Cosme, $$$
Daniel, $$$$
Diner, $$
Dirt Candy, $$
Edi & the Wolf, $$
Eleven Madison Park, $$$$
Estela, $$$
Frankie Spuntino 457, $$
Freemans, $$
Gotham Bar & Grill, $$$$
Isa, $$
Ivan Ramen, $$
Katz's Delicatessen, $$
Le Bernardin, $$$$
The Little Owl, $$$
Lupulo, $$

M. Wells Dinette, $$
Marea, $$$
Marlow & Sons, $$
Marta, $$
Mission Chinese, $$
Momofuku Ko, $$$$
Momofuku Noodle Bar, $$
The NoMad, $$$
Per Se, $$$$
Peter Luger Steak House, $$$$
Roberta's, $$
Saxon & Parole, $$
Semilla, $$$$
Shake Shack, $
SriPraPhai, $$
St. Anselm, $$
Sushi Nakazawa, $$$$

Best by Price

$

Burger Joint
The City Bakery
Dough
Gray's Papaya
Levain Bakery
The Meatball Shop
Mile End
Shake Shack

$$

Bubby's

Café Sabarsky
Candle 79
Fatty Crab
Katz's Delicatessen
M. Wells Dinette
Momofuku Noodle Bar
Somtum Der
Roberta's

$$$

ABC Kitchen
Babbo Ristorante
Balthazar
Bar Boulud
Marea
Minetta Tavern
The NoMad
Osteria Morini
The Standard Grill

$$$$

Craft
Eleven Madison Park
Jean-Georges
Le Bernardin
Per Se

Best by Cuisine

AMERICAN

ABC Kitchen
Cookshop
Craft

Eleven Madison Park
Gramercy Tavern
Hundred Acres
Per Se
The Red Cat

BARBECUE

Fette Sau
Hill Country

CHINESE

Grand Sichuan
Joe's Shanghai
Mission Chinese
Shun Lee Palace
Tasty Hand-Pulled Noodles
Xi'an Famous Foods

FRENCH

Bar Boulud
Daniel
Jean Georges
Lafayette Grand Café & Bakery
Le Bernardin

GREEK

Kefi
Pylos

INDIAN

Kati Roll Company
Tamarind

ITALIAN

Babbo Ristorante
Emporio
Lupa
Marea
Parm
Rubirosa

JAPANESE

Ippudo
Kurumazushi
Sushi Nakazawa
Sushi of Gari
Sushi Yasuda

MEDITERRANEAN

Aldea
Il Buco
The NoMad

MEXICAN

Empellón Taqueria
La Esquina
Maya
Mission Cantina
Toloache

PIZZA

Artichoke Pizza
Franny's
Keste Pizza & Vino
Lombardi's Pizza
Roberta's
Rubirosa

SEAFOOD

Grand Central Oyster
Bar & Restaurant
The John Dory
Marea
Mary's Fish Camp
Pearl Oyster Bar

SPANISH

Boqueria
Casa Mono
Tía Pol

STEAKHOUSE

BLT Prime
BLT Steak
Peter Luger Steak
House
Porter House New
York
Sparks Steakhouse

Best by Experience

BRUNCH

Balthazar
Bubby's
Cookshop
Harry's Café and
Steak
Sarabeth's Kitchen

CELEB-SPOTTING

ABC Kitchen
Balthazar
The Breslin Bar and
Dining Room
Café Boulud
DBGB Kitchen & Bar
Minetta Tavern
Nobu
The Standard Grill

CHILD-FRIENDLY

Bubby's
Carmine's
The City Bakery
Joe's Shanghai
Lombardi's Pizza
Odeon

GREAT VIEWS

Asiate
Marea
Michael Jordan's The
Steakhouse NYC
Per Se
Porter House New
York

LATE-NIGHT DINING

Balthazar
The Breslin Bar and
Dining Room
DBGB Kitchen & Bar
Emporio
Fatty Crab
Minetta Tavern
The Standard Grill

15

$
CAFÉ
✕ **Financier Patisserie.** On the cobblestone pedestrian street that has become the Financial District's restaurant row, this charming pâtisserie serves excellent pastries and delicious savory foods, like mushroom bisque, salads, and hot or cold sandwiches (we have cravings for the panini pressed with prosciutto, fig jam, mascarpone, and arugula). After lunch, relax with a cappuccino and a *financier* (almond tea cake), or an elegant pastry. In warm weather, perch at an outdoor table and watch Manhattanites buzz by. There are locations all over town. ⑤ *Average main: $7* ✉ *62 Stone St., between Mill La. and Hanover Sq., Financial District* ☎ *212/344–5600* ⊕ *www.financierpastries.com* ☾ *No dinner* ⌕ *Reservations not accepted* Ⓜ *2, 3 to Wall St.; 4, 5 to Bowling Green; J, Z to Broad St.* ✛ *1:E4.*

$$$
STEAKHOUSE
✕ **Harry's Café and Steak.** Its noise-dampening acoustics and maze of underground nooks combine to make Harry's Steak—the fine-dining half of the restaurant (Harry's Café is more casual, but the menu is the same)—one of the city's most intimate steak houses. Settle into a leather booth and start with a classic shrimp cocktail or the tomato trio, starring thick beefsteak slices topped with bacon and blue cheese, mozzarella and basil, and shaved onion with ranch dressing. The star attraction—prime aged porterhouse for two—is nicely encrusted with sea salt and a good match for buttery mashed potatoes infused with sweet roasted shallots and thick steak sauce spooned from Mason jars. Weekend brunch is popular, too. ⑤ *Average main: $35* ✉ *1 Hanover Sq., between Stone and Pearl Sts., Financial District* ☎ *212/785–9200* ⊕ *www.harrysnyc.com* ☾ *Closed Sun.* ⌕ *Reservations essential* Ⓜ *4, 5 to Bowling Green; 2, 3 to Wall St.; J, Z to Broad St.* ✛ *1:E4.*

$
AMERICAN
✕ **Ulysses'.** Squeezed between skyscrapers and the towering New York Stock Exchange, Stone Street is a two-block restaurant oasis that feels more like a village than the center of the financial universe. After the market closes, Wall Streeters head to Ulysses', a popular pub with 12 beers on tap and more than 50 bottled beers. Hungry? There are decent pub-grub options, like mini cheeseburgers, fried oysters, nachos, and wings. ⑤ *Average main: $10* ✉ *95 Pearl St., near Hanover Sq., Financial District* ☎ *212/482–0400* ⊕ *www.ulyssesnyc.com* Ⓜ *R to Whitehall St.; J, Z to Broad St.; 2, 3 to Wall St.* ✛ *1:E4.*

TRIBECA

TriBeCa and its restaurants are a playground for the rich and famous. Fortunately, glamorous dining rooms in converted warehouses have been joined in the last few years by more casual spots.

$$$
AUSTRIAN
FAMILY
✕ **Blaue Gans.** Chef Kurt Gutenbrunner, one of the most lauded Austrian chefs in New York, runs this sprawling brasserie like an all-day clubhouse. Pop in for a late-morning or early-afternoon snack—the coffee comes topped with *schlag*, the doughnuts filled with apricot jam. Or swing by in the evening for Central European standards like sausage, schnitzel, potato dumplings, and beef goulash. Wash it all down with a hoppy brew or a crisp Austrian white wine ⑤ *Average main: $25* ✉ *139 Duane St., near West Broadway, TriBeCa* ☎ *212/571–8880* ⊕ *www.kg-ny.com* Ⓜ *1, 2, 3, A, C to Chambers St.* ✛ *1:C1.*

$$
AMERICAN
FAMILY
✕ **Bubby's.** Neighborhood crowds clamoring for coffee and freshly squeezed juice line up for brunch at this TriBeCa mainstay, but Bubby's is good for lunch and dinner, too, if you're in the mood for comfort

food like mac 'n' cheese or fried chicken. The dining room is homey and cozy, with big windows; in summer, patrons sit at tables outside with their dogs. Brunch options include just about everything, including homemade granola, sour-cream pancakes with bananas and strawberries, and huevos rancheros with guacamole and grits. ⑤ *Average main: $18* ⊠ *120 Hudson St., at N. Moore St., TriBeCa* ☎ *212/219–0666* ⊕ *www.bubbys.com* Ⓜ *1 to Franklin St.* ✠ *1:C1.*

$$$ ✕ **Locanda Verde.** Chef Andrew Carmellini, first an acolyte of Daniel
ITALIAN   Boulud, and then a chef with a half dozen restaurants in his culinary arsenal, has definitely made a name for himself in New York City. This Robert De Niro–backed restaurant is still one of his best. The space at Locanda Verde is warm and welcoming, with accents of brick and wood and large windows that open to the street, weather permitting, while the menu is full of inspired Italian comfort food that hits the mark. Standouts include small plates like blue crab crostino with jalapeños and the pumpkin agnolotti in brown sage butter that diners reminisce about. Several draft beers, along with more than a dozen wines by the glass, make an already hopping bar scene even more of a draw. ⑤ *Average main: $27* ⊠ *377 Greenwich St., at N. Moore St., TriBeCa* ☎ *212/925–3797* ⊕ *www.locandaverdenyc.com* ⚟ *Reservations essential* Ⓜ *1 to Franklin St.* ✠ *1:B1.*

$$$$ ✕ **Nobu.** At this large, bustling TriBeCa dining room (or its sister loca-
JAPANESE   tion uptown), you might just spot a celeb or two. New York's famed Japanese restaurant has gained a lot of competition in recent years, but this is still the destination for the innovative Japanese cuisine Nobu Matsuhisa made famous (though he's rarely in attendance these days). Dishes like fresh yellowtail sashimi with jalapeño, rock shrimp tempura, or miso-marinated Chilean sea bass continue to draw huge crowds. Put yourself in the hands of the chef by ordering the tasting menu, or *omakase*, and specify how much you want to spend, then let the kitchen do the rest. Can't get reservations? Try your luck at the first-come, first-served **Nobu Next Door** (literally next door), with a similar menu plus a sushi bar. ⑤ *Average main: $38* ⊠ *105 Hudson St., at Franklin St., TriBeCa* ☎ *212/219–0500* ⊕ *www.myriadrestaurantgroup.com* ☽ *No lunch weekends* ⚟ *Reservations essential* Ⓜ *1 to Franklin St.* ✠ *1:B1.*

$$$ ✕ **Odeon.** New Yorkers change hangouts faster than they can speed-dial,
FRENCH   but this spot has managed to maintain its quality and flair for more
FAMILY   than 30 years. It still feels like *the* spot in TriBeCa to get a late-night bite. The neo–Art Deco room is still packed nightly with revelers, and the pleasant service and well-chosen wine list are always in style. Bistro menu highlights include frisée *aux lardons* (with bacon) with poached farm egg, grilled NY strip steak, and slow-cooked cod with baby leeks and fennel confit. ⑤ *Average main: $28* ⊠ *145 West Broadway, between Duane and Thomas Sts., TriBeCa* ☎ *212/233–0507* ⊕ *www. theodeonrestaurant.com* Ⓜ *1, 2, 3, A, C to Chambers St.* ✠ *1:C1; 2:D6.*

$$$ ✕ **Tamarind.** Many consider Tamarind to be one of Manhattan's best
INDIAN   Indian restaurants, and the elegant atmosphere makes it a different experience from many other NYC Indian eateries. Forsaking the usual brass, beads, sitar, and darkness, the dining room is sleek and modern. Welcoming host and owner Avtar Walia practically reinvents charm.

15

The busy kitchen prepares multiregional dishes, some familiar (tandoori chicken, a searing lamb vindaloo), some unique (succulent venison chops in a vigorously spiced cranberry sauce, she-crab soup with saffron, nutmeg, and ginger juice). The more intriguing a dish sounds, the better it turns out to be. $ *Average main: $26* ✉ *99 Hudson St., at Franklin St., TriBeCa* ☎ *212/775–9000* ⊕ *www.tamarindrestaurantsnyc.com* Ⓜ *1 to Franklin St.; A, C, E to Canal St.* ⊹ *2:C6.*

SOHO, NOLITA, LITTLE ITALY, AND CHINATOWN

SOHO

Sure, eating in SoHo may not feel very low-key, with mostly pricey eateries full of fashionistas and the "see and be seen" crowd, but the restaurants here are worth the fight for a table.

$$
AMERICAN
✗ **Back Forty West.** Chef Peter Hoffman was doing sustainable farm-to-table fare long before it became a near-obligatory restaurant trend in the Big Apple. The original Back Forty was in the East Village, but the current location just makes it more convenient for neighborhood denizens and shoppers to access the well-executed comfort food. The menu changes with the season, but expect dishes like coconut-milk-spiked scallop ceviche, pumpkin hummus, a very good grass-fed burger, and grilled trout from the Catskills, served alongside quality cocktails and a short but excellent list of beer and wine. Add in the rustic, homey decor, and you'll feel like you're hundreds of miles from that shopping mecca known as SoHo. $ *Average main: $20* ✉ *70 Prince St., at Crosby St., SoHo* ☎ *212/219–8570* ⊕ *www.backfortynyc.com* ☾ *No dinner Sun.* Ⓜ *B, D, F, M to Broadway–Lafayette St.; N, R to Prince St.; 6 to Spring St.* ⊹ *2:E3.*

$$$
FRENCH
✗ **Balthazar.** Even with long waits and excruciating noise levels, most out-of-towners agree that it's worth making reservations to experience restaurateur Keith McNally's flagship, a painstakingly accurate reproduction of a Parisian brasserie with an insider New York feel. Like the decor, entrées re-create French classics: Gruyère-topped onion soup, steak frites, and icy tiers of crab, oysters, and other pristine shellfish. Brunch is still one of the toughest tables in town. The best strategy to experience this perennial fave is to go at off-hours or on weekdays for breakfast to miss the crush. $ *Average main: $28* ✉ *80 Spring St., between Broadway and Crosby St., SoHo* ☎ *212/965–1414* ⊕ *www.balthazarny.com* ✍ *Reservations essential* Ⓜ *6 to Spring St.; N, R to Prince St.; B, D, F, M to Broadway–Lafayette St.* ⊹ *2:E4.*

$$
BAKERY
✗ **Balthazar Bakery.** Follow the beguiling scent of fresh-baked bread to Balthazar Bakery, next door to Keith McNally's always-packed Balthazar restaurant. Choices include fresh-baked baguettes and other varieties of French breads, as well as gourmet sandwiches, soups, and memorable pastries to take out (there is no seating). Try the berry noisette tart or coconut cake, or keep it simple with an eggy canelé or a buttery lemon or chocolate madeleine. $ *Average main: $23* ✉ *80 Spring St., near Crosby St., SoHo* ☎ *212/965–1785* ⊕ *www.balthazarbakery. com* ☾ *No dinner* ✍ *Reservations not accepted* Ⓜ *6 to Spring St.; N, R to Prince St.; B, D, F, M to Broadway–Lafayette St.* ⊹ *2:E4.*

$$$
MODERN
AMERICAN

✕ **Blue Ribbon.** After over 25 years, Blue Ribbon still has a reputation not just as an eclectic, top-notch seafood joint, but also as a serious late-night foodie hangout. Join the genial hubbub for midnight noshing, namely the beef marrow with oxtail marmalade and renowned raw-bar platters. Trustafarians, literary types, chefs, and designers—a good-looking gang—generally fill this dark box of a room until 4 am. The menu appears standard at first blush, but it's not. Try the duck club sandwich or matzo ball soup; the latter is a heady brew filled with the sacrilegious combo of seafood and traditional Jewish dumplings. ⑤ *Average main: $33* ✉ *97 Sullivan St., between Prince and Spring Sts., SoHo* ☎ *212/274–0404* ⊕ *www.blueribbonrestaurants.com* ☾ *No lunch* ✍ *Reservations essential* Ⓜ *C, E to Spring St.; N, R to Prince St.* ✦ *2:D3.*

$$$
JAPANESE

✕ **Blue Ribbon Sushi.** Sushi, like pizza, attracts plenty of opinionated fanatics, and Blue Ribbon Sushi gets consistent raves for its überfresh sushi and sashimi. Stick to the excellent raw fish and specials here if you're a purist, or branch out and try one of the experimental rolls: the Blue Ribbon—lobster, *shiso* (Japanese basil), and black caviar—is popular. The dark, intimate nooks, minimalist design, and servers with downtown attitude attract a stylish crowd who don't mind waiting for a table or chilled sake. Between the quality and the location, it's not cheap. ⑤ *Average main: $27* ✉ *119 Sullivan St., between Prince and Spring Sts., SoHo* ☎ *212/343–0404* ⊕ *www.blueribbonrestaurants.com* ✍ *Reservations not accepted* Ⓜ *C, E to Spring St.; N, R to Prince St.* ✦ *2:D3.*

15

$$$
AMERICAN

✕ **The Dutch.** Perpetually packed with the "see and be seen" crowd, chef Andrew Carmellini's homage to American cuisine is really an encapsulation of recent food and dining trends: there's an excellent burger (and at $23 it should be), a Kentucky-size bourbon collection behind the bar, greenmarket-driven comfort-food dishes like fried chicken, and bacon paired with things you would have not likely seen a couple of decades ago (in this case, scallops with bacon jam). And it all works well at this SoHo restaurant—so much so that you might consider returning for weekend brunch when the house-made bologna sandwich or cornmeal flapjacks appear on the menu. ⑤ *Average main: $29* ✉ *131 Sullivan St., at Prince St., SoHo* ☎ *212/677–6200* ⊕ *www.thedutchnyc. com* ✍ *Reservations essential* Ⓜ *C, E to Spring St.* ✦ *2:D3.*

$$$
MODERN
AMERICAN

✕ **Hundred Acres.** Set on a quiet block on the border of SoHo and Greenwich Village, the rustic, farmhouse-slash-greenhouse that is Hundred Acres is a lovely place to while away a long lunch or quiet dinner. The market-driven creative comfort food keeps the neighborhood patrons and out-of-towners-in-the-know coming back. The menu is loaded with all the items you'd expect from a farm-to-table affair: oysters, deviled eggs, broccoli rabe, and, yes, kale. Mains run the gamut from fish to meat: think a luscious pork shank with polenta and rhubarb chutney; shrimp and grits; or a classic burger made from pasture-raised beef, topped with Vermont cheddar and served with fries and Vidalia onion mayonnaise. Weekend brunch stands out, with variations on a Bloody Mary theme, and treats like a country pâté sandwich and goat-cheese-and-sage bread pudding. ⑤ *Average main: $27* ✉ *38 MacDougal St., between Houston and Prince Sts., SoHo* ☎ *212/475–7500* ⊕ *www.hundredacresnyc.com* Ⓜ *1 to Houston St.; C, E to Spring St.; N, R to Prince St.* ✦ *2:D3.*

$$ ✕**Lucky Strike.** Whether you're lucky enough to nab a table at this scene-
BISTRO y SoHo bistro at 1 pm or 1 am, Lucky Strike always seems like the place
to be. Bedecked in classic bistro trappings—hammered-copper stools,
mirrors with menu items scrawled on them—the restaurant would look
just as perfect in the Bastille neighborhood of Paris as it does in this
swanky part of the Big Apple. The kitchen offerings are straightforward:
croque monsieur, grilled salmon, and salade niçoise are old standbys,
with a turkey burger thrown in to accommodate the *Americain* palate.
Ⓢ *Average main: $19* ⊠ *59 Grand St., between West Broadway and
Wooster St., SoHo* ☎ *212/941–0772* ⊕ *www.luckystrikeny.com* ⚊ *No
credit cards* Ⓜ *1, A, C, E to Canal St.* ✛ *2:D4.*

$$$ ✕**Lure Fishbar.** Decorated like the clubby interior of a sleek luxury liner,
SEAFOOD Lure serves oceanic fare in multiple culinary styles. From the sushi
bar, feast on options like the Lure House Roll—a shrimp tempura roll
crowned with spicy tuna and Japanese tartar sauce—or opt for creative
dishes from the kitchen, like steamed branzino with oyster mushrooms,
scallions, and ponzu sauce, or Manila clams over pancetta-studded
linguine. For an all-American treat, you can't go wrong with a classic
lobster roll on brioche. The dark subterranean bar is a good spot for
cocktails and a snack. Brunch is served on weekends. Ⓢ *Average main:
$29* ⊠ *142 Mercer St., at Prince St., SoHo* ☎ *212/431–7676* ⊕ *www.
lurefishbar.com* Ⓜ *B, D, F, M to Broadway–Lafayette St.; N, R to Prince
St.* ✛ *2:E3.*

$$ ✕**MarieBelle.** Practically invisible from the front of the chocolate empo-
CAFÉ rium, the back entry to the Cacao Bar opens into a sweet, high-ceiling,
FAMILY 12-table hot-chocolate shop. Most people order the Aztec, European-
style (that's 65% Colombian chocolate mixed with hot water—no
cocoa powder here!). The first sip is startlingly rich but not too dense;
American-style, made with milk, is sweeter. Not to worry if you're vis-
iting in spring or summer: you can opt for Aztec iced chocolate—the
warm-weather version of the decadent cacao elixir—or the house-made
chocolate gelato. For more substantial snacking, choose a salad or sand-
wich from the dainty lunch menu. Ⓢ *Average main: $13* ⊠ *484 Broome
St., between West Broadway and Wooster St., SoHo* ☎ *212/925–6999*
⊕ *www.mariebelle.com* ☽ *No dinner* ⚌ *Reservations not accepted* Ⓜ *6
to Spring St.; A, C, E to Canal St.* ✛ *2:D4.*

$$$ ✕**The Mercer Kitchen.** Part of Alsatian superchef Jean-Georges Vongeri-
ASIAN FUSION chten's culinary empire, the celebrity-laden front room of this SoHo
spot in the Mercer Hotel is as much about scene as cuisine, which isn't
a bad thing. Dishes here look toward Asia (as is the proclivity of Mr.
Vongerichten), using simple ingredients and pairings. Think scallops
with lentils and pancetta or crispy squid with black-olive tartar sauce.
It's all good enough to make you feign disinterest over the A-list celeb
who just walked in. Ⓢ *Average main: $30* ⊠ *Mercer Hotel, 99 Prince
St., at Mercer St., SoHo* ☎ *212/966–5454* ⊕ *www.themercerkitchen.
com* ⚊ *No credit cards* Ⓜ *6 to Spring St.; N, R to Prince St.; B, D, F, M
to Broadway–Lafayette St.* ✛ *2:E3.*

$$$ ✕**Osteria Morini.** Less formal than chef Michael White's other renowned
ITALIAN Italian restaurants (like Marea in Midtown West), the atmosphere at
Osteria Morini is lively and upbeat, with communal tables at the center

and a rock 'n' roll sound track. The food nevertheless steals the show. Start with a selection of cheeses and cured meats, then move on to hearty pastas—a lusty ragù Bolognese or garganelli with prosciutto and truffle butter, for example—and main courses like oven-baked polenta accompanied by either sausage or mushrooms. Waits can be long, so try to come early or late, or grab one of the few bar seats for an inventive cocktail or a glass of Italian wine. Brunch is served weekends. $ *Average main: $26* ⊠ *218 Lafayette St., between Spring and Broome Sts., SoHo* ☎ *212/965–8777* ⊕ *www.osteriamorini.com* ☚ *Reservations essential* Ⓜ *6 to Spring St.* ✛ *2:E4.*

$$$ ✕ **Raoul's.** One of the first trendy spots in SoHo, this arty French res-
FRENCH   taurant has yet to lose its touch, either in the kitchen or atmosphere. Expect a chic bar scene—especially late at night—filled with polished PYTs, amazing photos on every piece of available wall space, and a lovely back room that you reach through the kitchen. The winding stairs to the upstairs dining room are narrow and a bit treacherous if wearing your highest heels. The food is bistro inspired, with oysters and salads to start, and pastas, fish, and meat options for mains. $ *Average main: $30* ⊠ *180 Prince St., between Sullivan and Thompson Sts., SoHo* ☎ *212/966–3518* ⊕ *www.raouls.com* ▬ *No credit cards* ◷ *No lunch weekdays* Ⓜ *C, E to Spring St.* ✛ *2:D3.*

NOLITA

In NoLIta, SoHo's trendy next-door neighborhood, the spirit of old, pre-chain-store SoHo prevails. Diminutive eateries, squeezed between up-and-coming designer boutiques, flank the narrow streets of this atmospheric neighborhood.

$ ✕ **Black Seed Bagels.** New York is known for bagels, which tend to be
CANADIAN   large and doughy and delicious. Montreal-style bagels, which is what
FAMILY   you'll find at Black Seed, have a denser, sweeter dough. The "toppings" (sesame, poppy seed, salt, everything) are more generous than on the New York bagels. The all-day menu here includes sandwich options with cream cheese, smoked salmon, whitefish salad, or baked eggs; the lunch menu adds a BLT with spicy mayo, roast beef with horseradish cream cheese, and a tuna melt to the mix, among others. Order at the counter and eat in if you can get a seat: the dark-wood-paneled café makes this one of the classiest bagel joints around. There's also a location at 176 1st Avenue (between E. 10th and 11th Streets) in the East Village. $ *Average main: $9* ⊠ *170 Elizabeth St., NoLIta* ☎ *212/730–1950* ⊕ *www.blackseedbagels.com* Ⓜ *6 to Spring St.* ✛ *2:F4.*

$$ ✕ **Café Habana.** The Mexican-style grilled corn, liberally sprinkled with
MEXICAN   chili powder, lime, and cotija cheese is undoubtedly worth getting your
FAMILY   hands dirty at this crowded, hip luncheonette. Follow up with a classic Cuban sandwich (roast pork, ham, Swiss cheese, pickles, and chipotle mayo), fish tacos, or one of the innovative salads. Be prepared for a wait at lunchtime or on weekend afternoons. The cocktails are good, too. There's a take-out shop with a few seats down the street at 229 Elizabeth Street. $ *Average main: $14* ⊠ *17 Prince St., at Elizabeth St., NoLIta* ☎ *212/625–2001* ⊕ *www.cafehabana.com* ☚ *Reservations not accepted* Ⓜ *6 to Spring St.; N, R to Prince St.; J, Z to Bowery* ✛ *2:F3.*

15

$$$
FRENCH

✕ Cherche Midi. Restaurateur Keith McNally's signature is restaurants that become perpetually "see and be seen" spots (cases in point: Odeon, Minetta Tavern, Balthazar, Schiller's Liquor Bar, etc.). This French bistro opened in 2014 but fits in so well with the neighborhood that it seems like it's been anchored on this corner for decades. The menu of classic French fare blends well with the rustic decor: as with most McNally restaurants, the culinary wheel is not being reinvented. Expect the classics—pan-roasted foie gras, steak tartare, steak frites, and lobster ravioli—executed very well. The wine list, French and Italian, includes ample amounts of affordable but delicious options. $ *Average main: $26* ✉ *282 Bowery, NoLIta* ☏ *212/226–3055* ⊕ *www.cherchemidiny. com* Ⓜ *6 to Bleecker St.; B, D, F, M to Broadway–Lafayette St.; F to 2nd Ave.* ✛ *2:F3.*

$$
ITALIAN

✕ Emporio. The brick-lined front room of this homey Roman eatery in NoLIta is a gathering spot for early-evening happy hour at the bar, where you'll find an appetizing selection of free small bites like frittata, white-bean salad, and ham-and-spinach *tramezzini* (finger sandwiches). The centerpiece of the large, skylighted back room is a wood-fired oven that turns out crisp, thin-crust pizzas topped with quality ingredients like prosciutto and buffalo mozzarella. Service is solicitous but not speedy, so you can linger over a bottle of wine from the copious selection. House-made pastas like garganelli with pork sausage and house ragù, and entrées like whole roasted fish with grilled lemon, are also excellent. $ *Average main: $23* ✉ *231 Mott St., between Prince and Spring Sts., NoLIta* ☏ *212/966–1234* ⊕ *www.emporiony.com* Ⓜ *B, D, F, M to Broadway–Lafayette St.; N, R to Prince St.; 6 to Bleecker St.* ✛ *2:F3.*

$$$
MEDITERRANEAN
Fodor'sChoice
★

✕ Estela. Long before Mr. and Mrs. Obama ate dinner here in late 2014, this second-floor restaurant had been on the map for those in the know. Ignacio Mattos is the commander-in-chief, and his creations have a tendency to sneak up on the diner: Is that rye matzo bread under the mashed salt cod? And are those sunchoke chips folded into the sumptuous beef tartare? Are scallops and lardo a good paring on the plate? The answer is "yes" to all of the above. The wine list is compact yet sprinkled with some great off-the-radar European gems. The minimalist room is a fitting space for the deceptively simple cooking going on here. $ *Average main: $27* ✉ *47 E. Houston St., NoLIta* ☏ *212/219–7693* ⊕ *www.estelanyc.com* ⊗ *No lunch weekdays* ⌾ *Reservations essential* Ⓜ *6 to Bleecker St.; B, D, F, M to Broadway–Lafayette St.* ✛ *2:F3.*

$$
MEDITERRANEAN

✕ Gato. When an orange cat crossed celebrity-chef Bobby Flay's path while he was waiting for the real estate agent to show him this space, he decided right then to call this restaurant Gato (Spanish for cat). And a sly cat it is. Despite the name, the menu goes beyond Spain to cover large culinary swaths of the Mediterranean. Sit at the bar and nosh on roasted octopus deliciously paired with bacon, garlic-bread-topped crab risotto, and Brussels sprouts sprinkled with pomegranates and pistachios. It all makes you feel like one lucky cat. $ *Average main: $21* ✉ *324 Lafayette St., NoLIta* ☏ *212/334–6400* ⊕ *www.gatonyc. com* ⊗ *No lunch* Ⓜ *6 to Bleecker St.; B, D, F, M to Broadway–Lafayette St.* ✛ *2:E3.*

$$ ✕ **La Esquina.** Anchoring a downtown corner under a bright neon sign,
MEXICAN La Esquina looks like nothing more than a fast-food taquería, with
cheap tacos sold to go until 2 in the morning. Just around the corner,
though, is a modestly priced café serving those same tacos along with
more ambitious fare like chiles rellenos (stuffed peppers) and carne
asada (grilled meat). The real draw, however, is hidden from sight: the
basement brasserie, like a Mexican speakeasy, is accessible by reser-
vation only, through an unmarked door just inside the ground-floor
taquería. Inside, discover a buzzy subterranean scene with pretty people
drinking potent margaritas and dining on upscale Mexican fare. Prices
downstairs are high, but portions are large. ⑤ *Average main: $20* ✉ *106
Kenmare, between Cleveland Pl. and Lafayette St., NoLIta* ☎ *646/613–
7100* ⊕ *www.esquinanyc.com* Ⓜ *6 to Spring St.* ✛ *2:E4.*

$$ ✕ **Lombardi's Pizza.** Brick walls, red-and-white-checker tablecloths, and
PIZZA the aroma of thin-crust pies emerging from the coal oven set the mood
FAMILY for dining on some of the best pizza in Manhattan. Lombardi's has
served pizza since 1905 (though not in the same location), and business
doesn't seem to have died down one bit. The mozzarella is always fresh,
resulting in a nearly greaseless slice, and the toppings, such as meatballs,
pancetta, or imported anchovies, are also top quality. The clam pizza,
with freshly shucked clams, garlic oil, pecorino-Romano cheese, and
parsley, is well-known among aficionados. ⑤ *Average main: $17* ✉ *32
Spring St., at Mott St., NoLIta* ☎ *212/941–7994* ⊕ *www.firstpizza.com*
🖎 *Reservations not accepted* ▭ *No credit cards* Ⓜ *6 to Spring St.; J, Z
to Bowery; N, R to Prince St.* ✛ *2:F4.*

$ ✕ **Parm.** There's more to this casual NoLIta eatery than the namesake
ITALIAN Italian sandwich for which the budding chainlet is named. Founded by
chefs Rich Torrisi and Mario Carbone (who are behind other hits like
Dirty French, Carbone, and Torrisi Italian Specialties, right next door),
Parm's menu also includes large Caesar salads, baked clams, and garlic
bread. And, of course, there are variations on the eponymous sandwich, including eggplant, meatball, turkey, and chicken. Affordable
bottles and glasses of wine invite you to stick around awhile. There
are other locations in Battery Park City and on the Upper West Side.
⑤ *Average main: $12* ✉ *248 Mulberry St., NoLIta* ☎ *212/993–7189*
⊕ *www.parmnyc.com* Ⓜ *B, D, F, M to Broadway/Lafayette; N, R to
Prince St.* ✛ *2:F3.*

$$$ ✕ **Public.** To start with, the space here is complex and sophisticated, with
ECLECTIC soaring ceilings and whitewashed brick walls, skylights, fireplaces, three
dining areas, and a vast bar. You've come for the food, though, and
you won't be disappointed. The menu flaunts its nonconformity, and
dishes, like the Australian barramundi fish, served with vanilla-celeriac
puree and braised garlic greens, demonstrate a light yet adventurous
touch. Brunch at Public is a local favorite, with exotic selections like
coconut pancakes topped with fresh ricotta, mango, and lime syrup, and
a juicy venison burger. Standout desserts include a chocolate mousse
with tahini ice cream and sesame candy. ⑤ *Average main: $26* ✉ *210
Elizabeth St., between Prince and Spring Sts., NoLIta* ☎ *212/343–7011*
⊕ *www.public-nyc.com* ☾ *Closed Mon.* Ⓜ *6 to Spring St.; N, R to
Prince St.; J, Z to Bowery* ✛ *2:F3.*

15

$$ ╳ **Rubirosa.** Named for a jet-setting Dominican playboy, this Rubirosa
ITALIAN is only Latin and lascivious in name. Locals have shown an insatiable
appetite for this exciting Italian-American eatery, so be prepared to wait
for a table. The kitchen isn't trying to reinvent anything here; it simply
serves high-quality classic Italian dishes, from pasta with red sauce or a
fork-tender veal chop Milanese to the thin-crust pizza (the recipe for the
latter comes from the late owner's parents, who have run the popular
Staten Island pizza joint, Joe & Pat's, since anyone can remember). You
don't have to be a jet-setter or a playboy to love this place. Just come
hungry. ⑤ *Average main: $19* ⊠ *235 Mulberry St., between Prince and
Spring Sts., NoLIta* ☎ *212/965–0500* ⊕ *www.rubirosanyc.com* ⊟ *No
credit cards* Ⓜ *6 to Spring St.; N, R to Prince St.* ⊹ *2:F3.*

$$ ╳ **The Smile.** Subterranean and almost hidden, the Smile turns frowns
AMERICAN upside down, if you like hipsters and celebrities, and, most especially,
hipster celebrities. Lounge among the fashion-conscious clientele (who
are trying oh-so-hard to not look that way) and munch on breakfast-y
items (served until 4:30 pm) like chunky granola, or go for one of the
giant sandwiches, or spaghetti with heirloom-tomato sauce. Dinner
options, like whole trout, brisket, hanger steak, or roasted chicken,
are more ambitious. Just be sure you wear shoes that scream "this
season." ⑤ *Average main: $16* ⊠ *26 Bond St., between Lafayette St. and
the Bowery, NoLIta* ☎ *646/329–5836* ⊕ *www.thesmilenyc.com* Ⓜ *B, D,
F, M to Broadway–Lafayette St.; 6 to Bleecker St.* ⊹ *2:E2.*

$$ ╳ **Uncle Boon's.** If you're looking for quality Thai in Manhattan, a good
THAI choice is Uncle Boon's in NoLIta. The chefs are a husband-and-wife
team who originally met in the kitchen at Michelin-starred Per Se. You
won't find evidence of über-haute cuisine here, but the simple, tasty
Thai fare is very good. Skip the green papaya salad—usually a must,
but somehow bland here—and go right for hearty entrées, such as the
khao soi, an ultra-tender chicken leg doused in a deliciously tangy yel-
low curry, or anything that's grilled. ⑤ *Average main: $23* ⊠ *7 Spring
St., near Elizabeth St., NoLIta* ☎ *646/370–6650* ⊕ *www.uncleboons.
com* ⊟ *No credit cards* Ⓜ *J, Z to Bowery; 6 to Spring St.* ⊹ *2:F3.*

CHINATOWN

Chinatown beckons adventurous diners with restaurants representing
numerous regional cuisines of China, including Cantonese, Sichuan,
Hunan, Fujian, Shanghai, and Hong Kong–style cooking. Malaysian
and Vietnamese restaurants also have taken root here, and the neighbor-
hood continues to grow rapidly, encroaching into what was Little Italy.

$$ ╳ **456 Shanghai Cuisine.** Come to this Chinatown eatery for above-aver-
CHINESE age Chinese fare, such as General Tso's chicken, pork buns, and cold
sesame noodles, but do yourself a favor and order soup dumplings (*xiao
long bao*) as soon as you sit down. You won't regret it. The dumplings,
doughy and thin on the outside, encase morsels of crab swimming in a
bold porky broth, truly a wonder of the culinary world—and 456 does
them as well as (or better than) anyone in the city. ⑤ *Average main: $14*
⊠ *69 Mott St., between Canal and Bayard Sts., Chinatown* ☎ *212/964–
0003* ⊟ *No credit cards* Ⓜ *6, J, N, Q, R, Z to Canal St.* ⊹ *2:F5.*

$ ✗**Great New York Noodletown.** Although the soups and noodles are
CHINESE unbeatable at this no-frills restaurant, what you should really order
FAMILY are the window decorations—the hanging lacquered ducks and roasted
pork, listed on a simple board hung on the wall and superbly served
with pungent garlic-and-ginger sauce on the side. Seasonal specialties
like duck with flowering chives and salt-baked soft-shell crabs are excellent. So is the congee, or rice porridge, available with any number of
garnishes. Solo diners may end up at a communal table. Noodletown
is open late—till 4 am on Friday and Saturday. ⑤ *Average main: $11*
✉ *28 Bowery, at Bayard St., Chinatown* ☎ *212/349–0923* ⊕ *www.
greatnynoodletown.com* ▭ *No credit cards* Ⓜ *6, J, N, Q, R, Z to Canal
St.; B, D to Grand St.; F to East Broadway* ✛ *2:G5.*

$$ ✗**Jing Fong.** On weekend mornings people pack this vast dim sum pal-
CHINESE ace, so be prepared to wait. Once your number is called, take the escala-
FAMILY tor up to the carnivalesque third-floor dining room, where servers push
carts crammed with tasty goodness. Expect to be plied with delights like
steamed dumplings, crispy spring rolls, barbecue pork buns, and shrimp
balls. For adventurous eaters, there's chicken feet, tripe, and snails.
Arrive early for the best selection, and save room for mango pudding.
⑤ *Average main: $16* ✉ *20 Elizabeth St., 2nd fl., between Bayard and
Canal Sts., Chinatown* ☎ *212/964–5256* ⊕ *www.jingfongny.com* Ⓜ *6,
J, N, Q, R, Z to Canal St.; B, D to Grand St.* ✛ *2:F5.*

$$ ✗**Joe's Shanghai.** Joe opened his first Shanghai restaurant in Queens in
CHINESE 1995, but buoyed by the accolades showered on his steamed soup dump-
FAMILY lings—filled with a rich, fragrant broth and ground pork or a pork-
crabmeat mixture—several Manhattan outposts soon followed. The trick
is to take a bite of the dumpling and slurp out the soup, then eat the
rest. There's almost always a wait, but the line moves fast. The soup
dumplings are a must, but you can fill out your order from the extensive
menu. There's another Joe's Shanghai in Midtown, at 24 West 56th Street,
between 5th and 6th Avenues (where credit cards are accepted). ⑤ *Average main: $16* ✉ *9 Pell St., between the Bowery and Mott St., Chinatown*
☎ *212/233–8888* ⊕ *www.joeshangbairestaurants.com* ▭ *No credit cards*
Ⓜ *6, J, N, Q, R, Z to Canal St.; B, D to Grand St.* ✛ *2:F5.*

$$ ✗**Mission Chinese Food.** When Oklahoma-born hipster chef Danny
CHINESE Bowien imported his wildly popular Sichuan spot from San Francis-
Fodor's Choice co's Mission District to lower Manhattan, an instant classic was born.
★ Celebrities, food writers, and foodies alike gravitate to Mission Chinese
nightly for Bowien's not-necessarily-authentic take on Sichuan cuisine.
Kung pao pastrami? Thrice-cooked bacon? Who cares if you can't find
these dishes in mainland China when they taste this amazing. Sip on
a signature cocktail—first-timers should initiate themselves with the
gin-and-coconut-spiked Phil Khallins—while eating your way through
tender pork jowl, fried chicken (served like Hainanese chicken rice you
can find at Hawker Centres in Singapore), and fall-off-the-bone cumin
ribs. Irony has never tasted this good. ⑤ *Average main: $20* ✉ *171
E. Broadway, Chinatown* ☎ *212/746–2986* ⊕ *www.mcfny.com* ☾ *No
lunch* ⌑ *Reservations not accepted* Ⓜ *F to East Broadway* ✛ *2:H5.*

$$ ✗**New Malaysia.** This Malaysian restaurant is a real find. Literally. You
MALAYSIAN could stroll right by it and never know it existed. That's because it's

15

in a passageway between the Bowery and Elizabeth Street. It's worth the trouble, though, as the menu is loaded with Malaysian favorites like roti flatbread with curry and delicious red-bean and coconut-milk drinks. The atmosphere is casual and table service is relaxed, which means you might need to flag down your server. $ *Average main: $14* ✉ *48 Bowery, near Canal St., Chinatown* ☎ *212/964–0284* ⊕ *www. newmalaysiarestaurant.com* Ⓜ *6, J, N, Q, R, Z to Canal St.; B, D to Grand St.* ✛ *2:G5.*

$$ ✕ **Peking Duck House.** This Chinatown institution is the place to go in
CHINESE New York for authentic Peking duck. Although the restaurant serves a full Chinese menu, everyone—and we mean everyone—orders the duck. Begin, as most tables do, with an order of Shanghai soup dumplings, then move on to the bird. It's carved table-side with plenty of fanfare—crisp burnished skin separated from moist flesh. Roll up the duck, with hoisin and scallions, in tender steamed pancakes. The menu at the Midtown location (236 E. 53rd Street) is a bit pricier. $ *Average main: $20* ✉ *28 Mott St., at Mosco St., Chinatown* ☎ *212/227–1810* ⊕ *www.pekingduckhousenyc.com* Ⓜ *6, J, N, Q, R, Z to Canal St.; B, D to Grand St.* ✛ *2:F5.*

$ ✕ **Tasty Hand-Pulled Noodles.** The name says it all. The open kitchen
CHINESE at this salt-of-the-earth Chinatown restaurant (located on charming, curved Doyers Street) means you can watch the noodle-slinger in action while awaiting your bowl of, um, tasty hand-pulled noodles. Just choose your ingredients—beef, pork, oxtail, eel, chicken, lamb, or shrimp, among others—and prepare to eat the most delicious bowl of $6 noodles since that last trip to Shanghai. The restaurant is small so be prepared to possibly share a table with a fellow noodle slurper. $ *Average main: $6* ✉ *1 Doyers St., at Bowery, Chinatown* ☎ *212/791–1817* ⊕ *www.tastyhandpullednoodles.com* ▬ *No credit cards* Ⓜ *6, J, N, Q, R, Z to Canal St.; B, D to Grand St.* ✛ *2:F6.*

$ ✕ **Vanessa's Dumpling House.** One of the best deals in Chinatown can
CHINESE be found here. Sizzling pork-and-chive dumplings are four for a buck. There are also vegetarian options. The restaurant is very casual: order at the counter and then grab a table, if you can find one. Vanessa's is especially popular with Lower East Side revelers looking to pad their stomachs before the night's debauchery. $ *Average main: $8* ✉ *118 Eldridge St., near Broome St., Chinatown* ☎ *212/625–8008* ⊕ *www. vanessasdumplinghouse.com* ⌔ *Reservations not accepted* Ⓜ *B, D to Grand St.* ✛ *2:G4.*

$ ✕ **Xe Lua.** A good Vietnamese restaurant in Manhattan is hard to find,
VIETNAMESE which is why you should seek out Xe Lua, in Chinatown just below Little Italy. Quick service and the marathon-length menu should satisfy any palate, but the real standouts are the clay-pot dishes: cooked and served in—you guessed it—a clay pot, the pork, chicken, veggies, or whatever you order become slightly caramelized, giving a subtle sweetness to the dish. The pho (the soupy national dish of Vietnam) is also a good bet, as the broth has a bolder flavor here than at other places. $ *Average main: $11* ✉ *86 Mulberry St., between Canal and Bayard Sts., Chinatown* ☎ *212/577–8887* ⊕ *www.xeluarestaurantnyc.com* ▬ *No credit cards* Ⓜ *6, J, N, Q, R, Z to Canal St.; B, D to Grand St.* ✛ *2:F5.*

GETTING CAFFEINATED IN NYC

There might be a chain coffee shop on every corner in New York City, but you won't find many locals there. The so-called "city that never sleeps" is fueled with coffee, but not just any coffee. We're a bit particular, some might say downright snobbish, about coffee, so—even if we're in a rush, which, of course, we are—we'll wait those few extra minutes for the best freshly roasted beans and pour-over brews. If you want to join discerning locals, look for outposts of Blue Bottle Coffee, Everyman Espresso, Joe Coffee, La Colombe, Ninth Street Espresso (which has locations other than 9th Street), Stumptown, and Third Rail Coffee all over Manhattan (and Brooklyn). Most spots offer the added bonus of homemade baked goods, and some also have light snacks, but don't expect that it'll be easy to find a seat.

$ ✕ **Xi'an Famous Foods.** Serving the very underrepresented cuisine of west-
CHINESE ern China, Xi'an Famous Foods serves food like you might not have tasted before. The restaurant first made a name for itself at its original location, in the dingy basement food court of a mall in Flushing, Queens, but this spot—shinier, brighter, and cleaner—serves the same exciting fare. First-timers should try the spicy cumin lamb burger, which is mouthwateringly delicious. Some of the dishes challenge the bounds of adventurousness in eating (lamb offal soup, anyone?), but don't let that scare you off. It's cheap enough to experiment, so tuck into that bowl of oxtail noodle soup and enjoy. **$** *Average main: $10* ✉ *67 Bayard St., between Mott and Elizabeth Sts., Chinatown* ☎ *212/608–4170* ⊕ *www.xianfoods.com* ▭ *No credit cards* Ⓜ *6, J, N, Q, R, Z to Canal St.; B, D to Grand St.* ✛ *2:F5.*

EAST VILLAGE AND LOWER EAST SIDE

EAST VILLAGE

This neighborhood, once a grungy ghetto for punk rockers and drug addicts, has gotten itself into shape, with great restaurants on every block—from amazing, inexpensive Asian spots to Michelin-starred destinations. St. Mark's Place is the center of New York's downtown Little Tokyo, and East 6th Street is its Indian Row.

$ ✕ **Artichoke Pizza.** Grab a gargantuan slice at this popular take-out joint,
PIZZA or order whole pies in the small, adjacent no-frills dining room. In the
FAMILY wee hours, lines often snake out the door for the artichoke-spinach slice, which tastes like cheesy dip on thick, crusty crackers. Those in the know opt for the less greasy margherita slice. Make sure you're hungry, and be prepared to stand in line awhile. For shorter lines, stop into the Greenwich Village location at 111 MacDougal Street. Or try the more formal Artichoke outpost underneath the High Line at 114 10th Avenue. **$** *Average main: $5* ✉ *328 E. 14th St., between 1st and 2nd Aves., East Village* ☎ *212/228–2004* ⊕ *www.artichokepizza.com* ▭ *No credit cards* ⌕ *Reservations not accepted* Ⓜ *L to 1st Ave.* ✛ *3:H4.*

$$ ✕ **Cafe Mogador.** An East Village dining institution if there ever was one,
MOROCCAN Cafe Mogador is a frequent stop for locals and, for some, a hip place

Restaurant Chains Worth a Taste

When you're on the go or don't have time for a leisurely meal, there are several very good chain restaurants and sandwich bars that have popped up around New York City. Those listed below are usually reasonably priced and the best in their category.

Dos Toros. Fresh and inexpensive tacos, burritos, and salads are the calling card at this local minichain with several locations in Manhattan and one in Brooklyn. The brothers who run the joint moved to NYC from San Francisco and were disappointed with the taquería options here, so they took matters into their own hands. Order at the counter and grab a seat. ⊕ www.dostoros.com.

Le Pain Quotidien. Part bakery, part café, this Belgian chain with locations throughout the city serves fresh salads and sandwiches at lunch and is great for breakfast. You can grab a snack to go or stay and eat breakfast, lunch, or dinner with waiter service. There are more than 20 locations throughout Manhattan,

including one in Central Park. ⊕ www.lepainquotidien.com.

Pret A Manger. This sandwich shop started in London in 1986 and opened its first American outpost in 2000. These days you can find one in various locations around NYC— there are several in Midtown, catering to the bustling lunch crowds. The sandwiches are excellent, and the salads are good, too. ⊕ www.pret.com.

Shake Shack. This homegrown chain has expanded across the United States and beyond, but it got its start in Madison Square Park. There are multiple locations in Manhattan and Brooklyn to enjoy burgers, hot dogs, and shakes. ⊕ www.shakeshack.com.

'wichcraft. Tom Colicchio may be best known these days as head judge of Bravo's *Top Chef*, but his fine-dining restaurants Craft and Craftbar are also well-known around Manhattan and beyond. At 'wichcraft, the sandwich shop he started with several partners back in 2003, the creations have his deliciously distinctive touch. ⊕ www.wichcraftnyc.com.

to be seen. Since 1983, the restaurant has been serving above-average Moroccan cuisine in a date-friendly, candlelit atmosphere. Finish off that creamy hummus before the chicken tagine arrives, nurse that glass of Italian wine, and ponder the fact that most of the people around you were barely walking when this family-run restaurant first fired up its couscous-cooking burners. $ *Average main: $16* ⊠ *101 St. Marks Pl., near 2nd Ave., East Village* ☎ *212/677–2226* ⊕ *www.cafemogador.com* ▭ *No credit cards* Ⓜ *L to 1st Ave.* ✛ *2:G1.*

$ ✕ **Crif Dogs.** Gluttony reigns at Crif Dogs, where you can indulge in
FAST FOOD creative—and delicious—hot dog creations. Try the Chihuahua, bacon
FAMILY wrapped and layered with avocado and sour cream, or the Tsunami, bacon wrapped with pineapple and teriyaki. (There are vegetarian dogs, too.) The tater tots banish all memories of the high school cafeteria. And that phone booth in the corner? Use that to enter secret, chic cocktail bar PDT (where there are more hot dogs available to pair with craft

cocktails). $ *Average main: $6* ✉ *113 St. Marks Pl., at Ave. A, East Village* ☎ *212/614–2728* ⊕ *www.crifdogs.com* Ⓜ *L to 1st Ave.* ✛ *3:H5.*

$$$
FRENCH

✕ **DBGB Kitchen & Bar.** The downtown arm of Daniel Boulud's New York City restaurant fleet, DBGB forgoes the white tablecloths, formal service, and steep prices found at the famed chef's fancier digs, and instead pays homage to the grittier, younger feel of its Lower East Side location. (The name is a wink at the legendary rock club CBGB.) Lined with shelves of pots, plates, and pans (not to mention copperware donated by renowned chefs from around the world), the dining room gives way to a partially open kitchen where you can catch the chefs preparing Boulud's take on French- and German-inspired pub fare. The menu features a handful of different varieties of sausages, decadent burgers (including the aptly named "piggy" burger, a juicy beef patty topped with a generous portion of pulled pork, jalapeño mayonnaise, and mustard-vinegar slaw on a cheddar bun), and classic entrées like steak frites and lemon-and-rosemary roasted chicken. $ *Average main: $28* ✉ *299 Bowery, between Houston and 1st Sts., East Village* ☎ *212/933–5300* ⊕ *www. dbgb.com* ⌕ *Reservations essential* Ⓜ *F to 2nd Ave.* ✛ *2:F2.*

$$
AUSTRIAN
Fodor's Choice
★

✕ **Edi & the Wolf.** For those who have always wanted to spend an evening in a countryside Austrian pub—and who hasn't?—but can't hop on a plane to Vienna, there's Edi & the Wolf, an outstanding restaurant deep in the section of the East Village called Alphabet City. The rustic interior (usually crammed with stylish thirtysomethings) is the perfect venue to sample dishes like honey-and-beer-accented ribs, pork-belly-laced poached eggs, and, of course, Wiener schnitzel, which is supertender and refreshingly free of grease. The well-curated beer selection focuses on Central Europe. Try the dark Czech brew, Krusovice (pronounced Kroo-sho-veetzay) $ *Average main: $22* ✉ *102 Ave. C, at 7th St., East Village* ☎ *212/598–1040* ⊕ *www.ediandthewolf.com* ☾ *No lunch weekdays* Ⓜ *F to 2nd Ave., L to 1st Ave.* ✛ *2:H1.*

$$
ITALIAN

✕ **Gnocco.** Owners Pierluigi Palazzo and Gianluca Giovannetti named their restaurant not after gnocchi but a regional Italian specialty—deep-fried dough bites typically served with northern Italian sliced meats like capicola, salami, and aged prosciutto. The gnocchi are certainly good, but the menu has so many other options you'll be forgiven if you skip them in favor of the house-made pasta specials; pizza topped with mozzarella, truffles, and mushrooms; hearty entrées like pork tenderloin in a balsamic emulsion with flakes of Grana Padano cheese; and salads—preferably all enjoyed in the roomy, canopied garden out back. $ *Average main: $20* ✉ *337 E. 10th St., between Aves. A and B, East Village* ☎ *212/677–1913* ⊕ *www.gnocco.com* Ⓜ *L to 1st Ave., 6 to Astor Pl.* ✛ *2:H1.*

$$
CHINESE

✕ **Grand Sichuan.** Yes, it's a local Chinese chainlet, and no, you don't come here for the ambience, but the food—like fiery Sichuan *dan dan* noodles, kung pao chicken, double-cooked pork, or crab soup dumplings—is good and inexpensive. $ *Average main: $18* ✉ *19–23 St. Marks Pl., near 3rd Ave., East Village* ☎ *212/529–4800* ⊕ *www. grandsichuanstmarks.com* Ⓜ *6 to Astor Pl.* ✛ *2:F1.*

$$
MEXICAN

✕ **Hecho en Dumbo.** "Made in Dumbo"—referring to the restaurant's former location in Brooklyn—specializes in *antojitos,* or "little cravings."

15

The result is something equivalent to Mexican comfort food for the hip thirtysomethings who frequent this restaurant on the Bowery. Variations on the taco theme may dominate the menu, but Hecho shines with house dishes like Berkshire pork shank and roasted scallops paired with bone marrow salsa. Pair your meal with one of the delicious margaritas (no bottled mix used here), sangria, or perhaps a *michelada*—beer and tomato juice on ice with lime and a salted rim. $ *Average main: $17* ⊠ *354 Bowery, between Great Jones and 4th Sts., East Village* ☎ *212/937–4245* ⊕ *www.hechoendumbo.com* ⊟ *No credit cards* Ⓜ *6 to Astor Pl.; N, R to 8th St.–NYU* ✛ *2:F2.*

$$$ ✕ **Il Buco.** The unabashed clutter of vintage kitchen gadgets and table-
ITALIAN ware harks back to Il Buco's past as an antiques store and affects a romantic country-house feel with excellent food—this is a favorite for a cozy, intimate meal. The menu focuses on meat and produce from local farms, with several excellent pasta choices, and a variety of Mediterranean tapas-like appetizers. Call ahead to book the intimate wine cellar for dinner. Il Buco Alimentari & Vineria, around the corner at 53 Great Jones Street, is a more casual setting, with a small market up front selling gourmet cheese and house-cured meats, and a wine bar in the back. $ *Average main: $28* ⊠ *47 Bond St., between the Bowery and Lafayette St., East Village* ☎ *212/533–1932* ⊕ *www.ilbuco.com* ☉ *No lunch Sun.* Ⓜ *6 to Bleecker St.; B, D, F, M to Broadway–Lafayette St.* ✛ *2:F2.*

$$ ✕ **Ippudo.** Crowds wait hours for the ramen noodles at Ippudo, the first
JAPANESE American branch of the Japanese chain. Loyal patrons say it's all about the rich, pork-based broth—there is a vegetarian version available but it lacks the depth of flavor. Those really in the know, though, make sure to order sleeper-hit appetizers like the peppery chicken wings or pork buns. It's not a hole-in-the-wall ramen spot, so although a meal here is relatively inexpensive, it's not dirt cheap. There's a newer Ippudo outpost in Midtown at 321 West 51st Street. $ *Average main: $16* ⊠ *65 4th Ave., between 9th and 10th Sts., East Village* ☎ *212/388–0088* ⊕ *www.ippudony.com* ⊜ *Reservations not accepted* Ⓜ *6 to Astor Pl.; N, R to 8th St.–NYU* ✛ *3:G5.*

$$$$ ✕ **Jewel Bako.** Arguably the best sushi restaurant in the East Village, this
JAPANESE tiny space gleams in a minefield of cheap, often inferior sushi houses. The futuristic bamboo tunnel of a dining room is gorgeous, but try to nab a place at the sushi bar and put yourself in the hands of sushi master Yoshi Kousaka. The five-course omakase, or chef's menu, starts at $125. (A less expensive sushi or sashimi omakase is $75.) You are served only what's freshest and best. $ *Average main: $50* ⊠ *239 E. 5th St., between 2nd and 3rd Aves., East Village* ☎ *212/979–1012* ⊕ *www. jewelbakosushi.com* ☉ *Closed Sun. No lunch* ⊜ *Reservations essential* Ⓜ *6 to Astor Pl.; N, R to 8th St.–NYU* ✛ *3:G6.*

$$$ ✕ **Lafayette Grand Cafe & Bakery.** Food-media darling, chef Andrew Car-
FRENCH mellini (of Locanda Verde, Bar Primi, and the Dutch) goes Gallic here. After nearly a decade of Italian dominance on the Big Apple restaurant scene, French is back in vogue again, and Lafayette is a return to Carmellini's roots: the kitchens of his mentor, the great Daniel Boulud. There's no culinary trickery happening here, just straightforward and very satisfying bistro fare. Creamy duck-confit-spiked pumpkin risotto,

a silky beef tartare, and steak frites are all excellent. So is the people-watching at this hip spot. $ *Average main: $25* ⊠ *380 Lafayette St., at Great Jones St., East Village* ☎ *212/533–3000* ⊕ *www.lafayetteny. com* Ⓜ *6 to Bleecker St.; B, D, F, M to Broadway–Lafayette St.; N, R to 8th St.–NYU* ✛ *3:F6.*

$ ✕ **Mamoun's Falafel.** This hole-in-the-wall institution, bustling day and
MIDDLE EASTERN night, is the place to go for speedy, hot, supercheap, and delicious
FAMILY Middle Eastern food. Tahini-topped pitas are packed with fresh, green-on-the-inside falafel balls. Be warned: the hot sauce is incendiary. The small space has a few tables, but this is food you can easily eat on the go. Best of all, it's open every night until at least 4 am. The original Mamoun's is still at 119 MacDougal Street, near Washington Square Park in Greenwich Village. $ *Average main: $7* ⊠ *22 St. Marks Pl., between 2nd and 3rd Aves., East Village* ☎ *212/387–7747* ⊕ *www. mamouns.com* ⚐ *Reservations not accepted* ▭ *No credit cards* Ⓜ *6 to Astor Pl.; N, R to 8th St.–NYU* ✛ *3:G5.*

$ ✕ **Mile End.** Named for a neighborhood in Montreal where the city's
DELI famed bagel bakeries exist, Mile End has became one of the darlings of the city's fooderati since it opened in Brooklyn several years ago. By the time this Manhattan location began rolling out its light, chewy, and slightly sweet Montreal bagels, the place was already an institution. The bagels are authentic, but the real reason to come here is for the impressive deli fare, including pastrami, roast beef, and smoked-meat sandwiches. The poutine—french fries with cheese curds and gravy—is a delicious mess. Once standing-room only, there's now seating in the long, narrow room, as well as dinner service. Dinner is also served at the original Brooklyn location in Boerum Hill, at 97A Hoyt Street. $ *Average main: $10* ⊠ *53 Bond St., near the Bowery, East Village* ☎ *212/529–2990* ⊕ *www.mileenddeli.com* ▭ *No credit cards* ☉ *No dinner Sun. and Mon.* Ⓜ *6 to Bleecker St.; B, D, F, M to Broadway–Lafayette St.* ✛ *2:F2.*

$$ ✕ **Minca.** It may have received less fanfare than some other East Village
JAPANESE noodle bars, but the ramen at this tiny, cramped spot is among the best in the city; the fact that visiting Japanese students eat here is a good sign. Try to get a seat at the bar, where you can watch the chefs prepare your food. Start with homemade *gyoza* dumplings, then dive your spoon and chopsticks into one of the many types of ramen. The shoyu (soy sauce) Minca ramen is unfailingly good, but anything with pork is also a good bet. $ *Average main: $14* ⊠ *536 E. 5th St., between Aves. A and B, East Village* ☎ *212/505–8001* ⊕ *www.newyorkramen.com* ⚐ *Reservations not accepted* ▭ *No credit cards* Ⓜ *F to 2nd Ave.* ✛ *2:H2.*

$$$$ ✕ **Momofuku Ko.** After a move to this quaint alleyway near where the
ASIAN Bowery and 1st Street meet, Momofuku Ko is still firing on all cylinders.
Fodor's Choice At James Beard Award–winning chef David Chang's most formal din-
★ ing option, diners sit at the bar to see Ko's chefs in action or opt for a standalone table. The menu is prix fixe only: 20 courses for $195. And it's worth it for the complex flavor strata that Chang builds. Reservations can be made online only, no more than 15 days ahead for dinner, and are extremely difficult to get. Log on at 10 am (a credit card number is required just to get into the system), when new reservations are available,

15

and keep hitting reload. ⑤ *Average main: $100* ⌑ *8 Extra Pl., at 1st St., East Village* ☎ *212/203–095* ⊕ *www.momofuku.com* ◷ *Closed Mon. No lunch* ⌑ *Reservations essential* Ⓜ *F to 2nd Ave.* ✛ *3:G6.*

$ ✕ **Momofuku Milk Bar.** This combination bakery, ice-cream parlor, and
CAFÉ   sandwich shop boasts quick-serve access to chef David Chang's cult-
FAMILY   ish pork buns, along with some truly psychedelic treats by pastry chef
Christina Tosi. Swing by for a kimchi croissant and glass of "cereal"
milk, or for treats like the curiously flavored soft-serve ice cream (cereal
milk, lemon verbena), "candy bar pie" (a sweet bomb of caramel, peanut-butter nougat, and pretzels atop a chocolate-cookie crust), one of
the addictive cookies (try the "compost" cookies, with pretzels, chocolate chips, and whatever inspires the bakers that day), or any of the
intriguing savories (the "volcano" is a cheese-and-potato pastry that is
impossible to eat daintily). ⑤ *Average main: $7* ⌑ *251 E. 13th St., East
Village* ☎ *347/577–9504* ⊕ *www.milkbarstore.com* ⌑ *Reservations not
accepted* Ⓜ *L to 3rd Ave.* ✛ *3:G4.*

$$ ✕ **Momofuku Noodle Bar.** Chef and owner David Chang has created a
ASIAN   shrine to ramen with this stylish 70-seat restaurant. His riff on the
Fodor'sChoice   Japanese classic features haute ingredients like Berkshire pork, free-
★   range chicken, and organic produce—though there are plenty of other
innovative options on the menu. His modern take on pork buns with
cucumber and scallions is phenomenal—alone worth the trip. You'll
probably have to wait if you go at regular meal times, but seats at
the long counter open up fairly quickly, and the lively atmosphere is
part of the fun. The excellent fried-chicken meal includes both triple-
fried Korean-style and Old Bay Southern-style chicken with a variety
of accoutrements, and feeds four to eight people (available by special
reservations only on the website). ⑤ *Average main: $17* ⌑ *171 1st Ave.,
between 10th and 11th Sts., East Village* ☎ *212/777–7773* ⊕ *www.
momofuku.com* ⌑ *Reservations not accepted* Ⓜ *L to 1st Ave.* ✛ *3:H5.*

$$ ✕ **Momofuku Ssäm Bar.** New York foodies have been salivating over chef
ASIAN   David Chang's Asian-influenced fare since he opened Noodle Bar in
2004. Ssäm Bar, with a more extensive menu, is equally worth the raves.
The restaurant is packed nightly with downtown diners cut from the
same cloth as the pierced and tattooed waitstaff and cooks. The no-
reservations policy (except for large parties or special dinners) means
having to wait in line for a chance to try Chang's truly inventive flavor combinations. The menu is constantly changing but the not-to-be-
missed riff on the classic Chinese steamed pork bun is almost always
available. Have a nightcap at Chang's inventive cocktail bar, Booker
& Dax, around the corner. ⑤ *Average main: $24* ⌑ *207 2nd Ave., at
13th St., East Village* ☎ *212/254–3500* ⊕ *www.momofuku.com/ssam*
Ⓜ *L to 1st Ave.* ✛ *3:G4.*

$$ ✕ **Motorino Pizza.** The Manhattan branch of the Williamsburg origi-
PIZZA   nal has brought its impossibly high standards—and long lines—to a
new borough. The authentic Neapolitan pies are made with glutinous,
dough-friendly double-zero flour and San Marzano tomatoes, and the
crusts are lightly charred. You can't go wrong with any of the signature
traditional pizzas, like marinara; margherita with fresh tomatoes, moz-
zarella, and basil; or a pie with spicy sopressata, sausage, and garlic; but

the seasonal selections are also tempting. Check out the brunch pizza (with egg and pancetta) on weekends. Antipasti like octopus and fingerling potato salad with celery-chili oil, and cockle-clam crostini round out the menu. The weekday lunchtime prix-fixe means pizza and salad is a bargain at $14 per person. [$] *Average main: $17* ⊠ *349 E. 12th St., at 1st Ave., East Village* ☎ *212/777–2644* ⊕ *www.motorinopizza.com* ⌲ *Reservations not accepted* [M] *L to 1st Ave.* ✛ *3:H4.*

$ ✕ **Porchetta.** Super-succulent Italian roast pork—dusted in fennel pol-
ITALIAN len and covered in crisp cracklin' skin—is the star attraction here. It is, in fact, just about the only thing on the menu of this tiny spot. Order your pork in a sandwich or as a platter with stewed greens and roasted potatoes. There's not much room for dining on-site, but the benches out front are ideal when the weather cooperates. [$] *Average main: $11* ⊠ *110 E. 7th St., near 1st Ave., East Village* ☎ *212/777–2151* ⊕ *www. porchettanyc.com* ⌲ *Reservations not accepted* [M] *6 to Astor Pl.; L to 1st Ave.* ✛ *3:H5.*

$$$ ✕ **Pylos.** The perfect setting for a relaxed dinner or an intimate spe-
GREEK cial occasion, this tastefully refined, light-filled East Village restaurant emphasizes rustic cooking from all over Greece. There are delicious versions of hearty comfort-food dishes like pastitsio and moussaka on the menu, but the lighter dishes—especially fish—let the flavors shine through. There is an extensive selection of interesting hot and cold mezes—start with the traditional trio of *tzatziki, taramosalata* (lemony fish roe dip), and *melitzanosalata* (an eggplant-based dip) and explore from there. Accompany your meal with some *vino* from the all-Greek wine list; the light white Atlantis wine from the island of Santorini is particularly enjoyable, and affordable. [$] *Average main: $26* ⊠ *128 E. 7th St., near Ave. A, East Village* ☎ *212/473–0220* ⊕ *www. pylosrestaurant.com* ⊗ *No lunch Mon. and Tues.* [M] *F to 2nd Ave.; L to 1st Ave.* ✛ *3:H5.*

$$ ✕ **Saxon & Parole.** One of the hottest spots on this burgeoning stretch of
MODERN the Bowery, this eatery may be named for two 19th-century racehorses,
AMERICAN but the food—and the extremely good-looking crowd—is nothing you'd
Fodor's Choice find in a barnyard. Settle into this cozy, sceney spot, order a cocktail,
★ and peruse a menu loaded with the Zeitgeist dishes of New York dining: roasted bone marrow, Brussels sprouts, pork belly, chicken-liver mousse, and, of course, an overpriced but excellent burger. The kitchen executes it all to complete deliciousness. The bar scene is lively, so come early for a cocktail. [$] *Average main: $23* ⊠ *316 Bowery, at Bleecker St., East Village* ☎ *212/254–0350* ⊕ *www.saxonandparole.com* ⊗ *No lunch* [M] *B, D, F, M to Broadway–Lafayette St.; 6 to Bleecker St.; F to 2nd Ave.* ✛ *2:F2.*

$$ ✕ **Somtum Der.** Once upon a time, New Yorkers had to venture to Queens
THAI to get good Thai food, but that's no longer the case. Not only have a handful of great Thai restaurants opened in Manhattan in recent years, but many of them hail from Isaan, a region in northeast Thailand that emphasizes light, spicy fare. Somtum Der, originally based in Bangkok, is one of the best. Start with the namesake *somtum*, a palate-singeing green papaya salad, before moving on to the *larb moo*, a mound of minced pork mixed with veggies and chilies. Also worth trying is the

15

fried chicken, which makes you question the Southern United States' monopoly on crispy bird. The restaurant is small and can get quite noisy. $ *Average main: $15* ⊠ *85 Ave. A, East Village* 🕾 *212/260–8570* ⊕ *www.somtumder.com* ▭ *No credit cards* Ⓜ *F to 2nd Ave.; L to 1st Ave.* ✛ *3:H6.*

$ ✕ **Veniero's Pasticceria.** Since 1894, this bustling bakery-café has sold
CAFÉ   every kind of Italian *dolce* (sweet), from cherry-topped cookies to
FAMILY   creamy cannoli and flaky *sfogliatelle* (shell-shape, filled pastry). Cheese-
cake lovers rejoice in Veniero's ricotta-based version. In all, a hungry visitor with a serious sweet tooth can choose from more than 150 different types of desserts. A wine license means you can top off your evening with a bottle of red. Veniero's is worth a look—check out the pressed-tin ceiling, marble floors, and stained glass—even if you're not hungry. $ *Average main: $5* ⊠ *342 E. 11th St., near 1st Ave., East Village* 🕾 *212/674–7070* ⊕ *www.venierospastry.com* ⌲ *Reservations not accepted* Ⓜ *6 to Astor Pl.; L to 1st Ave.* ✛ *3:H5.*

$ ✕ **Veselka.** Potato pierogi are available 24 hours a day at this East Vil-
EASTERN   lage stalwart, which opened in 1954. The name means "rainbow" in
EUROPEAN   Ukrainian. The authentic Ukrainian-slash-diner food is the perfect stick-
FAMILY   to-your-ribs ending to a night on the town—or beginning to a new day,
as the restaurant serves a full array of breakfast staples. It's a neighborhood experience, with tables of families sharing space with the hipsters. The spacious, sunny interior, with giant wall paintings to please the eye, is great for people-watching; don't take the servers' studied indifference personally. $ *Average main: $12* ⊠ *144 2nd Ave., at 9th St., East Village* 🕾 *212/228–9682* ⊕ *www.veselka.com* ⌲ *Reservations not accepted* Ⓜ *6 to Astor Pl.; N, R to 8th St.–NYU; L to 1st Ave.* ✛ *3:H5.*

$$ ✕ **Zum Schneider.** Located in Alphabet City, this garrulous Teutonic spot
GERMAN   teaches the ABCs of beer drinking and hearty eating. Grab a table outside when the weather's nice, among the young hipsters who frequent the spot, and get ready for some kraut-laden fun. After quaffing a liter-size stein of the sudsy stuff, you may crave food, and the menu, naturally, is a veritable sausage-palooza. In addition to the usual meaty fare, such as Wiener schnitzel and goulash, there are, well, more sausages. The crispy potato pancakes are a good bet, too. $ *Average main: $16* ⊠ *107 Ave. C, at 7th St., East Village* 🕾 *212/598–1098* ⊕ *www.zumschneider.com* ☾ *No lunch* Ⓜ *L to 1st Ave.; F to 2nd Ave.* ✛ *2:H1.*

LOWER EAST SIDE

The Lower East Side, home to generations of immigrant newcomers, has become quite the culinary hub over the last 15 years, with everything from molecular gastronomy to hipster Chinese cuisine. You can't walk a block without hitting a place that makes your stomach growl.

$$ ✕ **Clinton St. Baking Co.** There was a time when this Lower East Side
AMERICAN   restaurant was *the* place to come for brunch. Specifically, it was *the*
Fodor'sChoice   place to eat blueberry pancakes, which many regulars professed were
★   the best in the city, if not the state, or the whole country. But all that changed when owners Neil Kleinberg and DeDe Lahman added lunch and dinner to the menu. Oh, it's still a great place for brunch, but now you can eat those pancakes (along with a good Black Angus burger or crab-cake sandwich) anytime. February is pancake month when, in

addition to the blueberry, every weekday brings a special incarnation of the pancake. $ *Average main: $19* ⌗ *4 Clinton St., near Houston St., Lower East Side* ☎ *646/602–6263* ⊕ *www.clintonstreetbaking.com* ⊗ *No dinner Sun.* Ⓜ *F to 2nd Ave.; J, M, Z to Essex St.* ✛ *2:H2.*

$$ ✕ **Congee Village.** Don't be put off by the name—this boisterous China-
CHINESE town icon serves much more than the eponymous rice porridge. Indeed, the menu is enormous, covering an encyclopedic range of unusual Cantonese classics. The bamboo-cloaked dining room is great with a group of people, but being wedged in at a communal table with a boisterous family is part of the experience. If feeling adventurous, try the duck tongues in XO sauce or salt-and-pepper frog, or stick to familiar classics. Either way, the congee is a great way to start. $ *Average main: $15* ⌗ *100 Allen St., near Delancey St., Lower East Side* ☎ *212/941–1818* ⊕ *www.congeevillagerestaurants.com* Ⓜ *F to Delancey St.; J, M, Z to Essex St.; B, D to Grand St.* ✛ *2:G3.*

$$ ✕ **Dirt Candy.** One of the best, most inspired vegetarian restaurants out-
VEGETARIAN side California, Dirt Candy shines thanks to chef Amanda Cohen, who
Fodor's Choice knows how to coax every bit of flavor out of a vegetable, allowing said
★ veggies to shine and sparkle on the plate and the palate. First-timers shouldn't ignore the jalapeño hush puppies (with maple butter), the cauliflower curry (with a green-pea paneer), and the Brussels sprouts tacos, which are the best—and perhaps, the only—Brussels sprouts tacos you'll ever eat. Make reservations at least a week in advance or be prepared to wait with the waiflike regulars. $ *Average main: $17* ⌗ *86 Allen St., Lower East Side* ☎ *212/228–7732* ⊕ *www.dirtcandynyc. com* ⊗ *Closed Mon. No lunch* ⌂ *Reservations essential* Ⓜ *F to Delancey St.* ✛ *2:G4.*

$$$ ✕ **Dirty French.** Rich Torrisi and Mario Carbone, the chefs who created
FRENCH a small empire of Italian-American restaurants (Parm, Carbone, ZZ's Clam Bar) go Gallic at this Lower East Side bistro in the Ludlow Hotel. The name says it all: while the fare from the kitchen is French, the team put their own spin on it, taking many of the dishes on a tour of places like North Africa and Louisiana before they land on your table. Porgy is dusted with Cajun spices and the duck à l'orange is spiked with Moroccan *ras el hanout* spice blend. The long, all-French wine list includes some nice bottles from off-the-radar regions. $ *Average main: $30* ⌗ *Ludlow Hotel, 180 Ludlow St., Lower East Side* ☎ *212/254–3000* ⊕ *www.dirtyfrench.com* Ⓜ *F to 2nd Ave.* ✛ *2:G3.*

$ ✕ **Doughnut Plant.** If you want to know what it feels like to eat a dough-
CAFÉ nut for the first time, head to the Doughnut Plant, where the all-Amer-
FAMILY ican junk-food staple is elevated to high art. Fresh seasonal ingredients go into these decadent treats, with real fruit and imported chocolate mixed into the batter. Traditionalists croon over the vanilla-bean doughnut, but there are plenty of exotic flavors to tempt taste buds: the dense, fudgy Blackout is covered in crumb topping; carrot-cake doughnuts have a cream-cheese filling. The Lower East Side location is open every day from 6:30 am to 8 pm ('til 9 pm Friday and Saturday). There's a second location in Chelsea, next to the Chelsea Hotel; doughnuts are also available around the city at Dean & DeLuca and Zabar's. $ *Average main: $5* ⌗ *379 Grand St., Lower East Side* ☎ *212/505–3700* ⊕ *www.*

15

doughnutplant.com ⚲ *Reservations not accepted* ⊟ *No credit cards* Ⓜ *F to Delancey St.; J, M, Z to Essex St.; B, D to Grand St.* ✛ *2:G4.*

$$ **✕ The Fat Radish.** The phrase "seasonal British" might have once seemed
BRITISH   puzzling, but with seasonal ingredients very much in vogue and British cui-
sine making a name for itself, this handsome, hip, and sceney Lower East
Side (almost Chinatown) restaurant is worth a visit. The menu is eclectic
but full of excellent choices. Expect to be confronted by a lot of kale and
other en-vogue ingredients. Green curried monkfish, a cheeseburger served
with duck-fat fries, pork sausage and mussel stew, and roasted Peking
duck breast are just a few of the menu showstoppers. Match that with
quality craft British brews and potent cocktails and you'll be championing
English cuisine in no time. ⑤ *Average main: $22* ✉ *17 Orchard St., near
Canal St., Lower East Side* ☏ *212/300–4053* ⊕ *www.thefatradishnyc.com*
☽ *No lunch Mon.* Ⓜ *F to East Broadway* ✛ *2:G5.*

$$ **✕ Freemans.** It's hard to believe now, but there was once a time when
AMERICAN   New York restaurant interiors were trying hard not to look cool, with
Fodor'sChoice   no taxidermy or ironic tchotchkes littered around the room, or lodge-ish
★   dishes like hunters stew, potted pork, and grilled trout on the menu. But
we have Freemans to thank for the change, and their equally inspired
cocktails menu. Down a little-used alleyway on the Lower East Side,
trendsetting Freemans is as hip and popular as when it opened in 2004.
Just don't try too hard to look cool. ⑤ *Average main: $22* ✉ *End of
Freeman Alley, near Rivington St., Lower East Side* ☏ *212/420–0012*
⊕ *www.freemansrestaurant.com* ⚲ *Reservations not accepted* Ⓜ *F to
2nd Ave.; J, Z to Bowery* ✛ *2:F3.*

$$ **✕ Ivan Ramen.** Ivan Orkin's improbable but true story is one of the
JAPANESE   many layers that make New York City's restaurant scene so exciting,
Fodor'sChoice   authentic, and delicious: the self-described "Jewish kid from Long
★   Island" moved to Tokyo and became a ramen-making master, achiev-
ing near legendary status in the Japanese capital. In 2014 he opened this
Lower East Side temple to ramen and it's been packed since day one.
First-timers should try the triple pork, triple garlic *mazemen*, a type of
near-brothless ramen. The spicy red-chili ramen, filled to the rim with
chicken broth, a smashed egg, minced pork, and rye noodles, lives up to
its name. It all goes well with a pint of craft beer or a can of sake. ⑤ *Av-
erage main: $17* ✉ *25 Clinton St., Lower East Side* ☏ *646/678–3859*
⊕ *www.ivanramen.com* Ⓜ *F to 2nd Ave.; J, M, Z to Essex St.* ✛ *2:G3.*

$$ **✕ Katz's Delicatessen.** Everything and nothing has changed at Katz's since
DELI   it first opened in 1888, when the neighborhood was dominated by Jew-
Fodor'sChoice   ish immigrants. The rows of Formica tables, the long self-service coun-
★   ter, and such signs as "Send a salami to your boy in the army" are all
completely authentic. The lines still form on the weekends for giant, succulent hand-carved corned beef and pastrami sandwiches, soul-warming
soups, juicy hot dogs, and crisp half-sour pickles. Weeknights are more
laid-back. You get a ticket when you walk in and then get it punched
at the various stations where you pick up your food; don't lose it or
you'll have to pay the lost ticket fee. ⑤ *Average main: $16* ✉ *205 E.
Houston St., at Ludlow St., Lower East Side* ☏ *212/254–2246* ⊕ *www.
katzsdelicatessen.com* Ⓜ *F to 2nd Ave.* ✛ *2:G2.*

$$ **✗ Loreley Restaurant & Biergarten.** Beer gardens once dotted the New York
GERMAN City landscape in the way that Starbucks does now, but after World War
I and Prohibition, most of these outdoor drinking spots vanished. Then
in 2003 came Loreley (which eventually kicked off a new beer-garden
craze in the city). Don't mistake this Lower East Side hot spot for a place
where geriatrics in lederhosen swing their plus-size steins of beer to polka
music. Instead, there's a better-than-good chance of finding a gaggle of
hipsters nursing German craft beers while bobbing their heads to the
new Radiohead album and munching on plates of sausage, meatballs,
or schnitzel. The space out back may be more concrete than garden, but
it's a pleasure on a mild evening. $ *Average main: $17* ✉ *7 Rivington St.,
near the Bowery, Lower East Side* ☎ *212/253–7077* ⊕ *www.loreleynyc.
com* Ⓜ *J, Z to Bowery; B, D to Grand St.; F to 2nd Ave.* ✛ *2:F3.*

$ **✗ The Meatball Shop.** New York's first full-service meatball restaurant has
ITALIAN a pedigree chef, a professional waitstaff, a wine list, and a hip crowd.
FAMILY And the meatballs, oh, the meatballs: choose beef, pork, chicken, veg-
gie, or "special" ball options that range from chili cheese to Greek lamb
and Buffalo chicken; then decide if you want them served simply as is,
in sliders or a hero, as a salad, or a platter—all with an appropriate
choice of sauce and cheese. The meatball concept quickly caught on,
and there are now six locations: five in Manhattan and one in Wil-
liamsburg. Mix 'n' match ice-cream sandwiches—choose your flavor
and cookie—are worth saving room for. $ *Average main: $11* ✉ *84
Stanton St., near Allen St., Lower East Side* ☎ *212/982–8895* ⊕ *www.
themeatballshop.com* ✍ *Reservations not accepted* Ⓜ *F to 2nd Ave.; J,
Z to Bowery* ✛ *2:G3.*

$$ **✗ Mission Cantina.** Chef Danny Bowien rocked the New York dining
MEXICAN scene when he imported his San Francisco hit Mission Chinese Food
here, and then added another local favorite with this Mexican eatery.
The menu changes seasonally, but expect adventurous taco creations
with creative ingredient pairings: beef tongue sprinkled with peanuts,
and fresh tuna with wasabi are standouts. There are also huge burritos
stuffed with chorizo, lamb, and rotisserie chicken. There's an additional non-Mexican menu of Chinese staples available, too. The floor-
to-ceiling windows are excellent for people-watching. $ *Average main:
$14* ✉ *172 Orchard St., Lower East Side* ☎ *212/254–2233* ⊕ *www.
missioncantinany.com* Ⓜ *F to 2nd Ave.* ✛ *2:G3.*

$$ **✗ Schiller's Liquor Bar.** It may not be as hard to get in as it was back in
BISTRO 2003, when Keith McNally first opened this sceney hangout on the
FAMILY Lower East Side, but it still has the allure, with excellent bistro fare, sexy
cocktails, and the kind of atmosphere that is as comfortable for celebri-
ties as for parents with strollers. This is vintage Parisian à la McNally:
verdigris mirrored panels, forever-in-style subway tiles, a tin ceiling,
and a checkered floor, while Cuban sandwiches and steak frites reveal
a steady hand in the kitchen. This is also the place for a late-night bite,
since the kitchen is open until midnight every night (until 3 am Friday
and Saturday). Breakfast is served weekdays until 4 pm, with brunch
on weekends. $ *Average main: $20* ✉ *131 Rivington St., at Norfolk
St., Lower East Side* ☎ *212/260–4555* ⊕ *www.schillersny.com* Ⓜ *F to
Delancey St.; J, M, Z to Essex St.* ✛ *2:G3.*

15

$$ ✕ **Shopsin's.** Don't ask for substitutions or sauce on the side at New
ECLECTIC   York's most eccentric eatery, because Kenny Shopsin, owner and chef,
FAMILY   may really toss you out or ban you for life; somehow the attitude is part
of the appeal here. Though the eclectic menu runs to literally hundreds
of items—from pumpkin pancakes to chilaquiles, and from chili cheese-
burgers to lamb-curry soups—even the strangest foods conjured up in
his tight diner kitchen taste pretty great. The mac 'n' cheese pancakes
have loyal followers (they're even better with hot sauce). The space in
the Essex market is tiny, so expect to wait. Parties of more than four
aren't accepted. ⑤ *Average main: $17* ✉ *Essex Market, 120 Essex St.,
near Rivington St., Lower East Side* ⊕ *www.shopsins.com* ⊘ *Closed
Mon. and Tues. No dinner* ⚲ *Reservations not accepted* ▬ *No credit
cards* Ⓜ *F to Delancey St.; J, M, Z to Essex St.* ✛ *2:G3.*

$$ ✕ **The Stanton Social.** This swanky Lower East Side favorite lures crowds
ECLECTIC   with an expansive and eclectic small-plates menu, accompanied by a
perfectly calibrated cocktail list. Come before 7 if you want to be able
to hear your companion speak, but the people-watching and shared
dishes are good at any hour. Try the gooey, Gruyère-topped onion soup
dumplings, juicy Kobe beef sliders, and wasabi-crusted salmon. Downstairs feels like a more traditional dining room, whereas the second
level features a buzzy bar. The late-night lounge area, decorated with
cherry-blossom wallpaper and red leather upholstery, turns more night-
clubby the later it gets. Brunch—with options like spicy lobster Benedict—might blow your mind. Whatever time you come, save room for
the fresh doughnuts. ⑤ *Average main: $20* ✉ *99 Stanton St., between
Ludlow and Orchard Sts., Lower East Side* ☎ *212/995–0099* ⊕ *www.
thestantonsocial.com* ⊘ *No lunch* ⚲ *Reservations essential* Ⓜ *F to 2nd
Ave.; J, M, Z to Essex St.* ✛ *2:G3.*

$ ✕ **Sugar Sweet Sunshine.** The brainchild of two former Magnolia Bakery
CAFÉ   employees, Sugar Sweet's cupcakes are far superior; try the chocolate-
FAMILY   almond Gooey Gooey, or the cream cheese frosting–topped pumpkin flavor. The real showstopper? Swoon-inducing banana pudding,
with slices of ripe fruit and crumbled Nilla wafers suspended in decadent vanilla pudding. Cupcakes are the perfect on-the-go treat, but if
you prefer to hang out, there are cozy couches. ⑤ *Average main: $5*
✉ *126 Rivington St., between Essex and Norfolk Sts., Lower East Side*
☎ *212/995–1960* ⊕ *www.sugarsweetsunshine.com* ⚲ *Reservations not
accepted* Ⓜ *F to Delancey St.; J, M, Z to Essex St.* ✛ *2:G3.*

GREENWICH VILLAGE AND THE WEST VILLAGE

GREENWICH VILLAGE

Greenwich Village's bohemian days may have faded, but the romantic
allure of its tiny bistros, bars, and cafés remains. Around New York
University, shabby-chic eateries and take-out joints cater to students,
but there is a growing number of more sophisticated dining spots, too.

$$ ✕ **Arturo's.** Few guidebooks list this classic New York pizzeria, but the
PIZZA   jam-packed room and pleasantly smoky scent foreshadow a satisfying
FAMILY   meal. There's a full menu of Italian classics, but don't be fooled: pizza is
the main event. The thin-crust beauties are cooked in a coal-fired oven,

and emerge sizzling with simple toppings like pepperoni, sausage, and eggplant. Monday through Thursday, you can call ahead to reserve a table; weekends, be prepared to wait and salivate. If you like the whimsical paintings that plaster the walls, ask the waiter the price: they're for sale. ⑤ *Average main: $19* ✉ *106 W. Houston St., near Thompson St., Greenwich Village* ☎ *212/535–4480* ☉ *No lunch weekends* Ⓜ *1 to Houston St.; B, D, F, M to Broadway–Lafayette St.* ⊹ *2:D3.*

$$$
ITALIAN
Fodor'sChoice
★

✕ **Babbo Ristorante.** It shouldn't take more than one bite of the ethereal homemade pasta or tender barbecue squab with roast beet farrotto for you to understand why it's so hard to get a reservation at Mario Batali's casually elegant restaurant. The menu strays widely from Italian standards and hits numerous high points, in particular with the "mint love letters": ravioli filled with pureed peas, ricotta, and fresh mint, finished with spicy lamb sausage ragout; and rabbit with Brussels sprouts, housemade pancetta, and carrot vinaigrette. This is the perfect spot for a raucous celebratory dinner with flowing wine and festive banter. But be forewarned: if anyone in your party is hard of hearing, or bothered by loud rock music, choose someplace more sedate. ⑤ *Average main: $30* ✉ *110 Waverly Pl., between MacDougal St. and 6th Ave., Greenwich Village* ☎ *212/777–0303* ⊕ *www.babbonyc.com* ☉ *No lunch Sun. and Mon.* ⌂ *Reservations essential* Ⓜ *A, B, C, D, E, F, M to W. 4th St.* ⊹ *2:C1.*

$$$
MODERN
AMERICAN

✕ **Blue Hill.** This tasteful, sophisticated den of a restaurant—formerly a speakeasy—on a quiet side street maintains an impeccable reputation for excellence and consistency under the leadership of chef Dan Barber. The Obamas even stopped here for dinner, shutting down the street for one of their "date nights." Part of the slow-food, sustainable agriculture movement, Blue Hill mostly uses ingredients grown or raised within 200 miles, including the Four Season Farm at Stone Barns Center for Food and Agriculture, Barber's second culinary project in nearby Westchester County. The chefs produce precisely cooked and elegantly constructed food such as wild striped bass with potato-and-clam chowder and house-cured *guanciale* (pork jowl), and a smoked-tomato soup with American caviar. ⑤ *Average main: $32* ✉ *75 Washington Pl., between Washington Sq. W and 6th Ave., Greenwich Village* ☎ *212/539–1776* ⊕ *www.bluehillfarm.com* ☉ *No lunch* ⌂ *Reservations essential* Ⓜ *A, B, C, D, E, F, M to W. 4th St.* ⊹ *2:C1.*

$$$$
ITALIAN

✕ **Carbone.** It seems like Mario Carbone and Rich Torrisi can do no wrong. Case in point: Carbone. The achingly popular place not only sticks to the Italian-American formula that has won it (and their earlier restaurant Torrisi) acclaim, but goes one step further: the white-tableclothed Greenwich Village restaurant successfully emulates the Big Apple Italian restaurants of the 1950s, with revived dishes like veal marsala, rib-eye Diana, and baked clams. It's not cheap, but portions are generous. ⑤ *Average main: $45* ✉ *181 Thompson St., between Bleecker and Houston Sts., Greenwich Village* ☎ *212/254–3000* ⊕ *www.carbonenewyork.com* ☉ *No lunch weekends* ⌂ *Reservations essential* Ⓜ *A, B, C, D, E, F, M to W. 4th St.* ⊹ *2:D2.*

15

$$$
ITALIAN
Fodor's Choice
★

$\times$**Charlie Bird.** Perpetually packed since the day it opened in the spring of 2013, Charlie Bird is the love child of sommelier Robert Bohr, who was in charge of wine at vino-mad Cru, and chef Ryan Hardy, who made a name for himself at Little Nell in Aspen and, more recently, sharpened his skills as private chef for food-loving Jay-Z and Beyoncé—it's no coincidence the restaurant has a hip-hop theme (expect old-school and '90's rap on the hi-fi). The Italian-leaning menu is divided into small and large plates, vegetables, a "raw" section, and pasta. The uni-loaded duck-egg spaghetti marries surf 'n' turf in a deeply satisfying way, while the scallops are subtly laced with lardo, giving them an umami boost. ⑤ *Average main: $32* ⊠ *5 King St., at 6th Ave., Greenwich Village* ☎ *212/235–7133* ⊕ *www.charliebirdnyc.com* ▬ *No credit cards* ⌲ *Reservations essential* Ⓜ *C, E to Spring St.; 1 to Houston St.* ✛ *2:C3.*

$
INDIAN

$\times$**Kati Roll Company.** You can think of a kati roll as a South Asian taco: griddled parathas stuffed with savory-spiced grilled meat, shrimp, paneer, chickpea mash, or spiced mashed potato. They're the only things sold at this tiny, popular lunch spot cheerfully festooned with Bollywood posters. This is an excellent and inexpensive lunch option, but be warned that lines often form at weekday lunch, and there are only a few seats, so a good plan is to take your kati roll to a nearby park bench. There is also a location at 39th Street and 6th Avenue. ⑤ *Average main: $7* ⊠ *99 MacDougal St., near Bleecker St., Greenwich Village* ☎ *212/730–4280* ⊕ *www.thekatirollcompany.com* ⌲ *Reservations not accepted* Ⓜ *A, B, C, D, E, F, M to W. 4th St.* ✛ *2:D2.*

$$
ITALIAN

$\times$**Lupa.** Even the most hard-to-please connoisseurs have a soft spot for Lupa, Mario Batali and Joseph Bastianich's "downscale" Roman trattoria. Rough-hewn wood, great Italian wines, and simple preparations with top-quality ingredients define the restaurant, along with the "gentle" prices. People come repeatedly for dishes such as ricotta gnocchi with sweet-sausage ragout, house-made salumi, and sardines with golden raisins and pine nuts. The restaurant is split into two rooms: a boisterous space up front, with plenty of natural light, where walk-ins are welcome; and for those with reservations, an intimate back room, like a culinary cocoon in the best sense. ⑤ *Average main: $23* ⊠ *170 Thompson St., between Bleecker and Houston Sts., Greenwich Village* ☎ *212/982–5089* ⊕ *www.luparestaurant.com* Ⓜ *A, B, C, D, E, F, M to W. 4th St.* ✛ *2:D3.*

$$
SEAFOOD

$\times$**Mermaid Oyster Bar.** If you're craving a great raw bar, lobster roll, or soft-shell crab sandwich (in season), Mermaid Oyster Bar gives nearby classics Mary's Fish Camp and Pearl Oyster Bar a run for their money. Almost every dish is a winner here, but the lobster bisque laced with Manzanilla sherry and toasted pumpkin seeds, the blackened striped bass with roasted squash and Swiss chard, and the spicy seafood bucatini fra diavolo are all standouts. From the bar, try something from the list of perfect-pitch cocktails, like a Dark and Stormy, made with black rum and ginger beer, or a Pimm's Cooler with refreshing pieces of cucumber. There are two other locations in Manhattan, on the Upper West Side and in the East Village. ⑤ *Average main: $23* ⊠ *79 MacDougal St., at Houston St., Greenwich Village* ☎ *212/260–0100* ⊕ *www.themermaidnyc.com* ☾ *No lunch* Ⓜ *1 to Houston St.; A, B, C, D, E, F, M to W. 4th St.* ✛ *2:D2.*

$$$
MODERN
AMERICAN

✕**Minetta Tavern.** By converting a moribund 80-year-old Italian restaurant into a cozy hot spot, restaurateur Keith McNally created yet another hit. Try early and often to score reservations, so that you can sample creations like buttery trout meunière, bone marrow on toast, expertly aged steaks, and the celebrated Black Label burger, a gorgeous assembly of meat topped with caramelized onions and—for the brave—an added layer of cheese. The barroom, with its original details intact, is great for people-watching. Landing a table in the back room, with its original mural depicting West Village life and wall-to-wall photos of famous and infamous customers from eras gone by, makes sweet-talking the reservationist a worthy endeavor. ⑤ *Average main: $28* ✉ *113 MacDougal St., between Bleecker and 3rd Sts., Greenwich Village* ☎ *212/475–3850* ⊕ *www.minettatavernny.com* ⊘ *No lunch Mon. and Tues.* ⚑ *Reservations essential* Ⓜ *A, B, C, D, E, F, M to W. 4th St.* ✛ *2:D2.*

$$
BURGER

✕**Umami Burger.** Known as the "sixth taste," *umami* is the sensation on our palate when we eat something savory. It's also the name of this restaurant minichain whose Manhattan location serves one of the best burgers in the city. The signature burger looks like any other (except for the "u" branded into the top of the buns), but looks are deceiving. Dig, if you will, the umami-building process: caramelized onions are doused with star anise, the sweet-accented ketchup is made in-house, and the patty is sprinkled with sea-kelp powder and bonito flake, then sprayed with an oyster extract. The Manly Burger goes a step further, adding beer cheddar and bacon lardons. Starters include salads, fries, truffle fries, sweet potato fries, and onion rings. ⑤ *Average main: $14* ✉ *432 6th Ave., near 10th St., Greenwich Village* ☎ *212/677–8626* ⊕ *www.umami.com* Ⓜ *A, B, C, D, E, F, M to W. 4th St.* ✛ *3:D5.*

WEST VILLAGE

The West Village has mastered the art of destination restaurants that feel like neighborhood eateries. Places here are homey, yet remarkable enough to attract diners from all over the city.

$$$
ASIAN

✕**Annisa.** "Annisa" may mean "the women" in Arabic, but the top-notch food at this sedate West Village restaurant is inspired by Asia. Chef Anita Lo, one of the most underrated chefs in New York, cooks up miraculous dishes like foie gras soup dumplings, barbecue squid with basil and peanuts, and Japanese curry-spiked rabbit. Be sure to save room for dessert: the pecan and salted butterscotch beignets with bourbon ice cream are good enough to make you want to come back a second or third time. ⑤ *Average main: $30* ✉ *13 Barrow St., between 4th St. and 7th Ave. S, West Village* ☎ *212/741–6699* ⊕ *www.annisarestaurant.com* ⊘ *No lunch* Ⓜ *1 to Christopher St.–Sheridan Sq.; A, B, C, D, E, F, M to W. 4th St.* ✛ *2:C2.*

$$
ISRAELI

✕**Bar Bolonat.** Chef Einat Admony, who runs the show at Taïm and Balaboosta, has devised an intriguing menu at this sleek West Village spot that serves dishes that represent the Jewish diaspora around the Mediterranean. Sit at the bar and watch the kitchen in action or dine at a two-top in the dark-hued dining room—either way you can munch on tender lamb neck in a chickpea purée or the palate-tantalizing yellow Yemenite curry bedecked with shrimp. The wine list goes beyond the diaspora, but there are some interesting bottles from Israel and Morocco. ⓢ *Average main: $21* ✉ *611 Hudson St., West Village* ☎ *212/390–1545* ⊕ *www.barbolonatny.com* ⊘ *No lunch* Ⓜ *A, C, E to 14th St.; L to 8th Ave.* ✛ *3:B5.*

$$　✕ **Barbuto.** Chef Jonathan Waxman made a name for himself with his

ITALIAN　French-inspired California cuisine. Barbuto specializes in rustic preparations with bright flavors, like house-made duck sausage with creamy polenta, red-wine-braised short ribs, and pasta carbonara, though the menu changes daily, depending on what's available. The chef's acclaimed roasted chicken is usually on the menu in one form or another. The airy, sophisticated space gets busy, so make a reservation. The restaurant is particularly pleasant in nice weather when the giant garage-door-like windows open onto the street—watch the neighborhood go by. ⓢ *Average main: $20* ✉ *775 Washington St., between Jane and 12th Sts., West Village* ☎ *212/924–9700* ⊕ *www.barbutonyc.com* Ⓜ *A, C, E to 14th St.; L to 8th Ave.; 1 to Christopher St.–Sheridan Sq.* ✛ *3:B5.*

$$$　✕ **Blue Ribbon Bakery.** A neighborhood standard for good, if expensive,

ECLECTIC　food, this outpost of the Blue Ribbon empire has an eclectic menu with substantial sandwiches on homemade bread (freshly baked in the oven downstairs), small plates, legendary bread pudding, and entrées that span the globe, from hummus to grilled catfish with sautéed collards and sweet potatoes. The cavelike basement dining room is dark and intimate; upstairs is more open and light filled, with large windows looking out onto a pretty West Village corner. Brunch is notoriously crowded. ⓢ *Average main: $25* ✉ *35 Downing St., at Bedford St., Greenwich Village* ☎ *212/337–0404* ⊕ *www.blueribbonrestaurants.com* Ⓜ *1 to Houston St.; A, B, C, D, E, F, M to W. 4th St.* ✛ *2:C2.*

$$$　✕ **dell'anima.** Lines still snake out the door of this neighborhood favor-

ITALIAN　ite, so it's a good idea to make a reservation. Once you're in, check out the open kitchen, where the stylish crowd converges to watch chefs prepare authentic Italian dishes with a modern twist. Starters might include sweetbreads, bone marrow, or charred octopus with chorizo, while traditional first courses like pasta alla carbonara with *speck* (smoked and cured pork), egg, and pecorino are impeccable. The signature *pollo al diavolo* (spicy chicken) is seared with enough smoke and heat for all seasons. Anfora, their wine bar next door, is good for an after-dinner drink, if you want to linger in the area. ⓢ *Average main: $26* ✉ *38 8th Ave., at Jane St., West Village* ☎ *212/366–6633* ⊕ *www.dellanima.com* ⊘ *No lunch weekdays* Ⓜ *1, 2, 3, A, C, E to 14th St.; L to 8th Ave.* ✛ *3:C5.*

$$　✕ **Ditch Plains.** Named for a surf spot in Montauk, this laid-back neigh-

SEAFOOD　borhood restaurant serves an eclectic bill of beachfront fare—from fish tacos, lobster rolls, and fish 'n' chips to clam chowder and crab dip. There are options for landlubbers and vegetarians, too. It's not quite a beach shack, but the food and setting, with an upbeat rock sound track, are designed for conviviality, and the wine-list prices are extremely friendly, with whole and half bottles sold just above cost. The Bloody Marys are recommended, too. Breakfast/brunch is served every day from 11 am and dinner served until 2 am nightly. ⓢ *Average main: $19* ✉ *29 Bedford St., near Downing St., West Village* ☎ *212/633–0202* ⊕ *www.ditch-plains. com* ⌦ *Reservations not accepted* Ⓜ *1 to Houston St.* ✛ *2:C3.*

$$ ✕**Do Hwa.** If anyone in New York is responsible for making Korean
KOREAN food cool and user-friendly, it is the mother-daughter team behind this
chic and perennially popular restaurant. Jenny Kwak and her mother,
Myung Ja, serve home cooking in the form of *kalbi jim* (braised short
ribs), *bibimbop* (a spicy, mix-it-yourself vegetable-and-rice dish), and
other favorites that may not be as pungent as in Koreatown but are
satisfying nevertheless—in a far more sophisticated atmosphere. The
bar area, where movies are projected onto a side wall, gets pretty hap-
pening, too. $ *Average main: $23* ⊠ *55 Carmine St., between Bedford
St. and 7th Ave. S, West Village* ☎ *212/414–1224* ⊕ *www.dohwanyc.
com* ⊗ *No lunch weekends* Ⓜ *1 to Houston St.; A, B, C, D, E, F, M to
W. 4th St.* ✢ *2:C2.*

$ ✕**Dominique Ansel Kitchen.** Cronut? What cronut? Don't come looking
BAKERY for French baker Dominique Ansel's insanely popular Franken-pastry
here because you won't find it (for that, head to his other bakery in
SoHo). Instead, at this West Village spot the cutting-edge baker/wiz-
ard conjures up other edible oddities such as garlic bread croissants,
a French toast-like croque monsieur, and beignets sprinkled and filled
with matcha powder (the dust of these explodes like a green-spewing
volcano with each bite). In the warm-weather months, the outdoor
tables are much more pleasant than the uncomfortable stadiumlike
seating setup on the inside. Nothing here will ever match the phenom-
enon of the cronut, but given the much shorter lines at this location,
that's a good thing. $ *Average main: $8* ⊠ *137 7th Ave. S, West Village*
☎ *212/242–5111* ⊕ *www.dominiqueanselkitchen.com* ⌕ *Reservations
not accepted* Ⓜ *1 to Christopher St./Sheridan Square* ✢ *2:C1.*

$$ ✕**Empellón Taquería.** Chef Alex Stupak worked for years as the wiz-
MEXICAN ardlike pastry chef at the now-closed wd-50, New York's first intro-
duction to molecular gastronomy, so when he left to open—wait for
it—a taquería, many Manhattan diners either scratched their heads or
wondered if they'd be served deconstructed tacos. Instead, they got
simple yet well-executed fare using top-notch ingredients. There are
straightforward options—fish tempura, lamb, steak—as well as surprising variations, like a taco with sweetbreads and a chorizo gravy poured
over it. There are also several variations on the margarita theme, including one using the Japanese citrus, *yuzu*. Empellón isn't really south-of-
the-border authentic, but when it's this good, who cares? $ *Average
main: $24* ⊠ *230 W. 4th St., at 10th St., West Village* ☎ *212/367–0999*
⊕ *www.empellon.com* ⊗ *No lunch Mon.–Thurs.* Ⓜ *1 to Christopher
St.–Sheridan Sq.* ✢ *2:B1.*

$$ ✕**Fatty Crab.** This rustic Malaysian cantina showcases the exciting cui-
MALAYSIAN sine of chef Zak Pelaccio, who spent years cooking at famous French
restaurants before escaping to Southeast Asia for a year, where he fell
in love with the flavors of the region. Start with the addictive pickled
watermelon and crispy pork salad, an improbable combination that's
both refreshing and decadent. The can't-miss signature dish is chili
crab—cracked Dungeness crab in a pool of rich, spicy chili sauce, served
with bread for dipping. It's messy for sure, but worth rolling up your
sleeves. The small space fills up quickly, and be warned that the tables
are practically on top of each other, but it's lots of fun. $ *Average main:*

15

$22 ✉ *643 Hudson St., between Gansevoort and Horatio Sts., West Village* ☎ *212/352–3592* ⊕ *www.fattycrab.com* ⚑ *Reservations essential* Ⓜ *A, C, E to 14th St.; L to 8th Ave.* ✛ *3:C5.*

$$ ✕ **Frankies Spuntino.** The Frankies—that is, owners and chefs Frank Falcinelli and Frank Castronovo—have a winning formula at their West Village restaurant: serve hearty not-necessarily-by-the-book Italian-inflected fare using local, organic, and humanely raised ingredients in a laid-back atmosphere. Most menu items change seasonally, but expect pasta dishes like pappardelle with mushrooms and chestnuts; black spaghetti with mussels, cockles, and pistachios; and sweet-potato gnocchi with oxtail ragout. The large menu also includes crostini, fresh salads, cured meats, and cheese plates. It's a casual, family-friendly, neighborhood spot. ⑤ *Average main: $20* ✉ *570 Hudson St., at 11th St., West Village* ☎ *212/924–0818* ⊕ *www.frankiesspuntino.com* Ⓜ *A, C, E to 14th St.; L to 8th Ave.* ✛ *2:B1.*

ITALIAN

$$$ ✕ **I Sodi.** In a city that seems like a million Italian restaurants, this minimalist-design Tuscan-focused eatery in the West Village is a real find. Spiky-haired owner Rita Sodi, a Florentine who formerly worked in the fashion industry, ensures the traditional fare coming from the kitchen is satisfying. The menu changes weekly based on seasonal ingredients, but expect a bevy of pasta dishes topped with good stuff like duck ragout, and artichoke-laced lasagna, as well as not-very-Lipitor-friendly pancetta-wrapped pork and rabbit. Hoist a glass of grappa at the end of the meal, and be happy you're in the right place. Chef Sodi also runs the excellent Via Carota around the corner on Grove Street. ⑤ *Average main: $27* ✉ *105 Christopher St., between Bleecker and Hudson Sts., West Village* ☎ *212/414–5774* ⊕ *www.isodinyc.com* ☾ *No lunch* Ⓜ *1 to Christopher St.–Sheridan Sq.* ✛ *2:B2.*

ITALIAN

$ ✕ **Joe's Pizza.** You might recognize this Greenwich Village institution from its frequent cameos in TV and film (in *Spider-Man*, Tobey Maguire's Peter Parker was a Joe's delivery boy). But it's the classic gooey New York slice, dripping melted cheese onto paper plates, that *really* makes the place famous. And in a city brimming with by-the-slice spots, the crispy-bottomed slices here are the best. ⑤ *Average main: $6* ✉ *7 Carmine St., near Bleecker St., West Village* ☎ *212/366–1182* ⊕ *www. joespizzanyc.com* ⚑ *Reservations not accepted* ⊟ *No credit cards* Ⓜ *A, B, C, D, E, F, M to W. 4th St.* ✛ *2:C2.*

PIZZA
FAMILY

$$ ✕ **Keste Pizza & Vino.** At the back of the long, narrow Keste Pizza & Vino restaurant is a beautiful, tiled, wood-fired oven that cooks what might be Manhattan's most authentic Neapolitan pies at 1,000° F. Blistered and chewy around the edges, the margherita pie gives way to a softer center pooled with San Marzano tomato sauce and house-made mozzarella. There are numerous pizza options, including white pies and gluten-free crusts. This is a definite contender for best pizza in New York. The dining room is casual, and the location means it's almost always busy. ⑤ *Average main: $17* ✉ *271 Bleecker St., between 6th and 7th Aves., West Village* ☎ *212/243–1500* ⊕ *www.kestepizzeria.com* ⚑ *Reservations not accepted* Ⓜ *1 to Christopher St.–Sheridan Sq.; A, B, C, D, E, F, M to W. 4th St.* ✛ *2:C2.*

PIZZA

$$$
MODERN
AMERICAN
Fodor'sChoice
★
✕ **The Little Owl.** This tiny neighborhood joint, with seating for 28 people, is exceptionally eager to please—and this attitude, plus the food, is a winning combination. The menu is just as small, which actually makes it easier to decide what you want. And what you want are the pork-veal-beef-pecorino-cheese meatball "sliders," or miniburgers. The unusually juicy pork loin chop, served with Parmesan butter beans and wild dandelion greens, is gigantic and hugely satisfying. Raspberry-filled beignets, served with a ramekin of warm Nutella, are otherworldly. It's quintessential West Village: quirky and wonderful. Fans of the sitcom *Friends* might recognize the apartment building that houses the restaurant. ⑤ *Average main: $25* ✉ *90 Bedford St., at Grove St., West Village* ☎ *212/741–4695* ⊕ *www.thelittleowlnyc.com* ⌲ *Reservations essential* Ⓜ *1 to Christopher St.–Sheridan Sq.; A, B, C, D, E, F, M to W. 4th St.* ✛ *3:D6.*

$$
SEAFOOD
✕ **Mary's Fish Camp.** Diners still line up down the street before the restaurant opens for dinner to get a table at this small but bustling seafood shack. The result of a split between Pearl Oyster Bar's partners, Mary's is a more intimate space, but the two have similar menus: excellent fried oysters, chowders, and, of course, the sweet lobster roll with crisp fries, all of which have you licking your fingers. The killer hot fudge sundae is worth saving room for. The staff here are warm and friendly, too. This is the kind of place everyone wishes was in their neighborhood. ⑤ *Average main: $23* ✉ *64 Charles St., at 4th St., West Village* ☎ *646/486–2185* ⊕ *www.marysfishcamp.com* ◷ *No dinner Sun.* ⌲ *Reservations not accepted* Ⓜ *1 to Christopher St.–Sheridan Sq.* ✛ *2:B1.*

$$
MIDDLE EASTERN
✕ **Moustache.** There's typically a crowd waiting outside for one of the copper-top tables at this casual Middle Eastern neighborhood restaurant. The focal point is the perfect pita that accompanies tasty salads like lemony chickpea and spinach, hearty lentil and bulgur, or falafel. Also delicious is *lahambajin*, spicy ground lamb on a crispy flat crust. For entrées, try the leg of lamb, the juicy baby lamb sandwich, or merguez sausage sandwiches. Service is slow but friendly. There are also locations in the East Village and East Harlem. ⑤ *Average main: $13* ✉ *90 Bedford St., between Barrow and Grove Sts., West Village* ☎ *212/229–2220* ⊕ *www.moustachepitza.com* ⌲ *Reservations not accepted* Ⓜ *1 to Christopher St.–Sheridan Sq.; A, B, C, D, E, F, M to W. 4th St.* ✛ *2:B2.*

$$$
SEAFOOD
✕ **Pearl Oyster Bar.** There have been many imitators and few real competitors to this West Village seafood institution. Since 1997, Rebecca Charles has been serving arguably the best lobster roll in New York City in a no-frills space down charming, restaurant-lined Cornelia Street—and expanded next door to accommodate the throngs. But that's not the only reason you should cast your net here. Pan-roasted sea scallops and plus-size crab cakes compete with the legendary lobster roll for your taste buds' attention. Service is very efficient—you might even say rushed. ⑤ *Average main: $26* ✉ *18 Cornelia St., between 4th and Bleecker Sts., West Village* ☎ *212/691–8211* ⊕ *www.pearloysterbar.com* ◷ *Closed Sun. No lunch Sat.* Ⓜ *A, B, C, D, E, F, M to W. 4th St.* ✛ *2:C2.*

$$$
CHINESE
✕ **RedFarm.** Conceived and run by Ed Schoenfeld, an expert on Chinese cuisine, and Joe Ng, known as the dumpling king of New York, this

15

West Village restaurant specializes in—you guessed it—Chinese-style dumplings. At least partly. The menu focuses mostly on dim sum—small plates and snacks (often in dumpling form)—as well as Chinese-American dishes like three-chili chicken and chicken in garlic sauce. The lobster dumplings and the crab and pork soup dumplings are culinary wonders and nearly obligatory for first-timers. But come with a wallet the size of China itself because the dishes add up. Also consider trying the restaurant's duck-themed restaurant, Decoy, in the basement. There's also a location of RedFarm on Broadway and West 76th Street. ⑤ *Average main: $30* ⊠ *529 Hudson St., between 10th and Charles Sts., West Village* ☎ *212/792–9700* ⊕ *www.redfarmnyc.com* ⊗ *No lunch* Ⓜ *1 to Christopher St.–Sheridan Sq.* ⊕ *2:B2.*

$$$
BRITISH
✕ **The Spotted Pig.** Part cozy English pub, part laid-back neighborhood hangout, part gastronome's lure, the Spotted Pig showcases the impeccable food of the now-legendary London chef April Bloomfield (Mario Batali and his partners advised on the menu). Dishes like arugula salad with tangy radishes and Parmesan, and smoked-haddock-and-corn chowder with homemade crackers are studies in texture and flavor contrast. Shoestring potatoes accompany the Roquefort cheeseburger. Chase it with a foam-crowned glass of Old Speckled Hen. This neighborhood hangout still packs them in, so come early, or late. The Breslin, at the Ace Hotel, is another of Bloomfield's standout New York restaurants with an überclubby feel. ⑤ *Average main: $26* ⊠ *314 W. 11th St., at Greenwich St., West Village* ☎ *212/620–0393* ⊕ *www.thespottedpig. com* ⌕ *Reservations not accepted* Ⓜ *1 to Christopher St.–Sheridan Sq.; 2, 3 to 14th St.; L to 8th Ave.* ⊕ *2:A1.*

$$$$
JAPANESE
Fodor's Choice
★
✕ **Sushi Nakazawa.** Daisuke dreams of sushi. Fans of the acclaimed 2011 documentary *Jiro Dreams of Sushi* may remember Daisuke Nakazawa, the apprentice to the great Tokyo-based sushi master Jiro Ono, who spent the near-entirety of the film trying to perfect the egg custard. He finally succeeded, just as he has succeeded in wooing even the most finicky New York diners. It's all omakase (a tasting menu set by the chef) here, so sit back and enjoy two hours of being fed by one of the best sushi chefs in New York. Mr. Nakazawa practices an old Tokyo style of sushi making—putting all his highly fresh fish on a thumb-size bundle of rice. (Sorry, sashimi fans.) Reserve at least a month in advance, or try to get a table in the à la carte, no-reservations room adjacent to the restaurant. ⑤ *Average main: $170* ⊠ *23 Commerce St., near Bedford St., West Village* ☎ *212/924–2212* ⊕ *www.sushinakazawa.com* ⊗ *No lunch* ⌕ *Reservations essential* Ⓜ *1 to Christopher St.–Sheridan Sq.; A, B, C, D, E, F, M to W. 4th St.* ⊕ *3:D6.*

$
MIDDLE EASTERN
✕ **Taïm.** There's a real chef behind this tiny sliver of a restaurant, New York's only gourmet falafel stand. *Taïm* means "tasty" in Hebrew, and Tel Aviv transplant Einat Admony's fried chickpea balls are delicious, and available in several beguiling flavors (try them infused with spicy harissa sauce) along with a tantalizing display of à la carte salads (the carrots with Moroccan spices is a standout). There's another location in NoLIta, on Spring Street between Mott and Mulberry, as well as a food truck that makes its way around the city (you can find it via Twitter). ⑤ *Average main: $9* ⊠ *222 Waverly Pl., near Perry St., West*

Village ☎ *212/691–1287* ⊕ *www.taimfalafel.com* ⌕ *Reservations not accepted* Ⓜ *1, 2, 3 to 14th St.; L to 8th Ave.* ✛ *2:B1.*

$$$
AUSTRIAN
✕**Wallsé.** The modern Austrian menu at Kurt Gutenbrunner's lovely, light-filled neighborhood restaurant has a strong emphasis on Austrian tradition and urban New York attitude. It's hard to argue with such dishes as Wiener schnitzel with potato-cucumber salad and lingonberries, or venison goulash with spaetzle and Brussels sprouts, and it's often lighter than you'd think Austrian food would be. Desserts do Vienna proud: apple-walnut strudel is served with apple sorbet. The atmosphere is casual but sophisticated—perfect for either a weeknight dinner or a special occasion. Ⓢ *Average main: $33* ✉ *344 W. 11th St., at Washington St., West Village* ☎ *212/352–2300* ⊕ *www.wallse.com* ☾ *No lunch* ⌕ *Reservations essential* Ⓜ *1 to Christopher St.–Sheridan Sq.; A, C, E to 14th St.; L to 8th Ave.* ✛ *3:B6.*

$$
AMERICAN
FAMILY
✕**Westville.** If New York's neighborhoods were small country towns, they'd all have restaurants just like Westville. These adorable spots— with branches in the East and West Village, Chelsea, and west SoHo— serve simple, wholesome fare, at reasonable prices. Salads, grilled chicken, burgers, and chops are all good, but the seasonal sides, which change daily based on what's fresh at the market, are the real star attraction (the "Market Plate" with any three sides is a popular dinner option). Dessert is worth saving room for, too, especially the daily pie selections. Expect a wait on weekend nights. Ⓢ *Average main: $13* ✉ *210 W. 10th St., near Bleecker St., West Village* ☎ *212/741–7971* ⊕ *www.westvillenyc.com* Ⓜ *1 to Christopher St.–Sheridan Sq.* ✛ *3:C6.*

CHELSEA AND THE MEATPACKING DISTRICT

CHELSEA

Several big-name chefs have moved to the western part of this neighborhood in recent years, putting Chelsea on the dining map. For a tasty quick bite or a gift for your favorite foodie, stop by **Chelsea Market.**

$$
PIZZA
✕**Co.** "Company," as it's pronounced, took the New York pizza scene by red-sauce-scented storm when it opened in early 2009. Bread master Jim Lahey, who made a name for himself at the Sullivan Street Baking Company, crafts simple but memorable pies, the dough and crust of which play a starring role. The simple margherita (tomato sauce, mozzarella, basil) is a good way to sample Co.'s fare, but diners are always tempted by unorthodox pizzas like the caramelized-onion-and-walnut-purée pie or the béchamel-and-Parmesan-topped version. If you can, take a few friends, and order several pies. But it's not all pizza: the delicious veal meatballs and chicken-liver toast tempt even the most die-hard pizza lover to stray. Ⓢ *Average main: $19* ✉ *230 9th Ave., at 24th St., Chelsea* ☎ *212/243–1105* ⊕ *www.co-pane.com* ☾ *No lunch Mon.* Ⓜ *C, E to 23rd St.* ✛ *3:B2.*

$$$
AMERICAN
✕**Cookshop.** One of far-west Chelsea's first hot restaurants, Cookshop manages a casual elegance while focusing on seasonal, farm-fresh cuisine that continues to wow. Outdoor seating on 10th Avenue is quite peaceful in the evening; during the day you can survey a cross-section of gallery-hoppers and shoppers. Divine cocktails, made with fresh fruit

15

juices, are veritable elixirs of well-being. Line up early for brunch; it's worth the wait for dishes like baked eggs over duck and Swiss chard, or the fluffiest pancakes in town. Dinner is also a triumph, with a variety of perfectly prepared dishes like whitefish with lemony asparagus and hen-of-the-woods mushrooms, or a simple roasted chicken. $ *Average main: $26* ☒ *156 10th Ave., at 20th St., Chelsea* ☎ *212/924–4440* ⊕ *www.cookshopny.com* Ⓜ *A, C, E to 23rd St.* ✛ *3:B3.*

$$
ECLECTIC
╳ **Coppelia.** Named for a legendary ice-cream shop in Havana, Coppelia is neither Cuban nor an ice-cream parlor. At least not strictly speaking. Chef Julian Medina has created a 24-hour pan-Latin diner that works on many levels—for a quick breakfast, casual lunch, or late-night bite. The continent-sized menu emphasizes comfort food, with satisfying dishes like the pork-belly-spiked mac 'n' cheese, mountainous nachos, grilled cheese with jalapeño and bacon, and even kimchi-stuffed tacos. If you did have your *corazón* set on ice cream, there's plenty of it on the dessert menu. $ *Average main: $16* ☒ *207 W. 14th St., between 7th and 8th Aves., Chelsea* ☎ *212/858–5001* ⊕ *www.ybandco.com* Ⓜ *1, 2, 3, A, C, E, F, M to 14th St.; L to 8th Ave.* ✛ *3:C4.*

$$
CHINESE
╳ **Legend.** Sure, there's nothing Chinese about the generic name; and the location, on a stretch of 7th Avenue in Chelsea, is flanked by forgettable eating options. But do your taste buds a favor and eat at this affordable Sichuan spot, whose quiet opening was followed by a lot of buzz among New York's fooderati. The long menu is not for the indecisive, but nearly anything is a hit, including the double-cooked bacon, the massive and flaky whole roasted fish, and the ultraspicy *ma po* tofu. Dishes here lean toward the fiery side. $ *Average main: $15* ☒ *88 7th Ave., between 15th and 16th Sts., Chelsea* ☎ *212/929–1778* ⊕ *www.legendrestaurant88.com* Ⓜ *1, 2, 3, A, C, E, F, M to 14th St.; L to 8th Ave.* ✛ *3:D4.*

$$
PORTUGUESE
Fodor's Choice
★
╳ **Lupulo.** Michelin-starred chef George Mendes's homage to Portuguese tavern cuisine is a delicious escape amid the bustle of 6th Avenue. Unlike Aldea, Mendes's more formal eatery, Lupulo (which means "hops" in Portuguese) is a laid-back spot, featuring a long craft-beer list (even though there are few Portuguese beers on it). Pull up a seat at the island bar or snag a table next to the floor-to-ceiling windows and dig into Iberian comfort food like plates of salty grilled sardines, crispy shrimp turnovers, oven-baked octopus, and salt cod casserole for two. If beer isn't your thing, the all-Portuguese wine menu, which includes a few bottles of refreshing Vinho Verde, is a guaranteed palate cleanser. $ *Average main: $19* ☒ *835 6th Ave., Chelsea* ☎ *212/290–7600* ⊕ *www. lupulonyc.com* Ⓜ *B, D, F, M to 34th St.–Herald Square* ✛ *3:D1.*

$$$
MODERN
AMERICAN
╳ **The Red Cat.** Elegant yet unpretentious, a lovely neighborhood spot *and* a destination restaurant, the Red Cat is a great place to chat with a friend, celebrate an auspicious occasion, have a business dinner, or just enjoy an excellent meal. The American-meets-Mediterranean menu changes frequently, based on what's in season, but expect an eclectic menu of well-executed pastas, burgers, saffron-laced seafood, and meaty numbers. Factor in the affordable wine list and you'll most definitely feel like one lucky cat. $ *Average main: $27* ☒ *227 10th*

Ave., between 23rd and 24th Sts., Chelsea ☎ *212/242–1122* ⊕ *www. redcatrestaurants.com* Ⓜ *C, E to 23rd St.* ✛ *3:A2.*

$$ ✕ **Tía Pol.** It may be sardine-can small and dark, but that doesn't stop
SPANISH this popular tapas bar from being packed most nights. This is one of the best tapas spots in town, with a welcoming vibe, a dozen reasonably priced Spanish wines by the glass, and charm to spare. One of the most original tapas has become a signature here: bittersweet chocolate smeared on a baguette disc and topped with salty Spanish chorizo. *Patatas bravas* (rough-cut potatoes served with spicy aioli) are so addictive, you won't want to share them. The pork loin, piquillo pepper, and mild tetilla cheese sandwich is scrumptious, and so is the Galician octopus terrine. Tía Pol is also a great spot to stop and snack midway through a High Line jaunt. Ⓢ *Average main: $14* ✉ *205 10th Ave., between 22nd and 23rd Sts., Chelsea* ☎ *212/675–8805* ⊕ *www.tiapol.com* ⊘ *No lunch Mon.* ⚑ *Reservations essential* Ⓜ *C, E to 23rd St.* ✛ *3:A2.*

$$$ ✕ **Tipsy Parson.** If New York's Chelsea neighborhood were magically
SOUTHERN transported to the American South, the food might taste something like it does at this hip, Southern-accented eatery with a menu of artery-hardening delights. Named for a boozy Southern dessert, the Tipsy Parson and its menu are all about comfort in the belly and soul: fried pickles, homemade peanut butter with crackers, bourbon-laced chicken-liver mousse, and seafood potpie are designed to make you full and happy. The restaurant's close proximity to the High Line, the elevated park and greenway, means you can walk it all off afterward. Ⓢ *Average main: $25* ✉ *156 9th Ave., between 19th and 20th Sts., Chelsea* ☎ *212/620–4545* ⊕ *www.tipsyparson.com* ⊘ *No lunch Mon. and Tues.* Ⓜ *C, E to 23rd St.* ✛ *3:B3.*

$$ ✕ **Trestle on Tenth.** Cozy and warm with an inviting exposed-brick inte-
SWISS rior, this Swiss brasserie is a true west Chelsea neighborhood spot. Locals and gallery-hoppers quaff foamy beers and glasses of wine from the reasonable list while awaiting hearty Alpine-inspired dishes. Crispy duck necks, calves' liver with potato *rösti*, and butter lettuce with bacon are favorites. It's not art—for that, hit up one of the many galleries in the neighborhood—but it makes you yearn for Alpine landscapes. The location is convenient to the High Line. Ⓢ *Average main: $20* ✉ *242 10th Ave., at 24th St., Chelsea* ☎ *212/645–5659* ⊕ *www.trestleontenth. com* Ⓜ *C, E to 23rd St.* ✛ *3:A2.*

$$ ✕ **Txikito.** After being wined and dined at this popular Chelsea Spanish
SPANISH restaurant, you'd never guess that chef Alexandra Raij is from very un-Spanish Minneapolis. Her husband and business partner is, though, and the duo put on an impressive show. The theme is *cucina vasca*, or Basque cuisine, one of the most exciting regions in Iberia for eating. Raij captures the moment by serving standouts like juicy lamb meatballs in a minty broth, crispy beef tongue, and an addictive crabmeat gratin. The wine list at Txikito (pronounced Chi-kee-toe) is loaded with great bottles of Rioja and other tempranillos, many of which are from Basque winemakers. Ⓢ *Average main: $16* ✉ *240 9th Ave., at 25th St., Chelsea* ☎ *212/242–4730* ⊕ *www.txikitonyc.com* ⊘ *No lunch* Ⓜ *C, E to 23rd St.* ✛ *3:B2.*

15

MEATPACKING DISTRICT

Europeans, models, actors, and the people who love them stroll the sidewalk like they're on a catwalk, going from one hot restaurant to the next in this cobblestone-laden neighborhood, which has become almost too sceney for its own good. There's plenty of great eating here—you just might have to wait awhile (or impersonate a celebrity) to get a table.

$$$$ ✕ **Del Posto.** Much more formal than Babbo, Del Posto is Mario Batali's

ITALIAN grown-up venue (in partnership with Lidia and Joe Bastianich), and the dining room—with its sweeping staircase, formal decor, and live music from a baby grand—has the feel of an opulent hotel lobby. This is one of the most consistently dazzling special-occasion spots in the city, and the food is stellar. There are a variety of set menus to choose from ($149 for five courses; $179 for eight), plus à la carte options for parties of four and under. Pitch-perfect risotto is made fresh to order for two people or more, meat dishes like roasted veal chops are standouts, and pastas are ethereal—all with old-world table-side service. For a smaller taste of the experience, come for a cocktail and sample the bargain bar menu. $ *Average main: $65* ✉ *85 10th Ave., between 15th and 16th Sts., Meatpacking District* ☎ *212/497–8090* ⊕ *www.delposto.com* ◷ *No lunch weekends* ⌂ *Reservations essential* Ⓜ *A, C, E to 14th St.; L to 8th Ave.* ✛ *3:A4.*

$$$ ✕ **La Sirena.** The latest Batali and Bastianich temple of Italian gastron-

ITALIAN omy, La Sirena combines excellent Italian fare with the trendy ambience of the Maritime Hotel (which houses the restaurant). The huge 200-seat space (with a long 38-seat bar) is highlighted by wavy Roman-inspired black-and-white floor tiles and globe-shaped wall lights that help keep the space relatively dim. The menu stretches from the tip to top of the boot with dishes like short-rib carpaccio sprinkled with black truffles, and pastas filled with rich edible jewels such as duck and pancetta. Ballers might opt for the $120 lardo-encrusted, dry-aged, bone-in New York strip for two. The wine list, separated by the regions of Italy, offers some surprisingly affordable bottles. $ *Average main: $30* ✉ *88 9th Ave., Meatpacking District* ☎ *212/977–6096* ⊕ *www.lasirena-nyc.com* ⌂ *Reservations essential* Ⓜ *A, C, E to 14th St.* ✛ *3:B4.*

$$ ✕ **Spice Market.** Set in a cavernous space amid embroidered curtains and

ASIAN artifacts from Burma, India, and Malaysia, chef Jean-Georges Vongerichten's playful take on Southeast Asian street food keeps you asking the waiters, "What exactly was in that?" Sometimes the playfulness works, sometimes it doesn't, but don't miss the steamed lobster with garlic, ginger, and dried chili, or the squid salad with papaya and cashews. This may not be the hottest new restaurant on the block anymore, but it's still a fun Meatpacking venue with food that doesn't disappoint. $ *Average main: $23* ✉ *403 W. 13th St., at 9th Ave., Meatpacking District* ☎ *212/675–2322* ⊕ *www.spicemarketnewyork.com* ⌂ *Reservations essential* Ⓜ *A, C, E to 14th St.; L to 8th Ave.* ✛ *3:B4.*

$$$ ✕ **The Standard Grill.** Hotelier Andre Balazs created a scene for celebs,

AMERICAN fashion-industry insiders, and the common folk, too, who all cluster at this buzzy restaurant inside the Standard Hotel. In warm weather, the spacious outdoor seating area is perfect for sampling creative cocktails; there's an indoor bar, too, and two dining rooms—a casual one in front and a larger room in back, with a floor whimsically made up of thousands of glittering pennies. The menu is comfort-luxe, with dishes like roast chicken for two in a cast-iron skillet and delicious moist trout with a currant-and-pine-nut relish. For dessert, there's a nearly obscene chocolate mousse that comes with silicone spatulas in lieu of spoons. A late-night menu is served until 4 am. $ *Average main: $30* ⊠ *848 Washington St., between Little W. 12th and 13th Sts., Meatpacking District* ☎ *212/645–4100* ⊕ *www.thestandardgrill.com* Ⓜ *A, C, E to 14th St.; L to 8th Ave.* ✛ *3:B4.*

$$$ ✗ **Untitled at the Whitney.** Located in the handsome Renzo Piano–designed
AMERICAN Whitney Museum of American Art at the southern end of the High Line, restaurateur Danny Meyer's Untitled isn't necessarily the masterpiece in his collection of great restaurants, but the minimalist-design eatery is definitely worth a look (and a bite). Chef Michael Anthony (who does double duty here and at the outstanding Gramercy Tavern) puts his usual (and admirable) spin on everything: namely, deceptively simple dishes that explode with flavor. Roasted fried chicken paired with polenta, and fettuccine with bacon and white cheddar are just a couple of the artistically tasty dishes worth trying. $ *Average main: $25* ⊠ *Whitney Museum of American Art, 99 Gansevoort St., Meatpacking District* ☎ *212/570–3670* ⊕ *www.untitledatthewhitney.com* Ⓜ *A, C, E to 14th St.* ✛ *3:B5.*

UNION SQUARE WITH THE FLATIRON DISTRICT AND GRAMERCY

UNION SQUARE

Once the main spot in New York to go for protests, Union Square is now the stage for another type of communal experience: breaking bread. There is no shortage of appealing options at any price range (including picnic provisions from the wonderful greenmarket, open Monday, Wednesday, Friday, and Saturday).

$$$ ✗ **All'onda.** While this stylish restaurant bills itself as serving "modern
ITALIAN Venetian cuisine," it's more as if Japanese chefs quietly invaded Venice and begin updating the dishes. Chef Chris Jaeckle sneaks Asian elements into the otherwise Italian menu, emboldening the dishes to the tune of utter deliciousness. Truffle risotto has sake mash, crab-loaded garganelli has just the right touch of yuzu, and thick bucatini noodles are interlaced with fresh uni. There is, of course, more to the Japanese-accented Italian menu than just pasta: the juicy porchetta (laced with a seaweed salsa verde, naturally) and the tender short rib, paired with saffron risotto, are winning entrées. You'll want to say "*grazie*" or perhaps "*arigato*" to the chef on your way out. $ *Average main: $26* ⊠ *22 E. 13th St., Union Square* ☎ *212/231–2236* ⊕ *www.allondanyc.com* ☾ *Closed Mon.* Ⓜ *4, 5, 6, L, N, Q, R to 14th St.–Union Square* ✛ *3:F4.*

$$$$ ✗ **Gotham Bar & Grill.** A culinary landmark, Gotham Bar & Grill is every
AMERICAN bit as thrilling as when it opened in 1984. Celebrated chef Alfred Por-
Fodor'sChoice tale, who made the blueprint for "architectural food"—that is, towers
★ of stacked ingredients—builds on a foundation of simple, clean flavors. People come for Portale's transcendent preparations: no rack of lamb is more tender, no seafood salad sweeter. The stellar 20,000-bottle cellar provides the perfect accompaniments—at a price. The three-course

15

$38 greenmarket-driven prix-fixe lunch, served weekdays from noon to 2:15, is a steal, even if it's not as sophisticated as dinner. Take a stroll through the Union Square Greenmarket before or after lunch to see the chef's inspirations. Desserts are also memorable. ⑤ *Average main: $42* ⊠ *12 E. 12th St., between 5th Ave. and University Pl., Union Square* ☎ *212/620–4020* ⊕ *www.gothambarandgrill.com* ⊘ *No lunch weekends* Ⓜ *4, 5, 6, L, N, Q, R to 14th St.–Union Sq.* ⊹ *3:E4.*

$$ ╳ **Republic.** When Republic first opened, it was one of very few places
ASIAN to get an Asian-style noodle bowl with a stylish edge. Many have followed in its footsteps—and some are better—but for window-shoppers, greenmarketers, and anyone else in the Union Square area, this is a fun stop for a meal. The look is a cross between a downtown art gallery and a Japanese school cafeteria, and the young waitstaff dressed in black T-shirts and jeans hold remote-control ordering devices to accelerate the already speedy service. Sit at the long, bluestone bar or at the picnic-style tables, and order appetizers such as smoky grilled eggplant and luscious fried wontons. Spicy coconut chicken soup and Vietnamese-style barbecue pork are menu standouts. ⑤ *Average main: $15* ⊠ *37 Union Sq. W, between 16th and 17th Sts., Union Square* ☎ *212/627–7172* ⊕ *www.thinknoodles.com* ⌖ *Reservations not accepted* Ⓜ *4, 5, 6, L, N, Q, R to 14th St.–Union Sq.* ⊹ *3:F4.*

$$$ ╳ **Rosa Mexicano.** The idea that you can't find good south-of-the-border
MODERN cuisine in the Big Apple is quickly fading, thanks in part to this Union
MEXICAN Square restaurant (there are several other locations in the city too, including ones at Lincoln Center and TriBeCa). Although the spacious, colorfully lighted interior might tip you off that authenticity is best sought elsewhere, if you're looking for high-quality, well-executed Mex-flavored fare, step right up, hombre. Start with an order of guac (made table-side), moving on to the pork belly and scallop tacos, soul-comforting chicken tortilla pie, or the crispy pork shank—all of which taste better with a margarita. The daily happy hour at the bar is a great deal but gets crowded. ⑤ *Average main: $28* ⊠ *9 E. 18th St., between 5th Ave. and Broadway, Union Square* ☎ *212/533–3350* ⊕ *www.rosamexicano. com* Ⓜ *4, 5, 6, L, N, Q, R to 14th St.–Union Sq.* ⊹ *3:F3.*

$$$ ╳ **Tocqueville.** Hidden just steps from busy Union Square, this refined din-
MODERN ing oasis is a secret even to many New Yorkers. Enter through the aus-
AMERICAN tere reception area, past the heavy curtains and six-seat bar, and find the intimate dining area where chef and owner Marco Moreira's signature starter is the unctuous angel hair sea-urchin carbonara. Main courses are steeped in French tradition, with international flavors like saffron-and-fennel-spiked grilled octopus, and smoked duck breast paired with baby bok choy and Asian pear. The three-course $29 prix-fixe lunch is the ultimate deal. Jacket and tie are recommended. ⑤ *Average main: $32* ⊠ *1 E. 15th St., between 5th Ave. and Union Sq. W, Union Square* ☎ *212/647–1515* ⊕ *www.tocquevillerestaurant.com* ⊘ *No lunch Sun.* ⌖ *Reservations essential* Ⓜ *4, 5, 6, L, N, Q, R to 14th St.–Union Sq.* ⊹ *3:E4.*

FLATIRON DISTRICT

The popular Union Square Greenmarket has done wonders for the dining landscape in the area. Chefs, wanting to be close to the green bounty, have opened up restaurants nearby, particularly in the Flatiron District.

$$$
AMERICAN

× **ABC Kitchen.** Much more than a shopping break, Jean-Georges Vong-erichten's popular restaurant, inside posh housewares emporium ABC Carpet and Home, is more like a love letter to greenmarket cuisine. Underneath the exposed concrete beams, a chic crowd devours fresh, flavorful appetizers like the roasted carrot salad with avocado, crème fraîche, and toasted pumpkin seeds, or pretzel-dusted calamari. Winning entrées include roast suckling pig with smoked bacon marmalade and sea bass with chilies and herbs. The restaurant is committed to all the right causes—environmentalism, sustainability, supporting local farmers—all of which are announced in a near manifesto-length list on the back of the menu; thankfully, ABC Kitchen pulls it off without seeming patronizing or preachy. $ *Average main: $29* ⊠ *35 E. 18th St., between Broadway and Park Ave. S, Flatiron District* ☎ *212/475–5829* ⊕ *www.abckitchennyc.com* ⚓ *Reservations essential* Ⓜ *4, 5, 6, L, N, Q, R to 14th St.–Union Sq.* ✛ *3:F3.*

$$$
PORTUGUESE

× **Aldea.** Bouley alumnus George Mendes's popular restaurant relies on his Portuguese heritage as inspiration, which he elevates to new heights. Although there are no bad seats in this sleek bi-level space decorated with wood, glass, and blue accents, watching Mendes work in his spotless tiled kitchen from one of the seats at the chef's counter in the back is undeniably exciting. *Petiscos* (small bites) like cubes of crisp pork belly with apple cider reveal sophisticated cooking techniques and flavors. A delicate matsutake mushroom broth floated with a slow-poached egg is edged with a subtle brace of pine, while sea-salted cod reveals a deep, satisfying flavor strata. $ *Average main: $34* ⊠ *31 W. 17th St., between 5th and 6th Aves., Flatiron District* ☎ *212/675–7223* ⊕ *www. aldearestaurant.com* ☽ *Closed Sun. No lunch* ⚓ *Reservations essential* Ⓜ *4, 5, 6, L, N, Q, R to 14th St.–Union Sq.; F, M to 14th St.* ✛ *3:E3.*

$$
SPANISH

× **Boqueria.** Perennially packed, this convivial tapas spot has leather banquettes lining the main room and a few seats at the bar, but if you want to make friends, opt for the communal table running down the center of the dining room—if you can get a seat. Fried quail eggs and chorizo on roasted bread are even better than they sound, and the mushroom and ham croquettes are a mainstay. Traditional churros come with a thick hot chocolate for dipping. The original spot in the Flatiron District was so popular it spawned an offshoot in SoHo, at 171 Spring Street. $ *Average main: $20* ⊠ *53 W. 19th St., between 5th and 6th Aves., Flatiron District* ☎ *212/255–4160* ⊕ *www.boquerianyc. com* ⚓ *Reservations not accepted* Ⓜ *1 to 18th St.; F, M to 14th St.; L to 6th Ave.; N, R to 23rd St.* ✛ *3:E3.*

$$$
BRITISH
Fodor's Choice
★

× **The Breslin Bar and Dining Room.** A sceney meatopia inside the ever-trendy Ace Hotel, the Breslin is not for the Lipitor crowd. English chef April Bloomfield, who also runs the John Dory right next door and the excellent Spotted Pig in the West Village, hardens arteries with peanuts fried in pork fat, whipped lardo on pizza bianca, blood sausage accompanied by a fried duck egg, and a delicious feta-topped lamb burger. The dimly lighted, wood-bedecked interior is like a culinary womb, inspiring thoughts of planting yourself there all day or night nursing pints of cask-conditioned ale or scotch-based cocktails—you wouldn't be the first (or last). $ *Average main: $30* ⊠ *16 W. 29th St.,*

15

at Broadway, Flatiron District ☎ *212/679–1939* ⊕ *www.thebreslin.com* Ⓜ *N, R to 28th St.* ✛ *3:E1.*

$ ✕**The City Bakery.** This self-service bakery-restaurant has the urban
AMERICAN aesthetic to match its name. Chef and owner Maury Rubin's baked
FAMILY goods—giant cookies; addictively flaky, salty-sweet pretzel croissants;
elegant caramel tarts—are unfailingly rich and delicious, but another
major draw is the salad bar. It may seem overpriced, but the large selection of impeccably fresh food, including whole sides of baked salmon,
roasted vegetables, soups, and several Asian-accented dishes, delivers a
lot of bang for the buck. Much of the produce comes from the nearby
farmers' market. In winter, the bakery hosts a hot-chocolate festival;
in summer, it's lemonade time. ⑤ *Average main: $12* ⊠ *3 W. 18th St.,
between 5th and 6th Aves., Flatiron District* ☎ *212/366–1414* ⊕ *www.
thecitybakery.com* ☾ *No dinner* ⚇ *Reservations not accepted* Ⓜ *4, 5, 6,
L, N, Q, R to 14th St.–Union Sq.; F, M to 14th St.* ✛ *3:E3.*

$$$ ✕**The Clocktower.** Located in an actual clocktower (which also houses
BRITISH the New York EDITION Hotel), this Madison Square Park spot is
helmed by British superchef Jason Atherton who presides over the high-
ceilinged, dark-hued dining room that feels like an adult clubhouse. Best
described as elevated tavern fare, the menu offers diners choices like the
supertender red-wine-braised beef cheeks and comforting oxtail-spiked
mac 'n' cheese. Skip the overpriced wine list (unless, of course, you're
on an expense account) and head straight for the handful of signature
cocktails. The Milk Punch is loaded with cognac, applejack, and but-
termilk, and served in a plastic cup reminiscent of a cardboard milk
container—just in case you started to feel too adult here. ⑤ *Average
main: $33* ⊠ *Metropolitan Life Insurance Co. Tower, 5 Madison Ave.,
2nd fl., Flatiron District* ☎ *212/413–4300* ⊕ *www.theclocktowernyc.
com* Ⓜ *N, R to 23rd St.* ✛ *3:F2.*

$$$ ✕**Cosme.** When Enrique Olvera, chef at Pujol, arguably Mexico's best
MEXICAN restaurant, announced he was coming north of the border, New York
Fodor's Choice foodies went loco. Olvera's haute touch to his native cuisine is magic and,
★ coupled with the sleek design (soft lighting, minimalist decor), Cosme
makes for one fine dining experience. Sip an Expat martini (it comes with
a pickled tomatilla pepper floating in it) and peruse the menu of small
plates: start with the hamachi crudo, impossibly complex, with lime and
chili bringing out a charge in the fish; and move on to lobster pibil with
chorizo, which beautifully marries the surf-and-turf concept. ⑤ *Average
main: $31* ⊠ *35 E. 21st St., Flatiron District* ☎ *212/913–9659* ⊕ *www.
cosmenyc.com* ⚇ *Reservations essential* Ⓜ *N, R, 6 to 23rd St.* ✛ *3:F3.*

$$$$ ✕**Craft.** A meal here is like a luscious choose-your-own-adventure game
MODERN since every delectable dish comes à la carte. Craft is the flagship of *Top
AMERICAN Chef* head judge Tom Colicchio's mini-empire of excellent restaurants
around the country, including the upscale Craftbar and Craftsteak
brands, as well as grab-and-go sandwich bars called 'wichcraft. Just about
everything here is exceptionally prepared with little fuss, from simple
yet intriguing starters (like harissa-spiked octopus) and sides (including
the justly famous variety of roasted mushrooms, with oysters, trumpets,
chanterelles, and hen-of-the-woods) to desserts (warm chocolate tart with
buttermilk ice cream, cinnamon custard, and cashews). The serene dining

room of burnished dark wood and dangling radiant bulbs is more welcoming than it sounds. ⑤ *Average main: $40* ⊠ *43 E. 19th St., between Broadway and Park Ave. S, Flatiron District* ☎ *212/780–0880* ⊕ *www.craftrestaurant.com* ⊘ *No lunch weekends* ⚏ *Reservations essential* Ⓜ *4, 5, 6, L, N, Q, R to 14th St.–Union Sq.* ✛ *3:F3.*

$$$ ✕ **Craftbar.** This casual sibling to Tom Colicchio's Craft is a bargain
MODERN by comparison but still not cheap, though the food continues to gar-
AMERICAN ner raves and the service is consistently excellent. The menu features assertive seasonal cooking similar to what you can find at the upscale flagship just around the corner. The small-plates category on the menu elevates tiny nibbles like sausage-stuffed fried sage leaves or addictive fluffy salt-cod croquettes to temptations that make you forget the main course entirely. The rest of the menu is eclectic enough to satisfy. ⑤ *Average main: $27* ⊠ *900 Broadway, between 19th and 20th Sts., Flatiron District* ☎ *212/461–4300* ⊕ *www.craftbarnyc.com* ⚏ *Reservations essential* Ⓜ *4, 5, 6, L, N, Q, R to 14th St.–Union Sq.* ✛ *3:F3.*

$ ✕ **Dough.** There's a reason why these doughnuts in multilicious flavors
BAKERY have become a signature at so many cafés throughout Manhattan and
FAMILY Brooklyn—they are the perfect combination of light and airy, with enough substance to not be overwhelmed by toppings. And at the Manhattan outpost of the Bed-Stuy original, you can get them fresh out of the oven. Can't decide what kind? The hibiscus has just the right amount of tart fruitiness to balance the sweetness of the dough; other favorites include passion fruit, salted chocolate, and cinnamon and sugar. The coffee's good and the rustic benches mean you can linger long enough to think about going back for another (they taste good the next day, too). ⑤ *Average main: $4* ⊠ *14 W. 19th St., Flatiron District* ☎ *212/243–6844* ⊕ *www.doughdoughnuts.com* Ⓜ *N, R to E. 23rd St.* ✛ *3:E3.*

$$$ ✕ **Eataly.** The cavernous Eataly, from Mario Batali & Co., is a temple
ITALIAN to all things Italian. Ignore the overpriced produce market by the front
FAMILY entrance and make a beeline for La Piazza for sandwiches made with meticulously sourced ingredients (you can eat at the stand-up tables nearby). There's also a full-service pizza and pasta restaurant, a raw bar and fish eatery, and a wine bar for quaffing glass pours and beers on tap. Gourmet Italian chocolates, coffees, gelati, and pastries are all delicious for take-away, too, though still not cheap. Upstairs, the covered, rooftop birreria is open in all weather and serves hearty Austrian and German food as well as Italian specialties—and excellent beer, of course. ⑤ *Average main: $25* ⊠ *200 5th Ave., at 23rd St., Flatiron District* ☎ *646/398–5100* ⊕ *www.eataly.com* ⚏ *Reservations not accepted* Ⓜ *N, R, 6 to 23rd St.* ✛ *3:E2.*

$$$$ ✕ **Eleven Madison Park.** Luxury, precision, and creativity are the driving
MODERN forces at this internationally renowned restaurant overlooking Madison
AMERICAN Park. Swiss-born chef Daniel Humm oversees the kitchen, concocting
Fodor's Choice unexpected dishes that change often. It's entirely prix fixe, and dishes are
★ kept minimalist, giving Humm and company maximum latitude to work their magic on the plate. Not that they're resting on their laurels and accolades: the restaurant seems to reinvent itself when you least expect it, and its most recent incarnation focuses on elevated versions of classic New York fare. Think cognac-doused, truffle-sprinkled foie gras and Sichuan

15

peppercorn–encrusted duck. Reservations should be made two months in advance. $ *Average main: $225* ✉ *11 Madison Ave., at 24th St., Flatiron District* ☏ *212/889–0905* ⊕ *www.elevenmadisonpark.com* ⊘ *No lunch Sun.–Wed.* ⚲ *Reservations essential* Ⓜ *N, R, 6 to 23rd St.* ✛ *3:F2.*

$$ ✕ **Hill Country.** This enormous barbecue joint is perfect for big groups
BARBECUE   and carnivorous appetites. The beef-centric Texas-sized menu features meaty ribs and exceptionally succulent slow-smoked brisket (check your diet at the door and go for the moist, fatty option). Plump pork sausages, in regular and jalapeño cheese versions, are flown in directly from Kreuz Market in Lockhart, Texas. The market-style setup can mean long lines for meat, sold by the pound, or ribs at cutter-manned stations. Bring your tray downstairs for a fine bourbon selection and nightly live music. There's also an outpost in Brooklyn at 345 Adams Street. $ *Average main: $21* ✉ *30 W. 26th St., between Broadway and 6th Ave., Flatiron District* ☏ *212/255–4544* ⊕ *www.hillcountryny.com* Ⓜ *N, R, 6 to 28th St.; F, M to 23rd St.* ✛ *3:E2.*

$$ ✕ **The John Dory.** Chef April Bloomfield and former rock-band manager
SEAFOOD   turned restaurateur Ken Friedman can do no wrong. After winning taste buds and palates with gastropub Spotted Pig and the Breslin, the duo turned their attention to the sea. Fish tanks with brightly colored reefs and floor-to-ceiling windows create an eye-pleasing venue for the seafood feast that awaits those who snagged tables at this restaurant off the lobby of the hip Ace Hotel. The menu is dominated by small plates—chorizo-stuffed squid, an excellent lobster roll—but focuses on *crudo* (raw) dishes. The happy-hour special of $2 oysters and half off certain wines and beers is the perfect start to an evening. $ *Average main: $22* ✉ *1196 Broadway, at 29th St., Flatiron District* ☏ *212/792–9000* ⊕ *www.thejohndory.com* ⚲ *Reservations not accepted* Ⓜ *N, R to 28th St.* ✛ *3:E1.*

$$$ ✕ **The NoMad.** Named for the hotel, which itself is named for the up-
MODERN   and-coming neighborhood north of Madison Square Park, the NoMad
AMERICAN   is brought to you by Daniel Humm and Will Guidara, the masterminds
Fodor's Choice   behind much-lauded Eleven Madison Park. The atmosphere is a blend of
★   lively and sophisticated: plush velvet chairs and drapes for the hip young crowd that frequent the place. The food is similarly vibrant yet simple: seared scallops are paired with pumpkin, juicy suckling pig goes very nicely with pear confit and mustard. The poached-egg-and-quinoa dish unexpectedly transforms into a stew once the yolks are broken. The restaurant's pièce de résistance is the whole roasted chicken for two, which looks basic until the foie gras and black truffles are uncovered. Have a nightcap in the dimly lit and atmospheric Library Bar, which has floor-to-ceiling bookshelves and comfy chairs. $ *Average main: $34* ✉ *1170 Broadway, at 28th St., Flatiron District* ☏ *347/472–5660* ⊕ *www. thenomadhotel.com* ⚲ *Reservations essential* Ⓜ *N, R to 28th St.* ✛ *3:E2.*

$ ✕ **Shake Shack.** Although there are other locations of Danny Meyer's
AMERICAN   patties 'n' shakes joint around town (including Brooklyn), this is where
Fodor's Choice   it all began. Here in Madison Square Park, there's no indoor seating—
★   just snaking outdoor lines. Check the "Shack Cam" from their website to gauge your wait. Fresh Angus beef burgers are ground daily, and a single will run you from $5.29 to $9.64, depending on what you

want on it. For a burger on the go, they're decidedly tasty. For a few more bucks you can order a double, a stack, or a vegetarian 'Shroom Burger—a superrich, melty, Muenster-and-cheddar-stuffed fried portobello, topped with lettuce, tomato, and Shack sauce. The menu also offers "beef and bird" (chicken) hot dogs, french fries, and a variety of delicious frozen custard desserts, and—of course—shakes. $ *Average main: $7* ⊠ *Madison Square Park, near Madison Ave. and 23rd St., Flatiron District* ☎ *212/889–6600* ⊕ *www.shakeshack.com* Ⓜ *N, R, 6 to 23rd St.* ✛ *3:F2.*

$$$ ╳**Upland.** This collaboration between prolific Philly/NYC restaurateur
ITALIAN Stephen Starr and erstwhile Il Buco chef Justin Smilie tastes as if California and Italy miraculously collided. Marrying organic and in-season ingredients with Italian recipes, Upland's standouts include bucatini alla carbonara that could pass muster with discriminating eaters in the Eternal City or, um, the City of Angels. Of the three Neapolitan-style pizzas on the menu, you have to try the meaty 'nduja; just try to resist drinking your way through the Italian and California wine list so much that you can't pronounce it. $ *Average main: $26* ⊠ *345 Park Ave. S, Flatiron District* ☎ *212/686–1006* ⊕ *www.uplandnyc.com* Ⓜ *6 to 28th St.* ✛ *3:F2.*

GRAMERCY

This leafy, high-rent neighborhood, which has an old-world, old-money feel, is home to a few gems, tucked away down the long blocks of brownstones. Gramercy is a great place for a stroll before dinner.

$$$$ ╳**BLT Prime.** A masculine, vivacious space is the showcase for bold,
STEAKHOUSE appealing Franco-American cuisine. Menu specials are scrawled on a blackboard. Everything is served à la carte, and prices are high, but so is the quality of every dish. Although there are poultry, veal, and lamb dishes on the menu—from lemon-rosemary chicken to a lamb T-bone—steaks are the main event. The dry-aged USDA prime steaks—pulled from a 30-foot-wide dry-aging room—are broiled at 1,700°F, spread lightly with herb butter, and served with a choice of sauce (the béarnaise is perfection). $ *Average main: $40* ⊠ *111 E. 22nd St., between Lexington and Park Aves., Gramercy* ☎ *212/995–8500* ⊕ *www.bltprime. com* ☾ *No lunch* ⌕ *Reservations essential* Ⓜ *N, R, 6 to 23rd St.* ✛ *3:F2.*

$$ ╳**Casa Mono.** Andy Nusser put in his time cooking Italian under Mario
SPANISH Batali at Babbo before an obsession with Spain landed him his own acclaimed Iberian niche. The perennially cramped and crowded Casa Mono sends patrons to Bar Jamón, the wine-and-ham-bar annex next door, where you can pick at plates of *jamón serrano* while awaiting the main feature. Our favorite seats are at the Casa Mono counter overlooking the chef's open kitchen. Though most menu items are delectably shareable, of particular note are all things seared *à la plancha* (grilled on a metal plate), including blistered peppers and garlic-kissed mushrooms. Like his mentor, Nusser has a weakness for the neglected cuts of meat, so check your food fears at the door. $ *Average main: $21* ⊠ *52 Irving Pl., at 17th St., Gramercy* ☎ *212/253–2773* ⊕ *www.casamononyc.com* Ⓜ *4, 5, 6, L, N, Q, R to 14th St.–Union Sq.* ✛ *3:G3.*

$$$$ ╳**Gramercy Tavern.** Danny Meyer's intensely popular restaurant
AMERICAN tops many a New Yorker's list of favorite dining spots. In front, the

first-come, first-served tavern has a lighter menu—including a value-packed three-course prix fixe—along with great craft beers and cocktails scrawled on a board at the bar. The more formal dining room has a prix-fixe American menu, where choices include seasonal dishes such as marinated sea scallops with pickled peppers and fresh grapes, and rack of lamb with sunchokes, hazelnuts, and exotic mushrooms. Meyer's restaurants—he owns several well-regarded eateries in the city—are renowned for their food and hospitality, and Gramercy Tavern sets the standard. $ *Average main: $37 ⊠ 42 E. 20th St., between Broadway and Park Ave. S, Gramercy* 🕾 *212/477–0777* ⊕ *www.gramercytavern. com* ⌕ *Reservations essential* Ⓜ *N, R, 6 to 23rd St.* ✛ *3:F3.*

$$$ ✕ **Maialino.** Named for its signature dish—suckling pig—the perpetually
ROMAN   packed restaurant in the Gramercy Park Hotel is what it might look like if Manhattan and Rome collided: fashionable people eating in an Eternal City ambience. If you haven't been to the Italian capital in a while, there's plenty to reintroduce your taste buds to *la dolce vita*: excellent fried artichokes, spaghetti alla carbonara (made with guanciale, or pig cheek, just like in Rome), and sausage-studded pasta dish *lumaconi alla Norcia*. It's enough to make a toast to the good life—that is, if your dining companions can hear you over the chatter of the fashion models and bankers at surrounding tables. $ *Average main: $27 ⊠ 2 Lexington Ave., at 21st St., Gramercy* 🕾 *212/777–2410* ⊕ *www.maialinonyc.com* ⌕ *Reservations essential* Ⓜ *6 to 23rd St.* ✛ *3:G3.*

MIDTOWN EAST WITH MURRAY HILL

MIDTOWN EAST

Midtown East's streets are relatively quiet at night and on weekends, but during the week, the restaurants are filled with expense-account diners celebrating their successes. Indeed, some of the most formal dining rooms and most expensive meals in town can be found here.

$$$$ ✕ **Aquavit and Aquavit Café.** This elegant and refined Scandinavian res-
SCANDINAVIAN   taurant has seen a transition in the kitchen these last few years, going from Marcus Samuelsson to Marcus Jernmark, until he, too, exited. The place is now in steady hands with Emma Bengtsson at the helm. The elegant atmosphere features warm woods and modern Scandinavian design. There are a few options here: a $145 eight-course meal, $95 three-course affair, and a $115 six-course dinner that changes according to the season. Standout dishes include foie gras paired with licorice, sweetbreads paired with sauerkraut, venison tartare, and for dessert, smoked vanilla crème brûlée. Head to the sumptuous bar area to sample house-made aquavit. $ *Average main: $75 ⊠ 65 E. 55th St., between Madison and Park Aves., Midtown East* 🕾 *212/307–7311* ⊕ *www. aquavit.org* ☾ *Closed Sun. No lunch Sat.* ⌕ *Reservations essential* Ⓜ *E, M to 5th Ave./53rd St.* ✛ *4:F2.*

$$$ ✕ **BLT Steak.** Chef Laurent Tourondel may no longer be involved with his
STEAKHOUSE   namesake steak house, but this classy space, decked out in beige with resin-top black tables, still draws crowds. As soon as you're settled, puffy Gruyère popovers arrive still steaming. The no-muss, no-fuss menu is nonetheless large, and so are the portions of supple crab cakes

with celery-infused mayonnaise and luscious ruby tuna tartare with avocado, ramped up with soy-lime dressing. A veal chop crusted with rosemary and Parmesan lends new depth to the meat. Sides and desserts, like a killer peanut-butter chocolate mousse with banana ice cream, are all superior. ⑤ *Average main: $35* ⊠ *106 E. 57th St., between Lexington and Park Aves., Midtown East* ☎ *212/752–7470* ⊕ *www.bltsteak.com* ⊗ *No lunch weekends* ⚶ *Reservations essential* Ⓜ *4, 5, 6, N, R, Q to 59th St./Lexington Ave.* ✛ *4:F1.*

$$$ ✕ **Grand Central Oyster Bar & Restaurant.** Deep in the belly of Grand
SEAFOOD Central Station, the vast Oyster Bar has been a worthy seafood destination since 1913. Sit at the counter for the fried oyster po'boy or to slurp an assortment of bracingly fresh oysters before a steaming bowl of clam chowder, washed down with an ice-cold beer. This is also the place to experience the pleasure of fresh, unadorned seafood, such as lobster with drawn butter or grilled herring in season—generally better options than anything that sounds too complicated, like a cream-smothered seafood pan roast. ⑤ *Average main: $30* ⊠ *Grand Central Terminal, dining concourse, 42nd St. at Vanderbilt Ave., Midtown East* ☎ *212/490–6650* ⊕ *www.oysterbarny.com* ⊗ *Closed Sun.* Ⓜ *4, 5, 6, 7, S to Grand Central–42nd St.* ✛ *4:F4.*

$$$$ ✕ **Kurumazushi.** Only a small sign in Japanese indicates the location of
JAPANESE this extraordinary restaurant that serves sushi and sashimi exclusively. Bypass the tables, sit at the sushi bar, and put yourself in the hands of Toshihiro Uezu, the chef and owner. Among the selections are hard-to-find fish that Uezu imports directly from Japan. The most attentive, pampering staff in the city completes the wildly expensive experience. The showstopping chef's omakase, priced at whatever the market dictates and the type of fish on offer, could run as much as $300, but it's a multicourse feast you'll never forget. ⑤ *Average main: $175* ⊠ *7 E. 47th St., 2nd fl., between 5th and Madison Aves., Midtown East* ☎ *212/317–2802* ⊕ *www.kurumazushi.com* ⊗ *Closed Sun.* ⚶ *Reservations essential* Ⓜ *4, 5, 6, 7, S to Grand Central–42nd St.* ✛ *4:E3.*

$$$$ ✕ **Le Cirque.** Impresario-owner Sirio Maccioni still presides over this din-
FRENCH ing room, filled nightly with a "who's who" of politics, business, and society—regulars who've table-hopped from Le Cirque's first incarnation to its latest, in a glass-enclosed aerie on the ground floor of the Bloomberg headquarters. The menu strikes a balance between the creative and classic: Dover sole, filleted table-side, gives way to more avant-garde preparations like foie-gras ravioli. Desserts, too, have a split personality, with the menu divided into the "classic" and "new." The foot-tall napoleon that seems to arrive at every second table is an old favorite, but newer creations like the praline tortellini with exotic fruit also satisfy. Though jackets are still required in the dining room, things are more relaxed in the casual wine lounge. ⑤ *Average main: $60* ⊠ *151 E. 58th St., at Lexington Ave., Midtown East* ☎ *212/644–0202* ⊕ *www.lecirque.com* ⊗ *Closed Sun. No lunch Sat.* ⚶ *Reservations essential* Ⓜ *4, 5, 6 to 59th St.; N, Q, R to Lexington Ave./59th St.* ✛ *4:F1.*

$$$ ✕ **Michael Jordan's The Steakhouse NYC.** Don't be dissuaded by the fact
STEAKHOUSE that this place is technically part of a chain: there's nowhere remotely like it. The handsomely appointed space in Grand Central Terminal,

hung with gracious filigree chandeliers, overlooks one of the most famous interiors in America. Start with the stack of soft, toasted bread soldiers in a pool of hot Gorgonzola fondue. Pristine oysters make a great prelude for a prime dry-aged rib eye or a 2½-pound lobster, grilled, steamed, sautéed, or broiled. Sides, like creamy mac 'n' cheese and a crispy rosemary hash-brown cake, are equally tempting. $ *Average main: $34* ⊠ *Grand Central Terminal, West Balcony, 23 Vanderbilt Ave., between 43rd and 44th Sts., Midtown East* ☎ *212/655–2300* ⊕ *www.michaeljordansnyc.com* ⊙ *No lunch weekends* ⚑ *Reservations essential* Ⓜ *4, 5, 6, 7, S to Grand Central–42nd St.* ✛ *4:F4.*

$$ ✕ **Mint Restaurant & Lounge.** With a delightful dining room splashed with bright colors and flattering lighting, and executive chef and owner Gary Sikka's brightly seasoned dishes, Mint has joined the ranks of the best Indian restaurants in town. The large menu includes rarely encountered specialties from Goa and Sikkim. Freshly grilled, moist ground lamb kebabs deliver a slow burn to the palate. Chili heat punctuates other spices in the lamb vindaloo, resulting in a well-rounded array of savory flavors. Finish with carrot pudding with saffron and coconut flakes. $ *Average main: $22* ⊠ *150 E. 50th St., Midtown East* ☎ *212/644–8888* ⊕ *www.mintny.com* Ⓜ *6 to 51st St.; E, M to Lexington Ave./53rd St.* ✛ *4:G3.*

INDIAN

$$ ✕ **P. J. Clarke's.** This East Side institution has been dispensing burgers and beer for more than a century. Despite renovations and several owners over the years, the original P. J. Clarke's (there are offshoots in Lincoln Square and Chelsea) maintains the beveled-glass and scuffed-wood look of an old-time saloon. Many of the bartenders and patrons are as much a part of the decor as the light fixtures. More civilized at lunchtime, the bar area heaves with an after-work mob on weekday evenings. Pull up a stool if you can for superlative bar food, like clams casino and the signature burger smothered in creamy béarnaise. $ *Average main: $18* ⊠ *915 3rd Ave., at 55th St., Midtown East* ☎ *212/317–1616* ⊕ *www.pjclarkes.com* Ⓜ *E, M to 5th Ave./53rd St.; N, Q, R to Lexington Ave./59th St.; 4, 5, 6 to 59th St.* ✛ *4:G2; 1:B3; 5:C5.*

AMERICAN

$$$ ✕ **Shun Lee Palace.** If you want inexpensive Cantonese food without pretensions, head to Chinatown. If you prefer to be pampered and don't mind spending a lot of money, then this is the place, which has been elegantly serving classic Chinese fare for more than four decades. Supposedly the dish orange beef was first made here. Indeed, it's certainly worth a sample, but there's so much more. Beijing panfried dumplings make a good starter, and rack of lamb Sichuan-style, grilled with scallions and garlic, is a popular entrée. The "Lion's Head," a slow-baked pork dish, is one of the most tender porky things you'll eat. Beijing duck, served table-side with thin pancakes, is a signature dish here—and for good reason. $ *Average main: $29* ⊠ *155 E. 55th St., between Lexington and 3rd Aves., Midtown East* ☎ *212/371–8844* ⊕ *www.shunleepalace.net* ⚑ *Reservations essential* Ⓜ *N, Q, R to Lexington Ave./59th St.; 4, 5, 6 to 59th St.* ✛ *4:G2.*

CHINESE

$$$$ ✕ **Sparks Steakhouse.** Fans of mob history recognize Sparks as the spot where, in 1985, members of the Gambino crime family were gunned down under the orders of John Gotti. Today it's less about the mob connections and more about the food here, but still be sure to bring a

STEAKHOUSE

wad of cash. Magnums of wines that cost more than most people earn in a week festoon the large dining rooms of this classic New York steak house. Tasty, fresh seafood is given more than fair play on the menu, and the extra-thick lamb and veal chops are also noteworthy—but Sparks is really about dry-aged steak. Classic sides of hash browns, creamed spinach, sautéed mushrooms, and grilled onions are all you need to complete the experience—plus maybe a martini. $ *Average main: $42* ⊠ *210 E. 46th St., between 2nd and 3rd Aves., Midtown East* ☎ *212/687–4855* ⊕ *www.sparkssteakhouse.com* ⊙ *Closed Sun. No lunch Sat.* ⌲ *Reservations essential* Ⓜ *4, 5, 6, 7, S to Grand Central–42nd St.* ✛ *4:G4.*

$$$
JAPANESE
✕ **Sushi Yasuda.** Devotees mourned the return of namesake chef Naomichi Yasuda to Japan, but things are in able hands with his hand-picked successor, Mitsuru Tamura. Whether using fish flown in daily from Japan or the creamiest sea urchin, the chef makes sushi so fresh and delicate it melts in your mouth. A number of special appetizers change daily (crispy fried eel backbone is a surprising treat), and the fine selection of sake and beer complements the lovely food. The sleek, bamboo-lined interior is as elegant as the food. Try to sit at the bar, which was handcrafted by Yasuda from imported Japanese materials. $ *Average main: $33* ⊠ *204 E. 43rd St., between 2nd and 3rd Aves., Midtown East* ☎ *212/972–1001* ⊕ *www.sushiyasuda.com* ⊙ *Closed Sun. No lunch Sat.* Ⓜ *4, 5, 6, 7, S to Grand Central–42nd St.* ✛ *4:G4.*

MURRAY HILL

This area has a residential feel with plenty of bistros perfect for a casual meal. Lexington Avenue's "Curry Hill" section between 27th and 29th Streets is home to Indian spice shops, cafés, and restaurants.

$$
ITALIAN
Fodor's Choice
★
✕ **Marta.** The excellent cracker-thin crust of the Roman-style pizzas at Marta are a refreshing break from the thicker crust of the Neapolitan pizzas that have overtaken Manhattan in recent years, and we have beloved restaurateur Danny Meyer to thank for it. The high-ceiling dining room belies the casual fare, but the menu is a love letter to salt-of-the-earth Roman food, from the baseball-sized *suppli* (fried rice balls) to fried squash to those excellent thin pizzas topped with tangy tomato sauce and delicious items like guanciale (pork jowl) and arugula. $ *Average main: $20* ⊠ *29 E. 29th St., at Madison Ave., Murray Hill* ☎ *212/651–3800* ⊕ *www.martamanhattan.com* Ⓜ *6 to 28th St.* ✛ *3:F1.*

$$
DELI
✕ **2nd Ave Deli.** It may no longer be on 2nd Avenue, but the most recent incarnation of this East Village institution—about a mile uptown, in Midtown—still delivers on its longtime traditional matzo-ball soup, overstuffed three-decker sandwiches filled with house-cured pastrami, and other old-world specialties. Hot open-face sandwiches, like juicy beef brisket served with gravy and french fries, may be a heart attack on a plate, but hey, you only live once. Even better, you can now get your fill of kasha *varnishkes,* carrot tzimmes, and potato kugel until the wee hours of the night. There's also an outpost on the Upper East Side. $ *Average main: $23* ⊠ *162 E. 33rd St., between Lexington and 3rd Aves., Murray Hill* ☎ *212/689–9000* ⊕ *www.2ndavedeli.com* Ⓜ *6 to 33rd St.* ✛ *4:G6.*

15

MIDTOWN WEST

It's true that tourist traps abound on Broadway, but fortunately you needn't head far from Times Square to score a stellar meal. Just move away from the bright lights and unrelenting foot traffic that clogs the area. On calmer side streets and in adjoining Hell's Kitchen there are excellent dining options for budget travelers and expense-account diners alike. Some of the best steak houses and Italian restaurants are here, and many eateries offer budget pretheater dinners and prix-fixe lunch menus to draw in new business.

$$$$
MODERN
AMERICAN

✕**Aureole.** An island of fine dining just a stone's throw from bustling Times Square, Aureole is the second act of a New York classic from Charlie Palmer and his executive chef, Marcus Gleadow-Ware. From the street, a curved second-story corridor hosting the restaurant's storied wine collection beckons. A welcoming front barroom serves a more casual, yet still refined menu with dishes like a cheddar-bacon burger with pickled-ramp mayonnaise. The dining room, with its abundance of flowers, is the place to hobnob with expense-account diners and pretheater revelers. For dinner, starters like the pumpkin risotto with shrimp is a treat, and the $148 "parallel tasting" has the menu's greatest hits. There is no à la carte option in the main dining room. ⑤ *Average main: $50* ⊠ *135 W. 42nd St., between Broadway and 6th Ave., Midtown West* ☎ *212/319–1660* ⊕ *www.charliepalmer.com* ☯ *No lunch weekends* ⌕ *Reservations essential* Ⓜ *B, D, F, M to 42nd St.–Bryant Park; 1, 2, 3, 7, N, Q, R, S to Times Sq.–42nd St.* ✛ *4:D4.*

$$$$
SOUTHERN

✕**Bar Americain.** Celeb-chef Bobby Flay's largest Manhattan restaurant is the soaring Bar Americain. The 200-seat, two-story space looks like a dining room on a luxury liner. This is not food for the faint of heart: Flay piles on the butter, cream, and endless varieties of bacon. Southern-inflected brasserie fare includes deviled eggs with smoked shrimp, "secret recipe" fried chicken with black-pepper biscuit, and duck confit flavored with bourbon-based sauce and fig chutney. Slightly naughtier are the éclairs piped with whiskey-infused pastry cream and burnished with a burnt-sugar glaze. Brunch, featuring dishes like biscuits and cream gravy with sausage and scrambled eggs, is delicious. ⑤ *Average main: $36* ⊠ *152 W. 52nd St., between 6th and 7th Aves., Midtown West* ☎ *212/265–9700* ⊕ *www.baramericain.com* ⌕ *Reservations essential* Ⓜ *B, D, E to 7th Ave.; 1, C, E to 50th St.; N, Q, R to 49th St.* ✛ *4:C2.*

$$$
FRENCH

✕**Benoit.** Who needs to go to Paris when the world's most famous French chef, Alain Ducasse, can come to you? The interior of Ducasse's imported Right Bank bistro—cozy red-velour banquettes and wall lamps illuminating each table—is plucked straight from the City of Light. So is the menu, which doesn't reinvent anything as much as it replicates. And that's okay, especially when the fennel-inflected *loup de mer* (sea bass) or the tender roasted veal loin are so well executed. It's not exactly cheap for simple bistro fare. Then again, neither is a round-trip ticket to Paris. ⑤ *Average main: $29* ⊠ *60 W. 55th St., between 5th and 6th Aves., Midtown West* ☎ *646/943–7373* ⊕ *www.benoitny.com* ▭ *No credit cards* Ⓜ *N, Q, R to 5th Ave./59th St.; F to 57th St.* ✛ *4:D2.*

$$$
BRASSERIE

✕**Brasserie Ruhlmann.** In a plush 120-seat dining room with just enough Art Deco touches to harmonize with its Rockefeller Center setting, sublime French bistro cookery is on display. The room has a refined air but the staff is so friendly that the place could never be stuffy. The raw bar, with its selection of pedigreed oysters, is a great way to begin, or opt for a blue crab salad over mâche with a honey-lime vinaigrette. If it's on the menu, order braised rabbit nestled in mustard cream on a bed of fresh pappardelle, sprinkled with pitted cherries. Desserts like Floating Island—delicately baked meringue floating on a pond of crème anglaise—are embellished with a flurry of spun sugar. $ *Average main: $29* ⊠ *45 Rockefeller Plaza, 50th St. between 5th and 6th Aves., Midtown West* ☎ *212/974–2020* ⊕ *www.brasserieruhlmann.com* ☾ *No dinner Sun.* ⚏ *Reservations essential* Ⓜ *B, D, F, M to 47th–50th Sts./ Rockefeller Center; E, M to 5th Ave./53rd St.* ✛ *4:D3.*

$ ✕ **Burger Joint.** What's a college burger bar, done up in particleboard
BURGER and rec-room design straight out of *Happy Days,* doing inside a five-
Fodor's Choice star Midtown hotel? This tongue-in-cheek lunch spot, hidden behind a
★ heavy red-velvet curtain in the Parker Meridien hotel, does such boister-
ous midweek business that lines often snake through the lobby (which means you're best off coming at noon or earlier). Behind the curtain you can find baseball-cap-wearing, grease-spattered cooks dispensing paper-wrapped cheeseburgers and crisp, thin fries. Forget Kobe beef or foie gras—these burgers are straightforward, cheap, and delicious. There's a second location, serving inferior burgers, at 33 West 8th Street in Greenwich Village. $ *Average main: $9* ⊠ *Le Parker Meridien, 119 W. 56th St., between 6th and 7th Aves., Midtown West* ☎ *212/708–7414* ⊕ *www.burgerjointny.com* Ⓜ *N, Q, R to 57th St.–7th Ave.; F to 57th St.* ✛ *4:D1.*

$$$ ✕ **Carmine's.** Savvy New Yorkers line up early for the affordable fam-
ITALIAN ily-style meals at this large, busy Midtown eatery. Family photos line
FAMILY the walls, and there's a convivial feeling amid all the Times Square
hubbub. Don't be fooled: Carmine's may be huge, but it fills up with families carbo-loading for a day of sightseeing or a night of theater on Broadway. Hungry diners are rewarded with mountains of such popular, toothsome viands as fried calamari, linguine with white clam sauce, chicken parmigiana, and veal saltimbocca. $ *Average main: $25* ⊠ *200 W. 44th St., between Broadway and 8th Ave., Midtown West* ☎ *212/221–3800* ⊕ *www.carminesnyc.com* Ⓜ *A, C, E to 42nd St.–Port Authority; 1, 2, 3, 7, N, Q, R, S to Times Sq.–42nd St.* ✛ *4:C4; 6:A5.*

$$ ✕ **Danji.** Diminutive and dark, Danji is no ordinary Korean restaurant.
KOREAN Helmed by talented chef Hooni Kim, this Hell's Kitchen spot stands
out among the rows of restaurants that attract theatergoing tourists to the neighborhood. That's because Kim's take on Korean cuisine is inventive and inspired. The menu is split up between small, medium, and large plates, each category a combination of traditional Korean fare and more experimental dishes. Indulge in everything from taste-bud-burning Korean chicken wings to unctuous pork-belly sliders. Then count your blessings that you're not eating a mediocre meal like the rest of the out-of-town visitors in the neighborhood. $ *Average main: $20* ⊠ *346 W. 52nd St., between 8th and 9th Aves., Midtown West* ☎ *212/586–2880* ⊕ *www.danjinyc.com* ☾ *Closed Sun. No lunch Sat.* Ⓜ *C, E to 50th St.* ✛ *4:B2.*

15

$$$ ✕ **db Bistro Moderne.** Daniel Boulud's "casual bistro" (it's neither, actu-
FRENCH   ally) consists of two elegantly appointed dining rooms. The menu features
classic dishes like Nantucket Bay scallops or hanger steak exquisitely pre-
pared. Ever the trendsetter, Boulud's $35 "db" hamburger stuffed with
braised short ribs, foie gras, and black truffles, is the patty credited with
kick-starting the whole gourmet burger trend. Although it may not be the
trendy destination it once was, it's still a treat and worth every penny. The
service is friendly without being overbearing. ⑤ *Average main: $33* ✉ *55
W. 44th St., between 5th and 6th Aves., Midtown West* ☎ *212/391–2400*
⊕ *www.dbbistro.com* 🕭 *Reservations essential* Ⓜ *B, D, F, M to 42nd
St.–Bryant Park; 7 to 5th Ave.* ✛ *4:D4.*

$$ ✕ **Ellen's Stardust Diner.** If you haven't had enough Broadway singing and
AMERICAN   dancing, you'll get a kick out of Ellen's, a retro, 1950s-style diner, com-
FAMILY   plete with a singing waitstaff. The menu focuses on all-American classics like meat loaf and chicken potpie, and the waiters and waitresses
serenading you on roller skates have the talent to prove this restaurant is
right on Broadway. It's the kind of over-the-top family fun you'd expect
from the Times Square location, so don't expect a sophisticated—or
quiet—dining experience. ⑤ *Average main: $20* ✉ *1650 Broadway, at
51st St., Midtown West* ☎ *212/956–5151* ⊕ *www.ellensstardustdiner.
com* Ⓜ *1 to 50th St.; B, D, E to 7th Ave.* ✛ *4:C3.*

$$$ ✕ **Esca.** The name is Italian for "bait," and this restaurant, courtesy of
SEAFOOD   partners Mario Batali, Joe Bastianich, and longtime chef David Pas-
ternack, lures diners in with delectable crudo preparations—such as
tilefish with orange and Sardinian oil or pink snapper with a sprinkle
of crunchy red clay salt—and hooks them with entrées like whole, salt-
crusted branzino, sea bass for two, or bucatini pasta with spicy baby
octopus. The menu changes daily. Bastianich is in charge of the wine
cellar, so expect an adventurous list of Italian bottles. ⑤ *Average main:
$34* ✉ *402 W. 43rd St., at 9th Ave., Midtown West* ☎ *212/564–7272*
⊕ *www.esca-nyc.com* ☾ *No lunch Sun.* 🕭 *Reservations essential* Ⓜ *A,
C, E to 42nd St.–Port Authority* ✛ *4:A4.*

$$ ✕ **Five Napkin Burger.** This perennially packed Hell's Kitchen burger
BURGER   place and brasserie has been a magnet for burger lovers since day one.
Bottles of Maker's Mark line the sleek, alluringly lighted bar in the
back, a collection of antique butcher's scales hangs on a tile wall near
the kitchen, and meat hooks dangle from the ceiling between light fixtures. Though there are many menu distractions—deep-fried pickles
and warm artichoke dip, to name a few—the main attractions are the
juicy burgers, like the original 10-ounce chuck with a tangle of onions,
Gruyère cheese, and rosemary aioli. There's a patty option for everyone, including a ground lamb *kofta* and an onion-ring-topped ahi tuna
burger. For dessert, have an überthick black-and-white malted milk
shake. ⑤ *Average main: $16* ✉ *630 9th Ave., at 45th St., Midtown
West* ☎ *212/757–2277* ⊕ *www.5napkinburger.com* Ⓜ *A, C, E to 42nd
St.–Port Authority* ✛ *4:B4.*

$$$$ ✕ **The Lambs Club.** Restaurateur Geoffrey Zakarian's opulent supper
MODERN   club on the ground floor of the Chatwal Hotel has superb Art Deco
AMERICAN   detailing, blood-red leather banquettes, and a roaring fireplace. Cock-
tails are concocted by hipster mixologist Sasha Petraske, who eschews

the experimental in favor of classics like the sidecar and the martini, done well. The food is typical Zakarian, meaning new American cuisine with luxe touches in dishes like veal sweetbreads with peppered jus and grilled Treviso lettuce, or seared scallops with porcini mushrooms and Indian-spiced sauce. The lunchtime menu is padded with appealing choices, but the sleeper meal here is breakfast. Dishes like a house-made biscuit with fried egg, bacon, and cheddar, or fluffy lemon-ricotta pancakes, fill you up for the rest of the day. $ *Average main: $36* ✉ *132 W. 44th St., between 6th Ave. and Broadway, Midtown West* ☎ *212/997–5262* ⊕ *www.thelambsclub.com* Ⓜ *1, 2, 3, 7, N, Q, R, S to Times Sq.–42nd St.; B, D, F, M to 47th–50th Sts./Rockefeller Center* ✛ *4:D4.*

$$$$ ✕ **Le Bernardin.** Owner Maguy LeCoze presides over the teak-panel din-
SEAFOOD ing room at this trendsetting French seafood restaurant, and chef and
Fodor's Choice partner Eric Ripert works magic with anything that swims—preferring
★ at times not to cook it at all. Deceptively simple dishes such as poached lobster in rich coconut-ginger soup or crispy spiced black bass in a Peking duck bouillon are typical of his style. It's widely agreed that there's no beating Le Bernardin for thrilling cuisine, seafood or otherwise, coupled with some of the finest desserts in town and a wine list as deep as the Atlantic. It's prix-fixe only, and there are nonfish options (pasta and meat) available on request. $ *Average main: $155* ✉ *155 W. 51st St., between 6th and 7th Aves., Midtown West* ☎ *212/554–1515* ⊕ *www.le-bernardin.com* ☾ *Closed Sun. No lunch Sat.* 🏛 *Jacket required* Ⓜ *1 to 50th St.; N, Q, R to 49th St.; B, D, E to 7th Ave.* ✛ *4:C2.*

$$ ✕ **Le Pain Quotidien.** This international Belgian chain brings its home-
BAKERY land ingredients with it, treating New Yorkers to crusty organic breads, jams, chocolate, and other specialty products. You can grab a snack to go or stay and eat breakfast, lunch, or dinner at communal or private tables with waiter service. Come for a steaming latte and croissant in the morning or a tartine (open-faced sandwich) at noon. There are more than 20 locations throughout Manhattan, including in Central Park. $ *Average main: $14* ✉ *1271 6th Ave., at 50th St., Midtown West* ☎ *646/462–4165* ⊕ *www.lepainquotidien.com* Ⓜ *B, D, F, M to 47th–50th Sts./Rockefeller Center; N, Q, R to 49th St.; 1 to 50th St.* ✛ *4:D3.*

$$ ✕ **Lugo Cucina Italiana.** The area around Madison Square Garden is a
ITALIAN restaurant wasteland with the rare sparkling exception of Lugo Cucina Italiana, founded by an Italian menswear line. Locals rejoiced at the introduction of this spacious Italian "brasserie," serving comfort food with a dolce-vita twist all day long. Stop by for an espresso and pastry in the morning. Later, a single menu presents lunch, *aperitivo,* and dinner options, which include grazing portions of salumi, cheeses, and vegetable dishes like eggplant caponata, Tuscan white-bean salad, and grilled zucchini with pine nuts. Fuller meals of Neapolitan-style pizzas, house-made pastas, and grilled meats and fish also are commendable. $ *Average main: $24* ✉ *1 Penn Plaza, 33rd St. and 8th Ave., Midtown West* ☎ *212/760–2700* ⊕ *www.lugocaffe.com* ☾ *Closed weekends* Ⓜ *1, 2, 3, A, C, E to 34th St.–Penn Station* ✛ *4:C6.*

$$$
ASIAN

✕**Má Pêche.** Starkly decorated in the basement of the Chambers Hotel, Má Pêche is just blocks from MoMA. As the largest restaurant in David Chang's empire, you've got a decent shot of nabbing a seat. The menus are a bit more refined (and expensive) than those at Momofuku Noodle Bar and Ssäm Bar, with elegantly composed plates that might include lamb shank accompanied by eggplant, raisins, and rice, or seared swordfish with black beans, braised celery, and crisped shallots. On the way out you can pick up sweets from the uptown offshoot of Momofuku Milk Bar, like the addictive, buttery Crack Pie or intriguingly flavored soft-serve. ⑤ *Average main: $28* ✉ *15 W. 56th St., between 5th and 6th Aves., Midtown West* ☎ *212/757–5878* ⊕ *www.momofuku.com/ma-peche* Ⓜ *F to 57th St.; N, Q, R to 5th Ave./59th St.* ✛ *4:E1.*

$$$
SEAFOOD
Fodor's Choice
★

✕**Marea.** Carefully sourced, meticulously prepared fish and seafood take center stage at this well-pedigreed restaurant. Large picture windows in the dining room look out to expansive views of Central Park South, and silver-dipped shells on pedestals decorate the dining room. No expense is spared in importing the very best of the ocean's bounty, beginning with crudo dishes—think scallops with orange, wild fennel, and arugula—that are becoming the restaurant's signature. You'd be remiss, though, if you skipped the pastas that made chef Michael White famous. They're served here in lusty iterations like rich fusilli with octopus and bone marrow, and spaghetti with sea urchin. Whole fish like roasted turbot and salt-baked snapper are equally showstopping. Service is flawless. ⑤ *Average main: $27* ✉ *240 Central Park S, between Broadway and 7th Ave., Midtown West* ☎ *212/582–5100* ⊕ *www.marea-nyc.com* ⌦ *Reservations essential* Ⓜ *1, A, B, C, D to 59th St.–Columbus Circle* ✛ *4:B1.*

$$
MEDITERRANEAN

✕**Marseille.** With great food and a convenient location near several Broadway theaters, Marseille is perpetually packed. The Mediterranean creations are continually impressive, including the bouillabaisse, the signature dish of the region for which the restaurant is named—a mélange of mussels, shrimp, and whitefish in a fragrant broth, topped with a garlicky crouton and served with rouille on the side. Also worth a bite or two is the charred octopus with fennel and tomatoes. Leave room for the spongy beignets with chocolate and raspberry dipping sauces. ⑤ *Average main: $24* ✉ *630 9th Ave., at 44th St., Midtown West* ☎ *212/333–2323* ⊕ *www.marseillenyc.com* ⌦ *Reservations essential* Ⓜ *A, C, E to 42nd St.–Port Authority* ✛ *4:B4.*

$$$
SEAFOOD

✕**Oceana.** Entering this restaurant is like walking into the dressy stateroom of a modern luxury ocean liner. Floor-to-ceiling windows look out north and west, and the arrestingly designed raw bar backed with Mediterranean-hue ceramics serves stunningly fresh choices—you would expect gorgeous oysters at a restaurant called Oceana, and you get them. Chef Ben Pollinger has the skill and confidence to serve some of the most vivid and delicious seafood in town. A contemporary appetizer section includes items like marinated cucumber with apple and toasted spices. Grilled whole fish like halibut, swordfish, and crispy wild striped bass are served with a perfect rotating roster of sauces that includes a classic romesco and a grilled pineapple salsa. ⑤ *Average main: $34* ✉ *120 W. 49th St., at 6th Ave., Midtown West*

☎ *212/759–5941* ⊕ *www.oceanarestaurant.com* ⊘ *No breakfast or lunch weekends* ⌆ *Reservations essential* Ⓜ *B, D, F, M to 47th–50th Sts./Rockefeller Center* ⊹ *4:D3.*

$$$
BRAZILIAN
✗**Plataforma Churrascaria Rodizio.** This sprawling, boisterous shrine to meat, with its all-you-can-eat, prix-fixe menu, is best experienced with a group of ravenous friends. A caipirinha, featuring cachaça sugarcane liquor, sugar, and lime, kicks things off nicely. Follow up with a trip to the fabulous salad bar, piled with vegetables, meats, and cheeses—but remember, there's about to be a parade of all manner of grilled meats and poultry, from pork ribs to chicken hearts, delivered to the table on long skewers. Everyone at the table gets a coaster-size disc that's red on one side and green on the other: turn the green side up when you're ready for more. Pace yourself so you can try all the different delicacies; it's definitely a fun evening, but make sure to come hungry. ⑤ *Average main: $34* ⌧ *316 W. 49th St., between 8th and 9th Aves., Midtown West* ☎ *212/245–0505* ⊕ *www.plataformaonline.com* ⌆ *Reservations essential* Ⓜ *C, E to 50th St.* ⊹ *4:B3.*

$$
ECLECTIC
✗**Plaza Food Hall by Todd English.** At the Plaza Food Hall in the basement of the Plaza Hotel, celeb-chef Todd English oversees a series of minirestaurants, each with its own counter and seating ideal for a quick snack or a full-fledged meal. Entry is a little confusing: though the place is made up of individual food concepts, you are seated by a hostess at any available counter. Once settled, get up and survey your choices, then sit down and order from your waiter. There's a glistening raw bar, a burger joint, and a wood-fired pizza station where you can sample some of English's iconic pies, such as fig and prosciutto. It's one of the most varied and affordable daytime food options in an area of town that can still feel like a lunchtime wasteland. ⑤ *Average main: $18* ⌧ *Plaza Hotel, 1 W. 59th St., at 5th Ave., Midtown West* ☎ *212/986–9260* ⊕ *www.theplazany.com/dining/foodhall* Ⓜ *N, Q, R to 5th Ave./59th St.* ⊹ *4:E1.*

$$$$
STEAKHOUSE
✗**Quality Meats.** The handsome design at Quality Meats is inspired by classic New York City butcher shops in its use of warm wood, stainless steel, and white marble. Sit at the bar to peruse the extensive menu of wines and single-malt scotches, or sip a classic martini. Then retire to the dining room for memorable fare like the massive chunky crab cake, seared scallops, and sophisticated riffs on steak-house classics like beef Wellington. The grilled bacon, peanut butter, and apple starter is a must for any first-timer. The wine list emphasizes big bold reds, the perfect companion to a rich chunky steak. ⑤ *Average main: $37* ⌧ *57 W. 58th St., near 6th Ave., Midtown West* ☎ *212/371–7777* ⊕ *www.qualitymeatsnyc.com* ⊘ *No lunch weekends* ⌆ *Reservations essential* Ⓜ *F to 57th St.; N, Q, R to 5th Ave./59th St.* ⊹ *4:D1.*

$$
MEXICAN
✗**Toloache.** Make a quick detour off heavily trafficked Broadway into this pleasantly bustling Mexican cantina for one of the best dining options around Times Square. The bi-level eatery has a festive, celebratory vibe, with several seating options: bar, balcony, main dining room, and ceviche bar. Foodies flock here for three types of guacamole (traditional, fruited, and spicy), a trio of well-executed ceviches, and Mexico City–style tacos with Negra Modelo–braised brisket, and quesadillas studded with black truffle and *huitlacoche* (a corn fungus known as the

"Mexican truffle"). There's an extensive tequila selection—upward of 100 brands. Adventurous palates are drawn to tacos featuring chili-studded dried grasshoppers, lobes of seared foie gras, and caramelized veal sweetbreads. There are two other locations, in Greenwich Village and on the Upper East Side. ⑤ *Average main: $20* ⊠ *251 W. 50th St., near 8th Ave., Midtown West* ☎ *212/581–1818* ⊕ *www.toloachenyc. com* Ⓜ *1, C, E to 50th St.; N, Q, R to 49th St.* ✛ *4:B3.*

$$$$ ✕ **'21' Club.** Tradition's the thing at this town house landmark, a former
AMERICAN speakeasy that opened in 1929. Chef Sylvain Delpique tries to satisfy everyone with standards like the famous '21' burger and Dover sole with brown butter, as well as more modern dishes, such as sautéed pork belly with butternut squash puree, but the food is almost secondary to the restaurant's storied past. Belongings donated by famous patrons—for example, John McEnroe's tennis racket or Howard Hughes's model plane—hang from the ceiling. ⑤ *Average main: $42* ⊠ *21 W. 52nd St., between 5th and 6th Aves., Midtown West* ☎ *212/582–7200* ⊕ *www.21club.com* ⊘ *Closed Sun. No lunch Sat.* 🍴 *Jacket required* Ⓜ *E, M to 5th Ave./53rd St.; B, D, F, M to 47th–50th Sts./Rockefeller Center* ✛ *4:D2.*

$$$$ ✕ **Uncle Jack's Steakhouse.** Surpassing even its celebrated flagship restau-
STEAKHOUSE rant in Bayside, Queens, Uncle Jack's soars directly into the pantheon of the best steak houses in Manhattan. The space is vast and gorgeously appointed, and service is swift and focused. USDA prime steaks are dry aged for 21 days. Australian lobster tails are so enormous, they have to be served carved, yet the flesh is meltingly tender. Humongous pork chops, dripping with juice, are accompanied by chipotle sauerkraut. Desserts include an excellent 18-year Macallan-scotch-laced bread pudding. It's hard to go wrong at Jack's. ⑤ *Average main: $67* ⊠ *440 9th Ave., between 34th and 35th Sts., Midtown West* ☎ *212/244–0005* ⊕ *www.unclejacks.com* 🍴 *Reservations essential* Ⓜ *A, C, E to 34th St.–Penn Station* ✛ *4:B6.*

UPPER EAST SIDE

Long viewed as an enclave of the privileged, the Upper East Side has plenty of elegant, pricey eateries that serve the society "ladies who lunch" and bankers looking forward to a steak and single-malt scotch at the end of the day. However, visitors to Museum Mile and 5th Avenue shopping areas need not be put off. Whether you're looking to celebrate a special occasion or just want to grab a quick bite, there is something here for almost any budget.

$$$$ ✕ **Café Boulud.** Manhattan's "who's who" in business, politics, and the
FRENCH art world come to hobnob at Daniel Boulud's café-in-name-only, where the food and service are top-notch. The menu is divided into four parts: under La Tradition are classic French dishes such as roasted duck breast Montmorency with cherry chutney, green Swiss chard, and baby turnips, or guinea hen terrine with pear, rutabaga, and foie gras; Le Potager tempts with lemon ricotta ravioli; La Saison follows the rhythms of the season; and Le Voyage reinterprets cuisines of the world. Start with a drink at the chic Bar Pleiades. ⑤ *Average main: $43* ⊠ *Surrey*

Hotel, 20 E. 76th St., between 5th and Madison Aves., Upper East Side ☎ *212/772–2600* ⊕ *www.cafeboulud.com* ⌦ *Reservations essential* Ⓜ *6 to 77th St.* ✛ *5:F3.*

$$ ✕ **Café Sabarsky.** In the Neue Galerie, this stately coffeehouse is meant to
AUSTRIAN duplicate the Viennese café experience and does a good job of it, with
FodorśChoice Art Deco furnishings, a selection of daily newspapers, and cases filled
★ with cakes, strudels, and Sacher tortes. Museumgoers and locals love
to linger here over coffee. In fact, so much so it's sometimes a challenge
to find a seat (there's a slightly less aesthetically pleasing outpost of the
café in the basement). There is also a menu of heartier fare—created by
Michelin-starred Austrian chef Kurt Gutenbrunner—of goulash, sand-
wiches, smoked-pork-stuffed potato dumplings, and variations on a
sausage theme. $ *Average main: $18* ⊠ *Neue Galerie, 1048 5th Ave.,
near 86th St., Upper East Side* ☎ *212/240–9557* ⊕ *www.neuegalerie.org*
🕙 *Closed Tues. No dinner Mon. and Wed.* Ⓜ *4, 5, 6 to 86th St.* ✛ *6:E6.*

$$ ✕ **Candle 79.** The Upper East Side may seem like an unlikely place for
VEGETARIAN gourmet vegan fare, but the people behind Candle 79 have found a for-
FodorśChoice mula that would work in any neighborhood. The elegant, bi-level space,
★ done in warm, autumnal tones, is far from the health-food stereotype.
Appetizers like rice balls with tempeh bacon may sound like hippie
throwbacks but taste more like well-executed trattoria fare. Signature
dishes include the seitan piccata, which replaces the usual protein with
a vegetarian substitute and is so well made that you would never miss
the meat. Salads, soups, desserts, and entrées are all fresh and made
with local, organic, seasonal produce. There's also an impressive list of
organic wines and sakes. $ *Average main: $22* ⊠ *154 E. 79th St., at
Lexington Ave., Upper East Side* ☎ *212/537–7179* ⊕ *www.candle79.
com* Ⓜ *6 to 77th St.* ✛ *5:G2.*

$$ ✕ **Cascabel Taqueria.** Wrestling-theme design sets a whimsical back-
MEXICAN drop at this reasonably priced Mexican restaurant, where the tacos
are inventive, but don't veer too far from the comfort-food norm. The
Camaron scatters plump roasted shrimp among fresh oregano, garlic
oil, and black beans. The beef tongue is slow braised, then topped
with spring onion and serrano chilies. There's also fresh, creamy gua-
camole with house-fried chips, pert tortilla soup with queso fresco and
chicken, and dinner-only platters like adobe-marinated Berkshire pork
butt. At lunchtime, sandwiches—like shredded chicken with mango and
smashed avocado—hit the spot with a cold Mexican beer. Inside seating
is limited, but in temperate weather the outdoor tables expand your
possibilities. $ *Average main: $13* ⊠ *1538 2nd Ave., between 80th and
81st Sts., Upper East Side* ☎ *212/717–8226* ⊕ *www.cascabeltaqueria.
com* Ⓜ *6 to 77th St.* ✛ *5:H2.*

$$$ ✕ **Central Park Boathouse Restaurant.** There are plenty of pushcarts dis-
AMERICAN pensing hot dogs and sodas, but if you're looking to soak up Central
Park's magical ambience in an elegant setting, head for the Central
Park Boathouse, which overlooks the gondola lake. There you can
relax on the outdoor deck with a glass of wine and a cheese plate, or
go for a more formal meal inside the restaurant. In warmer months the
restaurant can get crowded, so aim for a late lunch or early-evening
cocktail. Note that dinner is not served in the winter months. $ *Average*

15

main: $30 ⊠ *E. 72nd St., at Park Dr. N, Upper East Side* ☎ *212/517–2233* ⊕ *www.thecentralparkboathouse.com* ⊗ *No dinner Dec.–Mar.* ⌚ *Reservations not accepted* Ⓜ *6 to 77th St.* ✛ *5:E3.*

$$$$
FRENCH
Fodor's Choice
★

✕**Daniel.** Celebrity-chef Daniel Boulud has created one of the most elegant dining experiences in Manhattan. The prix-fixe menu (there are à la carte selections in the elegant lounge and bar) is predominantly French, with such modern classics as turbot on Himalayan salt with an ale-and-gingerbread sauce, and a duo of dry-aged Angus black beef featuring meltingly tender red-wine-braised short ribs and seared rib eye with black trumpet mushrooms and Gorgonzola cream. Equally impressive are the serious artwork, professional service, extensive wine list, and masterful cocktails. Don't forget the decadent desserts and overflowing cheese trolley. A three-course vegetarian menu is also available. ⑤ *Average main: $125* ⊠ *60 E. 65th St., between Madison and Park Aves., Upper East Side* ☎ *212/288–0033* ⊕ *www.danielnyc.com* ⊗ *Closed Sun. No lunch* ⌚ *Reservations essential* 🏛 *Jacket required* Ⓜ *6 to 68th St.–Hunter College* ✛ *5:F5.*

$$
DINER
FAMILY

✕**Lexington Candy Shop.** Established in 1925, this corner luncheonette still sports 1940s-era milk-shake mixers, coffee urns, and a soda fountain. Enjoy the epic collection of Coca-Cola memorabilia along with fresh-made sodas, burgers, classic sandwiches, and breakfast all day. This is serious old-school New York City at its best. ⑤ *Average main: $15* ⊠ *1226 Lexington Ave., at E. 83rd St., Upper East Side* ☎ *212/288–0057* ⊕ *www.lexingtoncandyshop.net* Ⓜ *4, 5, 6 to 86th St.* ✛ *5:G1.*

$$$
MEXICAN

✕**Maya.** The upscale-hacienda appearance of this justifiably popular restaurant showcases some of the best Mexican food in the city, courtesy of pioneering Mexican chef Richard Sandoval. Begin with a fresh mango mojito, then tuck into delicious roasted corn soup with huitlacoche dumplings, stuffed poblano peppers, and a smoky filet mignon taco with jalapeño *escabeche* (a type of marinade). Next indulge in the tender roasted pork carnitas or the spicy chipotle shrimp. The bottomless-margarita brunch on weekends can get loud, but local Upper East Siders still enjoy it. ⑤ *Average main: $26* ⊠ *1191 1st Ave., between 64th and 65th Sts., Upper East Side* ☎ *212/585–1818* ⊕ *www.modernmexican.com* Ⓜ *4, 5, 6 to 59th St.; N, Q, R to Lexington Ave./59th St.* ✛ *5:H5.*

$$$$
FRENCH

✕**Rotisserie Georgette.** The Georgette in question is Georgette Farkas, who spent 17 years as chef Daniel Boulud's marketing and PR person. She's now branched out on her own and is set to show the culinary world how high rotisserie chicken can be elevated. This elegant spot with an altarlike rotisserie in the back of the room might spin the best fowl in the city. For a splurge, order the "Poule de Luxe," a whole chicken stuffed with foie gras. The creamy burrata and the smoked salmon with fennel are fine starters. ⑤ *Average main: $39* ⊠ *14 E. 60th St., between 5th and Madison Aves., Upper East Side* ☎ *212/390–8060* ⊕ *www.rotisserieg.com* ⊗ *No lunch Sun.* Ⓜ *4, 5, 6 to 59th St.; N, Q, R to 5th Ave./59th St.* ✛ *5:F6.*

$$$
JAPANESE

✕**Sushi of Gari.** Options at this popular sushi restaurant range from the ordinary (California roll) to the exotic like tuna with creamy tofu sauce, miso-marinated cod, or Japanese yellowtail with jalapeño. Japanese noodles (udon or soba) and meat dishes such as teriyaki and *negimaki* (scallions rolled in thinly sliced beef) are well prepared. Some of the inventive nonsushi items on the menu are worth a try, especially the fried cream-cheese dumplings. Reservations are recommended. There are other locations, too, including one across the park on Columbus Avenue, in Hell's Kitchen, and in TriBeCa. ⑤ *Average main: $25* ⊠ *402 E. 78th St., at 1st Ave., Upper East Side* ☎ *212/517–5340* ⊕ *www. sushiofgari.com* ⊗ *Closed Mon. No lunch* Ⓜ *6 to 77th St.* ✛ *5:H2.*

UPPER WEST SIDE

The area around Lincoln Center is a fine-dining hub; as you head north you'll find a mix of casual and sophisticated neighborhood spots.

$$$$
ASIAN
✕ **Asiate.** The unparalleled view is reason enough to visit Asiate's pristine dining room, perched on the 35th floor of the Time Warner Center in the Mandarin Oriental Hotel. Artfully positioned tables and minimalist decor help direct eyes to the windows, which peer over Central Park. At night, crystalline lights reflect in the glass, creating a magical effect. The kitchen turns out contemporary dishes with an Asian influence that pair unlikely ingredients: think foie gras and hazelnut brittle, or branzino and truffles. Professional, attentive service helps foster an atmosphere of dreamlike luxury. The restaurant has prix-fixe menus only, and an illustrious wine collection housing 2,000 bottles. ⑤ *Average main: $100* ⊠ *Mandarin Oriental Hotel, 80 Columbus Circle, 35th fl., at 60th St., Upper West Side* ☎ *212/805–8881* ⊕ *www.mandarinoriental.com* Ⓜ *1, A, B, C, D to 59th St.–Columbus Circle* ✛ *5:C6.*

$$$
FRENCH
Fodor's Choice
★
✕ **Bar Boulud.** Acclaimed French chef Daniel Boulud, known for upscale New York City eateries Daniel and Café Boulud, shows diners his more casual side with this lively contemporary bistro and wine bar. The long, narrow space accommodates 100 people. The menu emphasizes char-cuterie, including terrines and pâtés designed by Parisian charcutier Gilles Verot, who relocated just to work with Boulud, as well as tradi-tional French bistro dishes like steak frites and *poulet rôti à l'ail* (roast chicken with garlic mashed potatoes). The 500-bottle wine list is heavy on wines from Burgundy and the Rhône Valley. A pretheater three-course menu starts at $48, and weekend brunch has four courses plus coffee for $32. ⑤ *Average main: $29* ⊠ *1900 Broadway, between 63rd and 64th Sts., Upper West Side* ☎ *212/595–0303* ⊕ *www.barboulud. com* Ⓜ *1 to 66th St.–Lincoln Center; 1, A, B, C, D to 59th St.–Colum-bus Circle* ✛ *5:B5.*

$$
AMERICAN
✕ **Barney Greengrass.** At this Upper West Side landmark brusque wait-ers send out stellar smoked salmon, sturgeon, and whitefish to a happy crowd packed to the gills at small Formica tables. Split a fish platter with bagels, cream cheese, and other fixings, or get your velvety nova scrambled with eggs and buttery caramelized onions. If still hungry, go for a plate of cheese blintzes or the to-die-for chopped liver. Be warned that the weekend brunch wait can exceed an hour, so you're better off coming during the week. ⑤ *Average main: $18* ⊠ *541 Amsterdam Ave., between 86th and 87th Sts., Upper West Side* ☎ *212/724–4707* ⊕ *www. barneygreengrass.com* ⊗ *Closed Mon. No dinner* ⌚ *Reservations not accepted* ▭ *No credit cards* Ⓜ *1, B, C to 86th St.* ✛ *6:B6.*

15

$$ ✕**Bouchon Bakery.** Never mind that you're in the middle of a shopping
CAFÉ mall under a Samsung sign—soups and sandwiches don't get much
more luxurious than this. Acclaimed chef Thomas Keller's low-key
lunch spot (one floor down from his extravagant flagship, Per Se) draws
long lines for good reason. Share a mason jar of salmon rillettes—an
unctuous spread of cooked and smoked salmon folded around crème
fraîche and butter—then move on to one of the fork-and-knife open-
face tartines, like the tuna niçoise. When a sandwich has this much pedi-
gree, $16 is actually a bargain. Grab dessert, a fresh macaron or éclair,
from the nearby bakery window. Ⓢ *Average main: $17* ✉ *Time Warner
Center, 10 Columbus Circle, 3rd fl., Upper West Side* ☎ *212/823–9366*
⊕ *www.bouchonbakery.com* Ⓜ *1, A, B, C, D to 59th St.–Columbus
Circle* ✛ *5:C6.*

$$ ✕**Café Luxembourg.** The old soul of the Lincoln Center neighborhood
FRENCH seems to inhabit the tiled and mirrored walls of this lively, cramped
restaurant, where West End Avenue regulars—including lots of on-air
talent from nearby ABC News—are greeted with kisses, and musicians
and audience members pack the room after a concert. The bar's always
hopping, and the menu (served until 11 pm Sunday through Tuesday
and until midnight from Wednesday through Saturday) includes classics
like steak tartare and lobster roll alongside more contemporary dishes
like pan-seared trout with haricots verts, hazelnuts, and tomato-caper
compote. Ⓢ *Average main: $23* ✉ *200 W. 70th St., between Amster-
dam and West End Aves., Upper West Side* ☎ *212/873–7411* ⊕ *www.
cafeluxembourg.com* ⌂ *Reservations essential* Ⓜ *1, 2, 3, B, C to 72nd
St.* ✛ *5:A4.*

$$ ✕**Carmine's.** Set on a nondescript block of Broadway, this branch of
ITALIAN the Italian mainstay is a favorite for families celebrating special occa-
FAMILY sions, pre-prom groups of teens, and plain-old folks who come for the
tried-and-true items like fried calamari, linguine with white clam sauce,
chicken parmigiana, and veal saltimbocca, all served in mountainous
portions. Family photos line the walls, an antipasti table groans under
the weight of savory meats, cheese, and salads, and there's a convivial
feeling amid the organized chaos. Ⓢ *Average main: $24* ✉ *2450 Broad-
way, between 90th and 91st Sts., Upper West Side* ☎ *212/362–2200*
⊕ *www.carminesnyc.com* Ⓜ *1, 2, 3 to 96th St.* ✛ *6:A6.*

$$$$ ✕**Dovetail.** Inside Dovetail, chef and owner John Fraser's subdued
AMERICAN town-house restaurant, cream-color walls and maple panels create a
warm, soothing atmosphere. The menu, which changes daily based on
seasonal and available ingredients, features refined but hearty dishes.
Seek solace from winter temperatures with the earthy gnocchi topped
with matsutake mushrooms, poppy seeds, and lemon. Tender lamb
is heightened by potatoes, artichokes, and olives. The feast continues
with pastry chef Italivi Reboreda's luscious Brie crème brûlée paired
with buttermilk sherbet. Ⓢ *Average main: $41* ✉ *103 W. 77th St., at
Columbus Ave., Upper West Side* ☎ *212/362–3800* ⊕ *www.dovetailnyc.
com* ☉ *No lunch* Ⓜ *1 to 79th St.; B, C to 81st St.–Museum of Natural
History* ✛ *5:B2.*

$$ ✕**Fairway Market Café.** Fairway is a neighborhood institution, liv-
CAFÉ ing up to its reputation for great prices on gourmet products—and

shopping-cart jockeying down the narrow aisles. Upstairs, though, is the respite of Fairway Market Café, a large, brick-walled room with windows overlooking Broadway. Up front you can grab a pastry and coffee to go, but there's a full menu of fairly priced entrées as well. The place is run by Mitchell London, who's known for his juicy, well-marbled steaks—try the rib eye and you may never go back to Brooklyn's Peter Luger steak house again. ⑤ *Average main: $23* ⊠ *2127 Broadway, between 74th and 75th Sts., Upper West Side* ☎ *212/595–1888* ⊕ *www. fairwaymarket.com* Ⓜ *1, 2, 3 to 72nd St.* ✛ *5:A3.*

$ ✕ **Gray's Papaya.** It's a stand-up, take-out dive. And yes, limos do some-
FAST FOOD times stop here for these legendary hot dogs—they are delicious, and quite the economical meal. The recession special is two hot dogs and a drink for $6. There are cheap breakfast offerings, too, like the quintessential egg and cheese on a roll. Although there used to be several locations of Gray's Papaya throughout the city, this is the only one left. ⑤ *Average main: $5* ⊠ *2090 Broadway, at 72nd St., Upper West Side* ☎ *212/799–0243* ⊕ *www.grayspapayanyc.com* ⚐ *Reservations not accepted* ⊟ *No credit cards* Ⓜ *1, 2, 3 to 72nd St.* ✛ *5:B4.*

$$ ✕ **Isabella's.** Set in the shadow of the Museum of Natural History, Isa-
AMERICAN bella's has been a brunch-and-beyond stalwart for decades. Brunch
FAMILY time is especially busy, even though the restaurant is large; lunch is less crowded, and a great time to try neighborhood-institution salads like the seafood-loaded Cobb or grilled artichoke hearts with Parmesan and lemon-thyme vinaigrette. Another winner: the crab-cake sandwich layered with lush avocado. For dinner, don't skip the pine-nut-sprinkled mushroom ravioli. Try for a table outside when the weather's nice; it's a great perspective on the neighborhood and great for people-watching. ⑤ *Average main: $22* ⊠ *359 Columbus Ave., at 77th St., Upper West Side* ☎ *212/724–2100* ⊕ *www.isabellas.com* Ⓜ *B, C to 81st St.–Museum of Natural History* ✛ *5:B3.*

$$$$ ✕ **Jean-Georges.** This culinary temple in the Trump International Hotel
FRENCH and Towers focuses wholly on chef célèbre Jean-Georges Vongerichten's spectacular creations. The chef may now have restaurants sprinkled around the globe, but this is the spot in his culinary empire where you want to be. Some dishes approach the limits of the taste universe, like foie-gras brûlée with spiced fig jam and ice-wine reduction. Others are models of simplicity, like slow-cooked cod with warm vegetable vinaigrette. Exceedingly personalized service and a well-selected wine list contribute to an unforgettable meal. It's prix-fixe only. For Jean-Georges on a budget, try the prix-fixe lunch in the front room, Nougatine. ⑤ *Average main: $125* ⊠ *1 Central Park W, at 60th St., Upper West Side* ☎ *212/299–3900* ⊕ *www.jean-georges.com* ⚐ *Reservations essential* ⟠ *Jacket required* Ⓜ *1, A, B, C, D to 59th St.–Columbus Circle* ✛ *5:C6.*

$$ ✕ **Kefi.** *Kefi* is Greek for the bliss that accompanies a bacchanalia. At
GREEK Michael Psilakis's Upper West Side eatery—a giant homage to his grandmother's Greek cooking—it's not hard to achieve such a euphoric state. Among the mezes, the meatballs with roasted garlic, olives, and tomato stand out; the flavorful roast chicken with potatoes, red peppers, garlic, and thyme makes for a winning entrée; and the béchamel-rich Kefi mac 'n' cheese is irresistible. Reasonable prices make it easy to stick

15

around for a piece of traditional walnut cake with walnut ice cream. Ⓢ *Average main: $18* ✉ *505 Columbus Ave., between 84th and 85th Sts., Upper West Side* ☎ *212/873–0200* ⊕ *www.kefirestaurant.com* Ⓜ *1, B, C to 86th St.* ✛ *5:B1.*

$
BAKERY
FAMILY

✕ **Levain Bakery.** Completely unpretentious and utterly delicious, Levain Bakery's cookies are rich and hefty (they clock in at 6 ounces each). Choose from the chocolate-chip walnut, dark-chocolate chocolate chip, dark-chocolate peanut-butter chip, or oatmeal raisin. Batches are baked fresh daily and taste best when they're warm and melty right out of the oven. Levain's also bakes artisanal breads, including banana chocolate chip and pumpkin-ginger spice, sour-cream coffee cake, chocolate-chip and cinnamon brioche, sourdough rolls stuffed with Valrhona chocolate, blueberry muffins, a variety of scones, and bomboloncini—their unique jelly doughnuts. Ⓢ *Average main: $9* ✉ *167 W. 74th St., near Amsterdam Ave., Upper West Side* ☎ *212/874–6080* ⊕ *www.levainbakery.com* ◷ *No dinner* Ⓜ *1, 2, 3 to 72nd St.* ✛ *5:B3.*

$$$
BISTRO
FAMILY

✕ **Nice Matin.** If the Upper West Side and the French Riviera melded into one, it might look a little bit like Nice Matin. This is a longtime neighborhood favorite, particularly in warm-weather months, when regulars plant themselves at sidewalk tables and gawk at passersby while munching on Gallic fare like monkfish wading in sweet potato purée and garlicky mussels, and, of course, steak frites. The novel-size wine list boasts more than 2,000 bottles, so bring your reading glasses. Be sure to dress for the people-watching, particularly at the popular weekend brunch. Ⓢ *Average main: $25* ✉ *201 W. 79th St., at Amsterdam Ave., Upper West Side* ☎ *212/873–6423* ⊕ *www.nicematinnyc. com* ▭ *No credit cards* Ⓜ *1 to 79th St.* ✛ *5:A2.*

$$$$
AMERICAN
Fodor's Choice
★

✕ **Per Se.** The New York interpretation of what many consider one of America's finest restaurant (the Napa Valley's French Laundry), Per Se is chef Thomas Keller's Broadway stage. The large dining room is understated and elegant, with touches of wood, towering florals, and sweeping windows with views of Central Park. Keller embraces seasonality and a witty playfulness that speaks to his confidence in the kitchen, and some of his dishes are now world-renowned, such as the tiny cones of tuna tartare topped with crème fraîche, and the "oysters and pearls"—tiny mollusks suspended in a creamy custard with tapioca. Dessert service is a multicourse celebration of all things sweet, including a choice of 27 house-made chocolates. Service is sublime, as you'd expect. An à la carte "salon" menu is available in the front barroom, but let's face it: if you manage to snag a reservation, there's nothing else to do but submit to the $325 prix fixe. It's best to make reservations at least two months in advance. Ⓢ *Average main: $90* ✉ *Time Warner Center, 10 Columbus Circle, 4th fl., at 60th St., Upper West Side* ☎ *212/823–9335* ⊕ *www.perseny.com* ◷ *No lunch Mon.–Thurs.* ⌂ *Reservations essential* ⌂ *Jacket required* Ⓜ *1, A, B, C, D to 59th St.–Columbus Circle* ✛ *5:C6.*

$$$$
STEAKHOUSE

✕ **Porter House New York.** With clubby interiors by Jeffrey Beers and an adjoining lounge area, Porter House is helmed by veteran chef Michael Lomonaco. Filling the meat-and-potatoes slot in the Time Warner Center's upscale "Restaurant Collection," this masculine throwback highlights American wines and pedigreed supersize meat. The neighborhood, long underserved on the steak-house front, has warmed to Lomonaco's simple, solid American fare. Begin with his smoky clams casino or rich roasted marrow bones. Steaks are huge and expertly seasoned, and come with the usual battery of à la carte sides—creamed spinach, roasted mushrooms, and truffle mashed potatoes. ⑤ *Average main: $47* ⊠ *Time Warner Center, 10 Columbus Circle, 4th fl., at 60th St., Upper West Side* ☎ *212/823–9500* ⊕ *www.porterhousenewyork.com* Ⓜ *1, A, B, C, D to 59th St.–Columbus Circle* ✛ *5:C6.*

$$ **✗ Sarabeth's Kitchen.** Lining up for brunch here is as much an Upper
AMERICAN West Side tradition as taking a sunny Sunday afternoon stroll in nearby Riverside Park. Locals love the bric-a-brac-filled restaurant for sweet morning-time dishes like lemon ricotta pancakes and comforting dinners. The afternoon tea includes buttery scones with Sarabeth's signature jams, savory nibbles, and outstanding baked goods. Dinner entrées include chicken potpie and truffle mac 'n' cheese. There are several other locations around town, including one at Chelsea Market on 10th Avenue and West 15th Street. ⑤ *Average main: $19* ⊠ *423 Amsterdam Ave., at 80th St., Upper West Side* ☎ *800/773–7378* ⊕ *www.sarabeth. com* Ⓜ *1 to 79th St.* ✛ *5:B2.*

$$$ **✗ Telepan.** The greenmarket-driven menu at chef Bill Telepan's epon-
AMERICAN ymous eatery is heavy on the veggies (the seasonal vegetable starter wakes your palate right up), but fish lovers and first-timers should hook into the signature starter: smoked trout paired with sweet apple sour cream. Anything on the menu that contains eggs, like the "egg-in-a-hole" served with spinach and hen-of-the-woods mushrooms, is worth a try. There's the usual presence of foie gras and pork belly, but Telepan does seafood very well (try the scallops). For dessert, a crunchy peanut-butter-and-gianduja duo with peanut-brittle ice cream is sublime. ⑤ *Average main: $31* ⊠ *72 W. 69th St., between Columbus Ave. and Central Park W, Upper West Side* ☎ *212/580–4300* ⊕ *www. telepan-ny.com* ⊗ *No lunch* Ⓜ *1 to 66th St.–Lincoln Center; 2, 3 to 72nd St.; B, C to 72nd St.* ✛ *5:B4.*

HARLEM

Harlem culinary renaissance? Yes, indeed. This historic northern neighborhood has seen an infusion of fantastic restaurants in the last five years or so. There are still the standby Southern and soul-food restaurants but also newer arrivals, making your journey northward even more worthwhile.

$$$ **✗ The Cecil.** You might feel like you've stepped into a private club after
AFRICAN a pleasant doorman ushers you into this dimly lit space filled with red-
Fodor'sChoice leather banquettes and eye-pleasing art on the walls, but at the same
★ time, the Cecil feels very welcoming. The menu is influenced by the African diaspora, so there's a blend of culinary cultures—expect to be wowed. Heaping bowls of udon noodles are tangled around braised goat and edamame, all of which have been dunked in an African peanut sauce. Oxtail dumplings wade in a green-apple curry sauce. A tender lamb shank sits upon coconut-spiked grits. This is a club you want to be a part of. ⑤ *Average main: $30* ⊠ *210 W. 118th St., at St. Nicholas*

15

Ave., Harlem ☎ *212/866–1262* ⊕ *www.thececilharlem.com* ⊗ *No lunch Mon.–Wed.* Ⓜ *2, 3, B, C to 116th St.* ✛ *6:D1.*

$$ × **Chez Lucienne.** French Harlem? Not exactly, but Chez Lucienne is
BISTRO as close as you can get without leaving the comfortable confines of this historic neighborhood. If you can't get into the Red Rooster next door, grab a seat at the baby-blue banquette or relax at an outdoor table where locals come to sip coffee or wine, dogs at their side. The menu looks to Lyon with classics like sautéed foie gras and steak au poivre by a chef who logged time in the kitchen with famed chef Daniel Boulud. ⑤ *Average main: $20* ✉ *308 Lenox Ave., between 125th and 126th Sts., Harlem* ☎ *212/289–5555* ⊕ *www.chezlucienne.com* Ⓜ *2, 3 to 116th St.* ✛ *6:D1.*

$$$ × **Red Rooster Harlem.** Marcus Samuelsson, who earned his celebrity
AMERICAN chefdom at Aquavit in Midtown for his take on Ethiopian-accented Scandinavian cuisine (fusing the food of his birthplace with that of where he grew up), moved way uptown to Harlem in 2010, where he has created a culinary hot spot for the ages. The comfort-food menu jumps all over the place, reflecting the ethnic diversity that is modern-day New York City (and the patrons who regularly come here), from plantain-loaded oxtail to fried chicken to the tender meatballs (with lingonberry sauce) that he served at Aquavit. Expect a wait for Sunday brunch, with its gospel music, boozy cocktails, and modern takes on dishes like chicken and waffles. ⑤ *Average main: $26* ✉ *310 Lenox Ave., between 125th and 126th Sts., Harlem* ☎ *212/792–9001* ⊕ *www. redroosterharlem.com* ⊟ *No credit cards* Ⓜ *2, 3 to 125th St.* ✛ *6:D1.*

$$ × **Sylvia's.** This Harlem mainstay has been serving soul-food favorites
SOUTHERN like smothered chicken, barbecue ribs, collard greens, and mashed pota-
FAMILY toes to a dedicated crowd of locals, tourists, and college students since 1962. Owner Sylvia Woods may have passed on in the summer of 2012, but her restaurant and signature sauces, jarred and sold online and in the restaurant, are more popular than ever. Some say it's overly touristy—as the busloads attest—but it's still worth the experience. For the ultimate experience, come for Sunday gospel brunch; singing and eating were never a more delicious combination. ⑤ *Average main: $24* ✉ *328 Lenox Ave., near 127th St., Harlem* ☎ *212/996–0660* ⊕ *www. sylviasrestaurant.com* Ⓜ *2, 3 to 125th St.* ✛ *6:D1.*

BROOKLYN

BROOKLYN HEIGHTS

Brooklyn may be the place to eat these days, but Brooklyn Heights has always been more pleasing to the eye than to the taste buds.

$$ × **Colonie.** The key to this perpetually popular restaurant's success lies
MODERN in its use of ultrafresh ingredients, sourced from local purveyors and
AMERICAN presented with style in an upscale-casual space that honors its neigh-
Fodor's Choice borhood's historical roots. There's always an oyster special, along
★ with a selection of small plates like octopus with chorizo, duck egg with farro, and carrots with sunflower and candied garlic. The main courses, among them roast chicken and a sizable pork chop, tend to be hearty, though whole fish, fresh from the market, is on the menu as

well. Dessert options include a sticky date cake, Vermont cheeses, and rich, sweet wines. $ *Average main: $20* ⊠ *127 Atlantic Ave., Brooklyn Heights* ☎ *718/855–7500* ⊕ *www.colonienyc.com* ☾ *No lunch weekdays* Ⓜ *2, 3, 4, 5 to Borough Hall; R to Court St.* ✛ *7:A4.*

$$$$ ✕ **The River Café.** A deservedly popular special-occasion destination, this

MODERN AMERICAN waterfront institution complements its exquisite Brooklyn Bridge views with memorable top-shelf cuisine served by an unfailingly attentive staff. Lobster, lamb, duck, and strip steak are among the staples of the prix-fixe menu ($120 for dinner, $42 for Saturday lunch, $55 for Sunday brunch). The chocolate Brooklyn Bridge mousse delivers the perfect ending to dinner. Jackets are required for men after 5 pm. $ *Average main: $255* ⊠ *1 Water St., Brooklyn Heights* ☎ *718/522–5200* ⊕ *www. therivercafe.com* ☾ *No lunch weekdays* Ⓜ *2, 3 to Clark St.; A, C to High St.; F to York St.* ✛ *7:B2.*

DOWNTOWN BROOKLYN

Filled with neoclassical courthouse buildings and glass skyscrapers, there isn't much reason to come to downtown Brooklyn—unless, of course, you managed to nab a reservation at the borough's only three-Michelin-starred restaurant, Brooklyn Fare.

$$$$ ✕ **Chef's Table at Brooklyn Fare.** Should you manage to snag one of the

ECLECTIC 18 seats at Brooklyn's only Michelin three-star restaurant, you're in for a treat. Chef Cesar Ramirez prepares 20-plus courses of French- and Japanese-influenced raw and cooked seafood small plates. The extravaganza feels like dining in a secret enclave of sophisticates; note-taking, photography, and mobile phone use are discouraged to keep the focus on the meal, which costs $255 per person, exclusive of wine, tax, and tip. Every Monday at 10:30 am, reservations open for the entire week that's six weeks ahead. Seats fill up very quickly. Jackets are required for men. $ *Average main: $250* ⊠ *200 Schermerhorn St., near Hoyt St., Downtown Brooklyn* ☎ *718/243–0050* ⊕ *www.brooklynfare.com* ☾ *Closed Sun. and Mon. No lunch* ⌂ *Reservations essential* Ⓜ *2, 3 to Hoyt St.; 2, 3, 4, 5 to Nevins St.; A, C, G to Hoyt–Schermerhorn Sts.; B, Q, R to DeKalb Ave.* ✛ *7:B4.*

$ ✕ **Junior's.** Famous for its thick slices of cheesecake, Junior's has been

DINER FAMILY the quintessential Brooklyn diner since 1950. Classic cheeseburgers looming over little cups of coleslaw and thick french fries are first-rate, as are the sweet-potato latkes and pretty much all the breakfast offerings. You haven't truly arrived in the borough until you've sunk into one of the vinyl booths and eaten comforting diner classics in this brightly lit space. $ *Average main: $10* ⊠ *386 Flatbush Ave. Extension, Downtown Brooklyn* ☎ *718/852–5257* ⊕ *www.juniorscheesecake.com* Ⓜ *2, 3, 4, 5 to Nevins St.; B, Q, R to DeKalb Ave.; A, C, G to Hoyt–Schermerhorn Sts.* ✛ *7:C4.*

DUMBO

Once upon a time, the primary reason for a hungry person to come to DUMBO was to eat pizza at Grimaldi's. The past few years have seen the growing gentrification of these loft-strewn cobblestone streets, though, today sprinkled with toothsome eateries and cute boutiques.

Now that the Brooklyn waterfront has been fully developed you can walk off your meal on a romantic stroll.

$$
PIZZA
FAMILY
✗ **Juliana's.** Pizza pioneer Patsy Grimaldi's eponymous pie shops checker the city, but Juliana's is the latest in his thin-crust, coal-fired history. The restaurant is hidden in plain sight alongside neighboring Grimaldi's, where the lines are twice as long and the pizzas not as good. Patsy himself has severed ties with Grimaldi's, so do like the locals do and sample his classic white and margherita pies, homemade soups, and Brooklyn Ice Cream Factory desserts in this bright, bustling space. ⑤ *Average main: $20* ⊠ *19 Old Fulton St., DUMBO* ☎ *718/596–6700* ⊕ *www. julianaspizza.com* Ⓜ *2, 3 to Clark St.; A, C to High St.; F to York St.* ⊹ *7:B3.*

$$$
MODERN
AMERICAN
✗ **Vinegar Hill House.** DUMBO's top dining destination is well worth the sloping walk up from the waterfront. Those who make the trek are rewarded with candlelit tables, seasonal menus, and a twinkling rear patio lined with cherry trees. Word gets out about a scene this good, so the wait for one of the 40 tables can be considerable, particularly during weekend brunch. Bide your time at the cozy bar, which pours potent cocktails, local beer, and wine by the glass. ⑤ *Average main: $25* ⊠ *72 Hudson Ave., between Front and Water Sts., DUMBO* ☎ *718/522–1018* ⊕ *www.vinegarhillhouse.com* Ⓜ *F to York St.* ⊹ *7:C2.*

CARROLL GARDENS

Carroll Gardens has standout restaurants, which lure even those Manhattanites who might be loathe to cross the river.

$$
SEAFOOD
Fodor's Choice
★
✗ **Bergen Hill.** Seafood specialist Bergen Hill has earned a cult following among the neighborhood's discerning diners (many of the city's top food writers call the neighborhood home). Chef Andrew D'Ambrosi, a memorable *Top Chef* contestant, combines precisely cut raw fish with nontraditional flavors (perhaps tuna with green olive, currant, and jalapeño, or poached octopus with onion, raisin, and harissa). The toasts are a must—crunchy bread topped with lobster salad or perfectly seasoned roasted eggplant. The best seat is at the tiny chef's bar, where he might tell you about a recent trip to Barcelona or slide you a sample of his latest creation. The wine list is mostly old-world and adventurous; cocktails lean alternately classic and interpretive. ⑤ *Average main: $18* ⊠ *387 Court St., Carroll Gardens* ☎ *718/858–5483* ⊕ *www.bergenhill. com* ☽ *No lunch* Ⓜ *F, G to Carroll St.* ⊹ *7:A5.*

$$
AMERICAN
✗ **Buttermilk Channel.** *Food Network*–famous fried chicken and waffles have earned this Southern-accented new American bistro epic brunch lines and a legion of neighborhood regulars with their kids (the Clown Sundae is legendary among Carroll Gardens third-graders). But when day turns to night, Buttermilk Channel transforms into a surprisingly serious restaurant with an excellent, mostly American wine list and satisfying entrées including steaks, pan-roasted fish, and an outstanding warm lamb-shoulder salad. Vegetarians are certainly accommodated at many Brooklyn restaurants, but here they get a special menu. ⑤ *Average main: $22* ⊠ *524 Court St., at Huntington St., Carroll Gardens* ☎ *718/852–8490* ⊕ *www.buttermilkchannelnyc.com* ☽ *No lunch weekdays* Ⓜ *F, G to Smith–9th Sts.* ⊹ *7:A5.*

$$ ✕ **Frankies Spuntino 457.** When Frank Castronovo and Frank Falcinelli
ITALIAN opened this pioneering Italian-American restaurant in a former social
Fodor's Choice club, Carroll Gardens was a culinary backwater. Much has evolved in
★ the decade-plus since, but what hasn't changed is the small but well-
conceived menu of shareable salads (many with vegetables roasted or
marinated with the Frankies' own Sicilian olive oil), handmade pastas
like the cavatelli with hot sausage and browned sage butter, and crusty
sandwiches that ask to be split and shared. When the weather's nice, try
to score a seat in the gravel-lined backyard. $ *Average main: $16* ✉ *457
Court St., near Luquer St., Carroll Gardens* ☎ *718/403–0033* ⊕ *www.
frankiesspuntino.com* Ⓜ *F, G to Carroll St. or Smith–9th Sts.* ⊹ *7:A5.*

$$ ✕ **Nightingale 9.** Though it's named after an old Brooklyn telephone
VIETNAMESE code, Nightingale 9 takes its culinary inspiration from "long distance":
Vietnam. This smartly designed Smith Street favorite is a must for lem-
ongrass-grilled pork chops or the steamed rice crêpes called *banh cuon*,
stuffed with minced pork, chicken pâté, and cucumber. Chef Rob New-
ton visits Vietnam often and brings back authentic recipes that he sometimes reimagines with his Arkansas childhood in mind, such as smoked
pork sausage served with rice cakes and shrimp paste. Catfish is fried
with turmeric and spices, and served with a unique combination of dill
and peanuts. $ *Average main: $17* ✉ *329 Smith St., Carroll Gardens*
☎ *347/689–4699* ⊕ *www.nightingale9.com* ⊙ *Closed Mon.* Ⓜ *F, G to
Carroll St.* ⊹ *7:B5.*

$$$ ✕ **Prime Meats.** Steak, sausages, and serious Prohibition-era cocktails:
STEAKHOUSE it's a winning combination for Frank Castronovo and Frank Falcinelli,
who opened this Frankies offshoot as a tribute to turn-of-the-century
New York dining rooms. Try a chilled iceberg-lettuce salad with Maytag
blue cheese and a Vesper or dry martini to start, followed by a grilled
heritage pork chop or perhaps an order of steak frites—though there
are many other options, including a number of Teutonic dishes like
herb-and-Gruyère spätzle and house-made weisswurst. $ *Average main:
$26* ✉ *465 Court St., at Luquer St., Carroll Gardens* ☎ *718/254–0327*
⊕ *www.frankspm.com* ⌂ *Reservations not accepted* Ⓜ *F, G to Carroll
St. or Smith–9th Sts.* ⊹ *7:A5.*

WILLIAMSBURG

Still probably the hippest, happening-est neighborhood in the five bor-
oughs, Williamsburg is also one of the hottest destinations on the culi-
nary landscape. You'll find plenty of decadent twists on farm-to-table
cuisine, dressed-up comfort-food classics, and killer cocktails.

$$ ✕ **Diner.** The word "diner" might evoke a greasy spoon, but this trend-
AMERICAN setting restaurant under the Williamsburg Bridge is nothing of the sort.
Fodor's Choice Andrew Tarlow—the godfather of Brooklyn's farm-to-table culinary
★ renaissance—opened it in 1999 and launched an entire movement. The
restaurant occupies a 1927 dining car, and foodies cram into the tiny
booths to sample the daily changing menu. Your waiter will scrawl the
offerings on your paper tablecloth: expect two or three meat options, a
fish or two, and veggies (asparagus in spring, delicata squash in fall) from
farms in the Greater New York area. $ *Average main: $21* ✉ *85 Broadway, at Berry St., South Williamsburg* ☎ *718/486–3077* ⊕ *www.dinernyc.
com* ⌂ *Reservations not accepted* Ⓜ *J, M, Z to Marcy Ave.* ⊹ *7:D2.*

15

$$
BARBECUE

✕**Fette Sau.** It might seem odd to go to a former auto-body repair shop to feast on meat, but the funky building and courtyard are just the right setting for the serious barbecue served here. A huge wood-and-gas smoker delivers brisket, sausages, ribs, and even duck—all ordered by the pound. Sides include potato salad, broccoli salad, and baked beans, but meat is the main event. Pair your meal with one of the more than 40 American whiskeys and 10 microbrews. Come early, as tables fill up quickly, and even at 700 pounds of meat a night, the good stuff sometimes runs out by 9. ⑤ *Average main: $13* ⊠ *354 Metropolitan Ave., at Havemeyer St., North Williamsburg* ☎ *718/963–3404* ⊕ *www. fettesaubbq.com* ⊘ *No lunch Mon.–Thurs.* Ⓜ *L to Lorimer St.; G to Metropolitan Ave.* ✛ *7:E2.*

$$
MEDITERRANEAN
Fodor's Choice
★

✕**Isa.** Entering this restaurant on a rather barren block feels like walking into a modern farmhouse. Whitewashed walls, wood in geometric patterns, and a terra-cotta floor set the tone for Brooklyn-meets-Mediterranean fare, which means Tuscan-kale Caesar salads and wood-fired breakfast pizza with pancetta, fontina, salsa verde, and an egg. The food is sourced as locally as possible, and the wine list features many organic bottles from France and Italy. Ask for a seat near the open kitchen if you want to see what the chefs are up to, or sit on the other side and watch the bartenders shake cocktails using herbs from the rooftop garden. ⑤ *Average main: $24* ⊠ *348 Wythe Ave., at S. 3rd St., South Williamsburg* ☎ *347/689–3594* ⊕ *www.isa.gg* Ⓜ *L to Bedford Ave.; J, M, Z to Marcy Ave.* ✛ *7:D1.*

$$
FRENCH

✕**Le Barricou.** The team behind nearby Maison Premiere operates this Parisian-style brasserie serving escargots, coq au vin, and other French bistro classics. Diners sit at rustic wooden tables, and the walls are collaged with vintage French newspapers. Come for brunch if you've been searching for perfect eggs Benedict: the version here is drizzled with hollandaise and accompanied by salad and home fries (there are no reservations at brunch, so come early or expect to wait). ⑤ *Average main: $18* ⊠ *533 Grand St., between Lorimer St. and Union Ave., South Williamsburg* ☎ *718/782–7372* ⊕ *www.lebarricouny.com* Ⓜ *L to Lorimer St.; G to Metropolitan Ave.* ✛ *7:E2.*

$$
AMERICAN
Fodor's Choice
★

✕**Marlow & Sons.** With its green-and-white-striped awning, you might easily mistake this buzzy bistro for an old-timey grocery store, but this is a wood-panel dining room packed nightly with foodies for remarkable locavore cuisine. Part of the Andrew Tarlow empire, Marlow & Sons serves food that sounds simple until you take that first bite. A starter the menu lists as burrata with radishes, for example, emerges from the kitchen as a complex dish of melt-in-your-mouth cheese with thin slices of the root vegetable and a crunchy topping of golden raisin bread toasted with olive oil. The entrées are equally inspired, thanks to the creative use to which the chefs put fresh, seasonal ingredients. The must-do dessert, the salted chocolate caramel tart, represents decadence at its flawless best. ⑤ *Average main: $23* ⊠ *81 Broadway, at Berry St., South Williamsburg* ☎ *718/384–1441* ⊕ *www.marlowandsons.com* ☖ *Reservations not accepted* Ⓜ *J, M, Z to Marcy Ave.; L to Bedford Ave.* ✛ *7:D2.*

$$$$
STEAKHOUSE
Fodor'sChoice
★

✕ **Peter Luger Steak House.** Steak lovers come to Peter Luger for the exquisite dry-aged meat and the casual atmosphere. You can order individual steaks, but the porterhouse is highly recommended and served only for two, three, or four people. Make reservations as far ahead as possible as prime dining times fill up more than a month in advance. The lunch-only burger is beloved by those in the know, as is the bacon appetizer, available by the slice. ⑤ *Average main: $50* ✉ *178 Broadway, at Driggs Ave., South Williamsburg* ☎ *718/387–7400* ⊕ *www.peterluger.com* ⚏ *Reservations essential* ▭ *No credit cards* Ⓜ *J, M, Z to Marcy Ave.* ✛ *7:D2.*

$$
SOUTHERN

✕ **Pies 'N' Thighs.** Opened by three Diner alums, this little restaurant takes its moniker seriously, serving famously delicious fried chicken and pies made with organic and local ingredients. Perched on chairs from an elementary school, diners enjoy Southern-style meals that come with a protein (catfish and pulled pork for those who don't want chicken) and two sides (grits, mac 'n' cheese, and biscuits are favorites). Save room for pie: perhaps guava, key lime, banana cream, bourbon pecan, or many other varieties. There is also a location in lower Manhattan. ⑤ *Average main: $13* ✉ *166 S. 4th St., at Driggs Ave., South Williamsburg* ☎ *347/529–6090* ⊕ *www.piesnthighs.com* Ⓜ *J, M, Z to Marcy Ave.* ✛ *7:D2.*

$$$
MODERN
AMERICAN

✕ **Reynard.** The largest of Andrew Tarlow's Williamsburg restaurants (which include Diner and Marlow & Sons), Reynard has all the hallmarks of a Tarlow venture. Farm-to-table fare highlights the season's freshest ingredients, and everything is made in-house, even the granola. The grass-fed burger is always available, but the rest of the menu changes often enough that you'll want to come back to try it all. ⑤ *Average main: $26* ✉ *Wythe Hotel, 80 Wythe Ave., at N. 11th St., Williamsburg* ☎ *718/460–8004* ⊕ *www.reynardnyc.com* Ⓜ *L to Bedford Ave.* ✛ *7:D1.*

$$$$
AMERICAN
Fodor'sChoice
★

✕ **Semilla.** If dining has become a lot like theater then consider this Off-Off-Broadway sensation in Williamsburg to be about as entertaining on the taste buds as they come. The director, or, um, chef here is Jose Ramirez-Ruiz and he subverts the dominant dining paradigm by pushing vegetables out to the center stage, and putting meat on the sidelines as supporting cast. The $85 prix-fixe menu changes nightly based on the chef's mood and the availability of ingredients, but if you can nab one of the 18 seats that surround the long, U-shaped table in the diminutive dining room, your palate is in store for one delicious show. ⑤ *Average main: $85* ✉ *160 Havemeyer St., No. 5, Williamsburg* ☎ *718/782–3474* ⊕ *www.semillabk.com* ☾ *Closed Sun. and Mon.* ⚏ *Reservations essential* Ⓜ *J, M, Z to Marcy Ave.* ✛ *7:D2.*

$$
STEAKHOUSE
Fodor'sChoice
★

✕ **St. Anselm.** This modest spot grills high-quality meat and fish, all sustainably and ethically sourced, and at very reasonable prices. The sides, ordered à la carte, deserve special attention: the spinach gratin is dependably hearty, and the seasonal special of delicata squash with manchego (cheese from sheep's milk) is divine. Come early or risk a long wait, though you can get a drink from the owners' bar, Spuyten Duyvil, next door. St. Anselm is also open for brunch on weekends. ⑤ *Average main: $19* ✉ *355 Metropolitan Ave., at Havemeyer St., North Williamsburg* ☎ *718/384–5054* ⊕ *www.stanselm.net* ☾ *No lunch weekdays* ⚏ *Reservations not accepted* Ⓜ *L to Lorimer St.; G to Metropolitan Ave.* ✛ *7:E1.*

15

BUSHWICK

The big draw in Bushwick is Roberta's. The neighborhood is still pretty industrial, but there are new restaurants and bars out here creating a scene.

$
ETHIOPIAN

✕ **Bunna Cafe.** The best way to sample the diverse flavors, many quite spicy, of Ethiopian cuisine at this stellar restaurant are the combination platters—for one or to share—though you can also order individual dishes. If the delicious, seasonal *duba wot* (spiced pumpkin) is available, definitely include it in your platter. Everything is served with *injera*, a sourdough flatbread used to scoop up the various stews. The drink menu includes traditional *t'ej* (honey wine), cocktails, and wine and beer from Ethiopia and elsewhere. The namesake *bunna*—Ethiopian coffee brewed with cardamom and cloves—is worth a try, too. There's a special menu for brunch. $ *Average main: $11* ✉ *1084 Flushing Ave., at Porter Ave., Bushwick* 🕾 *347/295–2227* ⊕ *www.bunnaethiopia.net* Ⓜ *L to Morgan Ave.* ✛ *7:G2.*

$$
ITALIAN
Fodor's Choice
★

✕ **Roberta's.** A neighborhood groundbreaker since it opened in 2008, this restaurant in a former garage is a must-visit, especially for pizza connoisseurs. The menu emphasizes hyperlocal ingredients—there's a rooftop garden—and the wood-fired pizzas have innovative combinations of toppings like fennel, pork sausage, and pistachio. There are also pastas and meaty mains, along with a vegetarian-friendly option or two. In summer service extends to a hip patio tiki bar. Roberta's is wildly popular, so either come early or try for a table at lunch or brunch, which isn't as hectic. Blanca, the two-Michelin-starred tasting-menu-only ($195, Wed.–Sat., waitlist@blancanyc.com) restaurant on the Roberta's property serves innovative new American food. It's by reservation only. $ *Average main: $16* ✉ *261 Moore St., at Bogart St., Bushwick* 🕾 *718/417–1118* ⊕ *www.robertaspizza.com* Ⓜ *L to Morgan Ave.* ✛ *7:F2.*

FORT GREENE

Fort Greene has become one of the most desirable neighborhoods in Brooklyn, the lovely brownstone apartments attracting young professionals and many of the borough's established writers and artists. It's also a garden of culinary delights with restaurants leading the locavore farm-to-table movement. And who knows? Maybe even a famous director or author will be sitting at the table next to you.

$$$
ITALIAN

✕ **Roman's.** Part of an all-star Brooklyn restaurant group that includes Williamsburg favorites Diner and Marlow & Sons, this seasonally focused eatery has an Italian accent. Menus change daily and include farm-fresh fare like wintry fennel salads or pork meatballs *in brodo*, or delicacies like artichoke-studded house-made spaghetti in summer. When weather permits, request one of the candlelit alfresco tables: there's no better perch from which to soak up the Fort Greene scene. $ *Average main: $26* ✉ *243 DeKalb Ave., near Vanderbilt Ave., Fort Greene* 🕾 *718/622–5300* ⊕ *www.romansnyc.com* ☽ *No lunch weekdays* Ⓜ *C to Lafayette Ave.; G to Clinton–Washington Aves.* ✛ *7:D4.*

$$
AMERICAN

✕ **Walter's.** A sister restaurant to Williamsburg's Walter Foods, this buzzy bistro has a seasonal menu, a comely crowd, and rosy-hued lighting that gives the space a glamorous vibe. Stop in for a cocktail after a day in Fort Greene Park, or come for a heartier repast courtesy of Walter's raw bar, satisfying main dishes (the fried chicken with garlic mashed potatoes is a consistent winner), and market-fresh veggie sides. $ *Average main: $20* ⊠ *166 DeKalb Ave., Fort Greene* ☎ *718/488–7800* ⊕ *www.walterfoods.com/walters* Ⓜ *B, Q, R to DeKalb Ave.; C to Lafayette Ave.; G to Fulton St.* ✛ *7:C4.*

PARK SLOPE

Park Slope's reputation precedes it: this handsome, gay-friendly family neighborhood also happens to be a great place to fill the tummy. Restaurant-crammed 5th Avenue is not for the indecisive; there's everything from Mexican to Italian to Thai, and it's all quite good.

$$ ✕ **al di là Trattoria.** Roughly translated as "the great beyond," al di là has been consistently packed since it opened in 1998, and it's easy to understand why: perfectly prepared dishes from northern Italy served at affordable prices, in a relaxed atmosphere. The warm farro salad with seasonal ingredients and goat cheese is perfectly al dente; the hand-pinched ravioli are deliciously homemade; and meatier entrées like braised rabbit, pork loin scaloppine, and charcoal-grilled young Bo Bo chicken are highlights. The wine bar is a good spot to wait for a table. $ *Average main: $24* ⊠ *248 5th Ave., at Carroll St., Park Slope* ☎ *718/783–4565* ⊕ *www.aldilatrattoria.com* Ⓜ *R to Union St.* ✛ *7:C5.*

ITALIAN

$$ ✕ **Franny's.** Local, organic, sustainable, and high quality are the watchwords at this lively spot known for delicious wood-fired pizzas and inventive southern Italian dishes. The menu is gently priced, but portions run small. Seasonal flourishes might include ramps, roasted fennel, or whipped eggplant, and pizza toppings feature unusual cheeses like nutty grana padano, peppery pecorino, and sharp Ragusano D.O. caciocavallo: all pair well with the extensive list of Italian wines. Watch the crew at work through the open kitchen. $ *Average main: $18* ⊠ *348 Flatbush Ave., between Sterling Pl. and 8th Ave., Park Slope* ☎ *718/230–0221* ⊕ *www.frannysbrooklyn.com* ☾ *No lunch Mon.– Thurs.* Ⓜ *2, 3 to Grand Army Plaza; B, Q to 7th Ave.* ✛ *7:C5.*

ITALIAN

$$ ✕ **Talde.** *Top Chef* alumnus Dale Talde has created a showstopping menu of Asian-American comfort foods at this casual neighborhood restaurant. Taste the bold flavors of staples like the crispy pretzel pork and chive dumplings, tangy kung pao chicken wings with cilantro and peanuts, Filipino pork shoulder with pickled papaya, and Korean fried chicken with a kimchi-yogurt sauce cooled by sliced grapes. If the Filipino *halo-halo* dessert is on the menu, you're in for a sugar rush: it's shaved ice with sweetened condensed milk, coconut, tapioca, seasonal fruit, and Cap'n Crunch. Distract yourself with a cocktail at the bar if there's a wait for a table. $ *Average main: $23* ⊠ *369 7th Ave., at 11th St., Park Slope* ☎ *347/916–0031* ⊕ *www.taldebrooklyn.com* Ⓜ *F, G to 7th Ave.* ✛ *7:C6.*

ASIAN FUSION

PROSPECT HEIGHTS

Once referred to as the "new Park Slope," the neighborhood on the other side of Flatbush has come into its own. Leafy, brownstone-laden streets are increasingly filled with great restaurants.

$$ ✕ **Bar Corvo.** On the Crown Heights–Prospect Heights border (*corvo* means "crow" in Italian, as in Crow Hill, this area's old name) and a

ITALIAN

stone's throw from the Brooklyn Museum, this handmade-pasta specialist is an offshoot of Park Slope's renowned al di là. Like its sibling, Bar Corvo offers rustic decor alongside refined starches and salads—squid-ink spaghetti with octopus, *malfatti* gnocchi with walnuts, and an impeccable warm farro salad (the fried spicy chickpeas, billed a "snack," are highly addictive). For weekend museumgoers, Bar Corvo's brunch is a refined alternative to Tom's more casual diner fare up the block. $ *Average main: $18* ⊠ *791 Washington Ave., at Lincoln Pl., Prospect Heights* ☎ *718/230–0940* ⊕ *www.barcorvo.com* ☾ *No lunch weekdays* Ⓜ *2, 3 to Eastern Pkwy.–Brooklyn Museum; 2, 3, 4, 5 to Franklin Ave.; S to Botanic Garden* ✛ *7:D5.*

$$ ✕ **Chuko.** Whether it's because of the miniscule size of the restaurant or
JAPANESE   the habit-forming flavors of the noodle bowls, there's always a crowd outside this ramen storefront. Since opening in 2011 as an offshoot of Manhattan's Morimoto, Chuko has become a Prospect Heights institution with a small, reliably tasty menu—the signature ramen comes in a simple selection of broths and toppings. The Brooklyn flagship has since spawned Bar Chuko, a block away, which has a wider selection of *izakaya* small plates—Japanese bar food like yakitori skewers and clams with XO sauce. Wander over there if the mothership is mobbed or to enjoy a shochu cocktail while you wait. $ *Average main: $14* ⊠ *552 Vanderbilt Ave., at Dean St., Prospect Heights* ☎ *718/576–6701* ⊕ *www.barchuko.com* Ⓜ *2, 3 to Bergen St.; A, C to Clinton–Washington Aves.; B, Q to 7th Ave.* ✛ *7:D5.*

CONEY ISLAND

It's no longer an island, but this amusement park on the sea is salt-of-the-earth paradise. Think pizza and hot dogs and calorie-laden carnival fare. If you're in town during July 4, a Big Apple must-see is the annual Nathan's Famous hot-dog-eating contest where hundreds of people gather to watch "professional" eaters scarf down tubular meat.

$$ ✕ **Totonno's Pizzeria Napolitana.** Thin-crust pies judiciously topped with
PIZZA   fresh mozzarella and tangy, homemade tomato sauce, then baked in
FAMILY   a coal oven—at Totonno's you're not just eating pizza, you're biting into a slice of New York history. Not much has changed since Anthony (Totonno) Pero first opened the pizzeria, in 1924, right after the subways started running to Coney Island—the restaurant is at the same location and run by the same family, who use ingredients and techniques that have been handed down through four generations. The casual dining room is old-school, too, with checkerboard linoleum flooring, red-top tables, and wall-to-wall autographed photos, historic news clippings, and awards and accolades (including the James Beard American Classic). $ *Average main: $17* ⊠ *1524 Neptune Ave., between 15th and 16th Sts., Coney Island* ☎ *718/372–8606* ⊕ *www.totonnosconeyisland. com* ☾ *Closed Mon.–Wed.* ▭ *No credit cards* Ⓜ *D, F, N, Q to Coney Island–Stillwell Ave.* ✛ *7:G6.*

BRIGHTON BEACH

The subway trains that shuttle people out to this beachside neighborhood could be nicknamed the "time machine" because strolling the wide boardwalk along the sea feels like you've dropped into another time and space. Odessa in the 1980s comes to mind. After all, it was around that time when a mass migration of Russian immigrants settled in Brighton Beach. Today you'll hear more Slavic than English and you'll most certainly be tempted by the vodka and highly entertaining Russian restaurants that line the boardwalk.

$ ✕ **Cafe Kashkar.** Uyghur cuisine, from the Chinese region of Xinjiang, is
ASIAN   the focus of the menu at this postage-stamp-size café. Standouts include *naryn* (lamb dumplings), *samsa* (empanada-like lamb pies), pickles, vinegary salads, and clay-oven-baked bread. The few Uzbek dishes on the menu are recommended, in particular the pilaf and the lamb and vegetable *dymlama*—a meat-and-potato stew that's sometimes made with vegetables and fruit. The portions are definitely shareable. $ *Average main: $6* ✉ *1141 Brighton Beach Ave., at Brighton 15th St., Brighton Beach* ☎ *718/743–3832* ⊕ *www.kashkarcafe.com* Ⓜ *B, Q to Brighton Beach* ✛ *7:H6.*

$$ ✕ **Tatiana Restaurant and Night Club.** There are two prime times at Tatiana's: day and night. Sitting at a boardwalk-side table on a summer
RUSSIAN   afternoon, enjoying the breezes and the views of the Atlantic while eating lunch alfresco, is a quintessential Brighton Beach experience. After dark, a flashier crowd arrives, especially on weekends when Tatiana's hosts an extravagant floor show, with plenty of dancing, costumes, and acrobatics. The menu has a bit of everything: the Ukrainian specialties, like the sweet and savory *vareniki*, a pierogi-like dumpling that's considered Ukraine's national dish, are especially good, as are the herring, the homemade lox, and the caviar platters. Vodka can be ordered like wine—by the bottle. No sneakers are allowed in the evenings. $ *Average main: $22* ✉ *3152 Brighton 6th St. (or enter from boardwalk), Brighton Beach* ☎ *718/891–5151* ⊕ *www.tatianarestaurant.com* Ⓜ *B, Q to Brighton Beach* ✛ *7:H6.*

QUEENS

ASTORIA

After you're finished with the sights, why head back to Manhattan? End your day with dinner at one of Astoria's legendary Greek restaurants (on or near Broadway), or venture to the Middle Eastern restaurants farther out on Steinway Street.

$$ ✕ **Taverna Kyclades.** The current powerhouse of Hellenic eats in the
GREEK   neighborhood, Taverna Kyclades serves Greek classics at a higher level than you'd expect, given the simple decor and unassuming location. Fried calamari and grilled octopus make appearances at rock-bottom prices, despite their obvious quality, as do more out-of-the-ordinary dishes like "caviar dip" and swordfish kebabs. Lamb chops drip with juice, and grilled sardines are so fresh you'd swear they were just pulled from the sea. Be prepared to wait for a table at peak times, as they don't take reservations. There's also a Manhattan outpost on 1st Avenue

and East 13th Street in the East Village. $ *Average main: $17* ✉ *33-07 Ditmars Blvd., Astoria* ☎ *718/545–8666* ⊕ *www.tavernakyclades.com* ⌂ *Reservations not accepted* Ⓜ *N, Q to Astoria–Ditmars Blvd.* ✛ *7:F1.*

FLUSHING

Manhattan may be known for its fine four-star restaurants, but food lovers know there's one train to take to some of the best eats in the city. The 7 snakes its way through the middle of Queens, and conveniently through some of the best dining neighborhoods in New York. At the end of the line is Flushing, home to the second-largest Chinatown in the United States. (First is San Francisco's.) Wide streets have few tourists and many interesting stores and restaurants, making the long trip worth it. A couple of tips: bring cash, because not many of these restaurants accept credit cards, and be prepared to encounter language difficulties, as English speakers are in the minority. In Manhattan, catch the 7 train at Times Square or Grand Central Terminal.

$ ✕ **Spicy and Tasty.** Flushing is crammed with quality salt-of-the-earth
CHINESE   Chinese eateries, but Spicy and Tasty is the place to go for standout Chinese, particularly if you're a first-timer to the neighborhood. The restaurant lives up to its name with numbing Sichuan peppercorns and slicks of red chili oil. Tea-smoked duck has crispy skin and smoky, salty meat. Eggplant with garlic sauce tastes of ginger, tomatoes, and red chilies. Cool it all down with a Tsingtao beer. The $6.50 lunch special—weekdays only—is quite the deal. $ *Average main: $10* ✉ *39-07 Prince St., at 39th Ave., Flushing* ☎ *718/359–1601* ⊕ *www.spicyandtasty.com* ▭ *No credit cards* Ⓜ *7 to Flushing–Main St.* ✛ *7:H1.*

LONG ISLAND CITY

Long Island City began attracting more visitors when MoMA PS1 opened in the 1970s, and today it's getting more popular thanks to its hip but down-to-earth eateries and awesome views of the Manhattan skyline.

$$ ✕ **M. Wells Dinette.** When the original version of this beloved and experi-
CANADIAN   mental restaurant in Long Island City lost its lease and had to shut
Fodor'sChoice   down, a swath of New York eaters let out a collective groan. But they
★   didn't have to go too long without their foie-gras fix because French-Canadian chef Hugue Dufour reopened the restaurant at MoMA PS1. The menu changes depending on the season but diners might find dishes like veal cheek stroganoff, with thick bucatini, or bone marrow and escargot. Finish off with a slice of maple pie and a shot of maple bourbon. Then wander the gallery trying to make sense of the art (and your meal). The restaurant currently closes at 6 pm, leaving time for a leisurely lunch but not dinner. $ *Average main: $18* ✉ *MoMA PS1, 22–25 Jackson Ave., at 46th Ave., Long Island City* ☎ *718/786–1800* ⊕ *www.momaps1.org/about/mwells* ◷ *No dinner. Closed Tues. and Wed.* ⌂ *Reservations not accepted* Ⓜ *7, G to Court Sq.; E, M to Court Sq.–23rd St.* ✛ *7:F1.*

$$$$ ✕ **M. Wells Steakhouse.** From the team that made Long Island City a
STEAKHOUSE   dining destination with the original M. Wells and then the M. Wells Dinette inside MoMA PS1 comes this mecca devoted to meat. Once you find the door—go through the gate, then walk across the small courtyard—settle in at a table in the industrial space, order a cocktail (the

Canadian sidecar just means there's maple in the classic), and peruse the menu. There are some good but gimmicky options—a bone-in burger, the short or tall stack of pork chops, foie gras gnocchi—but we say stick to the steak, particularly the thick, juicy côte de boeuf, and you'll leave a happy diner. $ *Average main: $40* ⊠ *43-15 Crescent St., Long Island City* ☎ *718/786–9060* ⊕ *www.magasinwells.com* ۞ *Closed Sun.–Wed. No lunch* Ⓜ *7, N, Q to Queensboro Plaza; E, M, R to Queens Plaza* ✛ *7:F1.*

JACKSON HEIGHTS

One of the most ethnically diverse parts of New York City, Jackson Heights is home to a United Nations of cuisine: from outstanding Indian and Pakistani places to surprisingly excellent taco carts. Most recently, Tibetans and Nepalese have been moving into the neighborhood, setting up small shops selling juicy meat-filled *momos* (dumplings) and other Himalayan treats.

$ ✕ **Phayul.** Step through the doorway with the Himalayan eyebrow
TIBETAN threading sign above it, head up the twisting and turning stairway, then enter through a beaded curtain and you'll find yourself something of a delicious culinary anomaly: Tibetan-Sichuan cuisine. The traditional momos (Tibetan dumplings stuffed with meat) are worth trying, but the most exciting fare here lies in the fusion of the two cultures, like spicy blood sausage or tofu in a fiery chili sauce. The funky beef-studded Tibetan yak-cheese soup is for adventurous eaters. $ *Average main: $9* ⊠ *37-65 74th St., Jackson Heights* ☎ *718/424–1869* ▭ *No credit cards* Ⓜ *7 to 74th St.–Broadway; E, F, M, R to Jackson Heights–Roosevelt Ave.* ✛ *7:F1.*

WOODSIDE

It has long been said that to get great Thai food in the Big Apple, you have to go to Queens. While the Thai dining landscape has improved in other parts of the city, Woodside is still its epicenter. But to only associate Woodside with just Thai cuisine is underselling it; you'll find a variety of ethnic eateries here, including Ecuadorian and Italian.

$$ ✕ **SriPraPhai.** The main reason foodies flock to Woodside is to go to
THAI SriPraPhai (pronounced "See-PRA-pie"). It's widely considered the
Fodor's Choice best Thai restaurant in New York. Don't be overwhelmed by the huge
★ menu—it's hard to go wrong. Crispy watercress salad, *larb* (ground pork salad with mint and lime juice), sautéed chicken with cashews and pineapple, *kao-soy* (curried egg noodles), and roasted-duck green curry are a few standouts. If you go with a few people, order the delicately flavored whole steamed fish. There's a large separate menu for vegetarians. But prepare your palate: your mouth might feel like a five-alarm fire by the time you're finished. $ *Average main: $13* ⊠ *64-13 39th Ave., Woodside* ☎ *718/899–9599* ⊕ *www.sripraphairestaurant.com* ▭ *No credit cards* ۞ *Closed Wed.* Ⓜ *7 to 69th St.* ✛ *7:H1.*

15

THE BRONX

People don't really wander into this borough—like they do into Brooklyn and even Queens, hoping to stumble on some gem of an ethnic eatery—but the Bronx actually has a lot going for it, if you know where to look. Dotted throughout the borough are some great Mexican taquerías, African eateries, and old-school Italian joints. Skip Manhattan's Little Italy and head to the Bronx's Arthur Avenue for a real red-sauce treat; it's a much more authentic Italian-American neighborhood and a great place to carb-load.

$$ × **Antonio's Trattoria.** Antonio's bills itself as "an Italian restaurant serving simple food," but it's underselling itself. This is fantastic salt-of-the-earth Italian fare at its best. Start with the mini-meatballs wading in a marinara sauce and move on to baked clams, house-made ravioli, fettuccine carbonara, or excellent pizza, baked in a brick oven in the Neapolitan manner. Only the red-and-white checked tablecloths are missing. It's a bit off the main "Little Italy" strip, but worth the trek. And if you haven't eaten enough, expect a server to come by, prodding you with "*Mangia, mangia!*" $ *Average main: $22* ⊠ *2370 Belmont Ave., Belmont* ☎ *718/733–6630* ⊕ *www.antoniostrattoria.com* Ⓜ *B, D to 182nd–183rd Sts.*

ITALIAN

$$ × **Zero Otto Nove.** Though insiders who can get a table swear by Rao's on 114th Street in Manhattan, Zero Otto Nove chugs along as one of the best Italian restaurants north of 96th Street. The draw? A menu that nicely balances authentic Italian fare with good Italian-American classics. Try a wood-oven-fired pizza, perfectly chewy and loaded with buffalo mozzarella. The San Matteo, which adds broccoli rabe to the mix, is just as addictive as the plain-Jane margherita. Pasta dishes are worthy of your attention, too: the malfade with chickpeas, crispy pancetta, and bread crumbs might make you want to skip the pizza pie for now. For those who don't feel like a trek to the Bronx, there's another outpost in Chelsea. $ *Average main: $16* ⊠ *2357 Arthur Ave., Belmont* ☎ *718/220–1027* ⊕ *www.roberto089.com* ⊘ *Closed Mon.* ⚑ *Reservations not accepted* Ⓜ *B, D to 182nd–183rd Sts.*

ITALIAN

STATEN ISLAND

There's not much reason for tourists to spend time in New York's often-forgotten fifth borough, but if you made your way here on the free ferry from Whitehall Terminal and want to explore, you'll find plenty of homespun, no-frills eateries, including some of the best pizza in the city.

$$ **Denino's Pizzeria & Tavern.** Arguably the best pizzeria in the borough, Denino's has been run by the same Sicilian family for more than 75 years. Baking thin-crust pizzas in their current location since 1937, this Staten Island institution is worth the trip from St. George (half an hour by bus; 15-minute drive). For dessert, try Ralph's Famous Italian Ices and Ice Cream, conveniently located across the street. $ *Average main: $17* ⊠ *524 Port Richmond Ave., Staten Island* ☎ *718/442–9401* ⊕ *www.deninos.com* ▭ *No credit cards* Ⓜ *S44 or S94 bus from Staten Island Ferry Terminal (30 mins).*

ITALIAN
FAMILY

NEW YORK CITY DINING AND LODGING ATLAS

KEY

☐ Hotels
■ Restaurants
■ Restaurant in Hotel
1,2,3,A,B,C
Ⓜ ⟍ Station
NYC MTA Subway

Map 3

- Chelsea
- East Village
- Flatiron
- Gramercy Park
- Greenwich Village
- Meatpacking District
- Murray Hill
- Union Square

A   **B**   **C**   **D**

MAIN POST OFFICE

MADISON SQUARE GARDEN

PENN STATION

1

W. 31st St.
W. 30th St.   The Eventi
Riff Chelsea   W. 29th St.   **Lupulo**
                      E. 28th St.
Hotel Americano   Chelsea Park   W. 27th St.
                                 W. 26th St.   Hilton New York
Franklin Terrace   W. 25th St.   Fashion District

2

Tenth Avenue
Ninth Avenue
Eighth Avenue
Seventh Avenue
Eleventh Avenue
Ave. of the Americas
(6th Avenue)

Trestle on Tenth   ■ **Txikito**
                       ■ **Co.**   W. 24th St.
CHELSEA
The Red Cat ■   W. 23rd St.   C,E   F,M
Tía Pol ■
                  Clement Clark Moore Park   W. 22nd St.
                  High Line Hotel   W. 21st St.   The GEM Hotel Chelsea
                                             W. 20th St.
■ **Cookshop**   **Tipsy Parson**   W. 19th St.

3

West Side Highway
West St.
Tenth Avenue

                                             W. 18th St.
                                             W. 17th St.
La Sirena
The Maritime Hotel | W. 16th St.
■ **Del Posto**   W. 15th St.   ■ **Legend**

4

                        ■ **Mulino a Vino**   **Coppelia**
MEATPACKING DISTRICT   A,C,E,L   W. 14th St.   1,2,3   F,L,M
                        Spice Market ■
                        Gansevoort Meatpacking NYC   W. 13th St.
The Standard Grill
The Standard, High Line
Little W. 12th St.   **Fatty Crab** ■
Untitled at the Whitney
                                    ■ **dell'anima**

5

Hudson River Park
9A
Hudson River

Gansevoort St.
Horatio St.
Jane St.
Greenwich St.
Eighth Ave.
W. 4th St.
Greenwich Ave.
Waverly Pl.

■ **Bar Bolonat**   **Umami Burger** ■
□ The Jane   ■ **Barbuto**   Abingdon Square
W. 12th St.   **WEST VILLAGE**   Perry St.   Charles St.   W. 10th St.   Gay St.
Bethune St.
Bank St.   Hudson St.   **Westville** ■   Sheridan Square   A,B,C D,E,F,M
W. 11th St.   ■ **Wallsé**

6

Washington St.
Greenwich St.
West St.
West Side Highway
Christopher St.
Grove St.
Bedford St.
Jones St.
Cornelia St.
Bleecker St.
Carmine St.

                              The Little Owl ■
                              ■ **Sushi Nakazawa**

0 _____ 1,000 ft
0 _____ 300 m

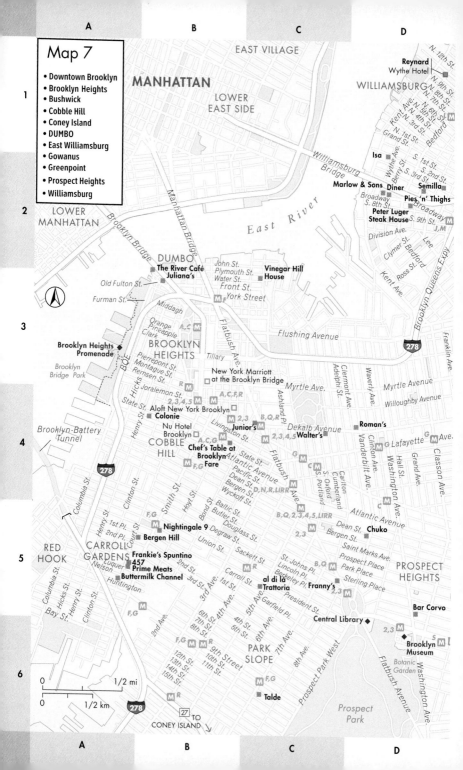

Map 7

- Downtown Brooklyn
- Brooklyn Heights
- Bushwick
- Cobble Hill
- Coney Island
- DUMBO
- East Williamsburg
- Gowanus
- Greenpoint
- Prospect Heights
- Williamsburg

EAST VILLAGE

MANHATTAN

LOWER EAST SIDE

LOWER MANHATTAN

East River

Brooklyn Bridge

Manhattan Bridge

Williamsburg Bridge

WILLIAMSBURG

Reynard
Wythe Hotel

N. 12th St.
N. 9th St.
N. 8th St.
N. 7th St.
N. 6th St.
N. 5th St.
N. 4th St.
N. 3rd St.
N. 1st St.
Grand St.
S. 1st St.
S. 2nd St.
S. 3rd St.

Kent Ave.
Wythe Ave.
Berry St.
Bedford

Isa

Marlow & Sons   Diner   Semilla
Broadway   Pies 'n' Thighs
S. 8th St.
Peter Luger   S. 9th St.
Steak House   J, M

Division Ave.
Clymer St. Bedford
Ross St. Lee

Kent Ave.

Brooklyn Queens Expy.

Franklin Ave.

DUMBO
The River Café
Juliana's
Old Fulton St.
Furman St.

John St.
Plymouth St.
Water St.
Front St.
York Street

Vinegar Hill House

Flushing Avenue

278

Brooklyn Heights Promenade

Brooklyn Bridge Park

BQE

Middagh

Orange
Pineapple
Clark   A, C
BROOKLYN HEIGHTS
Pierrepont St.
Montague St.
Remsen St.
Joralemon St.
Hicks St.
State St.
Henry St.

Tillary

Flatbush Ave.

New York Marriott at the Brooklyn Bridge

Myrtle Ave.

Ashland Pl.

Clermont Ave.
Adelphi St.
Waverly Ave.

Myrtle Avenue

Willoughby Avenue

A, C, F, R

2, 3, 4, 5

Aloft New York Brooklyn
Colonie
Nu Hotel Brooklyn

COBBLE HILL

A, C, G

Chef's Table at Brooklyn Fare
F, G

Livingston St.

A, C, G

Junior's   B, Q, R
2, 3   **Walter's**
2, 3, 4, 5

Roman's

Dekalb Avenue

Clinton Ave.
Vanderbilt Ave.
Hall St.
Washington Ave.
Grand Ave.
Classon Ave.

G

G   Lafayette   G   Ave.

Brooklyn-Battery Tunnel

RED HOOK

278

Columbia St.
Clinton St.
Hicks St.
Henry St.
Bay St.
Henry St.

1st Pl.
2nd Pl.

Smith St.
Hoyt St.
Bond St.
Court St.

State St.
Atlantic Avenue
Pacific St.
Dean St.
Bergen St.
Wyckoff St.
Baltic St.
Butler St.
Degraw St.
Union St.
Sackett St.
Carroll St.

Atlantic Avenue

C

Carlton Ave.
Cumberland
S. Oxford
S. Portland

Dean St.
Bergen St.

C   M

Chuko

D, N, R, LIRR

B, Q, 2, 3, 4, 5, LIRR

2, 3

PROSPECT HEIGHTS

CARROLL GARDENS
Luquer
Nelson
Huntington

Nightingale 9
F, G
Bergen Hill

Frankie's Spuntino 457
Prime Meats
Buttermilk Channel
F, G

1st St.
2nd St.
3rd St.
4th St.
5th St.
6th St.
7th St.
8th St.

3rd Ave.
4th Ave.
5th Ave.

St. Johns Pl.
Lincoln Pl.
Berkeley Pl.
Garfield Pl.
President St.

al di là Trattoria

St. Marks Ave.
Prospect Place
Park Place
Sterling Place

B, Q

Franny's
2, 3

Bar Corvo

2, 3

Central Library

9th Street
10th St.
11th St.
12th St.
13th St.
14th St.
15th St.

F, G   M

F, G   M

F, G

R

27
TO
CONEY ISLAND

PARK SLOPE

6th Ave.
7th Ave.
8th Ave.
Prospect Park West

Talde

Brooklyn Museum

2, 3   M

S

Botanic Garden
Flatbush Avenue
Washington Ave.

Prospect Park

0   1/2 mi

0   1/2 km

278

WHERE TO STAY

Updated by
Jessica Colley
Clarke

There are more hotel rooms than ever in New York City, as exciting new properties continue to open their doors not only in Manhattan but in Brooklyn and the outer boroughs as well. But does that mean that New York is cheap? Well, we wouldn't say *cheap*, but you can still find some deals, especially if you're not set on a specific property or neighborhood, and if you don't mind a few extra minutes of commuting time.

Hotels continue to slash rates based on market sensitivity—especially if you and all of those other Internet-savvy shoppers are willing to wait until the last minute. That said, if you want to stay in a specific place and the rate seems reasonable, book it—it's just as likely to go up, especially during peak seasons (spring and fall).

How to choose? The first thing to consider is location (*Check out our "Where Should I Stay?" chart*). Many New York City visitors insist on staying in the hectic Midtown area—and options are improving there—but other neighborhoods are often just as convenient. Less touristy areas, such as Gramercy, the Lower East Side, the Upper West Side—even Brooklyn—provide a far more realistic sense of New York life.

Also consider timing: the least expensive months to book rooms in the city are January and February. If you're flexible on dates, ask the reservationist if there's a cheaper time to stay during your preferred traveling month—that way you can avoid peak dates, like Fashion Week and the New York City Marathon. Be sure to ask about possible weekend packages that could include a third night free. (The Financial District in particular can be a discount gold mine on weekends.)

Another source of bargains? Chain hotels. Many have moved into the city and charge reasonable room rates. In addition to favorites like the Sheraton, Hilton, and Hyatt brands, there are Best Westerns, Days Inns, and Comfort Inns. These rates aren't as low as you find outside Manhattan, but they're certainly getting closer.

PLANNER

NEED A RESERVATION?

Hotel reservations are a necessity when planning your trip to New York. Competition for clients also means properties must undergo frequent improvements, especially during July and August, so when booking, ask about any renovations, lest you get a room within earshot of noisy construction, or temporarily (and inconveniently) without amenities such as room service or spa access.

SERVICES

Unless otherwise noted, all hotels listed have private baths, central heating, air-conditioning, and private phones. Many now have wireless Internet (Wi-Fi) available, though it's not always free. Most large hotels have video or high-speed checkout capability, and many can arrange babysitting. Pools are a rarity, but most properties have gyms or health clubs, and sometimes full-scale spas; hotels without facilities usually have arrangements for guests at nearby gyms, sometimes for a fee.

FAMILY TRAVEL

New York has gone to great lengths to attract family vacationers, and hotels have followed the family-friendly trend. Some properties provide such diversions as Web TV and in-room video games. Most full-service Manhattan hotels provide roll-away beds, babysitting, and stroller rental, but be sure to make these arrangements when booking, not when you arrive.

DOES SIZE MATTER?

If room size is important to you, ask how many square feet a room has, not just if it's big. A hotel room in New York is considered large if it's 500 square feet. Very large rooms are 600 square feet. To stay anywhere larger, book a multiroom suite. Small rooms are a tight 150 to 200 square feet, sometimes less.

PRICES

There's no denying that New York City hotels are expensive, but rates run the full range. For high-end hotels like the Mandarin Oriental at Central Park, prices start at $895 a night for a standard room in high season, which runs from September through December. At the low end of the spending spectrum, a bunk at the Jane starts at $99 for a single. But don't be put off by the prices printed here—many hotels slash their rates significantly for promotions and Web-only deals.

Prices in the reviews are the lowest cost of a standard double room in high season.

WHAT IT COSTS				
	$	$$	$$$	$$$$
FOR TWO PEOPLE	under $300	$300–$449	$450–$600	over $600

Prices are for a standard double room, excluding 14.75% city and state taxes.

16

WHERE SHOULD I STAY?

	Neighborhood Vibe	Pros	Cons
Lower Manhattan	Mostly skyscraper hotels in an area that buzzes with activity during weekday hours, but can be eerily quiet at night.	Low crime area; easy subway access to uptown sights; great walking paths along the waterfront and in Battery Park.	Construction and congestion near World Trade Center site; limited choice of restaurants and shopping.
SoHo and NoLIta (with Little Italy)	Swanky, high-end hotels with hip restaurants and lounges patronized by New Yorkers and travelers alike.	Scores of upscale clothing boutiques and art galleries nearby; safe area for meandering walks; easy subway access.	Not budget-friendly; streets are crowded on weekends; few major sites nearby.
East Village and the Lower East Side	The epicenter of edgy New York, great for travelers looking to party.	Great low-cost options for young generation. Great restaurants and independent boutiques.	One of the least subway-accessible Manhattan 'hoods; expect late-night noise.
Greenwich Village and the West Village	Hotels in this part of town are few and far between. The ones that are here are small and boutiquey.	Easy subway access to anywhere in town; great shopping, dining, and drinking venues.	Winding streets can be tough to navigate; most hotels are on the pricey side.
Chelsea and the Meatpacking District	More hotels are opening in one of the city's trendiest restaurant and nightlife areas.	"See and be seen"; lots of great shopping.	This is a trendy and pricey neighborhood for hotels. Most hotel bars are a real scene.
Union Square, Flatiron District, and Gramercy	A relatively quiet residential area.	Patches of calm respite from the hustle and bustle of downtown and Midtown; low crime area.	Limited subway access as you move east; Gramercy may be too quiet for some.
Midtown East and West, and Murray Hill	Mostly big-name hotel chains and luxury business suites around Times Square; lots of tourists.	Near Broadway theaters; budget options are available in chain hotels and indies alike.	Streets are often packed with pedestrians; area around Port Authority is gritty. Murray Hill is pretty quiet.
Upper East Side	Well-heeled residential neighborhood near many museums.	Removed from Midtown hustle; near tourist attractions like Central Park.	Streets are quiet after 9 pm; few budget dining options; limited subway access (just the 6 line).
Upper West Side	Hotels in a residential neighborhood near Central Park, Lincoln Center, and some museums.	Lovely tree-lined streets; laid-back neighborhood eateries.	Weekend trains can be slow; most hotels are on the pricey side.
Brooklyn	Brooklyn has a bit of everything so it depends on where you end up. Williamsburg is all about hipsters, while other neighborhoods are quite residential.	You'll find generally smaller boutique-style hotels with personalized service and character, and rates worth traveling for. Plus, a whole new borough to explore.	If you're out late in Manhattan, it'll be a subway or a relatively pricey taxi back to Brooklyn.

HOTEL REVIEWS

Listed alphabetically within neighborhoods. Please visit Fodors.com for expanded reviews. Use the coordinate (✛ 1:B2) at the end of each listing to locate a property on the corresponding map preceding this chapter.

LOWER MANHATTAN

FINANCIAL DISTRICT

$$ **Andaz Wall Street.** If space is a priority, head to the southern tip of **HOTEL** Manhattan: this sleek hotel has generous rooms with large windows, **Fodor's Choice** oak floors, and extra-large bathrooms. **Pros:** free Wi-Fi, bikes, snacks, ★ and nonalcoholic beverages; excellent, intuitive lighting controls; good value. **Cons:** limited choice for restaurants and nightlife in the neighborhood; in-house restaurant not open every day. ⑤ *Rooms from: $395* ✉ *75 Wall St., Financial District* ☎ *212/590–1234* ⊕ *www.newyork. wallstreet.andaz.hyatt.com* ⇝ *213 rooms, 40 suites* ⦿*No meals* Ⓜ *2, 3 to Wall St.* ✛ *1:E4.*

$$$ **Gild Hall.** Captains of Industry, here's a boutique hotel for you: oper- **HOTEL** ated by the owners of the several Thompson Hotels around the United States and beyond, Gild Hall aggressively courts clientele with a Y chromosome. **Pros:** central Financial District location; eye-popping lobby; stylish room design. **Cons:** small rooms for the price; untraditional location. ⑤ *Rooms from: $499* ✉ *15 Gold St., at Platt St., Financial District* ☎ *212/232–7700, 800/268–0700* ⊕ *www.thompsonhotels.com* ⇝ *116 rooms, 10 suites* ⦿*No meals* Ⓜ *2, 3, 4, 5, A, C, J, Z to Fulton St.* ✛ *1:E3.*

$$$ **The W New York Downtown.** In the heart of the Financial District, this **HOTEL** W outpost juxtaposes the gritty feel of the Financial District with sleek surfaces. **Pros:** near popular tourist attractions; restaurant offers some surprisingly affordable fare; modern workout room. **Cons:** scaffolding-dense neighborhood; not family-friendly. ⑤ *Rooms from: $499* ✉ *123 Washington St., at Albany St., Financial District* ☎ *646/826–8600* ⊕ *www.wnewyorkdowntown.com* ⇝ *214 rooms, 3 suites* ⦿*No meals* Ⓜ *1, R to Rector St.; 4, 5 to Wall St.* ✛ *1:C4.*

TRIBECA

$$$ **Conrad New York.** A pleasant surprise in a quiet Battery Park City **HOTEL** location, this hotel has many coveted amenities: significant square foot- **FAMILY** age, a breezy rooftop bar, and access to green space in nearby Hudson River Park. **Pros:** spacious rooms with separate living space; emphasis on art and design; near movie theater and restaurants; near downtown attractions. **Cons:** daily fee for Wi-Fi; removed from Midtown attractions; expensive. ⑤ *Rooms from: $499* ✉ *102 North End Ave., between Vesey and Murray Sts., TriBeCa* ☎ *212/945–0100* ⊕ *www. conradnewyork.com* ⇝ *463 suites* ⦿*No meals* Ⓜ *1, 2, 3, A, C to Chambers St.; E to World Trade Center* ✛ *1:B3.*

$$ **The Cosmopolitan Hotel.** For a bargain room in a great downtown **HOTEL** neighborhood, it's hard to beat this cost-conscious favorite. **Pros:** friendly staff; great location for power shoppers; recent refresh with New York–inspired design. **Cons:** sometimes noisy location; small

16

rooms. $⑤ Rooms from: $369 ⊠ 95 West Broadway, at Chambers St., TriBeCa ☎ 212/566–1900 ⊕ www.cosmohotel.com ⤵ 130 rooms, 1 suite ⚐ No meals Ⓜ 1, 2, 3, A, C to Chambers St. ✛ 1:C2.

$$
HOTEL

Ⓣ **Duane Street Hotel.** Amid TriBeCa's historic warehouses and trendy art galleries sits this boutique hotel, a fashionable addition to the neighborhood. **Pros:** great location; free Wi-Fi; stylish rooms; good pick for the allergy conscious. **Cons:** off-site gym; no 24-hour room service. ⑤ Rooms from: $399 ⊠ 130 Duane St., TriBeCa ☎ 212/964–4600 ⊕ www.duanestreethotel.com ⤵ 41 rooms, 2 suites ⚐ No meals Ⓜ 1, 2, 3, A, C to Chambers St. ✛ 1:C1; 2:D6.

$$$$
HOTEL
Fodor's Choice
★

Ⓣ **The Greenwich Hotel.** This understated, inviting hotel manages to fly under the radar even though Robert De Niro is an owner. **Pros:** fabulous restaurant (Locanda Verde, also available for room service); gorgeous pool; excellent service; luxurious bathrooms. **Cons:** some plumbing noise; high prices. ⑤ Rooms from: $625 ⊠ 377 Greenwich St., TriBeCa ☎ 212/941–8900 ⊕ www.thegreenwichhotel.com ⤵ 75 rooms, 13 suites ⚐ No meals Ⓜ 1 to Franklin St. ✛ 1:B1.

$$$$
HOTEL
FAMILY

Ⓣ **The Ritz-Carlton New York, Battery Park.** If you're staying this far downtown, the Ritz is your top choice. **Pros:** excellent service; best upscale base for downtown exploring; pet- and kid-friendly; Statue of Liberty views. **Cons:** removed from Midtown tourist sights; limited nighttime activities; few neighborhood options for dining and entertainment. ⑤ Rooms from: $650 ⊠ 2 West St., at Battery Park, TriBeCa ☎ 212/344–0800, 800/241–3333 ⊕ www.ritzcarlton.com/batterypark ⤵ 258 rooms, 40 suites ⚐ No meals Ⓜ 1, R, J to Rector St.; 4, 5 to Bowling Green ✛ 1:C5.

$$$
HOTEL

Ⓣ **The Roxy.** Formerly the Tribeca Grand, the Roxy is a fresh downtown property with an emphasis on art, music, and culture. **Pros:** great dining and bar scene; central downtown location; fun social atrium; pet-friendly. **Cons:** rooms get noise from restaurant below; bathrooms have slightly cold design. ⑤ Rooms from: $499 ⊠ 2 6th Ave., between Walker and White Sts., TriBeCa ☎ 212/519–6600, 800/965–3000 ⊕ www.roxyhotelnyc.com ⤵ 186 rooms, 15 suites ⚐ No meals Ⓜ A, C, E to Canal St. ✛ 2:D5.

$$
HOTEL

Ⓣ **Smyth, a Thompson Hotel.** Located almost on top of a convenient subway stop, this thoroughly modern hotel makes TriBeCa a welcoming landing spot for visitors. **Pros:** great service; good restaurant; excellent subway access. **Cons:** Wi-Fi not free; only a frosted-glass partition divides bathroom from sleeping area; bathrooms could have better lighting. ⑤ Rooms from: $375 ⊠ 85 West Broadway, between Chambers and Warren Sts., TriBeCa ☎ 212/587–7000 ⊕ www.thompsonhotels. com/hotels/smyth-tribeca ⤵ 96 rooms, 4 suites ⚐ No meals Ⓜ 1, 2, 3, A, C to Chambers St. ✛ 1:C2.

SOHO AND NOLITA

SOHO

$
HOTEL

Ⓣ **The Broome Hotel.** A Federal-style building from 1825 has been transformed into this boutique property with a special attention to quality service that can sometimes be neglected in SoHo. **Pros:** excellent location for SoHo's shopping and dining; free continental breakfast served on charming patio; good value for the neighborhood. **Cons:** no full-service restaurant on-site. $ *Rooms from: $209* ✉ *431 Broome St., SoHo* ☎ *212/431–2929* ⊕ *www.thebroomenyc.com* ↘ *10 rooms, 4 suites* ⏀ *Breakfast* Ⓜ *6 to Spring St.* ✛ *2:E4.*

$$$$ ⛁ **Crosby Street Hotel.** This whimsical boutique hotel, the first branch
HOTEL of a U.K. chain to open in the United States, has excellent SoHo views.
Fodor'sChoice **Pros:** unique, fun design; big, bright rooms; great bar. **Cons:** small gym.
★ $ *Rooms from: $675* ✉ *79 Crosby St., between Prince and Spring Sts., SoHo* ☎ *212/226–6400* ⊕ *www.firmdalehotels.com* ↘ *69 rooms, 17 suites* ⏀ *No meals* Ⓜ *6 to Spring St.; N, R to Prince St.; B, D, F, M to Broadway–Lafayette St.* ✛ *2:E3.*

$$ ⛁ **Hotel Hugo.** Those who dream of coming home to a SoHo loft will be
HOTEL drawn to this stylish property, inspired by the neighborhood's indus-
trial-chic residences. **Pros:** great location for walks along the Hudson River; stylish on-site dining and drinking options; rooftop with fantastic views. **Cons:** space in rooms is tight; not in the prime heart of SoHo, but on the edge of it. $ *Rooms from: $400* ✉ *525 Greenwich St., SoHo* ☎ *212/608–4848* ⊕ *www.hotelhugony.com* ↘ *120 rooms, 2 suites* ⏀ *No meals* Ⓜ *1 to Houston St.* ✛ *2:B4.*

$$ ⛁ **The James Hotel New York.** This hotel on the edge of SoHo never
HOTEL sacrifices comfort for style, so it's no wonder there's a high percentage
FAMILY of return customers: creative types, businesspeople, fashionistas, and
Fodor'sChoice anyone else with deep pockets. **Pros:** stellar service; fabulous views;
★ cool SoHo location. **Cons:** rooftop bar is expensive. $ *Rooms from: $429* ✉ *27 Grand St., between Thompson St. and 6th Ave., SoHo* ☎ *212/465–2000* ⊕ *www.jameshotels.com* ↘ *109 rooms, 5 suites* ⏀ *No meals* Ⓜ *1, A, C, E to Canal St.* ✛ *2:D4.*

$$$$ ⛁ **The Mercer.** Owner André Balazs has a knack for dating Hollywood
HOTEL starlets and channeling a neighborhood sensibility, and here it's SoHo
loft all the way. **Pros:** great location; sophisticated design touches; celebrity sightings in lobby. **Cons:** service inconsistent; some tight rooms. $ *Rooms from: $695* ✉ *147 Mercer St., at Prince St., SoHo* ☎ *212/966–6060, 888/918–6060* ⊕ *www.mercerhotel.com* ↘ *68 rooms, 7 suites* ⏀ *No meals* Ⓜ *N, R to Prince St.; B, D, F, M to Broadway–Lafayette St.* ✛ *2:E3.*

$$ ⛁ **NOMO SOHO.** Snazzy, fairy-tale-inspired style and a chic SoHo vibe
HOTEL make this property a winner for anyone looking for a decadent down-
Fodor'sChoice town New York experience. **Pros:** stylish rooms; friendly to electronics
★ addicts; fabulous views from floor-to-ceiling windows. **Cons:** elevators can be slow; standard rooms are on the small side. $ *Rooms from: $449* ✉ *9 Crosby St., SoHo* ☎ *212/389–1000* ⊕ *www.nomosoho.com* ↘ *263 rooms, 43 suites* ⏀ *No meals* Ⓜ *6, J, N, Q, R, Z to Canal St.* ✛ *2:E4.*

$$$$ ⛁ **SIXTY SoHo.** Formerly SoHo icon 60 Thompson, this hotel received
HOTEL a renovation and rebranding in 2014. **Pros:** central to SoHo night-
life; good gym; some rooms have balconies. **Cons:** not family-oriented; no pets allowed. $ *Rooms from: $689* ✉ *60 Thompson St., between Broome and Spring Sts., SoHo* ☎ *212/431–0400, 877/431–0400* ⊕ *www.thompsonhotels.com* ↘ *97 rooms, 10 suites* ⏀ *No meals* Ⓜ *C, E to Spring St.* ✛ *2:D4.*

16

$$ SoHo Grand. Once pioneering, now expensive, and with a vaguely
HOTEL creative vibe—the SoHo Grand defines what SoHo is today. **Pros:** fash-
ionable, laid-back sophistication; great service; surprisingly discreet set-
ting; diverse eating and drinking options. **Cons:** closer to Canal Street
than prime SoHo; rooms on small side. *Rooms from: $329 ✉ 310
West Broadway, at Grand St., SoHo ☎ 212/965–3000, 800/965–3000
⊕ www.sohogrand.com ⌁ 341 rooms, 12 suites ⏐○⏐ No meals Ⓜ 1, A,
C, E to Canal St. ✛ 2:D4.*

NOLITA

$$ The Nolitan Hotel. A welcome addition to an underserved neighbor-
HOTEL hood, the Nolitan combines a hip, slightly gritty feel with some luxe
touches, but don't expect a lot of space to spread out. **Pros:** cool vibe;
fun location convenient to lower Manhattan and Brooklyn; fabulous
views from rooftop and some rooms. **Cons:** smallish rooms; gym access
five-minute walk away; some street noise. *Rooms from: $409 ✉ 30
Kenmare St., NoLIta ☎ 212/925–2555 ⊕ www.nolitanhotel.com ⌁ 56
rooms, 1 suite ⏐○⏐ No meals Ⓜ J, Z to Bowery; 6 to Spring St. ✛ 2:F4.*

EAST VILLAGE AND THE LOWER EAST SIDE

EAST VILLAGE

$$$ The Bowery Hotel. Warmed by rich tapestries and fireplaces, the Bow-
HOTEL ery Hotel is like an English hunting lodge in Manhattan—and there's no
Fodor'sChoice shortage of Brits, who flock to the property. **Pros:** quirky, fun location;
★ happening bar and lobby-lounge area; celebrity sightings; interesting
views. **Cons:** gritty neighbors; rooms lack luxe touches expected at
this price. *Rooms from: $535 ✉ 335 Bowery, at 3rd St., East Village
☎ 212/505–9100 ⊕ www.theboweryhotel.com ⌁ 135 rooms, 25 suites
⏐○⏐ No meals Ⓜ 6 to Bleecker St.; B, D, F, M to Broadway–Lafayette
St. ✛ 2:F2.*

$$$ The Standard, East Village. A jarring, 21-story glass-and-steel finger
HOTEL rising up in the low-rise East Village, this hotel was never going to pass
under the radar—and that's guaranteed now that André Balazs and
company have taken over. **Pros:** stylish, sunny rooms with great views;
central location for downtown exploring; free Wi-Fi. **Cons:** out of character with the area; rooms on the small side. *Rooms from: $495 ✉ 25
Cooper Sq., between 5th and 6th Sts., East Village ☎ 212/475–5700
⊕ www.standardhotels.com/eastvillage ⌁ 145 rooms, 8 suites ⏐○⏐ No
meals Ⓜ 6 to Astor Pl.; N, R to 8th St.–NYU ✛ 2:F2.*

LOWER EAST SIDE

$ Hotel Indigo. Smack in the center of a dynamic residential neighbor-
HOTEL hood, this hotel offers a fantastic launching pad for restaurants, nightlife, and people-watching, though it will be hard to beat the sweeping
city views from the 14th-floor lobby's large windows. **Pros:** local flavor
with emphasis on art; rooftop swimming pool; sleek dining and drinking options. **Cons:** street noise is common in this all-night neighborhood.
*Rooms from: $285 ✉ 171 Ludlow St., Lower East Side ☎ 212/237–
1776 ⊕ www.ihg.com/hotelindigo/hotels/us/en/reservation ⌁ 293 rooms,
5 suites ⏐○⏐ No meals Ⓜ F to 2nd Ave.; J, M, Z to Essex St. ✛ 2:G3.*

$$$
HOTEL
Fodor'sChoice
★

Hotel on Rivington. A pioneer when it opened back in 2004, this glass-walled hotel on the Lower East Side is still a great choice if you want to be in the thick of the neighborhood's dining and nightlife scene. **Pros:** cool location and vibe; huge windows with wonderful New York views; many rooms have balconies; seriously luxurious bathrooms. **Cons:** feels clubby on weekends; isolated from some subway lines. ⑤ *Rooms from: $455* ✉ *107 Rivington St., between Ludlow and Essex Sts., Lower East Side* ☎ *212/475–2600, 800/915–1537* ⊕ *www.hotelonrivington. com* ⌁ *90 rooms, 18 suites* Ⓞ *No meals* Ⓜ *F to Delancey St.; J, M, Z to Essex St.* ✛ *2:G3.*

$$
HOTEL

The Ludlow. A stylish creation from hotelier Sean MacPherson, this hotel embodies the effortless cool attitude of the Lower East Side, from its cozy lounge with limestone fireplace to the romantic trellis-covered garden. **Pros:** hot restaurant and bar scene; some rooms have terraces and great views; gorgeous bathrooms. **Cons:** lounge and courtyard can get crowded. ⑤ *Rooms from: $325* ✉ *180 Ludlow St., Lower East Side* ☎ *212/432–1818* ⊕ *www.ludlowhotel.com* ⌁ *175 rooms* Ⓞ *No meals* Ⓜ *F to 2nd Ave.; J, M, Z to Essex St.* ✛ *2:G3.*

$$$
HOTEL

Sixty LES. This hotel is a great embodiment of the neighborhood inhabitants: hip, but friendly when you get to know it. **Pros:** in the heart of downtown scene; great views from suites; hip rooftop bar and pool. **Cons:** occasionally snobby staff; rooms are stylish but dark. ⑤ *Rooms from: $529* ✉ *190 Allen St., between Houston and Stanton Sts., Lower East Side* ☎ *877/460–8888* ⊕ *www.sixtyhotels.com/lowereastside* ⌁ *141 rooms, 10 suites* Ⓞ *No meals* Ⓜ *F to Delancey St.; J, M, Z to Essex St.* ✛ *2:G3.*

16

GREENWICH VILLAGE AND THE WEST VILLAGE

GREENWICH VILLAGE

$$$
HOTEL

The Jade. Among the ghosts of the literary salons and speakeasies of Greenwich Village is the Jade, a boutique property on a tree-lined street with an Art Deco sensibility. **Pros:** delivers a true Greenwich Village experience; cozy fireplaces; quiet neighborhood location. **Cons:** small rooms; no connecting rooms. ⑤ *Rooms from: $450* ✉ *52 W. 13th St., between 5th and 6th Aves., Greenwich Village* ☎ *212/375–1300* ⊕ *www.thejadenyc.com* ⌁ *109 rooms, 4 suites* Ⓞ *No meals* Ⓜ *1, 2, 3, F, M to 14th St.; L to 6th Ave.* ✛ *3:E4.*

$
HOTEL

The Marlton. Built in 1900 and once home to Jack Kerouac, this hotel has been renovated into a stylish boutique with a residential feel. **Pros:** fresh property with luxurious touches; spacious lobby with coffee bar; great Greenwich Village location; value with style. **Cons:** very small rooms; no work desks; no room service. ⑤ *Rooms from: $250* ✉ *5 W. 8th St., Greenwich Village* ☎ *212/321–0100* ⊕ *www.marltonhotel. com* ⌁ *105 rooms, 2 suites* Ⓞ *Breakfast* Ⓜ *A, B, C, D, E, F, M to W. 4th St.* ✛ *3:E5.*

$$
HOTEL

Washington Square Hotel. This low-key hotel in Greenwich Village is popular with visiting New York University parents—the location is also near Washington Square Park and its magnificent arch (and just down the street from Mario Batali's Babbo restaurant). **Pros:**

park-side location; deluxe rooms are charming; great hotel bar; free Wi-Fi. **Cons:** NYU students everywhere in the neighborhood; rooms are small. $\boxed{\$}$ *Rooms from: $315* ✉ *103 Waverly Pl., at MacDougal St., Greenwich Village* ☎ *212/777–9515, 800/222–0418* ⊕ *www. washingtonsquarehotel.com* ⤴ *152 rooms* ⫯⊙⫯ *Breakfast* Ⓜ *A, B, C, D, E, F, M to W. 4th St.* ✛ *2:D1.*

WEST VILLAGE

$ 🖳 **The Jane.** To some, the Jane is impossibly chic; to others, the rooms
HOTEL   are reminiscent of Sing Sing. **Pros:** extraordinary value for the neighborhood; hot bar scene; gorgeous decor in lounge; great branch of weekend-brunch favorite Café Gitane; convenient neighborhood for downtown sightseeing. **Cons:** impossibly tiny standard rooms; some rooms have shared bathrooms; noise from the bar. $\boxed{\$}$ *Rooms from: $125* ✉ *113 Jane St., at West St., West Village* ☎ *212/924–6700* ⊕ *www. thejanenyc.com* ⤴ *174 rooms* ⫯⊙⫯ *No meals* Ⓜ *A, C, E to 14th St.; L to 8th Ave.* ✛ *3:B5.*

CHELSEA AND THE MEATPACKING DISTRICT

CHELSEA

$$ 🖳 **The GEM Hotel Chelsea.** At this stylish, well-priced boutique hotel,
HOTEL   the modern rooms are small but designed to make the most of limited space. **Pros:** great Chelsea location; close to several subway lines; in-room coffeemakers. **Cons:** gym and business center, both on the lower level, feel like a work in progress; rooms may be too small for some. $\boxed{\$}$ *Rooms from: $349* ✉ *300 W. 22nd St., Chelsea* ☎ *212/675–1911* ⊕ *www.thegemhotel.com* ⤴ *81 rooms* ⫯⊙⫯ *No meals* Ⓜ *1, C, E to 23rd St.* ✛ *3:C3.*

$$ 🖳 **High Line Hotel.** A late-19th-century, redbrick, Gothic-style building
HOTEL   on the landscaped grounds of a former seminary was transformed into
Fodor's Choice   this lovely hotel, full of original architectural details like stained-glass
★   windows and pine floors. **Pros:** historic property with lots of character; gorgeous design from top to bottom; peaceful garden; quality coffee bar in the lobby. **Cons:** doesn't have the best subway access. $\boxed{\$}$ *Rooms from: $400* ✉ *180 10th Ave., at 20th St., Chelsea* ☎ *212/929–3888* ⊕ *www.thehighlinehotel.com* ⤴ *60 rooms, 4 suites* ⫯⊙⫯ *No meals* Ⓜ *C, E to 23rd St.* ✛ *3:A3.*

$ 🖳 **Hilton New York Fashion District.** Fashion is the theme at this Hilton,
HOTEL   located in the emerging Fashion District neighborhood (previously known as the garment district) on the upper edge of Chelsea. **Pros:** reasonable prices for a good location; rooftop lounge with great skyline views. **Cons:** small closets; trying to be trendy. $\boxed{\$}$ *Rooms from: $299* ✉ *152 W. 26th St., between 6th and 7th Aves., Chelsea* ☎ *212/858–5888* ⊕ *www3.hilton.com* ⤴ *280 rooms* ⫯⊙⫯ *No meals* Ⓜ *1 to 28th St.; C, E to 23rd St.* ✛ *3:D2.*

$$ 🖳 **Hotel Americano.** This boutique property, which overlooks the High
HOTEL   Line, captures the artistic and stylish spirit of Chelsea. **Pros:** year-round rooftop pool and bar; views overlooking the High Line; near the thriving gallery scene in Chelsea. **Cons:** low beds; bathrooms lack privacy; some furniture is form over function. $\boxed{\$}$ *Rooms from: $395* ✉ *518*

W. 27th St., between 10th and 11th Aves., Chelsea ☎*212/216–0000* ⊕*www.hotel-americano.com* ➳*49 rooms, 7 suites* ⦿*No meals* Ⓜ*C, E to 23rd St.* ✛*3:A1.*

$$ 🖥 **The Maritime Hotel.** The Maritime's white-ceramic tower, the former
HOTEL   HQ for the National Maritime Union, was the first luxury hotel to be opened in the Chelsea gallery district, and the property still feels a bit nautical: the small rooms resemble modern ship cabins, with burnished teak paneling, sea-blue drapes and bed accents, and 5-foot "portholes" that face the Hudson River skyline. **Pros:** fun rooms with big porthole windows; great location near Chelsea Market and the Chelsea galleries. **Cons:** street noise; small rooms. ⑤*Rooms from: $425* ✉*363 W. 16th St., at 9th Ave., Chelsea* ☎*212/242–4300* ⊕*www.themaritimehotel. com* ➳*121 rooms, 5 suites* ⦿*No meals* Ⓜ*A, C, E to 14th St.; L to 8th Ave.* ✛*3:B4.*

$ 🖥 **Riff Chelsea.** Formerly the Chelsea Star, this new hotel has a rich music
HOTEL   history (Madonna crashed here in the '80s) and a creative spirit, from the rock-star-inspired rooms to the ground-floor art gallery. **Pros:** central location near Penn Station; good value option; fresh, bold decor. **Cons:** some rooms have shared bathrooms. ⑤*Rooms from: $149* ✉*300 W. 30th St., Chelsea* ☎*212/244–7827* ⊕*www.riffhotels.com* ➳*36 rooms, 7 suites* ⦿*No meals* Ⓜ*1, 2, 3, A, C, E to 34th St.–Penn Station* ✛*3:C1.*

MEATPACKING DISTRICT

$$$ 🖥 **Gansevoort Meatpacking NYC.** Though the nearby Standard New York
HOTEL   has stolen some of its thunder, there's still plenty to draw guests to this chic Meatpacking District pioneer, starting with the sleek rooms that overlook the city or the Hudson River and the rooftop deck with a 45-foot heated pool. **Pros:** rooftop pool; wonderful art collection; great location for restaurants and shopping. **Cons:** location can seem too trendy, especially at night; service can be slipshod. ⑤*Rooms from: $485* ✉*18 9th Ave., at 13th St., Meatpacking District* ☎*212/206–6700* ⊕*www.hotelgansevoort.com* ➳*164 rooms, 22 suites* ⦿*No meals* Ⓜ*A, C, E to 14th St.; L to 8th Ave.* ✛*3:B4.*

$$$ 🖥 **The Standard, High Line.** André Balazs's architectural statement on
HOTEL   the West Side is still one of New York's hottest hotels. **Pros:** beautiful
Fodor'sChoice   building with sweeping views; beautiful people; impressive restaurant
★   space. **Cons:** noisy at night; tight rooms; can be too sceney. ⑤*Rooms from: $495* ✉*848 Washington St., between 13th and Little W. 12th Sts., Meatpacking District* ☎*212/645–4646* ⊕*www.standardhotels. com* ➳*334 rooms, 4 suites* ⦿*No meals* Ⓜ*A, C, E to 14th St.; L to 8th Ave.* ✛*3:B4.*

UNION SQUARE, FLATIRON DISTRICT, AND GRAMERCY

UNION SQUARE

$$ 🖥 **Hyatt Union Square New York.** Experiencing a bit of "real" New York
HOTEL   (and getting away from Midtown) got easier when this Hyatt opened
Fodor'sChoice   just south of Union Square in a newly built tower with three restaurants,
★   an on-site gym, and bikes and scooters to borrow. **Pros:** convenient and vibrant location; buzzy dining and drinking outlets. **Cons:** charge for

16

Internet; some standard rooms are small. $ *Rooms from: $400* ✉ *134 4th Ave., Union Square* ☎ *212/253–1234* ⊕ *www.unionsquare.hyatt. com* ⌁ *176 rooms, 2 suites* |○| *No meals* Ⓜ *4, 5, 6, L, N, Q, R to 14th St.–Union Sq.* ✢ *3:F4.*

$$$$ ⛼ **W New York Union Square.** The W chain's iconic New York City prop-
HOTEL erty continues to attract a mix of trendsetters and tourists, thanks to its downtown location and funky style. **Pros:** fashionable location; great restaurant. **Cons:** noisy lobby. $ *Rooms from: $650* ✉ *201 Park Ave. S, at 17th St., Union Square* ☎ *212/253–9119, 877/946–8357* ⊕ *www. wnewyorkunionsquare.com* ⌁ *254 rooms, 16 suites* |○| *No meals* Ⓜ *4, 5, 6, L, N, Q, R to 14th St.–Union Sq.* ✢ *3:F3.*

FLATIRON DISTRICT

$$ ⛼ **Ace Hotel.** The Ace is not your ordinary boutique hotel; the lively
HOTEL lobby melds Ivy League library with curiosity cabinet—taxidermy,
Fodor's Choice mosaic tile floors, wooden bookcases, antique sofas—while the staff
★ wear custom Levi's and Converse sneakers. **Pros:** in-house destina-
tion restaurants; supercool but friendly vibe; unfussy yet stylish. **Cons:**
dark lobby; caters to a young crowd; may be too sceney for some.
$ *Rooms from: $399* ✉ *20 W. 29th St., at Broadway, Flatiron District* ☎ *212/679–2222* ⊕ *www.acehotel.com* ⌁ *280 rooms, 8 suites* |○| *No meals* Ⓜ *N, R to 28th St.* ✢ *3:E1.*

$ ⛼ **Carlton Arms.** Europeans and students know about the chipper, win-
HOTEL ning attitude of this friendly, no-frills hotel, where the rooms are painted
by artists on a rotating basis. **Pros:** rock-bottom prices; friendly atti-
tude; quieter residential location. **Cons:** no elevator; many rooms have
shared baths. $ *Rooms from: $120* ✉ *160 E. 25th St., at 3rd Ave., Flat-
iron District* ☎ *212/684–8337, 212/679–0680 for reservations* ⊕ *www. carltonarms.com* ⌁ *54 rooms (20 with private bath)* |○| *No meals* Ⓜ *6 to 23rd St.* ✢ *3:G2.*

$$ ⛼ **The Eventi.** This hotel adds a touch of style just below Penn Station
HOTEL in an area desperately in need of new lodging options. **Pros:** great loca-
FAMILY tion; relaxing spa; nice gym. **Cons:** crowded lobby. $ *Rooms from: $350* ✉ *851 6th Ave., at 30th St., Flatiron District* ☎ *212/564–4567* ⊕ *www.eventihotel.com* ⌁ *239 rooms, 53 suites* |○| *No meals* Ⓜ *N, R to 28th St.* ✢ *3:D1.*

$$ ⛼ **Gansevoort Park Avenue NYC.** A downtown-hip hotel on the edge of
HOTEL lower Midtown, the Gansevoort Park Avenue improves upon its hard-
living Meatpacking District sibling by several degrees. **Pros:** happening
bar and rooftop; location convenient to Union Square; friendly staff.
Cons: if you want peace and quiet, this hotel is not for you. $ *Rooms
from: $445* ✉ *420 Park Ave. S, at 29th St., Flatiron District* ☎ *212/317–
2900* ⊕ *www.gansevoortpark.com* ⌁ *213 rooms, 36 suites* |○| *No meals*
Ⓜ *6 to 28th St.* ✢ *3:F1.*

$$ ⛼ **Hotel Giraffe.** A consistent property with friendly service, large rooms,
HOTEL and lots of repeat customers (particularly business travelers) Hotel
Giraffe pleases with nice extras such as a complimentary nightly wine-
and-cheese reception. **Pros:** rooftop terrace for guests; quiet hotel; nice
extras like free breakfast and coffee all day. **Cons:** street noise near
lower levels. $ *Rooms from: $400* ✉ *365 Park Ave. S, at 26th St.,*

Flatiron District ☎ *212/685–7700, 877/296–0009* ⊕ *www.hotelgiraffe. com* ⇋ *51 rooms, 21 suites* ⍩ *Breakfast* Ⓜ *6 to 28th St.* ✛ *3:F2.*

$$ **HOTEL** **Fodor's Choice** **★**

⬚ **The NoMad Hotel.** Named for the emerging "North of Madison" (that is, Madison Square Park) neighborhood in which it's located, this upscale-bohemian property was one of the most buzzed-about hotel openings of 2012. **Pros:** 24-hour room service; free Wi-Fi; quality, trendy on-site dining and drinking; central location. **Cons:** exposed bathtubs lack privacy. Ⓢ *Rooms from: $445* ✉ *1170 Broadway, at 28th St., Flatiron District* ☎ *212/796–1500* ⊕ *www.thenomadhotel. com* ⇋ *154 rooms, 14 suites* ⍩ *No meals* Ⓜ *N, R to 28th St.* ✛ *3:E2.*

$ **HOTEL**

⬚ **Park South Hotel.** In this beautifully transformed 1906 office building, rooms feel smartly contemporary, though they've retained some period details; request one with a view of the Chrysler Building to avoid overlooking noisy 27th Street and the bar on the ground floor. **Pros:** free breakfast and Internet; turndown service; good value. **Cons:** some noisy rooms; small rooms and bathrooms. Ⓢ *Rooms from: $299* ✉ *124 E. 28th St., between Lexington and Park Aves., Flatiron District* ☎ *212/448–0888, 800/315–4642* ⊕ *www.parksouthhotel.com* ⇋ *128 rooms, 3 suites* ⍩ *Breakfast* Ⓜ *6 to 28th St.* ✛ *3:F2.*

$ **HOTEL**

⬚ **The Paul.** Another stylish addition to an increasingly trendy neighborhood, this 21-floor hotel has comfortable, modern rooms with big warehouse-style windows and some fun touches like bedside dictionaries (why not learn a new word before calling it a day?) and Rolodexes full of neighborhood tips and staff picks. **Pros:** fun, developing neighborhood; fresh, stylish rooms with big windows; rooftop bar. **Cons:** rooms on small side. Ⓢ *Rooms from: $259* ✉ *32 W. 29th St., between Broadway and 6th Ave., Flatiron District* ☎ *212/204–5750* ⊕ *www. thepaulnyc.com* ⇋ *122 rooms, 3 suites* ⍩ *No meals* Ⓜ *1, N, R to 28th St.* ✛ *3:E1.*

$$ **HOTEL**

⬚ **The Roger.** A colorful choice in a rather plain neighborhood, the Roger continues to have a following among repeat visitors to New York, especially since its 2012 redesign. **Pros:** colorful room decor; friendly service; good value. **Cons:** no room service; tiny bathrooms. Ⓢ *Rooms from: $399* ✉ *131 Madison Ave., at 31st St., Flatiron District* ☎ *212/448–7000, 877/847–4444* ⊕ *www.therogernewyork.com* ⇋ *192 rooms, 2 suites* ⍩ *No meals* Ⓜ *6 to 33rd St.* ✛ *3:F1.*

16

GRAMERCY PARK

$$$$ **HOTEL**

⬚ **Gramercy Park Hotel.** Ian Schrager, boutique hotelier extraordinaire, decorated this property with contemporary art by the likes of Andy Warhol and Jean-Michel Basquiat. **Pros:** trendy bar scene; opulent rooms; great restaurant; park-side location. **Cons:** inconsistent service; expensive bar. Ⓢ *Rooms from: $629* ✉ *2 Lexington Ave., at Gramercy Park, Gramercy Park* ☎ *212/920–3300* ⊕ *www.gramercyparkhotel. com* ⇋ *139 rooms, 46 suites* ⍩ *No meals* Ⓜ *6 to 23rd St.* ✛ *3:G3.*

$$$ **HOTEL** **Fodor's Choice** **★**

⬚ **The Inn at Irving Place.** Fantasies of Old New York—Manhattan straight from the pages of Edith Wharton and Henry James, an era of genteel brick town houses and Tiffany lamps—spring to life at this discreet, romantic inn. **Pros:** romantic and charming; big rooms; excellent breakfast and tea service; Mario Batali's Casa Mono is downstairs. **Cons:** rooms show some wear; some street noise. Ⓢ *Rooms* *from: $449* ✉ *56 Irving Pl., between 17th and 18th Sts., Gramercy Park* ☎ *212/533–4600, 800/685–1447* ⊕ *www.innatirving.com* ⤳ *5 rooms, 6 suites* ⍾○⍾ *Breakfast* Ⓜ *4, 5, 6, L, N, Q, R to 14th St.–Union Sq.* ✛ *3:G3.*

$ | ⓣ **Marcel at Gramercy.** The chic, affordable Marcel gives guests both
HOTEL | style and substance in a prime location. **Pros:** outdoor patio has spectacular views of the city; good value. **Cons:** elevators are slow; some rooms are tight on space; decor not to everyone's taste. Ⓢ *Rooms from: $299* ✉ *201 E. 24th St., Gramercy Park* ☎ *212/696–3800* ⊕ *www. themarcelatgramercy.com* ⤳ *136 rooms* ⍾○⍾ *No meals* Ⓜ *6 to 23rd St.* ✛ *3:G2.*

MIDTOWN EAST AND MURRAY HILL

MIDTOWN EAST

$$$ | ⓣ **Andaz 5th Avenue.** The serene and spacious rooms at this chic, modern
HOTEL | property evoke that coveted New York loft feel, with floor-to-ceiling windows that look out over 5th Avenue and the New York Public Library. **Pros:** spacious and stylish; big, luxurious bathrooms; good dining and drinking options; suites have outdoor space. **Cons:** pricey; busy location might not suit all guests. Ⓢ *Rooms from: $525* ✉ *485 5th Ave., at 41st St., Midtown East* ☎ *212/601–1234* ⊕ *newyork.5thavenue. andaz.hyatt.com* ⤳ *148 rooms, 36 suites* ⍾○⍾ *No meals* Ⓜ *4, 5, 6, 7, S to Grand Central–42nd St.* ✛ *4:E5.*

$$ | ⓣ **The Benjamin.** NYC is often called the city that never sleeps, but if
HOTEL | a good night's rest is essential for your visit, the Benjamin may be
FAMILY | your choice accommodation—with a menu of 12 pillows to choose from (including buckwheat, water, and Swedish memory varieties), white-noise machines, and 500-thread-count sheets, they've got it covered. **Pros:** sleep-friendly; great location; gracious staff; kitchenettes in big rooms; pets stay for free. **Cons:** paid Internet and Wi-Fi; boring views; dull neighborhood after dark. Ⓢ *Rooms from: $389* ✉ *125 E. 50th St., at Lexington Ave., Midtown East* ☎ *212/715–2500* ⊕ *www. thebenjamin.com* ⤳ *113 rooms, 96 suites* ⍾○⍾ *No meals* Ⓜ *6 to 51st St.; E, M to Lexington Ave./53rd St.* ✛ *4:F3.*

$$ | ⓣ **FIFTY NYC.** This popular hotel attracts business travelers but it's also
HOTEL | comfortable for families or leisure travelers—especially the studios and
FAMILY | spacious suites, which have full kitchens and a clean, playful design that incorporates oversize chairs and couches. **Pros:** apartment-style living; large rooms; good value; kid- and pet-friendly. **Cons:** pricey Wi-Fi unless you get an online deal; neighborhood can be quiet after dark. Ⓢ *Rooms from: $329* ✉ *155 E. 50th St., at 3rd Ave., Midtown East* ☎ *212/751– 5710, 800/637–8483* ⊕ *www.affinia.com/fifty* ⤳ *251 rooms, 46 suites* ⍾○⍾ *No meals* Ⓜ *6 to 51st St.; E, M to Lexington Ave./53rd St.* ✛ *4:G3.*

$$$$ | ⓣ **Four Seasons Hotel.** For better or worse, the Four Seasons remains the
HOTEL | blueprint for what a Manhattan luxury hotel should be. **Pros:** spacious and comfortable rooms; perfect concierge and staff service; afternoon tea in the lobby lounge. **Cons:** pricey; confusing room controls; some furniture could use updating. Ⓢ *Rooms from: $995* ✉ *57 E. 57th St., between Park and Madison Aves., Midtown East* ☎ *212/758–5700,*

800/487–3769 ⊕ *www.fourseasons.com/newyork* ➷ *293 rooms, 75 suites* ⦿❘ *No meals* Ⓜ *4, 5, 6 to 59th St.; N, Q, R to Lexington Ave./59th St.* ✛ *4:F1.*

$$ 🏨 **The Gotham Hotel.** This sleek hotel has a lot going for it, but a clincher
HOTEL is that every room has outdoor space. **Pros:** welcoming staff; central location; every room has a balcony. **Cons:** no on-site gym. Ⓢ *Rooms from: $350* ⊠ *16 E. 46 St., between 5th and Madison Aves., Midtown East* ☎ *212/490–8500* ⊕ *www.thegothamhotelny.com* ➷ *66 rooms, 10 suites* ⦿❘ *No meals* Ⓜ *B, D, F, M to 47th–50th Sts./Rockefeller Center; 4, 5, 6, 7, S to Grand Central–42nd St.* ✛ *4:E4.*

$ 🏨 **Grand Hyatt New York.** This historic hotel has been transformed
HOTEL into a sleek and modern central hub. **Pros:** comfy beds; light-filled gym on a high floor; refreshing modern design; large, well-planned rooms. **Cons:** no in-room minibar; Wi-Fi not free. Ⓢ *Rooms from: $239* ⊠ *109 E. 42nd St., between Park and Lexington Aves., Midtown East* ☎ *212/883–1234, 800/233–1234* ⊕ *www.grandnewyork.hyatt. com* ➷ *1,306 rooms, 43 suites* ⦿❘ *No meals* Ⓜ *4, 5, 6, 7, S to Grand Central–42nd St.* ✛ *4:F4.*

$$$ 🏨 **Hotel Elysée.** This intimate hotel is a favorite for travelers looking
HOTEL for good value in a desirable Midtown location. **Pros:** complimentary snacks and Wi-Fi; individually decorated rooms; cute library. **Cons:** underwhelming lobby; slightly outdated decor. Ⓢ *Rooms from: $495* ⊠ *60 E. 54th St., between Madison and Park Aves., Midtown East* ☎ *212/753–1066, 800/535–9733* ⊕ *www.elyseehotel.com* ➷ *87 rooms, 16 suites* ⦿❘ *Breakfast* Ⓜ *E, M to 5th Ave./53rd St.* ✛ *4:F2.*

$$$ 🏨 **The Kitano.** As you might guess from the name, the Kitano imports
HOTEL much of its sensibility from Japan, with touches that include a bilingual concierge and a high-concept Japanese restaurant—it also makes for a notably service-oriented stay. **Pros:** extra soundproofing in guest rooms; cute mezzanine bar area; good value; excellent live jazz. **Cons:** lower-floor views are limited; expensive restaurant. Ⓢ *Rooms from: $499* ⊠ *66 Park Ave., at 38th St., Midtown East* ☎ *212/885–7000, 800/548–2666* ⊕ *www.kitano.com* ➷ *149 rooms, 18 suites* ⦿❘ *No meals* Ⓜ *4, 5, 6, 7, S to Grand Central–42nd St.* ✛ *4:F5.*

$$$$ 🏨 **Langham Place, Fifth Avenue.** Setting new standards for luxury, the
HOTEL towering, limestone-clad Langham Place, Fifth Avenue (formerly the Setai Fifth Avenue) was conceived as an opulent crash pad for wealthy overseas tourists, captains of industry on long-term stays, and anyone in need of some serious pampering. **Pros:** attentive service; gorgeous spa; great location; quality dining. **Cons:** street noise reported by guests on lower floors. Ⓢ *Rooms from: $745* ⊠ *400 5th Ave., Midtown East* ☎ *212/695–4005* ⊕ *www.langhamhotels.com* ➷ *157 rooms, 57 suites* ⦿❘ *No meals* Ⓜ *B, D, F, M, N, Q, R to 34th St.–Herald Sq.* ✛ *4:E5.*

$$ 🏨 **Library Hotel Manhattan.** Bookishly handsome, this stately landmark
HOTEL brownstone, built in 1900, is inspired by the nearby New York Public
Fodor'sChoice Library—each of its 10 floors is dedicated to one of the 10 categories
★ of the Dewey Decimal System and is stocked with art and books relevant to subtopics such as erotica, astronomy, or biography—let your interests guide your room choice. **Pros:** fun rooftop bar; playful book themes; stylish rooms. **Cons:** rooftop sometimes reserved for events;

16

more books in rooms themselves would be nice. ⑤ *Rooms from: $399* ✉ *299 Madison Ave., at 41st St., Midtown East* ☎ *212/983–4500, 212/983–4500* ⊕ *www.libraryhotel.com* ⌨ *60 rooms* ❂ *Breakfast* Ⓜ *4, 5, 6, 7, S to Grand Central–42nd St.* ✛ *4:E4.*

$$ ⊞ **Loews Regency Hotel.** This snazzy, spacious Park Avenue hotel has
HOTEL   state-of-the-art technology, a 10,000-square-foot spa, and bright, taste-
fully appointed rooms with notably comfortable beds. **Pros:** friendly
and helpful staff; fresh, recently renovated property; huge spa and fit-
ness center; appealing, buzzy bar and restaurant. **Cons:** on the expen-
sive side. ⑤ *Rooms from: $399* ✉ *540 Park Ave., at 61st St., Midtown
East* ☎ *212/759–4100, 800/233–2356* ⊕ *www.loewshotels.com* ⌨ *321
rooms, 58 suites* ❂ *No meals* Ⓜ *4, 5, 6 to 59th St.; N, Q, R to Lexing-
ton Ave./59th St.* ✛ *5:F6.*

$$$ ⊞ **Marmara Park Avenue.** A popular pick for extended-stay travelers, this
HOTEL   sleek property impresses with large rooms complete with conveniences
of home, like wet bars or fully equipped kitchens. **Pros:** lots of amenities
in rooms; serene lap pool, sauna, and steam room; many suites have
private terraces. **Cons:** neighborhood isn't the most exciting. ⑤ *Rooms
from: $500* ✉ *114 E. 32nd St., Midtown East* ☎ *212/603–9000* ⊕ *park.
marmaranyc.com* ⌨ *128 rooms, 3 suites* ❂ *No meals* Ⓜ *6 to 33rd St.*
✛ *3:F1.*

$$$ ⊞ **New York Palace.** From the moment you enter the gilded gates of these
HOTEL   connected mansions, originally built in the 1880s by railroad baron
Henry Villard, you know you're somewhere special; there's a reason
this is called the Palace. **Pros:** fresh property after extensive renova-
tion; great service; unmatched views of St. Patrick's Cathedral. **Cons:**
high prices; harried staff. ⑤ *Rooms from: $599* ✉ *455 Madison Ave.,
at 50th St., Midtown East* ☎ *212/888–7000, 800/697–2522* ⊕ *www.
newyorkpalace.com* ⌨ *822 rooms, 87 suites* ❂ *No meals* Ⓜ *6 to 51st
St.; E, M to Lexington Ave./53rd St.* ✛ *4:E3.*

$ ⊞ **One UN New York.** In a sky-high tower near the landmark United
HOTEL   Nations building, the One UN New York starts on the 28th floor and
has fabulous views—ask for a room facing west, toward Manhattan's
skyline. **Pros:** unbeatable East River and city views; good value; great
front-door and bell staff. **Cons:** a far walk to the subway; pricey Inter-
net access. ⑤ *Rooms from: $220* ✉ *1 United Nations Plaza, 44th St.
and 1st Ave., Midtown East* ☎ *212/758–1234, 866/866–8086* ⊕ *www.
millenniumhotels.com/usa/oneunnewyork* ⌨ *439 rooms, 34 suites*
❂ *No meals* Ⓜ *4, 5, 6, 7, S to Grand Central–42nd St.* ✛ *4:H4.*

$$$$ ⊞ **The Peninsula.** Stepping through the Peninsula's Beaux Arts facade
HOTEL   onto the grand staircase overhung with a monumental chandelier, you
Fodor's Choice know you're in for a glitzy treat. **Pros:** brilliant service; fabulous rooms
★   with convenient controls; unforgettable rooftop bar. **Cons:** expensive.
⑤ *Rooms from: $1045* ✉ *700 5th Ave., at 55th St., Midtown East*
☎ *212/956–2888, 800/262–9467* ⊕ *www.peninsula.com* ⌨ *185 rooms,
54 suites* ❂ *No meals* Ⓜ *E, M to 5th Ave./53rd St.* ✛ *4:E2.*

$ ⊞ **Pod 51.** If cramped quarters don't bother you, this is one of the best
HOTEL   deals in town. **Pros:** great prices; fun design; buzzy on-site dining and
drinking. **Cons:** not for claustrophobes; some shared baths. ⑤ *Rooms
from: $129* ✉ *230 E. 51st St., between 2nd and 3rd Aves., Midtown*

East ☎ 212/355–0300, 800/742–5945 ⊕ www.thepodhotel.com ⌨ 345 rooms (189 with private bath) ⏀ No meals Ⓜ 6 to 51st St.; E, M to Lexington Ave./53rd St. ✛ 4:G2.

$$ ⌂ **Roger Smith.** This quirky choice is one of the better affordable stays
HOTEL in the city. **Pros:** good location near Grand Central; intimate atmosphere; free Wi-Fi. **Cons:** street noise; small bathrooms. ⑤ Rooms from: $389 ✉ 501 Lexington Ave., between 47th and 48th Sts., Midtown East ☎ 212/755–1400, 800/445–0277 ⊕ www.rogersmith.com ⌨ 102 rooms, 28 suites ⏀ No meals Ⓜ 6 to 51st St.; E, M to Lexington Ave./53rd St. ✛ 4:F3.

$ ⌂ **The Roosevelt Hotel.** Named after Teddy, not Franklin, this Midtown
HOTEL icon just steps from Grand Central has an ornate lobby with cushy couches and an old-school bar detailed in heavy wood that makes the place feel like it's from another time, and it is—the property dates from 1924. **Pros:** great public areas; big bathrooms; comfortable rooftop lounge. **Cons:** dated design; limited in-room amenities. ⑤ Rooms from: $299 ✉ 45 E. 45th St., at Madison Ave., Midtown East ☎ 888/833–3969, 212/661–9600 ⊕ www.theroosevelthotel.com ⌨ 967 rooms, 48 suites ⏀ No meals Ⓜ 4, 5, 6, 7, S to Grand Central–42nd St. ✛ 4:F4.

$ ⌂ **70 Park Avenue.** A Midtown business-traveler favorite, the lobby and
HOTEL rooms here are infused with a bright color palette and modern furniture. **Pros:** complimentary evening wine reception; polite service; simple rooms and hotel layout. **Cons:** small rooms; design and art might not suit all tastes. ⑤ Rooms from: $299 ✉ 70 Park Ave., at 38th St., Midtown East ☎ 212/973–2400, 800/707–2752 ⊕ www.70parkave.com ⌨ 201 rooms, 4 suites ⏀ No meals Ⓜ 4, 5, 6, 7, S to Grand Central–42nd St. ✛ 4:F5.

$$$$ ⌂ **The Sherry-Netherland.** It may come as a surprise to learn that this
HOTEL stately part of the New York landscape is essentially a tall, luxurious apartment building that also has 50 hotel rooms and suites. **Pros:** gorgeous lobby; commanding, impeccable location; Cipriani access. **Cons:** small check-in area; rooms vary in taste and decor; nonsuites are on the small side; interior rooms lack views; guests sometimes feel the cold shoulder from the full-time residents. ⑤ Rooms from: $649 ✉ 781 5th Ave., at 59th St., Midtown East ☎ 212/355–2800, 800/247–4377 ⊕ www.sherrynetherland.com ⌨ 26 rooms, 24 suites ⏀ No meals Ⓜ N, Q, R to 5th Ave./59th St. ✛ 5:E6.

$$$$ ⌂ **The St. Regis.** World-class from head to toe, this 5th Avenue Beaux
HOTEL Arts landmark comes as close to flawless as any hotel in New York, with
Fodor'sChoice tech-savvy rooms, historic touches, and the iconic King Cole Bar. **Pros:**
★ classic NYC favorite; rooms combine true luxury with helpful technology; easy-access butler service; superb in-house dining; prestigious location. **Cons:** expensive; too serious for families seeking fun. ⑤ Rooms from: $995 ✉ 2 E. 55th St., at 5th Ave., Midtown East ☎ 212/753–4500, 877/787–3447 ⊕ www.stregisnewyork.com ⌨ 171 rooms, 67 suites ⏀ No meals Ⓜ E, M to 5th Ave./53rd St. ✛ 4:E2.

$$ ⌂ **W Hotel New York.** A hopping bar and sunken lounge in the reception
HOTEL area, funky decor touches like window boxes filled with grass, and guest

16

rooms that hew to the classic brand formula—they're small but they look good—make this a quintessential W property. **Pros:** central location; great-looking rooms; Bliss Spa in hotel. **Cons:** thin walls; small rooms; inconsistent service. ⑤ *Rooms from: $329* ✉ *541 Lexington Ave., between 49th and 50th Sts., Midtown East* ☎ *212/755–1200, 877/946–8357* ⊕ *www.wnewyork.com* ⬎ *696 rooms, 60 suites* ⑩ *No meals* Ⓜ *6 to 51st St.; E, M to Lexington Ave./53rd St.* ✛ *4:F3.*

$$ ⊡ **Waldorf-Astoria.** The Waldorf is undeniably historic, and while we'd
HOTEL   definitely recommend a cocktail at the classic Bull and Bear Bar downstairs, a night in one of the small standard rooms can feel a bit oppressive (and quite out of date) due to extensive use of floral patterns. **Pros:** historic Art Deco building filled with NYC's aristocratic, gangster, and jazz histories; best Waldorf salad in town; knowledgeable doormen. **Cons:** rooms not up-to-date; more about the name than the experience; in-hotel Starbucks costs twice as much as those around the corner. ⑤ *Rooms from: $399* ✉ *301 Park Ave., between 49th and 50th Sts., Midtown East* ☎ *212/355–3000, 800/925–3673* ⊕ *www. waldorfnewyork.com* ⬎ *1,027 rooms, 208 suites* ⑩ *No meals* Ⓜ *6 to 51st St.; E, M to Lexington Ave./53rd St.* ✛ *4:F3.*

$$ ⊡ **The William.** What was once two connected brownstones home to
HOTEL   a social club for Williams College has now been transformed into a modern, extended-stay hotel. **Pros:** convenient fully equipped kitchens; central location near Grand Central; good eating and drinking options. **Cons:** color and design may be too bright and modern for some guests. ⑤ *Rooms from: $395* ✉ *24 E. 39th St., between Park and Madison Aves., Midtown East* ☎ *646/922–8600* ⊕ *www.thewilliamnyc. com* ⬎ *33 rooms* ⑩ *No meals* Ⓜ *4, 5, 6, 7, S to Grand Central–42nd St.* ✛ *4:F5.*

MURRAY HILL

$$ ⊡ **The Carlton Hotel.** From the two-story lobby designed by David
HOTEL   Rockwell to still-intact, original 1904 Beaux Arts details such as the stained-glass dome (created by workers from the Tiffany glass factory), a 40-foot ceiling in the lobby, and a soaring crystal chandelier, the Carlton is a refurbished gem. **Pros:** spectacular lobby; stylish rooms. **Cons:** expensive bar; small rooms; dimly lit bathrooms. ⑤ *Rooms from: $449* ✉ *88 Madison Ave., between 28th and 29th Sts., Murray Hill* ☎ *212/532–4100, 800/601–8500* ⊕ *www.carltonhotelny.com* ⬎ *294 rooms, 23 suites* ⑩ *No meals* Ⓜ *6 to 28th St.; N, R to 28th St.* ✛ *3:F1.*

$ ⊡ **The Herald Square Hotel.** The sculpted cherubs on the facade and the
HOTEL   vintage magazine covers adorning the common areas hint that the great-value Herald Square Hotel used to be *Life* magazine's headquarters. **Pros:** affordable prices; centrally located. **Cons:** unattractive lobby; readers report inconsistent service. ⑤ *Rooms from: $199* ✉ *19 W. 31st St., between 5th Ave. and Broadway, Murray Hill* ☎ *212/279–4017, 800/727–1888* ⊕ *www.heraldnyc.com* ⬎ *100 rooms* ⑩ *No meals* Ⓜ *B, D, F, M, N, Q, R to 34th St.–Herald Sq.* ✛ *3:E1.*

$ ⊡ **Pod 39.** This cheap and cheerful sibling of the Pod Hotel on 51st
HOTEL   Street has tight quarters and trendy amenities. **Pros:** quality taco and cocktail spot; big rooftop with gorgeous views; lobby lounge with Ping-Pong table. **Cons:** tight quarters; buzzy lobby and restaurant might not

suit all guests. $\boxed{\$}$ *Rooms from: $229 $\boxtimes$ 145 E. 39th St, between Lexington and 3rd Aves., Murray Hill* $\boxtimes$ *212/865–5700* $\oplus$ *www.thepodhotel. com* $\rightleftharpoons$ *366 rooms* $\lvert\bigcirc\rvert$ *No meals* $\boxed{M}$ *4, 5, 6, 7, S to Grand Central–42nd St.* $\oplus$ *4:G5.*

$$$ $\boxed{\text{T}}$ **The Tuscany.** This historic building in Murray Hill was originally
HOTEL   apartments—which explains the generous space—and is now a family-
FAMILY   friendly hotel in a convenient location near Grand Central. **Pros:** very
large rooms for New York; fresh design and furnishings; art installa-
tions featuring local artists. **Cons:** on the expensive side. $\boxed{\$}$ *Rooms from:
$495 $\boxtimes$ 120 E. 39th St., between Park and Lexington Aves., Murray
Hill* $\boxtimes$ *212/686–1600* $\oplus$ *www.stgiles.com* $\rightleftharpoons$ *116 rooms, 8 suites* $\lvert\bigcirc\rvert$ *No
meals* $\boxed{M}$ *4, 5, 6, 7, S to Grand Central–42nd St.* $\oplus$ *4:F5.*

MIDTOWN WEST

$$$ $\boxed{\text{T}}$ **The Algonquin.** One of Manhattan's most historic properties, the
HOTEL   Algonquin is a landmark of literary history—think oak paneling and
pillars in the lobby—but with modernized rooms and contemporary
comforts. **Pros:** free Internet; friendly, knowledgeable staff; central location. **Cons:** some small rooms. $\boxed{\$}$ *Rooms from: $459 $\boxtimes$ 59 W. 44th St.,
between 5th and 6th Aves., Midtown West* $\boxtimes$ *212/840–6800, 800/555–
8000* $\oplus$ *www.algonquinhotel.com* $\rightleftharpoons$ *156 rooms, 25 suites* $\lvert\bigcirc\rvert$ *No meals*
$\boxed{M}$ *7 to 5th Ave.; B, D, F, M to 42nd St.–Bryant Park* $\oplus$ *4:D4.*

$$ $\boxed{\text{T}}$ **Archer Hotel.** Rooftop bar Skyglass, with its killer view of the Empire
HOTEL   State Building, is the star of this quirky new-build property just south
of Bryant Park. **Pros:** rooftop bar; whimsical design and ambience;
reasonably priced for Manhattan. **Cons:** small rooms; lack of amenities
including gym or spa; convenient but unglamorous location. $\boxed{\$}$ *Rooms
from: $379 $\boxtimes$ 45 W. 38th St., Midtown West* $\boxtimes$ *212/719–4100* $\oplus$ *www.
archerhotel.com* $\rightleftharpoons$ *180 rooms* $\lvert\bigcirc\rvert$ *No meals* $\boxed{M}$ *B, D, F, M, 7 to 42nd
St.–Bryant Park* $\oplus$ *4:D5.*

$$$$ $\boxed{\text{T}}$ **Baccarat Hotel & Residences.** This polished property provides pure
HOTEL   luxury at every corner, from the emphasis on quality service to the
glamorous salon and bar filled with fresh flowers where all the drinks
are served in Baccarat glassware. **Pros:** glamorous dining and drinking
options; excellent, prompt room service; serene swimming pool and
hot tub; all rooms are stocked with Baccarat glassware. **Cons:** very
expensive. $\boxed{\$}$ *Rooms from: $1,000 $\boxtimes$ 28 W. 53rd St., Midtown West*
$\boxtimes$ *212/790–8800* $\oplus$ *www.baccarathotels.com* $\rightleftharpoons$ *88 rooms, 26 suites*
$\lvert\bigcirc\rvert$ *No meals* $\boxed{M}$ *E, M to 5th Ave./53rd St.* $\oplus$ *4:D2.*

$$ $\boxed{\text{T}}$ **Belvedere Hotel.** Built during the 1920s, the Belvedere's main draw
HOTEL   is its Times Square/Theater District location; the rooms tend to be
FAMILY   dark with a dull design, although they are spacious and have kitch-
enettes with a microwave, mini-refrigerator, and coffeemaker. **Pros:**
good rates available; renovated rooms are good value. **Cons:** can be
loud with street noise; slow elevators; Wi-Fi free in only some room
categories. $\boxed{\$}$ *Rooms from: $329 $\boxtimes$ 319 W. 48th St., between 8th and
9th Aves., Midtown West* $\boxtimes$ *212/245–7000, 888/468–3558* $\oplus$ *www.
belvederehotelnyc.com* $\rightleftharpoons$ *352 rooms* $\lvert\bigcirc\rvert$ *No meals* $\boxed{M}$ *C, E to 50th St.*
$\oplus$ *4:B3.*

16

$$$
HOTEL
FAMILY

🔲 **The Blakely New York.** It may be a tried-and-true design motif, but it's hard to resist the English gentlemen's club when it's done right. **Pros:** all rooms have kitchenettes; central location; good-size rooms; acclaimed restaurant. **Cons:** rooms facing 54th Street can be noisy; some rooms have little natural light; expensive. $ *Rooms from: $529* ✉ *136 W. 55th St., between 6th and 7th Aves., Midtown West* ☎ *212/245–1800, 800/735–0710* ⊕ *www.blakelynewyork.com* ⤶ *60 rooms, 58 suites* ⚅| *Breakfast* Ⓜ *N, Q, R to 57th St.–7th Ave; F to 57th St.* ✛ *4:C2.*

$$
HOTEL

🔲 **Bryant Park Hotel.** A New York landmark that towers over the New York Public Library and Bryant Park, this sleek hotel is still a Midtown hot spot. **Pros:** gorgeous building; fashionable crowd and setting; across from pretty Bryant Park; free Wi-Fi. **Cons:** expensive; Cellar Bar frequently booked for events. $ *Rooms from: $445* ✉ *40 W. 40th St., between 5th and 6th Aves., Midtown West* ☎ *212/869–0100, 877/640–9300* ⊕ *www.bryantparkhotel.com* ⤶ *112 rooms, 16 suites* ⚅| *No meals* Ⓜ *B, D, F, M to 42nd St.–Bryant Park; 7 to 5th Ave.* ✛ *4:D5.*

$$
HOTEL

🔲 **Casablanca Hotel.** A favorite for the comfortable rooms and great location, the Casablanca evokes the sultry Mediterranean. **Pros:** great access to the Theater District; free continental breakfast and evening wine-and-cheese reception; free Wi-Fi. **Cons:** exercise facilities at nearby New York Sports Club, not on premises; heavy tourist foot traffic. $ *Rooms from: $439* ✉ *147 W. 43rd St., Midtown West* ☎ *212/869–1212* ⊕ *www.casablancahotel.com* ⤶ *39 rooms, 6 suites* ⚅| *Breakfast* Ⓜ *1, 2, 3, 7, N, Q, R, S to Times Sq.–42nd St.* ✛ *4:C4.*

$$$$
HOTEL
Fodor's Choice
★

🔲 **The Chatwal New York.** A lavishly refurbished reincarnation of a classic Manhattan theater club, the Chatwal delivers a stylish, luxury experience with a matching price tag. **Pros:** gorgeous lobby; state-of-the-art room controls and amenities; excellent service; quality dining, bar, and spa. **Cons:** some visitors may find the price too high for the Times Square location. $ *Rooms from: $795* ✉ *130 W. 44th St., between 5th and 6th Aves., Midtown West* ☎ *212/764–6200* ⊕ *www.thechatwalny. com* ⤶ *50 rooms, 26 suites* ⚅| *No meals* Ⓜ *B, D, F, M to 42nd St.–Bryant Park; 1, 2, 3, N, Q, R, S to Times Sq.–42nd St.; 7 to 5th Ave.* ✛ *4:D4.*

$
HOTEL

🔲 **Citizen M.** A stylish property with a refreshing attitude in Midtown, this hotel is all about giving you everything you need and nothing you don't. **Pros:** all-season rooftop bar; cozy lobby full of books and magazines; 20th floor gym with great views. **Cons:** rooms are tight on space. $ *Rooms from: $199* ✉ *218 W. 50th St., Midtown West* ☎ *212/461–3638* ⊕ *www.citizenm.com* ⤶ *230 rooms* ⚅| *No meals* Ⓜ *1, C, E to 50th St.; N, Q, R to 49th St.* ✛ *4:C3.*

$$
HOTEL

🔲 **City Club Hotel.** Oceanliner-inspired rooms at the City Club are brisk, bright, and masculine: they're also about the same size as a room on a cruise ship—that means tight quarters, matey, no matter how much you enjoy sharing space with Jonathan Adler ceramics. **Pros:** free Wi-Fi; great restaurant; personal service. **Cons:** no gym; tiny lobby. $ *Rooms from: $400* ✉ *55 W. 44th St., between 5th and 6th Aves., Midtown West* ☎ *212/921–5500* ⊕ *www.cityclubhotel.com* ⤶ *62 rooms, 3 suites* ⚅| *No meals* Ⓜ *B, D, F, M to 42nd St.–Bryant Park; 7 to 5th Ave.* ✛ *4:D4.*

$$ 🖼 **The Distrikt.** Rising high above Port Authority, the Distrikt tries to
HOTEL approximate the boutique hotel experience in an area of town best
known for its bus depot, and for the most part, it succeeds. **Pros:** central location; friendly staff; good Midtown views from higher floors.
Cons: on a gritty block right across from Port Authority; noisy on
lower floors. ⑤ *Rooms from: $429* ✉ *342 W. 40th St., between 8th
and 9th Aves., Midtown West* ☎ *212/706–6100* ⊕ *www.distrikthotel.
com* 🛏 *155 rooms* ⑩ *No meals* Ⓜ *A, C, E to 42nd St.–Port Authority* ✛ *4:B5.*

$$ 🖼 **DoubleTree Suites by Hilton Hotel New York City–Times Square.** Space is
HOTEL the draw at this 45-story Times Square top dog; every room is a suite,
FAMILY with a separate bedroom and living room (each with a big flat-screen
TV), occupying about 400 square feet overlooking Times Square and
Broadway—an especially desirable location during the New Year's Eve
ball drop. **Pros:** free 24-hour gym and Wi-Fi in public areas; extremely
helpful, informed concierge; convenient to the Theater District; very
quiet considering location. **Cons:** paid Wi-Fi in guest rooms; pricey
for a DoubleTree. ⑤ *Rooms from: $349* ✉ *1568 Broadway, at 47th
St., Midtown West* ☎ *212/719–1600* ⊕ *doubletree3.hilton.com* 🛏 *460
suites* ⑩ *No meals* Ⓜ *B, D, F, M to 42nd St.–Bryant Park; N, Q, R to
49th St.* ✛ *4:C3.*

$$ 🖼 **Dream New York.** Part hotel, part Kafkaesque dream, this Midtown
HOTEL spot specializes in style over comfort but is still quite livable, despite
some over-the-top design features—and noise from the scenesters
headed to the rooftop bar. **Pros:** AVA Lounge penthouse bar; large spa;
up-to-the-minute electronics. **Cons:** small rooms; spotty service; might
be too sceney for some. ⑤ *Rooms from: $345* ✉ *210 W. 55th St., at
Broadway, Midtown West* ☎ *212/247–2000* ⊕ *www.dreamhotels.com/
midtown* 🛏 *204 rooms, 12 suites* ⑩ *No meals* Ⓜ *N, Q, R to 57th St.–
7th Ave.* ✛ *4:C2.*

$ 🖼 **Hilton Times Square.** A glass-and-steel skyscraper atop a
HOTEL 335,000-square-foot retail complex that includes a movie theater and
Madame Tussauds Wax Museum, the Hilton Times Square soars 44 stories above Manhattan and overlooks New York City's famous skyline
and the Hudson River. **Pros:** great location for Times Square entertainment; convenient to public transportation; big rooms. **Cons:** impersonal
feel; nickel-and-dime charges and overpriced food and drink, especially
breakfast. ⑤ *Rooms from: $299* ✉ *234 W. 42nd St., between 7th and
8th Aves., Midtown West* ☎ *212/840–8222, 800/445–8667* ⊕ *www.
hilton.com* 🛏 *460 rooms, 2 suites* ⑩ *No meals* Ⓜ *1, 2, 3, 7, N, Q, R,
S to Times Sq.–42nd St.; A, C, E to 42nd St.–Port Authority* ✛ *4:C4.*

$$ 🖼 **Hotel Metro.** With mirrored columns and elegant black and white
HOTEL photos in the lobby, the Hotel Metro feels distinctively retro. **Pros:**
complimentary coffee and tea 24/7; renovated exercise room has flat-screen TVs; free Wi-Fi in rooms. **Cons:** noise seeps in from outside;
rooms are tasteful but spartan. ⑤ *Rooms from: $309* ✉ *45 W. 35th St.,
between 5th and 6th Aves., Midtown West* ☎ *212/947–2500* ⊕ *www.
hotelmetronyc.com* 🛏 *162 rooms, 20 suites* ⑩ *Breakfast* Ⓜ *B, D, F, M,
N, Q, R to 34th St.–Herald Sq.* ✛ *4:D6.*

16

$$ 🏨 **Hudson New York Hotel.** Budget fashionistas are drawn to the this
HOTEL   affordable hotel. **Pros:** fabulous, elegant bar; gorgeous Francesco Clem-
ente fresco in lobby; breathtaking Sky Terrace. **Cons:** staff can be conde-
scending; tiny rooms; overpriced cocktails. $ *Rooms from: $339* ✉ *356
W. 58th St., between 8th and 9th Aves., Midtown West* ☎ *212/554–
6000* ⊕ *www.hudsonhotel.com* ⏎ *878 rooms, 67 suites* ❍| *No meals*
Ⓜ *1, A, B, C, D to 59th St.–Columbus Circle* ⊕ *4:B1.*

$ 🏨 **Hyatt Herald Square New York.** Business travelers, tourists, and families
HOTEL   alike appreciate this fresh property a stone's throw from Penn Station
with a scenic rooftop bar featuring Empire State Building views. **Pros:**
fresh, stylish rooms with coffeemakers; friendly and efficient service;
location in the thick of it. **Cons:** small workout room; location can be
noisy. $ *Rooms from: $219* ✉ *30 W. 31st St., between 5th Ave. and
Broadway, Midtown West* ☎ *212/330–1234* ⊕ *heraldsquare.hyatt.com/
en/hotel/home.html* ⏎ *121 rooms, 1 suite* ❍| *No meals* Ⓜ *B, D, F, M,
N, Q, R to 34th St.–Herald Sq.* ⊕ *3:E1.*

$ 🏨 **Ink48.** If you want to be near Midtown but a bit removed from the
HOTEL   hustle and bustle, this Kimpton hotel is a great option. **Pros:** friendly
FAMILY staff; great views; large rooms; beautiful rooftop. **Cons:** out-of-the-way
location; lobby can feel overly quiet; street noise in lower-floor rooms.
$ *Rooms from: $299* ✉ *653 11th Ave., at 48th St., Midtown West*
☎ *212/757–0088* ⊕ *www.ink48.com* ⏎ *194 rooms, 24 suites* ❍| *No
meals* Ⓜ *C, E to 50th St.* ⊕ *4:A3.*

$$$ 🏨 **InterContinental New York Times Square.** A central location mere blocks
HOTEL   from the heart of Broadway, Times Square, and restaurant-rich Hell's
Kitchen makes the InterContinental a conveniently located draw. **Pros:**
central for transportation and entertainment; in-house restaurant
helmed by celebrity chef; attentive staff. **Cons:** fee for Internet. $ *Rooms
from: $459* ✉ *300 W. 44th St., between 8th and 9th Aves., Midtown
West* ☎ *877/331–5888,* ⊕ *www.interconny.com* ⏎ *578 rooms, 4 suites,
25 studios* ❍| *No meals* Ⓜ *A, C, E to 42nd St.–Port Authority* ⊕ *4:B4.*

$$$ 🏨 **JW Marriott Essex House.** With Central Park views and an Art Deco
HOTEL   masterpiece of a lobby, the JW Marriott Essex House is a comfortable
Midtown hotel full of character. **Pros:** great service; amazing views;
impressive restaurant. **Cons:** overly complex room gadgetry; expen-
sive bar. $ *Rooms from: $499* ✉ *160 Central Park S, between 6th and
7th Aves., Midtown West* ☎ *212/247–0300, 800/937–8461* ⊕ *www.
marriott.com* ⏎ *511 rooms, 117 suites* ❍| *No meals* Ⓜ *N, Q, R to 57th
St.–7th Ave.; F to 57th St.* ⊕ *4:C1.*

$$$ 🏨 **The Knickerbocker.** An oasis of elegant, urban sophistication in the
HOTEL   heart of Times Square, the Knickerbocker is a soothing counterpoint
to the mass of people, lights, and excitement that converge at the crossroads of Broadway and 42nd Street. **Pros:** in Times Square but aestheti-
cally apart from it; spacious gym; fabulous rooftop bar. **Cons:** nearby
dining isn't that exciting; small lobby. $ *Rooms from: $489* ✉ *6 Times
Sq., entrance on 42nd St., east of Broadway, Midtown West* ☎ *212/204–
4980* ⊕ *www.theknickerbocker.com* ⏎ *299 rooms, 31 suites* ❍| *No
meals* Ⓜ *1, 2, 3, 7, N, Q, R, S to Times Sq.–42nd St.* ⊕ *4:C4.*

$ 🏨 **La Quinta Inn Manhattan.** Smack in the middle of Koreatown and
HOTEL   close to Penn Station, this budget-friendly hotel in a cheerful old Beaux

Arts building may be one of the best deals in town. **Pros:** self-check-in machines; gift shop on the premises for necessities; relaxed rooftop bar; complimentary continental breakfast. **Cons:** no room service; no frills. ⑤ *Rooms from: $180* ✉ *17 W. 32nd St., between 5th Ave. and Broadway, Midtown West* ☎ *212/736–1600* ⊕ *www.laquintamanhattanny.com* ⇄ *182 rooms* ⑩ *Breakfast* Ⓜ *B, D, F, M, N, Q, R to 34th St.–Herald Sq.* ✛ *4:E6.*

$$ ⑪ **Le Parker Meridien.** Combining the comforts of a dependable large
HOTEL hotel with whimsical elements, this hotel keeps visitors coming back
FAMILY with its iconic patty-palace Burger Joint, which serves one of the city's best no-frills burgers from behind a velvet curtain. **Pros:** lively, animated vibe; best hotel gym in the city; fun dining; tech-friendly rooms. **Cons:** lobby is a public space and gets crowded at peak times; small bathrooms. ⑤ *Rooms from: $425* ✉ *119 W. 56th St., between 6th and 7th Aves., Midtown West* ☎ *212/245–5000, 800/543–4300* ⊕ *www.parkermeridien.com* ⇄ *513 rooms, 216 suites* ⑩ *No meals* Ⓜ *N, Q, R to 57th St.–7th Ave.; F to 57th St.* ✛ *4:D1.*

$$$ ⑪ **The London NYC.** Stylish and sophisticated, the London NYC merges
HOTEL the flair of both its namesake cities in spacious, tech-savvy suites that
Fodor'sChoice are some of the largest in New York, starting at 500 square feet. **Pros:**
★ posh atmosphere without prissiness; great fitness club; generous rooms; free Wi-Fi. **Cons:** no bathtubs in most rooms; expensive dining options. ⑤ *Rooms from: $599* ✉ *151 W. 54th St., between 6th and 7th Aves., Midtown West* ☎ *866/690–2029, 212/307–5000* ⊕ *www.thelondonnyc.com* ⇄ *562 suites* ⑩ *No meals* Ⓜ *B, D, E to 7th Ave.; N, Q, R to 57th St.–7th Ave.* ✛ *4:C2.*

$$$$ ⑪ **Mandarin Oriental.** The Mandarin's commitment to excess is evident
HOTEL in the lobby, on the 35th floor of the Time Warner Center, where dra-
Fodor'sChoice matic floor-to-ceiling windows look out over Columbus Circle and
★ Central Park. **Pros:** fantastic views from rooms, lounges, and pool; all the resources of the Time Warner Center; expansive suites; gorgeous, upscale restaurant with more amazing views. **Cons:** Trump hotel blocks some park views; expensive; mall-like surroundings. ⑤ *Rooms from: $895* ✉ *80 Columbus Circle, at 60th St., Midtown West* ☎ *212/805–8800* ⊕ *www.mandarinoriental.com/newyork* ⇄ *198 rooms, 46 suites* ⑩ *No meals* Ⓜ *1, A, B, C, D to 59th St.–Columbus Circle* ✛ *4:B1; 5:C6.*

$$ ⑪ **The Mansfield.** They sweat the small stuff at the Mansfield: Wi-Fi
HOTEL is free, bathroom products are from Aveda, and even the key cards are snazzily embossed with scenes of old-timey New York. **Pros:** free Wi-Fi; business center; 24-hour gym; great bar. **Cons:** small rooms and bathrooms; air-conditioners are window units. ⑤ *Rooms from: $319* ✉ *12 W. 44th St., between 5th and 6th Aves., Midtown West* ☎ *212/277–8700, 800/255–5167* ⊕ *www.mansfieldhotel.com* ⇄ *99 rooms, 27 suites* ⑩ *No meals* Ⓜ *B, D, F, M to 42nd St.–Bryant Park; 7 to 5th Ave.* ✛ *4:E4.*

$$ ⑪ **The Michelangelo.** Italophiles feel like they've been transported to
HOTEL the good life in the Mediterranean at this deluxe hotel, where the long, wide lobby lounge is clad with multihue marble and Veronese-style oil paintings. **Pros:** good location; spacious rooms. **Cons:** noisy

16

air-conditioning units; some rooms have limited views; small closets; in-room fixtures need some updating. $ *Rooms from: $399* ✉ *152 W. 51st St., at 7th Ave., Midtown West* ☎ *212/765–1900, 800/237–0990* ⊕ *www.michelangelohotel.com* ⤳ *123 rooms, 56 suites* ⦿No meals Ⓜ *B, D, E to 7th Ave.; 1 to 50th St.* ✛ *4:C3.*

$$ 🛏 **Muse Hotel.** Surrealist prints and busts of Thalia, the muse of comedy, adorn the lobby of this polished Kimpton property, a good pick for guests looking for a Midtown boutique-hotel experience. **Pros:** contemporary interiors; good Midtown location; pet-friendly; complimentary morning coffee and tea. **Cons:** street noise; small gym. $ *Rooms from: $389* ✉ *130 W. 46th St., between 6th and 7th Aves., Midtown West* ☎ *212/485–2400, 877/692–6873* ⊕ *www.themusehotel.com* ⤳ *181 rooms, 19 suites* ⦿No meals Ⓜ *B, D, F, M to 47th–50th Sts./Rockefeller Center* ✛ *4:C4.*

HOTEL

$$$ 🛏 **1 Hotel Central Park.** A commitment to next-level eco-friendly policies is evident in the smallest details at this hotel, from in-room chalkboards (instead of notepads) to triple-filtered water straight from the taps that eliminates the need for bottled water. **Pros:** committed to green policies; each room has a living wall at the entrance; cozy window seats with great city views; surprisingly quiet. **Cons:** some service inconsistencies. $ *Rooms from: $499* ✉ *1414 Avenue of the Americas, Midtown West* ☎ *212/703–2001* ⊕ *1hotels.com/central-park* ⤳ *206 rooms, 23 suites* ⦿No meals Ⓜ *F to 57th St; N, Q, R to 5th Ave./59th St.* ✛ *4:D1.*

HOTEL

$$ 🛏 **The OUT Hotel.** Billed as a straight-friendly "urban resort" in one of New York's most happening gay neighborhoods, the OUT is the incarnation of all things hip and modern. **Pros:** centrally located; affordable; friendly staff. **Cons:** can be noisy at night. $ *Rooms from: $359* ✉ *510 W. 42nd St., between 10th and 11th Aves., Midtown West* ☎ *212/947–2999* ⊕ *www.theoutnyc.com* ⤳ *87 rooms, 10 suites, 8 quads* ⦿No meals Ⓜ *A, C, E to 42nd St.–Port Authority* ✛ *4:A4.*

HOTEL
Fodor'sChoice
★

$$$$ 🛏 **Park Hyatt New York.** Occupying the first 25 floors of a towering Midtown skyscraper, this hotly anticipated luxury property is the new flagship of the global Park Hyatt brand. **Pros:** large guest rooms; luxurious furnishings; stunning decor and art collection. **Cons:** disappointing views from guest rooms; street noise is audible on lower floors; expensive. $ *Rooms from: $795* ✉ *153 W. 57th St., between 6th and 7th Aves., Midtown West* ☎ *646/774–1234* ⊕ *www.newyork.park.hyatt.com* ⤳ *115 rooms, 95 suites* ⦿No meals Ⓜ *N, Q, R to 57th St.–7th Ave.* ✛ *4:C1.*

HOTEL
Fodor'sChoice
★

$$$$ 🛏 **The Plaza.** Eloise's adopted home on the corner of Central Park, the Plaza is one of New York's most storied hotels, hosting all manner of dignitaries, moneymakers, and royalty. **Pros:** historic property; lavish rooms. **Cons:** rooms aren't that big for the money. $ *Rooms from: $895* ✉ *768 5th Ave., at Central Park, Midtown West* ☎ *212/759–3000* ⊕ *www.theplazany.com* ⤳ *180 rooms, 102 suites* ⦿No meals Ⓜ *N, Q, R to 5th Ave./59th St.* ✛ *4:E1.*

HOTEL
Fodor'sChoice
★

$$$ 🛏 **The Quin.** This luxury hotel just south of Central Park once housed artists like Marc Chagall and Georgia O'Keeffe. **Pros:** bright fitness center; spacious rooms; close to neighborhood destinations like Carnegie Hall. **Cons:** 57th Street location might be too chaotic for some.

HOTEL

⑤ *Rooms from: $599* ⊠ *101 W. 57th St., at 6th Ave., Midtown West* ☎ *212/245–7846* ⊕ *www.thequinhotel.com* ⤣ *208 rooms, 28 suites* ⊙| *No meals* Ⓜ *N, Q, R to 57th St.–7th Ave.; F to 57th St.* ✛ *4:D1.*

$$$
HOTEL
Fodor's Choice
★

⊡ **Refinery Hotel.** Set in a former hat factory, this hotel has a gorgeous year-round rooftop, impressively spacious rooms, and several buzzing bars and restaurants. **Pros:** lots of character and lovely, detailed design; rooftop lounge with great views; excellent bars and restaurant. **Cons:** limited dining and nightlife options nearby. ⑤ *Rooms from: $599* ⊠ *63 W. 38th St., between 5th and 6th Aves., Midtown West* ☎ *646/664–0310* ⊕ *www.refineryhotelnewyork.com* ⤣ *197 rooms* ⊙| *No meals* Ⓜ *B, D, F, M to 42nd St.–Bryant Park; 7 to 5th Ave.* ✛ *4:D5.*

$$$
HOTEL

⊡ **Renaissance Hotel.** After a shift from all-business to a more design-centric approach, the Renaissance is enjoying a renaissance of its own. **Pros:** contemporary design; latest in-room technology. **Cons:** rooms can be a bit noisy. ⑤ *Rooms from: $539* ⊠ *714 7th Ave., between 47th and 48th Sts., Midtown West* ☎ *212/765–7676, 800/628–5222* ⊕ *www.renaissancehotels.com* ⤣ *305 rooms, 5 suites* ⊙| *No meals* Ⓜ *N, Q, R to 49th St.; 1 to 50th St.; B, D, F, M to 47th–50th Sts./Rockefeller Center* ✛ *4:C3.*

$$$$
HOTEL
FAMILY
Fodor's Choice
★

⊡ **The Ritz-Carlton New York, Central Park.** It's all about the park views here, though the above-and-beyond service, accommodating to a fault, makes this renowned property popular with celebs and other demanding guests. **Pros:** great concierge; personalized service; stellar location; park views. **Cons:** pricey; limited common areas. ⑤ *Rooms from: $895* ⊠ *50 Central Park S, at 6th Ave., Midtown West* ☎ *212/308–9100, 866/671–6008* ⊕ *www.ritzcarlton.com* ⤣ *259 rooms, 47 suites* ⊙| *No meals* Ⓜ *F to 57th St.; N, Q, R to 5th Ave./59th St.* ✛ *4:D1.*

16

$$
HOTEL
FAMILY

⊡ **Room Mate Grace.** A favorite of European visitors and business travelers who work in fashion and entertainment, Grace delivers high-design lodgings on a budget. **Pros:** cool swimming pool lounge; friendly, helpful staff. **Cons:** small rooms; little in-room privacy (no door separating shower from main room). ⑤ *Rooms from: $319* ⊠ *125 W. 45th St., Midtown West* ☎ *212/354–2323* ⊕ *www.room-matehotels.com* ⤣ *139 rooms* ⊙| *No meals* Ⓜ *B, D, F, M to 47th–50th Sts./Rockefeller Center* ✛ *4:D4.*

$$
HOTEL

⊡ **The Royalton.** Back in the 1990s, the Royalton's lobby bar was one of the prime meeting spots for local A-listers, and a redesign has attracted a new generation of movers and shakers—be prepared to run the gauntlet of the buzzing lounge before reaching your room—but the helpful staff have ensured a smooth transition. **Pros:** hip lobby scene; luxurious beds and bathrooms; helpful service. **Cons:** dark hallways; lighting verges on eye-strainingly dim. ⑤ *Rooms from: $399* ⊠ *44 W. 44th St., between 5th and 6th Aves., Midtown West* ☎ *212/869–4400, 800/697–1791* ⊕ *www.royaltonhotel.com* ⤣ *141 rooms, 27 suites* ⊙| *No meals* Ⓜ *B, D, F, M to 42nd St.–Bryant Park; 7 to 5th Ave.* ✛ *4:D4.*

$
HOTEL

⊡ **The Shoreham.** In a neighborhood packed with generic hotels, the Shoreham sports a welcome dose of style, along with proximity to Midtown's attractions. **Pros:** tech-friendly rooms; pet-friendly attitude; stylish decor. **Cons:** not designed for families; limited space. ⑤ *Rooms from: $259* ⊠ *33 W. 55th St., between 5th and 6th Aves., Midtown West*

☎ *212/247–6700, 877/847–4444* ⊕ *www.shorehamhotel.com* ⟿ *177 rooms, 42 suites* ⦿| *No meals* Ⓜ *E, M to 5th Ave./53rd St.; F to 57th St.* ✛ *4:D2.*

$$ 🏨 **6 Columbus.** This boutique-style hotel in the shadow of the towering
HOTEL Time Warner Center has the vibe and amenities of downtown lodging
with a convenient Midtown location. **Pros:** convenient location; fun in-
hotel restaurant; reasonably priced for neighborhood; family-friendly.
Cons: rooms on lower floors facing 58th Street can be noisy. Ⓢ *Rooms
from: $399* ⊠ *6 Columbus Circle, 58th St. between 8th and 9th Aves.,
Midtown West* ☎ *877/626–5862* ⊕ *www.sixtyhotels.com/6columbus*
⟿ *88 rooms, 10 suites* ⦿| *No meals* Ⓜ *1, A, B, C, D to 59th St.–Colum-
bus Circle* ✛ *4:B1.*

$$ 🏨 **Sofitel New York.** With bilingual signage throughout the hotel, plenty
HOTEL of velvet in the lobby, and European modern design in the rooms—
think blond wood and fresh flowers—the Sofitel brings a Gallic flair to
Midtown West. **Pros:** central location; great beds; some suites with terraces and views. **Cons:** room views vary. Ⓢ *Rooms from: $350* ⊠ *45 W.
44th St., between 5th and 6th Aves., Midtown West* ☎ *212/354–8844*
⊕ *www.sofitel.com* ⟿ *346 rooms, 52 suites* ⦿| *No meals* Ⓜ *B, D, F, M
to 42nd St.–Bryant Park; 7 to 5th Ave.* ✛ *4:E4.*

$$ 🏨 **The Time Hotel.** One of the neighborhood's first boutique hotels, this
HOTEL spot half a block from the din of Times Square is a recently refreshed
and contemporary retreat. **Pros:** acclaimed and popular Serafina res-
taurant downstairs; surprisingly quiet for Times Square location; good
turndown service. **Cons:** service is inconsistent. Ⓢ *Rooms from: $349*
⊠ *224 W. 49th St., between Broadway and 8th Ave., Midtown West*
☎ *212/246–5252, 877/846–3692* ⊕ *www.thetimeny.com* ⟿ *167 rooms,
26 suites* ⦿| *No meals* Ⓜ *1, C, E to 50th St.; N, Q, R to 49th St.* ✛ *4:C3.*

$$$ 🏨 **Viceroy New York.** Handsome and finely tailored, this hotel has func-
HOTEL tional, tech-focused rooms and lots of amenities. **Pros:** comfortable,
quiet library with "cartender" mixing drinks in late afternoon; generous rooftop space with views of Central Park; appealing restaurant.
Cons: small, crowded lobby; busy 57th Street location might not suit
all guests. Ⓢ *Rooms from: $559* ⊠ *120 W. 57th St., Midtown West*
☎ *212/830–8000* ⊕ *www.viceroyhotelsandresorts.com/newyork* ⟿ *197
rooms, 43 suites* ⦿| *No meals* Ⓜ *N, Q, R to 57th St.–7th Ave.; F to
57th St.* ✛ *4:D1.*

$$ 🏨 **W Times Square.** Although it opened back in 2001, the W Times
HOTEL Square still stands out in the craziness of Times Square, thanks to its
iconic, 57-story exterior—if you want to be in the thick of the action,
this is a fun place to stay. **Pros:** bustling nightlife and happy-hour
scene; sleek rooms. **Cons:** if you want quiet, head elsewhere; no bath-
tubs in the smaller rooms. Ⓢ *Rooms from: $379* ⊠ *1567 Broadway,
at 47th St., Midtown West* ☎ *212/930–7400, 877/946–8357* ⊕ *www.
wnewyorktimessquare.com* ⟿ *466 rooms, 43 suites* ⦿| *No meals* Ⓜ *N,
Q, R to 49th St.* ✛ *4:C3.*

$$ 🏨 **Warwick.** This grande dame was built by William Randolph Hearst
HOTEL in 1926 for his mistress, Hollywood actress Marion Davies, and it's
hosted many from Tinseltown since then, including Cary Grant in
the Presidential Suite for 12 years. **Pros:** excellent restaurant and bar;

historic property; spacious suites. **Cons:** some rooms could use a refresh; no a/c in the hallways. ⑤ *Rooms from: $399* ✉ *65 W. 54th St., at 6th Ave., Midtown West* ☎ *212/247–2700, 800/223–4099* ⊕ *www.warwickhotels.com/new-york* ↳ *359 rooms, 67 suites* ⦿ *No meals* Ⓜ *F to 57th St.; B, D, E to 7th Ave.* ✛ *4:D2.*

$ ⚐ **Wellington Hotel.** A few blocks south of Central Park and Columbus
HOTEL Circle, the Wellington is a good base for visitors who want to see the
FAMILY sights in Midtown and the Upper West Side. **Pros:** central location; chipper, helpful staff; good for big families. **Cons:** dark, often small bathrooms; limited breakfast options. ⑤ *Rooms from: $275* ✉ *871 7th Ave., at 55th St., Midtown West* ☎ *212/247–3900, 800/652–1212* ⊕ *www.wellingtonhotel.com* ↳ *515 rooms, 85 suites* ⦿ *No meals* Ⓜ *N, Q, R to 57th Ave.–7th Ave.* ✛ *4:C2.*

$ ⚐ **Westin New York at Times Square.** This giant Midtown hotel has all the
HOTEL amenities and service you expect from a reliable brand, at fairly reasonable prices. **Pros:** central for Midtown attractions; big rooms; great gym. **Cons:** congested area near Port Authority; not the best location for prime dining and nightlife. ⑤ *Rooms from: $299* ✉ *270 W. 43rd St., at 8th Ave., Midtown West* ☎ *212/201–2700, 866/837–4183* ⊕ *www.westinny.com* ↳ *873 rooms* ⦿ *No meals* Ⓜ *A, C, E to 42nd St.–Port Authority* ✛ *4:B4.*

$ ⚐ **Yotel.** Look beyond the gimmicks (a luggage-storing robot, the futur-
HOTEL istic white design scheme) and discover one of New York's best-run, most functional lodgings. **Pros:** great value; large common outdoor space; access to West Side piers and Javits Center. **Cons:** rooms may be small for some; limited luggage storage and hanging space; 10th Avenue is a bit remote. ⑤ *Rooms from: $149* ✉ *570 10th Ave., at 42nd St., Midtown West* ☎ *646/449–7700* ⊕ *www.yotelnewyork.com* ↳ *647 rooms, 22 suites* ⦿ *Breakfast* Ⓜ *A, C, E to 42nd St.–Port Authority* ✛ *4:A4.*

UPPER EAST SIDE

$$$$ ⚐ **The Carlyle, A Rosewood Hotel.** On the well-heeled corner of Madison
HOTEL Avenue and 76th Street, the Carlyle's fusion of venerable elegance and
Fodor's Choice Manhattan swank calls for the aplomb of entering a Chanel boutique:
★ walk in chin high, wallet out, and ready to impress (and be impressed).
Pros: perhaps NYC's best Central Park views; refined service; delightful array of dining and bar options; chic shopping in the neighborhood; great bathtubs. **Cons:** removed from touristy Manhattan; stuffy vibe may not work for families; every room is different, limiting consistency. ⑤ *Rooms from: $800* ✉ *35 E. 76th St., between Madison and Park Aves., Upper East Side* ☎ *212/744–1600* ⊕ *www.thecarlyle.com* ↳ *121 rooms, 73 suites* ⦿ *No meals* Ⓜ *6 to 77th St.* ✛ *5:F3.*

$ ⚐ **The Franklin.** The best luxury boutique hotel north of 57th Street,
HOTEL this nine-story town house is a gem in a decidedly residential neighborhood. **Pros:** neighborhood-y location; free Wi-Fi and generous breakfast; pet-friendly. **Cons:** far from many tourist sights except Museum Mile; small rooms. ⑤ *Rooms from: $279* ✉ *164 E. 87th St., between Lexington and 3rd Aves., Upper East Side* ☎ *212/369–1000, 800/607–4009* ⊕ *www.franklinhotel.com* ↳ *50 rooms* ⦿ *Breakfast* Ⓜ *4, 5, 6 to 86th St.* ✛ *6:G6.*

16

$$$$ ⊞ **Hôtel Plaza Athénée.** Positioned unobtrusively by Central Park on the
HOTEL   Upper East Side, the Plaza Athénée (now related in name only to its
Parisian cousin) makes stellar service a priority, with a personal sit-
down check-in off to the side of the lobby, and extravagant in-room
dining service with an old-world feel: white tablecloths, candles, and
flowers are part of the deal. **Pros:** discerning service; fabulous hotel bar.
Cons: lobby can feel dark; Wi-Fi costs extra; expensive. Ⓢ *Rooms from:*
$695 ⊠ *37 E. 64th St., at Madison Ave., Upper East Side* ☎ *212/734–*
9100, 212/606–4600 ⊕ *www.plaza-athenee.com* ⇲ *117 rooms, 25*
suites ⦿*No meals* Ⓜ *6 to 68th St.–Hunter College; F to Lexington*
Ave./63rd St. ✛ *5:F5.*

$$ ⊞ **Hotel Wales.** A favorite for in-the-know travelers, the Wales is a pleas-
HOTEL   ant if unassuming hotel in a sedate neighborhood. **Pros:** on-site fitness
FAMILY   facilities; great neighborhood feel; roof garden. **Cons:** standard rooms
are tight on space; if seeking nightlife go elsewhere. Ⓢ *Rooms from:*
$395 ⊠ *1295 Madison Ave., between 92nd and 93rd Sts., Upper East*
Side ☎ *212/876–6000* ⊕ *www.hotelwalesnyc.com* ⇲ *46 rooms, 43*
suites ⦿*No meals* Ⓜ *6 to 96th St.* ✛ *6:F5.*

$$$$ ⊞ **The Lowell.** Steps from Madison Avenue shopping and the Museum
HOTEL   Mile, this old-money refuge on a leafy residential block was built as an
upscale apartment hotel in the 1920s and still delivers genteel sophistica-
tion and pampering service in an unbeatable location. **Pros:** great loca-
tion; service with a personal touch; charming decor; some suites with
wood-burning fireplaces. **Cons:** cramped lobby; expensive. Ⓢ *Rooms*
from: $800 ⊠ *28 E. 63rd St., between Madison and Park Aves., Upper*
East Side ☎ *212/838–1400, 800/221–4444* ⊕ *www.lowellhotel.com*
⇲ *27 rooms, 47 suites* ⦿*No meals* Ⓜ *N, Q, R to 5th Ave./59th St.; F*
to Lexington Ave./63rd St. ✛ *5:F6.*

$$$$ ⊞ **The Mark.** The Mark is the perfect combo of uptown panache and
HOTEL   downtown chic. **Pros:** hip design; cavernous closet space; great service;
Fodor's Choice   scene-making restaurant and bar. **Cons:** expensive; limited budget-din-
★   ing options in neighborhood. Ⓢ *Rooms from: $725* ⊠ *25 E. 77th St., at*
Madison Ave., Upper East Side ☎ *212/744–4300* ⊕ *www.themarkhotel.*
com ⇲ *106 rooms, 51 suites* ⦿*No meals* Ⓜ *6 to 77th St.* ✛ *5:F2.*

UPPER WEST SIDE

$$$ ⊞ **The Empire Hotel.** In a prime Upper West Side spot, the sophisticated
HOTEL   Empire Hotel attracts locals for views from the rooftop pool and lounge
area underneath the hotel's iconic red neon sign, while guests appreciate
the rooms, which are a comfortable and chic escape from the bustle of
the city. **Pros:** great location next to Lincoln Center and blocks from
Central Park; beautiful rooftop pool and bar; nice turndown service.
Cons: rooftop bar brings foot traffic through hotel lobby, plus noise
to some rooms; some rooms could use a refresh; bathrooms are nicely
designed but tiny; pool is quite small. Ⓢ *Rooms from: $499* ⊠ *44 W.*
63rd St., at Columbus Ave., Upper West Side ☎ *212/265–7400* ⊕ *www.*
empirehotelnyc.com ⇲ *376 rooms, 50 suites* ⦿*No meals* Ⓜ *1, A, B,*
C, D to 59th St.–Columbus Circle ✛ *5:C5.*

$ ⊞ **The Excelsior Hotel.** Directly across the street from the Ameri-
HOTEL   can Museum of Natural History, this well-kept, old-school spot is

Lodging Alternatives

CLOSE UP

APARTMENT RENTALS VS. SUITE HOTELS

For your trip to New York, you may want a little more space than the city's typically tiny hotel rooms provide. Some travelers consider apartment rentals, but there are many good reasons to stick to hotel suites instead. Why? First, apartment rentals of less than 30 days—with some very limited exceptions—are illegal in New York City, though Airbnb's attempts to change the New York State housing laws continue. Furthermore, apartment-rental scams are an issue. In some published reports, potential guests have arrived to find that the apartment they rented does not exist, or that they are paying for an illegal sublet. In some cases, travelers have lost their deposit or their prepaid rent (note: never wire money to an account).

Suite hotels and bed-and-breakfasts with apartmentlike accommodations are always a good option, but if you want a short-term apartment rental, consider one of the legal providers, and be sure to read reviews of individual apartments for firsthand feedback from fellow travelers.

Abode Limited. ☎ 800/835-8880, 212/472-2000 ⊕ www.abodenyc.com.

Suite hotels like the **Conrad New York**, the **DoubleTree Suites by Hilton Hotel New York City-Times Square**, and **The London NYC**—all in Manhattan—as well as the **Box House Hotel**, in Brooklyn, are definitely on the spacious side. **The Affinia** hotel group (⊕ www.Affinia.com), which includes the **FIFTY NYC**, has many suites as well. **Milburn Hotel** (⊕ www.milburnhotel.com) and the **Salisbury Hotel** (⊕ www.nycsalisbury.com) are some of the more popular independent budget options.

BED-AND-BREAKFASTS

B&Bs booked through a service may be either hosted (you're the guest in someone's quarters) or unhosted (you have full use of someone's vacated apartment, including kitchen privileges). Reservation services:

Bed and Breakfast Network of New York. ✉ 134 W. 32nd St., Suite 602, between 6th and 7th Aves., New York ☎ 212/645-8134, 888/707-4626 ⊕ www.bedandbreakfastnetwork.com.

City Lights Bed and Breakfast. ☎ 212/737-7049 ⊕ www.citylightsbedandbreakfast.com.

16

comfortable but has occasionally inconsistent staff. **Pros:** excellent neighborhood-y Upper West Side location near Central Park; near foodie mecca Zabar's and popular burger joint Shake Shack; tranquil environment. **Cons:** spotty front-desk staff; rooms are inconsistent; Wi-Fi is not free. ⑤ *Rooms from: $289* ✉ *45 W. 81st St., between Central Park W and Columbus Ave., Upper West Side* ☎ *212/362-9200* ⊕ *www.excelsiorhotelny.com* ⊷ *120 rooms, 80 suites* ⦿ *No meals* Ⓜ *B, C to 81st St.–Museum of Natural History* ✛ *5:C2.*

$$
HOTEL
FAMILY

🏨 **Hotel Beacon.** A neighborhood favorite for a reason, this Upper West Side hotel is three blocks from Central Park, 10 blocks from Lincoln Center, and steps from great gourmet grocery stores—Zabar's, Fairway, and Citarella. **Pros:** kitchenettes in all rooms; great UWS location;

affordable; great service. **Cons:** though comfortable and spacious, rooms aren't winning any design awards. $ *Rooms from: $319* ✉ *2130 Broadway, at 75th St., Upper West Side* ☎ *212/787–1100, 800/572–4969* ⊕ *www.beaconhotel.com* ⇆ *140 rooms, 137 suites* ⏐○⏐ *No meals* Ⓜ *1, 2, 3 to 72nd St.* ✛ *5:A3.*

$$ ⚇ **The Lucerne.** Service is the strong suit at this landmark-facade hotel,
HOTEL whose exterior has more pizzazz than the predictable guest rooms deco-
FAMILY rated with dark-wood reproduction furniture and chintz bedspreads.
Pros: free Wi-Fi; clean; great gym; close to Central Park. **Cons:** incon-
sistent room size; some guests report uncomfortable pillows. $ *Rooms
from: $309* ✉ *201 W. 79th St., at Amsterdam Ave., Upper West Side*
☎ *212/875–1000, 800/492–8122* ⊕ *www.thelucernehotel.com* ⇆ *165
rooms, 37 suites* ⏐○⏐ *No meals* Ⓜ *1 to 79th St.* ✛ *5:A2.*

$ ⚇ **Milburn Hotel.** Several hotel features that are tough to find in Man-
HOTEL hattan—generous space, kitchenettes, and a quiet night's sleep—are
FAMILY all available here at this welcoming property. **Pros:** peaceful location
near Central Park; free continental breakfast; free Wi-Fi; rooms have
kitchenettes and coffeemakers. **Cons:** traditional style may not suit the
taste of all guests. $ *Rooms from: $289* ✉ *242 W. 76th St., Upper West
Side* ☎ *212/362–1006* ⊕ *www.milburnhotel.com* ⇆ *62 rooms, 62 suites*
⏐○⏐ *Breakfast* Ⓜ *1 to 79th St.* ✛ *5:A3.*

$$ ⚇ **NYLO New York City.** Bringing modern style to the sometimes stodgy
HOTEL Upper West Side, this hotel nods to the jazz era—think raucous bar,
decadent living room with a fireplace, and tempting restaurants. **Pros:**
short walk from Central Park; quiet, safe location; excellent dining and
drinking options; rooms with terraces and dynamite views. **Cons:** lobby
might be too hectic for some; Upper West Side location removed from
some attractions. $ *Rooms from: $349* ✉ *2178 Broadway, Upper West
Side* ☎ *212/362–1100* ⊕ *www.nylohotels.com* ⇆ *258 rooms, 33 suites*
⏐○⏐ *No meals* Ⓜ *1 to 79th St.* ✛ *5:A3.*

$$$$ ⚇ **Trump International Hotel and Towers.** This iconic New York property's
HOTEL incomparable views of Central Park has interior design to match, conceived with the help of the Donald's daughter, Ivanka. **Pros:** fine service;
stellar views; discerning treatment. **Cons:** expensive. $ *Rooms from:
$800* ✉ *1 Central Park W, between 59th and 60th Sts., Upper West
Side* ☎ *212/299–1000, 888/448–7867* ⊕ *www.trumphotelcollection.
com* ⇆ *35 rooms, 141 suites* ⏐○⏐ *No meals* Ⓜ *1, A, B, C, D to 59th
St.–Columbus Circle* ✛ *5:C6.*

HARLEM

$ ⚇ **Aloft Harlem.** A reasonably priced option in an increasingly popular
HOTEL area of Harlem (Marcus Samuelsson's hot Red Rooster restaurant is
nearby), this branch of the Aloft chain delivers with cheerful service
and a fun atmosphere. **Pros:** good room size for the price; convenient
to subways; ever-increasing local shopping and dining options. **Cons:**
rooms have minimal space for hanging clothes; rooms get some street
noise. $ *Rooms from: $289* ✉ *2296 Frederick Douglass Blvd., between
123th and 124th Sts., Harlem* ☎ *212/749–4000* ⊕ *www.aloftharlem.
com* ⇆ *124 rooms* ⏐○⏐ *No meals* Ⓜ *A, B, C, D to 125th St.* ✛ *6:C1.*

BROOKLYN

DOWNTOWN BROOKLYN

$$ **Aloft New York Brooklyn.** A funky boutique operation in the heart of
HOTEL   Downtown Brooklyn, Aloft is a lively yet comfortable space. **Pros:** easy
FAMILY subway access; reasonable prices; guests have access to the adjacent
Sheraton's indoor swimming pool and room service. **Cons:** construction behind the hotel is noisy. *$ Rooms from: $359 ⊠ 216 Duffield
St., between Willoughby St. and Fulton Mall, Downtown Brooklyn
☎ 718/256–3833 ⊕ www.aloftnewyorkbrooklyn.com ⌂ 170 rooms,
6 suites ❙❍❙ No meals Ⓜ 2, 3 to Hoyt St.; A, C, F, N, R to Jay St.–
MetroTech ✛ 7:B4.*

$$ **New York Marriott at the Brooklyn Bridge.** The rooms at this well-situated hotel are classic Marriott—large and enhanced by high ceilings,
HOTEL
FAMILY massaging shower heads, rolling desks, and other nice touches. **Pros:**
near some of Brooklyn's hipper neighborhoods; traditional full-service
hotel. **Cons:** on a busy downtown street. *$ Rooms from: $369 ⊠ 333
Adams St., between Johnson and Willoughby Sts., Downtown Brooklyn ☎ 718/246–7000 ⊕ www.marriott.com/nycbk ⌂ 638 rooms, 28
suites ❙❍❙ No meals Ⓜ 2, 3, 4, 5 to Borough Hall; A, C, F, N, R to Jay
St.–Metro Tech ✛ 7:B3.*

BOERUM HILL

$ **NU Hotel Brooklyn.** The hip-yet-affordable NU, on one of Brooklyn's
HOTEL main nightlife and shopping streets, is perfect for visitors seeking a
perch near the best of the borough. **Pros:** great Brooklyn launching pad;
knowledgeable staff; 24-hour fitness center. **Cons:** subway or cab ride
to anything in Manhattan; bar area can be a little too quiet; limited
in-room amenities. *$ Rooms from: $299 ⊠ 85 Smith St., Boerum Hill
☎ 718/852–8585 ⊕ www.nuhotelbrooklyn.com ⌂ 87 rooms, 6 suites
❙❍❙ Breakfast Ⓜ F, G to Bergen St.; A, C, G to Hoyt-Schermerhorn Sts.
✛ 7:B4.*

WILLIAMSBURG

$ **Hotel Le Jolie.** This no-frills favorite has excellent service and is convenient not only to Williamsburg's arts, culture, and dining scenes,
HOTEL
but also to the subway and the Brooklyn-Queens Expressway, the latter handy should you want to get into Manhattan via car. **Pros:** good
value; free parking on a first-come, first-served basis; convenient part
of Brooklyn. **Cons:** proximity to highway can mean noise; can feel
remote even though near to subways. *$ Rooms from: $199 ⊠ 235
Meeker Ave., between Lorimer St. and Union Ave., Williamsburg
☎ 718/625–2100 ⊕ www.hotellejolie.com ⌂ 52 rooms ❙❍❙ Breakfast
Ⓜ L to Lorimer St. ✛ 7:E1.*

$$ **McCarren Hotel and Pool.** With funky design details like an underfoot,
HOTEL glass-encased river in the lobby (plus a fireplace), and a plum location
overlooking McCarren Park, this hotel sizzles with scenester savvy.
Pros: high hip factor; quality rooftop restaurant-bar; close to main thoroughfare Bedford Avenue. **Cons:** potential for noise from concerts in
McCarren Park; some room details like lighting controls could be more
user-friendly. *$ Rooms from: $315 ⊠ 160 N. 12th St., between Bedford
and Berry Sts., Williamsburg ☎ 718/218–7500 ⊕ www.chelseahotels.*

16

com/us/brooklyn/mccarren-hotel-and-pool/about ⌁ *60 rooms, 4 suites* ⓘ *No meals* Ⓜ *L to Bedford Ave.* ✛ *7:E1.*

$ ⊡ **Urban Cowboy B&B.** Williamsburg's only B&B, which occupies a
B&B/INN   newly renovated 100-year-old town house, combines the neighbor-
Fodor'sChoice   hood's renegade spirit with an eye for design. **Pros:** beautiful design with
★   personal touches; backyard Jacuzzi; personable staff. **Cons:** most rooms
share a bathroom. ⑤ *Rooms from: $200* ⊠ *111 Powers St., North Wil-*
liamsburg ☎ *347/840–0525* ⊕ *www.urbancowboybnb.com* ⌁ *4 rooms*
(3 with shared bath), 1 cabin ⓘ *Breakfast* Ⓜ *L to Lorimer St.; G to*
Metropolitan Ave. ✛ *7:E2.*

$$ ⊡ **Wythe Hotel.** A former cooperage on the Brooklyn waterfront has
HOTEL   found new life as the Wythe Hotel, a stunner for its Manhattan-skyline
Fodor'sChoice   views, locally sourced design touches and amenities, and supercool
★   restaurant (Reynard) and bar (Ides). **Pros:** unique building history;
excellent entry into fun neighborhood; Brooklyn-based design and envi-
ronmentally friendly products; fabulous views from rooms or rooftop
bar; destination-worthy restaurant. **Cons:** somewhat removed from the
subway; no room service. ⑤ *Rooms from: $300* ⊠ *80 Wythe Ave., at N.*
11th St., Williamsburg ☎ *718/460–8001* ⊕ *www.wythehotel.com* ⌁ *66*
rooms, 4 suites ⓘ *No meals* Ⓜ *L to Bedford Ave.* ✛ *7:D1.*

QUEENS

$ ⊡ **The Boro Hotel.** The boroughs beyond Manhattan beckon for space
HOTEL   and views. **Pros:** complimentary breakfast; fantastic views of Man-
hattan skyline; rooftop with lounge chairs. **Cons:** isolated location.
⑤ *Rooms from: $299* ⊠ *38-28 27th St., Long Island City* ☎ *718/433–*
1375 ⊕ *www.borohotel.com* ⌁ *108 rooms* ⓘ *Breakfast* Ⓜ *N, Q to*
39th Ave. ✛ *7:F1.*

$ ⊡ **The Paper Factory Hotel.** Space, style, access to intriguing local neigh-
HOTEL   borhoods, and seriously good value—this paper factory turned chic
FAMILY   hotel provides many reasons to stay in Queens. **Pros:** excellent value;
one-minute walk to subway; stylish rooms and restaurant; generous
space. **Cons:** some street noise reaches rooms. ⑤ *Rooms from: $199*
⊠ *37-06 36th St., Astoria* ☎ *718/392–7200* ⊕ *www.paperfactoryhotel.*
com ⌁ *123 rooms, 10 suites* ⓘ *No meals* Ⓜ *M, R to 36th St.* ✛ *7:H1.*

SHOPPING

Updated by
Kate Thorman

The Big Apple is one of the best shopping destinations in the world, rivaled perhaps only by London, Paris, and Tokyo. Its compact size, convenient subway system, and plentiful cabs (or Uber or Lyft rides) make it easy to navigate with plenty of bags in tow. But what it really comes down to is the staggering number and variety of stores. If you can't find it in New York, it probably doesn't exist.

If you like elegant flagships and money is no object, head to Midtown, where you'll find international megabrands like Louis Vuitton, Yves Saint Laurent, and Gucci, as well as famed department stores Bergdorf Goodman and Barneys. Nearby Madison Avenue has couture from Carolina Herrera and Vera Wang, and 5th Avenue is lined with famous jewelry stores like Tiffany, Van Cleef & Arpels, and Harry Winston. This is also the neighborhood to indulge in bespoke goods, such as handmade shoes from John Lobb. If you like designer pieces but can't afford them, don't despair—there are plenty of upscale consignment shops around the city where you can find last season's Chanel suit or a vintage YSL jacket.

The small, independent shops that once lined SoHo have largely been displaced by the likes of J.Crew and UNIQLO, but if you want to hit the chains, this is a great place to do it, because the neighborhood also provides high-quality people-watching and superb lunches. Poke around on the side streets and in nearby NoLIta for outposts of smaller local and foreign designers and, if you're craving some of old SoHo's artistic spirit, don't discount the street vendors' stalls, which sell handmade jewelry and simple cotton dresses. You never know—you might buy something from a soon-to-be-famous designer.

The East Village and Lower East Side are hotbeds of creativity and quirky coolness, with little boutiques selling everything from retro furniture to industrial-inspired jewelry tucked among bars and old tenement buildings. The Meatpacking District is another great shopping destination to find chic designer stores like Diane von Furstenberg and Catherine Malandrino along with independently owned boutiques.

LOWER MANHATTAN

FINANCIAL DISTRICT

Known primarily as the home of Wall Street, the Financial District isn't the best place for browsing.

BARGAIN SHOPPING

Fodor'sChoice
★

Century 21. For many New Yorkers this downtown fixture remains the mother lode of discount shopping. Seven floors are crammed with everything from Marc Jacobs shoes and half-price cashmere sweaters to Donna Karan sheets, though you have to sift through racks and fight crowds to find the gems. Best bets for men are shoes and designer briefs; the full floor of designer women's wear can yield some dazzling finds. Don't miss the children's section either, for brands like Ralph Lauren and Diesel. ■TIP→ **If you're on the Upper West Side, you can check out more discount shopping at the Broadway and 66th location.** ⊠ *22 Cortlandt St., between Broadway and Church St., Lower Manhattan* ☎ *212/227–9092* ⊕ *www.c21stores.com* Ⓜ *R to Cortlandt St.*

CLOTHING

Judith & Charles. The only New York outpost of this chic Canadian import is an ideal place to shop for work clothes that have an edge (think shift dresses in bold stripes). The clothing here is separated by color and style, so it's easy to peruse the racks of blazers, office-appropriate dresses, and well-cut tees. ⊠ *Brookfield Place, 250 Vesey St., between North End Ave. and West St., Financial District* ☎ *212/945–3100* ⊕ *www.judithandcharles.com* Ⓜ *A, C, E to Chambers St.*

Kamakura Shirts. Located amidst the high-rise office buildings of the Financial District, it's only appropriate that the recently opened, high-end Brookfield Place shopping center would be home to the second U.S. outpost of boutique Japanese shirtmakers Kamakura Shirts. Priding itself on impeccable service and timeless style, the designer offers both made-to-measure and ready-to-wear men's dress shirts, as well as custom ties. ⊠ *Brookfield Place, 225 Liberty St., between South End Ave. and West St., Financial District* ☎ *212/619–2484* ⊕ *www. kamakurashirts.com* Ⓜ *R to Cortlandt St.; 2, 3, 4, 5, A, C, J, Z to Fulton St.*

GIFTS AND SOUVENIRS

City Store. The official store of NYC sells anything and everything having to do with the city, from books and pamphlets to fun gifts. Pick up NYPD T-shirts, taxicab medallions, garbage truck toys, and dish towels silk-screened with the skyline. The store shuts at 5 pm weekdays and is closed weekends. ⊠ *1 Centre St., at Chambers St., Financial District* ☎ *212/386–0007* ⊕ *a856-citystore.nyc.gov/* Ⓜ *4, 5, 6 to Brooklyn Bridge–City Hall.*

TRIBECA

Known for its multimillion-dollar lofts and celebrity residents, TriBeCa is home to some of the most interesting boutiques in the city, though most are geared toward deep pockets, especially the design and clothing stores. Specialty shops such as Korin or J.Crew Men's Shop at the Liquor Store are worth a visit.

17

CLOSE UP

Deals and Steals

Everyone loves a bargain—including a temporary New Yorker. Scoring a good deal is a rite of passage, and the city is home to everything from low-cost department stores like Century 21 to hawkers of pseudo-Rolex watches and Kate Spade bags stationed at street corners and Canal Street stalls. Then there are the sample sales.

If a seasonal sale makes New Yorkers' eyes gleam, a sample sale throws them into a frenzy. With so many designer flagships and corporate headquarters in town, merchandise fallout periodically leads to tremendous deals. Although technically the term "sample sale" refers to stock that's a sample design, show model, leftover, or already discounted item, the term is now also used for sales of current-season goods. Location adds a bit of an illicit thrill to the event: sales are held in hotels, warehouses, offices, or loft spaces, where items both incredible and unfortunate jam a motley assortment of racks, tables, and bins. Generally, there is a makeshift communal dressing room, but mirrors are scarce, so veteran sample-sale shoppers come prepared for wriggling in the aisles; some wear tank tops with tights or leggings for modest quick changes. Two rules of thumb: grab first and inspect later, and call in advance to find out what methods of payment are accepted. One of the ultimate experiences is the Barneys Warehouse Sale, traditionally held in February and August in Chelsea (though the sale didn't happen in 2015—which is a good reminder to check on specific sales before you go). Other luscious sales include the Vera Wang bridal-gown sale (summer and early winter) and ABC Carpet & Home (winter and summer).

How to find out about these events? The level of publicity and regularity of sales vary. The print and online versions of *New York* magazine are always worth checking for sample-sale tip-offs, as are regular bulletins on **Racked** (⊕ *www.racked.com*). If you're interested in specific designers, call their shops and inquire—you may get lucky.

CHILDREN'S CLOTHING

FAMILY **Shoofly.** Stylish children's shoes and accessories imported from all over the world are the name of the game here. Choose from ballet flats, trendy sneakers, and motorcycle boots along with pom-pom hats, brightly patterned socks, eclectic toys, and jewelry. ⊠ *42 Hudson St., between Thomas and Duane Sts., TriBeCa* ☎ *212/406–3270* ⊕ *www. shooflynyc.com* Ⓜ *1, 2, 3 to Chambers St.*

CLOTHING

Fodor'sChoice **Issey Miyake.** This flagship, designed by Frank Gehry, attracts a non-
★ fashion crowd who come just to gawk at his undulating, 25-foot-high titanium sculpture, *The Tornado*. Miyake's signature style has clothes that are sleek and slim fitting, and made from polyester or ultra-high-tech textiles. This flagship carries the entire runway collection, as well as Pleats Please and Issey Miyake Fete. ⊠ *119 Hudson St., at N. Moore St., TriBeCa* ☎ *212/226–0100* ⊕ *www.tribecaisseymiyake.com* Ⓜ *1 to Franklin St.*

J.Crew Men's Shop at the Liquor Store. It would be easy to walk right past this place and think it's a bar rather than an outpost of J.Crew for men, because it's filled with manly knickknacks like old Jack Kerouac books and vintage photographs. Some of the best finds are the limited-edition suits and cashmere sweaters, as well as non–J.Crew items like Barbour jackets and Ray-Bans. ⊠ *235 West Broadway, at White St., TriBeCa* ☎ *212/226–5476* ⊕ *www.jcrew.com* Ⓜ *1 to Franklin St.*

La Garçonne. The popular online shop finally has a brick-and-mortar space to display its curated collection of clean-lined designer duds in monochromatic hues—unlike the Web store, though, this one only carries women's clothes. Brands like Alexander Wang, Rachel Comey, and Isabel Marant are perennial favorites. The minimalist, loftlike space also sells some home decor and beauty products. ⊠ *465 Greenwich St., between Watts and Desbrosses Sts., TriBeCa* ☎ *646/553–3303* ⊕ *www. lagarconne.com* Ⓜ *1 to Canal St.*

Nili Lotan. This Israeli-born designer worked for Ralph Lauren and Nautica before launching her own collection for women. Nili Lotan is known for her knitwear, drapey coats, and love of solid colors. Her whitewashed retail space also sells rare books. ⊠ *188 Duane St., between Greenwich and Hudson Sts., TriBeCa* ☎ *212/219–8794* ⊕ *www.nililotan.com* Ⓜ *1, 2, 3 to Chambers St.*

Steven Alan Annex. This TriBeCa flagship sells casual, cool sportswear. Steven Alan is the place to come if your preferred uniform is a cashmere beanie, untucked plaid shirt, and skinny jeans. The rustic space stocks clothing for men and women and sells its own line of clothing, as well as beauty products and home accessories. The designer also recently opened a new, stand-alone home design store down the street at 158 Franklin. ⊠ *103 Franklin St., TriBeCa* ☎ *212/343–0692* ⊕ *www. stevenalan.com* Ⓜ *1 to Franklin St.*

17

HOME DECOR

Korin. If you're serious about cooking, head to this specialty knife store in TriBeCa. Previously only open to the trade, it is one of the best places to shop for top-quality knives imported from Japan. ⊠ *57 Warren St., between West Broadway and Church St., TriBeCa* ☎ *212/587–7021* ⊕ *www.korin.com* Ⓜ *1, 2, 3 to Chambers St.*

JEWELRY AND ACCESSORIES

Ten Thousand Things. You might find yourself wishing for 10,000 things from the showcases in this elegant boutique, which recently moved to TriBeCa from its old Meatpacking District haunt. Designs run from delicate gold and silver chains to long Peruvian opal earrings. Many shapes are abstract reflections of natural forms, like twigs or seedpods. Prices start around $180 but quickly rise. ⊠ *7 Harrison St., between Greenwich and Staple Sts., TriBeCa* ☎ *212/352–1333* ⊕ *www. tenthousandthingsnyc.com* Ⓜ *1 to Franklin St.*

SHOES, HANDBAGS, AND LEATHER GOODS

Matt Bernson. Thankfully, the footwear at designer Matt Bernson's TriBeCa flagship store is both beautiful and blister-proof. Though the native New Yorker's comfy, affordable sandals are staples at the likes of Bloomingdale's, this shop is his first stand-alone venture. His shop also stocks accessories such as jewelry and handbags. Don't miss the design-er's dog, Abraham, who accompanies him to work every day. ✉ *20 Har-rison St., between Greenwich and Staple Sts., TriBeCa* ☎ *212/941–7634* ⊕ *www.mattbernson.com* Ⓜ *1 to Franklin St.*

Fodor's Choice **Shinola.** This World War II–era shoe polish brand, proudly based in Detroit,
★   has been relaunched as a company that builds handcrafted watches, bicy-cles, leather goods, journals, and pet accessories. Shinola's TriBeCa flag-ship store also sells American-made products from other brands, such as Filson. ✉ *177 Franklin St., between Greenwich and Hudson Sts., TriBeCa* ☎ *917/728–3000* ⊕ *www.shinola.com* Ⓜ *1 to Franklin St.*

WINE

24 Hubert Wines. Run by the former wine director of the Michelin-starred restaurant at Napa's iconic Meadowood resort, this sleek neighborhood wine shop emphasizes California wines as much as European. It culti-vates a welcoming, unpretentious atmosphere at its regular tasting and winemaker events, most of which are open to the public and listed on the website. ✉ *24 Hubert St., at Greenwich St., TriBeCa* ☎ *212/810–2899* ⊕ *www.24hubert.com* Ⓜ *A, C, E to Canal St.; 1 to Franklin St.*

SOHO AND NOLITA

SOHO

Head to SoHo for both the cheap and the hyperchic. The narrow side-walks get very busy, especially on weekends, but this is a fun "see-and-be-seen" neighborhood. There are plenty of familiar high-fashion names like Prada, Chanel, and Louis Vuitton, as well as several less expensive chains, like Banana Republic and Sephora, which have made landgrabs on Broadway. But you can still hit a few clothing and housewares bou-tiques not found elsewhere in this country. The hottest shopping area runs west from Broadway over to 6th Avenue, between West Houston and Grand Streets. Don't overlook a couple of streets east of Broadway, too: Crosby and Lafayette have several intriguing shops.

BEAUTY

Fodor's Choice **Birchbox.** Cult favorite beauty-subscription service Birchbox now has
★   a retail space. Visitors to its SoHo store can stock up on best-selling products here, which range from $5–$200 and include everything from lip balm and stylish mugs to curling irons, headphones, and fragrance. There's also a BYOB (Build Your Own Birchbox) section, where users create their own box full of samples. The store also has a separate floor set aside for makeup, hair, and nail services. ✉ *433 West Broad-way, between Spring and Prince Sts., SoHo* ☎ *646/589–8500* ⊕ *www.birchbox.com* Ⓜ *N, R to Prince St.*

MiN. If the selection of grooming products at Duane Reade isn't arti-sanal or exotic enough for you, head to MiN. This wood-paneled shop is decidedly masculine in flavor, with leather couches and exposed-brick walls, though the products appeal to all. Shop for unusual scents from Santa Maria Novella and L'Artisan Parfumeur, shaving products from Old Bond Street, or quirkier items like mustache wax. ✉ *117 Crosby St., between Prince and Houston Sts., SoHo* ☎ *212/206–6366* ⊕ *min.com* Ⓜ *N, R to Prince St.*

BOOKS AND STATIONERY

Housing Works Bookstore Cafe. Operated by a nonprofit that puts all proceeds towards combating AIDS and homelessness, this New York institution has an impressive collection of used and donated books. Its café is a popular spot for laptop-toting creatives, and literary and cultural events are held here almost nightly; a full calendar is available on the store's website. ☒ *126 Crosby St., between Prince and Houston Sts., SoHo* ☎ *212/334–3324* ⊕ *www.housingworks.org/bookstore* Ⓜ *B, D, F, M to Broadway–Lafayette St.; N, R to Prince St.*

CHILDREN'S CLOTHING

FAMILY **Giggle.** This high-end baby store is often gridlocked with strollers but stocks nearly everything a stylish parent (and baby) could ever need. The Giggle flagship carries all the gear and accessories to build a chic nursery, including Dwell bedding, plush toys, and bold kids' clothing. Basic gear such as high chairs and strollers are also sold, and the staff makes sure parents know how to fold that complicated stroller before leaving the store. Additional Giggle outlets are located on the Upper West and Upper East Sides. ☒ *451 West Broadway, between Prince and W. Houston Sts., SoHo* ☎ *212/334–5817* ⊕ *www.giggle.com* Ⓜ *C, E to Spring St.*

FAMILY **J.Crew.** If you want to pick up stylish clothing for yourself as well as your children, head to this location of J.Crew, which stocks women's clothing as well its Crewcuts line. Stocking pint-size versions of the preppy classic clothes the brand is famous for, this shop is replete with cords, cashmere sweaters, and blazers for the junior set as well as stylish moms. The SoHo men's store is located a few blocks away on Broadway, and the 5th Avenue store offers a wider selection for all three demographics. ☒ *99 Prince St., between Greene and Mercer Sts., SoHo* ☎ *212/966–2739* ⊕ *www.jcrew.com* Ⓜ *C, E to Spring St.*

FAMILY **Les Petits Chapelais.** Designed and made in France, these clothes for kids (from newborn up to age 12) are cute and stylish but also practical. Corduroy outfits have details like embroidered flowers and contrasting cuffs, and soft, fleecy jackets are reversible. There's also a line of sailor-inspired clothes. ☒ *146 Sullivan St., between Houston and Prince Sts., SoHo* ☎ *212/625–1023* ⊕ *lespetitschapelais-nyc.com* Ⓜ *C, E to Spring St.*

CLOTHING

& Other Stories. The first U.S. outpost of this popular shop owned by Swedish megastore H&M focuses on midrange clothes and bold twists on staples designed in Paris and Stockholm. Come here to browse chunky sweaters, pointy-toed flats, and printed coats. Don't miss the designer collaborations and beauty section. ☒ *575 Broadway, between Houston and Prince Sts., SoHo* ☎ *646/767–3063* ⊕ *www.stories.com/us* Ⓜ *N, R to Prince St.*

A Bathing Ape. Known simply as BAPE to devotees, this exclusive label has a cult following in its native Tokyo. At first it may be hard to see what the fuss is about. A small selection of camouflage gear and limited-edition T-shirts for men, women, and children is placed throughout the minimalist space; the real scene stealers are the flashy retro-style

CLOSE UP

Street Vendor Shopping

If you're looking for original or reproduced artwork, the two areas to visit for street vendors are the stretch of 5th Avenue in front of the Metropolitan Museum of Art (roughly between 81st and 82nd Streets) and the SoHo area of West Broadway, between Houston and Broome Streets. In both areas, dozens of artists sell original paintings, drawings, and photographs (some lovely, some lurid), as well as photo reproductions of famous New York scenes (the Chrysler Building, South Street Seaport). Prices can start as low as $15, but be sure to haggle.

The east–west streets in SoHo are an excellent place to look for handmade crafts: Spring and Prince Streets, especially, are jammed with tables full of beaded jewelry, tooled leather belts, cotton sundresses, and homemade hats and purses. These streets are also great places to find deals on art books; several vendors have titles featuring the work of artists from Diego Rivera to Annie Leibovitz, all for about 20% less than

you pay at a chain. It's best to know which books you want ahead of time, though; street vendors wrap theirs in clear plastic, and can get testy if you unwrap them but don't wind up buying.

Faux-designer handbags, sunglasses, wallets, and watches are some of the most popular street buys in town—but crackdowns on knockoffs have made them harder to find. The hub used to be Canal Street, roughly between Greene and Lafayette Streets, but many vendors there have swept their booths clean of fake Vuitton, Prada, Gucci, and Fendi merchandise. You might have better luck finding one near Herald Square or Madison Square Garden, and good fake handbags are still sold by isolated vendors around such shopping areas as Rockefeller Center and the lower stretch of 5th Avenue, near Union Square. If you're looking for bargain luggage, skip Canal Street, as the bags there might not last beyond the flight home, and instead pick up a bargain at Marshalls, TJ Maxx, or Century 21.

---

sneakers in neon colors. ⊠ *91 Greene St., between Prince and Spring Sts., SoHo* ☎ *212/925–0222* ⊕ *www.bape.com* Ⓜ *N, R to Prince St.*

Fodor'sChoice
★ **Agent Provocateur.** If Victoria's Secret is too tame for you, try this British lingerie shop, which has a naughty twist. Showpieces include boned corsets, lace sets with contrast-color trim, bottoms tied with satin ribbons, and a few fetish-type leather ensembles. A great selection of stockings is complemented by the garter belts to secure them. ⊠ *133 Mercer St., between Prince and Spring Sts., SoHo* ☎ *212/965–0229* ⊕ *www.agentprovocateur.com* Ⓜ *N, R to Prince St.*

Alexander Wang. *Vogue* darling Alexander Wang's boutique is as unfussy and cool as his clothes. In between browsing for perfectly slouchy tank tops, sheath dresses, or edgy ankle boots, shoppers should check out the rotating display of luxe objects tucked inside the store's cage, which has included furry punching bags and marbleized surfboards. ⊠ *103 Grand St., between Greene and Mercer Sts., SoHo* ☎ *212/977–9683* ⊕ *www.alexanderwang.com* Ⓜ *6, J, N, Q, R, Z to Canal St.*

Luxe shops line the streets of SoHo.

Allan & Suzi. The duo behind Allan & Suzi has been selling pristine vintage clothing to celebrities for years—and has also outfitted the cast of *Sex and the City.* Their downtown store sells a mix of new and vintage finds, ranging from the elegant to the wacky. Dig, and you may find a Gaultier gown or a Pauline Trigère dress, along with crazy disco gear. ✉ *237 Centre St., between Grand and Broome Sts., SoHo* ☎ *212/724–7445* ⊕ *allanandsuzi.com* Ⓜ *6, J, N, Q, R, Z to Canal St.*

American Two Shot. This boutique sells a carefully curated mix of contemporary designs for men and women, including clothing from Timo Weiland, Lazy Oaf, and Nanushka, as well as rare vintage finds. The displays are fun and witty (you might see a voodoo doll). The space also functions as an art gallery and includes an outpost of Cafe Integral for shoppers in need of a caffeine fix. The shop recently launched its own clothing line, which is made in L.A. ✉ *135 Grand St., between Crosby and Lafayette Sts., SoHo* ☎ *212/925–3403* ⊕ *www.americantwoshot. com* Ⓜ *6, J, N, Q, R, Z to Canal St.*

Anna Sui. The violet-and-black salon, with its Victorian rock-chick vibe, is the ideal setting for Sui's bohemian and rocker-influenced designs and colorful beauty products. ✉ *484 Broome St., between West Broadway and Wooster St., SoHo* ☎ *212/941–8406* ⊕ *www.annasui.com* Ⓜ *C, E to Spring St.*

A.P.C. This hip French boutique sells deceptively simple clothes in an equally understated setting. Choose from sharply cut gabardine and corduroy suits to dark denim jeans and jackets. For women, best bets include striped sweaters and skinny jeans. ✉ *131 Mercer St., between*

Prince and Spring Sts., SoHo ☎ *212/966–9685* ⊕ *usonline.apc.fr* Ⓜ *6 to Spring St.; N, R to Prince St.; B, D, F, M to Broadway–Lafayette St.*

Balenciaga. This glossy new flagship is sheathed in acres of green marble and limestone. The two-story space has a minimalist design, all the better to show off creative director Alexander Wang's structured designs. Don't miss the luxurious handbags and leather shoes. ✉ *148 Mercer St., between Houston and Prince Sts., SoHo* ☎ *212/206–0872* ⊕ *www. balenciaga.com* Ⓜ *N, R to Prince St.*

Christopher Fischer. Featherweight cashmere sweaters, wraps, and throws in every hue, from Easter-egg pastels to rich jewel tones, have made Fischer the darling of the men and women of the preppy set. His shop also carries leather accessories, housewares, and baby clothes. ✉ *80 Wooster St., between Spring and Broome Sts., SoHo* ☎ *212/965–9009* ⊕ *www.christopherfischer.com* Ⓜ *N, R to Prince St.*

Fodor's Choice   **Comptoir des Cotonniers.** The "cotton counter" angles for multigen-
★   erational shopping, lining up stylish, comfortable basics for babies, twentysomethings, ladies of a certain age, and everyone in between. There's a subtle Parisian vibe to the understated tunics, dresses, and separates; colors tend to be muted. The brand's first U.S. branch has a nature-friendly, minimalist look, with pale-wood floors and lots of natural light. ✉ *155 Spring St., between West Broadway and Wooster St., SoHo* ☎ *212/274–0830* ⊕ *www.comptoirdescotonniers.com* Ⓜ *C, E to Spring St.*

Costume National. Everything about this Italian designer boutique is sexy and minimalist, with a rock'n'roll edge. Both clothes—and lighting—are dark; shoppers find sharply tailored wool pants for men and silky tops for women in muted shades of black, gray, and charcoal, along with motorcycle boots and leather gloves. ✉ *150 Greene St., between Houston and Prince Sts., SoHo* ☎ *212/431–1530* ⊕ *www.costumenational. com* Ⓜ *N, R to Prince St.*

Emporio Armani. At this middle child of the Armani trio, the clothes are elegant without ever being fussy, and frequently stocked in cream, muted blues, and ever-cool shades of taupe. Fashion-conscious men, women, and children are all catered to. ✉ *410 West Broadway, at Spring St., SoHo* ☎ *646/613–8099* ⊕ *www.armani.com/us/emporioarmani* Ⓜ *C, E to Spring St.*

Etro. This Italian fashion house is known for its trademark paisleys and bold patterns, which cover everything from suits and dresses to lustrous pillows. Etro's downtown location combines the best of Italy with a SoHo loft, with high tin ceilings, brightly colored rugs, and industrial lighting. ✉ *89 Greene St., between Spring and Prince Sts., SoHo* ☎ *646/329–6929* ⊕ *www.etro.com* Ⓜ *N, R to Prince St.*

French Connection. This British-owned company stocks an impressive collection of on-trend clothing for men and women at reasonable prices. Some of the best bets are the sharply tailored trench coats and jeans, as well as dresses. For men, try the cashmere sweaters and skinny trousers. ✉ *435 West Broadway, at Prince St., SoHo* ☎ *212/219–1197* ⊕ *www. frenchconnection.com* Ⓜ *C, E to Spring St.*

Fodor's Choice ★ **Isabel Marant.** If you're after that casually glamorous Parisian vibe, look no further than Isabel Marant. Long a favorite of globe-trotting fashionistas, the French designer opened her first U.S. retail store in the heart of SoHo. The tailored jackets, shorts, and flirty dresses are eclectic and sophisticated, with textured, deeply hued fabrics. ⊠ *469 Broome St., at Greene St., SoHo* ☎ *212/219–2284* ⊕ *www.isabelmarant.com* Ⓜ *N, R to Prince St.*

Kiki de Montparnasse. Named for Man Ray's mistress and muse from the 1940s, this upscale lingerie store serves up decadent styles in a seductive but artistic setting. Shoppers find exquisitely made corsets, bra and underwear sets, and luxe bondage kits, but a large portion of the store is used as a rotating art gallery for erotic art. ⊠ *79 Greene St., at Spring St., SoHo* ☎ *212/965–8150* ⊕ *www.kikidm.com* Ⓜ *N, R to Prince St.*

Kirna Zabête. Think of this space as a mini department store for some of the biggest names in fashion, including Alexander Wang, Azzedine Alaïa, Roland Mouret, and Valentino Garavani. The multilevel store has a fun, pop art–inspired design, complete with neon signs suggesting that shoppers "leave looking lovely" and that "life is short, buy the shoes." ⊠ *477 Broome St., between Greene and Wooster Sts., SoHo* ☎ *212/941–9656* ⊕ *www.kirnazabete.com* Ⓜ *N, R to Prince St.*

Marc Jacobs. One of Marc Jacobs' various NYC boutiques, this location, housed in a former garage, retails crisply tailored designs for men and women in luxurious fabrics: silk, cashmere, wool bouclé, and tweeds ranging from the demure to the flamboyant. The details, though—oversize buttons, circular patch pockets, and military-style grommet belts—add a sartorial wink. The shoe selection is not to be missed. ⊠ *163 Mercer St., between Houston and Prince Sts., SoHo* ☎ *212/343–1490* ⊕ *www.marcjacobs.com* Ⓜ *N, R to Prince St.*

17

Marni. If you're a fan of the boho-chic look, stock up on Consuelo Castiglioni's brightly colored clothes at the designer's SoHo outpost. The collection features dresses and jackets in quirky prints, and many of the silhouettes are vintage inspired. Accessories are also eye-popping. ⊠ *161 Mercer St., between W. Houston and Prince Sts., SoHo* ☎ *212/343–3912* ⊕ *www.marni.com* Ⓜ *N, R to Prince St.*

Michael Kors. This designer keeps rolling out boutiques around the city, but this new flagship, opened in 2015, is the biggest and most impressive yet. A three-story temple to his clean-lined, classic clothing and accessories, the store is the first to dedicate a whole level to menswear, and even has its own signature suit design. ⊠ *520 Broadway, between Broome and Spring Sts., SoHo* ☎ *212/336–4501* ⊕ *www.michaelkors. com* Ⓜ *6 to Spring St.; N, R to Prince St.*

Miu Miu. Prada front woman Miuccia Prada established a secondary line (bearing her childhood nickname, Miu Miu) to showcase her more experimental ideas. Look for Prada-esque styles in more daring colors and cuts, such as high-waist skirts with scalloped edges, Peter Pan–collar dresses in bold patterns, and patent-leather pumps. ⊠ *100 Prince St., between Mercer and Greene Sts., SoHo* ☎ *212/334–5156* ⊕ *www. miumiu.com* Ⓜ *N, R to Prince St.*

Moncler. Many New York women swear by Moncler coats to keep them warm but still stylish throughout the winter. This store is the Italian brand's first foray into New York. The knee-length puffer is a firm favorite, but there are stylish ski jackets and accessories, along with pieces created in collaboration with designers like Giambattista Valli. ⊠ *90 Prince St., between Mercer St. and Broadway, SoHo* ☎ *646/350–3620* ⊕ *www.moncler.com* Ⓜ *N, R to Prince St.*

Nanette Lepore. Feminine and flirty are the best way to describe the line at this cheerful shop; skirts are pleated, shift dresses have lace appliqués, and fur shrugs have tiny sleeves. ⊠ *423 Broome St., between Lafayette and Crosby Sts., SoHo* ☎ *212/219–8265* ⊕ *www.nanettelepore.com* Ⓜ *6 to Spring St.*

Odin. Gentlemen, if you're tired of the corporate look, head to Odin to spruce up your weekend wardrobe. This boutique, which caters only to men, carries separates from cool brands including Rag & Bone, Thom Browne, and Band Of Outsiders. The cheerful and helpful staff guarantees you will leave looking hip—but not as if you're trying too hard. ⊠ *199 Lafayette St., between Broome and Kenmare Sts., SoHo* ☎ *212/966–0026* ⊕ *www.odinnewyork.com* Ⓜ *6 to Spring St.*

Fodor'sChoice ★ **Opening Ceremony.** Just like Colette in Paris, Opening Ceremony bills itself as a concept store, which means you never know what you'll find. The owners are constantly globe-trotting to soak up the work of foreign designers and bring back the best clothing, products, and vintage items to showcase in their store. Hong Kong, Japan, Brazil, and the United Kingdom have all been represented. The 35 Howard address includes shoes, kids' clothes, books, and women's wear, while 33 Howard, next door, is dedicated to menswear. Both spaces also double as galleries for modern art and installations. ⊠ *35 Howard St., between Broadway and Crosby St., SoHo* ☎ *212/219–2688* ⊕ *www.openingceremony.us* Ⓜ *6, J, N, Q, R, Z to Canal St.*

Paul Smith. Fans love Paul Smith for his classic-with-a-twist clothes, and this 5,000-square-foot flagship is a temple to his design ethos and inspirations. Victorian mahogany cases complement the dandyish British styles they hold. Embroidered vests; brightly striped socks, scarves, and shirts; and tongue-in-cheek cuff links are all signature Paul Smith looks, along with classic suits and outerwear for men and women. Shoppers also find furniture and a selection of photography books and ephemera. ⊠ *142 Greene St., between Houston and Prince Sts., SoHo* ☎ *646/613–3060* ⊕ *www.paulsmith.co.uk* Ⓜ *N, R to Prince St.*

Prada. This ultramodern flagship space, designed by Rem Koolhaas, incorporates so many technological innovations that it was written up in *Popular Science.* Dressing rooms' glass walls turn opaque at the touch of a button, and instead of mirrors, shoppers can check themselves out in large video panels. ⊠ *575 Broadway, at Prince St., SoHo* ☎ *212/334–8888* ⊕ *www.prada.com* Ⓜ *N, R to Prince St.*

R by 45rpm. This cult-favorite Japanese denim brand may be pricey, but fans love the label for its attention to detail, like hand-dyed denim woven on antique looms. The T-shirts are particularly stylish, the non-denim women's wear is ethereal and cozy, and the men's shirts and blazers are elegantly tailored. ⊠ *169 Mercer St., between Houston and Prince Sts., SoHo* ☎ *917/237–0045* ⊕ *www.rby45rpm.com* Ⓜ *N, R to Prince St.*

Reiss. Think of Reiss as the Banana Republic of Britain—a go-to place for casual-but-tailored clothes at a relatively gentle price. Kate Middleton is a loyal customer. Standouts for women include cowl-neck sweater dresses and A-line skirts. Men's wool combat trousers are complemented by shrunken blazers, military-inspired peacoats, and trim leather jackets. ⊠ *387 West Broadway, between Spring and Broome Sts., SoHo* ☎ *212/925–5707* ⊕ *www.reissonline.com* Ⓜ *N, R to Prince St.*

Saint Laurent Paris. This fabled French house is now under the direction of Hedi Slimane, who revitalized the brand and opened a new down-town flagship, with high ceilings and a monochromatic palette. The new Saint Laurent nods to the past, with a refined, polished elegance. Don't miss the sleek shoes and structured handbags. ⊠ *80 Greene St., between Spring and Broome Sts., SoHo* ☎ *212/431–3240* ⊕ *www.ysl. com* Ⓜ *N, R to Prince St.; 6 to Spring St.*

Saturdays Surf NYC. Who knew New York had a surfing scene? This almost painfully cool boutique brought the culture to the heart of SoHo with its boards, men's clothing, surf-focused fine art, and other hipster accessories. The shop also has a La Colombe coffee counter in the front and a quiet garden in the back. ⊠ *31 Crosby St., between Grand and Broome Sts., SoHo* ☎ *212/966–7875* ⊕ *www.saturdaysnyc.com* Ⓜ *6, N, Q, J, Z to Canal St.; 6 to Spring St.*

17

Sean. This French-pedigreed shop carries classic, understated mens-wear imported from Europe at reasonable prices. Linen and corduroy painter's coats are best sellers, along with V-neck sweaters and a respect-able collection of slim-cut suits. ⊠ *181 Prince St., between Sullivan and MacDougal Sts., SoHo* ☎ *212/598–5980* ⊕ *www.seanstore.com* Ⓜ *N, R to Prince St.*

Seize sur Vingt. Head to this boutique if you're ready to splurge on an exquisitely tailored shirt or suit. Men and women can pick out an off-the-rack item and have it tailored in-house for a perfect fit, or create a fully bespoke shirt from a mind-boggling array of fabrics (linen, broad-cloth oxford, flannel). To complete the look, sweaters, shoes, and acces-sories are also available. ⊠ *78 Greene St., between Spring and Broome Sts., SoHo* ☎ *212/625–1620* ⊕ *www.16sur20.com* Ⓜ *N, R to Prince St.*

7 for All Mankind. Whether you're hunting for superskinny, high-waisted, or boot-cut jeans in a dark or distressed finish, this temple to denim has it all. The jeans are a firm celebrity favorite (Cameron Diaz is a fan), but be warned: although they are guaranteed to make your derriere look good, they don't come cheap. You'll also find stylish and sexy dresses here, plus sweaters and jackets for men and women. ⊠ *394 West Broadway, between Broome and Spring Sts., SoHo* ☎ *212/226–8615* ⊕ *www.7forallmankind.com* Ⓜ *C, E to Spring St.*

Stella McCartney. McCartney's flagship store has a luxe look, thanks to parquet flooring and touches of gold found in the Art Deco sculptures and clothing racks. Her main collection, done mostly in gauzy, muted colors, is on the top floor, while children's, Adidas by Stella McCartney, and lingerie are on the lower level. In keeping with McCartney's vegetarianism, fur and leather are verboten. ⊠ *112 Greene St., between Spring and Prince Sts., SoHo* ☎ *212/255–1556* ⊕ *www.stellamccartney. com* Ⓜ *N, R to Prince St.*

Tess Giberson. This Rhode Island School of Design graduate has been making waves for her eponymous women's collection. The boutique has an airy, minimalist feel, with whitewashed walls and rotating art exhibits that perfectly match the clothing's pared-down aesthetic. Your best bets are floaty silk dresses and striking knitwear. ⊠ *97 Crosby St., between Prince and Spring Sts., SoHo* ☎ *212/226–1932* ⊕ *www. tessgiberson.com* Ⓜ *N, R to Prince St.*

Fodor'sChoice
★
3X1. In this huge denim shop, which doubles as a factory, customers can watch 3x1 jeans being made. The walls of the pristine white space are lined with an assortment of more than 600 varieties of selvedge denim. Those looking for a bespoke pair start by selecting the perfect denim. Jeans are hand-cut and sewn by the in-house seamstresses, who work in a glass-enclosed space. Shoppers can also buy off-the-rack jeans, with hems tailored on the spot (starting at $195). ⊠ *15 Mercer St., between Grand and Howard Sts., SoHo* ☎ *212/391–6969* ⊕ *www.3x1.us* Ⓜ *6, J, N, Q, R, Z to Canal St.*

Topshop. British cult favorite Topshop, which has only a handful of U.S. stores, is a master at pumping out of-the-minute-fashion at reasonable prices. It can be a madhouse, and items sell quickly, but it's worth fighting the crowds. Slinky dresses are around $130, and jeans and jumpsuits are about $90. Coats and shoes are also standouts. Male stylistas can browse through the ground-level Topman. ⊠ *478 Broadway, between Broome and Grand Sts., SoHo* ☎ *212/966–9555* ⊕ *www.topshop.com* Ⓜ *6 to Spring St.; N, R to Prince St.*

Trademark. Retail is in the blood of Trademark founders Pookie and Louisa Burch, the daughters of C. Wonder founder Chris Burch. Both their boutique and clothing line reflect a restrained American design aesthetic. Their collection ranges from boxy jackets to totes and turtleneck sweaters. ⊠ *95 Grand St., between Greene and Mercer Sts., SoHo* ☎ *646/559–4945* ⊕ *www.trade-mark.com* Ⓜ *6, J, N, Q, R, Z to Canal St.*

Vera Wang. Not content designing just wedding dresses, Wang is also a star at evening wear and casual-but-chic day wear. Her entire ready-to-wear collection is showcased here in this gleaming, all-white store. Choose from clothes ranging from sexy one-shouldered satin gowns to cashmere sweaters and wool pencil skirts. Don't miss the shoe collection. ⊠ *158 Mercer St., between Houston and Prince Sts., SoHo* ☎ *212/382–2184* ⊕ *www.verawang.com* Ⓜ *N, R to Prince St.*

Vivienne Tam. Known for her East-meets-West designs, Tam makes dresses, blouses, and trousers with clean lines and bold prints in luxurious fabrics like silk. ⊠ *40 Mercer St., at Grand St., SoHo* ☎ *212/966–2398* ⊕ *www.viviennetam.com* Ⓜ *N, R to Prince St.*

Fodor'sChoice
★
What Goes Around Comes Around. Professional stylists and celebrities flock here to dig up pristine vintage items like Levi's and Azzedine

Alaïa dresses, as well as Hermès scarves and Chanel jewelry. The vintage rock tees (think Black Sabbath, Mötley Crüe) are great finds but can set you back an eye-watering $300–$600. ✉ *351 West Broadway, between Broome and Grand Sts., SoHo* ☎ *212/343–1225* ⊕ *www. whatgoesaroundnyc.com* Ⓜ *6, J, N, Q, R, Z to Canal St.*

Woolrich. In a nod to this brand's almost 200-year history, Woolrich's first retail space is decorated with vintage shearing tools and catalogs from the original Pennsylvania mill. The space is cozy, thanks to throw rugs and industrial-style lighting, and the full Woolrich product line is sold here, from sweaters to blankets and thick winter coats. ✉ *125 Wooster St., between Prince and Spring Sts., SoHo* ☎ *646/371–9968* ⊕ *www.woolrich.com* Ⓜ *N, R to Prince St.*

CRAFTS

Fodor's Choice
★

Purl. Anyone with a crafty bent will fall in love with this colorful paradise of top-quality knitting and sewing supplies, gorgeous craft books, and much, much more. Prices aren't cheap but the salespeople are extra friendly and knowledgeable. It's worth a browse even if you're not planning to buy anything. ✉ *459 Broome St., between Mercer and Green Sts., SoHo* ☎ *212/420–8796* ⊕ *www.purlsoho.com* Ⓜ *6 to Spring St.*

FOOD AND TREATS

Fodor's Choice
★

Harney & Sons. Fancy a cuppa? Harney & Sons produces more than 250 varieties of loose tea, which can be sampled at its store and tea salon in SoHo. The design is sleek and dramatic, with a 24-foot-long tasting bar and floor-to-ceiling shelves stocked with tea. Shoppers find classic brews like English breakfast and oolong, along with interesting herbals (ginger and licorice, or mint verbena). Enjoy a cup with a scone or other light fare, available at the tea salon. ✉ *433 Broome St., between Broadway and Crosby St., SoHo* ☎ *212/933–4853* ⊕ *www.harney.com* Ⓜ *6 to Spring St.*

Fodor's Choice
★

Jacques Torres Chocolates. Visit the café and shop here and be literally surrounded by chocolate. The glass-walled downtown space also houses Torres's chocolate factory, so you can watch the goodies being made while sipping a richly spiced cocoa or nibbling on a Java Junkie bar. Signature taste: the "wicked" chocolate, laced with cinnamon and chili pepper. ✉ *350 Hudson St., at King St., SoHo* ☎ *212/414–2462* ⊕ *www. mrchocolate.com* Ⓜ *1 to Houston St.*

Kee's Chocolates. Owner Kee Ling Tong whips up delicious truffles and macaroons with unusual, Asian-inspired flavors. Try the ginger peach and rosewater lychee macaroons, or truffles flavored with lemongrass mint and tamarind. ✉ *80 Thompson St., between Spring and Broome Sts., SoHo* ☎ *212/334–3284* ⊕ *www.keeschocolates.com* Ⓜ *C, E to Spring St.*

MarieBelle. The handmade chocolates here are nothing less than works of art. Square truffles and bonbons—in flavors like Earl Grey, cappuccino, passion fruit, and saffron—are painted with edible dyes (cocoa butter dyed with natural coloring) so each resembles a miniature painting. Relax in the Cacao Bar and Tea Salon while sipping an Aztec hot chocolate, made from rich cacao, rather than cocoa powder. ✉ *484 Broome*

17

St., between West Broadway and Wooster St., SoHo ☎ *212/226–8901* ⊕ *www.mariebelle.com* Ⓜ *N, R to Prince St.; 6, C, E to Spring St.*

Fodor's Choice
★

Vosges Haut-Chocolat. This chandeliered salon lined with apothecary shelves takes a global approach to chocolate. Many of the creations are travel inspired: the Budapest bonbons combine dark chocolate and Hungarian paprika, while the Japanese-influenced Black Pearls contain wasabi. Don't miss the best-selling chocolate-bacon bars. ⊠ *132 Spring St., between Wooster and Greene Sts., SoHo* ☎ *212/625–2929* ⊕ *www. vosgeschocolate.com* Ⓜ *N, R to Prince St.*

HOME DECOR

de Vera. Owner Federico de Vera crisscrosses the globe searching for unique decorative products, so shoppers never know what might turn up here. Venetian glass vases, Thai Buddhas, and antique rose-cut diamond rings are typical finds. ⊠ *1 Crosby St., at Howard St., SoHo* ☎ *212/625–0838* ⊕ *www.deveraobjects.com* Ⓜ *6, J, N, Q, R, Z to Canal St.*

Jonathan Adler. Everything at this flagship store, housed in a former plumbing factory, is fun and happy. Adler boldly funks up midcentury modern design, with striped, striated, or curvy handmade pottery (ranging from a $30 vase to a chunky $400 lamp) and hand-loomed wool pillow covers, rugs, and throws. Pull up to the Gift Bar if you need inspiration for a present. ⊠ *53 Greene St., between Broome and Grand Sts., SoHo* ☎ *212/941–8950* ⊕ *www.jonathanadler.com* Ⓜ *6, J, N, Q, R, Z to Canal St.*

Fodor's Choice
★

Matter. This beautifully curated store appeals to fans of sleek, modern furniture—if money is no object. How about the iconic Tank armchair by Alvar Aalto for a cool $5,000? Or a smoked-glass coffee table by Established & Sons for $1,400? Even if your budget is limited, Matter is worth a visit for inspiration. ⊠ *405 Broome St., between Centre and Lafayette Sts., SoHo* ☎ *212/343–2600* ⊕ *www.mattermatters.com* Ⓜ *6 to Spring St.*

Michele Varian. This stylish textile designer's shop is a temple to independent designers and artists, featuring a curated collection of everything from furniture to jewelry to kids' toys. Many of the pieces are by local designers, but the boutique also regularly hosts pop-up shops for out-of-town brands. ⊠ *27 Howard St., at Crosby St., SoHo* ☎ *212/343–0033* ⊕ *www.michelevarian.com* Ⓜ *6, N, Q, J, Z to Canal St.*

Room & Board. Fans of streamlined, midcentury modern furniture ascend to heaven here. This location is stocked with sleek sofas, beds, and children's furniture as well as accessories like rugs and lamps—90% of it made in America. Design aficionados can choose from iconic pieces like seating cubes from Frank Gehry and Eames molded plywood chairs, or items from up-and-coming designers. ⊠ *105 Wooster St., between Spring and Prince Sts., SoHo* ☎ *212/334–4343* ⊕ *www.roomandboard. com* Ⓜ *N, R to Prince St.*

JEWELRY AND ACCESSORIES

Fodor's Choice
★

Alexis Bittar. This Brooklyn-born designer began selling his first jewelry line, made from Depression-era glass, on a corner in SoHo. Now, Bittar counts A-list celebs and fashion editors among his fans. He makes clean-line, big-statement jewelry from vermeil, colored Lucite, pearls, and vintage glass. The store mirrors this aesthetic with a mix of old and new, like antique-white Victorian-era lion's-claw tables and Plexiglas walls. ☒ *465 Broome St., between Mercer and Greene Sts., SoHo* ☏ *212/625–8340* ⊕ *www.alexisbittar.com* Ⓜ *N, R to Prince St.*

Fodor's Choice **Aurélie Bidermann.** This French jeweler's New York boutique is all white
★ with pops of color, and includes a mural commissioned from a street artist. Bidermann's signature look is bold and inspired by her travels and nature. Look out for lace filigree gold cuffs, large turquoise necklaces, and drop earrings in the shape of gingko leaves. ☒ *265 Lafayette St., between Prince and Spring Sts., SoHo* ☏ *212/335–0604* ⊕ *www. aureliebidermann.com* Ⓜ *N, R Prince St.*

Fodor's Choice **Broken English.** This L.A. favorite has now made its way to New York.
★ Owner Laura Freedman sells a well-curated selection of jewelry from designers including Anita Ko and Carla Amorim. Expect delicate and whimsical pieces, from diamond-encrusted ear cuffs to geometric rings. ☒ *56 Crosby St., between Spring and Broome Sts., SoHo* ☏ *212/219–1264* ⊕ *www.brokenenglishjewelry.com* Ⓜ *6 to Spring St.*

Stuart Moore. Everything about this boutique is minimalist, from the architecture to the jewelry. Most of the designs (from Henrich & Denzel to Beatrice Mueller) have a streamlined, almost industrial look: diamonds are set in brushed platinum, and gold bangles are impossibly delicate. ☒ *411 West Broadway, at Spring St., SoHo* ☏ *212/941–1023* ⊕ *www.stuartmoore.com* Ⓜ *C, E to Spring St.; N, R to Prince St.*

SHOES, HANDBAGS, AND LEATHER GOODS

Camper. Urbanites love this Spanish footwear company for its funky but comfortable shoes. The flagship store has an unusual pagoda-style roof, and inside the store, there's a vertical garden. All the slip-ons and lace-ups here have generously rounded toes and a springy feel. ☒ *110 Prince St., at Greene St., SoHo* ☏ *212/343–4220* ⊕ *www.camper.com* Ⓜ *N, R to Prince St.*

The Frye Company. This 6,000-square-foot mecca to boots has an old western feel, thanks to the exposed brick walls and reclaimed barn doors. Boots can be tattooed—or hot stamped—with your initials while you wait in the lounge. In addition to Frye's famed boots, shoppers can also pick from flats, oxfords, clogs, and mules. ☒ *113 Spring St., between Mercer and Greene Sts., SoHo* ☏ *212/226–3793* ⊕ *www. thefryecompany.com* Ⓜ *N, R to Prince St.*

Longchamp. Their Le Pliage foldable nylon bags may have become a preppy staple, but don't think this label is stuffy—or all about nylon. There's a wide selection of leather handbags as well as wallets, belts, and shoes. Kate Moss also designs a line for Longchamp. ☒ *132 Spring St., between Wooster and Greene Sts., SoHo* ☏ *212/343–7444* ⊕ *www. longchamp.com* Ⓜ *N, R to Prince St.*

NOLITA

NoLIta ("North of Little Italy") is a shopping mecca, thanks to the abundance of boutiques that range from quirky to elegant. Like SoHo, NoLIta has changed from an understated, locals-only area to a crowded weekend magnet, as much about people-watching as shopping. Still,

17

unlike those of its SoHo neighbor, these stores remain largely independent. Running along the parallel north–south spines of Elizabeth, Mott, and Mulberry Streets, between Houston and Kenmare Streets, NoLIta's boutiques tend to be small and, as real estate costs dictate, somewhat pricey.

BEAUTY

Fodor's Choice ★ **Le Labo.** If you're bored with the perfume stock at department stores, come to this tiny boutique with a rustic, industrial vibe and resident mixologist who helps create your ideal perfume. After you choose your favorite scents, the perfume is mixed and a personalized label created for your bottle. ✉ *233 Elizabeth St., between Prince and Houston Sts., NoLIta* ☎ *212/219–2230* ⊕ *www.lelabofragrances.com* Ⓜ *B, D, F, M to Broadway–Lafayette St.*

Fodor's Choice ★ **Santa Maria Novella.** A heavy, iron-barred door leads to a hushed, scented inner sanctum of beauty products. This location is one of only two U.S. outposts for the 600-year-old Florentine company that makes intriguingly archaic colognes, creams, and soaps such as Dental Elixir and rose rice powder according to both traditional and modern recipes. Everything is packaged in bottles and jars with antique-style apothecary labels. There's also a wide selection of fragrances. ✉ *285 Lafayette St., between Houston and Prince Sts., NoLIta* ☎ *212/271–0884* ⊕ *www.santamarianovellausa.com* Ⓜ *N, R to Prince St.*

BOOKS AND STATIONERY

Fodor's Choice ★ **McNally Jackson.** This cozy independent bookstore is a bibliophile's dream. The bright two-story space has hardwood floors, a café, and plenty of chairs for lounging and curling up with a book. More than 50,000 books are stocked and the literary section is organized geographically. Budding authors can self-print their tomes on a device called the Espresso Book Machine. ✉ *52 Prince St., between Lafayette and Mulberry Sts., NoLIta* ☎ *212/274–1160* ⊕ *www.mcnallyjackson.com* Ⓜ *N, R to Prince St.; 6 to Spring St.*

CLOTHING

Creatures of Comfort. Owner Jade Lai has brought her popular L.A. outpost to New York. The open, airy boutique racks cool clothes from emerging designers alongside products from around the world. Most of the colors are muted, and brands carried include Acne, Band of Outsiders, and the house label, Creatures of Comfort. There's also a small selection of shoes, as well as under-the-radar beauty products, such as Rodin hand cream. ✉ *205 Mulberry St., between Spring and Kenmare Sts., NoLIta* ☎ *212/925–1005* ⊕ *www.creaturesofcomfort. us* Ⓜ *6 to Spring St.*

Fodor's Choice ★ **Duncan Quinn.** Described as "Savile Row meets Rock 'n' Roll" by *GQ*, this designer provides full bespoke and ready-to-wear services for everything from chalk-stripe suits to cuff links and croquet shirts, all in a shop not much bigger than its silk pocket squares. Off-the-rack shirts are handmade in Italy, but if you want to splurge, get fitted for a shirt with mother-of-pearl buttons. ✉ *70–80 Kenmare St., between Mott and Mulberry Sts., NoLIta* ☎ *212/226–7030* ⊕ *www.duncanquinn.com* Ⓜ *6 to Spring St.; J, Z to Bowery.*

INA. The clothing at this couture consignment store harks back only one or two seasons, and in some cases, the items have never been worn. Browse through the racks to spot gems from Lanvin, Chanel, and Alexander McQueen. There are multiple locations around the city; technically in NoHo, this outpost carries offerings for both men and women. ✉ *15 Bleecker St., at Elizabeth St., NoLIta* ☎ *212/228–8511* ⊕ *www. inanyc.com* Ⓜ *6 to Bleecker St.*

Jay Kos. There aren't too many boutiques where the owner sometimes whips up a snack for customers in the boutique's custom kitchen, but this designer—famous for dressing Diddy and Johnny Depp—wanted his boutique to have a homey feel. The clothes veer toward the fabulous: suede shoes, linen suits, and cashmere sweaters, which are displayed in armoires. ✉ *293 Mott St., at Houston St., NoLIta* ☎ *212/319–2770* ⊕ *www.jaykos.com* Ⓜ *B, D, F, M to Broadway–Lafayette St.*

Fodor'sChoice
★
Malia Mills. Swimsuit-fit fanatics have met their match here—especially those gals who are different sizes on top and bottom (bikini tops go up to size E). Flattering bikini tops and bottoms are sold separately: halters, bandeaus, and triangle tops, plus boy-cut, side-tie, and low-ride bottoms. There's a collection of one-pieces as well. ✉ *199 Mulberry St., between Spring and Kenmare Sts., NoLIta* ☎ *212/625–2311* ⊕ *www. maliamills.com* Ⓜ *6 to Spring St.*

Margaret O'Leary. Born in Ireland but settled in California, O'Leary is known for her knitwear. Her NoLIta boutique stocks everything from cashmere to cable knit in sweaters, tunics, and capes. Come here when the temperature starts to drop and you want to feel cozy. ✉ *279 Mott St., between Prince and Houston Sts., NoLIta* ☎ *646/274–9498* ⊕ *www.margaretoleary.com* Ⓜ *N, R to Prince St.*

Oak. Most of the clothing here comes in black or leather, and the store carries high-end designers in addition to its own line. Come here for skinny jeans, capes, and draped jersey dresses. ✉ *28 Bond St., between Lafayette St. and Bowery, NoHo* ☎ *212/677–9312* ⊕ *www.oaknyc. com* Ⓜ *6 to Bleecker St.*

Resurrection. If you're serious about vintage—and have deep pockets—Resurrection stocks a treasure trove of pristine pieces from Chanel, Gucci, Halston, Alaïa, and YSL among others. Kate Moss is a fan, and designers like Marc Jacobs and Anna Sui have sought inspiration among the racks. ✉ *217 Mott St., between Prince and Spring Sts., NoLIta* ☎ *212/625–1374* ⊕ *www.resurrectionvintage.com* Ⓜ *6 to Spring St.*

Fodor'sChoice
★
Warm. If you want to feel the love, come to this little boutique owned by lifelong surfers Winnie Beattie and her husband Rob Magnotta. Everything has a sunny, beachy vibe, from leather sandals, bikinis, and bleached sweaters to handblown glass vases. There's also a collection of children's books, housewares, and menswear. ✉ *181 Mott St., between Kenmare and Broome Sts., NoLIta* ☎ *212/925–1200* ⊕ *www.warmny. com* Ⓜ *6 to Spring St.*

JEWELRY AND ACCESSORIES

Dinosaur Designs. This Australian-owned brand designs jewelry and housewares inspired by nature and organic shapes. Resin is used to craft jewelry and vases in bold colors like hot pink and orange. Don't

17

miss the striking tableware. ⊠ *211 Elizabeth St., at Prince St., NoLIta* ☎ *212/680–3523* ⊕ *www.dinosaurdesigns.com.au* Ⓜ *N, R to Prince St.*

Erica Weiner. This eponymous designer specializes in vintage-inspired jewelry and antiques: delicate Art Deco earrings, vintage lockets, and necklaces fashioned from antique charms. The Erica Weiner collection includes pieces under $200. ⊠ *173 Elizabeth St., between Kenmare and Spring Sts., NoLIta* ☎ *212/334–6383* ⊕ *www.ericaweiner.com* Ⓜ *6 to Spring St.; J, Z to Bowery.*

Me&Ro. Minimalist, Eastern styling has gained these designers a cult following. The Indian-inspired, hand-finished gold bangles, earrings, and necklaces are covered in delicate jewels. Although the fine jewelry is expensive, small sterling silver pendants start at around $170. ⊠ *241 Elizabeth St., between Houston and Prince Sts., NoLIta* ☎ *917/237–9215* ⊕ *www.meandrojewelry.com* Ⓜ *N, R to Prince St.*

SHOES, HANDBAGS, AND LEATHER GOODS

Fodor's Choice
★

Clare V. L.A.-based designer Clare Vivier's first New York store displays her signature simple-but-elegant leather fold-over clutches in every size and color, as well as understated totes and duffels. There is a line of men's accessories, plus iPad cases, sunglasses, and other sundries. ⊠ *239 Elizabeth St., between Houston and Prince Sts., NoLIta* ☎ *646/484–5757* ⊕ *www.clairevivier.com* Ⓜ *N, R to Prince St.*

High Way. The bags here marry form and function. Totes and messenger bags come in durable leather and nylon, and some handbags have a wealth of inner pockets. ⊠ *238 Mott St., between Prince and Spring Sts., NoLIta* ☎ *212/966–4388* ⊕ *www.highwaybuzz.com* Ⓜ *6 to Spring St.*

John Fluevog Shoes. The inventor of the "Angel" sole (protects against water, acid, and "Satan"), Fluevog designs chunky, funky shoes and boots for men and women that are popular with rock stars and those who want to look like one. ⊠ *250 Mulberry St., at Prince St., NoLIta* ☎ *212/431–4484* ⊕ *www.fluevog.com* Ⓜ *N, R to Prince St.*

Kathryn Amberleigh. This designer, a graduate of the Fashion Institute of Technology, has perfected the sexy-but-edgy look in her handcrafted shoes. There are simple flats and wedges along with peep-toe ankle boots and sky-high heels. Most designs hover around the $250 mark. ⊠ *219 Mott St., between Prince and Spring Sts., NoLIta* ☎ *212/842–2134* ⊕ *www.kathrynamberleigh.com* Ⓜ *6 to Spring St.*

Manhattan Portgage/Token. Although messenger bags are now ubiquitous, pay homage to the store that started it all. Super durable, they come in waxed canvas as well as nylon, and the line has expanded to include totes, duffels, and travel bags, all in unadorned, simple styles. ⊠ *258 Elizabeth St., between Houston and Prince Sts., NoLIta* ☎ *212/226–9655* ⊕ *www.manhattanportage.com* Ⓜ *N, R to Prince St.*

Sigerson Morrison. The details—just-right T-straps, small buckles, a perfectly pointy toe—make these women's shoes irresistible. Prices start around $300, so the sales are big events. ⊠ *28 Prince St., between Mott and Elizabeth Sts., NoLIta* ☎ *212/219–3893* ⊕ *www.sigersonmorrison. com* Ⓜ *6 to Spring St.; N, R to Prince St.*

EAST VILLAGE AND LOWER EAST SIDE

EAST VILLAGE

The East Village is a fabulous hunting ground for independent boutiques and jam-packed vintage stores.

ANTIQUES AND COLLECTIBLES

Lost City Arts. This sprawling shop is one of the best places to shop for 20th-century design furniture, lighting, and accessories. Lost City can also help you relive the Machine Age with an in-house, retro-modern line of furniture. ⊠ *18 Cooper Sq., at E 5th St., East Village* ☎ *212/375–0500* ⊕ *www.lostcityarts.com* Ⓜ *6 to Astor Pl.*

BEAUTY

Bond No. 9. Created by the same fragrance team as Creed, this line of scents is intended to evoke the New York City experience, with a scent for every neighborhood: Central Park, a men's fragrance, is woodsy and "green," and Park Avenue is discreet but not too sweet. This flagship also carries candles and body creams. ⊠ *9 Bond St., between Lafayette St. and Broadway, East Village* ☎ *212/228–1732* ⊕ *www.bondno9.com* Ⓜ *6 to Bleecker St.*

Fodor'sChoice ★ Kiehl's Since 1851. At this favored haunt of top models and stylists (and the brand's flagship), white-smocked assistants help you choose between the lotions and potions, all of which are packaged in simple-looking bottles and jars. Some of the products, such as the Ultra Facial Cream, Creme with Silk Groom hairstyling aid, and superrich Creme de Corps, have attained near-cult status among fans. ⊠ *109 E. 3rd Ave., at 13th St., East Village* ☎ *212/677–3171* ⊕ *www.kiehls.com* Ⓜ *L to 3rd Ave.*

CLOTHING

Cloak & Dagger. Come here if you like refined but on-trend looks. The racks are lined with tulip skirts, belted dresses, and trenches handpicked by owner and designer Brookelynn Starnes. ⊠ *334 E. 9th St., between 1st and 2nd Aves., East Village* ☎ *212/673–0500* ⊕ *www.cloakanddaggernyc.com* Ⓜ *6 to Astor Pl.*

Fodor'sChoice ★ John Varvatos. This menswear designer has long been inspired by rock 'n' roll. His ad campaigns have starred the likes of Franz Ferdinand and Green Day, so it's fitting that he transformed the former CBGB club into his New York flagship. The space is dotted with vintage pianos, guitars, and vinyl records. And the clothes? The jeans, leather pants, and suede shoes give you rock-star cred, but there are also classic, understated styles for the corporate set. ⊠ *315 Bowery, between E. 1st and 2nd Sts., East Village* ☎ *212/358–0315* ⊕ *www.johnvarvatos.com* Ⓜ *6 to Bleecker St.*

Pas de Deux. Fashion editors love this little boutique—which looks like it was imported straight from Paris—thanks to the marble checkerboard floor, chandeliers, and fine woodwork. The well-curated selection includes dresses, trench coats, and denim from Isabel Marant, Thakoon Panichgul, and Alexander Wang. There are also lots of lovely little accessories, like eyeglasses, cardholders, and delicate necklaces. ⊠ *328 E. 11th St., between 1st and 2nd Aves., East Village* ☎ *212/475–0075* ⊕ *www.pasdedeuxny.com* Ⓜ *6 to Astor Pl.; L to 1st Ave.*

Screaming Mimi's. Browse through racks bulging with vintage finds from the 1920s through '90s. Retro wear includes everything from dresses to soccer shirts and prom dresses. Although most of the non-designer finds are affordable, Screaming Mimi's also carries vintage designer duds from Valentino, Chloé, and Gaultier. ✉ *382 Lafayette St., between 4th and Great Jones Sts., East Village* ☎ *212/677–6464* ⊕ *www.screamingmimis.com* Ⓜ *6 to Bleecker St.*

Tokio 7. Even fashion designers like Alexander Wang have been known to pop into this high-end consignment store to browse. Racks are loaded with goodies from A-list designers such as Gucci, Stella McCartney, Diane von Furstenberg, and Phillip Lim, and the inventory changes almost daily. ✉ *83 E. 7th St., between 1st and 2nd Aves., East Village* ☎ *212/353–8443* ⊕ *www.tokio7.net* Ⓜ *6 to Astor Pl.*

Trash and Vaudeville. This punk mecca is famous for dressing stars like Debbie Harry and the Ramones back in the '70s, and its rock 'n' roll vibe lives on. Goths, punks, and pro wrestlers shop here for bondage-inspired pants and skirts, as well as vinyl corsets and mini kilts. ✉ *4 St. Marks Pl., between 2nd and 3rd Aves., East Village* ☎ *212/982–3590* ⊕ *www.trashandvaudeville.com* Ⓜ *6 to Astor Pl.*

HOME DECOR

White Trash. Looking for a midcentury modern Danish desk? This is your place. Owner Stuart Zamsky crams his store with surprisingly affordable pieces that are mostly from the '40s through '70s, including tables, lamps, and chairs. Quirkier pieces include paper mobiles from the '70s, old fondue sets, and antique medical-office cabinets. ✉ *304 E. 5th St., between 1st and 2nd Aves., East Village* ☎ *212/598–5956* ⊕ *www.whitetrashnyc.com* Ⓜ *6 to Astor Pl.*

JEWELRY AND ACCESSORIES

Verameat. All the jewelry here is handmade in New York City, and none of it is typical. Design motifs include wrenches, Big Macs, and grenades. Tilda Swinton is a fan. ✉ *315 E. 9th St., between 1st and 2nd Aves., East Village* ☎ *212/388–9045* ⊕ *www.verameat.com* Ⓜ *6 to Astor Pl.*

TOYS

Dinosaur Hill. Forget about Elmo and Barbie. This little shop is crammed with quirky gifts for kids like hand puppets and marionettes from Asia, telescopes, and wooden rattles. Don't miss the unusual instruments, such as a cedar kalimba. ✉ *306 E. 9th St., between 1st and 2nd Aves., East Village* ☎ *212/473–5850* ⊕ *www.dinosaurhill.com* Ⓜ *6 to Astor Pl.*

WINE

Astor Wines & Spirits. Stock up on wine, spirits, and sake at this beautiful shop; it often has the bottle you can't find anywhere else. To unwind and learn more about food and wine, there's a wine library and a kitchen for cooking classes. ✉ *399 Lafayette St., at E. 4th St., East Village* ☎ *212/674–7500* ⊕ *www.astorwines.com* Ⓜ *6 to Astor Pl.*

LOWER EAST SIDE

Head to the Lower East Side for excellent vintage finds and edgy looks. Once home to multitudes of Eastern European immigrants and crumbling tenement buildings, the Lower East Side has transformed from New York's bargain-hunting ground into a hotbed for indie design that includes everything from clothing to furniture. Ludlow and Orchard Streets are the main drags for boutiques, bars, and hip restaurants. Head here if you want to revamp your look with a trendier style. For the full scope of this area, prowl from Allen to Essex Streets, and south of Houston Street down to Broome.

ANTIQUES AND COLLECTIBLES

Las Venus. Fans of midcentury modern design and sleek lines need to make a beeline here. Las Venus stocks upscale vintage furniture and accessories in excellent condition. While most of the items are sleek, this is also the place to indulge in Lucite and zebra-print fantasies. ✉ *113 Stanton St., between Ludlow and Essex Sts., Lower East Side* ☎ *212/358–8000* ⊕ *www.lasvenus.com* Ⓜ *F to 2nd Ave.*

CLOTHING

Assembly New York. What started as a minimalist menswear boutique became a minimalist menswear designer, then added a minimalist women's wear line, and is now a surprisingly spacious shop full of architectural clothing and accessories from a range of international, independent designers. ✉ *170 Ludlow St., between Stanton and E. Houston Sts., Lower East Side* ☎ *212/253–5393* ⊕ *www.assemblynewyork.com* Ⓜ *F to 2nd Ave.*

Frankie. A trendy concept store by the same team behind the now-shuttered Lower East Side favorite Pixie Market, the Frankie Shop caters to fashion-conscious women with its clean-lined, modern styles in understated hues from international designers. Best of all, the upscale-casual clothes, trendy boots, and both decor and fashion accessories look more expensive than they are. ✉ *100 Stanton St., between Ludlow and Orchard Sts., Lower East Side* ☎ *212/253–0953* ⊕ *www. thefrankieshop.com* Ⓜ *F to 2nd Ave.*

Lost Weekend NYC. Surfers and wannabe surfers stock up on boutique surf gear, boards, and Lost Weekend's signature clothes at this coffee shop–cum–surfer lifestyle boutique. It also offers a collection of art books and surf photography, as well as men's grooming products. ✉ *45 Orchard St., between Hester and Grand Sts., Lower East Side* ☎ *917/261–2401* ⊕ *www.lostweekendnyc.com.*

The Rising States. This unassuming boutique from a lifelong fashion fan stocks a curated collection of ultrahip pieces for ladies—think quirky dresses, tailored pants, loose tops, and colorful heels and boots—by mostly local designers (like Samantha Pleet and Miranda Bennett) who often drop by the shop. ✉ *168 Ludlow St., between Stanton and E. Houston Sts., Lower East Side* ☎ *646/649–2410* ⊕ *www. therisingstatesnyc.com* Ⓜ *F to 2nd Ave.*

SHOES, HANDBAGS, AND LEATHER GOODS

Altman Luggage. Having trouble fitting all your purchases into your bag? Altman sells top-of-the-line luggage from Rimowa, Samsonite, and Tumi at discount prices. A selection of watches and cosmetic bags are also for sale. ✉ *135 Orchard St., between Delancey and Rivington Sts., Lower East Side* ☎ *212/254–7275* ⊕ *www.altmanluggage.com* Ⓜ *J, M, Z to Essex St.; F to Delancey St.*

17

GREENWICH VILLAGE AND WEST VILLAGE

GREENWICH VILLAGE

The Beats were born and raised in the Village, but today, the poets and artists have long been replaced by New York University buildings and apartments with sky-high rent. Still, if you know where to look, there are charmingly offbeat stores worth exploring here that retain the flavor of the glory days.

BEAUTY

C. O. Bigelow. Founded in 1838, this is the oldest apothecary-pharmacy in the United States; Mark Twain used to fill prescriptions here. They still fill prescriptions, but the real reason to come is for the hard-to-find brands like Klorane shampoo and Elgydium toothpaste. Bigelow also has its own line of products, including green-tea lip balm and quince hand lotion. ⊠ *414 6th Ave., between W. 8th and 9th Sts., Greenwich Village* ☎ *212/533–2700* ⊕ *www.bigelowchemists.com* Ⓜ *A, B, C, D, E, F, M to W. 4th St.*

CLOTHING

Denim & Supply. Owned by Ralph Lauren, this boutique has a rustic, utilitarian look, with distressed wood floors and plenty of Americana. Jeans, denim shirts, and jackets for men and women are available in every hue along with T-shirts, dresses, and cargo pants. ⊠ *99 University Pl., at E. 12th St., Greenwich Village* ☎ *212/677–1895* ⊕ *www. denimandsupply.com* Ⓜ *4, 5, 6, L, N, Q, R to 14th St.–Union Sq.*

La Petite Coquette. Everything at this lingerie boutique is unabashedly sexy, and the helpful staff can find the perfect fit. The store's own line of corsets, camisoles, and other underpinnings comes in a range of colors. ⊠ *51 University Pl., between E. 9th and 10th Sts., Greenwich Village* ☎ *212/473–2478* ⊕ *www.thelittleflirt.com* Ⓜ *N, R to 8th St.–NYU.*

Personnel of New York. "Lifestyle boutique" is an overused term, but it is the best way to describe this indie favorite, which specializes in men's and women's clothing from New York and L.A. designers. The boutique also stocks unusual home goods, such as bottle openers by Japanese designer Tadanori Baba and soap from Juniper Ridge. ⊠ *9 Greenwich Ave., between Christopher and 10th Sts., Greenwich Village* ☎ *212/924–0604* ⊕ *www.personnelofnewyork.com* Ⓜ *1 to Christopher St.–Sheridan Sq.; A, B, C, D, E, F, M to W. 4th St.*

WEST VILLAGE

One of the most picturesque neighborhoods in New York, the West Village is filled with charming boutiques, restaurants, and bars—many of which have retained their vintage charm thanks to exposed brick walls and pressed tin ceilings. Stroll around, get lost on a cobblestone street, and finish a day of shopping with a drink at a cozy bar.

Bleecker Street is a particularly good place to indulge all sorts of shopping appetites. Foodies love the blocks between 6th and 7th Avenues for the specialty purveyors like Murray's Cheese (⊠ *254 Bleecker St.*). Fashion fans forage along the stretch between West 10th Street and 8th Avenue. Hudson Street and Greenwich Avenue are also prime boutique-browsing territory. Christopher Street, true to its connection with the lesbian and gay community, has a handful of shops sporting rainbow flags.

ANTIQUES AND COLLECTIBLES

Kaas Glassworks. From the outside in, this shop is oh-so-charming, an old-fashioned sign and sandwich board welcoming shoppers and passersby. The specialty here is decoupage that has been turned into quirky trays and paperweights. Owner Carol Kaas uses antique prints, vintage postcards, historical maps, and ephemera in her work, and customizes decoupage trays from wedding invitations, photos, baby announcements, or other paper keepsakes. ⊠ *117 Perry St., between Greenwich and Hudson Sts., West Village* ☎ *212/366–0322* ⊕ *www.kaas.com* Ⓜ *1 to Christopher St.–Sheridan Sq.*

BEAUTY

Fodor'sChoice
★
Aedes Perfumery. Arguably the best place to buy fragrance in Manhattan, this boutique's super-knowledgeable staff helps shoppers find the perfect scent. High-end brands like L'Artisan Parfumeur and Annick Goutal are stocked, along with luxurious skin-care products, pricey candles, and room diffusers. The shop's signature gift wrap is as beautiful as what's inside the box. ⊠ *7 Greenwich Ave., at Christopher St., West Village* ☎ *212/206–8674* ⊕ *www.aedes.com* Ⓜ *1 to Christopher St.–Sheridan Sq.*

CAP Beauty. This is a one-stop shop for natural skin care, which means that 100% of its products are free from synthetic ingredients. Brands carried include Elizabeth Dehn, Tata Harper, and Ko Denmark. CAP also does spa treatments, facials, and acupuncture. ⊠ *238 W. 10th St., between Hudson and Bleecker Sts., West Village* ☎ *212/227–1088* ⊕ *www.capbeauty.com* Ⓜ *1 to Christopher St.–Sheridan Sq.*

Jo Malone. This crisp black-and-white boutique sets a serene backdrop for sampling tangy scents like lime blossom and mandarin, or Earl Grey and cucumber. Fragrances can be worn alone or layered. The U.S. flagship for the British brand also offers complimentary hand massages (by appointment) and has a sampling bar for creating a bespoke scent. ⊠ *330 Bleecker St., at Christopher St., West Village* ☎ *212/242–1454* ⊕ *www.jomalone.com* Ⓜ *1 to Christopher St.–Sheridan Sq.*

BOOKS AND STATIONERY

bookbook. This small, independent bookstore is crammed with the latest new releases as well as a thoughtful assortment of general nonfiction, guidebooks, and children's books. But when the weather cooperates, the real focus here is the carefully selected sale tables that spill out onto the sidewalk, with deals on everything from Graham Greene to Chuck Palahniuk. ⊠ *266 Bleecker St., between 6th and 7th Aves., West Village* ☎ *212/807–8655* ⊕ *www.bookbooknyc.com* Ⓜ *1 to Christopher St.–Sheridan Sq.; A, B, C, D, E, F, M to W. 4th St.*

Fodor'sChoice
★
Three Lives & Company. One of the city's best book selections is displayed on the tables and counters of this bookshop, which highlights the latest literary fiction and serious nonfiction, classics, quirky gift books, and gorgeously illustrated tomes. The staff members' literary knowledge is formidable, so don't be afraid to ask for their own picks. ⊠ *154 W. 10th St., at Waverly Pl., West Village* ☎ *212/741–2069* ⊕ *www.threelives. com* Ⓜ *1 to Christopher St.–Sheridan Sq.*

17

CLOTHING

Cynthia Rowley. This boutique delivers flirty, whimsical dresses that are perfect for cocktail parties. To complete the look, throw on some of the designer's colorful pumps and sharply tailored coats. ⊠ *376 Bleecker St., between Charles and Perry Sts., West Village* ☎ *212/242–3803* ⊕ *www.cynthiarowley.com* Ⓜ *1 to Christopher St.–Sheridan Sq.*

Hotoveli. This unprepossessing nook stocks some of the most elegant (and expensive) designers in the world, ranging from Alexander McQueen to Vivienne Westwood. If you have to ask how much an item costs, don't try it on. ⊠ *378 Bleecker St., between Charles and Perry Sts., West Village* ☎ *212/206–7475* ⊕ *www.hotoveli.com* Ⓜ *1 to Christopher St.–Sheridan Sq.*

Khirma Eliazov. This former magazine editor now designs an elegant line of handbags, clutches, and accessories that are favorites among stars like Blake Lively and J.Lo. She uses luxury materials, including python, alligator, crocodile, and stingray skins. ⊠ *102 Charles St., between Hudson and Bleecker Sts., West Village* ☎ *646/529–1408* ⊕ *www.khirmaeliazov.com* Ⓜ *1 to Christopher St.–Sheridan Square.*

FOOD AND TREATS

Li-Lac Chocolates. Feeding the Village's sweet tooth since 1923, Li-Lac indulges shoppers with its almond bark and coconut clusters as well as such specialty items as chocolate-molded Statues of Liberty. The coconut rolls and chocolate-covered graham crackers tempt even the most stubborn dieter. To see how the small-batch chocolates are made, visit Li-Lac's Brooklyn factory. ⊠ *40 8th Ave., at Jane St., West Village* ☎ *212/924–2280* ⊕ *www.li-lacchocolates.com* Ⓜ *A, C, E to 14th St.; L to 8th Ave.*

Sockerbit. Who knew Scandinavians were obsessed with candy? There's much more than Swedish fish at this gleaming white candy emporium that stocks hard candies, gummies, licorice, and chocolate. Have fun pronouncing the names of treats like Bumlingar Jordgubb and Zoo Klubba. ⊠ *89 Christopher St., between Bleecker and W. 4th Sts., West Village* ☎ *212/206–8170* ⊕ *www.sockerbit.com* Ⓜ *1 to Christopher St.–Sheridan Sq.*

SHOES, HANDBAGS, AND LEATHER GOODS

Fodor's Choice ★ **Flight 001.** Frequent flyers can one-stop shop at this travel-themed store that puts a creative spin on everyday accessories. Shop for bright luggage tags, passport holders, satin sleep masks, and innovative storage for everything from shoes to toiletries. ⊠ *96 Greenwich Ave., between W. 12th and Jane Sts., West Village* ☎ *212/989–0001* ⊕ *www.flight001.com* Ⓜ *1, 2, 3 to 14th St.*

Fodor's Choice ★ **Leffot.** This simple, understated store focuses on one thing: selling top-quality men's shoes. Owner Steven Taffel, who previously worked at Prada, has stocked his shop with selections from John Lobb, Church's, and Edward Green. These shoes are meant to last a lifetime, and many have a price tag to match. Bespoke footwear is also available. ⊠ *10 Christopher St., at Gay St., West Village* ☎ *212/989–4577* ⊕ *www.leffot.com* Ⓜ *1 to Christopher St.–Sheridan Sq.; A, B, C, D, E, F, M to W. 4th St.*

Lulu Guinness. Hit this black-and-white-boutique for cheerfully eccentric accessories such as handbags printed with images of lips, dolls, and cameos. Other accessories, including umbrellas and luggage, are equally fun. ⊠ *394 Bleecker St., between W. 11th and Perry Sts., West Village* ☎ *212/367–2120* ⊕ *www.luluguinness.com* Ⓜ *1 to Christopher St.–Sheridan Sq.*

CHELSEA AND THE MEATPACKING DISTRICT

CHELSEA

Chelsea offers one-stop shopping for some of the biggest retail brands, as well as quirky local boutiques.

BOOKS AND STATIONERY

FAMILY **Books of Wonder.** Readers young and old delight in Manhattan's oldest and largest independent children's bookstore. The friendly, knowledgeable staff can help select gifts for all reading levels. Don't miss the extensive Oz section, plus the collection of old, rare, and collectible children's books and original children's book art. ⊠ *18 W. 18th St., between 5th and 6th Aves., Chelsea* ☎ *212/989–3270* ⊕ *www.booksofwonder.com* Ⓜ *F, M to 14th St.; L to 6th Ave.*

Posman Books. Posman Books has an outstanding selection of contemporary and classic books across genres. Don't miss the cheeky and serious high-quality greeting cards. Look for a second location at 30 Rockefeller Plaza in Midtown West. ⊠ *Chelsea Market, 75 9th Ave., between 15th and 16th Sts., Chelsea* ☎ *212/627–0304* ⊕ *www.posmanbooks. com* Ⓜ *A, C, E to 14th St.; L to 8th Ave.*

CLOTHING

Comme des Garçons. The designs in this swoopy, gold-adorned space consistently push the fashion envelope with brash patterns, unlikely juxtapositions (tulle and neoprene), and cuts that are meant to be thought-provoking, not flattering. Architecture students come just for the interior design. ⊠ *520 W. 22nd St., between 10th and 11th Aves., Chelsea* ☎ *212/604–9200* ⊕ *www.comme-des-garcons.com* Ⓜ *C, E to 23rd St.*

Fisch for the Hip. This high-end consignment store sells carefully curated men's and women's clothing and accessories, from top designers including Tom Ford, Balenciaga, and Lanvin. Hermès bags are a specialty. ⊠ *88½ 7th Ave., between W. 15th and 16th Sts., Chelsea* ☎ *212/633–6965* ⊕ *www.fischforthehip.com* Ⓜ *A, C, E to 14th St.; L to 8th Ave.; 1 to 18th St.*

New York Vintage. Stylists to the stars, TV costumers, and the deep-pocketed descend upon this boutique to browse racks of prime vintage clothing. Everything is high-end, so don't expect any bargains. Take your pick from Yves Saint Laurent, Madame Grès, and Thierry Mugler items. There's a good selection of handbags and stilettos, too. ⊠ *117 W. 25th St., between 6th and 7th Aves., Chelsea* ☎ *212/647–1107* ⊕ *www. newyorkvintage.com* Ⓜ *F, M to 23rd St.*

17

Fodor's Choice   **Story.** Launched by former consultant Rachel Shechtman, Story is a con-
★   cept store with a twist. Every few weeks, it partners with a new sponsor
to develop a retail "story," like a magazine spread, which ranges from
wearable tech to "home for the holidays." Pop by often to admire the
artful displays, and you never know what will be for sale, from chocolates to clothing to books. Story also hosts events such as talks with
TED speakers. ⊠ *144 10th Ave., at 19th St., Chelsea* ☎ *212/242–4853*
⊕ *www.thisisstory.com* Ⓜ *A, C, E to 14th St.; L to 8th Ave.*

GIFTS AND SOUVENIRS

Eleni's. Take a bite out of the Big Apple—in cookie form—with these
perfectly decorated treats, shaped like yellow cabs, the New York skyline, and police cars. It's not just New York depicted here; the iced
cookies come in every design imaginable, from iPhones to bottles of
nail polish. Photos of loved ones can be transferred onto cupcakes—if
you don't mind taking a bite. ⊠ *Chelsea Market, 75 9th Ave., between
15th and 16th Sts., Chelsea* ☎ *212/255–7990* ⊕ *www.elenis.com* Ⓜ *A,
C, E to 14th St.; L to 8th Ave.*

MUSIC STORES AND MEDIA

Jazz Record Center. If you're seeking rare or out-of-print jazz recordings,
this is your one-stop shop. Long-lost Ellingtons and other rare pressings
come to light here; the jazz-record specialist also stocks books, collect-
ibles, DVDs, posters, CDs, and LPs. ⊠ *236 W. 26th St., 8th fl., between
7th and 8th Aves., Chelsea* ☎ *212/675–4480* ⊕ *www.jazzrecordcenter.
com* Ⓜ *1 to 28th St.*

WINE

Bottlerocket Wine & Spirit. Fun and approachable, this shop puts a new
spin on wine shopping. Vintages are organized by quirky factors like
their compatibility with Chinese takeout and whom they'd best suit as
gifts (ranging from "Third Date" to "The Boss"). A kids' play nook and
doggie area make the space extra welcoming. ⊠ *5 W. 19th St., between
5th and 6th Aves., Chelsea* ☎ *212/929–2323* ⊕ *www.bottlerocketwine.
com* Ⓜ *4, 5, 6, L, N, Q, R to 14th St.–Union Sq.*

MEATPACKING DISTRICT

For nearly a century, the industrial western edge of downtown Manhattan was defined by slaughterhouses and meatpacking plants,
blood-splattered cobblestone streets, and men lugging carcasses into
warehouses before dawn.

But in the late 1990s, the area bounded by 14th Street, Gansevoort
Street, Hudson Street, and 11th Avenue speedily transformed into
another kind of meat market. Many of the old warehouses now house
ultrachic shops, nightclubs, and restaurants packed with angular fashionistas. Jeffrey, a pint-sized department store, was an early arrival,
followed by bigger brands such as Diane von Furstenberg and a few
lofty furniture stores. Despite the influx of a few chains—albeit stylish
ones like Scoop—eclectic boutiques keep popping up. The one thing
that's hard to find here is a bargain.

CLOTHING

Fodor's Choice **Diane von Furstenberg.** At this light-filled New York flagship, try on the
★ iconic DVF wrap dress in myriad patterns. The blouses, shorts, and
skirts are equally feminine. ⊠ *874 Washington St., at 14th St., Meatpacking District* ☏ *646/486–4800* ⊕ *www.dvf.com* Ⓜ *A, C, E to 14th
St.; L to 8th Ave.*

Jeffrey. The Meatpacking District really arrived when this Atlanta-
based mini Barneys opened its doors. You can find an incredible array
of designer shoes—Valentino and red-soled Christian Louboutin are
some of the best sellers—plus top labels such as Yves Saint Laurent and
Lanvin. ⊠ *449 W. 14th St., between 9th and 10th Aves., Meatpacking
District* ☏ *212/206–1272* ⊕ *www.jeffreynewyork.com* Ⓜ *A, C, E to
14th St.; L to 8th Ave.*

Rebecca Taylor. This designer is known for her soft, feminine work, which
runs the gamut from sexy to understated, all with a slightly vintage
flair. Taylor's downtown location is a serene, spacious environment for
browsing racks of silky shirtdresses, embroidered tunics, and ruffled
overcoats. Her shoes, handbags, and jewelry are equally romantic. ⊠ *34
Gansevoort St., between Greenwich and Hudson Sts., Meatpacking
District* ☏ *212/243–2600* ⊕ *www.rebeccataylor.com* Ⓜ *A, C, E to 14th
St.; L to 8th Ave.*

Trina Turk. Make a beeline to this boutique if you like bright, happy
colors and 1970's-influenced clothing. The shop, designed by Jonathan Adler, showcases Turk's ready-to-wear clothing in a bright, airy
setting. Swimwear is a standout, and menswear is also sold here. ⊠ *67
Gansevoort St., between Washington and Greenwich Sts., Meatpacking District* ☏ *212/206–7383* ⊕ *www.trinaturk.com* Ⓜ *A, C, E to 14th
St.; L to 8th Ave.*

17

UNION SQUARE AND THE FLATIRON DISTRICT

UNION SQUARE

The several blocks around Union Square—which itself is home to the
city's best greenmarket, and a holiday market leading up to Christmas—just south of the Flatiron District, has large retail chains such as
J.Crew, Banana Republic, and Anthropologie.

BEAUTY

Fresh. Long a beauty favorite, with ingredients that are good enough to
eat (think brown sugar, soy, and black tea), the Fresh flagship has an
apothecary-inspired look, with beautifully packaged soaps displayed
like pastries in a glass case. Pull up a seat at the communal Kitchen
Table to try out a new product. ⊠ *872 Broadway, at 18th St., Union
Square* ☏ *212/477–1100* ⊕ *www.fresh.com* Ⓜ *4, 5, 6, L, N, Q, R to
14th St.–Union Sq.*

BOOKS AND STATIONERY

Fodor's Choice **The Strand.** Opened in 1927 and still run by the same family, this mon-
★ strous book emporium—home to 2 million volumes, or "18 Miles of
Books"—is a symbol of a bygone era, a mecca for serious bibliophiles,
and a local institution. The store has survived the Great Depression,

World War II, and competition from Barnes & Noble and the Kindle. The stock includes new and secondhand books, plus thousands of collector's items and merchandise. A separate rare-book room is on the third floor (it closes at 6:15 daily). The basement has discounted, barely touched review copies of new books, organized by author. If you're looking for souvenirs, visit the New York section of the bookstore for New York–centric literature, poetry, and cookbooks, as well as T-shirts and totes. Visitors should also check the Strand's events calendar and try to attend an author or artist event. Headliners have ranged from Anne Rice to James Franco. ⊠ *828 Broadway, at 12th St., Union Square* ☎ *212/473–1452* ⊕ *www.strandbooks.com* Ⓜ *4, 5, 6, L, N, Q, R to 14th St.–Union Sq.*

CLOTHING

Beacon's Closet. Brooklyn favorite Beacon's Closet now has a Big Apple outpost. This simple space, which is lit by multiple chandeliers, has a wide selection of gently used modern and vintage clothes. Comb through the racks and you might find pieces from Christian Dior, Marc Jacobs, or AllSaints as well as stylish items from under-the-radar labels. ⊠ *10 W. 13th St., between 5th and 6th Aves., Union Square* ☎ *917/261–4863* ⊕ *www.beaconscloset.com* Ⓜ *4, 5, 6, L, N, Q, R to 14th St.–Union Sq.*

J.Crew. This preppy-chic staple in so many people's closets continues to push the envelope under superstar Jenna Lyons. Yes, you can still get cardigans, cords, and tees in every pastel color of the rainbow, but the clothes today are sometimes downright sexy. The leather jackets and sequined skirts are also perfect for that casual, thrown-together look. This flagship carries women's, men's, and Crewcuts for children as well as a wedding gown collection. ⊠ *91 5th Ave., between 16th and 17th Sts., Union Square* ☎ *212/255–4848* ⊕ *www.jcrew.com* Ⓜ *4, 5, 6, L, N, Q, R to 14th St.–Union Sq.*

Journelle. This chic, New York–based boutique was started by two women who believed that sexy, pretty lingerie should be everyday wear—and comfortable, too. The staff is approachable and helpful. There are now a handful of stores around the city, including in SoHo and on the Upper East Side. ⊠ *3 E. 17th St., between Broadway and 5th Ave., Union Square* ☎ *212/255–7800* ⊕ *www.journelle.com* Ⓜ *4, 5, 6, N, Q, R, L to Union Sq.*

FOOD AND WINE

Max Brenner: Chocolate by the Bald Man. This shop and restaurant is all about a Wonka-ish sense of entertainment. The café encourages the messy enjoyment of gooey creations like chocolate pizzas for kids, but there are also savory options to soak up all that sugar. Take-away treats include caramelized pralines and tins of hot-chocolate mix. ⊠ *841 Broadway, between 13th and 14th Sts., Union Square* ☎ *646/467–8803* ⊕ *www.maxbrenner.com* Ⓜ *4, 5, 6, L, N, Q, R to 14th St.–Union Sq.*

Fodor'sChoice
★

Union Square Wine & Spirits. Tastings are easy at this well-stocked store, thanks to Enomatic machines. These card-operated contraptions let you sample dozens of wines. If machines don't do it for you, generous tastings are held most Fridays and Saturdays. ⊠ *140 4th Ave., at 13th St.,*

Union Square ☎ *212/675–8100* ⊕ *www.unionsquarewines.com* Ⓜ *4, 5, 6, L, N, Q, R to 14th St.–Union Sq.*

HOME DECOR

Fodor's Choice **ABC Carpet & Home.** If you love eclectic luxury home goods from around
★ the world, this is your place. Spread over 10 floors is a superb selection of rugs, antiques, textiles, furniture, and bedding, including sleek sofas and Balinese daybeds. The ground floor is a wonderland of silk pillows and jewelry. To refuel, there's an in-house restaurant from Jean-Georges Vongerichten. More rugs and carpets are unrolled across the street at 881 Broadway. ⊠ *888 Broadway, at 19th St., Union Square* ☎ *212/473–3000* ⊕ *www.abchome.com* Ⓜ *4, 5, 6, L, N, Q, R to 14th St.–Union Sq.*

JEWELRY AND ACCESSORIES

Beads of Paradise. Not your ordinary bead store, the baubles here are sourced from around the world. Shoppers can choose silver from Bali and Mexico and ancient glass beads from China, along with semiprecious stones. Sign up for a class to learn how to put it all together. The store also has a wide range of other trinkets from around the world, including Buddha figurines from Thailand, Madonna candles from Mexico, and Ganesha-printed hangings from India. ⊠ *16 E. 17th St., between 5th Ave. and Broadway, Union Square* ☎ *212/620–0642* ⊕ *www.beadsofparadisenyc.com* Ⓜ *4, 5, 6, L, N, Q, R to 14th St.– Union Sq.*

FLATIRON DISTRICT

The Flatiron District, north of Union Square, stretches from about 17th Street up to 29th Street, and between 6th Avenue and Lexington. This is one of the buzziest areas in New York, brimming with both large and small stores. Come here if you want to shop the big chains minus the Midtown tourist crowds.

BOOKS AND STATIONERY

Idlewild Books. Named for the pre-1960s JFK Airport, this travel-inspired bookstore is one of the last of its kind in America. They stock guidebooks, novels, and children's books grouped by destination, and also run foreign-language classes, ranging from Arabic to German. If those chairs look familiar, it may be because you huddled in one during a layover at the American Airlines terminal. ⊠ *12 W. 19th St., 2nd fl., between 5th and 6th Aves., Flatiron District* ☎ *212/414–8888* ⊕ *www. idlewildbooks.com* Ⓜ *4, 5, 6, L, N, Q, R to 14th St.–Union Sq.*

CHILDREN'S CLOTHING

FAMILY **Space Kiddets.** The funky (Elvis-print rompers, CBGB onesies) mixes with the old-school (retro cowboy-print pants, brightly colored clogs, Bruce Lee T-shirts) and the high-end (Lili Gaufrette, Kenzo, Boo Foo Woo from Japan) at this casual, trendsetting store. ⊠ *26 E. 22nd St., between Broadway and Park Ave., Flatiron District* ☎ *212/420–9878* ⊕ *www.spacekiddets.com* Ⓜ *6 to 23rd St.*

17

CLOTHING

Anthropologie. This popular women's clothing and home accessories chain epitomizes bohemian chic. ✉ *85 5th Ave., at 16th St., Flatiron District* ☎ *212/627–5885* ⊕ *www.anthropologie.com* Ⓜ *4, 5, 6, L, N, Q, R to 14th St.–Union Sq.*

Fodor's Choice ★ **Club Monaco.** In addition to the brand's signature clothing (think of a hipper Banana Republic), this flagship includes an outpost of Williamsburg favorite Toby's Estate Coffee, as well as a bookstore operated by the Strand and a flower shop operated by boutique florists Putnam & Putnam. ✉ *160 5th Ave., between 20th and 21st Sts., Flatiron District* ☎ *212/352–0936* ⊕ *www.clubmonaco.com* Ⓜ *N, R to 23rd St.*

Madewell. This J.Crew spinoff is ideal for casual women's staples like jeans, T-shirts, and sweaters with a vintage look. The two-story Manhattan flagship has a quirky, homespun design; merchandise is displayed on everything from old mill tables to meat hooks. Don't miss the shoe shop and home-goods collection. ✉ *115 5th Ave., between 18th and 19th Sts., Flatiron District* ☎ *212/228–5172* ⊕ *www.madewell.com* Ⓜ *4, 5, 6, L, N, Q, R to 14th St.–Union Sq.*

Fodor's Choice ★ **Maison Kitsuné.** This decades-old French fashion and music label made its stateside debut in this airy, sun-washed boutique for mens- and women's-wear classics with a stylish Gallic twist, ranging from cardigans and loafers to blazers and dresses. ✉ *NoMad Hotel, 1170 Broadway, at 28th St., Flatiron District* ☎ *212/481–6010* ⊕ *www.kitsune.fr* Ⓜ *N, R to 28th St.*

FOOD AND TREATS

Eataly. This sprawling Italian grocery, originally from Torino, has the best selection of imported foodstuffs in the city, as well as a variety of cafés and restaurants, set between the aisles and meat and cheese counters. Up on the roof, there's also a house brewery and beer garden. ✉ *200 5th Ave., at 24th St., Flatiron District* ☎ *212/229–2560* ⊕ *www.eataly.com* Ⓜ *N, R, 4, 5, 6 to 23rd St.*

HOME DECOR

Fodor's Choice ★ **Fishs Eddy.** The dishes, china, and glassware for resale come from all walks of crockery life, including corporate dining rooms and failed restaurants, so you never know what you might find. Fishs Eddy also sells its own lines of dishes, which have classic looks. ■TIP→ The shop is a great place to pick up New York–themed gifts, such as mugs and trays. ✉ *889 Broadway, at 19th St., Flatiron District* ☎ *212/420–9020* ⊕ *www.fishseddy.com* Ⓜ *4, 5, 6, L, N, Q, R to 14th St.–Union Sq.*

Marimekko. If you love bright, cheerful patterns, make a beeline to the Marimekko flagship. This 4,000-square-foot store is primarily white, so the colorful merchandise pops. Everything from pot holders and shower curtains to coats and dresses is available here in the Finnish brand's bold signature prints. If you're feeling crafty, pick up a few yards of fabric to create something of your own. ✉ *200 5th Ave., between 23rd and 24th Sts., Flatiron District* ☎ *212/843–9121* ⊕ *www.marimekko.com* Ⓜ *N, R to 23rd St.*

Holiday Markets

Between Thanksgiving and Christmas, holiday markets—rows of wooden stalls, many with red-and-white-stripe awnings—spring up around town. The gifts and goods vary from year to year, but there are some perennial offerings: colorful handmade knitwear and jewelry; sweet-smelling soaps, candles, and lotions with hand-lettered labels; glittery Christmas ornaments of every stripe; and New York–themed gift items.

While the holiday market in Grand Central Terminal's Vanderbilt Hall is indoors, most vendors set up outside. There's one every year at Columbus Circle, near the southwest entrance to Central Park, and another at Bryant Park, behind the New York City Public Library. The largest and most popular, however, is at the south end of Union Square, where you can go from the greenmarket to the stalls, just like the downtowners who meet in the afternoon or after work to look for unique or last-minute gifts.

TOYS

FAMILY **Kidding Around.** This independent shop is piled high with old-fashioned wooden toys, sturdy musical instruments, classic kids' books, and plenty of arts-and-crafts materials. The costume racks are rich with dress-up potential. ⊠ *60 W. 15th St., between 5th and 6th Aves., Union Square* ☎ *212/645–6337* ⊕ *www.kiddingaroundtoys.com* Ⓜ *F, M to 14th St.; 4, 5, 6, L, N, Q, R to 14th St.–Union Sq.*

17

MIDTOWN EAST

If money is no object, put on your best shopping shoes and most glamorous sunglasses and head to Midtown East. Some of the world's most luxurious brands—from Gucci to Christian Dior—have their flagship stores along 5th Avenue. All the stores *on* 5th Avenue are included in Midtown East, although some might be on the west side of the street and have West in their address.

ANTIQUES AND COLLECTIBLES

A La Vieille Russie. Antiques dealers since 1851, this shop specializes in European and Russian decorative arts, jewelry, and paintings. Behold bibelots by Fabergé and others, enameled or encrusted with jewels. If money is no object, there are also antique diamond necklaces and pieces of china once owned by Russian nobility. ⊠ *781 5th Ave., at 59th St., Midtown East* ☎ *212/752–1727* ⊕ *www.alvr.com* Ⓜ *N, Q, R to 5th Ave./59th St.*

The Chinese Porcelain Company. Though the name of this prestigious shop indicates one of its specialties, its stock covers more ground, ranging from lacquerware to Khmer sculpture, as well as work by contemporary Chinese artists. ⊠ *232 E. 59th St., between 2nd and 3rd Aves., Midtown East* ☎ *212/838–7744* ⊕ *www.chineseporcelaincompany.com/* Ⓜ *4, 5, 6 to 59th St.; N, Q, R to Lexington Ave./59th St.*

Flying Cranes Antiques. At this world leader in Japanese antiques, shoppers find rare, museum-quality pieces from the Meiji period, Japan's Golden Age. Items include ceramics, cloisonné, metalwork, baskets, and samurai swords and fittings. ⊠ *Manhattan Art and Antiques Center, 1050 2nd Ave., between 55th and 56th Sts., Midtown East* ☎ *212/223–4600* ⊕ *www.flyingcranesantiques.com* Ⓜ *E, M to Lexington Ave./53rd St.*

Leo Kaplan Ltd. The impeccable items here include Art Nouveau glass and pottery, porcelain from 18th-century England, antique and modern paperweights, and Russian art. ⊠ *114 E. 57th St., between Park and Lexington Aves., Midtown East* ☎ *212/355–7212* ⊕ *www.leokaplan. com* Ⓜ *4, 5, 6 to 59th St.; N, Q, R to Lexington Ave./59th St.*

Newel. This huge collection spans the Renaissance through the 20th century. The nonfurniture finds, from figureheads to bell jars, make for prime conversation pieces. Newel is a major supplier of antiques for Broadway shows and luxury department store windows. ⊠ *306 E. 61st St., 3rd fl., between 2nd Ave. and Ed Koch Queensboro Bridge Exit, Midtown East* ☎ *212/758–1970* ⊕ *www.newel.com* Ⓜ *4, 5, 6 to 59th St.; N, Q, R to Lexington Ave./59th St.*

BOOKS AND STATIONERY

Fodor's Choice ★ **Argosy Bookstore.** Family owned since 1925, Argosy is a charmingly old-fashioned place to browse for both bargain and priceless books. The shop keeps a scholarly stock of rare books and autographs. It's also a great place find low-price maps and prints for gifts. ⊠ *116 E. 59th St., between Park and Lexington Aves., Midtown East* ☎ *212/753–4455* ⊕ *www.argosybooks.com* Ⓜ *4, 5, 6 to 59th St.; N, Q, R to Lexington Ave./59th St.*

CAMERAS AND ELECTRONICS

Fodor's Choice ★ **Apple Store.** New York's flagship Apple Store features a 32-foot-high glass cube that appears to float over its subterranean entrance. The Apple-obsessed will be happy to know this location is open 24/7, holidays included. Make an appointment (well in advance) at the Genius Bar if you need tech help. There's also an Apple Store location in SoHo, in a converted historic post office building, as well as a handful of other branches around the city, including on the Upper West Side, on West 14th Street, and in Grand Central Station. ⊠ *767 5th Ave., at 59th St., Midtown East* ☎ *212/336–1440* ⊕ *www.apple.com* Ⓜ *N, Q, R to 5th Ave./59th St.*

Sony Store. Located on the ground floor of the Sony Building, this sunny space is a wonderland of electronics, with all the latest home-theater equipment, cameras, tablets, and smartphones. ⊠ *550 Madison Ave., at 55th St., Midtown East* ☎ *212/833–8800* ⊕ *www.store.sony.com* Ⓜ *E, M to 5th Ave./53rd St.*

CLOTHING

Abercrombie & Fitch. This brand is known for its casual preppy clothes for men, women, and kids—but brace yourself for the thumping club music and dim lighting. ⊠ *720 5th Ave., at 56th St., Midtown East* ☎ *212/306–0936* ⊕ *www.abercrombie.com* Ⓜ *F to 57th St.; N, Q, R to 5th Ave./59th St.*

Banana Republic. Although there are nearly a dozen Banana Republic stores around the city, come to the flagship for the biggest selection of clothing. Don't miss the Heritage collection or the big clearance racks. ⊠ *Rockefeller Center, 626 5th Ave., at 51st St., Midtown East* ☎ *212/974–2350* ⊕ *www.bananarepublic.com* Ⓜ *B, D, F, M to 47th–50th Sts./Rockefeller Center; E, M to 5th Ave./53rd St.*

Brooks Brothers. The clothes at this classic American haberdasher are, as ever, traditional, comfortable, and fairly priced. Summer seersucker, navy-blue blazers, and the peerless oxford shirts have been staples for generations; the women's and boys' selections have variations thereon. Get scanned by a digital tailor for precisely measured custom shirts or suits; an appointment is recommended. ⊠ *346 Madison Ave., at 44th St., Midtown East* ☎ *212/682–8800* ⊕ *www.brooksbrothers.com* Ⓜ *4, 5, 6, 7, S to Grand Central–42nd. St.*

Burberry. This six-story glass-and-stone flagship is a temple to all things plaid, British, and Cara Delevingne. The iconic trench coat can be made-to-measure here, and the signature plaid can be found on bikinis, scarves, and wallets. For children, there are mini versions of quilted jackets and cozy sweaters. ⊠ *9 E. 57th St., between 5th and Madison Aves., Midtown East* ☎ *212/407–7100* ⊕ *us.burberry.com* Ⓜ *N, Q, R to 5th Ave./59th St.*

Chanel. The Midtown flagship has often been compared to a Chanel suit—slim, elegant, timeless, and decorated in the signature black-and-white colors. Come here for the iconic suits and quilted handbags, along with other pillars of Chanel style: chic little black dresses, evening gowns, and yards of pearls. There's also a cosmetics area where you can stock up on the famed scents and nail polish. ⊠ *15 E. 57th St., between 5th and Madison Aves., Midtown East* ☎ *212/355–5050* ⊕ *www.chanel.com* Ⓜ *N, Q, R to 5th Ave./59th St.*

Christian Dior. This very white, very glossy space sets a serene background to showcase the luxe ready-to-wear collection along with handbags and accessories. If you're not in the market for an investment gown or fine jewelry, peruse the latest status bag. The Dior menswear boutique is next door; the cigarette-thin suits are often snapped up by women. ⊠ *21 57th St., between 5th and Madison Aves., Midtown East* ☎ *212/931–2950* ⊕ *www.dior.com* Ⓜ *N, Q, R to 5th Ave./59th St.*

Fodor's Choice ★ **Dover Street Market.** The New York location is the only U.S. outpost of Rei Kawakubo's Dover Street Market (the others are in London, Tokyo, and Beijing). It's basically a multilevel fashion emporium: each floor has mini boutiques from brands including Prada, Alaïa, and Alexander Wang, alongside lesser-known designers. The seven-story building is worth a look just for the people-watching. The in-house Rose Bakery is the perfect spot to refuel with an espresso or berry tart. ⊠ *160 Lexington Ave., at 30th St., Midtown East* ☎ *646/837–7750* ⊕ *newyork. doverstreetmarket.com* Ⓜ *6 to 28th St.*

Fodor's Choice ★ **Dunhill.** If you're stumped on what to buy the man in your life, head to Dunhill. The menswear is exquisitely tailored, and the accessories, like wallets and cuff links, are somewhat affordable. The walk-in humidor stores top-quality tobacco and cigars. ⊠ *545 Madison Ave., at 55th*

17

St., Midtown East ☎ *212/753–9292* ⊕ *www.dunhill.com* Ⓜ *E, M to 5th Ave./53rd St.*

Gucci. Located in the Trump Building, this 46,000-square-foot flagship with floor-to-ceiling glass windows is the largest Gucci store in the world. Here, shoppers find a special "heritage" department, plus goods exclusive to the store. The clothing is edgy and sexy. Skin-tight pants might be paired with a luxe leather jacket; silk tops leave a little more to the imagination. Many of the accessories, like wraparound shades or snakeskin shoes, have Gucci's signature horsebit detailing. ✉ *725 5th Ave., at 56th St., Midtown East* ☎ *212/826–2600* ⊕ *www.gucci.com* Ⓜ *N, Q, R to 5th Ave./59th St.*

H&M. Of-the-moment trends are packaged for the mass market at this affordable Swedish clothing chain, which has numerous stores in the city. H&M has collaborated with many designers, including Karl Lagerfeld and Isabel Marant. ✉ *589 5th Ave., between 47th and 48th Sts., Midtown East* ☎ *855/466–7476* ⊕ *www.hm.com* Ⓜ *B, D, F, M to 47–50th St./Rockefeller Center.*

Joe Fresh. Think of this brand as the Canadian version of H&M crossed with the Gap, selling stylish but classic clothes for men and women at affordable prices. The New York flagship stocks everything from sweaters and denim to button-down shirts and shoes in a rainbow of colors. Just about all items are under $100. ✉ *510 5th Ave., between 42nd and 43rd Sts., Midtown East* ☎ *212/764–1731* ⊕ *www.joefresh.com* Ⓜ *7 to 5th Ave.; B, D, F, M to 42nd St./Bryant Park.*

Massimo Dutti. Owned by Zara, this brand is that more ubiquitous one's older, more sophisticated sibling. The three-story space specializes in sleek basics that are perfect for work or the weekends, such as blazers, trench coats, and silky sweaters. ✉ *689 5th Ave., between 54th and 55th Sts., Midtown East* ☎ *212/371–2555* ⊕ *www.massimodutti.com* Ⓜ *E, M to 5th Ave./53rd St.*

Tommy Hilfiger. The global flagship oozes old-school Americana, with its dark-wood paneling, shirts displayed on bookshelves, and scattering of antiques. It's filled with tailored suits for men, smart sweater sets and pencil skirts for women, and evening wear along with sportswear, plus a whole floor devoted to denim. ✉ *681 5th Ave., between 53rd and 54th Sts., Midtown East* ☎ *212/223–1824* ⊕ *usa.tommy.com* Ⓜ *E, M to 5th Ave./53rd St.*

UNIQLO. At 89,000 square feet, this location is the biggest UNIQLO in the world (in New York, there are also branches in SoHo and near Herald Square). Shoppers can scoop up staples such as sweaters, skinny jeans, and button-down shirts in a rainbow of colors. Don't miss the limited-edition collaborations with big-name designers and stylists. The Heattech clothing range is always a big hit. Weekday mornings are the best time to avoid long lines for the dressing rooms. ✉ *666 5th Ave., at 53rd St., Midtown East* ☎ *877/486–4756* ⊕ *www.uniqlo.com* Ⓜ *E, M to 5th Ave./53rd St.*

Versace. The architecture here, with its marble floor and glittering chandeliers, provides the perfect backdrop for the outrageous designs and colors of Versace clothes. The brand's housewares and bedding collection are also available here. ✉ *647 5th Ave., between 51st and 52nd Sts., Midtown East* ☎ *212/317–0224* ⊕ *www.versace.com* Ⓜ *E, M to 5th Ave./53rd St.*

Zara. This massive store is one of Zara's biggest in the United States and the place to come for affordable, stylish fashion. New merchandise arrives twice a week and ranges from classics like blazers to edgier skinny trousers. There are also two lounge areas, in case you need a shopping break. ✉ *666 5th Ave., between 52nd and 53rd Sts., Midtown East* ☎ *212/765–0477* ⊕ *www.zara.com* Ⓜ *E, M to 5th Ave./53rd St.*

DEPARTMENT STORES

Bergdorf Goodman. This luxury department store is the ultimate shopping destination, offering ladies (and gentlemen) who lunch designer clothes, a stellar shoe department, and top-notch service. The fifth floor is where to go for contemporary lines. The range of products in the beauty department is unparalleled, and shoppers can complete their look with highlights at the in-house John Barrett salon. If you need to refuel, grab a bite at the seventh-floor BG Restaurant, with Central Park views, or a quick bite at the beauty-level Good Dish. ✉ *754 5th Ave., between 57th and 58th Sts., Midtown East* ☎ *212/753–7300* ⊕ *www. bergdorfgoodman.com* Ⓜ *N, Q, R to 5th Ave./59th. St.*

Fodor'sChoice
★
Bloomingdale's. Only a few stores in New York occupy an entire city block; the uptown branch of this New York institution is one of them. The main floor is a crazy, glittery maze of mirrored cosmetic counters and perfume-spraying salespeople. Once you get past this dizzying scene, you can find good buys on designer clothes, bedding, and housewares. ✉ *1000 3rd Ave., main entrance at 59th St. and Lexington Ave., Midtown East* ☎ *212/705–2000* ⊕ *bloomingdales.com* Ⓜ *4, 5, 6 to 59th St.; N, Q, R to Lexington Ave./59th St.*

17

Henri Bendel. Behind the graceful Lalique windows, discover a world of luxe accessories, all from Henri Bendel's own collection. Work your way through two floors of jewelry, scarves, handbags, and sunglasses. If you really want to pamper yourself, visit Frédéric Fekkai's hair salon on the fourth floor. ✉ *712 5th Ave., between 55th and 56th Sts., Midtown East* ☎ *212/247–1100* ⊕ *www.henribendel.com* Ⓜ *E, M to 5th Ave./53rd St.*

Lord & Taylor. This is not your mother's Lord & Taylor. The department store has been working hard to attract a younger, hipper crowd. Shoppers find classic brands like Coach and Ralph Lauren along with jeans from Seven for All Mankind and tops by Trina Turk. Don't miss the lovely ground-floor beauty department. Best of all, it isn't nearly as crowded as competitor Macy's. ✉ *424 5th Ave., between 38th and 39th Sts., Midtown East* ☎ *212/391–3344* ⊕ *www.lordandtaylor.com* Ⓜ *B, D, F, M to 42nd St.–Bryant Park.*

Saks Fifth Avenue. This iconic store has been upping its fashion stakes and revamping its résumé by adding more contemporary designer lines, such as Proenza Schouler and Victoria Beckham. The department store now has a designer sneaker shop, as well as an enormous Christian Louboutin shop-within-a-shop. The ground-floor beauty department stocks everything from the classics to the edgy. ✉ *611 5th Ave., between 49th and*

50th Sts., Midtown East ☎ *212/753–4000* ⊕ *www.saksfifthavenue.com* Ⓜ *E, M to 5th Ave./53rd St.; B, D, F, M to 47–50th St./Rockefeller Center.*

GIFTS AND SOUVENIRS

New York City Transit Museum Gallery Annex & Store. Located in the symbolic heart of New York City's transit system, the store features an eclectic array of merchandise all linked to the MTA (Metropolitan Transportation Authority), from straphanger ties to earrings made from old subway tokens. ⊠ *Grand Central Terminal, Vanderbilt Pl. and 42nd St., Shuttle Passage, Midtown East* ☎ *212/878–0106* ⊕ *www. nytransitmuseumstore.com* Ⓜ *4, 5, 6, 7, S to Grand Central–42nd St.*

HOME DECOR

Armani Casa. In keeping with the Armani aesthetic, the minimalist furniture and housewares here have a subdued color scheme (gold, gray, cream, and black). Big-ticket items include luxuriously upholstered sofas and sleek coffee tables. The desk accessories and throw pillows are equally understated. ⊠ *Decoration & Design Building, 979 3rd Ave., Suite 1424, between 58th and 59th Sts., Midtown East* ☎ *212/334–1271* ⊕ *www.armanicasa.com* Ⓜ *4, 5, 6 to 59th St.; N, Q, R to Lexington Ave./59th St.*

JEWELRY AND ACCESSORIES

Bulgari. This Italian company is certainly not shy about its name, which encircles gems, watch faces, and an ever-growing accessories line. There are ornate, weighty rings and other pieces mixing gold with stainless steel, porcelain, and the brand's signature cabochon multicolored sapphires. Wedding and engagement rings are slightly more subdued. ⊠ *730 5th Ave., at 57th St., Midtown East* ☎ *212/315–9000* ⊕ *www. bulgari.com* Ⓜ *N, Q, R to 5th Ave./59th St.*

Cartier. Established in 1914, this legendary French jeweler and firm favorite among royals and celebrities is the place to come for exquisite engagement rings, luxury watches, or cuff links. Cartier's iconic designs include the panther motif, the Trinity ring, and Tank watches. ⊠ *767 5th Ave., between 58th and 59th Sts., Midtown East* ☎ *212/457–3202* ⊕ *www.cartier.com* Ⓜ *N, Q, R to 5th Ave./59th St.*

H. Stern. Sleek designs pose in an equally modern 5th Avenue setting; smooth cabochon-cut stones, most from South America, glow in pale wooden display cases. The designers make notable use of semiprecious stones such as citrine, tourmaline, and topaz. ⊠ *645 5th Ave., between 51st and 52nd Sts., Midtown East* ☎ *212/655–3910* ⊕ *www.hstern.net* Ⓜ *E, M to 5th Ave./53rd St.*

Harry Winston. These jewels regularly adorn celebs at the Oscars, and you need an A-list bank account to shop here. The ice-clear diamonds are of impeccable quality and set in everything from emerald-cut solitaire rings to wreath necklaces resembling strings of flowers. No wonder the jeweler was immortalized in the song "Diamonds Are a Girl's Best Friend." ⊠ *718 5th Ave., at 56th St., Midtown East* ☎ *212/399–1000* ⊕ *www.harrywinston.com* Ⓜ *F to 57th St.; N, Q, R to 5th Ave./59th St.*

Mikimoto. The Japanese originator of the cultured pearl, Mikimoto presents a glowing display of high-luster pearls. Besides the creamy strands from their own pearl farms, check out diamond-and-pearl earrings, bracelets, and rings. ✉ *730 5th Ave., between 56th and 57th Sts., Midtown East* ☎ *212/457–4600* ⊕ *www.mikimotoamerica.com* Ⓜ *F to 57th St.; N, Q, R to 5th Ave./59th St.*

Tiffany & Co. It's hard to think of a more iconic New York jewelry store than Tiffany, along with its unmistakable blue box. Daydream among the displays of platinum-and-diamond bracelets and massive engagement rings, but head to the sterling-silver floor for more affordable baubles. The new Tiffany T line is streamlined and modern. ✉ *727 5th Ave., at 57th St., Midtown East* ☎ *212/755–8000* ⊕ *www.tiffany.com* Ⓜ *N, Q, R to 5th Ave./59th St.*

Van Cleef & Arpels. This French jewelry company is considerably more low-key than many of its blingy neighbors, in both design and marketing ethos (you won't see them opening a store in your average mall). Their best-known design is the cloverleaf Alhambra, which can be found on rings, necklaces, and earrings. ✉ *744 5th Ave., at 57th St., Midtown East* ☎ *212/896–9284* ⊕ *www.vancleefarpels.com* Ⓜ *N, Q, R to 5th Ave./59th St.*

SHOES, HANDBAGS, AND LEATHER GOODS

Bally. If you want to channel your inner princess, you can't go wrong with the ladylike pumps and high-heeled boots here. The accessories and clothing are equally tasteful. ✉ *628 Madison Ave., at 59th St., Midtown East* ☎ *212/751–9082* ⊕ *www.bally.com* Ⓜ *N, Q, R to 5th Ave./59th St.*

Bottega Veneta. The signature crosshatch weave graces leather handbags, slouchy satchels, and shoes; the especially satisfying brown shades extend from fawn to deep chocolate. The stylish men's and women's ready-to-wear collection is also sold here. ✉ *650 Madison Ave., between 59th and 60th Sts., Midtown East* ☎ *212/371–5511* ⊕ *www.bottegaveneta.com* Ⓜ *4, 5, 6 to 59th St.; N, Q, R to Lexington Ave./59th St.*

Cole Haan. This brand is known for its comfortable but stylish footwear—many shoes have Nike Air cushioning in the heel. Everything from sandals to boots and pumps is available. ✉ *Rockefeller Center, 620 5th Ave., between 49th and 50th Sts., Midtown East* ☎ *212/765–9747* ⊕ *www.colehaan.com* Ⓜ *B, D, F, M to 47–50th St./Rockefeller Center.*

Fendi. Once known for its furs, Fendi is now synonymous with decadent handbags, and its new Madison Avenue flagship is a temple to them. The purses are beaded, embroidered, and fantastically embellished within an inch of their lives. Buttery soft leathers, ladylike evening dresses, structured handbags, and other accessories are also available. ✉ *598 Madison Ave., between 57th and 58th Sts., Midtown East* ☎ *212/897–2244* ⊕ *www.fendi.com* Ⓜ *N, Q, R to 5th Ave./59th St.*

Fratelli Rossetti. Don't come here expecting sexy, skyscraper stilettos. This Italian leather-goods company excels at classic shoes. Riding boots are among the most popular items, but there are also pumps, loafers, and slouchy ankle boots. Men can choose from oxfords and boots. There's also a line of leather handbags. ✉ *625 Madison Ave., between E. 58th and E. 59th Sts., Midtown East* ☎ *212/888–5107* ⊕ *www. fratellirossetti.com* Ⓜ *N, R, Q, 5th Ave./59th St.; 4, 5, 6 to 59th St.*

17

Fodor's Choice ★ **Louis Vuitton.** In the mammoth 57th Street flagship, shoppers get their fill of LV-emblazoned handbags and accessories, as well as the more subtle Damier check pattern and colorful striated leathers. The clothes and shoes here are devastatingly chic. ⊠ *1 E. 57th St., at 5th Ave., Midtown East* ☎ *212/758–8877* ⊕ *www.louisvuitton.com* Ⓜ *N, Q, R to 5th Ave./59th St.*

Salvatore Ferragamo. Elegance and restraint typify these designs, from patent leather ballet flats to weekender ankle boots. The company has reworked some of its women's styles from previous decades, like the girlish Audrey (as in Hepburn) ballet flat, released seasonally for limited runs. Don't miss the silk ties for men. ⊠ *655 5th Ave., at 52nd St., Midtown East* ☎ *212/759–3822* ⊕ *www.ferragamo.com* Ⓜ *E, M to 5th Ave./53rd St.*

Stuart Weitzman. The broad range of shoe styles, from wing tips to strappy sandals, is enhanced by an even wider range of sizes and widths. Bridal shoes are hugely popular, if pricey. ⊠ *625 Madison Ave., between E. 58th and 59th Sts., Midtown East* ☎ *212/750–2555* ⊕ *www.stuartweitzman.com* Ⓜ *N, Q, R to 5th Ave./59th St.; 4, 5, 6 to 59th St.*

TOYS

FAMILY **American Girl Place.** Grade-school kids are crazy for American Girl dolls, whose lines range from historically accurate characters to contemporary girls with all the accompanying clothes and accessories. Bring your doll here for a doll hairdressing station, café, and Dress Like Your Doll shop. ⊠ *609 5th Ave., at 49th St., Midtown East* ☎ *212/371–2220* ⊕ *www.americangirl.com* Ⓜ *B, D, F, M to 47th–50th Sts./Rockefeller Center.*

MIDTOWN WEST

Stretching west from ritzy 5th Avenue, Midtown West covers everything from Herald Square to Times Square, and plenty in between. In other words, whether you're window-shopping or have money to burn, you'll no doubt find something to strike your fancy, from high-end designers to major retail brands.

CAMERAS AND ELECTRONICS

B&H Photo & Video. Low prices, good customer service, and a liberal return policy make this well-stocked emporium a favorite with pros and amateurs alike looking for audio and video equipment, new cameras, or laptops. Be sure to leave a few extra minutes for the checkout procedure; also, keep in mind that the store is closed Saturday. B&H is also known for its ceiling-height conveyor-belt system to move packages. ⊠ *420 9th Ave., between W. 33rd and 34th Sts., Midtown West* ☎ *212/239–7765* ⊕ *www.bhphotovideo.com* Ⓜ *1, 2, 3, A, C, E to 34th St.–Penn Station.*

CLOTHING

Forever 21. The pounding music, plethora of jeggings, and graffiti-covered NYC taxicabs parked inside appeal to tween shoppers. But even if you are older than 21, there's still reason to shop here. This location, clocking in at a whopping 90,000 square feet and perched right on Times Square, is crammed with supertrendy clothes that won't break the bank, such as slouchy sweaters, shirtdresses, and poofy skirts. Menswear and children's clothes are also sold here, and the jewelry is surprisingly well-done. There are several other locations in Manhattan, including Union Square and Herald Square. ⊠ *1540 Broadway, between W. 45th and 46th Sts., Midtown West* ☎ *212/302–0594* ⊕ *www.forever21.com* Ⓜ *N, Q, R to 49th St.; 1, 2, 3, N, Q, R, 7 to Times Square/42nd St.*

Gap. Gap may be as ubiquitous as Starbucks, but it is still a go-to place for classic denim, khakis, and sweaters in a rainbow of colors, as well as on-trend capsule collections from top designers. This Herald Square flagship also carries GapBody, GapMaternity, GapKids, and babyGap. ⊠ *60 W. 34th St., at Broadway, Midtown West* ☎ *212/760–1268* ⊕ *www.gap.com* Ⓜ *B, D, F, M, N, Q, R to 34th St.–Herald Sq.*

Norma Kamali. A fashion fixture from the 1980s, Norma Kamali has a thoroughly modern, though still '80s-influenced, line. Her luminously white store carries graphic bathing suits, Grecian-style draped dresses, and her signature poofy "sleeping-bag coats." The in-house Wellness Café sells olive oil–based beauty products. ⊠ *11 W. 56th St., between 5th and 6th Aves., Midtown West* ☎ *212/957–9797* ⊕ *www. normakamali.com* Ⓜ *N, Q, R 5th Ave./59th St.*

DEPARTMENT STORES

Macy's. Macy's iconic flagship has just emerged from a multiyear renovation, and visitors can now expect a glossier, grander look with acres of marble and new video screens. On both the cosmetics and clothing floors, the focus has been shifted to prestige brands like Gucci and Kate Spade. With over 1 million square feet of retail space at your feet, it's easy to spend an entire day shopping here. ⊠ *Herald Square, 151 W. 34th St., between Broadway and 7th Ave., Midtown West* ☎ *212/695–4400* ⊕ *www.macys.com* Ⓜ *B, D, F, M, N, Q, R to 34th St.–Herald Sq.*

FOOD AND TREATS

Morrell & Company. This high-end, sprawling wine shop also includes a wine bar and auction division. Come by for a free tasting or, if money is no object, head to the rare-wine vault. More than 100 fine wines are available by the glass at the store's café. ⊠ *1 Rockefeller Plaza, at W. 49th St., Midtown West* ☎ *212/688–9370* ⊕ *morrellwine.com* Ⓜ *B, D, F, M to 47th–50th Sts./Rockefeller Center.*

HOME DECOR

Muji. If you're into simple, chic, and cheap style, Muji has you covered. The name of this Japanese import translates to "no brand," and indeed, you don't find logos plastered on the housewares or clothes. Instead, their hallmark is a streamlined, minimalist design. The whole range of goods, from milky porcelain teapots to wooden toys, is invariably user-friendly. ⊠ *620 8th Ave., at W. 40th St., Midtown West* ☎ *212/382–2300* ⊕ *www.muji.us* Ⓜ *A, C, E to 42nd St.–Port Authority; 1, 2, 3, N, Q, R, 7 to Times Square–42nd St.*

JEWELRY AND ACCESSORIES

Skagen. Brave the crowds in Times Square to head to Skagen's flagship, which sells watches, handbags, and leather accessories inspired by Danish design. Many of the timepieces and satchels have a unisex design and

17

are logo-free. ✉ *1585 Broadway, between W. 47th and 48th Sts., Midtown West* ☎ *845/384–1221* ⊕ *www.skagen.com* Ⓜ *N, Q, R to 49th St.*

MUSEUM STORES

Museum of Arts and Design. This well-curated gift shop stocks crafts like beautiful handmade tableware, unusual jewelry, and rugs, often tied into ongoing exhibits. It's a great place to stock up on gifts. ✉ *2 Columbus Circle, at 8th Ave., Midtown West* ☎ *212/299–7700* ⊕ *thestore.madmuseum.org* Ⓜ *1, A, B, C, D to 59th St.–Columbus Circle.*

Museum of Modern Art Design and Book Store. MoMA's in-house shop stocks a huge selection of art reproductions and impressive coffee-table books about painting, sculpture, film, and photography. Across the street is the **MoMA Design Store,** where you can find Charles and Ray Eames furniture reproductions, vases designed by Alvar Aalto, and lots of clever toys. ✉ *11 W. 53rd St., between 5th and 6th Aves., Midtown West* ☎ *212/708–9700* ⊕ *www.moma.org/visit/plan/stores* Ⓜ *E, M to 5th Ave./53rd St.*

PERFORMING ARTS MEMORABILIA

Drama Book Shop. If you're looking for a script, be it a lesser-known Russian translation or Broadway hit, chances are you can find it here. The range of books spans film, music, dance, TV, and biographies. The shop also hosts Q&A's with leading playwrights. ✉ *250 W. 40th St., between 7th and 8th Aves., Midtown West* ☎ *212/944–0595* ⊕ *www.dramabookshop.com* Ⓜ *A, C, E to 42nd St.–Port Authority; 1, 2, 3, 7, N, Q, R, S to Times Sq.–42nd St.*

One Shubert Alley. This was the first store to sell Broadway merchandise outside of a theater. Today, souvenir posters, tees, and other knickknacks memorializing past and present Broadway hits still reign at this Theater District shop. ✉ *1 Shubert Alley, between W. 44th and 45th Sts., Midtown West* ☎ *212/944–4133* Ⓜ *1, 2, 3, 7, N, Q, R, S to Times Sq.–42nd St.*

Triton Gallery. Theatrical posters both large and small are available, and the selection is democratic, with everything from Marlene Dietrich's *Blue Angel* to recent Broadway shows represented. ✉ *The Film Center, 630 9th Ave., Suite 808, between W. 44th and 45th Sts., Midtown West* ☎ *212/765–2472* ⊕ *www.tritongallery.com* Ⓜ *A, C, E to 42nd St.–Port Authority.*

SHOES, HANDBAGS, AND LEATHER GOODS

Manolo Blahnik. These sexy status shoes are some of the most expensive on the market. The signature look is a pointy toe with a high, delicate heel, but there are also ballet flats, gladiator sandals, and over-the-knee dominatrix boots that cost nearly $2,000. Pray for a sale. ✉ *31 W. 54th St., between 5th and 6th Aves., Midtown West* ☎ *212/582–3007* ⊕ *www.manoloblahnik.com* Ⓜ *E, M to 5th Ave./53rd St.*

THE UPPER EAST SIDE

This well-heeled neighborhood is known for its antiques shops and high-end designers, such as Carolina Herrera, Oscar de la Renta, and Tom Ford. Shops are primarily sprinkled along Madison Avenue.

Outlet Shopping in NYC

Traditionally, dedicated bargain shoppers from around the world have devoted a day of their New York City trips to taking the bus to Woodbury Common Premium Outlets, an hour north of the city. But, as of November 2017, this time-honored pilgrimage will become unnecessary, when Empire Outlets opens on Staten Island.

Located on the waterfront, the outlets are next to the Staten Island Ferry Terminal, which has a 20-minute free ferry that travels between downtown Manhattan and Staten Island. The outlets will be home to Staten Island's first gourmet-food hall, the Marketplace at Empire Outlets, as well as dozens of premium outlets and a luxury hotel.

ANTIQUES AND COLLECTIBLES

Florian Papp. Established in 1900, this store has an unassailable reputation among knowledgeable collectors. Expect to find American and European antiques and paintings from the 18th to 20th centuries. Gilt mirrors, chandeliers, and mahogany tables abound. ⊠ *962 Madison Ave., between E. 75th and 76th Sts., Upper East Side* ☎ *212/288–6770* ⊕ *www.florianpapp.com* Ⓜ *6 to 77th St.*

Keno Auctions. Leigh Keno of *Antiques Roadshow* fame presides over this auction house, which specializes in Americana. As expected, he has a good eye and an interesting inventory; he's sold silver sauceboats from Paul Revere, masterpiece paintings, and Chippendale furniture. ⊠ *127 E. 69th St., between Park and Lexington Aves., Upper East Side* ☎ *212/734–2381* ⊕ *www.kenoauctions.com* Ⓜ *6 to 68th St.–Hunter College.*

BEAUTY

NARS. Women adore NARS for its iconic products such as Jungle Red lipstick and multiuse make-up sticks. The NARS flagship has glossy white walls and a red counter, and stocks the full NARS makeup range as well as a collection of "François' Favorite Things," which includes books, films, and photographs that have served as inspiration. ⊠ *971 Madison Ave., between E. 75th and 76th Sts., Upper East Side* ☎ *212/861–2945* ⊕ *www.narscosmetics.com* Ⓜ *6 to 77th St.*

BOOKS AND STATIONERY

Crawford Doyle Booksellers. You're as likely to see an old edition of Wodehouse as a best seller in the window of this shop. Bibliophiles find a high-quality selection of fiction, nonfiction, and biographies, plus some rare books on the balcony. Salespeople offer their opinions *and* ask for yours. ⊠ *1082 Madison Ave., between E. 81st and 82nd Sts., Upper East Side* ☎ *212/288–6300* ⊕ *www.crawforddoyle.com* Ⓜ *4, 5, 6 to 86th St.*

CHILDREN'S CLOTHING

FAMILY **Bonpoint.** Celebrities love this French children's boutique for the beautiful designs and impeccable workmanship—think pony-hair baby booties, hand-embroidered jumpers, and cashmere onesies. The flagship has a loftlike design with whimsical touches, such as a large indoor tree and a cloud sculpture. ☒ *805 Madison Ave., between E. 67th and 68th Sts., Upper East Side* ☎ *212/879–0900* ⊕ *www.bonpoint.com* Ⓜ *6 to 68th St.–Hunter College.*

FAMILY **Infinity.** Prep-school girls and their mothers giggle and gossip over the tween clothes (with more than a few moms picking up T-shirts and jeans for themselves) with Les Tout Petits dresses, Juicy Couture jeans, and tees emblazoned with Justin Bieber. ☒ *1116 Madison Ave., at E. 83rd St., Upper East Side* ☎ *212/734–0077* Ⓜ *4, 5, 6 to 86th St.*

CLOTHING

Fodor's Choice
★
Alexander McQueen. The New York flagship of this iconic fashion house is full of rich details, like intricately patterned floors, and tiny architectural details meant to draw the eye, such as feathers in the molding. Now under the helm of Sarah Burton, the designer sells both menswear and women's wear, in styles that lean towards edgy gothic. ☒ *747 Madison Ave., between E. 64th and 65th Sts., Upper East Side* ☎ *212/645–1797* ⊕ *www.alexandermcqueen.com* Ⓜ *6 to 68th St.–Hunter College.*

Barbour. The signature look here is the British company's waxed-cotton and quilted jackets, available for men and women. The quilted jackets, tweeds, moleskin pants, lamb's-wool sweaters, and tattersall shirts invariably call up images of country rambles. ☒ *1047 Madison Ave., at E. 80th St., Upper East Side* ☎ *212/570–2600* ⊕ *www.barbour.com* Ⓜ *6 to 77th St.*

BCBG Max Azria. This brand's initials are short for "bon chic, bon genre," which means stylish sportswear and embellished, embroidered evening dresses here. The collection ranges from leather pants to maxi dresses. ☒ *770 Madison Ave., at E. 66th St., Upper East Side* ☎ *212/717–4225* ⊕ *www.bcbg.com* Ⓜ *6 to 68th St.–Hunter College.*

Belstaff. Nearly a century old, this British brand specializes in motorcycle gear that has quite the pedigree—both Che Guevara and Steve McQueen have worn Belstaff. The relaunched company has expanded its collection to include luxury basics for men and women, including peacoats, waxed jackets, and body-hugging dresses with luxury touches like python and crocodile. ☒ *814 Madison Ave., between E. 68th and 69th Sts., Upper East Side* ☎ *212/897–1880* ⊕ *www.belstaff.com* Ⓜ *6 to 68th St.–Hunter College.*

Bra Smyth. Chic and sexy underthings in soft cottons and silks line the shelves of this longtime uptown staple. In addition to the selection of bridal-ready white bustiers and custom-fit swimsuits (made in bra-cup sizes), the store is best known for its knowledgeable staff, many of whom can give tips on proper fit and size you up on sight. Cup sizes run from AA to J. ☒ *905 Madison Ave., at E. 73rd St., Upper East Side* ☎ *212/772–9400* Ⓜ *6 to 68th St.–Hunter College.*

Calvin Klein. Though the namesake designer has bowed out, the label keeps channeling his particular style. This stark flagship store emphasizes the luxe end of the clothing line. Men's suits tend to be soft around the edges; women's evening gowns are often a fluid pouring of silk. There are also shoes, accessories, housewares, and makeup. ☒ *654 Madison Ave.,* *at E. 60th St., Upper East Side* 🕾 *212/292–9000* ⊕ *www.calvinklein.com* Ⓜ *4, 5, 6 to 59th St.; N, Q, R to Lexington Ave./59th St.*

Calypso St. Barth. Catch an instant island-vacation vibe from Calypso's colorful women's wear, which includes caftans, tunics, and dangly jewelry. To complete the look, there are also boho housewares at the brand's New York flagship, which has a suitably beachy vibe (check out the shell chandeliers). There are multiple branches throughout the city with different themes, including an outlet on Broome Street. ✉ *900 Madison Ave., between E. 72nd and 73rd Sts., Upper East Side* 🕾 *212/535–4100* ⊕ *www.calypsostbarth.com* Ⓜ *6 to 77th St.*

Carolina Herrera. A favorite of the high-society set (and A-list celebs), Herrera's designs are ladylike and elegant. Her suits, gowns, and cocktail dresses in luxurious fabrics make for timeless silhouettes. ✉ *954 Madison Ave., at E. 75th St., Upper East Side* 🕾 *212/249–6552* ⊕ *www. carolinaherrera.com* Ⓜ *6 to 77th St.*

Dolce & Gabbana. It's easy to feel like an Italian movie star amid these exuberant (in every sense) clothes. Corseted dresses are a favorite; the fabric could be sheer, furred, or leopard print. Men's suits are slim and sharp. ✉ *827 Madison Ave., at E. 69th St., Upper East Side* 🕾 *212/249– 4100* ⊕ *www.dolcegabbana.com* Ⓜ *6 to 68th St.–Hunter College.*

Fodor'sChoice ★ **Kate Spade.** The new Kate Spade flagship is located in a pretty uptown town house, so it feels like shopping in a well-appointed home—albeit one with oversized chandeliers and glamorous custom rugs. The nearly 8,000-square-foot space contains every Kate Spade product, from clothing to shoes and beauty. ✉ *789 Madison Ave., between E. 66th and 67th Sts., Upper East Side* 🕾 *212/988–0259* ⊕ *www.katespade.com* Ⓜ *6 to 68th St.–Hunter College.*

17

La Perla. If money is no object, shop here for some of the sexiest underthings around. The collection includes lace sets, corsets, and exquisite bridal lingerie. ✉ *803 Madison Ave., between 67th and 68th Sts., Upper East Side* 🕾 *212/570–0050* ⊕ *www.laperla.com* Ⓜ *6 to 68th St.–Hunter College.*

Fodor'sChoice ★ **Lanvin.** This French label has been around since 1889 and is the oldest French fashion house still in existence. With Alber Elbaz at the helm, Lanvin's signature look is fluid and sexy; think one-shouldered cocktail dresses, cigarette pants, and ruffled blouses. This elegant town house is the first U.S. outpost. The interior design itself is a showstopper; the three-story space oozes old money and glamour with its Art Deco chandeliers and soothing gray walls. And the clothes? Just as slinky. ✉ *815 Madison Ave., between 68th and 69th Sts., Upper East Side* 🕾 *646/439–0381* ⊕ *www.lanvin.com* Ⓜ *6 to 68th St.–Hunter College.*

Lisa Perry. This designer takes an artist's approach in her gleaming white space. She has created dresses printed with famous Andy Warhol photographs, such as the image of him drowning in a Campbell's Soup can. Pop art aside, her store is filled with a mix of '60s and '70s vintage clothes, as well as her own designs. ✉ *988 Madison Ave., at 77th St., Upper East Side* 🕾 *212/431–7467* ⊕ *www.lisaperrystyle.com* Ⓜ *6 to 77th St.*

Fodor's Choice
★ **Ludivine.** Make a beeline for this store if you love French designers. Owner Ludivine Grégoire showcases of-the-moment Gallic (and a few Italian) designers like Vanessa Bruno, Jerome Dreyfuss, and Carvin. ⊠ *1216 Lexington Ave., between E. 82nd and 83rd Sts., Upper East Side* ☎ *212/249–4053* ⊕ *www.boutiqueludivine.com* Ⓜ *4, 5, 6 to 86th St.*

Marina Rinaldi. If you are a curvy gal and want to celebrate your figure rather than hide it, shop here. A branch of Milanese fashion house Max Mara, Marina Rinaldi sells form-flattering knit dresses, wool trousers, and coats that are tasteful and luxurious. ⊠ *13 E. 69th St., between Madison and 5th Aves., Upper East Side* ☎ *212/734–4333* ⊕ *www.marinarinaldi.com* Ⓜ *6 to 68th St.–Hunter College.*

Max Mara. Think subtle colors and classics in plush fabrics—pencil skirts in heathered wool, tuxedo-style evening jackets, and wool and cashmere overcoats. The suits are exquisitely tailored. ⊠ *813 Madison Ave., at E. 68th St., Upper East Side* ☎ *212/879–6100* ⊕ *www.maxmara.com* Ⓜ *6 to 68th St.–Hunter College.*

Milly. These bright, cheerfully patterned clothes look as at home on the Upper East Side as they would in Palm Beach or Marrakech. At designer Michelle Smith's U.S. flagship, find flirty cocktail dresses, beach-ready maxis, and boldly patterned bathing suits. ⊠ *900 Madison Ave., at E. 73rd St., Upper East Side* ☎ *212/395–9100* ⊕ *www.milly.com* Ⓜ *6 to 77th St.*

Morgane Le Fay. The clothes here have a dreamy, ethereal quality that is decidedly feminine. Silk gowns are fluid and soft, while blazers and coats are more tailored. Her wedding dresses are also popular with brides who want a minimalist look. ⊠ *980 Madison Ave., between E. 76th and 77th Sts., Upper East Side* ☎ *212/879–9700* ⊕ *www.morganelefay.com* Ⓜ *6 to 77th St.*

Oscar de la Renta. Come here for the ladylike but bold runway designs of this upper-crust favorite. Skirts swing, ruffles billow, embroidery brightens up tweed, and even a tennis dress looks like something you could go dancing in. ⊠ *772 Madison Ave., at E. 66th St., Upper East Side* ☎ *212/288–5810* ⊕ *www.oscardelarenta.com* Ⓜ *6 to 68th St.–Hunter College.*

Otte. This stylish mini chain has outposts around the city, but the Upper East Side location has the biggest selection of clothing from on-trend designers such as Helmut Lang and Band of Outsiders, as well as its own line. If you want that nonchalant-chic look, like a tailored cape thrown over skinny jeans, this is your place. ⊠ *1232 3rd Ave., between E. 71 and 72nd Sts., Upper East Side* ☎ *212/744–4002* ⊕ *otteny.com* Ⓜ *6 to 68th St.–Hunter College.*

Fodor's Choice
★ **Ralph Lauren.** Even if you can't afford the clothes here, come just to soak up the luxe lifestyle. The designer's women's flagship is housed in a 22,000-square-foot building inspired by the avenue's historic Beaux Arts mansions, complete with it's own curving marble staircase and stone floors. In addition to the complete women's collection, the brand's lingerie, housewares, and fine-jewelry and watch salon are here. ⊠ *888 Madison Ave., at E. 72nd St., Upper East Side* ☎ *212/434–8000* ⊕ *www.ralphlauren.com* Ⓜ *6 to 68th St.–Hunter College.*

Roberto Cavalli. Rock-star style (at rock-star prices) means clothing decked out with fur, feathers, and lots of sparkle. Animal prints are big in this temple to the over-the-top. ✉ *711 Madison Ave., at E. 63rd St., Upper East Side* ☎ *212/755–7722* ⊕ *www.robertocavalli.com* Ⓜ *N, Q, R to 5th Ave./59th St.*

Tom Ford. Famous for revamping Gucci, Ford does not disappoint with his eponymous line. Women's stilettos and clutches are unabashedly sexy, while men's selections veer towards the traditional and are impeccably tailored. Shirts come in more than 300 hues, and off-the-rack suits start around $3,000. His Black Orchid unisex fragrance is a cult favorite. ✉ *845 Madison Ave., at E. 70th St., Upper East Side* ☎ *212/359–0300* ⊕ *www.tomford.com* Ⓜ *6 to 68th St.–Hunter College.*

Tomas Maier. The creative director of luxury Italian company Bottega Veneta now has an eponymous store in Manhattan. The elegant, wood-floored space showcases Tomas Maier's understated clothing for men and women as well as jewelry and home goods, such as candles. Best bets include classic black dresses and structured handbags. ✉ *956 Madison Ave., between E. 75th and 76th Sts., Upper East Side* ☎ *212/988–8686* ⊕ *www.tomasmaier.com* Ⓜ *6 to 77th St.*

Tory Burch. The global flagship of this preppy boho label is housed in an elegantly restored town house. The five-story space features Tory Burch's signature orange-lacquer walls, purple curtains, and gold hardware. If you already own her iconic ballet flats, browse through the ready-to-wear collection, handbags, shoes, and jewelry. ✉ *797 Madison Ave., between E. 67th and 68th Sts., Upper East Side* ☎ *212/510–8371* ⊕ *www.toryburch.com* Ⓜ *6 to 68th St.–Hunter College.*

17

Valentino. No one does a better red than Valentino, and the mix here at this four-story town house is at once audacious and beautifully cut; the fur or feather trimmings, low necklines, and opulent fabrics are about as close as you can get to celluloid glamour. Big spenders can request the VIP suite. ✉ *821 Madison Ave., between E. 68th and 69th Sts., Upper East Side* ☎ *212/772–6969* ⊕ *www.valentino.com* Ⓜ *6 to 68th St.–Hunter College.*

Vera Wang Bride. This celebrity wedding-dress designer churns out dreamy dresses that are sophisticated without being over-the-top. Choose from A-line and princess styles, as well as slinky sheaths. If money is no object, bespoke wedding dresses are available. An appointment is essential. ✉ *991 Madison Ave., at E. 77th St., Upper East Side* ☎ *212/628–3400* ⊕ *www.verawang.com* Ⓜ *6 to 77th St.*

Vilebrequin. Allow St-Tropez to influence your summer style. This iconic French swimwear designer began by making classic striped, floral, and solid-color trunks in sunny hues for both men and boys. Nowadays, it's expanded to include a women's line, resort wear, and summery accessories. ✉ *1007 Madison Ave., between E. 77th and 78th Sts., Upper East Side* ☎ *212/650–0353* ⊕ *us.vilebrequin.com* Ⓜ *6 to 77th St.*

DEPARTMENT STORES

Barneys New York. This luxury boutique-style department store continues to provide fashion-conscious and big-budget shoppers with irresistible, must-have items at its uptown flagship store. The extensive menswear selection has a handful of edgier designers, though made-to-measure is always an option. The women's department showcases posh designers of all stripes, from the subdued lines of Armani and Nina Ricci to the irrepressible Alaïa and Zac Posen. The shoe selection trots out Prada boots and strappy Blahniks; the cosmetics department keeps you in Kiehl's, Sue Devitt, and Chantecaille; jewelry runs from the whimsical (Jennifer Meyer) to the classic (Ileana Makri). ⊠ *660 Madison Ave., between E. 60th and 61st Sts., Upper East Side* ☎ *212/826–8900* ⊕ *www.barneys. com* Ⓜ *4, 5, 6 to 59th St.; N, Q, R to Lexington Ave./59th St.*

Fodor'sChoice ★ **Fivestory.** This luxurious mini department store, located inside an Upper East Side town house, carries clothing, accessories, shoes, and home decor for men, women, and children in an elegant setting (think marble floors and lots of velvet and silk). It specializes in independent designers but also showcases designs from heavy hitters such as Jason Wu and Lanvin. ⊠ *18 E. 69th St., at Madison Ave., Upper East Side* ☎ *212/288– 1338* ⊕ *www.fivestoryny.com* Ⓜ *6 to 68th St.–Hunter College.*

FOOD AND TREATS

FP Patisserie. Famed French patissier François Payard has multiple boutiques around the city but this location is the flagship. Chocolates, pastries, and macarons are displayed like jewels in glass cases. If you need to calm the sugar rush, there's a small dining area serving dishes like croque monsieur. ⊠ *1293 3rd Ave., between E. 74th and 75th Sts., Upper East Side* ☎ *212/717–5252* ⊕ *www.payard.com* Ⓜ *6 to 77th St.*

Fodor'sChoice ★ **La Maison du Chocolat.** Stop in at this artisan chocolatier's small tea salon to dive into a cup of thick, heavenly hot chocolate. The Paris-based outfit sells handmade truffles, chocolates, and pastries that could lull you into a chocolate stupor. ⊠ *1018 Madison Ave., between E. 78th and 79th Sts., Upper East Side* ☎ *212/744–7118* ⊕ *www.lamaisonduchocolat. com* Ⓜ *6 to 77th St.*

JEWELRY AND ACCESSORIES

Asprey. This luxury retailer's claim to fame is jewelry; its own eponymous diamond cut has A-shape facets, but the British brand caters to all tastes. Everything from leather goods and rare books to polo equipment and scarves are available. ⊠ *853 Madison Ave., between E. 70th and 71st Sts., Upper East Side* ☎ *212/688–1811* ⊕ *www.asprey.com* Ⓜ *6 to 68th St.–Hunter College.*

Fred Leighton. If you're in the market for vintage diamonds, this is the place, whether your taste is for tiaras, Art Deco settings, or sparklers once worn by a Vanderbilt. The skinny, stackable diamond eternity bands are hugely popular. ⊠ *773 Madison Ave., at E. 66th St., Upper East Side* ☎ *212/288–1872* ⊕ *www.fredleighton.com* Ⓜ *6 to 68th St.– Hunter College.*

MUSEUM STORES

Fodor's Choice ★ **Cooper Hewitt, Smithsonian Design Museum.** Prowl the shelves at this well-stocked museum shop for intriguing urban oddments and ornaments, like sculptural tableware, Alexander Girard dolls, housewares by Alessi, and Japanese notebooks by Postalco. ✉ *2 E. 91st St., at 5th Ave., Upper East Side* ☎ *212/849–8355* ⊕ *www.cooperhewitt.org* Ⓜ *4, 5, 6 to 86th St.*

Metropolitan Museum of Art Store. This sprawling museum shop has a phenomenal book selection, as well as posters, Japanese print note cards, and decorative pillows covered in William Morris prints. Reproductions of statuettes and other objets d'art fill the gleaming cases. Don't miss the jewelry selection, with its Byzantine- and Egyptian-inspired baubles. ✉ *1000 5th Ave., at E. 82nd St., Upper East Side* ☎ *212/570–3894* ⊕ *store.metmuseum.org* Ⓜ *4, 5, 6 to 86th St.*

Museum of the City of New York. Satisfy your curiosity about New York City's past, present, or future with the terrific selection of books, cards, toys, and photography posters. ✉ *1220 5th Ave., at E. 103rd St., Upper East Side* ☎ *917/492-3330* ⊕ *shop.mcny.org* Ⓜ *6 to 103rd St.*

Neue Galerie. Like the museum, the in-house bookshop and design store focuses on German, Austrian, and Central European art. Everything from children's toys to accessories and home decor is available here. ✉ *1048 5th Ave., at E. 86th St., Upper East Side* ☎ *212/628–6200* ⊕ *shop.neuegalerie.org* Ⓜ *4, 5, 6 to 86th St.*

SHOES, HANDBAGS, AND LEATHER GOODS

Anya Hindmarch. Although arguably most famous for her "I'm Not a Plastic Bag" tote, Hindmarch's real standouts are buttery leather shoulder bags and hobos, which are decidedly understated. Her designs run the gamut from cheeky to ladylike. Leather goods can be embossed with monograms, entire sentences, or a sketch. ✉ *795 Madison Ave., between E. 67th and 68th Sts., Upper East Side* ☎ *646/852-6233* ⊕ *www.anyahindmarch.com* Ⓜ *6 to 68th St.–Hunter College.*

Fodor's Choice ★ **Charlotte Olympia.** The Art Deco–inspired space at this British shoe store showcases very sexy and expensive stilettos, pumps, and flats. Accessories such as shoulder bags and clutches are also available. ✉ *22 E. 65th St., at Madison Ave., Upper East Side* ☎ *212/744-1842* ⊕ *www.charlotteolympia.com* Ⓜ *6 to 68th St.–Hunter College.*

Christian Louboutin. Lipstick-red soles are the signature of Louboutin's delicately sexy couture slippers and stilettos, and his pointy-toe creations come trimmed with beads, buttons, or "tattoos." ✉ *967 Madison Ave., between E. 75th and 76th Sts., Upper East Side* ☎ *212/396–1884* ⊕ *www.christianlouboutin.com* Ⓜ *6 to 77th St.*

Devi Kroell. You may have spotted her snakeskin hobo on celebs such as Halle Berry and Ashley Olsen. This serene space is a perfect backdrop for the designer's luxury handbags and shoes, which are crafted from premium leather. Roomy shoulder bags come in python and calf leather, and evening bags have a touch of sparkle. There's also a selection of jewelry and scarves. ✉ *717 Madison Ave., between E. 63rd and 64th Sts., Upper East Side* ☎ *212/644–4499* ⊕ *www.devikroell.com* Ⓜ *F to Lexington Ave./63rd St.*

17

Hermès. This legendary French retailer is best known for its iconic handbags, the Kelly and the Birkin, named for Grace Kelly and Jane Birkin, as well as its silk scarves and neckties. True to its roots, Hermès still stocks saddles and other equestrian items in addition to a line of beautifully simple separates. ⊠ *691 Madison Ave., at E. 62nd St., Upper East Side* ☎ *212/751–3181* ⊕ *www.hermes.com* Ⓜ *N, Q, R to 5th Ave./59th St.; F to Lexington Ave./63rd St.*

Fodor'sChoice
★ **Jack Rogers.** This brand, beloved by prepsters everywhere, is most famous for its Navajo sandal, worn by Jackie Onassis. You can still buy the Navajo at the Jack Rogers flagship store, as well as other footwear like loafers, boots, and wedges. ⊠ *1198 Madison Ave., between E. 87th and 88th Sts., Upper East Side* ☎ *212/259–0588* ⊕ *www.jackrogersusa.com* Ⓜ *4, 5, 6 to 86th St.*

Jimmy Choo. Pointy toes, low vamps, narrow heels, ankle-wrapping straps—these British-made shoes are sometimes more comfortable than they look. ⊠ *716 Madison Ave., between E. 63rd and 64th Sts., Upper East Side* ☎ *212/759–7078* ⊕ *www.jimmychoo.com* Ⓜ *F to Lexington Ave./63rd St.*

John Lobb. If you truly want to be well-heeled, pick up a pair of these luxury shoes, whose prices start at around $1,200. Owned by Hermès, John Lobb offers classic styles for men, such as oxfords, loafers, boots, and slippers. ⊠ *800 Madison Ave., between E. 67th and 68th Sts., Upper East Side* ☎ *212/888–9797* ⊕ *www.johnlobb.com* Ⓜ *6 to 68th St.–Hunter College.*

Robert Clergerie. Although best known for its chunky, comfy wedges, this French brand is not without its sense of fun. The sandal selection includes beaded starfish shapes, and for winter, the ankle boots have killer heels with padded soles. ⊠ *19 E. 62nd St., between 5th and Madison Aves., Upper East Side* ☎ *212/207–8600* ⊕ *www.robertclergerie.com* Ⓜ *N, Q, R to 5th Ave./59th St.; F to Lexington Ave./63rd St.*

Fodor'sChoice
★ **Smythson of Bond Street.** Although Smythson still sells stationery fit for a queen—check out the royal warrant from England's HRH—it is also a place to scoop up on-trend handbags, iPad cases, and wallets. The hues range from sedate brown and black to eye-popping tangerine. The softbound leather diaries, address books, and travel accessories make ideal gifts. ⊠ *667 Madison Ave., between E. 60th and 61st Sts., Upper East Side* ☎ *212/265–4573* ⊕ *www.smythson.com* Ⓜ *F to 57th St.; N, Q, R to 5th Ave./59th St.*

Tod's. These coveted driving moccasins, loafers, and boots are the top choice for jet-setters who prefer low-key, logo-free luxury goods. Though most of the women's selection is made up of low-heel or flat styles, an increasing number of high heels have been driving up sales. The leather handbags feature the same fine craftsmanship. ⊠ *650 Madison Ave., at E. 60th St., Upper East Side* ☎ *212/644–5945* ⊕ *www.tods.com* Ⓜ *N, Q, R to 5th Ave./59th St.*

THE UPPER WEST SIDE

Although largely a residential neighborhood, the Upper West Side has some excellent food (Zabar's) as well as smaller boutiques.

BOOKS AND STATIONERY

Westsider Books & Westsider Records. This wonderfully crammed space is a lifesaver on the Upper West Side. Squeeze in among the stacks of art books and fiction, or pop outside for the $1 bargains. Don't miss the rare-book collection. Nearby, at 233 West 72nd Street, the record shop has an equally impressive collection of vinyl and CDs. ✉ *2246 Broadway, between W. 80th and 81st Sts., Upper West Side* ☎ *212/362–0706* ⊕ *www.westsiderbooks.com* Ⓜ *1 to 79th St.*

CHILDREN'S CLOTHING

FAMILY **A Time for Children.** When you shop at this funky boutique, you'll also be doing some good, as 100% of the profits go to the Children's Aid Society. Choose from toys, books, and clothing, which include classic brands such as Petit Bateau as well as more whimsical choices like graphic-print footed PJs. ✉ *506 Amsterdam Ave., between W. 84th and 85th Sts., Upper West Side* ☎ *212/580–8202* ⊕ *www.atimeforchildren. org* Ⓜ *1 to 86th St.*

CLOTHING

BOC. Who needs to go downtown for cutting-edge designers? This store stocks sleek designs from the likes of Ulla Johnson, Loeffler Randall, and A.L.C. The selection of bags, shoes, and jewelry is just as stylish. ✉ *410 Columbus Ave., between W. 79th and 80th Sts., Upper West Side* ☎ *212/799–1567* ⊕ *www.bocnyc.com* Ⓜ *1 to 79th St.; B, C, to 81st St.–Museum of Natural History.*

Intermix. Whether you're looking for the perfect daytime dress, a pair of J Brand jeans, or a puffer coat that doesn't make you look like the Michelin man, Intermix sells a well-curated assortment of emerging and established designers. Expect to see designs from DVF, Rag & Bone, and Missoni. There are a number of locations in the city. ✉ *210 Columbus Ave., between W. 69th and 70th Sts., Upper West Side* ☎ *212/769–9116* ⊕ *www.intermixonline.com* Ⓜ *1, 2, 3, B, C to 72nd St.*

Mint. Trendy pieces that don't break the bank are what Mint is all about. The collection includes Alice & Olivia, Susana Monaco, and Joe's Jeans. The walls are painted, of course, in mint green. ✉ *448 Columbus Ave., between W. 81st and 82nd Sts., Upper West Side* ☎ *212/362–6250* ⊕ *www.shopmint.com* Ⓜ *1 to 79th St.; B, C to 81st St.–Museum of Natural History.*

Pachute. This cozy boutique, which means "simple" in Hebrew, specializes in stylish casual wear. If your weekend uniform consists of button-down shirts, understated jewelry, and espadrilles, then make a beeline here. ✉ *57 W. 84th St., between Columbus Ave. and Central Park W, Upper West Side* ☎ *212/501–9400* ⊕ *www.pachute.com* Ⓜ *B, C to 86th St.*

17

FOOD AND TREATS

Le Palais des Thés. If you prefer a mellower caffeine kick, come to this French-owned tea boutique. All varieties of black and green teas are available as well as rarer leaves and globally inspired blends, such as a Turkish hammam flavor that includes roses and dates. The box sets and canisters make excellent gifts. ⊠ *194 Columbus Ave., between W. 68th and 69th Sts., Upper West Side* ☎ *646/664–1902* ⊕ *www.palaisdesthes. com* Ⓜ *1 to 66th St.–Lincoln Center; B, C to 72nd St.*

Fodor'sChoice ★ **Zabar's.** When it comes to authentic New York food, it's hard to beat rugelach, bagels, or lox from this iconic, local-favorite specialty food emporium. ⊠ *2245 Broadway, at W. 80th St., Upper West Side* ☎ *212/787–2000* ⊕ *www.zabars.com* Ⓜ *1 to 79th St.*

SHOES, HANDBAGS, AND LEATHER GOODS

Fodor'sChoice ★ **Tani.** Fashionable Upper West Side ladies love this shoe store for its huge selection and patient staff. Tani's selection is mostly classic-with-a-twist, and shoppers find brands that are more cool than sexy, such as Dolce Vita and Camper. ⊠ *131 W 72nd St., between Columbus and Amsterdam Aves., Upper West Side* ☎ *212/595–1338* ⊕ *www.taninyc. com/* Ⓜ *1, 2, 3, B, C to 72nd St.*

BROOKLYN

BROOKLYN HEIGHTS

FOOD AND TREATS

FAMILY Fodor'sChoice ★ **Sahadi's.** Inhale the aromas of spices and dark-roast coffee beans as you enter this Middle Eastern trading post that's been selling bulk foods in Brooklyn since 1948. Bins and jars and barrels hold everything from nuts, dried fruit, olives, and pickled vegetables to cheeses, chocolate, candy, those intoxicating coffees, and all manner of spices. There's a large selection of prepared food and groceries as well. ⊠ *187 Atlantic Ave., Brooklyn Heights* ☎ *718/624–4550* ⊕ *www.sahadis.com* Ⓜ *2, 3, 4, 5 to Borough Hall; R to Court St.; A, C, F, R to Jay St.–MetroTech.*

DUMBO

BOOKS AND STATIONERY

FAMILY **powerHouse Arena.** Edgy art-book publisher powerHouse is a vision in concrete and steel at this bright showroom that sells illustrated titles, children's books, and works by authors from Joseph Mitchell to Gary Shteyngart. The space also hosts publishing parties, book launches, readings, and discussion groups. ⊠ *37 Main St., DUMBO* ☎ *718/666–3049* ⊕ *www.powerhousearena.com* Ⓜ *A, C to High St.; F to York St.*

CARROLL GARDENS

FOOD AND TREATS

Fodor'sChoice ★ **G. Esposito & Sons Jersey Pork Store.** The epitome of an old-school Italian butcher and specialty shop, Esposito's has been serving the area once known as South Brooklyn for almost 100 years. Brothers and co-owners John and George Esposito run the store their grandfather opened in 1922 and are still producing homemade sausages, dry-aged soppressata, and hero sandwiches made on Caputo's bread. Order up an Italian Combo with the works, or the habit-forming Santino's "Fluffy"

Combo, stuffed with chicken cutlets, sweet peppers, Asiago cheese, pesto, and oil and vinegar, and grab a seat in neighboring Carroll Park to chow down. ⊠ *357 Court St., Carroll Gardens* ☎ *718/875–6863* ⊘ *Closed most Sun. Aug. and Sept.* Ⓜ *F, G to Carroll St.*

GIFTS AND SOUVENIRS

FAMILY

Fodor'sChoice ★

By Brooklyn. The name says it all. This is the borough's prime purveyor of dry goods, gifts, and comestibles conceived of and created in Brooklyn. Fill a Maptote denim tote bag stamped "Brooklyn" (of course) with jewelry by Natural Abstract, Mike's Hot Honey (to garnish your favorite slice of pizza or create the perfect cocktail), and Apotheke soap. Other top picks include *The Roberta's Cookbook,* featuring recipes from Bushwick's revolutionary Neopolitan-style pizzeria, and the reclaimed-Brooklyn-slate cheese board by Brooklyn Slate Company. There's also a Williamsburg location at 142 Grand Street. ⊠ *261 Smith St., Carroll Gardens* ☎ *718/643–0606* ⊕ *shop.bybrooklyn.com* Ⓜ *F, G to Bergen St. or Carroll St.*

COBBLE HILL
BOOKS AND STATIONERY

FAMILY **BookCourt.** This wonderful, family-run shop has been a star on Court Street for more than 30 years. The tables and shelves are filled with books to browse, and the staff is happy to recommend titles. The shop stocks works by the neighborhood's many local writers, who often appear for readings and signings. ⊠ *163 Court St., Cobble Hill* ☎ *718/875–3677* ⊕ *www.bookcourt.com* Ⓜ *2, 3, 4, 5 to Borough Hall; F, G to Bergen St.*

17

CLOTHING

Bird. Looking for the chicest women's wear in Brooklyn? You'll find it at this beloved boutique known for its indie designers and high prices. Everything from knit sweaterdresses and cardigans to statement shoes and delicate gold jewelry share the cozy (and newly remodeled) space. There are a few items for men as well. ⊠ *220 Smith St., at Butler St., Cobble Hill* ☎ *718/797–3774* ⊕ *www.shopbird.com* Ⓜ *F, G to Bergen St.*

PARK SLOPE
GIFTS AND SOUVENIRS

FAMILY **Annie's Blue Ribbon General Store.** The perfectly giftable, Brooklyn-made products at this variety store include Apotheke candles and diffusers, Bellocq teas, Claudia Pearson's hand-drawn tea towels, and Bocce's Bakery lobster-roll treats for your favorite canine. Brooklyn-themed tchotchkes, eco-friendly cleaning supplies, stationery, and toys round out the selection. You can't go wrong gifting the mass-produced prank kit to any kid between the ages of 4 and 10. ⊠ *232 5th Ave., between President and Carroll Sts., Park Slope* ☎ *718/522–9848* ⊕ *www. blueribbongeneralstore.com* Ⓜ *R to Union St.*

TOYS

FAMILY

Fodor'sChoice ★

Brooklyn Superhero Supply Co. If you can't crack a smile in this store—where all proceeds from superhero costumes, gear, and secret identity kits benefit 826NYC's writing and tutoring programs for kids—step immediately into its Devillainizer cage. Once cleansed, browse the invisibility, dark matter, and cloning tools sold in plastic jugs and fake paint cans. The clever labels listing "ingredients" and "warnings" are worth every ounce of the tongue-in-cheek superpower products. ✉ *372 5th Ave., between 5th and 6th Sts., Park Slope* ☎ *718/499–9884* ⊕ *www. superherosupplies.com* Ⓜ *F, G to 4th Ave.; R to 9th St.*

CONEY ISLAND
FOOD AND TREATS

FAMILY **Williams Candy.** Selling homemade candy apples, marshmallow sticks, popcorn, nuts, and giant lollipops for more than 75 years, this old-school corner candy shop with the yellow awning is a Coney Island mainstay. Owner Peter Agrapides used to visit the store with his mother when he was a kid; he's been the proud owner for 30 years. ✉ *1318 Surf Ave., at W. 15th St., Coney Island* ☎ *718/372–0302* ⊕ *www. candytreats.com* Ⓜ *D, F, N, Q to Coney Island–Stillwell Ave.*

NIGHTLIFE

Updated by
Jessica Colley
Clarke

New Yorkers are fond of the "work hard, play hard" maxim, but the truth is, Gothamites don't need much of an excuse to hit the town. Any day of the week could easily be mistaken for a Friday or Saturday; the bottom line is that there's always plenty to do in this 24-hour city. Whether it's raising a glass in a divey 1930s saloon, a gay sports bar, the latest dimly lit cocktail den, or a swanky rooftop lounge; checking out the latest band; or laughing it up at a comedy show, it isn't hard for visitors to get a piece of the action.

The nightlife scene still resides largely downtown—in the dives of the East Village and Lower East Side, the classic jazz joints of the West Village, and the Meatpacking District's and Chelsea's "see-and-be-seen" clubs. Midtown, especially around Hell's Kitchen, has developed a vibrant scene, too, and plenty of preppy hangouts dot the Upper East and Upper West Sides. Brooklyn, especially Williamsburg, is the destination for hipsters.

Keep in mind that *when* you go is just as important as *where* you go. A club that is packed at 11 pm might empty out by midnight, and a bar that raged last night may be completely empty tonight. *Paper* magazine has a good list of roving parties. You can check its online nightlife guide, *PM*, via its website (⊕ *www.papermag.com*). Scour industry-centric websites, too, like *Eater* and *Grub Street,* which catalog the comings and goings of many a nightlife impresario. The *New York Times* has listings of cabaret and jazz shows, most comprehensively in its Friday and Sunday Arts sections. Bear in mind that a venue's life span is often measured in months, not years. Phone ahead or check online to make sure your target hasn't closed or turned into a polka hall (although, you never know—that could be fun, too).

LOWER MANHATTAN

FINANCIAL DISTRICT

BARS

Fodor's Choice ★ **The Dead Rabbit.** For exquisite cocktails without the dress code or pretentious door policy typical of some New York cocktail dens, venture to the tip of Manhattan for a night of Irish hospitality in a 19th-century-inspired saloon. The ground-floor taproom serves craft beers and whiskeys of the world, while the upstairs parlor shakes and stirs craft cocktails, many utilizing Irish whiskey—accompanied by ragtime music played live on the piano. ⊠ *30 Water St., Financial District* ☎ *646/422–7906* ⊕ *www.deadrabbitnyc.com* Ⓜ *1 to South Ferry; R to Whitehall St.*

TRIBECA

BARS

B-flat. The design is red-on-red here, and the Asian-style cocktails are particularly groovy (literally—one, with citrusy Japanese yuzu juice and vodka, has been dubbed the Groovy) at this Japan-meets-'50s-America lounge. Listen to live jazz while nibbling on American and Japanese-inflected treats. ⊠ *277 Church St., between Franklin and White Sts., TriBeCa* ☎ *212/219–2970* ⊕ *www.bflat.info* Ⓜ *1 to Franklin St.; A, C, E, J, N, Q, R, Z, 6 to Canal St.*

Brandy Library. Alas, the only book in this exquisite, wood-paneled room is the leather-bound menu listing hundreds of brandies and single-malt scotches. The bottles are on gorgeous backlighted "bookshelves," though, and you can learn what makes each of them special by chatting with the spirit sommelier—or by attending their Spirit School tasting classes. ⊠ *25 N. Moore St., between Varick and Hudson Sts., TriBeCa* ☎ *212/226–5545* ⊕ *www.brandylibrary.com* Ⓜ *1 to Franklin St.; A, C, E to Canal St.*

M1-5. For the more bohemian of TriBeCa pubgoers, this lipstick-red, high-ceiling spot is a vast playground (as in, billiards and darts). There is a reggae jukebox, huge screens for sports, live shows, and DJ nights on the weekends—all without a pesky cover charge. Extra points, too, for the bar's name, which cites TriBeCa's warehouse zoning law. ⊠ *52 Walker St., between Broadway and Church St., TriBeCa* ☎ *212/965–1701* ⊕ *www.m1-5.com* Ⓜ *A, C, E J, N, Q, R, Z, 6 to Canal St.*

Smith and Mills. Attractive scenesters frolic at this tiny gem of a gin mill, where mixologists who resemble Daniel Day-Lewis dispense elixirs (and caviar) from a bar hung with pots and pans. There are cozy table-nooks for couples, and while the food is worth a visit, many locals come here late when a cocktail craving hits. ⊠ *71 N. Moore St., between Hudson and Greenwich Sts., TriBeCa* ☎ *212/226–2515* ⊕ *www.smithandmills. com* Ⓜ *1 to Franklin St.; A, C, E to Canal St.*

Terroir Wine Bar. If the tag line—the Elitist Wine Bar for Everyone—isn't enough to get you in the door, the extensive wine list, including options by the glass, bottle, or adorable 3-ounce "taste" should do the trick. This low-lit neighborhood wine bar is easy to walk right by on charming Harrison Street, but once inside you will find seats at the bar for wine-centric conversations with the sharp staff or more private nooks

18

for a romantic evening of wine and cheese. ⊠ *24 Harrison St., TriBeCa* ☎ *212/625–9463* ⊕ *wineisterroir.com* Ⓜ *1 to Franklin St.*

Tiny's and the Bar Upstairs. This diminutive three-story town house in the heart of TriBeCa dates all the way back to 1810. The ground floor is home to a restaurant with a wood-burning fireplace in the back, and food is served until late; upstairs a pressed-copper bar provides an intimate place for cocktails and snacks. This is prime date territory, with several other neighborhood watering holes close by. ⊠ *135 W. Broadway, TriBeCa* ☎ *212/374–1135* ⊕ *tinysnyc.com* Ⓜ *1, 2, 3 to Chambers St.*

Ward III. You can get a solid Negroni or Manhattan at this exposed-brick watering hole, but where the bar really shines is in its bespoke cocktails. Fight for a seat at the bar if possible to watch the sharply clad mixologists whip up house specialties, or simply give them a few descriptive words ("spirit-forward," "something with bourbon," "light and refreshing") and let them create a cocktail on the spot to match your thirst. ⊠ *111 Reade St., between West Broadway and Church St., TriBeCa* ☎ *212/240–9194* ⊕ *www.ward3.com* Ⓜ *1, 2, 3 to Chambers St.; A, C to Chambers St.*

DANCE CLUBS AND DJ VENUES

Santos Party House. "Now *this* is what I call a dance club," says Arthur Baker, the legendary DJ (and record producer), about this glorious downtown dance club, where the velvet ropes part for everyone. Co-owned by rocker Andrew W. K., the bi-level Santos ain't fancy, but that's the point, and the customers are as eclectic as the DJs, including Mr. Baker, who flies in regularly from London. Hence the musical vibe—underground dance, mostly—is simply kaleidoscopic. ⊠ *96 Lafayette St., between White and Walker Sts., TriBeCa* ☎ *212/584–5492* ⊕ *www.santospartyhouse.com* Ⓜ *6, J, N, Q, R, Z to Canal St.*

CHINATOWN, NOLITA, AND SOHO

CHINATOWN

BARS

Apotheke. Tucked away down a winding lane deep in Chinatown, this cocktail apothecary is a surprising find in a neighborhood known more for soup dumplings than creative tipples. Influenced by the 19th-century absinthe parlors of Paris, this historically inflected spot is all about drama and presentation. Think more chemistry lab than traditional bar—the results are not only delicious, but a feast for the eyes. ⊠ *9 Doyers St., Chinatown* ☎ *212/406–0400* ⊕ *www.apothekenyc.com* Ⓜ *6, J, N, Q, R, Z to Canal St.; 4, 5, 6 to Brooklyn Bridge–City Hall.*

NOLITA

BARS

Madam Geneva. Adjacent to the stylish and packed restaurant Saxon + Parole, this gin den is named after the 18th-century English term for the clear spirit. The brick-lined, dimly lit bar and lounge is a natural spillover space after dinner next door; you can also nibble on Asian-inspired snacks here (from the same kitchen). The crowd is thirsty, polished, and often on the prowl. There's a DJ on weekends. ⊠ *4 Bleecker St., NoHo* ☎ *212/254–0350* ⊕ *www.madamgeneva-nyc.com* Ⓜ *6 to Bleecker St.; F to 2nd Ave.; B, D, F, M to Broadway–Lafayette St.*

Sweet and Vicious. This unpretentious lounge is high on the sweet factor and luckily low on the vicious attitudes. There's a lovely back garden that's more private than the sceney bars you might otherwise hit in SoHo and NoLIta. ⊠ *5 Spring St., between the Bowery and Elizabeth St., NoLIta* ☎ *212/334–7915* ⊕ *www.sweetandvicious.nyc* Ⓜ *6 to Spring St.; J, Z to Bowery.*

SOHO
BARS

City Winery. Is it the city's most creative wine bar? Or its most impressive concert space? Both, actually. Pairing killer music (Nick Lowe, Shawn Colvin, War, Los Lobos) with unique events (Klezmer Breakfast, Cheese Brunch, tours of its in-house winery, special "Vinofile" memberships, and a Twitter–wine-tasting party called Spit and Twit), the City Winery has ample room for customers with "good taste" in every sense of the term. ⊠ *155 Varick St., at Vandam St., SoHo* ☎ *212/608–0555* ⊕ *www. citywinery.com/newyork* Ⓜ *1 to Houston St.*

Ear Inn. Since the early 1800s this watering hole (at one time also a bordello) has been a sturdy New York landmark in a rapidly changing downtown. For those imbibers who prefer a pint of Guinness over the latest cocktail fads, this long wooden bar offers a cozy, unhurried place to raise a glass and rub elbows with New Yorkers. The benches outside are also a perfect spot to relax in the warmer weather. ⊠ *326 Spring St., between Greenwich and Washington Sts., SoHo* ☎ *212/226–9060* ⊕ *www.earinn.com* Ⓜ *1 to Houston St.; C, E to Spring St.*

Fanelli's. Linger over the *New York Times* at this terrific neighborhood bar and restaurant, a down-to-earth SoHo landmark that's been serving drinks (and solid cuisine—dig those burgers!) since 1847. Check out the hilarious old-timey photos on the walls, too. ⊠ *94 Prince St., at Mercer St., SoHo* ☎ *212/226–9412* Ⓜ *N, R to Prince St.; B, D, F, M to Broadway–Lafayette St.*

Jimmy. Located on the 18th floor of the trendy James Hotel, Jimmy is an all-season rooftop bar with stellar views and a cozy fireplace. Sit in a corner nook for Empire State Building vistas, or head toward the outdoor pool area to survey the bridges over the East River. Cocktails are a highlight, featuring seasonal ingredients and novelties like ice cubes made from cinnamon water. ⊠ *15 Thompson St., at Grand St., SoHo* ☎ *212/201–9118* ⊕ *www.jimmysoho.com* Ⓜ *C, E to Spring St.; A, C, E to Canal Street; 1 to Canal St.*

La Compagnie des Vins Surnaturels. Cheese, charcuterie, and chocolate are all temptations at this cozy wine bar, lined with exposed-brick walls and shelves stocked with wine (the complete list is over 600 bottles). This is the dimly lit sister property of a bar of the same name in Paris; the wine list leans heavily toward French options. ⊠ *249 Centre St., SoHo* ☎ *212/343–3660* ⊕ *www.compagnienyc.com* Ⓜ *6 to Spring St.*

18

Pegu Club. Modeled after an officers' club in Myanmar, the Pegu manages to feel expansive and calm even when packed. The well-dressed and flirtatious come here partly for the exotic surroundings, but primarily for the cocktails, which are innovative, prepared with superlative ingredients, and predictably pricey. ✉ *77 W. Houston St., 2nd fl., between West Broadway and Wooster St., SoHo* ☎ *212/473–7348* ⊕ *www.peguclub.com* Ⓜ *B, D, F, M to Broadway–Lafayette St.; 6 to Bleecker St.*

Fodor's Choice
★ **Pravda.** This Russian retreat has more than 70 different vodkas, including a dozen house-infused flavors from chili and horseradish to coffee. The speakeasy feel of this underground spot is comfortable enough to spend the entire night, and Russian-inspired nibbles including caviar with blini provide longevity to try yet another vodka variation, from cucumber-dill to ginger-infused flavors. ✉ *281 Lafayette St., between Houston and Prince Sts., SoHo* ☎ *212/226–4944* ⊕ *www.pravdany.com* Ⓜ *N, R to Prince St.; B, D, F, M to Broadway–Lafayette St.*

EAST VILLAGE AND LOWER EAST SIDE

EAST VILLAGE
BARS

Beauty Bar. Grab a seat in a barber chair or under a dryer at this made-over hair salon where, during happy hour, the manicurist will do your nails for a fee that includes a drink. (How's that for multitasking?) The DJ spins everything from Britpop to rock—a great sound track for primping. ✉ *231 E. 14th St., between 2nd and 3rd Aves., East Village* ☎ *212/539–1389* ⊕ *www.thebeautybar.com* Ⓜ *4, 5, 6, L, N, Q, R to 14th St.–Union Sq.*

Death + Company. Theater behind the bar, inventive cocktails, and decadent bar bites bring thirsty New Yorkers to the sister lounge of the equally imaginative and classy nearby bar Mayahuel. Check out the hilarious wall mural toward the rear, setting the tone for the tongue-in-cheek satanic vibe of this watering hole. ✉ *433 E. 6th St., between 1st Ave. and Ave. A, East Village* ☎ *212/388–0882* ⊕ *www.deathandcompany.com* Ⓜ *F to 2nd Ave., 6 to Astor Pl.*

Fodor's Choice
★ **Mayahuel.** The Agave goddess is behind the name of this cocktail den, where all manner of Aztec spirits (raspberry-tea-infused tequila, pineapple-infused mescal) make for the fiendishly rococo concoctions, courtesy of master mixologist Philip Ward. Equally good are snacks such as popcorn with lime, cheese, and chili. The bi-level setting conjures a south-of-the-border bordello feel. ✉ *304 E. 6th St., between 1st and 2nd Aves., East Village* ☎ *212/253–5888* ⊕ *www.mayahuelny.com* Ⓜ *F to 2nd Ave.; 6 to Astor Pl.; N, R to 8th St.–NYU.*

McSorley's Old Ale House. One of New York's oldest saloons (it claims to have opened in 1854) and immortalized by *New Yorker* writer Joseph Mitchell, McSorley's is a must-visit for beer lovers, even if only two kinds of brew are served: McSorley's Light and McSorley's Dark. It's also essential for blarney lovers, and much friendlier to women than it was before the '80s. (The motto here once was "Good ale, raw onions, and no ladies.") Go early to avoid the down-the-block lines on Friday

CLOSE UP

Kickin' Karaoke

If you're looking for a venue other than your shower to bust out a rendition of Queen's "Somebody to Love," you're in good company. Otherwise-jaded New Yorkers have become hooked on the goofy, addictive pleasure of karaoke. The K-word means "empty orchestra" in Japanese, and seems to tickle both downtown hipsters (who dig the irony of kitsch) and uptown financiers (who need a good rebel yell at the end of a workday), and everybody in between who loves to flex the golden pipes after a few drinks.

There are three ways of getting your lead-vocalist groove on: doing it in public at a barwide Karaoke Night; reserving a private space at a bar ("karaoke boxes," they're called), where only your friends can hear you scream—er, sing; and bounding up onstage in front of a live band.

The hard-core karaoke places tend to be either grungy or glitzy, with as many as 15 available boxes for rent by the hour or night (each box includes a music machine, microphones, and bar service), as well as up to 80,000 songs on tap for you to warble. (Don't worry, that figure includes stuff by Journey, REO Speedwagon, Britney Spears, and other grotesquely catchy Top 40 music.) There are two locations of **Sing-Sing** (✉ 9 St. Marks Pl. ☎ 212/387–7800, and ✉ 81 Ave. A ☎ 212/674–0700), a serving of cheesiness at Midtown's **Pulse** (✉ 135 W. 41st St., between Broadway and 6th Ave. ☎ 212/278–0090), and just about anywhere else in the unofficial Koreatown that sprawls around Herald Square is a blast—try **Karaoke Duet 35** (✉ 53 W. 35th St., 2nd fl., between 5th and 6th Aves. ☎ 646/473–0826).

For live-band karaoke, head to the Lower East Side's hottest songfest: Monday-night rock 'n' roll karaoke at **Arlene's Grocery** (✉ 95 Stanton St. ☎ 212/995–1652).

18

and Saturday nights. ✉ 15 E. 7th St., between 2nd and 3rd Aves., East Village ☎ 212/473–9148 Ⓜ 6 to Astor Pl.

Otto's Shrunken Head Tiki Bar & Lounge. Who says NYC doesn't appeal to all tastes? Should you get a sudden urge to visit a tiki bar while in the East Village—and who doesn't sometimes?—the ultrapopular Otto's is your ticket. You'll find more than just a bamboo bar here, namely fish lamps, a tattooed, punk-rock crowd, cute little banquettes, drinks served in shrunken-head mugs, beef jerky for sale, and DJs prone to spinning anything from '50s rock to "Soul Gidget" surf music. ✉ 538 E. 14th St., between Aves. A and B, East Village ☎ 212/228–2240 ⊕ www.ottosshrunkenhead.com Ⓜ L to 1st Ave.

PDT. Those who crave their cocktails with a little cloak-and-dagger really flip over PDT (which stands for "Please Don't Tell"). This pseudo-speakeasy can only be reached through a phone booth in Crif Dogs, an unassuming hot-dog joint. Patrons with phoned-in reservations are escorted through the phone booth's false back into the cocktail bar, which is decorated with warm wooden beams and tongue-in-cheek taxidermy. ✉ 113 St. Marks Pl., between 1st Ave. and Ave. A, East Village ☎ 212/614–0386 ⊕ www.pdtnyc.com Ⓜ 6 to Astor Pl.

Pouring Ribbons. This polished second-floor cocktail bar is named after the way a drink forms iridescent liquid ribbons when it is expertly poured. Coiffed bartenders shake or stir your concoction of choice from a grid-based menu that allows you to visualize just how "spirit-forward" or "refreshing" you want your drink to be. Elaborate cocktail garnishes on the bar look tempting enough to eat, but order some cheese and charcuterie to accompany your drinks instead. ⊠ *225 Ave. B, 2nd fl., between 13th and 14th Sts., East Village* ☎ *917/656–6788* ⊕ *www.pouringribbons.com* Ⓜ *L to 1st Ave.*

Temple Bar. Unmarked and famous for its classic cocktails and romantic atmosphere, the Temple is prime first-date territory, especially once you drift past the sleek bar to the back, where, swathed in almost complete darkness, you can lounge on a comfy banquette, order an old-fashioned, and do what people on first dates do. ⊠ *332 Lafayette St., East Village* ☎ *212/925–4242* ⊕ *www.templebarnyc.com* Ⓜ *B, D, F, M to Broadway–Lafayette St.; 6 to Bleecker St.*

CABARET AND PIANO BARS

Joe's Pub. Wood paneling, red-velvet walls, and comfy sofas make a lush setting for top-notch performers and the A-list celebrities who love them (or pretend to). Named for the Public Theater's near-mythic impresario Joe Papp, and located inside the Public, Joe's doesn't have a bad seat—but if you want to occupy one, buy tickets beforehand and/or arrive at least half an hour early for the Italian-inspired dinner menu. ⊠ *425 Lafayette St., between 4th St. and Astor Pl., East Village* ☎ *212/539–8778* ⊕ *www.joespub.com* Ⓜ *6 to Astor Pl.*

LOWER EAST SIDE

BARS

Back Room. The Prohibition-era atmospheric touches here include tin ceilings, chandeliers, velvet wallpaper, mirrored bars, an amply sized fireplace, and a "hidden" outdoor entrance (which you can find easily enough, through the back alley). The music consists of rock CDs rather than a live spinmeister, and the drinks come in old-fashioned teacups or wrapped in paper bags. These, and other prize quirks, attract a slightly older clientele than many of its rowdier neighbors. ⊠ *102 Norfolk St., between Delancey and Rivington Sts., Lower East Side* ☎ *212/228–5098* ⊕ *www.backroomnyc.com* Ⓜ *F to Delancey St.; J, M, Z to Essex St.*

Spitzer's Corner. No, you won't rub shoulders with ex-governor Eliot Spitzer here, but you can find 40 types of craft beer on tap plus a selection of the bottled variety, good food, floor-to-ceiling windows that pop open in fine weather, and wooden walls supposedly taken from pickle barrels (fortunately, the air is free of any scent from their former contents). ⊠ *101 Rivington St., at Ludlow St., Lower East Side* ☎ *212/228–0027* ⊕ *www.spitzerscorner.com* Ⓜ *F to Delancey St.; J, M, Z to Essex St.*

LIVE MUSIC VENUES

Arlene's Grocery. On Monday nights, crowds pack into this former Puerto Rican bodega for Rock 'n' Roll Karaoke, where they live out their rock-star dreams by singing favorite punk anthems onstage with a live band.

The other six nights of the week are for local bands, and accordingly hit-or-miss. ✉ *95 Stanton St., between Ludlow and Orchard Sts., Lower East Side* ☎ *212/358–1633* ⊕ *www.arlenesgrocery.net* Ⓜ *F to 2nd Ave.*

Bowery Ballroom. This theater with Art Deco accents is probably the city's top midsize concert venue. Packing in the crowds here is a rite of passage for musicians on the cusp of stardom, including the Gossip, Manic Street Preachers, and the exuberant Go! Team. Grab one of the tables on the balcony (if you can), stand (and get sandwiched) on the main floor, or retreat to the comfortable bar in the basement, which really fills up after each show. ✉ *6 Delancey St., between the Bowery and Chrystie St., Lower East Side* ☎ *212/533–2111* ⊕ *www. boweryballroom.com* Ⓜ *J, Z to Bowery.*

The Delancey. From the palm-studded rooftop deck (heated in winter, hosting barbecues in summer) down to the basement, where noisy rock and punk bands hold court, the multifaceted Delancey, at the foot of the Williamsburg Bridge, strikes an invigorating balance between classy and trashy. ✉ *168 Delancey St., between Clinton and Attorney Sts., Lower East Side* ☎ *212/254–9920* ⊕ *www.thedelancey.com* Ⓜ *F to Delancey St.; J, M, Z to Essex St.*

Mercury Lounge. You have to squeeze past all the sardine-packed hipsters in the front bar to reach the stage, but it's worth it. Not only does this top-quality venue, a "little sister to the Bowery Bar," specialize in cool bands on the indie scene, but it was also where the late, great Jeff Buckley used to stop by to do spontaneous solo shows. ✉ *217 E. Houston St., at Ave. A, Lower East Side* ☎ *212/260–4700* ⊕ *www. mercuryloungenyc.com* Ⓜ *F to 2nd Ave.*

Pianos. With two venues for live music and DJs—the Showroom downstairs and Lounge upstairs—as well as a full bar that serves food downstairs, there's something for everyone at this Lower East Side staple. It's a blast late nights. ✉ *158 Ludlow St., just south of Stanton St., Lower East Side* ☎ *212/505–3733* ⊕ *www.pianosnyc.com* Ⓜ *F to Delancey St.; J, M, Z to Essex St.*

Rockwood Music Hall. Musicians and DJs rev up the crowd seven days a week at this intimate, multistage venue. Performances start as early as 3 pm on the weekends and 6 pm during the week—meaning you can get your live music fix and catch up on your sleep, too. Many shows are free. ✉ *196 Allen St., Lower East Side* ☎ *212/477–4155* ⊕ *www. rockwoodmusichall.com* Ⓜ *F to 2nd Ave.; J, Z to Bowery.*

GREENWICH VILLAGE AND WEST VILLAGE

GREENWICH VILLAGE

BARS

124 Rabbit Club. Named for a 19th-century bar on, or near, its current site, this tiny-yet-charming exotic beer bar could easily steal the motto of the punk band the Germs: "What We Do Is Secret." There's such a hushed, sacred (yet low-rent) vibe to this subterranean space of baby chandeliers, scratchy wallpaper, and rabbit images that the glorious menu comes as a surprise: on it you find "autumnal ales,"

18

Trappist monk–made beers, and strange American concoctions on tap, plus fantastic beers from Belgium, Germany, Great Britain, and the Baltic region. ✉ *124 MacDougal St., between W. 3rd and Bleecker Sts., Greenwich Village* 🕾 *212/254–0575* Ⓜ *A, C, E, B, D, F, M to W. 4th St.*

Vol de Nuit. Tucked away from the street, the "Belgian Beer Bar" (as everybody calls it) features a European-style, enclosed outdoor courtyard and a cozy interior, all red light and shadows. NYU grad-student types come for the mammoth selection of beers on tap as well as the fries, which are served with Belgian flair, in a paper cone with an array of sauces on the side. ✉ *148 W. 4th St., at 6th Ave., Greenwich Village* 🕾 *212/982–3388* ⊕ *www.voldenuitbar.com* Ⓜ *A, B, C, D, E, F, M to W. 4th St.*

JAZZ VENUES

Fodor's Choice
★

Blue Note. Considered by many (not least its current owners) to be "the jazz capital of the world," the Blue Note was once the stomping ground for such legends as Dizzy Gillespie, and still hosts a variety of acts, from Chris Botti to the Count Basie Orchestra to Boz Scaggs. Expect a steep cover charge except for late shows on weekends, when the music goes from less jazzy to more funky. ✉ *131 W. 3rd St., near 6th Ave., Greenwich Village* 🕾 *212/475–8592* ⊕ *www.bluenote.net* Ⓜ *A, B, C, D, E, F, M to W. 4th St.*

Knickerbocker Bar and Grill. Jazz is on the menu Friday and Saturday nights at this old-fashioned steak house, a longtime staple of the city's more intimate music scene. ✉ *33 University Pl., at 9th St., Greenwich Village* 🕾 *212/228–8490* ⊕ *www.knickerbockerbarandgrill.com* Ⓜ *N, R to 8th St.–NYU; 6 to Astor Pl.*

LIVE MUSIC VENUES

(Le) Poisson Rouge. Underneath the site of the late, lamented Village Gate jazz emporium is this cutting-edge jewel of a place, whose name means "the Red Fish" (and whose parentheses around "Le" remain a mystery). Blending just the right mix of posh notes (lush decor, fine dining) and brave music programming (jazz, classical, electronic, cabaret, rock, folk—even, with the splendiferous Ralph's World, children's music), the Poisson is quite simply an essential NYC fixture. ✉ *158 Bleecker St., at Thompson St., Greenwich Village* 🕾 *212/505–3474* ⊕ *www. lepoissonrouge.com* Ⓜ *A, B, C, D, E, F, M to W. 4th St.*

WEST VILLAGE

BARS

Corner Bistro. Opened in 1961, this charming neighborhood saloon serves what many think are some of the best (and most affordable) burgers in town. Once you actually get a seat, the space feels nice and cozy, but until then, be prepared to drink a beer amid lively and hungry patrons. ✉ *331 W. 4th St., at 8th Ave., West Village* 🕾 *212/242–9502* ⊕ *www.cornerbistrony.com* Ⓜ *1, 2, 3, A, C, E to 14th St.; L to 8th Ave.*

Fodor's Choice
★

Employees Only. The dapper, white-coated bartenders (many of them impressively mustachioed) at this cocktail bar mix delicious, well-thought-out tipples with debonair aplomb and freshly squeezed mixers. Sip one in the dimly lit bar area and you might feel like you've stepped back in time—if it weren't for the crush of trendy West Village locals and visitors in the know at your back. Look for the green awning that says "EO" and the neon "Psychic" sign out front. Dinner is served in the restaurant at the back: it's quality, but pricey. ✉ *510 Hudson St., between Christopher and 10th Sts., West Village* ☎ *212/242–3021* ⊕ *www.employeesonlynyc.com* Ⓜ *1 to Christopher St.–Sheridan Sq.; A, B, C, D, E, F, M to W. 4th St.*

Hudson Bar and Books. Along with its sister branches—Beekman Bar and Books on Beekman Place and Lexington Bar and Books on, yep, Lexington—the Hudson reflects a literary bent in its cocktails, with names like the Dewey Decimal, the Cervantes Spritzer, and Alphabet Absinthe (topped off with floating letter-shape sugar cubes). Despite that, it's hardly a hushed library where well-read butlers serve you; the atmosphere here is more about book decor than serious literature. It's seriously clubby, with wood paneling and leather banquettes. And it's one of the few places where you can still smoke. ✉ *636 Hudson St., at Horatio St., West Village* ☎ *212/229–2642* ⊕ *www.barandbooks.cz/ hudson/* Ⓜ *A, C, E to 14th St.; L to 8th Ave.*

Fodor's Choice
★ **Little Branch.** Top-quality cocktails, dim lighting, and snug booths make this the ideal spot for a conversation with friends (that you can actually hear) or an intimate date. ✉ *20 7th Ave., at Leroy St., West Village* ☎ *212/929–4360* Ⓜ *1 to Houston St.*

Otheroom. Ever wish that the bar you're drinking in had something more interesting on its walls than Budweiser signs? Head to the far west Otheroom, art gallery by day, upscale drinking spot by night. The menu is pretty creative, too, with dozens of microbrews and American wines available by the glass. ✉ *143 Perry St., between Greenwich and Washington Sts., West Village* ☎ *212/645–9758* ⊕ *theotheroomnyc.com* Ⓜ *1 to Christopher St.–Sheridan Sq.*

White Horse Tavern. According to New York legend, writer Dylan Thomas drank himself to death in this historic West Village tavern founded in 1880. When the weather's nice, try to snag a seat at one of the sidewalk tables for prime—and, given the neighborhood, we do mean prime—people-watching. ✉ *567 Hudson St., at 11th St., West Village* ☎ *212/989–3956* Ⓜ *1 to Christopher St.–Sheridan Sq.*

Wilfie & Nell. Combine the cozy atmosphere and frothy pints standard at Irish pubs with a well-heeled West Village crowd and you get Wilfie & Nell, a candlelit bar full of communal tables for making new friends. This perpetually crowded neighborhood favorite, with its low ceilings and locally sourced food, is a popular singles spot as well as a good match for night owls: food and brews are served into the wee hours. ✉ *228 W. 4th St., between 10th St. and 7th Ave. S, West Village* ☎ *212/242–2990* ⊕ *www.wilfieandnell.com* Ⓜ *1 to Christopher St.–Sheridan Sq.; A, B, C, D, E, F, M to W. 4th St.*

CABARET AND PIANO BARS

The Duplex. No matter who's performing, the largely gay audience hoots and hollers in support of the often kitschy performers at this music-scene staple on busy Sheridan Square since 1951. Singers and comedians hold court in the cabaret theater, while those itching to take a shot at open mike head downstairs to the lively piano bar. ✉ *61 Christopher St., at 7th Ave. S, West Village* ☎ *212/255–5438* ⊕ *www.theduplex.com* Ⓜ *1 to Christopher St.–Sheridan Sq.*

18

GAY NIGHTLIFE

Cubbyhole. Early in the evening the crowd is mixed at this neighborhood institution, where the DJs, unpretentious decor, and inexpensive margaritas are popular. Later on, the women take charge. ✉ *281 W. 12th St., at W. 4th St., West Village* ☎ *212/243–9041* ⊕ *www.cubbyholebar. com* Ⓜ *1, 2, 3, A, C, E to 14th St.; L to 8th Ave.*

Fodor's Choice ★ **Henrietta Hudson.** The nightly parties at this laid-back West Village HQ for the Sapphic set attract young professional women, out-of-towners, and longtime regulars. Because the DJ and pool table quickly create a crowd, though, stake your claim to a spot early, especially on weekends. ✉ *438 Hudson St., at Morton St., West Village* ☎ *212/924–3347* ⊕ *www.henriettahudson.com* Ⓜ *1 to Christopher St.–Sheridan Sq.*

JAZZ VENUES

Fodor's Choice ★ **Village Vanguard.** This prototypical jazz club, tucked into a cellar in the Village since the 1940s, has been the haunt of legends like Thelonious Monk and Barbara Streisand. Today you can hear jams from the likes of Bill Charlap and Ravi Coltrane, and on Monday night the sizable resident Vanguard Jazz Orchestra blow their collective heart out. ✉ *178 7th Ave. S, between 11th and Perry Sts., West Village* ☎ *212/255–4037* ⊕ *www.villagevanguard.com* Ⓜ *1, 2, 3 to 14th St.*

LIVE MUSIC VENUES

SOB's. The initials stand for "Sounds of Brazil" (no, not what you—and everybody else—might think), and this is *the* place for reggae, African, and Latin music, with some jazz gigs sprinkled in. The late, great Cuban sensation Cachao used to hold court here, as does calypso's Mighty Sparrow when he's up north. Don't miss the Haitian dance parties, the after-work Latin-groove happy hour, or the bossa nova brunches. Dinner is served as well. ✉ *204 Varick St., West Village* ☎ *212/243–4940* ⊕ *www.sobs.com* Ⓜ *1 to Houston St.*

CHELSEA AND THE MEATPACKING DISTRICT

CHELSEA

BARS

Half King. Writer Sebastian Junger (*The Perfect Storm*) is one of the owners of this would-be literary mecca. We say "would-be," because the ambience can be more publike than writerly—and that's fine, since the King draws such a friendly crowd (media types, mostly). We like it best for its frequent readings, gallery exhibits, and Irish-American menu. ✉ *505 W. 23rd St., between 10th and 11th Aves., Chelsea* ☎ *212/462–4300* ⊕ *www.thehalfking.com* Ⓜ *C, E to 23rd St.*

Porchlight. At this southern-inflected bar you can have your cocktails and eat your fried oysters and smoked cheddar biscuits, too. Located in far West Chelsea (a little bit of a hike from the subway), this relaxed watering hole from New York restaurateur and hospitality king Danny Meyer is an intimate space to quaff and nibble the night away. ✉ *271 11th Ave., Chelsea* ☎ *212/981–6188* ⊕ *porchlightbar.com* Ⓜ *C, E to 23rd St.; 1 to 28th St.*

COMEDY CLUBS

Fodor's Choice ★ **Upright Citizens Brigade Theatre.** Raucous sketch comedy, audience-initiated improv, and classic stand-up take turns onstage here at the city's absolute capital for alternative comedy. There are classes available, too. ✉ *307 W. 26th St., between 8th and 9th Aves., Chelsea* ☎ *212/366–9176* ⊕ *www.ucbtheatre.com* Ⓜ *C, E to 23rd St.*

GAY NIGHTLIFE

Gym Sports Bar. At New York's first gay sports bar, the plentiful flat-screen TVs and cheap Budweisers draw athletic enthusiasts of every stripe, from athlete to armchair. Nobly, the bar sponsors—and frequently hosts parties for—a number of local gay sports teams. ✉ *167 8th Ave., at 18th St., Chelsea* ☎ *212/337–2439* ⊕ *www.gymsportsbar.com* Ⓜ *A, C, E to 14th St.; L to 8th Ave.; 1 to 18th St.*

THE MEATPACKING DISTRICT

BARS

Plunge. The Gansevoort Hotel's slick rooftop bar would be worth visiting even without its sweeping views. The adjectives sleek and glossy could easily be illustrated by Plunge, where the lighting is soft, the furnishings are cool and comfy (at least to a degree), the music isn't too loud, servers of both sexes are sexy, and there is ample space—indoors as well as out. ✉ *18 9th Ave., at 13th St., Meatpacking District* ☎ *212/660–6736* ⊕ *www.hotelgansevoort.com* Ⓜ *A, C, E to 14th St.; L to 8th Ave.*

The Standard Hotel Biergarten, Grill, and Living Room. Practically the official bar of the High Line park, the Standard Biergarten is a sprawling, riotous space complete with Ping-Pong tables and big steins of beer. There's also a grill bar and indoor Living Room lounge. As for the chic hot spot on the top floor, unofficially called the Boom Boom Room, it's currently the hardest door in town ("hardest," that is, to get through). ✉ *848 Washington St., at 13th St., Meatpacking District* ☎ *212/645–4646* ⊕ *www.standardhotels.com* Ⓜ *A, C, E to 14th St.; L to 8th Ave.*

DANCE CLUBS AND DJ VENUES

Cielo. Relatively mature clubgoers (if the word "mature" can ever be applied to such a crowd) gravitate to this small but sturdy Meatpacking District music-head mecca to toss back cocktails, dig the high-quality sound system, groove to top-flight DJs spinning soulful Latin beats and techno, boogie on the sunken dance floor, and smoke in the no-frills garden outside. Monday night is home to the award-winning Deep Space parties, where resident DJs (as well as guest spinmeisters like Dimitri from Paris) rev up the faithful with everything from dubstep to Stravinsky. ✉ *18 Little W. 12th St., between 9th Ave. and Washington St., Meatpacking District* ☎ *212/645–5700* ⊕ *www.cieloclub.com* Ⓜ *A, C, E to 14th St.; L to 8th Ave.*

18

UNION SQUARE, GRAMERCY, AND THE FLATIRON DISTRICT

UNION SQUARE

BARS

Rye House. A welcoming bar with slick cocktails and a clever take on comfort food, the Rye House beckons just steps from the chain-store overload of Union Square. From boiled peanuts and fried pickles to their own take on a Sazerac, the space is a welcome respite from the hustle and bustle outside. ⊠ *11 W. 17th St., between Broadway and 5th Ave., Union Square* ☎ *212/255–7260* ⊕ *www.ryehousenyc.com* Ⓜ *4, 5, 6, L, N, Q, R to 14th St.–Union Sq.*

GRAMERCY

BARS

Dear Irving. This cocktail parlor invites Gramercy locals inside with its name, the beginning of a letter to the lovely Irving Place on which the bar resides. Interiors are chic and refined, and just like at sister property Raines Law Room, there are private sections of tables and couches for intimate conversations. Reservations are recommended, especially during prime weekend hours, but must be made online. ⊠ *55 Irving Pl., between 17th and 18th Sts., Union Square* ⊕ *www.dearirving.com* Ⓜ *4, 5, 6, L, N, Q, R to 14th St.–Union Sq.*

Old Town Bar. The proudly unpretentious bi-level Old Town is redolent of old New York, and why not? It's been around since 1892. Tavern-style grub, mahogany everywhere, and atmosphere, atmosphere, atmosphere make this a fun stop on any pub crawl. Men: don't miss the giant, person-size urinals. ⊠ *45 E. 18th St., between Broadway and Park Ave. S, Gramercy* ☎ *212/529–6732* ⊕ *www.oldtownbar.com* Ⓜ *4, 5, 6, L, N, Q, R to 14th St.–Union Sq.*

Pete's Tavern. This historic landmark (where O. Henry was a loyal customer) is one of the bars that claims to be the oldest continuously operating watering hole in the city. Pete's has charm to spare, with its long wooden bar and cozy booths, where locals crowd in for a beer or a fantastic burger. When weather warms up, sidewalk tables with red-and-white-checker tablecloths on scenic Irving Place are a neighborhood favorite. ⊠ *129 E. 18th St., at Irving Pl., Gramercy* ☎ *212/473–7676* ⊕ *www.petestavern.com* Ⓜ *4, 5, 6, L, N, Q, R to 14th St.–Union Sq.*

JAZZ VENUES

FAMILY
Fodor's Choice
★

Jazz Standard. The Standard's sizable underground room draws top names in the business. As a part of Danny Meyer's southern-food restaurant Blue Smoke, it's one of the few spots where you can get dry-rubbed ribs to go with your bebop. Bring the kids for the Jazz Standard Youth Orchestra concerts every Sunday afternoon. ⊠ *116 E. 27th St., between Park and Lexington Aves., Gramercy* ☎ *212/576–2232* ⊕ *www.jazzstandard.com* Ⓜ *6 to 28th St.*

LIVE MUSIC VENUES

Fodor's Choice
★

Irving Plaza. This two-story venue is known for its solid rock performances, both indie (DJ Shadow and Sleater-Kinney) and more mainstream (Lenny Kravitz)—even if they can get a little pricey. Red walls and chandeliers add a Gothic touch. If the main floor gets too cramped, seek sanctuary in the chill bar upstairs. ✉ *17 Irving Pl., at 15th St., Gramercy* ☎ *212/777–6800* ⊕ *www.irvingplaza.com* Ⓜ *4, 5, 6, L, N, Q, R to 14th St.–Union Sq.*

FLATIRON DISTRICT

BARS

The Ace Hotel. A hot spot for the digital set, this hotel's lobby and adjoining restaurant spaces—the Breslin and the John Dory—have been packed since they opened at this Pacific Northwest import. If your bearded hipster friend came into some cash, his place would look like the lobby here, with reclaimed-wood tables, beer signs, and beautiful folks in oversize eyeglasses drinking coffee by day or a craft brew by night (while a DJ spins in the background). ✉ *20 W. 29th St., between Broadway and 5th Ave., Flatiron District* ☎ *212/679–2222* ⊕ *www. acehotel.com/newyork* Ⓜ *R to 28th St.*

Flatiron Lounge. Here, resident mixologists rely on the freshest (and sometimes most exotic) ingredients available. The cocktail menu changes often, but if you're stumped, tell the bartenders what you like and they'll happily invent a bespoke concoction on the spot. ✉ *37 W. 19th St., between 5th and 6th Aves., Flatiron District* ☎ *212/727–7741* ⊕ *www.flatironlounge.com* Ⓜ *1 to 18th St.; F, M to 14th St.; L to 6th Ave.; 6 to 23rd St.*

Fodor'sChoice
★ **The NoMad Bar.** A sultry space from the team behind the NoMad Hotel (with a separate entrance on 28th Street) this bi-level bar impresses with its inviting leather banquettes, extensive golden-lit bar, and tempting list of craft cocktails. The food leans towards comfort classics, such as chicken potpie and bacon-wrapped hot dogs, but the design is pure sophistication. ✉ *10 W. 28th St., at Broadway, Flatiron District* ☎ *347/472–5660* ⊕ *www.thenomadhotel.com* Ⓜ *N, R to 28th St.; 6 to 28th St.*

Raines Law Room. There's no phone number or big sign for this cocktail bar; just ring the bell to enter. Wood-burning fireplaces, deep banquettes, and curtains for privacy all contribute to the comfortable, living room–like vibe—perfect for a date or intimate group gathering. An outdoor, candlelit garden is functional, too: herbs grown here are used in the carefully crafted cocktails. ✉ *48 W. 17th St., Flatiron District* ⊕ *www.raineslawroom.com* Ⓜ *F, M to 14th St.; 4, 5, 6, L, N, Q, R to 14th St.–Union Sq.*

MIDTOWN EAST AND MURRAY HILL

MIDTOWN EAST

BARS

The Bar Downstairs. The bar without a name in the basement of the Andaz 5th Avenue may lack a moniker, but it certainly has pedigree. Alchemy Consulting, a joint venture from Chicago's Violet Hour and New York's Death and Co., designed the cocktails here; look for spins on the Negroni and Manhattan in the sleek subterranean space. The food menu is similarly upmarket, with a variety of nebulously Spanish small plates. ✉ *485 5th Ave., at 41st St., Midtown East* ☎ *212/601–1234* ⊕ *newyork.5thavenue.*

18

andaz.hyatt.com/en/hotel/dining/thebardownstairs.html Ⓜ *B, D, F, M to 42nd St.–Bryant Park; 7 to 5th Ave.; 4, 5, 6, S to Grand Central–42nd St.*

Fodor's Choice
★ **Campbell Apartment.** Commuters pack into this Grand Central Terminal bar on their way to catch trains home during the evening rush, but don't let the crush of humanity scare you away—you can have a romantic time here in one of Manhattan's more beautiful rooms. The restored space dates to the 1920s, when it was the private office of an executive named John W. Campbell, and as the exquisite decor suggests, old JWC knew how to live. Sample the good life as you knock back a well-built cocktail from an overstuffed chair. Just try to avoid that weekday evening rush. ⊠ *Grand Central Terminal, 15 Vanderbilt Ave. entrance, Midtown East* ☎ *212/953–0409* ⊕ *www.grandcentralterminal.com* Ⓜ *4, 5, 6, 7, S to Grand Central–42nd St.*

King Cole Bar. A justly beloved Maxfield Parrish mural of "Old King Cole" himself, as well as his psychedelic court, adds to the already considerable elegance at this romantic and essential Midtown meeting place. Try a Bloody Mary—this is where the drink was introduced to Americans. Be warned: prices for a single cocktail are steep. ⊠ *St. Regis Hotel, 2 E. 55th St., between 5th and Madison Aves., Midtown East* ☎ *212/339–6857* ⊕ *www.kingcolebar.com* Ⓜ *E, M to 5th Ave./53rd St.*

P. J. Clarke's. Mirrors and polished wood and other old-time flair adorn New York's most famous Irish bar. Steeped in Hollywood lore—Steve McQueen was once a regular, and scenes from the 1945 movie *Lost Weekend* were shot here—Clarke's draws in the after-work crowd that appreciates drinking beer, slurping oysters, and eating exceptionally juicy burgers while immersed in the place's history. ⊠ *915 3rd Ave., at 55th St., Midtown East* ☎ *212/317–1616* ⊕ *www.pjclarkes.com* Ⓜ *6 to 51st St.; E, M to Lexington Ave./53rd St.; 4, 5, 6 to 59th St.; N, Q, R to Lexington Ave./59th St.*

GAY NIGHTLIFE

Evolve Bar and Lounge. Rising from the ashes of a popular gay club on the same site, this glossy, raucous Chelsea-style bar–club gets Midtown East rocking, with its sexy-yet-genial staff and theme nights like Pop-off Thursday, Bulge Friday, and Disco Balls Sunday. ⊠ *221 E. 58th St., between 2nd and 3rd Aves., Midtown East* ☎ *212/355–3395* Ⓜ *4, 5, 6 to 59th St.; N, Q, R to Lexington Ave./59th St.*

Townhouse Bar. It's the elegant yin to the rowdy yang of **Evolve,** which is just across the block at East 58th Street. Distinguished mature men from the Upper East Side meet younger would-be versions of themselves at this "gentlemen's club," which looks like the home of a blueblood with superb taste. The attire is "uptown casual" if not fancier. ⊠ *236 E. 58th St., between 2nd and 3rd Aves., Midtown East* ☎ *212/754–4649* ⊕ *www.townhouseny.com* Ⓜ *4, 5, 6 to 59th St.; N, Q, R to Lexington Ave./59th St.*

MURRAY HILL

BARS

Middle Branch. Sasha Petraske's speakeasy-style cocktail bars have expanded into Murray Hill with Middle Branch, a two-story space and former antiques store with no sign outside to announce its presence.

Cocktail lovers find the brick town house anyway, and inside, linger over small plates, live jazz, and a long list of sophisticated drinks. ✉ *154 E. 33rd St., Murray Hill* ☎ *212/213–1350* Ⓜ *6 to 33rd St.*

MIDTOWN WEST

BARS

Cellar Bar. Underneath the Bryant Park Hotel—and a tiled, arched ceiling—is one of the more spectacular spaces in Midtown. As a DJ with a taste for classic R&B spins the night away, a fashion-industry crowd gets up to dance. ✉ *40 W. 40th St., between 5th and 6th Aves., Midtown West* ☎ *212/642–2211* ⊕ *www.cellarbarbryantparkhotel.com* Ⓜ *B, D, F, M to 42nd St.–Bryant Park; 7 to 5th Ave.*

Fodor'sChoice ★ **Joe Allen.** Everybody's en route either to or from a show at this "old reliable" on the boisterous Restaurant Row, celebrated in the musical version of *All About Eve*. Chances are you'll even spot a Broadway star at the bar or in the dining room. Still, our favorite thing about Joe's is not the show crowd but the hilarious "flop wall," adorned with posters from musicals that bombed, sometimes spectacularly. (Check out the ones for *Paradox Lust, Got Tu Go Disco,* and *Dude,* the unfortunate sequel to *Hair.*) ✉ *326 W. 46th St., between 8th and 9th Aves., Midtown West* ☎ *212/581–6464* ⊕ *www.joeallenrestaurant.com* Ⓜ *A, C, E to 42nd St.–Port Authority; N, Q, R to 49th St.*

Lantern's Keep. The elegance of cocktail culture from another era is alive and well at Lantern's Keep, an intimate lounge tucked behind the lobby of the Iroquois Hotel. Reservations are recommended for this watering hole, where plush seats are huddled around a fireplace. There is no standing room here, resulting in a luxurious, leisurely vibe. Cocktails are works of art and bartenders are helpful at identifying your perfect poison. ✉ *Iroquois Hotel, 49 W. 44th St., between 5th and 6th Aves., Midtown West* ☎ *212/453–4287* ⊕ *www.iroquoisny.com/lanternskeep* Ⓜ *B, D, F, M to 42nd St.–Bryant Park.*

The Rum House. Among the glittering lights of Broadway theaters, Rum House is a destination bar thanks to its attention to the craft of mixing cocktails. The sister property to downtown favorite Ward III, this bar has nightly live piano music and creative libations in addition to all the classic cocktails. ✉ *228 W. 47th St., between 7th and 8th Aves., Midtown West* ☎ *646/490–6924* ⊕ *therumhousenyc.com* Ⓜ *N, Q, R to 49th St.; A, C, E to 42nd St.–Port Authority.*

Russian Vodka Room. Forget **Russian Samovar** across the block—here's where the serious vodka drinking goes down. The Vodka Room features a glowing, sophisticated front room with nightly piano player (and the superlative Dmitri Kolesnik on Monday, free of charge), a more sumptuous back room, a generous Attitude Adjustment Hour (that's Russki for "Happy Hour"), and an impressive variety of infused vodkas (horseradish! ginger! pepper!). For those who crave variety, a vodka tasting menu is available, as are culinary standards like borscht. ✉ *265 W. 52nd St., between Broadway and 8th Ave., Midtown West* ☎ *212/307–5835* ⊕ *www.russianvodkaroom.com* Ⓜ *1, C, E to 50th St.*

18

Salon de Ning. Take a break from 5th Avenue shopping at this glass-lined penthouse bar on the 23rd floor of the ritzy Peninsula Hotel. Drinks are pricey, of course, but what isn't in this neighborhood? The views are worth it, especially from the rooftop terraces. ⌧ *Peninsula Hotel, 700 5th Ave., at 55th St., Midtown West* ☎ *212/956–2888* ⊕ *newyork. peninsula.com* Ⓜ *E, M to 5th Ave./53rd St.*

COMEDY CLUBS

Caroline's on Broadway. This high-gloss club presents established names as well as comedians on the edge of stardom. Janeane Garofalo, David Alan Grier, Colin Quinn, and Gilbert Gottfried have all headlined. ⌧ *1626 Broadway, between 49th and 50th Sts., Midtown West* ☎ *212/757–4100* ⊕ *www.carolines.com* Ⓜ *N, Q, R to 49th St.; 1 to 50th St.*

GAY NIGHTLIFE

Posh. Lest you think that Hell's Kitchen has no good gay lounges, Posh has walls covered in fine canvases by local artists, trophies over the bar, ample room for kibitzing and dancing, plenty of neon decor, and hours that are "4 pm to 4 am GUARANTEED." ⌧ *405 W. 51st St., at 9th Ave., Midtown West* ☎ *212/957–2222* ⊕ *www.poshbarnyc.com* Ⓜ *C, E to 50th St.*

JAZZ VENUES

Birdland. This place gets its name from saxophone great Charlie "Yard-bird" (or just "Bird") Parker, so expect serious musicians such as John Pizzarelli, the Dave Holland Sextet, and Arturo O'Farrill's Afro-Cuban Jazz Orchestra (on Sunday night). The dining room serves moderately priced American fare with a Cajun accent. ⌧ *315 W. 44th St., between 8th and 9th Aves., Midtown West* ☎ *212/581–3080* ⊕ *www. birdlandjazz.com* Ⓜ *A, C, E to 42nd St.–Port Authority.*

Dizzy's Club Coca Cola. For a night of jazz without the pretension, turn to Dizzy's, an intimate club with Manhattan skyline views and Southern-inflected cuisine (okra, fried chicken, catfish) and cocktails. Late-night sessions are ideal for an after-dinner nightcap; some of the drinks, such as the Dizzy Gillespie, are named after jazz legends. ⌧ *10 Columbus Circle, Midtown West* ☎ *212/258–9595* ⊕ *www.jazz.org/dizzys* Ⓜ *1, A, B, C, D to 59th St.–Columbus Circle.*

Iridium. This cozy, top-drawer club is a sure bet for big-name talent like the David Murray Black Saint Quartet and Michael Wolff. The sight lines are good, and the sound system was designed with the help of Les Paul, the inventor of the solid-body electric guitar, who used to play here every Monday night. The rest of the week sees a mix of artists like Chuck Mangione and the Eddie Daniels Band. ⌧ *1650 Broadway, at 51st St., Midtown West* ☎ *212/582–2121* ⊕ *www.theiridium.com* Ⓜ *1 to 50th St.; N, Q, R to 49th St.*

LIVE MUSIC VENUES

B. B. King Blues Club & Grill. This lavish Times Square club is vast, shiny, and hosts a range of musicians, from the Harlem Gospel Choir to George Clinton and the P-Funk All-Stars. It's also where surviving rock legends like Little Richard and Chuck Berry play as well. ⌧ *237 W. 42nd St., between 7th and 8th Aves., Midtown West* ☎ *212/997–4144* ⊕ *www.bbkingblues.com* Ⓜ *A, C, E to 42nd St.–Port Authority; 1, 2, 3, 7, N, Q, R, S to Times Sq.–42nd St.*

UPPER EAST SIDE

BARS

American Trash. You might tell from the name that this isn't exactly your granddad's UES drinking establishment. Bicycle tires, golf clubs, and other castoffs cover the walls and ceiling, ensuring that the Trash, a sanctum of sleaze, merits its descriptive name. Eight plasma TVs, three video games, a defiantly rock 'n' roll jukebox, and a pool table keep the neighborhood crowd (as well as stray bikers who hate them) busy. Some nights local bands play classic rock. ☒ *1471 1st Ave., between 76th and 77th Sts., Upper East Side* ☏ *212/988–9008* Ⓜ *6 to 77th St.*

Fodor'sChoice
★ **Auction House.** This Victorian-style lounge brings a touch of downtown chic to the sometimes suburban-feeling Upper East Side with candlelit tables, high tin ceilings, and velvet couches. Rap and hip-hop fans should look elsewhere (the only tunes coming out of this joint are alternative and rock), and baseball caps and sneakers are strictly forbidden, as are—at the other end of the spectrum—fur coats. ☒ *300 E. 89th St., between 1st and 2nd Aves., Upper East Side* ☏ *212/427–4458* ⊕ *auctionhousenyc.com* Ⓜ *4, 5, 6 to 86th St.*

Bar Pleiades. The cocktail bar companion to Café Boulud, also in the Surrey Hotel, Bar Pleiades is a livelier alternative to the more staid atmosphere at the Carlyle's Bemelmans Bar. The design is classic to a fault, employing a black-and-white theme that's positively Audrey Hepburn–esque. Drinks rotate seasonally, and there are tasty nibbles from the café kitchen. Though it doesn't have the same drink menu, the rooftop bar is a cozy aerie good for people- and skyscraper-watching. ☒ *Surrey Hotel, 20 E. 76th St., between 5th and Madison Aves., Upper East Side* ☏ *212/772–2600* ⊕ *www.barpleiades.com* Ⓜ *6 to 77th St.*

Opia. The motto for this upscale-yet-unpretentious bar-restaurant—"If you like us, tell your friends, and if you don't, tell your enemies!"— isn't necessary, given its manifold charms: a drop-dead-gorgeous design, plenty of space for canoodling and cavorting, a romantic balcony (though 57th Street isn't exactly a scenic beach), plus live jazz on Saturday nights. ☒ *130 E. 57th St., between Lexington and 3rd Aves., Upper East Side* ☏ *212/688–3939* ⊕ *www.opiarestaurant.com* Ⓜ *4, 5, 6 to 59th St.; N, Q, R to Lexington Ave./59th St.*

Seamstress. This dedicated cocktail den—complete with low lighting, exposed brick walls, and cozy booth seating—elevated the drinking options in what can feel like a quiet neighborhood. Cocktails (and the creative bartenders who invented them) may be the main draw here, but the food menu is worth a look, too. ☒ *339 E. 75th St., Upper East Side* ☏ *212/288–8033* ⊕ *seamstressny.com* Ⓜ *6 to 77th St.*

CABARET AND PIANO BARS

Fodor'sChoice
★ **The Carlyle.** The hotel's discreetly sophisticated Café Carlyle hosts such top cabaret and jazz performers as Christine Ebersole, John Pizzarelli, Steve Tyrell, and Woody Allen, who swings on the clarinet with the Eddy Davis New Orleans Jazz Band. The less fancy-schmancy (though still pricey) **Bemelmans Bar,** with a mural by the author of the *Madeline* books, features a rotating cast of pianist-singers. ☒ *35 E. 76th St.,*

18

between Madison and Park Aves., Upper East Side ☎ *212/744–1600* ⊕ *www.thecarlyle.com* Ⓜ *6 to 77th St.*

COMEDY CLUBS

Chicago City Limits. This crew tout themselves as performing in the longest-running improv show in the city. Heavy on audience participation, the improv shows take place Friday and Saturday nights and seldom fail to whip visitors into what the comics might call a "phun phrenzy." ⊠ *351 E. 74th St., at 1st Ave., Upper East Side* ☎ *212/888–5233* ⊕ *www.chicagocitylimits.com* Ⓜ *6 to 77th St.*

GAY NIGHTLIFE

Fodor's Choice
★

Brandy's Piano Bar. A singing waitstaff warm up the mixed crowd at this delightful and intimate Upper East Side lounge, getting everyone in the mood to belt out their favorite tunes. In fact, the Brandy's scene is so cheerful that some patrons call it musical Prozac, keeping depression at bay. ⊠ *235 E. 84th St., between 2nd and 3rd Aves., Upper East Side* ☎ *212/744–4949* ⊕ *www.brandyspianobar.com* Ⓜ *4, 5, 6 to 86th St.*

UPPER WEST SIDE

BARS

The Empire Hotel Rooftop Bar. The only thing better than hanging out in Lincoln Center on a lovely night is hanging out a dozen stories above Lincoln Center. Thanks to the radically refurbished Empire Hotel's sprawling rooftop bar, you can enjoy that pleasure even on nights that are less than lovely. We're talking thousands of square feet here, most of it outdoors, and heated in winter. ⊠ *44 W. 63rd St., between Broadway and Columbus Ave., Upper West Side* ☎ *212/265–7400* ⊕ *www.empirehotelnyc.com* Ⓜ *1 to 66th St.–Lincoln Center.*

JAZZ VENUES

Smoke. If you can't wait until sunset to get your riffs on, head uptown to this lounge near Columbia University, where the music starts as early as 6 pm. Performers include some of the top names in the business, including turban-wearing organist Dr. Lonnie Smith and the drummer Jimmy Cobb (who kept time on Miles Davis's seminal album *Kind of Blue*). ⊠ *2751 Broadway, between 105th and 106th Sts., Upper West Side* ☎ *212/864–6662* ⊕ *www.smokejazz.com* Ⓜ *1 to 103rd St.*

HARLEM

BARS

Corner Social. With nearly 20 beers on tap, sports on big screens, and bar food that's anything but boring, it's no surprise that this neighborhood favorite is packed on weekends. In warm weather an outdoor patio gives you a front-row seat to the scene on Lenox Avenue. ⊠ *321 Lenox Ave., at 126th St., Harlem* ☎ *212/510–8552* ⊕ *www.cornersocialnyc.com* Ⓜ *2, 3 to 125th St.*

Fodor's Choice
★

Ginny's Supperclub. Head downstairs from Marcus Samuelsson's renowned Red Rooster restaurant and find yourself in a glamorous lounge that seems right out of the 1920s. The cocktails are classic with a modern flair and there is live music and/or DJs most Saturday evenings and some weeknights, as well as a gospel brunch. ⊠ *310 Lenox Ave., at 125th St., Harlem* ☏ *212/421–3821* ⊕ *www.ginnyssupperclub.com* Ⓜ *2, 3 to 125th St.*

Harlem Public. A juicy burger, live music, and more than a dozen craft beers on tap make this the type of neighborhood watering hole every New Yorker wants on their corner. Plenty of stools fill the exposed brick space, along with a scattering of tables on the sidewalk during warm weather. It's an unfussy spot to raise a glass after a day of exploring vibrant Harlem. ⊠ *3612 Broadway, at 149th St., Harlem* ☏ *212/939–9404* ⊕ *www.harlempublic.com* Ⓜ *1, A, B, C, D to 145th St.*

Shrine. It doesn't look like much from the outside, but this small performance venue with a global slant hosts multiple events each night, including live music, DJs, spoken word, and dance. ⊠ *2271 Adam Clayton Powell Jr. Blvd., between 133rd and 134th Sts., Harlem* ☏ *212/690–7807* ⊕ *www.shrinenyc.com* Ⓜ *2, 3 to 135th St.*

JAZZ VENUES

Minton's. The jazz institution that once featured big-name performers such as Dizzy Gillespie and Duke Ellington has reopened as a sophisticated supper club with a roster of house-band jazz performers and featured musicians. The Southern-revival food is garnering acclaim (the kitchen is shared with the Cecil restaurant next door). It's not a cheap night out, but worth the splurge. Jackets are required for men. ⊠ *206 W. 118 St., near Adam Clayton Powell Jr. Blvd., Harlem* ☏ *212/243–2222* ⊕ *www.mintonsharlem.com* Ⓜ *2, 3, B, C to 116th St.*

BROOKLYN

18

CARROLL GARDENS

BARS

Fodor's Choice
★

Clover Club. Long recognized for excellent drinks—both classic and inspired by the classics—and a cozy vibe, this is one of the best cocktail bars in Brooklyn. The whole operation is thanks to Julie Reiner, a passionate mixologist and businesswoman who has long been a leader in the industry. Each quarter, she and her bar staff write a seasonal cocktail list, inspired perhaps by a spirit (Chartreuse, for example) or a classic drink style (like the flip). Weekends get busy; we recommend weekdays in the early evening when you can sit at the bar and call bartender's choice. Weekend brunch is very good, too, and not just for the Bloody Mary: the lamb burger is excellent, and there's a nice selection of baked eggs. ⊠ *210 Smith St., Carroll Gardens* ☏ *718/855–7939* ⊕ *www.cloverclubny.com* Ⓜ *F, G to Bergen St.*

DUMBO

BARS

Superfine. The narrow bar and bi-level floor plan might seem a little odd, but friendly service and a convivial crowd transform this renovated warehouse into a welcoming neighborhood spot. The kitchen's organic menu changes seasonally, but the real action is at the bar, where stiff libations are poured near the popular, orange-felt pool table. ⊠ *126 Front St., between Jay and Pearl Sts., DUMBO* ☏ *718/243–9005* ⊕ *superfine. nyc* Ⓜ *A, C to High St.; F to York St.*

WILLIAMSBURG

BARS

Barcade. Stop reminiscing about your arcade-loving youth and start playing the more than 30 vintage video games (most cost a mere quarter) lining the walls of this high-spirited bar-arcade. Challenge yourself with favorites like Ms. Pac-Man or rarities like Rampage. Barcade isn't just about the games, though: there's a good selection of microbrews, as well as snacks. ⊠ *388 Union Ave., between Ainslie and Powers Sts., North Williamsburg* ☎ *718/302–6464* ⊕ *www.barcadebrooklyn.com* Ⓜ *G to Metropolitan Ave.; L to Lorimer St.*

Fodor'sChoice **Ides Bar.** Without a doubt the buzziest bar in Williamsburg, the Ides
★ benefits from its privileged position on the Wythe Hotel's rooftop. Well-heeled patrons from all over the world line up for entry and the jaw-dropping views of the Manhattan skyline. It's a hot spot on weekends, and crowded—it's more than worth it to go early and have that memorable view all to yourself. ⊠ *Wythe Hotel, 80 Wythe Ave., 6th fl., North Williamsburg* ☎ *718/460–8006* ⊕ *www.wythehotel.com/the-ides* Ⓜ *L to Bedford Ave.*

Fodor'sChoice **Maison Premiere.** Step inside this buzzy bar and restaurant, marked only
★ by a small "Bar, Oysters" sign, and you'll instantly feel whisked away to New Orleans. Sip expertly made cocktails at the horseshoe-shape bar, or dine on platters of oysters at one of the café tables (there are full dinner and brunch menus as well). In spring and summer, the back garden is a lush oasis with cast-iron tables amid wisteria and palms. ⊠ *298 Bedford Ave., at S. 1st St., South Williamsburg* ☎ *347/335–0446* ⊕ *www.maisonpremiere.com* Ⓜ *L to Bedford Ave.*

Radegast Hall & Biergarten. The vibe is boisterous at this sprawling beer garden, with plenty of communal tables that foster a convivial atmosphere. The Central European beers on tap and in bottles pair well with hearty foods like schnitzel, goulash, and delicious hot pretzels. There's live music most nights. ⊠ *113 N. 3rd St., North Williamsburg* ☎ *718/963–3973* ⊕ *www.radegasthall.com* Ⓜ *L to Bedford Ave.*

Spuyten Duyvil. You might need to be a beer geek to recognize the obscure names of the more than 100 imported microbrews available here, but the connoisseurs behind the bar are more than happy to offer detailed descriptions and make recommendations. They'll also help you choose cheese and charcuterie platters to match your beverages. The space is narrow, with limited seating: all the more reason to take advantage of the huge backyard in summer. ⊠ *359 Metropolitan Ave., near Havemeyer St., North Williamsburg* ☎ *718/963–4140* ⊕ *www. spuytenduyvilnyc.com* Ⓜ *L to Lorimer St.; G to Metropolitan Ave.*

BREWERIES

Fodor'sChoice **Brooklyn Brewery.** When Brooklyn officially became part of New York
★ City, in 1898, it had almost 50 active brewery operations producing a startling 10% of American beer, but a hops blight and Prohibition put beer production here into serious decline through the 20th century. The Brooklyn Brewery stepped onto the scene in 1988, first bringing beer to Brooklyn from a brewery in upstate New York and then, in 1996, from this former matzo factory in Williamsburg. Free 15-minute guided

tours are offered on weekend afternoons, and there are always at least eight or 10 offerings in the convivial taproom: the signature lager is popular, as is the Belgian-inspired Local 1, or try one of the seasonal offerings. Note that no open-toed shoes are allowed on the tours. ⊠ *79 N. 11th St., between Berry St. and Wythe Ave., North Williamsburg* ☎ *718/486–7422* ⊕ *www.brooklynbrewery.com* Ⓜ *L to Bedford Ave.; G to Nassau Ave.*

LIVE MUSIC VENUES

Bembe. This steamy, bi-level lounge is Williamsburg's answer to Miami clubbing, though decorated with salvaged items including an old red-wood front door from a New York State winery. The crowd is as eclectic as the DJ-spun beats, from reggae to Brazilian—often accompanied by live drumming. The tropical bar menu adds to the place's Latin cred. ⊠ *81 S. 6th St., at Berry St., South Williamsburg* ☎ *718/387–5389* ⊕ *www.bembe.us* Ⓜ *J, M, Z to Marcy Ave.*

Music Hall of Williamsburg. This intimate, trilevel music venue in a former mayonnaise factory has excellent acoustics, so it's no surprise that it draws die-hard fans of rock and indie music. There's balcony seating and an additional bar upstairs. If you love Manhattan's Bowery Ballroom, you'll feel the same way about this venue; it's run by the bookers at Bowery Presents, so you can expect the same quality lineups. ⊠ *66 N. 6th St., near Wythe Ave., North Williamsburg* ☎ *718/486–5400* ⊕ *www.musichallofwilliamsburg.com* Ⓜ *L to Bedford Ave.*

Union Pool. This former pool-supply store is a funky multipurpose venue, complete with a corrugated tin–backed bar, a photo booth, a small stage for live music, and cheap PBR. It's a popular spot on the Friday-night circuit, especially for late-night dancing. The back patio has a taco truck and a fire pit. ⊠ *484 Union Ave., near Meeker Ave., North Williamsburg* ☎ *718/609–0484* ⊕ *www.union-pool.com* Ⓜ *G to Metropolitan Ave.; L to Lorimer St.*

BUSHWICK AND EAST WILLIAMSBURG

BARS

Fodor's Choice ★ **Featherweight.** The cocktail list at this small spot is full of the hits you'd expect at a bar run by the experts behind the two Weather Up spaces in Manhattan and Prospect Heights. Part of the allure, though, is that bartenders will mix a cocktail to your precise specifications. Prime time here is late night. Finding the entrance is part of the fun: look for the painted feather and the three-story-tall mural of a boxer. ⊠ *135 Graham Ave., at Johnson Ave., East Williamsburg* ☎ *202/907–3372* ⊕ *www. featherweightbk.com* Ⓜ *J, M to Lorimer St.; L to Montrose Ave.*

PARK SLOPE

BARS

Union Hall. This neighborhood standby has something going on just about every night. On the main floor, two bocce courts and a library nook with couches and fireplace are popular hangouts; downstairs, there are smart comedy shows featuring *Daily Show* and *Saturday Night Live* regulars, eclectic talks, or DJs spinning. The outdoor patio is open in good weather. The menu of perfectly tasty burgers, sandwiches, and bar snacks (the beer cheese is a highlight) means the patrons tend to

18

settle in for the evening. Events are either free or have a modest cover ($5 to $20). ✉ *702 Union St., at 5th Ave., Park Slope* ☎ *718/638–4400* ⊕ *www.unionhallny.com* Ⓜ *R to Union St.*

LIVE MUSIC VENUES

Fodor's Choice ★ **Barbès.** Outstanding regulars like the Django Reinhardt mantle-bearer Stephane Wrembel, western-swingers Brain Cloud, and Slavic Soul Party spin threads of folk and "ethnic" into 21st-century music, while the Erik Satie Quartet keeps Satie, Britten, and other classical composers relevant. Performances take place in the back room, where a pitcher is passed to collect the $10 suggested cover. Up front, the somewhat musty bar has a laid-back vibe and a full cocktail menu. ✉ *376 9th St., at 6th Ave., Park Slope* ☎ *347/422–0248* ⊕ *www.barbesbrooklyn.com* Ⓜ *F, G to 7th Ave.*

QUEENS

ASTORIA

BARS

Bohemian Hall & Beer Garden. Warm summer nights and cold beers have been savored by locals for over 100 years at the Bohemian Hall & Beer Garden. With pitchers of beer, picnic tables, live music, and Czech dishes from the kitchen, this sunny garden is an ideal spot for getting together with old friends—or making new ones over big mugs of Staropramen and Pilsner Urquell. ✉ *29-19 24th Ave., Astoria* ☎ *718/274–4925* ⊕ *www.bohemianhall.com* Ⓜ *N, Q to Astoria–Ditmars Blvd.*

LONG ISLAND CITY

BARS

Dutch Kills. The dark bar and cozy wooden booths at Dutch Kills—a cocktail den with a nod to the neighborhood's historic roots—serves up finely crafted drinks at a couple of dollars cheaper than similar Manhattan watering holes. Expect precisely chiseled chunks of ice and skilled bartenders who, with a few queries into your preferences and curiosities, can create a concoction just to your taste. ✉ *27-24 Jackson Ave., Long Island City* ☎ *718/383–2724* ⊕ *www.dutchkillsbar.com* Ⓜ *E, M, R to Queens Plaza; G to Court Sq.; 7, N, Q to Queensboro Plaza.*

PERFORMING ARTS

Updated by
Elissa Garay

"Where do you wait tables?" is the not-so-ironic question New York performers get when they say they're in the arts. Even more telling is that most of these struggling artists don't miss a beat when they respond with the restaurant's name. Fact is, if you're an aspiring performer here, you'd better be tough and competitive. There is a constant influx of artists from around the globe, and all these actors, singers, dancers, and musicians striving for their big break infuse the city with a crackling creative energy.

Just as tough are the audiences. Although costly ticket prices can make attending a Broadway show a less common outing for even the most devout theater-loving New Yorkers, that's not true of many other kinds of more affordable performances. Whether the audiences are primarily local or not, it's their discernment that helps drive the arts scene, whether they are flocking to a concert hall to hear a world-class soprano deliver a flawless performance, or crowding into a cramped café to support fledgling writers reading from their own work.

New York has upwards of 200 "legitimate" theaters (meaning those with theatrical performances, not movies), and many more ad hoc venues—parks, churches, lofts, galleries, rooftops, even parking lots. The city is also a revolving door of special events: summer jazz, one-act-play marathons, film festivals, and music and dance celebrations from the classical to the avant-garde, to name just a few. It's this unrivaled wealth of culture and art that many New Yorkers cite as the reason they're here, and the reason why millions more make the migration.

PLANNING

ARTS PLANNER

DANCE, OPERA, MUSIC, AND MORE

In addition to theater, New York is one of the premier cities in the world for ballet and contemporary dance, opera, and classical music. Start your search with a visit to the websites of three of the biggest performing arts centers: Lincoln Center (⊕ *www.lincolncenter.org*), Carnegie Hall (⊕ *www.carnegiehall.org*), and the Brooklyn Academy of Music (⊕ *www.bam.org*). They all have detailed events calendars, and their listings demonstrate the sheer depth of great performances available in New York. It's also helpful to consider the time you're visiting. Many arts groups schedule the bulk of their performances from September through May, with special holiday events planned in November and December. Although the number of performances in many venues tapers off in the dog days of summer, the period also brings lots of festivals and outdoor performances, many of them inexpensive or free. Finally, it's smart to also check out the websites of any museums you think you might want to visit while in town. The Frick, for instance, has been hosting world-class classical-music concerts in its 165-seat Music Room since 1938, while the Metropolitan Museum of Art periodically stages concerts and other performing arts events in locations like the Egyptian Temple of Dendur, or in its enviable gallery of musical instruments.

WHAT'S ON?

The *New York Times* (⊕ *www.nytimes.com/events*) listings are probably the single best place to find out what's happening in the city. The *New Yorker*'s Goings On About Town listings (⊕ *www.newyorker. com*) are more selective, while *New York* magazine (⊕ *www.nymag. com*) gives a slightly more opinionated spin on the performing arts. The theater sites ⊕ *www.playbill.com*, ⊕ *www.theatermania.com*, and ⊕ *www.offoffonline.com* (for Off-Off-Broadway) provide information like synopses, accessibility info, run times, seating charts, and links to buy tickets. Sites like ⊕ *www.broadway.org*, run by The Broadway League; ⊕ *www.offbroadway.com*, run by the League of Off-Broadway Theatres and Producers; and ⊕ *www.broadwaycollection.com*, geared toward the travel trade, but with information in multiple languages, are each a wealth of information.

BROADWAY AND OFF-BROADWAY—WHAT'S THE DIFFERENCE?

There are just over 40 Broadway theaters in New York, and although you might expect their shows to be the best ones in town, the definition depends on theater capacity (which must count at least 500 seats), not quality. Nearly all are within a few blocks of Times Square. A show must be performed in a Broadway theater as part of the eligibility requirements for a Tony Award. Off-Broadway theaters, which are scattered throughout the city, have 100 to 499 seats; Off-Off-Broadway venues seat fewer than 100.

BUYING TICKETS AT FULL PRICE

How much do tickets sell for, anyway? The average price paid for a Broadway show runs just over $100; not counting the limited "premium seat" category (or discount deals), the low end for musicals is in the

$25–$75 range. Nonmusical comedies and dramas start at about $25 and top out at about $160. Off-Broadway show tickets run $30–$90, and Off-Off-Broadway shows can run as low as $15–$25, or even less if you find a deal. Tickets to an opera start at about $25 for nosebleed seats and can soar to more than $400 for prime locations. Classical music concerts go for $25 to $100 or more, depending on the venue and the performers. Dance performances are usually in the $15 to $70 range, but expect choice seats for the ballet to cost more, especially around the holidays.

Scoring tickets is fairly easy, especially if you have some flexibility. Always start with the website of the venue or theater company to see what going rates are (and if any deals are available). If timing or cost is critical, the only way to ensure the seats you want is to make your purchase in advance—and that might be months ahead for a hit show. In general, tickets for Saturday evening and for weekend matinees, or for Broadway shows featuring big-name stars for limited runs, are the toughest to secure, and the priciest.

For smaller performing arts companies, and especially for Off-Broadway shows, try **Ticket Central**, on Theater Row; service charges are nominal here. **SmartTix** is a reliable resource for (usually) smaller performing arts companies, including dance and music; their service charges are nominal as well.

Sure bets for Broadway (and some other big-hall events) are the box office or either **Telecharge** or **Ticketmaster.** Virtually all larger shows are listed with one service or the other, but never both; specifying "premium" helps get elusive—and expensive—seats. A broker or your hotel concierge should be able to procure last-minute tickets, but many regard brokers as legal scalpers, and their prices may even exceed "premium" rates. Be prepared to pay steep add-on service fees for all ticketing services.

■TIP➔ Although online ticket services provide seating maps to help you choose, the advantage of going to the box office is twofold: there are no add-on service fees, and a ticket seller can personally advise you about sight lines—and knee room—for the seat location you are considering. Broadway box offices do not usually have direct phone lines; their walk-in hours are generally 10 am until curtain.

BUYING DISCOUNT TICKETS

The cheapest—though chanciest—ticket opportunities are found at participating theater box offices on the day of the performance. These rush tickets, usually about $25–$40, may be distributed by lottery and are usually for front-row (possibly neck-craning) seats, though it can vary by theater; there are also standing-room-only seats available on occasion (usually for under $30). Check the comprehensive planner on ⊕ *www.nytix.com* or go to the box office of the show you are interested in to discover whether they make such an offer and how to pursue it. Obstructed-view seats or those in the very rear balcony are sometimes available at deeply discounted rates, for advance purchase.

For advanced discount purchases, the best seating is likely available by using a discount code. Procure these codes, good for an average of 20% to 50% off, online. (You need to register on each website.) The excellent no-subscription-required ⊕ *www.broadwaybox.com* posts nearly all discount codes currently available for Broadway shows. As with the discount codes provided through online subscriber services—**Theater-Mania, Playbill,** and **Best of Off Broadway** among them—to avoid service charges, you must bring the printout to the box office, and make your purchase there.

For seats at up to 50% off the usual price, get same-day discount tickets by going to one of the **TKTS booths** (⊕ *www.tdf.org*): there's one in Times Square, another at South Street Seaport, and a third in downtown Brooklyn. Although they do tack on a $4.50-per-ticket service charge, and not all shows are predictably available, the broad choices and ease of selection—and, of course, the solid discount—make TKTS the go-to source for the flexible theatergoer. You can browse available shows for that day online or via a TKTS app (⊕ *www.tdf.org/tktsapp*), or check the electronic listings board near the ticket windows to mull over your options while you're in line. At the Times Square location (under the red glass staircase), there is a separate "Play Only" window (for nonmusical events) to further simplify (and expedite) things; they also offer a 7-Day Fast Pass, meaning if you buy tickets today, you can come back within the next seven days to make another purchase without having to wait on line. Times Square hours are: Monday and Wednesday–Saturday 3–8, and Tuesday 2–8 for evening performances; for Wednesday and Saturday matinees 10–2; for Sunday matinees 11–3; and for Sunday evening shows, from 3 until 7. The South Street Seaport location, at the corner of Front and John Streets, is open Monday–Saturday 11–6, and Sunday 11–4, except in winter. Brooklyn hours are Tuesday–Saturday 11–3 and 3:30–6. All ticket sales are for shows on that same day (one exception: the Brooklyn location's matinee tickets are for next-day performances only). Credit cards and cash are accepted at all locations. ■TIP➔ Ticket-booth hours may vary over holiday periods; also note that the longest lines are generally within the first hour of the booths' opening.

Contacts Best of Off Broadway. ⊠ *New York* ☎ *877/633–4746* ⊕ *www.bestofoffbroadway.com.* **Playbill.** ⊠ *New York* ⊕ *www.playbill.com.* **Smart-Tix.** ⊠ *New York* ☎ *212/868–4444* ⊕ *www.smarttix.com.* **Telecharge.** ⊠ *New York* ☎ *212/239–6200, 800/447–7400* ⊕ *www.telecharge.com.* **TheaterMania.** ⊠ *New York* ☎ *212/352–3101, 866/811–4111* ⊕ *www.theatermania.com.* **Ticket Central.** ⊠ *Playwrights Horizon, 416 W. 42nd St., between 9th and 10th Aves., Midtown West* ☎ *212/279–4200* ⊕ *www.ticketcentral.com* Ⓜ *A, C, E to 42nd St.–Port Authority.* **Ticketmaster.** ⊠ *New York* ☎ *866/448–7849 for automated service, 800/745–3000* ⊕ *www.ticketmaster.com.* **TKTS Downtown Brooklyn.** ⊠ *1 MetroTech Ctr., at corner of Myrtle St. Promenade and Jay St., Downtown Brooklyn* ☎ *212/912–9770* ⊕ *www.tdf.org/tkts* Ⓜ *A, C, F, R to Jay St.–MetroTech; 2, 3, 4, 5 to Borough Hall* ⊠ *South Street Seaport, John and Front Sts., near rear of 199 Water St., Financial District* ☎ *212/912–9770* ⊕ *www.tdf.org/tkts* Ⓜ *2, 3, 4, 5, A, C, J, Z to Fulton St.* **TKTS South Street Seaport.** ⊠ *South Street Seaport, John and Front Sts., near rear of 199 Water St., Financial District* ☎ *212/912–9770* ⊕ *www.tdf.org/tkts* Ⓜ *2, 3, 4, 5, A, C, J, Z to Fulton St.* **TKTS Times Square.** ⊠ *Duffy Sq., 47th St. and Broadway, Midtown West* ☎ *212/912–9770* ⊕ *www.tdf.org/tkts* Ⓜ *1, 2, 3, 7, N, Q, R, S to Times Sq.–42nd St.*

19

CLOSE UP

Best Tips for Broadway

Whether forking over hundreds of dollars for a top seat or shoestringing it with a standing-room ticket, you'll have better Broadway experiences to brag about if you take our advice.

Do your homework. Remember—your friend's must-see may not be yours. Subscribe to online newsletters ahead of your trip for access to show reviews, special ticket offers, and more. If it's a classic play or opera, you may enjoy it more if you've read a synopsis before you go.

Reserve and plan ahead. The TKTS booth is great if you're up for what the fates make available, but for must-sees, book early. While you're at it, ask whether the regular cast is expected. (An in-person stop at the box office is the most reliable way to score this information, but don't hold them to it unless it's the day of the performance. If there is a change then—and the replacement cast is not acceptable to you—you may get a refund.) For musicals, live music often adds a special zing; confirm when ticketing to avoid surprises on the rare occasion when recorded music is used.

Check theater seating charts. Front mezzanine is a great option; with seats that overhang the orchestra section, they can be better (though not always less expensive) than many orchestra seats. Book with a seating chart at hand (available online and at the box office). Check accessibility, especially at older theaters with multiple flights of stairs and few elevators.

Know when to go. Typically, Broadway shows give eight performances a week. There are nightly performances from Tuesday through Saturday night, and matinees at 2 pm on Wednesday and Saturday and at 3 pm on Sunday (on Monday most theaters are closed, or "dark"). Weekend shows, especially Saturday night, are the most difficult tickets to get. Tuesday is especially promising, and typically an earlier curtain—7 instead of the usual 8 pm—helps ensure a good night's sleep for your next day of touring.

Dress right. You can throw on jeans to go to the theater these days, but personally we feel shorts and sneakers have no place on Broadway (at least in the audience). Bring binoculars if your seats are up high, check bulky coats if a coat check is available, and drop bags and packages off at your hotel room in advance—theater seats tend to be narrow, with little leg room.

Travel smart. Trying to get to the show on time? Unless you don't mind watching the meter run up while you're stuck in traffic, avoid cabs into or out of Times Square. Walk, especially if you're within 10 blocks of the theater. Otherwise, take the subway; many train lines converge in the area.

Dine off Broadway. Dining well on a budget and doing Broadway right are not mutually exclusive. The key is to avoid eating in Times Square itself—even the national chains are overpriced. Consider eating earlier instead, in whatever neighborhood you're visiting that day. If you're already in Midtown, head west to 9th or 10th Avenue, where prix-fixe deals and ethnic eateries are plentiful and many actors and theater folk live. You never know whom you'll see on the street or at the next table.

PERFORMING ARTS IN NEW YORK CITY

Listings are alphabetical by neighborhood.

LOWER MANHATTAN

FINANCIAL DISTRICT
READINGS AND LECTURES
Poets House. Situated in a bright and airy building in the residential area of Battery Park City and near the Hudson River, this reading room is an open resource for all ages, with a 60,000-volume library, readings, and other poetry-centric events. ⊠ *Battery Park City, 10 River Terr., at Murray St., Financial District* ☎ *212/431–7920* ⊕ *www.poetshouse.org* Ⓜ *1, 2, 3, A, C to Chambers St.*

TRIBECA
MUSIC
FAMILY **Tribeca Performing Arts Center.** This center celebrates theater (with a clever children's series) and dance but is primarily known for jazz. Highlights in Jazz and Lost Jazz Shrines are two of its special series. ⊠ *199 Chambers St., between Greenwich and West Sts., TriBeCa* ☎ *212/220–1460 for tickets* ⊕ *www.tribecapac.org* Ⓜ *1, 2, 3, A, C to Chambers St.*

SOHO
READINGS AND LECTURES
Fodor's Choice **The Greene Space** (*Jerome L. Greene Performance Space*). The local ★ public radio stations WNYC and WQXR invite the public into their intimate (125 seats) studio for live shows featuring classical, rock, jazz, and new music; audio theater; conversation; and interviews. It's a great place to get up-close with writers and newsmakers, as well as musicians and actors who might be playing Carnegie Hall, Broadway, or the Met Opera a few days later. ⊠ *44 Charlton St., at Varick St., SoHo* ☎ *646/829–4000* ⊕ *www.thegreenespace.org* Ⓜ *C, E to Spring St.; 1 to Houston St.*

Housing Works Bookstore Cafe. Amid roughly 25,000 books and CDs for sale, Housing Works hosts a wide range of literary and cultural events, including quirky readings, sometimes with unannounced surprise guests; journal and book launches; and storytelling or music nights. This cozy store is staffed largely by volunteers, and all profits go toward fighting homelessness and HIV/AIDS. ⊠ *126 Crosby St., between Houston and Prince Sts., SoHo* ☎ *212/334–3324* ⊕ *www.housingworks.org/ bookstore* Ⓜ *N, R to Prince St.; B, D, F, M to Broadway–Lafayette St.*

Fodor's Choice **The Moth.** Dedicated to first-person storytelling, this roving series has ★ spread far beyond just New York, where it was founded in 1997 by the writer George Dawes Green. But it's still going strong here: the Mainstage shows bring together luminaries to tell their stories and maybe dish a little, too. At the much looser open-mike StorySLAMs, competitors are randomly selected and given just five minutes to tell their story, which must tie in with the night's theme. These tales get told at Housing Works and other venues downtown and in Brooklyn. ⊠ *Housing Works Bookstore Cafe, 126 Crosby St., between Houston and Prince*

19

Sts., SoHo ☎ *212/742–0551* ⊕ *themoth.org/events* Ⓜ *N, R to Prince St.; B, D, F, M to Broadway–Lafayette St.*

THEATER

HERE. Celebrating all manner of contemporary, genre-bending productions, the original home of Eve Ensler's *The Vagina Monologues* and Basil Twist's *Symphonie Fantastique* also houses art exhibitions and a café. ✉ *145 6th Ave., between Spring and Dominick Sts., SoHo* ☎ *212/647–0202, 212/352–3101 for tickets* ⊕ *www.here.org* Ⓜ *C, E to Spring St.*

EAST VILLAGE AND LOWER EAST SIDE

EAST VILLAGE

DANCE

Danspace Project. Founded to foster the work of independent choreographers such as Lucinda Childs and David Gordon, Danspace Project sponsors performances that are as fresh—and idiosyncratic—as the historic church space they occupy. Performance series curated by guest artists are also a regular part of the calendar. ✉ *St. Mark's Church in-the-Bowery, 131 E. 10th St., at 2nd Ave., East Village* ☎ *212/674–8112, 866/811–4111 for tickets* ⊕ *www.danspaceproject.org* Ⓜ *6 to Astor Pl.; N, R to 8th St.–NYU; L to 3rd Ave.*

FILM

Fodor's Choice ★ **Anthology Film Archives.** Dedicated to preserving and exhibiting independent and avant-garde film, Anthology Film Archives is made up of two screening rooms that seat 187 and 75 as well as a film repository, all inside a renovated redbrick courthouse. Cofounded in the 1960s by the downtown legend and filmmaker Jonas Mekas, Anthology remains a major destination for adventurous and unusual movies, new as well as old. The Essential Cinema series delves into the works of canonized, groundbreaking directors; the frequent festivals are more eclectic and may cover under-recognized auteurs, such as a series devoted to the director Edgar G. Ulmer, as well as hard-to-see films of all types. This is an experience for film lovers, not casual moviegoers, so don't expect the amenities you'd find at a multiplex. ✉ *32 2nd Ave., at 2nd St., East Village* ☎ *212/505–5181* ⊕ *www.anthologyfilmarchives.org* Ⓜ *F to 2nd Ave.*

MUSIC

SubCulture. With its exposed brick, structural pillars, theater-style seating, and industrial-chic bar, this intimate subterranean concert hall could just as easily be a cool lounge as a venue for classical (especially chamber), jazz, and new music. Series here have included in-the-round performances of all of Beethoven's string quartets; an annual PianoFest, which brings in some of the most exciting pianists from across many genres; and concerts from Tony Award–winning composer Jason Robert Brown, featuring guest appearances from various Broadway stars. The calendar also finds room for singer-songwriters, comedians, and performers of world music. ✉ *45 Bleecker St., between the Bowery and Lafayette St., East Village* ☎ *212/533–5470* ⊕ *www.subculturenewyork. com* Ⓜ *6 to Bleecker St.; B, D, F, M to Broadway–Lafayette St.*

READINGS AND LECTURES

KGB Bar. A nexus of the downtown literary scene, KGB keeps a busy calendar of readings and discussions: start with Sunday Night Fiction or KGB Poetry on Monday night. The name and the Soviet kitsch are a nod to the bar's history as a speakeasy for leftist Ukrainians. ⊠ *85 E. 4th St., between the Bowery and 2nd Ave., East Village* ☏ *212/505–3360* ⊕ *www.kgbbar.com* Ⓜ *F to 2nd Ave.; 6 to Bleecker St.*

Nuyorican Poets Cafe. The reigning arbiter of poetry slams, the Nuyorican Poets Cafe hosts open-mike events and the influential granddaddy (b. 1989) of the spoken-word scene, the Friday Night Poetry Slam. Other performances, including hip-hop open mikes, jazz acts, and theatrical performances, round out the schedule. Although tickets for many of the popular shows like the Friday Night Poetry Slam and the Monday-night open mikes can be purchased in advance online, it's still a good idea to line up early; the small venue can get packed to the point of standing-room only. ⊠ *236 E. 3rd St., between Aves. B and C, East Village* ☏ *212/780–9386* ⊕ *www.nuyorican.org* Ⓜ *F to 2nd Ave.; J, M, Z to Essex St.*

The Poetry Project. Launched in 1966, the Poetry Project has been a source of sustenance for poets (and their audiences) ever since. This place has seen performances by Allen Ginsberg, Amiri Baraka, Sam Shepard, Patti Smith, Anne Waldman, and many others. At current readings you might find artists of the same caliber. Prime times are Monday, Wednesday, and Friday. ⊠ *St. Mark's Church in-the-Bowery, 131 E. 10th St., at 2nd Ave., East Village* ☏ *212/674–0910* ⊕ *www. poetryproject.org* Ⓜ *N, R to 8th St.–NYU; 6 to Astor Pl.; L to 3rd Ave.*

THEATER

Classic Stage Company. At the CSC's cozy 199-seat theater you can see excellent revivals—such as Chekhov's *Three Sisters*, Shakespeare's *Romeo and Juliet*, or several plays of Euripides—often with a modern spin, reigning theatrical stars, and new scores. ⊠ *136 E. 13th St., between 3rd and 4th Aves., East Village* ☏ *212/677–4210* ⊕ *www. classicstage.org* Ⓜ *4, 5, 6, N, Q, R to 14th St.–Union Sq.; L to 3rd Ave.*

19

La MaMa E.T.C. Ellen Stewart (1919–2011) founded La MaMa E.T.C. in 1961 in a small Manhattan basement. Since that time, the Experimental Theatre Club has grown continuously, all the while taking risks on unknown works that cross cultures and performance disciplines (of note, Blue Man Group got its start here). In an effort to keep theater accessible, tickets are a bargain across the theater's four venues, ranging from just $10 to $25. ⊠ *66 and 74A E. 4th St., between the Bowery and 2nd Ave., East Village* ☏ *646/430–5374* ⊕ *www.lamama.org* Ⓜ *F to 2nd Ave.; 6 to Bleecker St.*

New York Theatre Workshop. Works by new and established playwrights anchor this theater's repertoire. Jonathan Larson's *Rent* got its start here before going to Broadway, as did the hit musical *Once*. Works by Tony Kushner (*Homebody/Kabul*), Caryl Churchill, Amy Herzog, and Paul Rudnick have also been staged here. Hit the box office for day-of CheapTix rush tickets; those seats are $25—in cash—as available, and are only on offer to young people (under 25), seniors (over 65), artists, and residents of the Lower East Side, with proper ID. ✉ *79 E. 4th St., between the Bowery and 2nd Ave., East Village* ☎ *212/460–5475* ⊕ *www.nytw.org* Ⓜ *F to 2nd Ave.; 6 to Astor Pl.*

Fodor's Choice
★ **The Public Theater.** Fresh theater, such as Lin-Manuel Miranda's current Broadway sensation *Hamilton,* and *Here Lies Love,* David Byrne and Fatboy Slim's "poperetta" about Imelda Marcos, keep people talking about the Public Theater. Many more noted productions that began here (*Hair, A Chorus Line*) went on to Broadway and beyond. Some shows release limited-availability $20 rush standby tickets at the box office (two tickets max; cash only). Check online for available performances. ✉ *425 Lafayette St., south of Astor Pl., East Village* ☎ *212/539–8500, 212/967–7555 for tickets* ⊕ *www.publictheater.org* Ⓜ *6 to Astor Pl.; N, R to 8th St.–NYU.*

Theater for the New City. This four-theater cultural complex stages three- or four-week-long runs of new shows by emerging and mid-career American playwrights. The socially conscious group also runs a free summer program of street theater, performed in all five boroughs. ✉ *155 1st Ave., between 9th and 10th Sts., East Village* ☎ *212/254–1109* ⊕ *www.theaterforthenewcity.net* Ⓜ *6 to Astor Pl.; L to 1st Ave.*

LOWER EAST SIDE
FILM
Sunshine Cinema. Talk about busy: according to a *Village Voice* article, this storied building, which reportedly dates back to 1844, has served as "a church, an immigrant meeting hall, a boxing venue, a nickel-odeon, a Yiddish vaudeville house, a hardware warehouse, a graffiti showcase, and an indie-rock playroom." Since 2001, it's been a great neighborhood theater showing a mix of art-house and smaller-release mainstream-independent films on five decent-size screens. Great mid-night movies play, too. ✉ *143 E. Houston St., between 1st and 2nd Aves., Lower East Side* ☎ *212/260–7289* ⊕ *www.landmarktheatres. com* Ⓜ *F to 2nd Ave.; J, Z to Bowery.*

THEATER
Dixon Place. Founded back in the 1980s, this small, nonprofit theater continues to host worthy, and frequently unconventional and hilarious, performances of theater, music, dance, and more, with a focus on new works. Its popular HOT! Festival of Queer Performance, held in July, is the longest-running LGBTQ festival in the world. Whatever you're seeing of the some 1,000 shows held here each year, the Lounge, Dixon Place's cheerful bar, is a great place to meet up before the show and connect with artists after. ✉ *161A Chrystie St., between Rivington and Delancey Sts., Lower East Side* ☎ *212/219–0736* ⊕ *www.dixonplace. org* Ⓜ *J, Z to Bowery; B, D to Grand St.*

GREENWICH VILLAGE AND WEST VILLAGE

GREENWICH VILLAGE

FILM

Angelika Film Center. Foreign, independent, and specialty films are screened here. Despite its (six) tunnel-like theaters, small screens, and the occasionally audible subway rumble below, it's usually packed with cinephiles; get a snack at the café while you wait for your movie to be called. ⊠ *18 W. Houston St., between Mercer St. and Broadway, Greenwich Village* ☎ *212/995–2570* ⊕ *www.angelikafilmcenter.com/nyc* Ⓜ *B, D, F, M to Broadway–Lafayette St.; 6 to Bleecker St.; N, R to Prince St.*

IFC Center. The IFC Center shows a mix of repertory and first-run independent, art-house, shorts (including cartoons), and foreign movies. Despite the modern wire-mesh facade, there are still clues that this was once the much-beloved Waverly Theater. ⊠ *323 6th Ave., at 3rd St., Greenwich Village* ☎ *212/924–7771* ⊕ *www.ifccenter.com* Ⓜ *A, B, C, D, E, F, M to W. 4th St.–Washington Sq.*

READINGS AND LECTURES

Center for Architecture. This contemporary glass-faced gallery near Washington Square hosts lively discussions (which may be accompanied by films or other visuals) on topics like radical architecture in Mexico City or what to expect when you renovate an apartment. ⊠ *536 LaGuardia Pl., between 3rd and Bleecker Sts., Greenwich Village* ☎ *212/683–0023* ⊕ *cfa.aiany.org* Ⓜ *A, B, C, D, E, F, M to W. 4th St.*

New York Studio School. The venerable New York Studio School hosts two—always free, almost always on Tuesday and Wednesday—evening lecture series on contemporary issues in art. Hear from both emerging and established artists and curators, as well as some of the biggest names in art history and criticism. The school building served as the original location of the Whitney Museum. ⊠ *8 W. 8th St., between 5th Ave. and Macdougal St., Greenwich Village* ☎ *212/673–6466* ⊕ *www. nyss.org* Ⓜ *A, B, C, D, E, F, M to W. 4th St.*

THEATER

FAMILY

Fodor's Choice

★

Monday Night Magic. Since 1997, Michael Chaut and three other magician producers have been running these weekly performances in and around Greenwich Village (they've been a permanent fixture at the Players Theatre since 2011). The acts, usually four per night on stage, come from all over the world and often include performers you'd see in much bigger theaters and clubs on other nights. The mind-reading and sleight-of-hand with birds, cards, balls, and handkerchiefs come at a fast pace. The magic continues even during intermission, when at least two additional magicians mingle with guests in the lobby and in the theater to perform card tricks and other "close-up magic." Although the acts are tailored for an adult audience, they're also suitable for younger viewers, ages 12 and older, especially on special family nights. ⊠ *Players Theatre, 115 MacDougal St., between 3rd and Bleecker Sts., Greenwich Village* ☎ *212/615–6432, 800/838–3006 for tickets* ⊕ *www. mondaynightmagic.com* Ⓜ *A, B, C, D, E, F, M to W. 4th St.*

19

FILM SERIES AND REVIVALS

Although many of the screens listed here show first-run releases, old favorites and rarities are the heart of their programing. These gems—which include just about every kind of film, from silent and noir to the most au courant experimental work—are frequently screened at museums, cultural societies, and other institutions, such as the **French Institute Alliance Française** (☎ 212/355–6100 ⊕ www.fiaf.org), **Scandinavia House** (☎ 212/779–3587 ⊕ www.scandinaviahouse.org), and major branches of the **New York Public Library** (☎ 917/275–6975 ⊕ www.nypl.org). A reliably creative range of repertory screenings can always be found at **Anthology Film Archives** (☎ 212/505–5181 ⊕ www.anthologyfilmarchives.org), **Film Forum** (☎ 212/727–8110 ⊕ www.filmforum.org), the **Museum of Modern Art (MoMA)** (☎ 212/708–9400 ⊕ www.moma.org), the **Museum of the Moving Image** (☎ 718/777–6888 ⊕ www.movingimage.us), the **Brooklyn Academy of Music** (☎ 718/636–4100 ⊕ www.bam.org), and the **Film Society of Lincoln Center** (☎ 212/875–5610 ⊕ www.filmlinc.com).

FAMILY **Skirball Center for the Performing Arts.** This pristine, wood-lined theater on the NYU campus supports emerging artists, with interesting dance, music, and theater events, often in collaboration with international companies. Conferences and even a circus or two round out the calendar, which also includes many family-friendly events. ⊠ 566 LaGuardia Pl., at Washington Sq. S, Greenwich Village ☎ 212/992–8484, 888/611–8183 for tickets ⊕ www.nyuskirball.org Ⓜ A, B, C, D, E, F, M to W. 4th St.; N, R to 8th St.–NYU.

WEST VILLAGE

FILM

Fodor's Choice ★ **Film Forum.** In addition to premiering new international features and documentaries that are otherwise hard to catch on the big screen, this nonprofit theater with three theaters hosts movies by canonized directors such as Hitchcock, Godard, and Bertolucci; in-depth film series devoted to particular actors or genres; and newly restored prints of classic works. The small café in the lobby serves tasty cakes and freshly popped popcorn. This is no megaplex; be prepared for small seats and screens and a cash-only box office (credit cards can be used to buy tickets online in advance). ⊠ 209 W. Houston St., between 6th Ave. and Varick St., West Village ☎ 212/727–8110 ⊕ www.filmforum.org Ⓜ 1 to Houston St.; C, E to Spring St.

CHELSEA

DANCE

Fodor's Choice ★ **Joyce Theater.** Set within a former Art Deco movie house in Chelsea, the 472-seat Joyce Theater has superb sight lines and presents a wide range of classical and contemporary dance during its 48-week season that includes a rotating roster of diverse international, national, and New York–based companies. ⊠ 175 8th Ave., at 19th St., Chelsea

☎ *212/691–9740, 212/242–0800 for tickets* ⊕ *www.joyce.org* Ⓜ *A, C, E to 14th St.; L to 8th Ave.; 1 to 18th St.*

New York Live Arts. This Chelsea space serves as the home stage for the innovative Bill T. Jones/Arnie Zane Dance Company. It's also a laboratory for new choreographers and artists in residence, and hosts non-choreographed events such as panel discussions. ⊠ *219 W. 19th St., between 7th and 8th Aves., Chelsea* ☎ *212/691–6500, 212/924–0077 for tickets* ⊕ *www.newyorklivearts.org* Ⓜ *1 to 18th St.; A, C, E, to 23rd St.*

THEATER

FAMILY **TADA!** Vibrant original musicals for family audiences are performed by a cast of talented kids (ages 8 to 18). Most shows are on weekends, and children's tickets start at $10. ⊠ *15 W. 28th St., 2nd fl., between Broadway and 5th Ave., Chelsea* ☎ *212/252–1619* ⊕ *www.tadatheater. com* Ⓜ *1, 6, N, R to 28th St.*

MIDTOWN WEST

FILM

Fodor's Choice
★
Museum of Modern Art (MoMA) films. You'll find some of the most engaging international film repertory around at Roy and Niuta Titus Theaters 1 and 2, in MoMA's lower level. Sometimes the films tie in with current art exhibitions; the Contenders series, which starts each fall, is a chance to catch up on the past year's releases that are likely to win awards, or at least stand the test of time. Movie tickets are available at the museum for same-day screenings (a limited number are released up to one week in advance). They're free if you have purchased museum admission ($25); otherwise they cost $12. ⊠ *11 W. 53rd St., between 5th and 6th Aves., Midtown West* ☎ *212/708–9400* ⊕ *www.moma.org/ calendar/film* Ⓜ *E, M to 5th Ave./53rd St.; B, D, F, M to 47th–50th Sts./ Rockefeller Center.*

19

The Paris Theatre. Across from the Plaza Hotel stands The Paris Theatre—a rare, stately remnant of the single-screen era. Opened in 1948, it retains its wide screen (and balcony) and is a fine showcase for new movies, often foreign and with a limited release. ⊠ *4 W. 58th St., between 5th and 6th Aves., Midtown West* ☎ *212/593–4872, 212/688–3800 for tickets* ⊕ *www.theparistheatre.com* Ⓜ *N, Q, R to 5th Ave./59th St.; F to 57th St.*

MUSIC

FAMILY
Fodor's Choice
★
Carnegie Hall. Carnegie Hall is, of course, one of the world's most famous concert halls. Its incomparable acoustics make it one of the best venues in the world to hear classical music, but it's also strong in jazz, pop, cabaret, and folk music. Since the opening-night concert on May 5, 1891, which Tchaikovsky conducted, virtually every important musician the world has known has performed in this Italian Renaissance–style building. Leonard Bernstein had his debut here; Vladimir Horowitz made his historic return to the concert stage here. The world's top orchestras perform in the grand and fabulously steep 2,804-seat **Isaac Stern Auditorium**; the 268-seat **Weill Recital Hall** often features young talents making their New York debuts; and the subterranean

599-seat **Judy and Arthur Zankel Hall** attracts big-name artists such as the Kronos Quartet and Milton Nascimento to its modern and stylish space. A noted roster of family concerts is also part of Carnegie's programming. The Carnegie box office releases $10 rush tickets for some shows on the day of performance, or you may buy partial-view seating in advance at 50% off the full ticket price. ✉ *881 7th Ave., at 57th St., Midtown West* ☎ *212/247–7800* ⊕ *www.carnegiehall.org* Ⓜ *N, Q, R to 57th St.–7th Ave.; B, D, E to 7th Ave.; F to 57th St.*

The Town Hall. Founded by suffragists and built in 1921 by famed architects McKim, Mead & White, The Town Hall has been part of NYC's cultural fabric for 95 years. Notable Town Hall claims include: Strauss, Stravinsky, and Isaac Stern's U.S. debuts; Marian Anderson's first NYC recital; Dizzy Gillespie and Charlie Parker's introduction of bebop to the world; and Bob Dylan's first major concert. More recently, their stage has welcomed musicians like Gilberto Gil, Joan Baez, Patti Smith, and Ray LaMontagne; comedians like Stephen Colbert and Larry David; live radio broadcasts of *A Prairie Home Companion* with Garrison Keillor; TED Talks Live; and more. ✉ *123 W. 43rd St., between 6th Ave. and Broadway, Midtown West* ☎ *212/997–6661, 800/982–2787 for tickets* ⊕ *www.thetownhall.org* Ⓜ *1, 2, 3, 7, N, Q, R, S to Times Sq.–42nd St.; B, D, F, M to 42nd St.–Bryant Park.*

PERFORMANCE CENTERS

Baryshnikov Arts Center. Famed dancer and actor Mikhail Baryshnikov's longtime vision came to fruition in this modern performing arts venue for contemporary dance, theater, music, and film. The center, set within the Hudson Yards neighborhood, hosts a range of resident artists, including dancers and musical groups, as well as productions by boundary-breaking international choreographers, playwrights, filmmakers, and musicians. The vibrant programming is presented in the center's 238-seat Jerome Robbins Theater and the 136-seat Howard Gilman Performance Space. ✉ *450 W. 37 St., between 9th and 10th Aves., Midtown West* ☎ *646/731–3200* ⊕ *www.bacnyc.org* Ⓜ *A, C, E to 34th St.–Penn Station; 7 to 34th St.–Hudson Yards.*

Fodor'sChoice ★ **New York City Center.** Pause as you enter this neo-Moorish building, built in 1923 for the Shriners (cousins of the Freemasons), and admire the ornate decorative details in the recently restored lobby and theater. City Center's 2,200-seat main stage is perfectly suited for dance and special theatrical events. The Tony Award–honored Encores! series, generally held in spring, revisits musicals of the past in a concert format—an event that has led to shows returning to Broadway, with the long-running *Chicago* among them. Tickets for City Center's annual Fall for Dance festival sell out quickly. ✉ *131 W. 55th St., between 6th and 7th Aves., Midtown West* ☎ *212/581–1212 for tickets* ⊕ *www.nycitycenter.org* Ⓜ *N, Q, R to 57th St.–7th Ave.; F to 57th St.*

Fodor'sChoice ★ **Radio City Music Hall.** This landmark was built shortly after the stock market crash of 1929; John D. Rockefeller wanted to create a symbol of hope in what was a sad, broke city. When it opened, some said Radio City Music Hall was so grand that there was no need for performances, because people would get more than their money's worth simply by

19

CLOSE UP

New York's Film Festivals

New York's extreme diversity is what makes it a cinephile's heaven: you'll find dozens of festivals for niche interests and those just wanting to be at the front end of what's out there. New releases and premieres dominate the festival scene, but the city has its share of retrospective events, especially in summer.

The city's preeminent film event is the annual **New York Film Festival** (⊕ *www.filmlinc.com*), presented by the Film Society of Lincoln Center, from late September into October. The lineup is announced about a month in advance, and screenings often sell out quickly (though standby tickets are available for most events). Film venues include Lincoln Center's Alice Tully Hall, Walter Reade Theater, and Elinor Bunin Munroe Film Center. In January, the Film Society join forces with the Jewish Museum to produce the **New York Jewish Film Festival** (⊕ *www.nyjff.org*); in March it joins MoMA to present **New Directors/ New Films** (⊕ *www.newdirectors.org*), and June brings their collaboration on the **Human Rights Watch Film Festival** (⊕ *ff.hrw.org*), among other festivals and repertory programming throughout the year.

The **Tribeca Film Festival** (⊕ *www. tribecafilm.com/festival*) takes place in mostly downtown venues for about two weeks starting mid-April and shows mainstream premieres along with indie flicks, television debuts, a conversation series, and more.

Fans also flock to other noteworthy annuals like the **New York Asian Film Festival** (⊕ *www.asiancinevision. org*) from late June to early July; and the **Margaret Mead Film Festival** (⊕ *www.amnh.org/explore/ margaret-mead-film-festival*) in October or November and **DOC NYC** (⊕ *www.docnyc.net*) in November, two fall festivals that focus on documentaries from all over.

For kids, the year-round programs of the **New York International Children's Film Festival (NYICFF** ⊕ *www.gkids.com*) peak in March with an extravaganza of about 100 new films for ages 3–18.

Summer in New York sees a bonanza of alfresco film; screenings are usually free (but arrive early to secure a space; screenings begin at dusk). The **HBO Bryant Park Summer Film Festival** (⊕ *www.bryantpark.org*) shows classic films at sundown on Mondays, June–August. The **Hudson RiverFlicks** (⊕ *www.riverflicks.org*) series in July and August has movies for grown-ups on Wednesday evening on Pier 63; Hudson RiverFlicks, Family Fridays for kids are at Pier 46. The Upper West Side has **Summer on the Hudson** (⊕ *www.nycgovparks. org*) with Wednesday-night screenings on Pier 1, near West 70th Street. **Rooftop Films'** (⊕ *www.rooftopfilms. com*) Underground Movies Outdoors is more eclectic than most other film series, with shows outdoors in summer on rooftops in all five boroughs. Check the schedule for off-season screenings as well. On Thursday evenings in July and August, check out **Movies with a View in Brooklyn Bridge Park** (⊕ *www. brooklynbridgepark.org*).

sitting there and enjoying the space. Despite being the largest indoor theater in the world with its city-block-long marquee, it feels warm and intimate. Seventy-five-minute "Stage Door" walking tours run year-round, but access is limited during show times. Day-of-tour tickets are sold at the Radio City Avenue Store; advance tickets are available by phone or through the website.

Although there are concerts and other events here year-round, the biggest draw is the Radio City Christmas Spectacular: more than a million visitors every year come to see the iconic Rockettes. Make reservations as early as possible, especially if you want to attend near Christmas or on a weekend. Certain dates and times tend to sell out, but you can usually find tickets for all shows until mid-October. Tickets start at $46 per person for the 90-minute show, although there are often promotions and deals available, especially for nonpeak times. ⊠ *1260 6th Ave., between 50th and 51st Sts., Midtown West* ☎ *212/247–4777, 866/858–0007 for tickets* ⊕ *www.radiocity.com* Ⓜ *B, D, F, M to 47th–50th Sts./Rockefeller Center; N, Q, R to 49th St.*

READINGS AND LECTURES

LIVE from the NYPL. The New York Public Library's discussion series includes a rich program of lectures and reading events from the biggest names in books and culture in general. Most programs are held at the famous main library. ⊠ *Stephen A. Schwarzman Building, 5th Ave. at 42nd St., Midtown West* ☎ *917/275–6975 for tickets, 888/718–4253 for tickets* ⊕ *www.nypl.org/live* Ⓜ *B, D, F, M to 42nd St.–Bryant Park; 7 to 5th Ave.*

THEATER

FAMILY **New Amsterdam Theatre.** In 1997 Disney refurbished the elaborate 1903 Art Nouveau New Amsterdam Theatre, where Bob Hope, Jack Benny, Fred Astaire, and the *Ziegfeld Follies* once drew crowds. *The Lion King* ruled here for the first nine years of its run, followed by *Mary Poppins* and then *Aladdin* starting in 2014. ⊠ *214 W. 42nd St., between 7th and 8th Aves., Midtown West* ☎ *866/870–2717 for tickets* ⊕ *www. disneyonbroadway.com* Ⓜ *1, 2, 3, 7, N, Q, R, S to Times Sq.–42nd St.; A, C, E to 42nd St.–Port Authority.*

FAMILY
Fodor's Choice
★
The New Victory Theater. In a magnificently restored space from 1900, The New Victory Theater presents an international roster of supremely kid-pleasing plays, music, dance, opera, puppetry, and circus performances. Through the organization's workshops and exhibits, children and their parents can also learn more about other parts of theater (writing, for instance) and kinds of performance, such as break dancing. Count on reasonable ticket prices, high-energy and high-class productions, and the opportunity for kids to chat with the artists after many performances. ⊠ *209 W. 42nd St., between 7th and 8th Aves., Midtown West* ☎ *646/223–3010* ⊕ *www.newvictory.org* Ⓜ *1, 2, 3, 7, N, Q, R, S to Times Sq.–42nd St.; A, C, E to 42nd St.–Port Authority.*

Playwrights Horizons. Known for its support of new work by American playwrights, this Off-Broadway theater was the first home for eventual Broadway hits such as *Grey Gardens* and Wendy Wasserstein's *Heidi Chronicles.* ⊠ *416 W. 42nd St., between 9th and 10th Aves., Midtown*

19

West ☎ *212/564–1235, 212/279–4200 for tickets* ⊕ *www.phnyc.org* Ⓜ *A, C, E to 42nd St.–Port Authority.*

Roundabout Theatre Company. This nonprofit theatrical company is known for its revivals of classic musicals and plays, including *Anything Goes* and *The Importance of Being Earnest.* Its main stage, the American Airlines Theatre, is the former Selwyn—the venerable home to the works of Coward, Kaufman, and Porter in their heyday. The Roundabout's other Broadway venues are Studio 54, which was the longtime home of its successful *Cabaret* revival, and the Stephen Sondheim Theatre. The two Off-Broadway stages at the Harold and Miriam Steinberg Center for Theatre show a mix of classics and works from up-and-coming playwrights. ✉ *American Airlines Theatre, 227 W. 42nd St., between 7th and 8th Aves., Midtown West* ☎ *212/719–1300* ⊕ *www.roundabouttheatre.org* Ⓜ *1, 2, 3, 7, N, Q, R, S to Times Sq.– 42nd St.; A, C, E to 42nd St.–Port Authority.*

Signature Theatre Company. Designed by the architect Frank Gehry, the company's Pershing Square Signature Center houses three theater spaces. The Tony Award–winning theater company provides a platform for both New York and world premieres, as well as revivals. All tickets are $25 for a show's initially announced run. A central space with a café and bookstore connects the theaters, so come early, or stay late; the café is open until midnight Tuesday through Sunday. ✉ *Pershing Square Signature Center, 480 W. 42nd St., between 9th and 10th Aves., Midtown West* ☎ *212/967–1913, 212/244–7529 for tickets* ⊕ *www. signaturetheatre.org* Ⓜ *A, C, E to 42nd St.–Port Authority.*

UPPER EAST SIDE

PERFORMANCE CENTERS

FAMILY **92nd Street Y.** Well-known soloists, jazz musicians, show-tune stylists, and chamber music groups perform in 92Y's 905-seat **Kaufmann Concert Hall.** But the programming is hardly limited to music—its online calendar bristles with popular lectures and readings series featuring big-name film and TV stars, authors, poets, playwrights, political pundits, and media bigwigs (many events are live streamed or archived online). Also worth the Upper East Side trek are the Harkness Dance Festival, film programs, and many family-friendly events. ✉ *1395 Lexington Ave., at 92nd St., Upper East Side* ☎ *212/415–5500 for tickets* ⊕ *www.92y.org* Ⓜ *6 to 96th St.; 4, 5, 6 to 86th St.*

Fodor'sChoice **Park Avenue Armory.** Completed in 1881 and occupying an entire city
★   block, this handsome Gothic-style brick building was used as the headquarters, drill hall, and social club for the Seventh Regiment, a National Guard unit called the "Silk Stocking" regiment because its members were mainly drawn from wealthy Gilded Age families. The sumptuous reception rooms on the first floor and Company Rooms on the second floor were designed by Louis Comfort Tiffany, Stanford White, and other fashionable designers of the time. The armory eventually fell into disrepair, and its opulent rooms were in danger of ruin. In 2007, help came in the form of a major restoration that is ongoing, and the armory was put back into service, but this time in the service of art. The

Jazz at Lincoln Center performs at Frederick P. Rose Hall next to Columbus Circle.

huge installations, plays, and immersive concerts here take advantage of the massive space its 55,000-square-foot drill hall provides. A couple of standouts: the Royal Shakespeare Company summerlong series of plays, performed inside a replica of its theater in Stratford-upon-Avon, and a collaboration between artist Douglas Gordon and pianist Hélène Grimaud that turned the hall into a massive reflecting pool. ⊠ *643 Park Ave., between 66th and 67th Sts., Upper East Side* ☎ *212/616–3930, 212/933–5812 for tickets* ⊕ *www.armoryonpark.org* Ⓜ *6 to 68th St.– Hunter College, F to Lexington Ave./63rd St.*

READINGS AND LECTURES

Works & Process. Insight into the creative process is what the Works & Process program at the Guggenheim is all about. Often drawing on dance and theater works-in-progress, the live performances are complemented by illuminating discussions with their choreographers, playwrights, and directors. There are very popular holiday concerts, too. ⊠ *Guggenheim Museum, 1071 5th Ave., between 88th and 89th Sts., Upper East Side* ☎ *212/423–3575* ⊕ *www.worksandprocess.org* Ⓜ *4, 5, 6 to 86th St.*

UPPER WEST SIDE

MUSIC

Great Music in a Great Space. This aptly named series of public concerts is inspired by a wide range of musical traditions and performed in St. John the Divine's massive, atmospheric, Gothic-style space. The program showcases composers and performers of choral and instrumental music, often to sold-out crowds. ⊠ *The Cathedral Church of St. John the Divine, 1047 Amsterdam Ave., at 112th St., Morningside Heights* ☎ *212/316–7540* ⊕ *www.stjohndivine.org* Ⓜ *1, B, C to Cathedral Pkwy.–110th St.*

FAMILY **Jazz at Lincoln Center.** A few blocks south of Lincoln Center itself, this Columbus Circle venue is almost completely devoted to jazz, with a sprinkling of other genres mixed in. Stages in Rafael Viñoly's crisply modern **Frederick P. Rose Hall** include the 1,200-seat **Rose Theater,** where a worthy Jazz for Young People series joins buoyant adult programming a few times each year. Also here is **The Appel Room,** an elegant theater with a glass wall overlooking Columbus Circle, and the smaller **Dizzy's Club Coca-Cola,** where there are two sets nightly, and often more that go late into the night. All are accompanied by a full bar and restaurant. ⊠ *Time Warner Center, 10 Columbus Circle, 5th fl., Broadway at 60th St., Upper West Side* ☎ *212/258–9800, 212/721–6500 for tickets* ⊕ *www.jazz.org* Ⓜ *1, A, B, C, D to 59th St.–Columbus Circle.*

Merkin Concert Hall at Kaufman Music Center. A destination for both old-school and cutting-edge musical performances, this concert hall around the corner from Lincoln Center is a lovely, acoustically advanced 450-seater that presents chamber pieces. It's also known for jazz, world, new music, and especially its Ecstatic Music Festival (from January through March), when an eclectic group of indie-classical artists more than lives up to its billing. ⊠ *129 W. 67th St., between Broadway and Amsterdam Ave., Upper West Side* ☎ *212/501–3300* ⊕ *www. kaufmanmusiccenter.org/mch* Ⓜ *1 to 66th St.–Lincoln Center.*

Miller Theatre. Adventurous programming of jazz, classical, early and modern music, and dance makes up the calendar at this Columbia University theater, founded in 1988. A well-designed 688-seater, this is a hall that rewards serious listeners. ⊠ *Columbia University, 2960 Broadway, at 116th St., Morningside Heights* ☎ *212/854–1633, 212/854–7799 for tickets* ⊕ *www.millertheatre.com* Ⓜ *1 to 116th St.–Columbia University.*

PERFORMANCE CENTERS

Fodor'sChoice **Lincoln Center.** A major cultural destination, attracting more than 5 mil-
★ lion visitors annually, the Lincoln Center complex is one of the most concentrated places for the performing arts in the nation, as home to 11 resident organizations, including: the Chamber Music Society of Lincoln Center, Film Society of Lincoln Center, Jazz at Lincoln Center, the Juilliard School, Lincoln Center for the Performing Arts, Lincoln Center Theater, Metropolitan Opera, New York City Ballet, New York Philharmonic, New York Public Library for the Performing Arts, and the School of American Ballet.

This massive white travertine-clad complex contains 23 theaters in all, part of a 16-acre campus that was planned by master architect Philip Johnson, and built as part of an urban-renewal effort that arose over the course of several years from 1962 to 1969; some 40 years later, it was given a thorough remodeling to better integrate it into the neighborhood.

Visitors today can enjoy more recent improvements like expanded public and green spaces, free Wi-Fi, and various dining options.

To get oriented, start across the street, on Broadway between 62nd and 63rd Streets, at the David Rubenstein Atrium. There you'll find free Wi-Fi, tables, a café, and that rarest of NYC commodities: a public restroom. In addition to free concerts on Thursdays (at 7:30 pm), a new schedule of free musical and dance performances, as well as discussions and spoken-word programs, has been added throughout the week. Day-of-show discounted tickets for many Lincoln Center venues may be purchased in person here; there is a limit of four tickets per customer, and the amount of discount depends on the performance. Because the box office is closed on Monday, any available tickets for Monday performances are sold on Sunday.

The acoustics in **Alice Tully Hall** are top-notch; the hall's home to the Chamber Music Society of Lincoln Center (*www.chambermusicsociety. org*). **David Geffen Hall** is the residence of the New York Philharmonic (*www.nyphil.org*); its season is September to June. Orchestra rehearsals are open to the public on selected weekday mornings ($20, plus fees; usually Wednesday or Thursday). A popular Young People's Concert series takes place Saturday afternoon, four times throughout the season. Lincoln Center presents its well-attended Great Performers, Lincoln Center Festival, Mostly Mozart Festival, and White Light Festival in these halls, too.

The largest hall, the **Metropolitan Opera House** is notable for its dramatic arched entrance, as well as its lobby's immense Swarovski crystal chandeliers and Marc Chagall paintings. The titan of American opera companies and an institution since its founding in 1883, the Metropolitan Opera (*www.metopera.org*) brings the world's leading singers to the vast stage here from September to May. All performances, including those sung in English, are subtitled on small screens on the back of the seat in front of you. A frequent resident of the Met (and sometimes, of the David H. Koch Theater) is the American Ballet Theatre (*www.abt. org*), renowned for its gorgeous full-program renditions of the 19th-century classics (*Swan Lake, Giselle, The Sleeping Beauty*) with choreography re-envisioned by 20th-century or contemporary masters. A limited number of same-day $20 rush orchestra seats are available at the Met's website. These tickets go on sale for Sunday through Friday evening performances at noon, for matinees four hours before curtain, and for Saturday evenings at 2 pm.

The **David H. Koch Theater,** considered of the world's top theaters for dance, is the home of the formidable New York City Ballet (*www. nycballet.com*), which has a roster of more than 90 dancers, a 62-piece orchestra, and an unmatched repertory of modern masterpieces, including landmark works by George Balanchine, Jerome Robbins, and Peter Martins. NYCB performs at the theater for 21 weeks each year, including fall, winter, and spring repertory seasons, with Thanksgiving through New Year's devoted to the beloved annual production of Balanchine's *The Nutcracker.* The theater also hosts a mix of other

19

internationally famous dance troupes throughout the year, as well as Lincoln Center Festival and White Light Festival performances.

The **Lincoln Center Theater** complex houses the Vivian Beaumont Theater, the smaller Mitzi E. Newhouse Theater, and the rooftop Claire Tow Theater, which has 131 seats and a small outdoor terrace.

The auditorium of the **Walter Reade Theater** (*www.filmlinc.com*) shows film series devoted to "the best in world cinema," including silents, documentaries, retrospectives, and recent releases, often on the same theme or from the same country. The Elinor Bunin Munroe Film Center has two small screening rooms, a café, and an amphitheater that hosts lectures and panel discussions.

In addition to extensive musical and theatrical holdings, the **New York Public Library for the Performing Arts** mounts periodic exhibitions related to major artists and composers. At the library's free year-round Silent Clowns series (*www.silentclowns.com*), held Saturday afternoons each month in its auditorium, rarely seen prints of the silent era's comedy masters are paired with live piano music.

Tours of Lincoln Center, including the Met, take place daily and leave from the atrium; reservations are recommended and can be made from the website (*atrium.lincolncenter.org*) or in person. Tours do not include backstage areas, but sometimes do visit parts of the auditoriums. Backstage tours of the Met ($22) are held during the performance season. ✉ *From 62nd to 66th St., between Broadway/Columbus and Amsterdam Aves., Upper West Side* ☏ *212/875–5000 for main switchboard, 212/721–6500 for tickets* ⊕ *www.lincolncenter.org* Ⓜ *1 to 66th St.– Lincoln Center.*

FAMILY **Symphony Space.** Although Symphony Space runs an energetic roster of classical, jazz, international, and other kinds of music, it also excels with many other kinds of art programming. On the literary front, its two halls—the **Peter Jay Sharp Theatre** and the **Leonard Nimoy Thalia**— host a celebrated roster of literary events, including Bloomsday on Broadway, the Thalia Book Club, and the famed Selected Shorts series: stories read by prominent actors and broadcast live on National Public Radio. There's also a popular comedy series, Uptown Showdown, as well as Performance in HD screenings from the National Theatre Live, Royal Shakespeare Company, and Royal Opera House. Plays, films, and "Thalia Docs" on Sunday (usually true-to-their-roots arthouse screenings) round out the adult programming. For the family, turn to the hugely popular **Just Kidding** lineup for a nonstop parade of zany plays, sing-alongs, midday Saturday (and sometimes Sunday) movies, and animation. ✉ *2537 Broadway, at 95th St., Upper West Side* ☏ *212/864–5400* ⊕ *www.symphonyspace.org* Ⓜ *1, 2, 3 to 96th St.*

THEATER

Fodor's Choice ★ **Shakespeare in the Park.** Some of the best things in New York are, indeed, free—including this summer festival presented by the Public Theater and performed at an open-air stage in Central Park. Many notable performers have appeared here, including Meryl Streep, Michelle Pfeiffer, Christopher Walken, Helen Hunt, Morgan Freeman, Al Pacino, Anne Hathaway, and Kevin Kline. The tickets are given out (limit two per person) starting at noon on the day of each show, and always sell out. What you save in money, you make up for in time and tedium—lines are usually *long*. Plan to line up by midmorning or earlier if there have been good reviews. The easiest way to score these scarce tickets is to register via an online lottery between midnight and noon on the day you'd like to attend; an email response after noon confirms (or denies) success. Making a donation to the Public Theater is one way to avoid the lines and be sure you get a ticket. ⊠ *Delacorte Theater, Central Park, Midpark, use 81st St. entrance at Central Park W, Upper West Side* ☎ *212/967–7555* ⊕ *www.publictheater.org* ☐ *Free* Ⓜ *B, C to 81st St.–Museum of Natural History.*

HARLEM

MUSIC

Apollo Theater. Michael Jackson, Ella Fitzgerald, and James Brown are just a few of the world-class performers who have appeared on this equally famed stage, which first opened back in 1934. If the Apollo's Amateur Night doesn't get you up to 125th Street on Wednesdays, consider the theater's intimate late-night music series, Apollo Music Café, events on select Friday and Saturday nights, featuring a variety of jazz, pop, hip-hop, and rock performers. ⊠ *253 W. 125th St., between Frederick Douglass and Adam Clayton Powell Jr. Blvds., Harlem* ☎ *212/531–5300, 800/745–3000 for tickets* ⊕ *www.apollotheater. org* Ⓜ *2, 3, A, B, C, D to 125th St.*

Harlem Stage. Set in a perfectly restored 1890 Croton Aqueduct facility, Harlem Stage is a cozy 192-seat uptown venue for jazz, world music, and dance. ⊠ *The Gatehouse, 150 Convent Ave., at 135th St., Harlem* ☎ *212/281–9240* ⊕ *www.harlemstage.org* Ⓜ *B, C to 135th St.; 1 to 137th St.–City College.*

BROOKLYN

FORT GREENE
PERFORMANCE CENTERS

Fodor's Choice ★ **Brooklyn Academy of Music (BAM).** Founded in 1861, BAM is a multi-use performing arts center spanning three Instagram-worthy edifices, including the Beaux Arts, seven-story Peter Jay Sharp building. Facilities include an unadorned "black box" theater, dance venues, a four-screen movie theater, an opera house, a ballroom, and a café. Cyclists park in style at the David Byrne–designed bike rack on Lafayette Avenue between St. Felix Street and Ashland Place. ⊠ *Peter Jay Sharp Building, 30 Lafayette Ave., between St. Felix St. and Ashland Pl., Fort Greene* ☎ *718/636–4100* ⊕ *www.bam.org* Ⓜ *2, 3, 4, 5, B, D, N, Q, R at Atlantic Ave.–Barclays Center; G to Fulton St.; C to Lafayette Ave.*

PARK SLOPE
THEATER

FAMILY **Puppetworks.** Finely detailed wooden marionettes and hand puppets are on the bill at Puppetworks. Kid-friendly performances like *Alice in Wonderland* or *Cinderella* come to life on weekends in this 75-seat

19

neighborhood theater. Reservations are required; credit cards are not accepted. ✉ *338 6th Ave., at 4th St., Park Slope* ☎ *718/965–3391* ⊕ *www.puppetworks.org* Ⓜ *F, G to 7th Ave.; R to 9th St.*

DUMBO
THEATER

Fodor's Choice
★

St. Ann's Warehouse. This veritable performing arts arena has commissioned cutting-edge theater, music, and a surprising amount of high-art puppeteering since 1980. The venue recently relocated to a stunningly refurbished, 1860 tobacco warehouse in the waterfront Brooklyn Bridge Park (in the shadow of the Brooklyn Bridge). The inaugural season at the new venue saw an all-female production of *Henry IV,* produced by London's Donmar Warehouse, and the American premiere of Irish playwright Enda Walsh's first opera, *The Last Hotel.* Previous productions at former locations were put on by the National Theatre of Scotland, Globe Theatre of London, Kneehigh Theatre, and more; the organization has also hosted musicians and comedians like Daniel Kitson, Marianne Faithfull, and the late David Bowie. ✉ *Tobacco Warehouse, 45 Water St., between Dock and Old Fulton Sts., DUMBO* ☎ *718/254–8779* ⊕ *stannswarehouse.org* Ⓜ *A, C to High St.; F to York St.*

BROOKLYN HEIGHTS
MUSIC

Bargemusic. This "cozy floating concert hall moored just south of the Brooklyn Bridge," as the *New York Times* once described it, keeps chamber music groups busy year-round on a renovated harbor barge that has a fabulous view of the Manhattan skyline. It even hosts free, family-friendly afternoon concerts on select Saturday afternoons. Note that the venue really is on the water, so you might want to skip it if you're susceptible to seasickness. ✉ *Fulton Ferry Landing, Old Fulton and Furman Sts., Brooklyn Heights* ☎ *718/624–4924* ⊕ *www.bargemusic.org* Ⓜ *A, C to High St.; F to York St.*

QUEENS

ASTORIA
FILM

Museum of the Moving Image films. This museum touts two theaters, including both a show palace and an intimate screening room, where classic Hollywood and foreign titles share the screen with experimental works, new films from the international festival circuit, live musical collaborations, and in-person appearances by moviemaker luminaries. Daily short films are screened in Tut's Fever Movie Palace, a fab Red Grooms and Lysiane Luong–designed installation. ✉ *36–01 35th Ave., between 36th and 37th Sts., Astoria* ☎ *718/777–6888* ⊕ *www.movingimage.us/films* Ⓜ *M, R to Steinway St.; N, Q to 36th Ave.*

TRAVEL SMART
NEW YORK CITY

GETTING HERE AND AROUND

New York City packs a staggering range of sights and activities into the 301 square miles of its five boroughs. You probably want to focus most of your visit in Manhattan, but with more time, taking a trip to Brooklyn or one of the other three boroughs (Queens, the Bronx, or Staten Island) is worthwhile.

If flying into one of the three major airports that service New York—John F. Kennedy (JFK), LaGuardia (LGA), or New Jersey's Newark (EWR)—pick your mode of transportation for getting to Manhattan before your plane lands. Tourists typically either take a car service or head to the taxi line, but those aren't necessarily the best choices, especially during rush hour. Consider public transportation, especially if you're traveling light and without young children—it's an inexpensive option.

Once you're in Manhattan, getting around can be a breeze when you get the hang of the subway system. Better yet, if you're not in a rush and the weather's cooperating, just walk—it's the best way to discover the true New York. Not quite sure where you are or how to get where you're headed? Ask a local. You may be surprised at how friendly the city's inhabitants are, debunking their reputation for rudeness. In the same getting-there-is-half-the-fun spirit, there are also boat and bus journeys that let you see the city from a whole new perspective.

■ AIR TRAVEL

Generally, international flights go in and out of John F. Kennedy or Newark airport, while domestic flights go in and out of both of these, as well as LaGuardia Airport.

AIRLINE SECURITY ISSUES

Transportation Security Administration (*TSA*). The TSA offers travel tips and has answers for almost every question about travel safety and security procedures. ⊕ *www.tsa.gov.*

AIRPORTS

The major air gateways to New York City are LaGuardia Airport (LGA) and JFK International Airport (JFK) in the borough of Queens, and Newark Liberty International Airport (EWR) in the state of New Jersey.

Airport Information JFK International Airport (*JFK*). ☎ *718/244–4444* ⊕ *www. jfkairport.com.* **LaGuardia Airport** (*LGA*). ☎ *718/533–3400* ⊕ *www.laguardiaairport. com.* **Newark Liberty International Airport** (*EWR*). ✉ *Newark* ☎ *973/961–6000* ⊕ *www. newarkairport.com.*

TRANSFERS—CAR SERVICES

Car services can be a great convenience, because the driver often meets you in the baggage-claim area and helps with your luggage. The flat rates are often comparable to taxi fares, but some car services charge for parking and wait time at the airport. To eliminate these expenses, other car services require you to telephone their dispatcher (or order a car through their app) when you land so they can send the next available car to pick you up. The New York City Taxi and Limousine Commission rules require all car services be licensed and pick up riders only by prior arrangement; if possible, call 24 hours in advance for reservations or at least a half day before your flight's departure. Drivers of nonlicensed vehicles ("gypsy cabs") often solicit fares outside the terminal in baggage-claim areas. Don't take them: you run the risk of an unsafe ride in a vehicle that may not be properly insured and will almost certainly pay more than the going rate. Getting a car via the Uber ride-sharing service or one of its competitors is another option.

For phone numbers, see Taxi Travel.

TRANSFERS—TAXIS AND SHUTTLES

Outside the baggage-claim area at each of New York's major airports are taxi stands where a uniformed dispatcher helps passengers find taxis (*see Taxi Travel*). Cabs are not permitted to pick up fares anywhere else in the arrivals area, so if you want a taxi, take your place in line. Shuttle services generally pick up passengers from a designated spot along the curb.

GO Airlink NYC, NYC Airporter, and SuperShuttle run vans and some buses from JFK, LaGuardia, and Newark (NYC Airporter does not run to Manhattan from Newark) airports to popular spots like Grand Central Terminal, the Port Authority Bus Terminal, Penn Station, and hotels in Manhattan. Fares on NYC Airporter, for instance, cost about $14–$17 one way and $26–$30 round-trip per person to or from JFK or LGA. Those rates are significantly cheaper than taking a taxi if you're on your own, but probably not if there are two or more of you traveling together. If you choose to use such services, keep in mind that customers' satisfaction with them is very mixed; online reviews often complain of rude employees and significant waits for vans to both arrive and reach their destinations. In any case, allow lots of time for the shuttle's other pickups and drop-offs along the way.

Shuttle Service GO Airlink NYC.
☎ 877/599–8200, 212/812–9000 ⊕ www.goairlinkshuttle.com. **NYC Airporter.**
☎ 718/777–5111 ⊕ www.nycairporter.com.
SuperShuttle. ☎ 800/258–3826 ⊕ www.supershuttle.com.

TRANSFERS FROM JFK INTERNATIONAL AIRPORT

The rate for traveling between JFK and Manhattan by yellow cab in either direction is a flat fee of $52.80 plus surcharges and tolls (which average about $6). The trip takes 35–60 minutes. Prices are roughly $25–$55 for trips to most other locations in New York City. You should also tip the driver for safe driving and good service.

JFK's AirTrain ($5) connects JFK Airport to the New York City Subway (A, E, J, and Z trains) and the Long Island Railroad (LIRR)—both of which take you to Manhattan or Brooklyn. The monorail system runs 24 hours. ■TIP→ Not sure which train to take? Check ⊕ *www.citymapper.com,* ⊕ *www.iridenyc.com,* or ⊕ *tripplanner.mta.info* (or their corresponding apps) for the best route to your destination. Subway travel between JFK and Manhattan takes less than an hour and costs $3.75 in subway fare (including $1 to buy a MetroCard) plus $5 for the AirTrain. The LIRR travels between JFK's AirTrain stop (Jamaica Station) and Penn Station in around 30 minutes, for about $17, including the AirTrain fee. When traveling *from* Manhattan to the Howard Beach station, be sure to take the A train marked "Far Rockaway" or "Rockaway Park," not "Lefferts Boulevard."

JFK Transfer Information AirTrain JFK.
☎ 877/535–2478 ⊕ www.airtrainjfk.com. **Long Island Railroad.** ☎ 511 ⊕ www.mta.info/lirr.

TRANSFERS FROM LAGUARDIA AIRPORT

Taxis cost $30–$50 (plus tip and tolls) to most destinations in New York City, and take at least 20–40 minutes.

For $2.75 (pay with a MetroCard or exact change in coins, no pennies) you can ride the Q70 bus to the Woodside–61st Street subway station (with connections to the 7 train, or to the LIRR, with service to Penn Station) or to the Jackson Heights–Roosevelt Avenue subway stop, where you can transfer to the E, F, M, R, and 7 trains and reach many points in Manhattan and Brooklyn. Another option is to take the M60 bus to its end point at 106th Street and Broadway on Manhattan's Upper West Side, with connections en route to several New York City Subway lines (2, 3, 4, 5, 6, A, B, C, D, N, and Q trains). Allow at least 60 minutes for the entire trip to Midtown, and perhaps a bit more during heavy traffic or rain.

TRANSFERS FROM NEWARK AIRPORT

Taxis to Manhattan cost $50–$70 plus tolls and tip and take 20–45 minutes in light traffic; inquire with the airport's taxi dispatcher about shared group rates, too. If you're heading to the airport from Manhattan, there's a $17.50 surcharge on top of the normal taxi rate, plus tolls and a customary tip.

AirTrain Newark, an elevated light-rail system, can take you from the airline terminal to the Newark Liberty International Airport Station. From here you can take New Jersey Transit (or, for a much higher price, Amtrak) trains heading to New York Penn Station. It's an efficient and low-cost way to get to New York City, particularly if you don't have many in your group and aren't carrying massive amounts of luggage. Total travel time to New York Penn Station via New Jersey Transit is approximately 30 minutes and costs $13. By contrast, a similar, slightly faster trip (about 25 minutes) via Amtrak costs roughly $28. The AirTrain runs every three minutes from 5 am to midnight and every 15 minutes from midnight to 5 am. Note that New Jersey Transit trains first make a stop at the confusingly named Newark Penn Station before they reach New York Penn Station, their final stop. If you're not sure when to get off the train, ask a conductor or fellow passenger.

Coach USA, with Olympia Trails, runs Newark Airport Express buses that leave for Manhattan and stop at Port Authority, Bryant Park (at 42nd Street and 5th Avenue), and Grand Central Terminal about every 15 to 30 minutes until midnight. The trip takes roughly 45 minutes, and the fare is $16 (plus a $1 administrative fee). Buses headed to Newark Airport depart at the same intervals, from the same Manhattan locations.

Newark Airport Transfer Information
AirTrain Newark. ☎ 888/397-4636 ⊕ www. airtrainnewark.com. **Coach USA—Newark Airport Express.** ☎ 877/863-9275, 908/354-3330 ⊕ newarkairportexpress.com.

TRANSFERS BETWEEN AIRPORTS
There are several transportation options for connecting to and from area airports, including shuttles, AirTrain and mass transit, and car service or taxi.

SuperShuttle and NYC Airporter run vans and buses between Newark, JFK, and LaGuardia airports. AirTrain provides information on how to reach your destination from any of New York's airports. Note that if you arrive after midnight at any airport, you may wait a long time for a taxi. There is also no shuttle service on NYC Airporter at that time.

Contacts AirTrain. ☎ 800/247-7433 ⊕ www.panynj.gov/airtrain.

▌ BOAT TRAVEL

The Staten Island Ferry runs across New York Harbor between Whitehall Street (next to Battery Park in Lower Manhattan) and St. George terminal in Staten Island. The free 25-minute ride gives you a view of the Financial District skyscrapers, the Statue of Liberty, and Ellis Island.

New York Water Taxi shuttles passengers to the city's many waterfront attractions between the Hudson River (on Manhattan's west side) and East River (on its east side), including stops in Lower Manhattan (for access to the 9/11 Memorial Museum) and the South Street Seaport, as well as two locations in Brooklyn.

An all-day pass on the water taxi is $30; a similar pass that also allows passengers to visit the 9/11 Memorial Museum as part of their sightseeing package is $54. Another package includes a visit to One World Observatory for $58.

Also consider NY Waterway, which runs ferry service across the Hudson River between Manhattan and New Jersey ports; it also operates on the East River, connecting Manhattan with Brooklyn, Queens, and, seasonally, with Governors Island (the ferries also connect several locations within Brooklyn and in Long Island City, Queens).

NY Waterway ferries offer single-trip ($4–$9), 10-trip (New Jersey routes only; $60–$83), and monthly passes ($160–$272), and their East River Ferry has all-day hop-on, hop-off passes ($12–$18).

Information New York Water Taxi (*NYWT*).
☎ *212/742–1969* ⊕ *www.nywatertaxi.com.*
NY Waterway. ☎ *800/533–3779* ⊕ *www.*
nywaterway.com. **Staten Island Ferry.** ☎ *311*
⊕ *www.siferry.com.*

▮ BUS TRAVEL

Most city buses in Manhattan follow easy-to-understand routes along the island's street grid. Routes go north and south on the avenues and east and west on the major two-way crosstown streets: 96th, 86th, 79th, 72nd, 66th, 57th, 42nd, 34th, 23rd, and 14th. Bus routes usually operate 24 hours a day, but service is infrequent late at night. Traffic jams can make rides maddeningly slow, especially along 5th Avenue in Midtown and on the Upper East Side. Certain bus routes provide "limited-stop service" during weekday rush hours, which saves travel time by stopping only at major cross streets and transfer points. A sign posted at the front of the bus indicates limited service; ask the driver whether the bus stops near where you want to go before boarding.

To find a bus stop, look for a light-blue sign (green for a "limited" bus, which skips more stops) on a green pole; bus numbers and routes are listed, with the stop's name underneath.

Bus fare is the same as subway fare: $2.75. Pay when you board with exact change in coins (no pennies, and no change is given) or with a MetroCard.

MetroCards (*see Public Transportation*) allow you one free transfer between buses or from bus to subway; when using coins on the bus, you can ask the driver for a free transfer coupon, good for one change to an intersecting route. Legal transfer points are listed on the back of the slip. Transfers generally have time limits of two hours.

Several routes in the city now have so-called Select Bus Service (SBS) rather than limited-stop service. These routes include those along 1st and 2nd Avenues and 34th Street in Manhattan, as well as the M60, which travels between LaGuardia Airport and 125th Street in Harlem. The buses, which are distinguished from normal city buses by signs identifying the bus as SBS on the front, make fewer stops. In addition, riders must pay for their rides before boarding with either a MetroCard or coins at a machine mounted on the street. The machine prints out a receipt. This receipt is the only proof of payment, so be sure to hold onto it for your entire SBS trip or risk a fine for fare evasion.

Bus route maps and schedules are posted at many bus stops in Manhattan, major stops throughout the other boroughs, and ⊕ *MTA.info*. Each of the five boroughs of New York has a separate bus map; they're available from some station booths, but rarely on buses. The best places to obtain them are the information kiosks in Grand Central Terminal and Penn Station, and the MTA's website. Additionally, the MTA Bus Time app ⊕ *bustime.mta.info* provides riders with real-time bus arrival information citywide.

Most buses that travel outside the city depart from the Port Authority Bus Terminal, on 8th Avenue between 40th and 42nd Streets. You must purchase your ticket at a ticket counter, not from the bus driver, so give yourself enough time to wait in line. The terminal is connected to the subway (A, C, E, N, Q, R, 1, 2, 3, and 7 lines), which offers direct travel on to Penn Station, Grand Central Terminal, and more. Several bus lines serving northern New Jersey and Rockland County, New York, make daily stops at the George Washington Bridge Bus Station from 5 am to 1 am. The station is connected to the 175th Street station on the A line of the subway, which travels down the west side of Manhattan.

A variety of discount bus services, including BoltBus and Megabus, run direct routes to and from cities such as Philadelphia, Boston, and Washington, D.C., with the majority of destinations along the East Coast. These budget options, priced from as little as $10 one way (sometimes even less, if you snag a deal), depart from locations throughout the city and can be more convenient than traditional bus services, although not always as comfortable.

Buses in New York Metropolitan Transportation Authority (MTA) Travel Information Line. ☎ *511* ⊕ *www.mta.info.*

Buses to New York BoltBus. ☎ *877/265– 8287* ⊕ *www.boltbus.com.* **Coach USA.** ☎ *800/877–1888* ⊕ *www.coachusa.com.* **Go Buses (by Academy Bus).** ☎ *855/888– 7160* ⊕ *www.gobuses.com.* **Greyhound.** ☎ *800/231–2222* ⊕ *www.greyhound.com.* **Megabus.** ☎ *877/462–6342* ⊕ *us.megabus. com.* **New Jersey Transit.** ☎ *973/275–5555* ⊕ *www.njtransit.com.* **Trailways.** ☎ *800/225– 6815* ⊕ *www.trailways.com.*

Bus Stations George Washington Bridge Bus Station. ✉ *4211 Broadway, between 178th and 179th Sts., Washington Heights* ☎ *800/221–9903* ⊕ *www.panynj.gov.* **Port Authority Bus Terminal.** ✉ *625 8th Ave., at 42nd St., Midtown West* ☎ *212/564–8484* ⊕ *www.panynj.gov.*

■ CAR TRAVEL

If you plan to drive into Manhattan, try to avoid the morning and evening rush hours and lunch hour. Tune in to traffic reports online or on the radio (e.g., WCBS 880 or 1010 WINS on the AM radio dial) before you set off, and don't be surprised if a bridge is partially closed or entirely blocked with traffic.

Driving within Manhattan can be a nightmare of gridlocked streets, obnoxious drivers, and seemingly suicidal jaywalkers and bicyclists. Narrow and one-way streets are common, particularly downtown, and can make driving even more difficult. The most congested streets of the city generally lie between 14th and 59th Streets and 3rd and 8th Avenues. In addition, portions of Broadway near Times Square (from 42nd to 47th Street) and Herald Square (33rd to 35th) are closed to motorized traffic. This can create gridlock and confusion in nearby streets.

GASOLINE

Gas stations are few and far between in Manhattan. If you can, fill up at stations outside Manhattan, where prices are generally cheaper. In Manhattan, you can refuel at stations along 10th and 11th Avenue south of West 57th Street, and along East Houston Street. Some gas stations in New York require you to pump your own gas; others provide attendants.

PARKING

Free parking is difficult to find in Midtown, and on weekday evenings and weekends in other neighborhoods. If you find a spot on the street, check parking signs carefully, and scour the curb for a faded yellow line indicating a no-parking zone, the bane of every driver's existence. Violators may be towed away or ticketed literally within minutes. If you do drive, use your car sparingly in Manhattan. If you can't find public parking, pull into a guarded parking garage; note that hourly rates (which can be $40 or more for just two hours) decrease somewhat if a car is left for a significant amount of time.
■ TIP➔ BestParking (⊕ *nyc.bestparking. com*) helps you find the cheapest parking-lot options for your visit; search by neighborhood, address, or attraction.

RULES OF THE ROAD

On city streets the speed limit is 25 mph, unless otherwise posted. No right turns on red are allowed within city limits, unless otherwise posted. Be alert for one-way streets and "no left turn" intersections.

The law requires that front-seat passengers wear seat belts at all times. Children under 16 must wear seat belts in both the front and back seats. Always strap children under age four into approved child-safety seats. It is illegal to use a handheld cell phone while driving in New York State. Police have the right to seize the car of anyone arrested for DWI (driving while intoxicated) in New York City.

CAR RENTALS

When you reserve a car, ask about cancellation penalties, taxes, drop-off charges (if you're planning to pick up the car in one destination and leave it in another), and surcharges (for being under or over a certain age, additional drivers, or driving across state or country borders or beyond a specific distance from your point of rental). All these things can add substantially to your costs. Request car seats and extras such as GPS when you book.

Rates are sometimes—but not always—better if you book in advance or reserve through a rental agency's website. There are other reasons to book ahead, though: for popular destinations (like NYC), during busy times of the year, or to ensure that you get certain types of cars (vans, SUVs, exotic sports cars).

■TIP➜ Make sure that a confirmed reservation guarantees you a car. Agencies sometimes overbook, particularly for busy weekends and holiday periods.

Rates in New York City average $70–$120 a day and $300–$500 a week (plus tax) for an economy car with air-conditioning, automatic transmission, and unlimited mileage. Rental costs are lower outside New York City, specifically in such places like Hoboken, New Jersey, and Yonkers, New York. If you already have a membership with short-term car-rental service like Zipcar, consider using them for your car needs in the city.

CAR-RENTAL INSURANCE

If you own a car and carry comprehensive car insurance for both collision and liability, your personal auto insurance probably covers a rental, but read your policy's fine print to be sure. If you don't have auto insurance, you should probably buy the collision- or loss-damage waiver (CDW or LDW) from the rental company. This eliminates your liability for damage to the car. Some credit cards offer CDW coverage, but it's usually supplemental to your own insurance and may not cover special vehicles (SUVs, minivans, luxury models, and the like). If your coverage is secondary, you may still be liable for loss-of-use costs from the car-rental company (again, read the fine print). If you're planning on using credit-card insurance, use that card for *all* transactions, from reserving to paying the final bill.

You may also be offered supplemental liability coverage. The car-rental company is required to carry a minimal level of liability coverage insuring all renters, but it may not be enough to cover claims in a really serious accident if you're at fault. Your own auto-insurance policy should also protect you if you own a car; if you don't, you have to decide whether you are willing to take the risk.

U.S. rental companies sell CDWs and LDWs for about $9 a day; supplemental liability is usually more than $10 a day. The car-rental company may offer you all sorts of other policies, but they're rarely worth the cost. Personal accident insurance, which is basic hospitalization coverage, is an especially egregious rip-off if you already have health insurance.

■TIP➜ You can decline insurance from the rental company and purchase it through a third-party provider such as AIG's Travel Guard (⊕ *www.travelguard.com*)—$9 per day for $35,000 of coverage.

■ PUBLIC TRANSPORTATION

When it comes to getting around New York, you have your pick of transportation in almost any neighborhood you're likely to visit. The subway and bus networks are extensive, especially in Manhattan, although getting across town can take some extra maneuvering. If you're not pressed for time, consider taking a public bus (*see Bus Travel*); they generally are slower than subways, but you can also see the city as you travel. Yellow cabs (*see Taxi Travel*) are abundant, except during the evening rush hour, when many drivers' shifts change, and in bad weather, when they get snapped up quickly. If it's late at night or you're outside Manhattan, using a ride-sharing service such as Lyft or Uber may be a good idea. Like a taxi ride, the subway (*see Subway Travel*) is a true New York City experience; it's also often the quickest way to get around. However, New York (especially Manhattan) is really a walking town, and depending on the time of day, the weather, and your destination, hoofing it could be the easiest and most enjoyable option.

During the height of weekday rush hours (especially from 7:30 am to 9:30 am and 5 pm to 7 pm) avoid Midtown if you can—subways and streets are jammed, and travel time on buses and taxis can easily double.

Subway and bus fares are $2.75 per ride. Reduced fares are available for senior citizens and people with disabilities during non–rush hours.

You pay for mass transit with a Metro-Card, a plastic card with a magnetic strip. There is a $1 fee for any new MetroCard purchase but there is an 11% bonus added to the card if you put $5.50 or more on the card. (There is a $5.50 minimum card purchase at station booths; this minimum does not apply at vending machines.) A Single Ride Ticket (sold only at Metro-Card vending machines) is $3. To help calculate the exact number of rides you need without having a balance left over, note that putting $9.91 on an existing MetroCard will get you $11 value, equal to 4 rides (add $1 for any new MetroCard purchase). As you swipe the card through a subway turnstile or insert it in a bus's card reader, the cost of the fare is automatically deducted. With the MetroCard, you can transfer free from bus to subway, subway to bus, or bus to bus, within a two-hour period.

MetroCards are sold at all subway stations and some stores—look for an "Authorized Sales Agent" sign. The MTA sells two kinds of MetroCards: unlimited-ride and pay-per-ride. Seven-day unlimited-ride MetroCards ($31) allow bus and subway travel for a week. If you expect to ride more than 11 times in one week, this is the card to get.

Unlike unlimited-ride cards, pay-per-ride MetroCards can be shared between riders. (Unlimited-ride MetroCards can be used only once at the same station or bus route in an 18-minute period.)

You can buy or add money to an existing MetroCard at a MetroCard vending machine, available at most subway station entrances (usually near the station booth). The machines accept major credit cards and ATM or debit cards. Many also accept cash, but note that the maximum amount of change they return is $6, which is doled out in dollar coins.

SUBWAY TRAVEL

The subway system operates on more than 840 miles of track 24 hours a day and serves nearly all the places you're likely to visit. It's cheaper than a cab, and during the workweek it's often faster than either taxis or buses. The trains are well lighted and air-conditioned. Still, the New York subway is hardly problem-free. Many trains are crowded, the older ones are noisy, the air-conditioning can break, and platforms can be dingy and damp. Homeless people sometimes take refuge from the elements by riding the trains, and panhandlers and buskers head there for a captive audience. Although trains usually run frequently, especially during rush hours, you never know when some incident somewhere on the line may stall traffic. In addition, subway construction sometimes causes delays or limitation of service, especially on weekends and after 10 pm on weekdays.

You can transfer between subway lines an unlimited number of times at any of the numerous stations where lines intersect. If you use a MetroCard (*see Public Transportation*) to pay your fare, you can also transfer to intersecting MTA bus routes for free. Such transfers generally have a time limit of two hours.

Most subway entrances are at street corners and marked by lampposts with an illuminated Metropolitan Transportation Authority (MTA) logo or globe-shape green or red lights—green means the station is open 24 hours and red means the station closes at night (though the colors don't always correspond to reality). Subway lines are designated by numbers and letters, such as the 3 line or the A line. Some lines run "express" and skip stops, and others are "local" and make all stops. Each station entrance has a sign indicating the lines that run through the station. Some entrances are also marked "uptown only" or "downtown only." Before entering subway stations, read the signs carefully. One of the most frequent mistakes visitors make is taking the train in the wrong direction. Maps of the full subway system are posted in every train car and usually on the subway platform (though these are sometimes out of date). You can usually pick up free maps at station booths.

For the most up-to-date information on subway lines, call the MTA's Travel Information line or visit its website. The MTA TripPlanner and Citymapper apps and websites are a good source for figuring out the best line to take to reach your destination, as is Google Maps. Alternatively, ask a station agent.

Pay your subway fare at the turnstile, using a MetroCard bought from a vending machine or booth attendant.

Schedule and Route Information Metropolitan Transportation Authority (MTA) Travel Information Line. ☎ 511 ⊕ *www.mta.info.*

Subway Information Citymapper. ⊕ *www.citymapper.com.* **MTA Trip Planner.** ☎ *511* ⊕ *tripplanner.mta.info.*

▌ TAXI TRAVEL

Yellow cabs are almost everywhere in Manhattan, cruising the streets looking for fares. They are usually easy to hail on the street or from a cabstand in front of major hotels, though finding one at rush hour or in the rain can take some time (and assertiveness). Even if you're stuck in a downpour or at the airport, do not accept a ride from a "gypsy cab." If a cab is not yellow and does not have a numbered aqua-color aluminum medallion bolted to the hood, you could be putting yourself (or at least your wallet) in danger by getting into the car.

You can see whether a taxi is available by checking its rooftop light. If the numbers are lit, the cab is available, and the driver is ready to take passengers—he or she is required to take passengers to any location in New York City as well as Newark Airport and two adjoining counties, although only NYC and Newark locations are metered. Once the meter is engaged (off-meter rates are prohibited; even JFK and out-of-town flat fares must be recorded by the meter for the passenger's protection), the fare is $2.50 just for entering the vehicle, which includes the first ⅕ mile, and 50¢ for each unit thereafter. A unit is defined as either ⅕ mile when the cab's cruising at 6 mph or faster or as 60 seconds when the cab is either not moving or moving at less than 6 mph. New York State adds 50¢ to each cab ride. There's also a 50¢ night surcharge added between 8 pm and 6 am, and a much-maligned $1 peak-hour surcharge is tacked on between 4 pm and 8 pm. Lastly, there is also a 30¢ "improvement surcharge" for all rides. All taxi drivers are required to accept credit cards as payment. On rare occasions, some who prefer cash claim their machines are broken when that isn't actually the case. If a driver waits until the end of the ride to mention a broken machine and you want to pay by credit card, you may wish to ask the driver to turn off the meter and drive you to an ATM to see if this extra hassle is worth it.

One taxi can hold a maximum of four passengers (an additional passenger under the age of seven is allowed if the child sits on someone's lap). You must pay any bridge or tunnel tolls incurred during your trip. In order to keep things moving quickly, all taxi drivers are required to use an E-ZPass in their cabs to automatically pay tolls, and they must pass the discounted toll rate along to the passenger; the total toll amount is added to the final fare. Taxi drivers expect a 10% to 20% tip, which should be rewarded for safe driving and good service.

To avoid unhappy taxi experiences, try to know where you want to go and how to get there before you hail a cab. ■TIP→ Know the cross streets of your destination (for instance, "5th Avenue and 42nd Street") before you enter a cab; a quick call to your destination will give you cross-street information, as will a glance at a map. Also, speak simply and clearly to make sure the driver has heard you correctly—few are native English-speakers, so it never hurts to make sure you've been understood. If headed for a far-flung location in Brooklyn or Queens, it can be helpful to pull up the location using Google Maps or a similar app, especially if the driver doesn't have GPS of his own. When you leave the cab, remember to take your receipt. It includes the cab's medallion number, which can help you track the cabbie down in the event that you've left your possessions in the cab or if you want to report an unpleasant ride (or even to compliment your driver for a great experience). Any charges, such as those for bridges, are itemized on the receipt; you can double-check to make sure you were charged correctly.

Yellow taxis can be difficult to find in parts of Brooklyn, Queens, the Bronx, and Staten Island. To help with this issue, in 2013 the city of New York created a brand-new class of taxi service:

apple-green Boro Taxis, which act like yellow taxis: they charge the same metered rates, accept credit cards, and must take you to any location within the city of New York. The difference is that green taxis are only allowed to pick up fares in non-Manhattan boroughs and in Manhattan locations above 96th Street.

If you're outside Manhattan and can't find a yellow or green taxi, you may have no choice but to call a car service. Locals and staff at restaurants and other public places can often recommend a reliable company. Always confirm the fee beforehand; a 10%–20% tip is customary.

Another increasingly popular option is booking a car through one of the car service apps like Uber, Lyft, Gett, or SheRides, which match passengers with potential car-service drivers. After booking a car through one of their respective apps, you can trace its journey to you via GPS, and you get a notification once it has arrived. These services are sometimes cheaper than a taxi (especially if the service allows for a carpool option that allows passengers to share rides at a discounted fare) but sometimes more, especially if "surge pricing" is in effect (when it's raining or at other high-demand times). The apps do let you get an estimate on rates before you book, but Gett is the only one that offers fixed "surge-free" rates regardless of demand, weather, or traffic. Payment and tipping (if applicable) is also done via the apps.

Car-Service Companies Boro Taxis information. ⊕ www.nyc.gov. **Carey.** ☎ 800/336–4646 ⊕ www.carey.com. **Carmel Car & Limousine Service.** ☎ 212/666–6666, 866/666–6666 ⊕ www.carmellimo.com. **Dial 7 Car Service.** ☎ 212/777–7777 ⊕ www.dial7. com. **London Towncars.** ☎ 212/988–9700, 800/221–4009 ⊕ www.londontowncars.com. **Gett.** ⊕ www.gett.com. **Lyft.** ⊕ www.lyft. com. **SheRides.** ⊕ www.shetaxis.com. **Uber.** ⊕ www.uber.com.

TRAIN TRAVEL

For information about the subway, see Subway Travel.

Metro-North Railroad trains take passengers from Grand Central Terminal to points north of New York City, both in New York State and Connecticut. Amtrak trains arrive at Penn Station. For trains from New York City to Long Island and New Jersey, take the Long Island Rail Road and New Jersey Transit, respectively; both operate from Penn Station. The PATH trains to New Jersey offer service to Newark, Jersey City, Harrison, and Hoboken; the main PATH stations are located at 33rd Street or the World Trade Center.

Information **Amtrak Pennsylvania Station.** ✉ *Midtown West* ☎ *800/872-7245* ⊕ *www. amtrak.com.* **Long Island Rail Road.** ✉ *Penn Station, Midtown West* ☎ *511* ⊕ *www.mta.info/ lirr.* **Metro-North Railroad.** ✉ *Grand Central Terminal, Midtown East* ☎ *212/532-4900, 511* ⊕ *www.mta.info/mnr.* **New Jersey Transit.** ✉ *Penn Station, Midtown West* ☎ *973/275-5555* ⊕ *www.njtransit.com.* **PATH.** ☎ *800/234-7284* ⊕ *www.panynj.gov/path.*

Train Stations **Grand Central Terminal.** ✉ *89 E. 42nd St., at Park Ave., Midtown East* ⊕ *www.grandcentralterminal.com.* **Penn Station.** ✉ *From 31st to 33rd St., between 7th and 8th Aves., Midtown West* ☎ *511.*

ESSENTIALS

▮ COMMUNICATIONS

INTERNET

You can check your email or surf the Internet at all public libraries, many cafés and public parks, and most hotels. In addition, all of New York's subway stations are on target to have both Wi-Fi and mobile service by 2017; about 150 stations in Manhattan and Queens currently have it. NYC & Company and Google Maps offer online maps that outline free Wi-Fi hot spots in the New York area; the app WiFi Finder can also help you track down hot spots.

Contacts NYC & Company. ⊕ *www.nycgo.com.*

▮ DISABILITIES AND ACCESSIBILITY

New York has come a long way in making life easier for people with disabilities. At most street corners, curb cuts allow wheelchairs to roll along unimpeded. Many restaurants, shops, and movie theaters with step-up entrances have wheelchair ramps. Though some New Yorkers may rush past those in need of assistance, you'll find plenty of people who are more than happy to help you get around.

NYC & Company's website has information on the accessibility of many landmarks and attractions in their free downloadable guide. The NYC Mayor's Office for People with Disabilities is another great resource outlining accessibility throughout the city. If you need to rent a wheelchair or scooter while in New York, Scootaround will deliver it to your hotel (or wherever you're staying); reservations can be made up to a year in advance.

Local Resources NYC & Company. ⊕ *www. nycgo.com/accessibility.* **NYC Mayor's Office for People with Disabilities** (*MOPD*). ☎ *311* ⊕ *www. nyc.gov/mopd.* **Scootaround.** ☎ *888/441–7575* ⊕ *locations.scootaround.com/nyc.*

LODGING

Despite the Americans with Disabilities Act (ADA), the level of accessibility seems to differ from hotel to hotel. Some properties may be accessible by ADA standards for people with mobility disabilities but not for people with hearing or vision impairments, for example.

If you have a hearing impairment, check whether the hotel has devices to alert you visually to the ring of the telephone, a knock at the door, and a fire/emergency alarm.

If you're bringing a service dog, you're not required to let the hotel staff know ahead of time (they must accommodate your service dog regardless); however, you may wish to notify them in advance as a courtesy.

SIGHTS AND ATTRACTIONS

Most public facilities in New York City, whether museums, parks, or theaters, are wheelchair-accessible. Some attractions have special programs for people with mobility, sight, or hearing, or cognitive disabilities.

TRANSPORTATION

Although the city is working to retrofit stations to comply with the ADA, not all stations, including many major ones, are accessible and unlikely to be so in the near future. Accessible stations are clearly marked on subway and rail maps. Visitors in wheelchairs have better success with public buses, all of which have wheelchair lifts and "kneelers" at the front to facilitate getting on and off. Bus drivers provide assistance.

Reduced fares are available to disabled passengers; if paying with cash, you need to present a Medicare card or Paratransit card. You may also apply for a Temporary Reduced-Fare MetroCard in advance of your visit. Visitors to the city are also eligible for the same Access-a-Ride program benefits as New York City residents.

Drivers with disabilities may use windshield cards from their own state or Canadian province to park in designated handicapped spaces.

The U.S. government's Disability.gov website is loaded with advice for travelers with disabilities, including an entire section devoted transportation. Visit ⊕ *www. disability.gov* for more information.

Information and Complaints Reduced-Fare MetroCard. ☎ *511* ⊕ *www.mta.info/ accessibility/transit.htm.*

▌ GAY AND LESBIAN TRAVEL

Attitudes toward same-sex couples are very tolerant in Manhattan and most other parts of the city. Hell's Kitchen, Chelsea, and Greenwich Village are some of the most prominently gay neighborhoods, but gays and lesbians feel at home almost everywhere. One of the world's oldest and largest gay-pride parades takes place on 5th Avenue the last Sunday in June.

PUBLICATIONS

For listings of gay events and places, check out *Next,* which is online and also distributed in many gay bars throughout Manhattan. *Time Out New York* (⊕ *www.timeout.com/newyork/lgbt*) magazine offers a gay-friendly take on what's happening in the city.

Gay Publications Gay City News. ⊕ *www. gaycitynews.com.* **Next.** ⊕ *www.nextmagazine. com.* **TimeOut NY LGBT.** ⊕ *www.timeout.com/ newyork/lgbt.*

Local Information The Center (*Lesbian, Gay, Bisexual & Transgender Community Center*). ✉ *208 W. 13th St., between 7th and 8th Aves., Greenwich Village* ☎ *212/620-7310* ⊕ *www. gaycenter.org.*

▌ KIDS IN NEW YORK

For listings of children's events, consult *Time Out New York, New York* magazine, and other local media. The Friday *New York Times* arts section also includes children's activities. Other good sources on happenings for youngsters are the websites NYMetroParents and New York Family (and their respective magazines). If you have access to cable television, check the local all-news channel New York 1, where you'll find a spot aired several times daily that covers current and noteworthy children's events. *Fodor's Around New York City with Kids* (available in most bookstores) can help you plan your days together.

LODGING

Before you consider using a cot or fold-out couch for your child, ask how large your hotel room is—New York City rooms are usually small. Many hotels in New York allow children under a certain age to stay in their parents' room at no extra charge, but others may charge for them; be sure to find out the cutoff age for children's comps or discounts before booking.

PUBLIC TRANSPORTATION

Up to four children shorter than 44 inches who are traveling with a paying adult ride for free on MTA buses and subways. If pushing a stroller, don't struggle through a subway turnstile; ask the station agent to buzz you through the gate (the attendant will ask you to swipe your MetroCard through the turnstile nearest the gate). Keep a sharp eye on your kids while in the subway; at some stations there is a gap between the train doors and the platform.

▌ MEDIA

NEWSPAPERS AND MAGAZINES

The major daily newspapers in New York are *The New York Times* and *Wall Street Journal,* both broadsheets, and the *Daily News* and *New York Post,* which are tabloids. The *Village Voice* is a free alternative weekly. Local magazines and websites include *The New Yorker* and *New York.* All of these are widely available online and at newsstands and shops around town.

▌ MONEY

In New York, it's easy to get swept up in a debt-inducing cyclone of $60-per-person dinners, $120 theater tickets, $20 nightclub covers, and $300 hotel rooms. But one of the good things about the city is that you can spend in some areas and save in others. Within Manhattan, a cup of coffee can cost from $1 to $4, a pint of beer from $5 to $8, and a sandwich from $6 to $10. Generally, prices in the other four boroughs are lower than those in Manhattan.

The most generously bequeathed treasure of the city is the arts. The stated admission fee at the Metropolitan Museum of Art is a suggestion; you can donate a lesser amount and not be snubbed. Many other museums in town have special times during which admission is free. The Museum of Modern Art, for instance, is free on Friday from 4 to 8. In summer a handful of free music, theater, and dance performances, as well as films (usually screened outdoors), fill the calendar each day.

Prices in this guide are given for adults. Reduced fees are typically available for children, students, and senior citizens.

CREDIT CARDS

Record all your credit card numbers—as well as the phone numbers to call if your cards are lost or stolen (there's a contact number typically listed on the back of the card)—in a safe place, so you're prepared should something go wrong.

Reporting Lost Cards American Express. ☎ 800/528–4800 ⊕ www.americanexpress. com. **Diners Club.** ☎ 800/234–6377 ⊕ www. dinersclub.com. **Discover.** ☎ 800/347–2683 ⊕ www.discovercard.com. **MasterCard.** ☎ 800/627–8372 ⊕ www.mastercard.com. **Visa.** ☎ 800/847–2911 ⊕ www.visa.com.

▌ RESTROOMS

Public restrooms in New York are few and far between. If you find yourself in need of a restroom, head for Midtown department stores, museums, or the lobbies of large hotels to find the cleanest bathrooms. Public atriums, such as those at the Citicorp Center and Trump Tower, also provide good public facilities, as do Bryant Park and the many Starbucks coffee shops in the city.

Restaurants usually allow only patrons to use their restrooms, but if you're dressed well and look as if you belong, you can often just sail right in. If too self-conscious for this brand of nonchalance, just ask the host or hostess nicely. Be aware that cinemas, Broadway theaters, and concert halls have limited amenities, and there are often long lines before performances/screenings and during intermissions.

▌ SAFETY

New York City is one of the safest large cities in the country. However, do not let yourself be lulled into a false sense of security. As in any large city, unsuspecting travelers in New York remain particularly easy marks for pickpockets and hustlers.

After the September 11, 2001, terrorist attacks, security was heightened throughout the city. Never leave any bags unattended, and expect to have yourself and your possessions inspected thoroughly in such places as airports, sports stadiums, city buildings, and sometimes even subway stations or museums.

Ignore the panhandlers on the streets and subways, people who offer to hail you a cab (they sometimes appear at transit hubs like Penn Station, the Port Authority, and Grand Central), and limousine and gypsy-cab drivers who (illegally) offer you a ride.

Keep jewelry out of sight on the street; better yet, leave valuables at home. Don't carry wallets, smartphones, or other gadgets in your back pockets, and make sure bags and purses stay closed.

Avoid deserted blocks in unfamiliar neighborhoods. A brisk, purposeful pace helps deter trouble wherever you go.

The subway runs around the clock and is generally well trafficked until midnight (and until at least 2 am on Friday and Saturday nights), and overall it is very safe. If you do take the subway late at night, ride in the center car, with the conductor. Watch out for unsavory characters lurking around the inside or outside of stations.

When waiting for a train, head to the center of the platform, and stand far away from its edge, especially when trains are entering or leaving the station. Once the train pulls into the station, avoid empty cars. While on the train, don't engage in verbal exchanges with aggressive riders. If a fellow passenger makes you nervous while on the train, trust your instincts and change cars. When disembarking, stick with the crowd until you reach the street.

Travelers Aid International helps stranded travelers, airport passengers, and unaccompanied children, and works closely with the police and other social service agencies.

■ TIP➔ Distribute your cash, credit cards, IDs, and other valuables between a deep front pocket, an inside jacket or vest pocket, and a hidden money pouch.

Information Travelers Aid International (JFK). ✉ JFK International Airport, Terminal 4, Queens ☎ 718/656–4870 ⊕ jfk.travelersaid. org ✉ Newark Liberty International Airport, Newark ☎ 973/623–5052 ⊕ www.travelersaid. org. **Travelers Aid International (EWR).** ✉ Newark Liberty International Airport, Newark ☎ 973/623–5052 ⊕ www.travelersaid.org

■ SENIOR-CITIZEN TRAVEL

The Metropolitan Transportation Authority (MTA) charges lower fares for passengers 65 and over.

To qualify for age-related discounts, mention your senior-citizen status up front when booking hotel reservations (not when checking out). Be sure to have identification on hand. When renting a car, ask about promotional car-rental discounts, too, which can be cheaper than senior-citizen rates.

THE FODORS.COM CONNECTION

Before your trip, be sure to check out what fellow travelers are saying in the Travel Talk forums on ⊕ www.fodors.com.

■ SPORTS AND THE OUTDOORS

The New York City Department of Parks & Recreation lists all of the recreational facilities and activities available throughout NYC's parks.

Contact Information NYC Department of Parks & Recreation. ☎ 311 ⊕ www. nycgovparks.org.

BASEBALL

The subway gets you directly to the stadiums of both New York–area major-league teams: the New York Mets play at Citi Field, at the next-to-last stop on the 7 train in Queens, while the Yankees defend their turf at Yankee Stadium in the Bronx, accessible via the B, D, and 4 trains. The Mets-affiliated minor-league Brooklyn Cyclones are named for Coney Island's famous wooden roller coaster. They play 38 home games at MCU Park, next to the boardwalk, with views of the Atlantic over the right-field wall and Luna Park amusement park over the left-field wall. Most people make a day of it, with time at the beach and amusement rides before an evening game. Take the D, F, N, or Q subway to the end of the line, and walk one block to the right of the original Nathan's Famous hot dog stand.

For another fun, family-oriented experience, check out the Staten Island Yankees, one of New York's minor-league teams, which warms up many future New York Yankees players. The stadium, a five-minute walk from the Staten Island Ferry terminal, has magnificent views of Lower Manhattan and the Statue of Liberty.

Contact Information Brooklyn Cyclones.
⊠ *MCU Park, 1904 Surf Ave., at 19th St., Coney Island* ☎ *718/372–5596, 718/507–8499 for tickets* ⊕ *www.brooklyncyclones.com* Ⓜ *D, F, N, Q to Coney Island–Stillwell Ave.* **New York Mets.** ⊠ *123-01 Roosevelt Ave., 126th St. and Roosevelt Ave., Flushing* ☎ *718/507–8499* ⊕ *www.mets.com* Ⓜ *7 to Mets–Willets Point.* **New York Yankees.** ⊠ *Yankee Stadium, 1 E. 161st St., at River Ave., Bronx* ☎ *718/293–6000* ⊕ *newyork.yankees.mlb.com* Ⓜ *4, B, D to 161st St.–Yankee Stadium.* **Staten Island Yankees.** ⊠ *Richmond County Bank Ballpark, 75 Richmond Terr., St. George* ☎ *718/720–9265* ⊕ *www.siyanks.com* Ⓜ *Staten Island Ferry.*

BASKETBALL

The New York Knicks arouse intense hometown passions, which means tickets for home games at Madison Square Garden are hard to come by. Try StubHub to score tickets. The Brooklyn Nets are across the river, in the swanky Barclays Center. The stadium is easily reachable by 11 different subway lines and the LIRR. The men's basketball season runs from late October through April. The New York Liberty, a member of the WNBA (Women's National Basketball Association), had its first season in 1997. The season runs from May through September, with home games played at Madison Square Garden.

Contact Information Brooklyn Nets.
⊠ *Barclays Center, 620 Atlantic Ave., at Flatbush Ave., Prospect Heights* ☎ *917/618–6700 for box office* ⊕ *www.nba.com/nets* Ⓜ *2, 3, 4, 5, B, D, N, Q, R to Atlantic Ave.–Barclays Center.* **Madison Square Garden.** ⊠ *4 Pennsylvania Plaza, near 32nd St., between 7th and 8th Aves. New York* ☎ *212/465–6741* ⊕ *www.msg.com* Ⓜ *1, 2, 3 to 34th St.–Penn Station.* **New York Knicks.** ☎ *212/465–5867* ⊕ *www.nba.com/knicks.* **New York Liberty.** ☎ *212/465–6073 for tickets, 212/465–6000 for fan hotline* ⊕ *www.nyliberty.com.*

BICYCLING

In recent years, bicycling the streets of Manhattan and many parts of Brooklyn has become more mainstream and much less the sole province of bike messengers and zealots. The city government and biking organizations have both helped make it safer, and drivers and pedestrians are more aware that bikes are likely to be on the road, too. Check the NYC Department of Transportation's website for a cycling map that shows the best routes and roads with designated bike lanes, as well as local road rules, including for taking a bike on public transit.

For biking under more controlled conditions, head to New York's major parks. Central Park has a 6-mile circular drive with a couple of decent climbs. North of 72nd Street, its roadways are permanently closed to car traffic, making cycling here particularly appealing; other sections are open to vehicular traffic on weekdays from 8 am to 10 am (the Central Drive/East Drive is open to cars from 7 am to 7 pm on weekdays).

Beware of renting a bike from the many illegal vendors that hang out on the streets near Central Park, especially by Columbus Circle. These bikes tend to be old and mismatched and are also sometimes stolen. Look for the one authorized Central Park bike vendor set up at Merchants' Gate Plaza (next to Columbus Circle at Central Park South and Central Park West); Central Park hosts additional seasonal bike rental locations within the park at the Loeb Boathouse (east side of park, between 74th and 75th Streets) or Tavern on the Green restaurant (west side, between 66th and 67th Streets). Otherwise, it's better to rent from someone with an actual storefront. Most bike-rental stores have copies of the very handy official NYC Bike Map, which is published annually and shows traffic flow and bike lanes for all of New York City.

The busy bike lane along the Hudson River Park's (rentals are also available within the park) esplanade parallels the waterfront from West 59th Street south to the esplanade of Battery Park City. The lane also heads north, connecting with the bike path in Riverside Park and the esplanade between West 72nd and West 100th Streets, continuing all the way to the George Washington Bridge. From Battery Park it's a quick ride up to the Wall Street area, which is relatively deserted on weekends, and over to the bike lane along the East River.

The 3.3-mile circular drive in Brooklyn's Prospect Park is closed to cars year-round except from 7 am to 9 am (on the northbound East Drive) on weekdays. It has a long, gradual hill that tops off near the Grand Army Plaza entrance.

Bike Rentals and Information Bicycle Rentals at Loeb Boathouse. ⊠ *East side of park between 74th and 75th Sts., Central Park* ☎ *212/517–2233 for Boathouse, 212/260–0400 for Tavern on the Green or Merchants' Gate Plaza* ⊕ *www.centralparknyc.org* Ⓜ *6 to 68th St.–Hunter College.* **Get Up and Ride.** ⊠ *330 S. 3rd St., near Keap St., Williamsburg* ☎ *646/801–2453* ⊕ *www.getupandride.com.* **New York City Department of Transportation.** ☎ *311* ⊕ *www.nyc.gov/bikes.* **Pedal Pusher Bike Shop.** ⊠ *1306 2nd Ave., at 69th St., Upper East Side* ☎ *212/288–5592* ⊕ *www.pedalpusherbikeshop.com* Ⓜ *6 to 68th St.–Hunter College.* **Toga Bike Shop.** ⊠ *110 West End Ave., at 64th St., Upper West Side* ☎ *212/799–9625* ⊕ *www.togabikes.com* Ⓜ *1 to 66th St.–Lincoln Center.* **Waterfront Bicycle Shop.** ⊠ *391 West St., between Christopher and 10th Sts., West Village* ☎ *212/414–2453* ⊕ *www.bikeshopny.com* Ⓜ *1 to Christopher St.–Sheridan Sq.*

CITI BIKE BICYCLING SHARE
New York's bike-sharing program debuted in 2013 with hundreds of stations, the majority in Manhattan south of Central Park and northern Brooklyn; hundreds more have been rolled out through 2016, with expansions further north in Manhattan, deeper into Brooklyn, and into Long Island City in Queens. The three-speed, 40-pound, bright-blue bikes, which are either charming or clunky depending on your perspective, are outfitted with lights and bungee cords to secure small bags and other items. They don't come with

helmets, though: wearing one is recommended but not mandatory.

After buying a Citi Bike pass, you are able to borrow an unlimited number of the bikes for either 24 hours ($9.95) or seven days ($25). What is limited is your time with a particular bike: the time between unlocking a bike at one station at returning it to another must be 30 minutes or under, or you face additional charges, and these overtime charges add up quickly (all the way to $1,200 for never returning a bike at all). As soon as you return one bike, you're free to get another—even one from the same location.

Before you pull a bike from one of the bays and start the 30-minute clock running, spend a little time planning your route. Citi Bike's apps are helpful with this, because they show which of the computerized outdoor stations have bikes available, and—just as important—which have empty bays available for when it's time to return your bike.

Contact Information Citi Bike. ☎ *855/245–3311 for customer service* ⊕ *www.citibikenyc.com.*

GROUP BIKE RIDES
Bike New York runs a 40-mile, five-borough bike ride the first Sunday in May. The Five Borough Bicycle Club organizes day and weekend rides. The New York Cycle Club sponsors regular rides for every level of ability. Time's Up!, a nonprofit advocacy group, leads free recreational rides and workshops for cyclists; the Central Park Moonlight Ride, departing from Columbus Circle at 10 pm the first Friday of every month, is a favorite.

Contact Information Bike New York. ☎ *212/870–2080* ⊕ *www.bike.nyc.* **Five Borough Bicycle Club.** ☎ *347/688–2925* ⊕ *www.5bbc.org.* **New York Cycle Club.** ☎ ⊕ *www.nycc.org.* **Time's Up!** ☎ *212/802–8222* ⊕ *www.times-up.org.*

BOATING, KAYAKING, AND PADDLEBOARDING

Central Park has rowboats (plus a Venetian gondola for evening glides) on the 22-acre Central Park Lake. Rent your rowboat, which holds up to four people, at Loeb Boathouse, near East 74th Street, from April through November ($15 an hour). Gondola rides (complete with gondolier) are available during the same period and can be reserved ($45 per half hour); the gondola hold up to six people.

Operated by Manhattan Community Boathouse is the Pier 96 Boathouse in Midtown West and the dock at West 72nd Street, where you can take a sturdy kayak out for a paddle for free on weekends and weekday evenings from mid-May through mid-October. This walk-up kayaking program is offered on a first-come, first-served basis (no reservations are taken in advance) and is suitable for people of all ages and abilities. Kayaks, paddles, life jackets, and basic instructions are provided. All participants must sign a liability waiver and know how to swim. The Downtown Boathouse, at Pier 26 in TriBeCa, has a similar season and services (though weekday evening rides are only available in July and August). Manhattan Kayak Company gives kayak and stand-up paddleboard (SUP) lessons for all levels and runs trips on the Hudson River between May and late September, including a fun New York After Dark tour for $80.

Contact Information Downtown Boathouse. ⊠ *Pier 26 Boathouse, Near N. Moore St. at the Hudson River, TriBeCa* ⊕ *www. downtownboathouse.org* Ⓜ *1 to Franklin St.; A, C, E to Canal St.* **Loeb Boathouse.** ⊠ *East side of park between 74th and 75th Sts., Central Park* ☎ *212/517–2233* ⊕ *www. thecentralparkboathouse.com/boats.php* Ⓜ *6 to 77th St.* **Manhattan Community Boathouse.** ⊠ *56th St. at the Hudson River, Midtown West* ⊕ *www.manhattancommunityboathouse. org* Ⓜ *1, A, B, C, D to 59th St.–Columbus Circle.* **Manhattan Kayak Company.** ⊠ *Pier 84, 555 12th Ave., at 44th St., Midtown West* ☎ *212/924–1788* ⊕ *www.manhattankayak.com* Ⓜ *A, C, E to 42nd St.–Port Authority.*

FOOTBALL

The football season runs from August through December. The enormously popular New York Giants play at MetLife Stadium in East Rutherford, New Jersey. Most seats for Giants games are sold on a season-ticket basis. However, single tickets are occasionally available at Giants. com or on ticket resale sites like the NFL Ticket Exchange (by Ticketmaster) or StubHub. The New York Jets also play at MetLife Stadium. Jets tickets are likewise hard to come by, with most snapped up by fans before the season opener.

Contact Information Metlife Stadium. ⊠ *One MetLife Stadium Dr., East Rutherford* ☎ *201/559–1515, 201/559–1300 for box office* ⊕ *www.metlifestadium.com.* **New York Giants.** ☎ *201/935–8222 for tickets* ⊕ *www.giants. com.* **New York Jets.** ☎ *800/469–5387 for tickets* ⊕ *www.newyorkjets.com.*

HOCKEY

The New York Rangers, one of the oldest teams in the National Hockey League, operate out of Madison Square Garden. The New York Islanders hockey team moved from their suburban Long Island arena to the Barclays Center in Brooklyn for the 2015–16 season. The regular season for hockey runs from October through early April and the playoffs go through June.

Contact Information New York Islanders. ⊠ *Barclays Center, 620 Atlantic Ave., at Flatbush Ave., Prospect Heights* ☎ *917/618–6700* ⊕ *islanders.nhl.com* Ⓜ *2, 3, 4, 5, B, D, N, Q, R to Atlantic Ave.–Barclays Center.* **New York Rangers.** ⊠ *Madison Square Garden, 4 Pennsylvania Plaza, near 32nd St., between 7th and 8th Aves. New York* ☎ *212/465–6000,* ⊕ *rangers. nhl.com* Ⓜ *1, 2, 3 to 34th St.–Penn Station.*

ICE-SKATING

The outdoor rink in Rockefeller Center, open from October through early April, is much smaller in real life than it appears on TV and in movies, with only 150 skaters permitted at a time—though it *is* as beautiful, especially when Rock Center's enormous Christmas tree towers above it. Reservations can be booked in advance via the website and are recommended—especially around the holidays. Otherwise, tickets are first-come, first-served, so be prepared to wait (early morning is the best time to get on the ice quickly). Be prepared to pay, too: skating rates are $25–$32 for adults, which doesn't include skate rental ($12). Central Park has two rinks, also open from late October through early April, including the beautifully situated Wollman Rink, which has skating until long after dark beneath the lights of the city. Be prepared for daytime crowds on weekends. The Lasker Rink, at the north end of Central Park, is usually less crowded than Wollman. Chelsea Piers' Sky Rink has two year-round indoor rinks overlooking the Hudson. Skate rentals are available at all rinks. The skating rink at the Winter Village at Bryant Park has "free" skating, although this doesn't include skate rental ($15–$19) or the likely fee to either buy a lock for a locker or have bags checked ($8–$10). Winter Village's rink is open from November through early March, daily from 8 am to 10 pm. A FastPass (available online, includes skate rental and bag check) allows you to skip the line; it costs $22–$28. ■TIP➔ **Every winter the trendy Standard Hotel, in the Meatpacking District near the High Line, makes its own tiny ice rink. Skate tickets are $13 and skate rental is $4; the rink, at 848 Washington Street at West 13th Street, is open from 9 am until at least midnight on weekends and from noon until midnight on weekdays. When you're done, hot toddies and Alpine-inspired snacks are ready to take the edge off any chill.**

Contact Information Lasker Rink.
✉ *Midpark near 106th St., Central Park* ⊕ *Park entrance at 110th St. and Lenox Ave.* ☎ *917/492–3856* ⊕ *www.laskerrink.com* Ⓜ *B, C to Cathedral Parkway–110th St.; 2, 3*

to Central Park North–110th St. **The Rink at Winter Village at Bryant Park.** ✉ *1065 6th Ave., between 40th and 42nd Sts., Midtown West* ☎ *212/661–6640* ⊕ *wintervillage.org/ skate* Ⓜ *B, D, F, M to 42nd St.–Bryant Park.* **Rockefeller Center.** ✉ *5th Ave., between 49th and 50th Sts., lower plaza, Midtown West* ☎ *212/332–7654* ⊕ *www.therinkatrockcenter. com* Ⓜ *B, D, F, M to 47th–50th Sts./Rockefeller Center; E, M to 5th Ave./53rd St.* **Sky Rink at Chelsea Piers.** ✉ *Pier 61, W. 21st St., at the Hudson River, Chelsea* ☎ *212/336–6100* ⊕ *www.chelseapiers.com/sr* Ⓜ *C, E to 23rd St.* **Wollman Skating Rink.** ✉ *North of 6th Ave. and Central Park S. entrance, between 62nd and 63rd Sts., Central Park* ☎ *212/439–6900* ⊕ *www.wollmanskatingrink.com* Ⓜ *1, A, B, C, D to 59th St.–Columbus Circle; N, Q, R to 5th Ave.–59th St.; F to 57th St.*

JOGGING

All kinds of New Yorkers jog, some with dogs or babies in tow, so you always have company on the regular jogging routes. What's not recommended is setting out on a lonely park path at dusk. Go running when and where everybody else does. On Manhattan streets, roughly 20 north–south blocks make a mile.

In Manhattan, Central Park is the busiest spot, specifically along the nearly 1.6-mile path circling the Jacqueline Kennedy Onassis Reservoir,. A runners' lane has been designated along park roads; the entire loop road is a hilly 6 miles. A good 1.75-mile route starts at the Tavern on the Green along the West Drive, heads south around the bottom of the park to the East Drive, and circles back west on the 72nd Street park road to your starting point. Riverside Park, along the Hudson River bank in Manhattan, is glorious at sunset. You can cover 3 miles by running from West 72nd to West 100th Streets and back, and the Greenbelt trail extends roughly 4 more miles north to the George Washington Bridge at 181st Street. Other favorite Manhattan circuits are the Battery Park City esplanade (just over a mile), which connects to 4 more miles of jogging paths in Hudson River Park, as well as to sections of the East River Esplanade.

∎ STUDENTS IN NEW YORK

New York is home to Columbia University, New York University, Fordham University, the City College of New York, and more. With other colleges scattered throughout the five boroughs, and a huge population of public and private high-schoolers, it's no wonder the city is rife with student discounts. Wherever you go, especially museums, sightseeing attractions, and performances, identify yourself as a student and ask if a discount is available, but be prepared to show your ID.

ArtsConnection Teen Programs/High 5 Tickets to the Arts is a great program for teens 13 and 18 (or anyone in middle or high school). Tickets to a wide variety of performances (though only rarely Broadway shows) and museum passes are sold for $5 online or by phone. And, for every student ticket, an adult can get a $5 ticket, too. Check the website to find out about upcoming events and offerings.

Contact Information ArtsConnection. ✉ *520 8th Ave., Suite 321, at 36th St., Midtown West* ☎ *212/302–7433* ⊕ *teens.artsconnection. org/faq-high5.* **STA Travel.** ✉ *722 Broadway, between Washington Pl. and Waverly Pl., West Village* ☎ *212/473–6100, 800/781–4040 for 24-hr service center* ⊕ *www.sta.com.*

∎ TAXES

A sales tax of 8.875% applies to almost everything you can buy retail, including restaurant meals. However, prescription drugs and nonprepared food bought in grocery stores are exempt. Clothing and footwear costing less than $110 are also exempt.

∎ TIPPING

The customary tipping rate for taxi drivers is 10%–20%; bellhops are usually given $2 per bag in luxury hotels, $1 per bag elsewhere. Hotel maids should be tipped $2 per day of your stay. A doorman who hails or helps you into a cab can be tipped $1–$2. You should also tip your hotel concierge for services rendered; the size of the tip depends on the difficulty of your request, as well as the quality of the concierge's work. Waiters should be tipped 15%–20%, though at higher-end restaurants, a solid 20% is more the norm. Tip $1 or $2 per drink you order at the bar, or possibly more if you're ordering something especially time-consuming to make.

∎ VISITOR INFORMATION

The Grand Central Partnership (a business-improvement district) operates a number of information kiosks in and around Grand Central Terminal. They're loaded with maps and helpful brochures on attractions throughout the city and staffed by friendly, knowledgeable, multilingual New Yorkers.

NYC & Company runs Official NYC Information Centers at Macy's Herald Square as well as in Lower Manhattan at City Hall Park and the South Street Seaport. Its official visitor guide and map, both downloadable from NYC & Company's website as well as in hard copies available around town, are both very useful.

The Downtown Alliance has information on the area encompassing City Hall south to Battery Park, and from the East River to West Street; the Times Square Alliance covers the Times Square area. For a free booklet listing New York State and New York City attractions and tour packages, contact the New York State Division of Tourism.

CONTACTS

City Information Downtown Alliance.
☎ *212/566-6700* ⊕ *www.downtownny.com.*
Grand Central Partnership. ☎ *212/883-*
2420 ⊕ *www.grandcentralpartnership.nyc.*
NYC & Company Information Center at
Macy's Herald Square. ✉ *151 W. 34th St.,*
between 7th Ave. and Broadway, Midtown
West ☎ *212/484-1222* ⊕ *www.nycgo.com*
Ⓜ *B, D, F, M, N, Q, R to 34th St.–Herald Sq.*
Times Square Alliance. ✉ *Midtown West*
☎ *212/768-1560* ⊕ *www.timessquarenyc.org.*

Statewide Information New York State
Division of Tourism. ☎ *800/225-5697*
⊕ *www.iloveny.com.*

INDEX

PHOTO CREDITS

Front cover: David Sucsy/iStockphoto [Description: Central Park and New York City Skyline, New York City, New York]. 1, Songquan Deng/Shutterstock. 2, Kord.com/age fotostock. Chapter 1: Experience New York City: 8-9, Sean Pavone / Shutterstock. 18 (left), Xuan Che/Flickr, [CC BY 2.0]. 18 (top center), Andreykr l Dreamstime.com. 18 (top right), Sylvian Granadam/age fotostock. 18 (bottom right), Dmitro2009 / Shutterstock. 19 (top left), Revoc9 l Dreamstime.com. 19 (bottom left), Craig Chesek/AMNH. 19 (right), Picture-Quest. Chapter 2: Lower Manhattan: 41, Sepavo l Dreamstime. com. 43, Cpenler l Dreamstime.com. 44, Chuck Pefley/Alamy. 49, Almaz 888 l Dreamstime.com. 54, Oscity l Dreamstime.com. 57, Estormiz/Wikimedia Commons. Chapter 3: SoHo, NoLIta, Little Italy, and Chinatown. 59, Littleny l Dreamstime.com. 61, Kmiragaya l Dreamstime.com. 62, Adeliepenguin l Dreamstime.com. 64, JayLazarin/iStockphoto. 67, Philip Lange/Shutterstock. Chapter 4: The East Village and the Lower East Side: 69, Robert K. Chin / Alamy. 71, Bruce Monroe/Flickr, [CC BY-SA 2.0]. 72, Tomás Fano/Flickr, [CC BY-SA 2.0]. 77, wdstock / iStockphoto. Chapter 5: Greenwich Village and the West Village: 79, Almaz888 l Dreamstime.com. 81, Evelyn Proimos/Flickr, [CC BY 2.0]. 82, wdstock/iStockphoto. 83, Ambient Images Inc./Alamy. 86, Jennifer Arnow. Chapter 6: Chelsea and the Meatpacking District: 89, Marco Rubino / Shutterstock. 91 and 92, Jennifer Arnow. 97, Hannoonnes l Dreamstime.com. 100, Nicolas McComber/iStockphoto. Chapter 7: Union Square, the Flatiron District, and Gramercy Park: 103, Sean Pavone / Shutterstock. 105, Kord.com/age fotostock. 106, Littleny l Dreamstime.com. 107, Natursports l Dreamstime.com. 109, Marco Rubino / Shutterstock. Chapter 8: Midtown East: 113, Kord.com/age Fotostock. 115, Jaap Hart/iStockphoto. 116, svlumagraphica/iStockphoto. 118, Jewelite l Dreamstime.com. 123, Stuart Monk/iStockphoto/Thinkstock. 124, Stuart Monk/Shutterstock. Chapter 9: Midtown West: 129, Dibrova l Dreamstime.com. 131, Ahavelaar l Dreamstime.com. 132, Alexpro9500 l Dreamstime.com. 133, Andykazie l Dreamstime.com. 136, oversnap/iStockphoto. 139, Berniephillips l Dreamstime.com. Chapter 10: The Upper East Side: 143, Nicholas Pitt/Alamy. 145, Kmiragaya l Dreamstime.com. 146, Superbo l Dreamstime.com. 150, Alexpro9500 l Dreamstime.com. Chapter 11: The Upper West Side: 155, Mary Robnett. 157, Momos/Wikimedia Commons. 158, Kord.com/age fotostock. 161, Jennifer Arnow. 165, Rabbit75 l Dreamstime.com. 169, Kmiragaya l Dreamstime.com. Chapter 12: Harlem: 171, Aijadream l Dreamstime.com. 173, Joe Malone/Agency Jon Arnold Images/age fotostock. 174, SuperStock/age fotostock. 177, Adam Reich. 179, Mark B. Schlemmer/Flickr, [CC BY 2.0]. Chapter 13: Brooklyn: 181, Olga Bogatyrenko/Shutterstock. 183, Jennifer Arnow. 184, Ace Stock Limited/Alamy. 187, Stocksnapper l Dreamstime.com. 195, Mary Robnett. 199, Littleny l Dreamstime.com. 202, pio3 / Shutterstock. Chapter 14: Queens, the Bronx, and Staten Island: 205, Sylvain Grandadam/age fotostock. 207, Michel Friang/Alamy. 208, Terry Robinson/Flickr, [CC BY-SA 3.0]. 213, Elizabeth Beller, via Wikimedia Commons [CC BY-SA 3.0]. 217, Ffooter l Dreamstime.com. 219, littleny / Shutterstock. 224, Jennifer Arnow. Chapter 15: Where to Eat: 227, Nick Solares. 228, The Spotted Pig. 229 (top), stocksolutions/Shutterstock. 229 (bottom), rakratchada/Shutterstock. 230, Ace Stock Limited/Alamy. Chapter 16: Where to Stay: 325, Adrian Gaut. 326, Park Hyatt New York. Chapter 17: Shopping: 357, Mary Robnett. 358, Richard Levine/Alamy. 365, Piero Ribelli. Chapter 18: Nightlife: 411, Michael Belardo/Alamy. 412, Jazz Guy /Flickr, [CC BY 2.0]. Chapter 19: The Performing Arts: 435, Brian Stanton. 436, Evan Joseph. 448, Jiawangkun l Dreamstime.com. 453, Jazz at Lincoln Center. Back cover, from left to right: Kan1234 l Dreamstime.com; Littleny l Dreamstime.com; Dave Winer/Flickr, [CC BY-SA 2.0]. Spine: AlexGul/Shutterstock.

NOTES

NOTES

ABOUT OUR WRITERS

Kelsy Chauvin is a freelance writer, editor, and photographer based in Brooklyn. Her work appears regularly in numerous print and digital publications, including *Condé Nast Traveler*, *The Points Guy*, *Rand McNally*, *Zagat*, *Gothamist*, *Passport*, *Curve Magazine*, and others. Follow her travels on Instagram and Twitter at @kelsycc.

Jessica Colley Clarke is a travel and food writer based in Harlem. She adores New York for its bubbling pizza pies, storied cobbled streets, and picnics on the bank of the Hudson River. Jessica shares her travels and New York tips on Twitter at @jessicacolley.

David Farley is the author of the award-winning travel memoir An Irreverent Curiosity and writes about food and travel for *AFAR* magazine, the *New York Times*, and *National Geographic Traveler*. He teaches writing at Columbia University and New York University.

Modern-day explorer and diligent travel scribe **Elissa Garay** has traveled to and reported on nearly 60 countries around the globe, though no place on the planet has captured her attention and affection like her New York City hometown. With 15 years experience as a travel editor and writer, she's served as a contributor to Fodor's since 2012, and has had hundreds of travel articles featured in major national publications like *Condé Nast Traveler*, *Travel + Leisure*, *Cruise Critic*, *The Huffington Post*, and more. Follow her on Twitter at @TravelSpiritNYC.

Laura Itzkowitz writes for *Travel + Leisure*, *Refinery29*, and *Saveur*, among others. She is the co-author of a forthcoming guide to New York City's hidden bars and restaurants. She lives in Greenpoint.

Kristin Iversen is a writer and editor who has lived in Brooklyn for 15 years. She is the managing editor for *Brooklyn* and *The L* magazines, and her work has appeared in the *New York Observer* and *The Nervous Breakdown*, among others.

Christina Knight has lived in Park Slope since 1995 and is a senior multimedia producer at WNET/Thirteen where she works with *American Masters*, *Great Performances*, and NYC-ARTS.org.

Megan Eileen McDonough splits her time between Brooklyn, San Francisco, and Hong Kong. She runs *Bohemian Trails*, a blog for the savvy traveler, and she also contributes to *The Huffington Post*, *WIRED*, and *Budget Travel*.

Marisa Meltzer is a writer based in Brooklyn. She currently resides in Red Hook but has also lived in Brooklyn Heights and Prospect Heights. Her work has appeared in the *New York Times*, *Elle*, *AFAR*, and others.

Chris Molanphy is a pop-chart analyst, feature writer, music critic, and Brooklyn native. His work has appeared in *Slate*, *Pitchfork*, the *Village Voice*, NPR Music's The Record, RollingStone.com, Billboard, and CMJ. He is a frequent guest on National Public Radio (All Things Considered, Soundcheck, On the Media). He lives in Brooklyn.

Irish-born writer **Jacinta O'Halloran** has been calling New York City home for more than two decades. She can walk the part (i.e., fast) and talk the part (i.e., when she's mad at cabdrivers, ordering bagels, or giving directions) of a local, but she still sees and feels the city like a visitor (i.e., she still looks up!).

Matt Rodbard lives in Carroll Gardens and writes about restaurants, chefs, drinks, music, and New York City as a place to enjoy all of it. He is the executive editor at Food Republic and is writing a book about Korean food in America.

Josh Rogol, a native of Stamford, Connecticut, now makes his home in Brooklyn. He is a licensed New York City tour guide, freelance travel writer, and a video producer for *USA Today Sports*. His quest to sample the best of New York's culinary world is a passion that spans all five boroughs.

Emily Saladino lives in Brooklyn's Clinton Hill neighborhood. She contributes food, culture, and travel stories to BBC, *Condé Nast Traveler*, *USA Today*, *Travel + Leisure*, and others.

Sarah Spagnolo is editor-at-large at Foursquare; before that spent a decade at *Travel + Leisure*. She's been based in Bed-Stuy since 2013.